PLANE SURVEYING

PLANE SURVEYING

THIRD EDITION

A M Chandra

Professor of Civil Engineering
Arba Minch University, Ethiopia
Formerly Professor of Civil Engineering
Geomatics Engineering Section
Indian Institute of Technology Roorkee, India

NEW AGE INTERNATIONAL (P) LIMITED, PUBLISHERS

LONDON • NEW DELHI • NAIROBI

Bangalore • Chennai • Cochin • Guwahati • Hyderabad • Kolkata • Lucknow • Mumbai

Visit us at **www.newagepublishers.com**

Published by New Age International (P) Ltd., Publishers
First Edition: 2002
Third Edition: 2015
Reprint: 2018

GLOBAL OFFICES

- **New Delhi** **NEW AGE INTERNATIONAL (P) LIMITED, PUBLISHERS**
  7/30 A, Daryaganj, New Delhi-110002, (INDIA)
  Tel.: (011) 23253771, 23253472, **Telefax:** 23267437, 43551305
  E-mail: contactus@newagepublishers.com • Visit us at www.newagepublishers.com
- **London** **NEW AGE INTERNATIONAL (UK) LTD.**
  27 Old Gloucester Street, London, WC1N 3AX, UK
  E-mail: info@newacademicscience.co.uk • Visit us at www.newacademicscience.co.uk
- **Nairobi** **NEW AGE GOLDEN (EAST AFRICA) LTD.**
  Ground Floor, Westlands Arcade, Chiromo Road (Next to Naivas Supermarket)
  Westlands, Nairobi, KENYA, **Tel.:** 00-254-713848772, 00-254-725700286
  E-mail: kenya@newagepublishers.com

BRANCHES

- **Bangalore** 37/10, 8th Cross (Near Hanuman Temple), Azad Nagar, Chamarajpet, Bangalore- 560 018
  Tel.: (080) 26756823, **Telefax:** 26756820, **E-mail: bangalore@newagepublishers.com**
- **Chennai** 26, Damodaran Street, T. Nagar, Chennai-600 017, **Tel.:** (044) 24353401, **Telefax:** 24351463
  E-mail: chennai@newagepublishers.com
- **Cochin** CC-39/1016, Carrier Station Road, Ernakulam South, Cochin-682 016, **Tel.:** (0484) 2377303, **Telefax:** 4051304
  E-mail: cochin@newagepublishers.com
- **Guwahati** Hemsen Complex, Mohd. Shah Road, Paltan Bazar, Near Starline Hotel, Guwahati-781 008,
  Tel.: (0361) 2513881, **Telefax:** 2543669, **E-mail: guwahati@newagepublishers.com**
- **Hyderabad** 105, 1st Floor, Madhiray Kaveri Tower, 3-2-19, Azam Jahi Road, Near Kumar Theater, Nimboliadda
  Kachiguda, Hyderabad-500 027, **Tel.:** (040) 24652456, **Telefax:** 24652457
  E-mail: hyderabad@newagepublishers.com
- **Kolkata** RDB Chambers (Formerly Lotus Cinema) 106A, 1st Floor, S N Banerjee Road, Kolkata-700 014
  Tel.: (033) 22273773, **Telefax:** 22275247, **E-mail: kolkata@newagepublishers.com**
- **Lucknow** 16-A, Jopling Road, Lucknow-226 001, **Tel.:** (0522) 2209578, 4045297, **Telefax:** 2204098
  E-mail: lucknow@newagepublishers.com
- **Mumbai** 142C, Victor House, Ground Floor, N.M. Joshi Marg, Lower Parel, Mumbai-400 013
  Tel.: (022) 24927869, **Telefax:** 24915415, **E-mail: mumbai@newagepublishers.com**
- **New Delhi** 22, Golden House, Daryaganj, New Delhi-110 002, **Tel.:** (011) 23262368, 23262370, **Telefax:** 43551305
  E-mail: sales@newagepublishers.com

ISBN: 978-81-224-3880-2
C-18-05-11420

Printed in India at Tanya Printers, Delhi.
Typeset at Aakriti Graphics, Delhi.

NEW AGE INTERNATIONAL (P) LIMITED, PUBLISHERS
7/30 A, Daryaganj, New Delhi-110002
Visit us at **www.newagepublishers.com**
(CIN: U74899DL1966PTC004618)

Preface to the Third Edition

This edition of the book has been thoroughly revised. Wherever necessary, the illustrations have been modified and explanations have been made more clear.

In Chapter 1, the "Map Numbering System" has been added. For some of the problems, alternate solutions have been provided to make the readers find alternate approaches to solve a problem. At the end an appendix on "Greek Alphabets" has been added to help the readers in correct identification of the alphabets by name.

The readers are welcome to give their suggestions if any, through the Publisher.

A.M. Chandra

Preface

The University of Roorkee, formerly known as Thomason College of Civil Engineering and now the Indian Institute of Technology Roorkee, was established in 1847 as Roorkee College with the objective of producing engineers who would one day build the edifice of their motherland. Rightly, the Institute and more notably its Department Civil Engineering can lay claim to be the cradle of engineering education and technology in the country of ours.

The first step in the engineering practice is surveying and the soundness of the former is dependent upon the reliability and accuracy of the latter. Therefore, it is imperative that a student of engineering has a good knowledge of surveying. With the above objective, the author delved into writing a book on the subject, knowing pretty well that many excellent books are available. The urge to write a book on this fascinating and mundane subject emanated from years of experience in teaching and its field application in various types of situations.

This revised edition on Plane Surveying contains the chapters on the topics of basic nature and are essentials for surveying. The subject matter has been thoroughly revised and arranged in a logical sequence such that the students acquire the fundamentals of surveying chapter by chapter as they proceed. Certain additions have also been included to enhance the productivity and potential of the book, in terms of more text, various other examples and lots of questionnaire in a lucid language and understanding manners.

The book contains 12 chapters. Chapter 1 is introductory, explains basic concepts of surveying and basic definitions. Chapter 2 explains the concept of errors in survey measurements and their propagation. A surveyor should understand the different types of errors, their sources and how they propagate and therefore this topic has been introduced in the beginning.

Basic survey measurements are covered in chapters 3 through 6. The topics included in these chapters are horizontal distance, vertical distance, slope, distance, elevation, angle and direction measurements. The measurement using stadia tacheometry has been discussed in chapter 8. Chapter 7 deals with contouring and uses of contours in civil engineering projects.

Chapters 9 and 10 constitute a part of survey operations. Traversing is covered in chapter 9. Chapter 10 deals with plotting of maps by plane tabling. The way use of tangent clinometer in plane tabling has been discussed in this book is normally not found in the available textbooks on the subject.

Calculation of areas and volumes from the survey measurements has been explained in chapter 11. The last chapter 12, deals in detail with setting out the various types of curves used to connect the straights. A special feature of this chapter is that it covers almost all the field problems in setting out the circular curves.

The book is intended for degree, diploma and A.M.I.E. students. The book will also be useful to the practising engineers and surveyors.

The author acknowledges the patience and support he received from his wife Archana Chandra, son Anshuman Chandra, and daughter Arushi Chandra through the long process of bringing this book to fruition. This book could not have seen the light of the day but for their encouragement.

Finally, the author wishes to record his gratitude to his almamatter, the University of Roorkee, which provided him with an intellectually stimulating environment and a working platform conducive to creativity.

In spite of every care taken, some errors might have crept in. The author will be grateful to the readers for bringing such errors to his notice. Any suggestions for improvement will be gratefully acknowledged.

It is worth to mention here that another book by the author covering the topics on triangulation, trilateration, adjustment of survey measurements, field astronomy, map projection, photogrammetry, photointerpretation, remote sensing, modern systems in surveying and mapping including the chapters on topographic surveying, hydrographic surveying, construction surveying, and route surveying is also available to the students interested in the topics on higher surveying.

A.M. Chandra

Contents

1

INTRODUCTION AND BASIC CONCEPTS

1.1 GENERAL

The plans or maps of areas are required for various purposes such as planning, design, and execution of engineering projects, location of different geological structures, showing the geographical boundaries of districts, states and countries too. The plans or maps are prepared by the method of surveying. *Surveying* is defined as an art of making such measurements of the relative positions of points on the surface of earth that on drawing them to scale, natural and artificial features are exhibited in their correct relative horizontal and vertical positions.

1.2 PRIMARY DIVISIONS OF SURVEYING

The earth has the approximate shape of an oblate ellipsoid of revolution. The Clark (1866) ellipsoid has polar axis of 12,713,168 m and an equatorial axis of 12,756,413 m. The difference in the two axes is only about 43 km.

The shape of the earth being close to an ellipsoid or spheroid, its surface has curvature. The curvature of the earth's surface is the main factor for the following divisions of surveying:

(*a*) Geodetic Surveying

(*b*) Plane Surveying.

In geodetic surveying, the curved shape of the earth is taken into account. It is usually of a rational character, and is undertaken by government agencies, *e.g.*, the U.S. National Geodetic Survey, the U.S. Coast and Geodetic Survey, the Ordinance Survey in the U.K., the Survey of India, and the Geological Survey of India. The aim may be purely scientific, that is to determine the size and shape of the earth, or it may be the production of accurate maps of large areas. Refined instruments and methods are used, and the absolute positions of a series of points on the earth's surface are determined. These points serve as control points for surveys covering smaller areas. When large areas are involved, the computations must be based on the mean spheroidal shape of the earth.

The sum of three angles of a triangle on a sphere, known as *spherical triangle*, is greater than that of the corresponding plane triangle, by an amount known as *spherical excess*. It is one second of arc for an area of about 200 sq. km on the earth. This indicates that plane surveying procedures are adequate up to 1000 sq. km, although no definite limit can be assigned.

The plane surveying is that type of surveying which does not take into account the curvature of the earth, and the surface of the earth is treated as a plane surface. If the area to be surveyed is more than

1000 km^2, the angles measured on the surface of the earth cannot be in a plane surface, but are in a curved surface, therefore, geodetic surveying must be employed to achieve precision for large areas. The plane surveying, thus, is valid for surveys of small extent, where the effect of curvature becomes negligible. Most ordinary surveys, such as location and construction surveys of highways, railways, canal and other civil engineering projects, fall in this category. They, may also be undertaken for scientific, geographical, navigational, and military purposes. In plane surveys the direction of plumb lines are considered parallel, at different points, and all angles are plane angles.

The operation of levelling to determine elevations is usually considered a division of plane surveying. However, the datum has to be a curved surface if the earth's shape is to be accounted for. The curvature of the earth's surface can be ignored in levelling operations which involve very small area and where rough values are adequate.

1.3 CLASSIFICATION OF SURVEYING

Broadly the classification of surveying may be based on

(*a*) the function of survey, and

(*b*) instruments employed.

Classification Based on Function of Surveying

The surveys can further be classified based on the purpose for which they are conducted. They are as follows.

Control surveying is for establishing the horizontal and vertical positions of widely spaced control points using geodetic methods.

Land surveying is for determining the boundaries and areas of parcels of land. It is also known as property survey, boundary survey, or cadastral survey.

City surveys are for urban planning. These are conducted within the limits of the city. These are required for the purpose of layout of buildings, streets, sewers, etc.

Topographic surveys are for depiction of topography of a region. It includes natural features such as hills, rivers, forest, and man-made features such as towns, villages, buildings, roads, transmission lines, canals, etc.

Engineering surveys are undertaken specifically for engineering purposes. It is for collection of requisite data for planning, design, and execution of engineering projects such as design of roads, bridges, dams, and transmission lines. There are further subdivisions as reconnaissance, preliminary surveys, and location surveys. The first is of exploratory nature, the second is to collect adequate data for design, and the third is to set out work on the ground.

Route surveys are primarily for planning, design, and execution of highways, railways, canals, pipelines, and other linear projects.

Construction surveys are those types of surveys which are required to establish points, lines, grades, and for staking out engineering works, after the plans have been prepared and the structural design has been done.

Astronomic surveys are conducted for the determination of latitudes, longitudes, azimuths, local time, etc., for various places by observing heavenly bodies such as Sun and stars.

Geological surveys are conducted to determine different strata of the earth's crust for geological studies.

Archaeological surveys have the primary objective of unearthing relics of antiquity.

Mine surveys are conducted for the exploration of mineral deposits, and to guide tunnelling and other operations associated with mining.

Satellite surveys are conducted to establish intercontinental, interdatum, and interisland geodetic ties all the world over by making observations on artificial satellites.

Military surveys are conducted for military purposes.

Classification Based on Instruments Employed

The surveying operations employ various kinds of instruments, and therefore, it is possible to classify surveys according to the principal instrument on which they are based as under.

Chain survey: This is the simplest type of surveying in which only linear measurements are made with a chain or tape, and no angular measurements are taken.

Compass survey: The horizontal angles are measured with the help of a magnetic compass. The linear measurements are also required which are taken with a chain or tape.

Plane-table survey: The map is prepared in the field itself by determining the directions of various lines making linear measurements, and plotting the details on paper using a plane table.

Levelling survey: This type of survey is used to determine the elevations and relative heights of points with the help of an instrument known as level.

Theodolite survey: Theodolite survey is primarily used in traversing and triangulation for providing controls. The horizontal and vertical angles are measured with the help of theodolite.

Tacheometric survey: A special type of theodolite known as tacheometer, is used to determine horizontal and vertical distances directly.

Photogrammetric survey: In this type of survey, the measurements are made with the help of photographs.

EDM survey: In this type of survey, the linear measurements are made with the help of EDM instruments. In trilateration, all the three sides of a triangle are measured with EDM instrument.

1.4 PRINCIPLES OF SURVEYING

The fundamental principles upon which the various methods of surveying are based, are very simple to understand. They involve

1. fixing a point in relation to points already fixed, and
2. working from the whole to the part.

Fixing a Point in Relation to Points Already Fixed

In Fig.1.1, the positions of two points *A* and *B* are already fixed. The third point *C* can be located in relation to *A* and *B*, by the following direct approaches:

(*a*) Measure the distances *AC* and *BC*, and locate *C* as the intersection point of the arcs with centres at *A* and *B*.

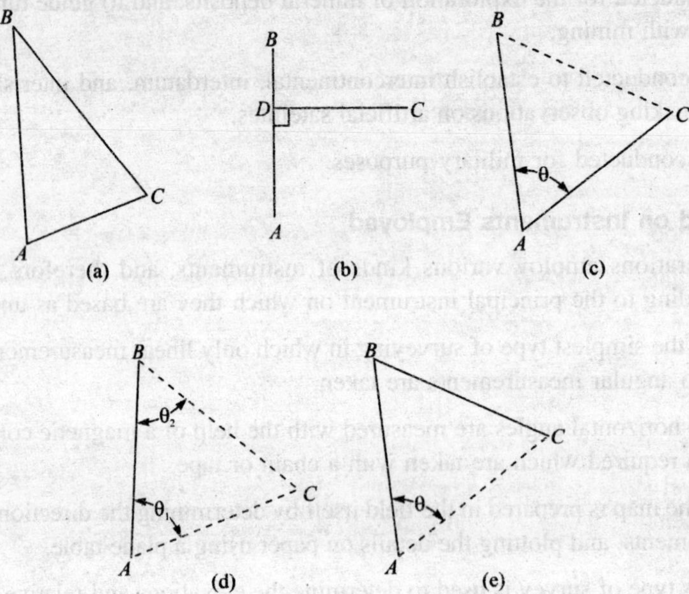

Fig. 1.1 Fixing a point in relation to points already fixed

(*b*) Measure the perpendicular distance *CD* of *C* from *AB*, and the distance *AD* or *BD*, to locate *C*.

(*c*) Measure the distance *AC* and angle *BAC*, to locate *C*.

(*d*) Measure the angles *BAC* and *ABC*, to locate *C*.

(*e*) Measure the angle *BAC* and the distance *BC*, to locate *C*.

The plotting of points on drawing sheet is done by scaling the measured distances.

The above methods, specially (*b*), (*c*), and (*d*) could also be employed for measuring the relative altitudes.

For a given survey work, depending on the purpose of the survey, the degree of accuracy required, the nature and the extent of the area, and the time available, a surveyor may adopt different combinations of the above approaches, and various types of available instruments for fixing horizontal and vertical locations of points.

The selection of a method best suited to a particular survey depends on the degree of skill acquired by the surveyor.

Working From the Whole to the Part

This is the ruling principle in surveying. The surveyor should first establish a sufficient number of points with high degree of precision in and around the area to be surveyed. Such points are known as *primary control points*. The gaps are then filled with a system of *secondary control points* at closer intervals with slightly less precision. Further gaps are then filled by *tertiary control points* at even closer intervals and with even less precision. For the surveys which are of ordinary nature, the tertiary control points are used to fix details on the ground. As a rule, the errors in survey details should be too small to plot, while the accuracy of the control points used for plotting the detail must be as high as possible.

The purpose of working from the whole to the part is mainly to localise the errors, *i.e.*, not to magnify and to control the accumulation of errors. In the reverse process of working from the part to the whole, the errors will get magnified.

The other points which must be kept in mind are:

(*a*) Choose a method of survey that is the most suitable for the purpose.

(*b*) Recording of data should be done carefully.

(*c*) Make provisions for adequate checks.

1.5 DEFINITIONS OF SOME BASIC TERMS

The following are some basic terms most commonly used in surveying:

Level surface: A level surface is the equipotential surface of the earth's gravity field. It is a curved surface, and every element of which is normal to plumb line. A body of still water provides the best example of a level surface.

Level line: A line lying in a level surface is a level line. It is thus a curved line normal to the plumb at all the points.

Horizontal plane: A horizontal plane is a plane which is tangential to a level surface at a particular point.

Horizontal line: A line tangent to a level surface is a horizontal line.

Horizontal angle: An angle measured between two intersecting lines lying in a horizontal plane, is defined as a horizontal angle.

Vertical line: A vertical line is a line perpendicular to the horizontal plane.

Vertical plane: A plane containing a vertical line is vertical plane.

Vertical angle: The angle between two intersecting lines in a vertical plane, is vertical angle.

Zenith angle: An angle between two lines in a vertical plane where one of the lines is directed towards zenith is known as zenith angle. A vertical line in the direction away from the centre of the earth and above the observer's head, is said to be directed towards zenith.

Horizontal distance: In plane surveying, distance measured along a level line is termed as horizontal distance.

Elevation: The vertical distance of a point from an assumed datum or mean sea-level is known as elevation.

Contour: A contour is an imaginary line of constant elevation on the surface of ground.

Grade or gradient: The slope of a line or rate of ascent or descent is termed as grade or gradient.

Latitude and departure: If the *x*-axis and *y*-axis in a cartesian coordinate system, are in east-west direction and north-south direction, respectively, the *y*-cordinate of point is its latitude and *x*-coordinate departure.

1.6 PHASES OF SURVEY WORK

A survey work has the following phases:

Planning, analysis and decision-making It involves the following:

(*i*) Selection of an appropriate method of surveying,

(*ii*) Selection of instruments and other equipments, and

(*iii*) Selection and fixing of survey stations.

Care and adjustment of instruments To ensure best results, the instruments must be kept in good working condition. The surveyor must check before use that the permanent adjustments of the instruments are not disturbed.

Field work It is the process of collecting field data by making linear and angular measurements, and recording them in a systematic manner.

Office work The office work involves:

(*i*) Computation of coordinates,

(*ii*) Data processing,

(*iii*) Preparing plans or maps to suitable scales, and

(*iv*) Computation of areas and volumes.

Setting out works It involves pegging out the structure on the ground before construction starts.

1.7 SCALE

Since the areas to be plotted are rather large compared to the size of the paper on which the map of the area is to be plotted, it is not possible to draw the measured distances directly. Actually, the measured distances are drawn to some scales.

The *scale* is defined as the ratio of the distance between two points on a map to the corresponding distance on the ground. Selection of a scale depends on the size of the area to be surveyed, purpose of survey, and required precision in plotting. Maps are generally classed as *large scale* when the scale is greater than 1 cm = 10 m, as *intermediate scale* when scale is between 1 cm = 10 m and 1 cm = 100 m, and as *small scale* when the scale is less than 1 cm = 100 m. In general, the scale should be as small as possible and still represent the detail with sufficient precision. Thus, it should not be necessary to read the scale closer than 0.25 mm or so.

Table 1.1 gives the recommended scales for different type of surveys.

Table 1.1 Scales for different type of surveys

Purpose of survey	Scale	R.F.
Building sites	1 cm = 10 m or less	$\frac{1}{1000}$ or less
Town planning, reservoir survey, etc.	1 cm = 50 m to 100 m	$\frac{1}{5000}$ to $\frac{1}{10,000}$
Route surveys	1 cm = 100 m	$\frac{1}{10,000}$
Longitudinal section		
I: Horizontal scale	1 cm = 100 m to 200 m	$\frac{1}{10,000}$ to $\frac{1}{20,000}$
II: Vertical scale	1 cm = 1 m to 2 m	$\frac{1}{100}$ to $\frac{1}{200}$
Cross sections (Both horizontal and vertical scales are equal)	1 cm = 1 m to 2 m	$\frac{1}{100}$ to $\frac{1}{200}$
Location surveys	1 cm = 50 m to 200 m	$\frac{1}{5000}$ to $\frac{1}{20,000}$
Land surveys	1 cm = 5 m to 50 m	$\frac{1}{500}$ to $\frac{1}{5,000}$
Topographic surveys	1 cm = 0.25 km to 2.5 km	$\frac{1}{25,000}$ to $\frac{1}{250,000}$
Cadastral surveys	1 cm = 5 m to 0.5 km	$\frac{1}{500}$ to $\frac{1}{50,000}$
Geographical surveys	1 cm = 5 km to 150 km	$\frac{1}{5,00,000}$ to $\frac{1}{150,00,000}$

Representation of Scale

A scale can be represented numerically or graphically. If a scale is represented as 1 cm = 50 m, for example, it is known as *Engineer's scale*. According to this scale a specified distance on the map (*i.e.*, 1 cm) represents the corresponding distance on the ground (*i.e.*, 50 m). The other way is to indicate the scale by a ratio known as *representative fraction*, abbreviated as R.F. For the scale 1 cm = 50 m,

$$\text{R.F.} = \frac{1 \text{ cm}}{(50 \text{ m} \times 100) \text{ cm}} = \frac{1}{5000}$$

or $$= 1 : 5000$$

In *graphical representation*, a line subdivided into plan distance corresponding to convenient units of length on the ground, is drawn on the map as shown in Fig. 1.2.

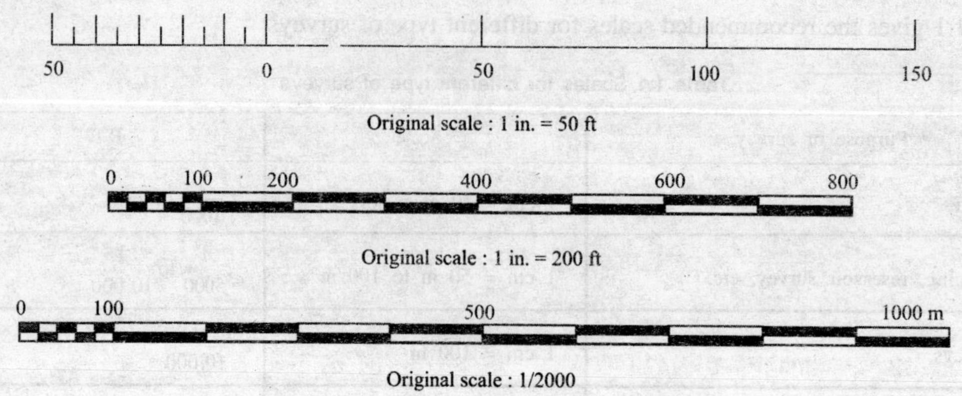

Fig. 1.2 Graphical scales

Since the distances on the maps can be determined by actual scaling, the graphical scale has advantage over the numerical scale that even when the map has been shrunk or has been reproduced to some other scale, they also change with the map, and therefore, the ratio of distances on the map to the distances on the ground are unaffected.

For detail plotting, the following two types of scales are used for linear measurements:

(*a*) Plain scale, and

(*b*) Diagonal scale.

Plain scale The *plain scale* is one which makes possible the measurement of some unit and its submultiples. Thus, if x is any unit then on a plain scale we can measure x and $(1/n)x$ where n is some suitable number. For example,

(*i*) Metre and one-tenth of a metre.

(*ii*) Kilometre and one-tenth of a kilometre.

(*iii*) 100 kilometre and one-fifth of 100 kilometres.

(*iv*) Hour and one-sixth of an hour.

If R.F. for a scale is 1:50 and maximum distance to be measured using the scale is 6 m then to construct a plain scale, steps to be followed are

50 units on the ground = 1 unit on the map

6 m on the ground $= \frac{6}{50}$ m on the map

= 12 cm on the map

Draw a line of 12 cm, and divide it equally into 6 parts. The first part *A* on the left side further divided into 10 equal parts to read $\frac{1}{10}$ m (Fig. 1.3).

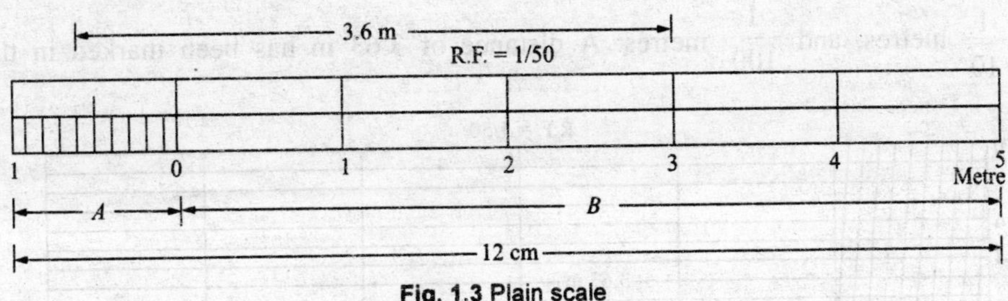

Fig. 1.3 Plain scale

Diagonal scale A *diagonal scale* reads some unit, its submultiples and further submultiples. Thus if x is any unit, the diagonal scale can measure x, $(1/n)x$ and $(1/m)(1/n)x$, where n and m are some suitable integer numbers. For example,

(*i*) Metre, one-tenth of a metre or decimetre, and one-tenth of decimetre.

(*ii*) Kilometres, 100 metres or hectometre and 10 metres or decametre.

The base of a diagonal scale is a plain scale where we have subdivisions in the part A, and the main unit of measurements in the part B as in a plain scale, shown in Fig. 1.3. To further divide the subdivisions of part A, help of diagonal is taken, as it is difficult to subdivide the divisions being small in length. This is explained in Fig. 1.4. Let the length AB is to be divided into n equal number of parts. Take a perpendicular AC at A, and divide it into n (=10) equal divisions Ca_1, a_1a_2, a_2a_3, etc. Draw a diagonal BC. From a_1, a_2, a_3, etc., draw lines parallel to AB, intersecting BC at b_1, b_2, b_3, etc., from where draw lines perpendicular to AB. These lines intersect AB dividing it in n (= 10) equal parts. In this figure, AB has been divided into 10 equal parts using the diagonal BC. The distances a_1b_1, a_2b_2, etc., are subdivisions of AB such that

$$a_1b_1 = \frac{1}{10} AB$$

$$a_2b_2 = \frac{2}{10} AB$$

$$a_3b_3 = \frac{3}{10} AB$$

$$\vdots \qquad \vdots$$

$$a_9b_9 = \frac{9}{10} AB$$

$$a_{10}b_{10} = \frac{10}{10} AB = AB.$$

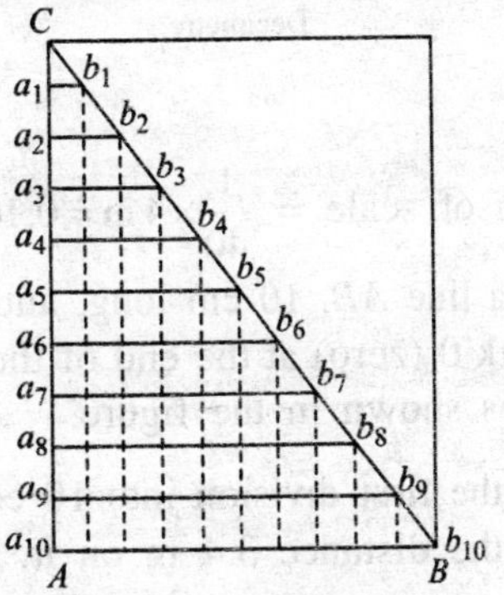

Fig. 1.4 Dividing a line with the help of a diagonal

Figure 1.5 shows that the plain scale shown in Fig. 1.3 has been converted into a diagonal scale to read $\frac{1}{10}\left[\frac{1}{10} \text{ m}\right]$, *i.e.*, $\frac{1}{100}$ m or 1 cm by subdividing the divisions of part A of the plain scale with the help of diagonals for each division. This diagonal scale can measure the distances in metres, $\frac{1}{10}$ metres, and $\frac{1}{100}$ metres. A distance of 3.63 m has been marked in the figure.

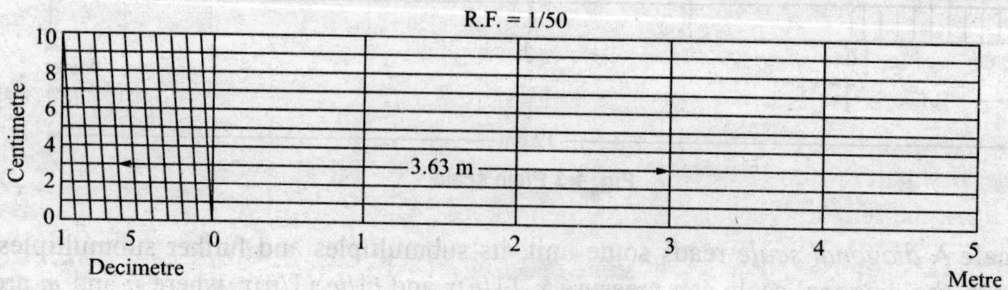

Fig. 1.5 Diagonal scale

ILLUSTRATIVE EXAMPLES

Example 1.1

Draw a plain scale of R.F. = 1/40 to show metres and decimetres, and long enough to measure up to 4 metres. Show a distance of 3.4 metres on it.

Solution (*Fig. 1.6*):

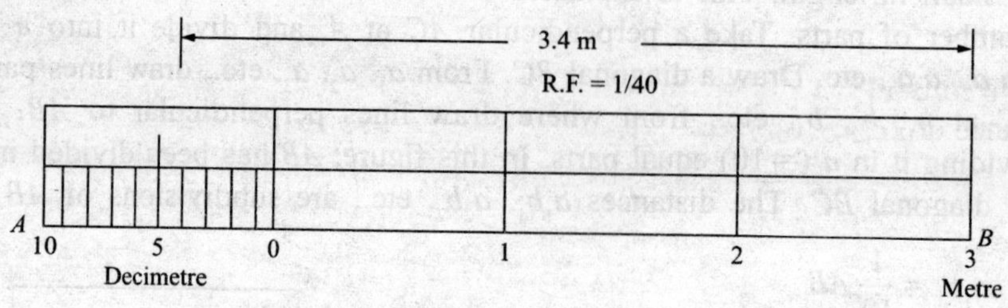

Fig. 1.6

$$\text{Length of scale} = \frac{1}{40} \times 4\text{ m} = 0.10\text{ m} = 10\text{ cm}$$

Draw a line *AB*, 10 cm long, and divide it into 4 equal parts, each part representing a single metre. Mark 0 (zero) at the end of the first division, and then 1, 2 and 3, at the end of subsequent divisions as shown in the figure.

Subdivide the first division into 10 equal parts to represent single decimetre. Complete the scale, and mark the distance 3.4 m on it.

Example 1.2

A rectangular plot of 25 km² in area is shown on a map by a similar rectangular area of 1 cm². Construct a plain scale to show units of ten kilometres and single kilometres. The scale should be long enough to read up to 50 km. Measure a distance of 37 km on it.

Solution (*Fig. 1.7*):

$$1\text{ cm}^2 = 25\text{ km}^2$$

or $$1\text{ cm} = 5\text{ km}$$

$$\text{R.F.} = \frac{1 \text{ cm}}{5 \times 1000 \times 100 \text{ cm}} = \frac{1}{500000}$$

$$\text{Length of scale} = \frac{1}{500000} \times 50 \text{ km} = 10 \text{ cm}$$

Therefore, draw a line 10 cm long, and divide it into 5 equal parts, each representing 10 km. Subdivide the first part in 10 equal divisions, each representing 1 km. Complete the scale as shown in the figure, and mark the required distance 37 km on it.

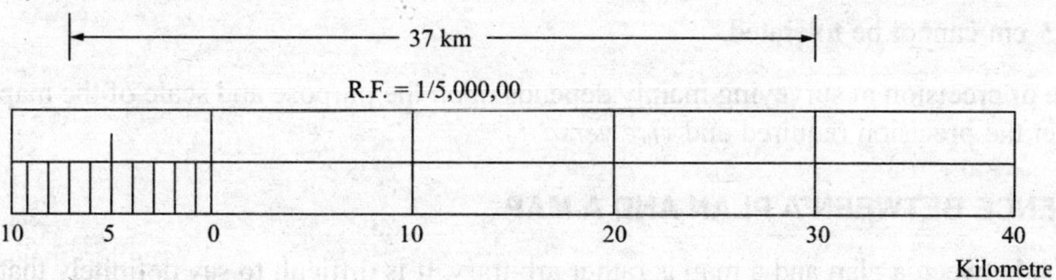

Fig. 1.7

Example 1.3

Draw a scale 1 cm = 3 m to read metres and decimetres, and to be long enough to read up to 30 m. Measure a distance of 22.3 m on it.

Solution (*Fig. 1.8*):

$$\text{R.F.} = \frac{1 \text{ cm}}{3 \times 100 \text{ cm}} = \frac{1}{300}$$

$$\text{Length of scale} = \frac{1}{300} \times 30 \text{ m} = 10 \text{ cm}$$

Draw a line of 10 cm length, and divide it into 3 equal parts, each division representing 10 m. Divide the first part into 10 equal parts, each division representing 1m. Then draw diagonals as shown in the figure to read 1/10 m, and mark the distance 22.3 m on the scale.

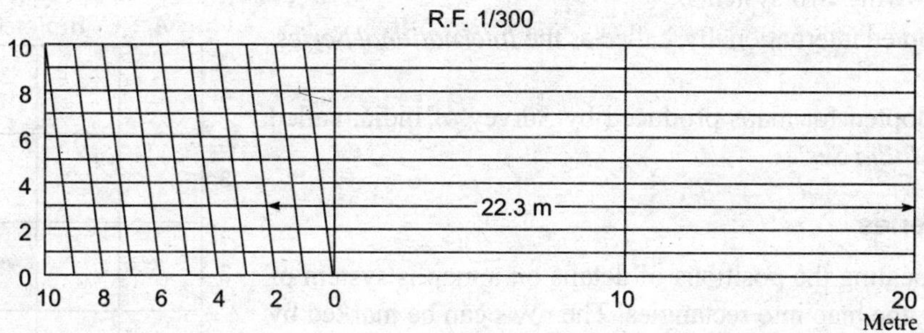

Fig. 1.8

1.8 PRECISION IN SURVEYING

The minimum distance which can be plotted on a map is 0.25 mm is the size of a dot. The permissible error in linear measurements on the ground, thus, depends upon the scale of plotting. In other words, the error in linear measurements which cannot be plotted on the map, is the permissible error. For example, if a map is required to be on scale 1 cm = 1 km, the error of $\frac{0.25 \times 1000}{10} = 25\,\text{m}$ will not affect the accuracy of the map as the linear measurements up to 25 m on the ground can be plotted as a dot. Since any plotting of size less than the size of dot is not possible, the measurements of lesser than 25 m length have no meaning. On the other hand, for the scale of 1 cm = 5 m of a map, the error more than $\frac{0.25 \times 50}{10} = 12.5$ cm cannot be tolerated.

The degree of precision in surveying mainly depends upon the purpose and scale of the map. Larger the scale better the precision required and *vice versa.*

1.9 DIFFERENCE BETWEEN A PLAN AND A MAP

The distinction between a plan and a map is rather arbitrary. It is difficult to say definitely that when a plan becomes a map.

Generally a plan is orthographic representation of features on or near the earth on a horizontal plane. Therefore, all the distances on a plan are horizontal distances to some scale. The earth's curvature is not taken into account, therefore, preferably the plans are prepared for smaller areas to avoid distortions due to curvature of the earth in the adopted projection system.

A map is also a graphical representation of features but differs from a plan when the scale is small and is constructed using a projection system other than orthographic. Generally, maps give some additional information such as about the topography with the help of contours.

1.10 MAP NUMBERING SYSTEM

Maps produced by different agencies of the world depict the features of the Earth's surface of certain area referred to some coordinate system. Thus to identify that a map belongs to which area on the Earth's surface, a map numbering system is required to immediately convey the information about the location of the area shown in that map.

Map numbering system

There are following two systems:

(*i*) System adopted internationally, called as the *International Series,* and

(*ii*) System adopted for maps produced by Survey of India, called as the *Survey of India Series.*

International Series

One way of locating the positions of details on a map is system of grids by dividing the map into rectangles. The rows can be marked by numbers and the columns by alphabets as shown in Fig. 1.9. Thus any rectangle can be designated by a number and a letter, for example 2C. To make the location still easier, a further division of the rectangles can be done.

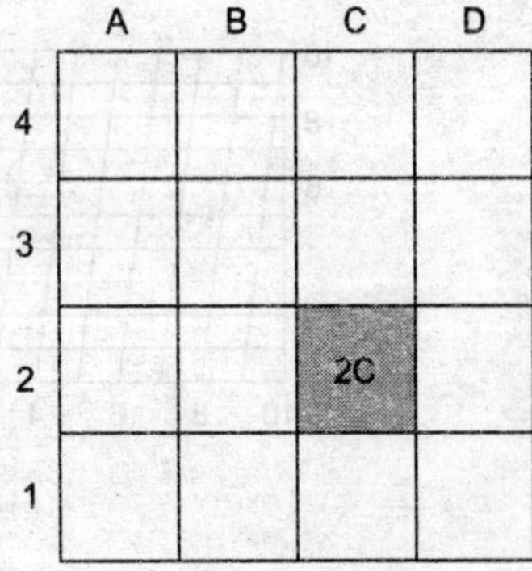

Fig. 1.9. System of grids

Another way of locating the details is by drawing a set of parallel lines on the map, the central one along the true meridian at the place. The lines at other places will deviate from the direction of central meridian due to the convergence of meridian as shown in Fig. 1.10. Taking these lines and the lines drawn perpendicular to them, grids are formed, and the locations of details are given with reference to these lines.

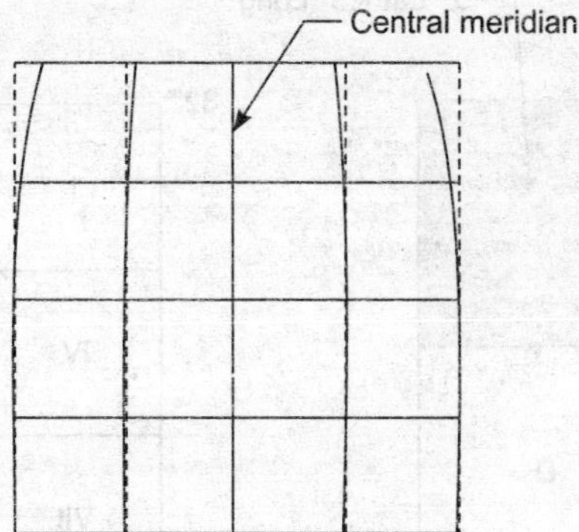

Fig. 1.10 System of converging parallels

Since the topographic maps usually cover large areas of the Earth's surface, the surface of earth has been divided into rectangles of 4° in latitude and 6° in longitude (Fig. 1.11). The strips of 6° longitude are numbered from 1 to 60 starting at 180° west and increasing towards east. These strips are divided into columns by parallels spaced at 4°, and indicated by alphabets A to V on either sides of equator, from 0° to 88° of latitude with polar regions lettered Z. A topographic map covering the area of 4° in latitude and 6° in longitude is 1 to 1 million (1:1,000,000) scale map. The map containing New Delhi has the number NH 43, where N means north of equator. Each such maps or sheets are also named after the most important places located in them for example; NH 43 is 'Delhi'.

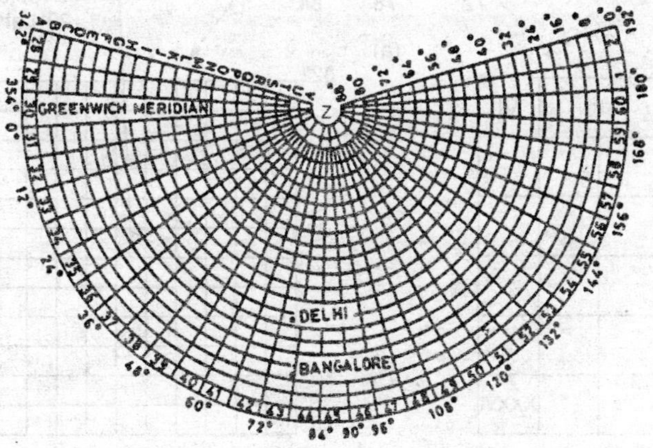

Fig. 1.11 Alphanumeric representation of 1:1,000,000 sheets

Further sub-divisions of 1:1,000,000 sheets have been shown in Fig. 1.12 and 1.13, to produce maps at different scales.

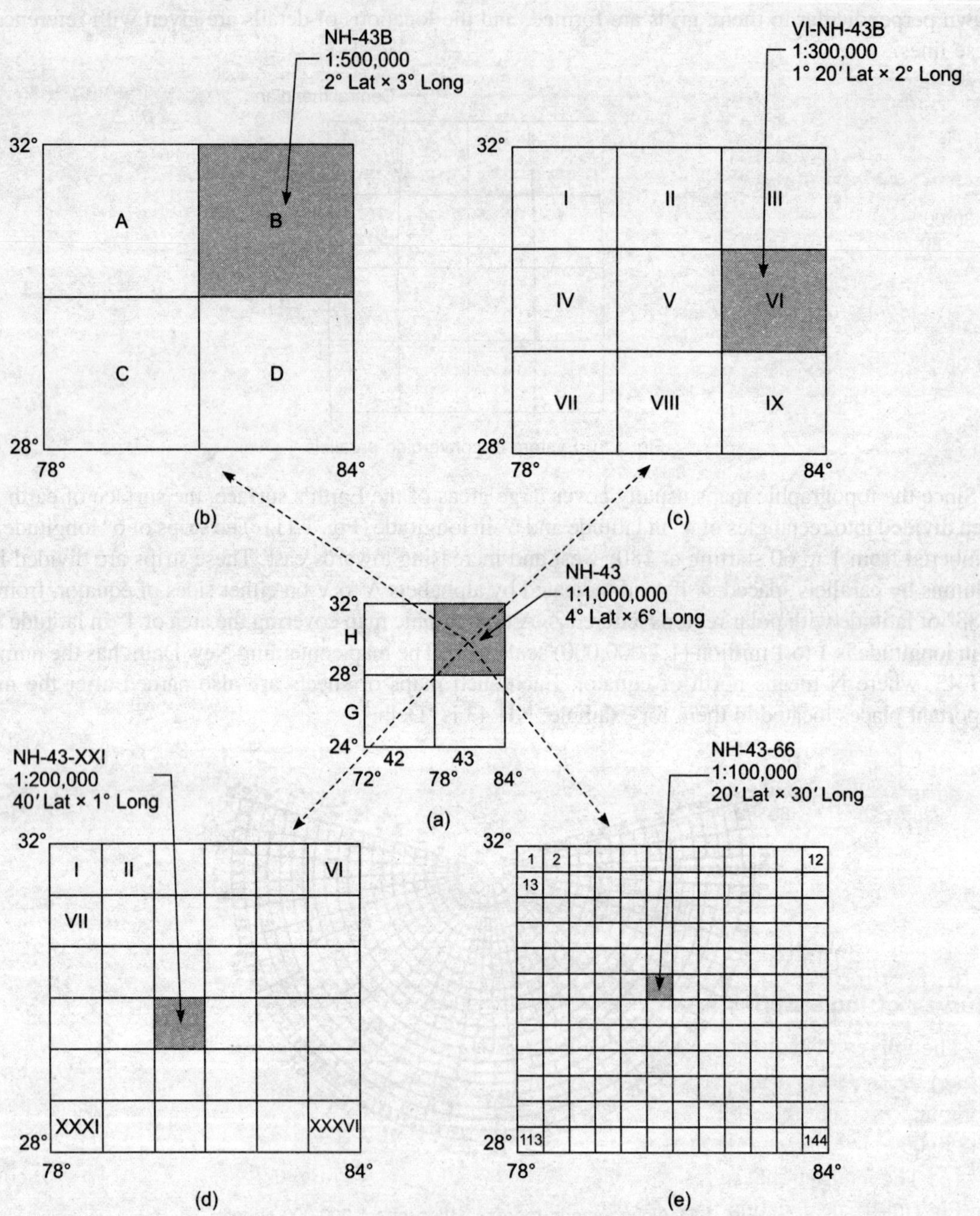

Fig. 1.12 Various sub-divisions of 1:1,000,000 sheets and their numbering, scale and area covered

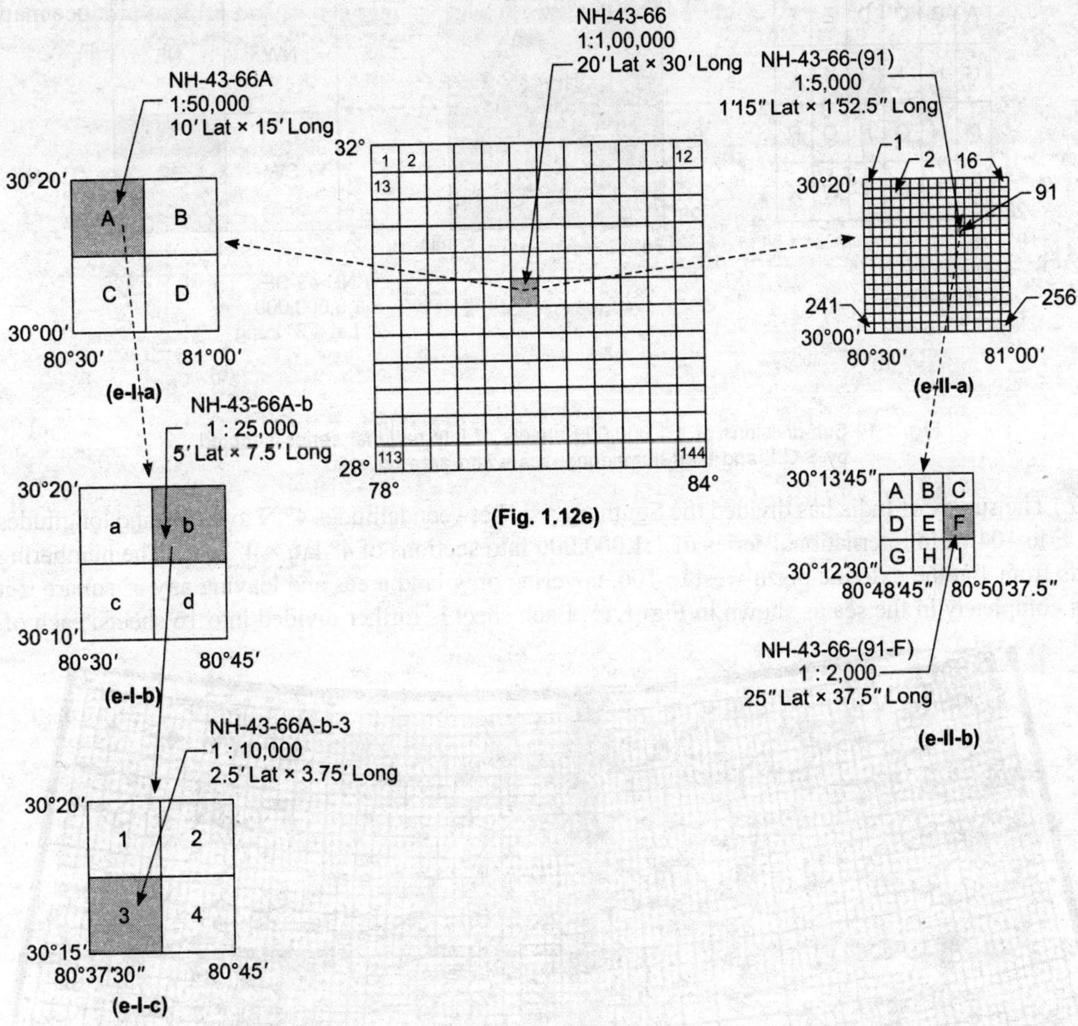

Fig. 1.13 Various sub-divisions of 1:100,000 sheets and their numbering, scale and area covered

Survey of India Series

The Survey of India has adopted the following systems of sheet numbering:

(*a*) The international series of 4° lat × 6° long is divided into 24 squares, each square of 1° lat × 1° long and designating from *A* to *X* as shown in Fig. 1.14a. Each square is a degree sheet at a scale of 1:250,000 (1 inch to 4 miles).

(*b*) The international series of 4° lat. × 6° long. is divided into four parts, each of 2° lat × 3° long, as in Fig. 1.14b, designating them by cardinal directions NW, NE, SW, and SE, the scale of these sheets being 1:500,000. Further divisions of 1:500,000 sheets are same as in the international series.

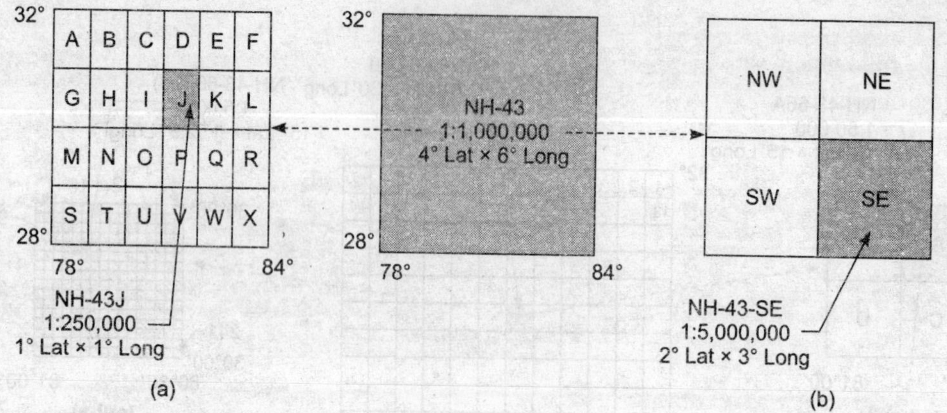

Fig. 1.14 Sub-divisions of 1:1,000,000 sheets of international series adopted by S.O.I. and their numbering, scale and area covered

(*c*) The survey of India has divided the Southern Asia between latitudes 4° N to 40° N and longitudes 44° E to 104° E in international series of 1:1,000.000 into sections of 4° lat. × 4° long. The numbering starts from 1 at the extreme north-west to 106, covering only land areas and leaving any 4° square if it falls completely in the sea as shown in Fig. 1.15. Each sheet is further divided into 16 sheets, each of

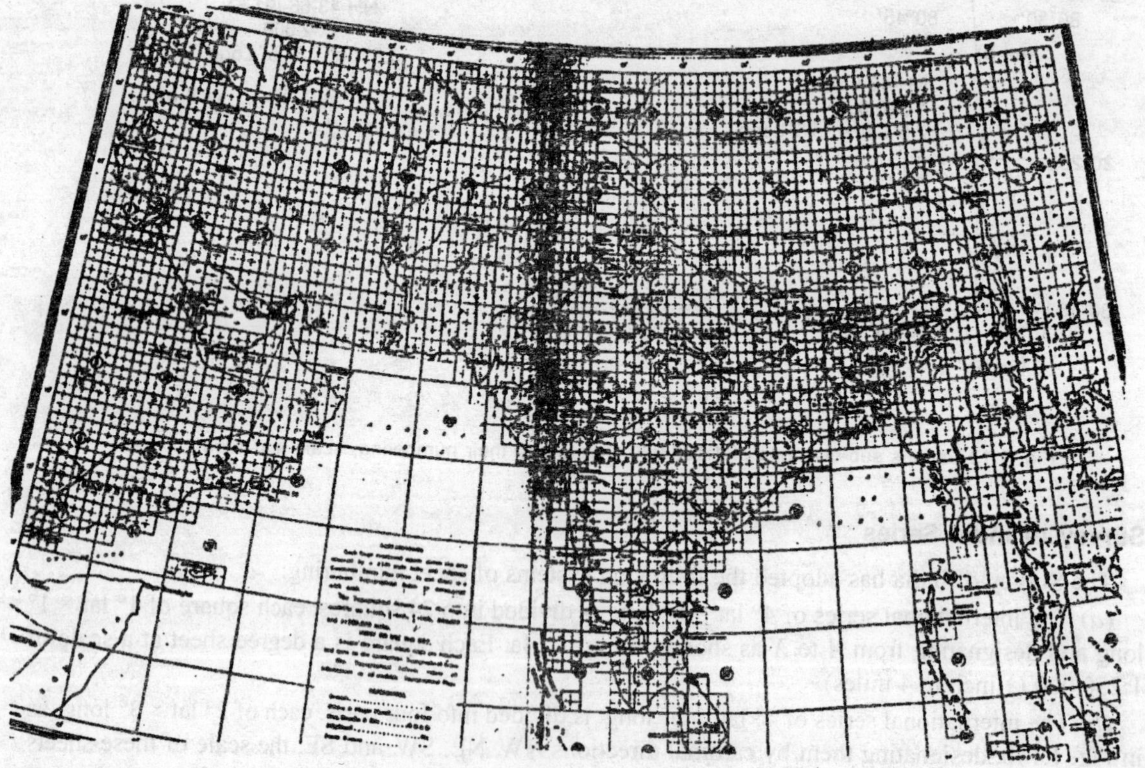

Fig. 1.15 Key to topographical indexes in Southern Asia

1° lat × 1° long, designated as Degree sheets (Fig. 1.16). These degree sheets were further sub-divided in the following ways:

(*i*) Degree sheets have been divided into four parts, each of 30′ lat × 30′ long, designating them by cardinal directions NW, NE, SW, and SE. Such sheets are identified as 57 M/SE (Fig. 1.16).

(*ii*) Degree sheets have also been divided into 16 sheets, each 15′ lat × 15′ long, as shown in Fig. 1.16. Such sheets are identified as 57 B/3, and they are at a scale of 1 : 50,000.

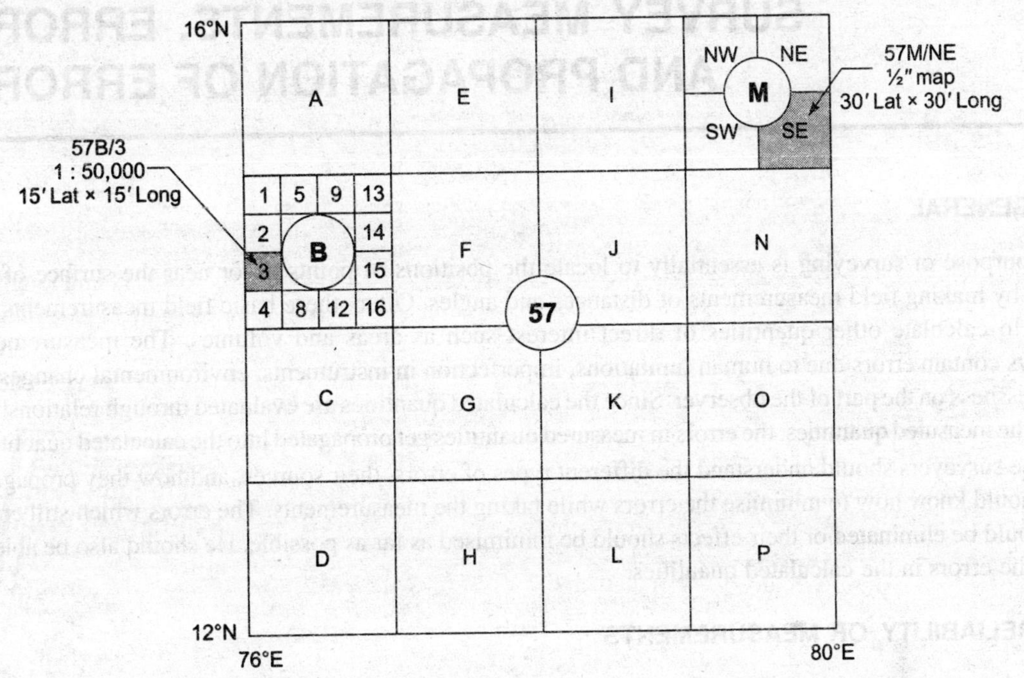

Fig. 1.16 S.O.I. sub-divisions of 1:1,000,000 sheets of international series

QUESTIONS

1.1 What is surveying? Explain its importance in civil engineering.

1.2 What are broad divisions of surveying? State their objectives.

1.3 Discuss the classifications of surveying based on
(*a*) the function of survey, and
(*b*) instrument employed.

1.4 Explain the fundamental principles of surveying.

1.5 What are the various phases of survey work? Discuss each briefly.

1.6 Explain the difference between a plain scale and a diagonal scale.

1.7 What would be the permissible error in making the linear measurements for a map on the scale 1 : 500000?

2

SURVEY MEASUREMENTS, ERRORS AND PROPAGATION OF ERRORS

2.1 GENERAL

The purpose of surveying is essentially to locate the positions of points on or near the surface of the earth by making field measurements of distances and angles. Often, these basic field measurements are used to calculate other quantities of direct interest such as areas and volumes. The measurements always contain errors due to human limitations, imperfection in instruments, environmental changes, or carelessness on the part of the observer. Since the calculated quantities are evaluated through relationships with the measured quantities, the errors in measured quantities get propagated into the calculated quantities.

The surveyors should understand the different types of errors, their sources, and how they propagate. He should know how to minimise the errors while taking the measurements. The errors which still creep in should be eliminated or their effects should be minimised as far as possible. He should also be able to find the errors in the calculated quantities.

2.2 RELIABILITY OF MEASUREMENTS

Several terms are used to express the reliability of measurements. The two most common are

1. Precision, and
2. Accuracy.

Precision is the degree of closeness or conformity of repeated measurements of the same quantity to each other whereas the *accuracy* is the degree of closeness or conformity of a measurement to its true value.

It is perfectly feasible to have a data set that is highly accurate but not very precise, and vice versa. The difference between accuracy and precision is best illustrated in Fig. 2.1, that is results of a shooting competition between four contestants *A*, *B*, *C*, and *D*. The shooting results indicate that

(*i*) Contestant *A* is accurate but not precise,

(*ii*) Contestant *B* is inaccurate and also not precise,

(*iii*) Contestant *C* is neither accurate nor precise, and

(*iv*) Contestant *D*, the winner, is both accurate and precise,

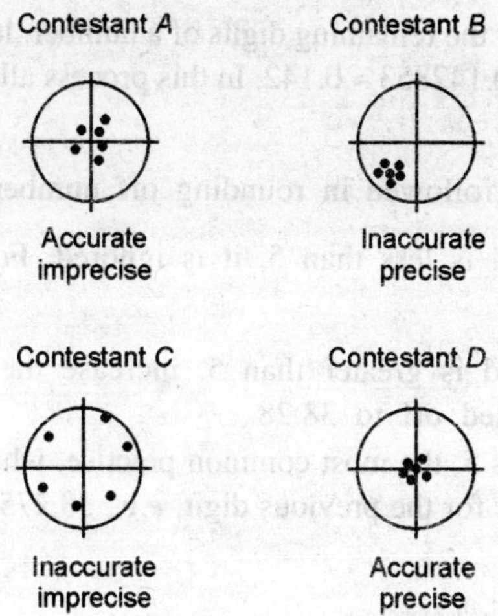

Fig. 2.1 Accuracy versus precision

Significant Figures

The number of digits or *significant figures* is an indication of the accuracy of a measurement. Only these digits in a measured number have significance. The number of significant figures in a numerical quantity equals "the number of digits in the quantity less all zero digits that are used to fix the position of the decimal point." The following examples make this clear.

Two significant figures : 32, 3.2, 0.32, 0.0032, 0.030
Three significant figures : 131, 13.1, 0.000131, 0.0320
Four significant figures : 3456, 34.56, 0.00003456, 32.00

The significant figures are very important from the following point of views.

(*i*) If large number of operations are required in computations, unnecessary digits retained after significant figures will take extra computation time resulting into wastage of time and money.

(*ii*) On the other hand, if one or two digits extra than required ones are not used in computations, the final computed values of a quantity are badly affected due to rounding off errors.

Rounding Off Numbers and Truncation

Dropping one or more digits from a number so that only significant ones or those that are necessary and sufficient for subsequent calculations, is known as *rounding off number*. If more digits have been dropped than the required ones, the result will have round-off errors or rounding error.

For example $\frac{1}{7}$ is equal to 0.142857142857, and we consider only 0.142857, then it is in error by 0.000000142857. In another example of $\sqrt[3]{2}$ which is 1.25992104989487316476...... if we consider 1.25992, there is an error of 0.00000104989487316476...... Double-rounding can increase the rounding off error. For example if the numeral 9.945309 is rounded to two decimal places (9.95) for data entry purposes, and then rounded again to one decimal place (10.0) for display purposes, the apparent round-off error is 10.0 – 9.945309 = 0.054691. If the original number was rounded to one decimal place in one step (9.9), the round-off error is only 9.9 – 9.945309 = 0.045309.

Truncation is simply chopping-off the remaining digits of a number. It is also called rounding to zero. For example, the truncated value of $0.142853 \approx 0.142$. In this process all significant digits after the third have been dropped.

The rules given below should be followed in rounding off numbers:

Rule 1: If the digit to be dropped is less than 5, it is ignored. For example, 38.274 is rounded off to 38.27.

Rule 2: If the digit to be dropped is greater than 5, increase the preceding digit by one. For example, 38.276 is rounded off to 38.28.

Rule 3: If the digit to be dropped is 5, the most common practice, which produces balanced result, is to use nearest even number for the previous digit, *e.g.*, 38.275 will become 38.28 and 38.285 will also be taken as 38.28.

2.3 CONCEPT OF ERRORS IN MEASUREMENTS

Different conditions discussed in Sec.2.1 under which the measurements are made, cause variations in measurements, and therefore, no measured quantity is completely determinable. A fixed value of a quantity concieved as its *true value*, can never be measured, as some errors will always creep in during its measurement, and what we get is nothing more than an *estimate* of the true value.

The difference between the measured quantity x and its true value τ is known as *error* ε, *i.e.*,

$$\varepsilon = x - \tau \qquad \text{...(2.1)}$$

Mathematically the measurement or observation is a variable, and study of observational errors and their behaviour is essentially the study of observations itself. *Theory of errors* deals with the study of observational errors.

Since the true value of a measurement cannot be determined, the exact value of ε can never be found out. However, if we can obtain a good estimate $\hat{x}$ of τ, then $\hat{x}$ can be used as a reference to express the variation in observed values x. Therefore, if we define υ as *residual*, then

$$\upsilon = \hat{x} - x \qquad \text{...(2.2)}$$

The residuals express the variations in the measurements. The quantity ($\hat{e}$) equal to ($-\upsilon$) is called *correction* to the measured quantity or *residual error, i.e.*,

$$(-\hat{e}) = \hat{x} - x$$

or Residual = $\hat{x} - x$

and residual error = $x - \hat{x}$.

2.4 TYPES OF ERRORS

Errors have been traditionally classified into the following three types:

1. Gross errors (blunders or mistakes),
2. Systematic errors, and
3. Random or accidental errors.

Gross Errors

Gross errors are, in fact, not errors at all, but results of mistakes that are due to the carelessness of the observer. Pointing on the wrong survey target, taking incorrect reading on the scale, reading on the wrong scale, and wrong recording the value of reading, are some examples of blunders or mistakes. The blunders or mistakes generally result into large errors which can easily be detected compared to small errors.

Good field procedures are designed to assist in detecting the gross errors. These may be

(*a*) Careful checking of all pointings on survey targets.
(*b*) Taking multiple readings on scales and checking for reasonable consistency.
(*c*) Verifying recorded data by reading scales.
(*d*) Taking repeated measurements independently and checking for consistency.
(*e*) Using simple geometric and algebraic checks such as sum of all the angles taken at a station is 360°, sum of three angles in a plane triangle is 180°.

The gross errors must be detected and eliminated from the survey measurements before such measurements can be used.

Systematic Errors

The errors which are systematic or follow some pattern, are termed as *systematic errors*. Such errors are always according to some deterministic system, and can be expressed by functional relationship. Measurement of distance by a too short tape and expansion of steel tape with respect to temperature, are the examples of systematic errors. Such errors are of a constant nature, and hence can be computed using the functional relationships, and the measurement can be corrected for them.

The personal bias of an observer, and imperfect conditions of the instruments also lead to systematic errors. Systematic errors also occur through simplification of geometry such as considering a plane triangle instead of spherical triangle.

Like the gross errors, the systematic errors must also be detected and eliminated from the survey measurements before adjusting the remaining errors.

Random Errors

After all mistakes are detected and removed, and the measurements are corrected for all known systematic errors, there will still remain some variations in measurements that result from observational errors. These errors do not have any known functional relationship based on a deterministic system and have random behaviour, and therefore, are known as *random errors*. As stated earlier that a measurement is looked upon mathematically as a variable, the measurement having a component of error which behaves like a random variable, itself becomes a random variable.

Random errors, often called as accidental errors, are unpredictable in regard to both size and algebraic sign. They are truely accidental and cannot be avoided. The general behaviour of the random errors is that

(*i*) a plus error will occur as frequently as will a minus error,
(*ii*) small errors will occur more frequently than large errors, and
(*iii*) very large errors do not occur at all, or their chance to occur is remote.

Whereas systematic errors are dealt with mathematically using functional relationships or models, random errors use probability models.

Theory of errors discussed in Chapter 2 of *Higher Surveying* by the author, deals with random errors.

2.5 CONCEPT OF PROBABILITY IN SURVEY MEASUREMENTS

A survey measurement finally left with only random errors, is a random variable just as number of dots on the top face of a dice. In order to understand the random nature of a survey measurement, it may be measured repeatedly, and its frequency distribution describing its random variation is studied. A distance of about 510 m is measured 200 times, and the measurements free of gross errors and corrected for systematic errors, are presented in Table 2.1.

Table 2.1 Repeated measurements of a distance

Measured values of distance (m)	Number of measurements (frequency = f)	Relative frequency ($R = f/\Sigma f$)
510.11	1	0.005
510.12	3	0.015
510.13	7	0.035
510.14	18	0.090
510.15	21	0.105
510.16	35	0.175
510.17	39	0.195
510.18	30	0.150
510.19	23	0.115
510.20	10	0.050
510.21	11	0.055
510.22	0	0.000
510.23	2	0.010
	$\Sigma f = 200$	$\Sigma R = 1$

In Table 2.1, the relative frequency for a given interval is an indication of probability implied by the following equation.

$$P(E) \text{ [probability of a favourable outcome]} = \frac{f \text{ [number of favourable outcomes]}}{n \text{ [number of all possible outcomes]}} \quad ...(2.3)$$

For example, for the inclusive interval 510.16 m to 510.169 m there are $f = 35$ observations. Therefore, the corresponding relative frequency R is

$$R = \frac{f}{n} = \frac{35}{200} = 0.175$$

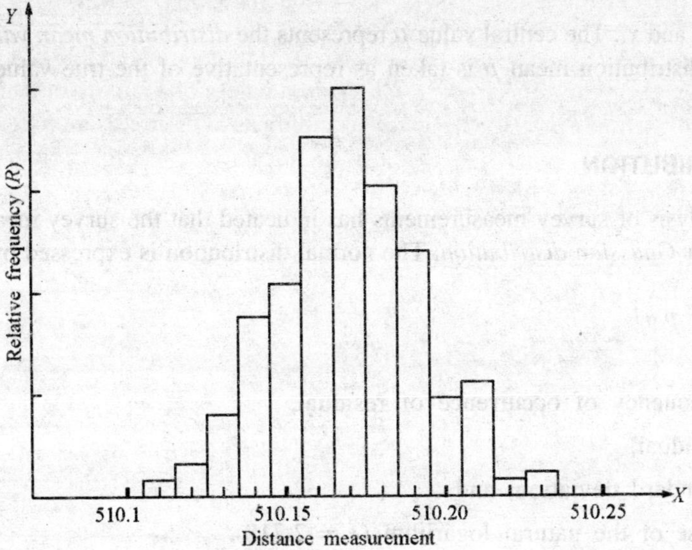

Fig. 2.2 Histogram

A diagram (Fig. 2.2), known as *frequency distribution* or more frequently *histogram,* can be constructed between the given class intervals and corresponding relative frequencies. It is found that the frequency distribution is centered on or near the value 510.175 m which is mean of all the readings. The highest frequencies of occurrence are at or near the central value. An interesting point to note is that the mean value has the highest relative frequency.

If the number of repeated measurements are increased to a very large number, and the class interval is made narrow, it will be found that each relative frequency approaches to a stable limit which is the *probability*. In such case the histogram approaches to the appearance of a curve, known as *probability distribution curve* or *probability density function curve* shown in Fig. 2.3. The area under the curve between two measured values of a distance, x_1 and x_2, is the probability of a measurement falling

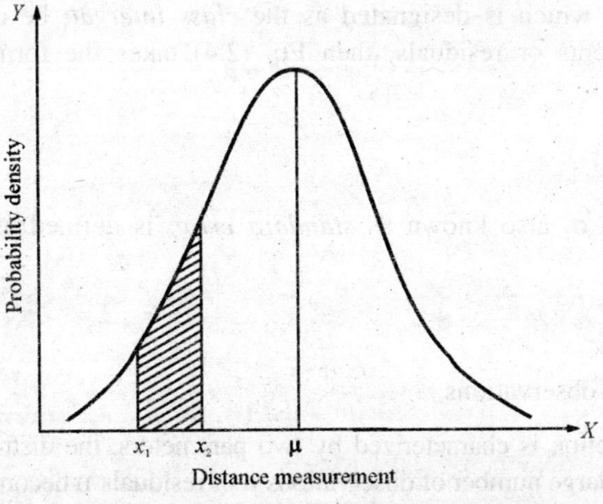

Fig. 2.3 Probability density function curve

between the values x_1 and x_2. The central value μ represents the *distribution mean value* of the distance measurements. The distribution mean μ is taken as representative of the true value of the measured distance.

2.6 NORMAL DISTRIBUTION

The statistical analysis of survey measurements has indicated that the survey measurements follow *normal distribution* or *Gaussian distribution*. The normal distribution is expressed by

$$y = \frac{1}{\sigma\sqrt{2\pi}} e^{-\frac{1}{2}\left(\frac{\upsilon}{\sigma}\right)^2} \qquad \text{...(2.4)}$$

where y = the frequency of occurrence of residual,

υ = the residual,

σ = the standard deviation, and

e = the base of the natural logarithm (e = 2.718).

Fig. 2.4 shows a normal distribution curve.

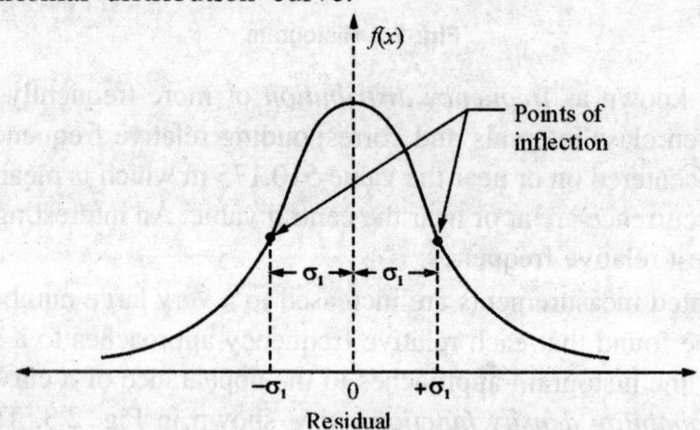

Fig. 2.4 Normal distribution curve

If the abscissa interval which is designated as the *class interval*, be denoted by *I*, and *n* be the number of measurements or residuals, then Eq. (2.4) takes the form

$$y = \frac{nI}{\sigma\sqrt{2\pi}} e^{-\frac{1}{2}\left(\frac{\upsilon}{\sigma}\right)^2} \qquad \text{...(2.5)}$$

The *standard deviation* σ, also known as *standard error,* is defined as

$$\sigma = \pm\sqrt{\frac{\Sigma\upsilon^2}{n-1}} \qquad \text{...(2.6)}$$

where n = number of observations.

The normal density function is characterized by two parameters, the distribution mean μ, and the standard deviation σ. For a large number of observations μ of residuals υ becomes zero. σ is also termed as *root-mean square* (R.M.S.) *error*. The square of standard deviation σ^2 is called the *variance*.

The standard deviation is a measure of the spread or dispersion of the probability distribution, and reflects the degree of variation in the measurement. If the repeated measurements are closely clustered together as shown in Fig. 2.5, they are said to have high precision and if they are widely spread apart, they have low precision.

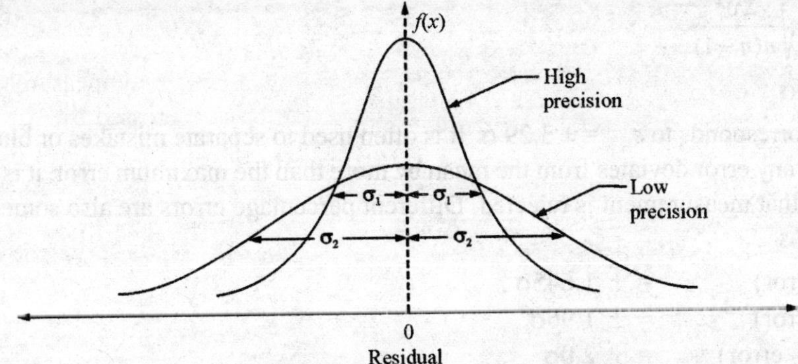

Fig. 2.5 Precision of measurements

There are some other indicators of precision, and are briefly given below.

Variance which is expressed as

$$V = \sigma^2$$

$$= \frac{\Sigma \upsilon^2}{n-1} \qquad \text{...(2.7)}$$

is also used as a measure of dispersion or spread.

Standard error of the mean expressed by

$$\sigma_m = \pm\sqrt{\frac{\Sigma \upsilon^2}{n\,(n-1)}}$$

$$= \pm\frac{\sigma}{\sqrt{n}} \qquad \text{...(2.8)}$$

is indicator of the limits of the errors found within which the true value of the mean will lie with a certainty of 68.3% of its being correct.

Standard error of the single measurement expressed by

$$\sigma_1 = \pm\sqrt{\frac{\Sigma \upsilon^2}{n-1}} \qquad \text{...(2.9)}$$

is equal to standard *error* σ. The two terms are used synonymously.

Most probable error expressed by

$$e = \pm\, 0.6745\sqrt{\frac{\Sigma \upsilon^2}{(n-1)}}$$

$$e = \pm\, 0.6745\,\sigma \qquad \text{...(2.10)}$$

is defined as the error for which there are equal chances of its being less than and more than the probable error. It is also called 50% error, and expressed as E_{50}.

Most probable error of the mean is expressed as

$$e_m = \pm 0.6745\sqrt{\frac{\Sigma \upsilon^2}{n(n-1)}}$$

$$= \pm 0.6745\sigma_m \qquad ...(2.11)$$

Maximum error corresponds to $e_{max} = \pm 3.29\,\sigma$. It is often used to separate mistakes or blunders from the random errors. If any error deviates from the mean by more than the maximum error, it is considered as a gross error, and that measurement is rejected. Different percentage errors are also sometimes used. They are expressed as

(*i*) E_{90} (90% error) $= \pm 1.645\sigma$ ...(2.12)
(*ii*) E_{95} (95% error) $= \pm 1.96\sigma$ ...(2.13)
(*iii*) $E_{95.5}$ (95.5% error) $= \pm 2.0\sigma$ ...(2.14)
(*iv*) $E_{99.7}$ (99.7% error) $= \pm 3.0\sigma$ ...(2.15)

ILLUSTRATIVE EXAMPLES

Example 2.1

The distance between two points *A* and *B* was measured 10 times under identical conditions, and the measured values were recorded as

53.56 m, 53.52 m, 53.54 m , 53.58 m, 53.55 m, 53.60 m, 53.54 m, 53.57 m, 53.54 m, 53.56 m.

Determine the following:

(*i*) The standard error
(*ii*) The standard error of the mean
(*iii*) The most probable error
(*iv*) The most probable error of the mean
(*v*) The variance
(*vi*) The maximum error.

Solution:

Determine the mean μ of the measurements, residuals υ, and υ^2 as shown in Table 2.2.

Number of observations $n = 10$

(*i*) Standard error or standard deviation (Eq. 2.6)

$$\sigma = \pm\sqrt{\frac{\Sigma \upsilon^2}{n-1}}$$

$$= \pm\sqrt{\frac{4.800 \times 10^{-3}}{10-1}} = \pm\ \mathbf{0.023\ m.}$$

Table 2.2

Measurements (x) (m)	Residuals ($\upsilon = \mu - x$)	υ^2
53.56	– 0.004	1.600×10^{-5}
53.52	0.036	1.296×10^{-3}
53.54	0.016	2.560×10^{-4}
53.58	– 0.024	5.760×10^{-4}
53.55	0.006	3.600×10^{-5}
53.60	– 0.044	1.936×10^{-3}
53.54	0.016	2.560×10^{-4}
53.57	– 0.014	1.960×10^{-4}
53.54	0.016	3.600×10^{-5}
53.56	– 0.004	1.960×10^{-4}
$\mu = \dfrac{535.56}{10} = 53.556$	$\Sigma\upsilon = -0.000$	$\Sigma\upsilon^2 = 4.800 \times 10^{-3}$

(*ii*) Standard error of the mean (Eq. (2.8))

$$\sigma_m = \pm\sqrt{\frac{\Sigma\upsilon^2}{n(n-1)}}$$

$$= \pm\sqrt{\frac{4.800\times10^{-3}}{10\times(10-1)}} = \pm\ \mathbf{0.007\ m.}$$

(*iii*) Most probable error (Eq. (2.10))

$$e = \pm 0.6745\sigma$$

$$= \pm 0.6745 \times 0.023 = \mathbf{\pm 0.016\ m.}$$

(*iv*) Most probable error of the mean (Eq. (2.11))

$$e_m = \pm\ 0.6745\ \sigma_m$$

$$= \pm\ 0.6745 \times 0.007 = \mathbf{\pm 0.005\ m.}$$

(*v*) Variance (Eq. (2.7))

$$V = \sigma^2$$

$$= (\pm\ 0.023)^2 = \mathbf{0.0005\ m^2.}$$

(*vi*) Maximum error

$$e_{\max} = \pm\ 3.29\sigma$$

$$= \pm\ 3.29 \times 0.023 = \pm\ \mathbf{0.076\ m.}$$

Example 2.2

The following eight measurements of a horizontal angle were made:

S.No.	Horizontal angle (*A*)
1	32°22′10″
2	32°21′50″
3	32°21′40″
4	32°22′00″
5	32°21′50″
6	32°22′00″
7	32°22′10″
8	32°22′20″

Compute the standard deviation, the most probable error, and the maximum error.

Solution:

The mean, $\mu = \frac{\Sigma A}{n} = 32°22'00''$

The residuals can be computed from

$\upsilon = \mu - A$, thus

$\upsilon_1 = +10'', \upsilon_2 = -10'', \upsilon_3 = -20'', \upsilon_4 = 0'', \upsilon_5 = -10'', \upsilon_6 = 0'', \upsilon_7 = +10'', \upsilon_8 = +20''$

$\Sigma\upsilon^2 = 1200$

The standard deviation from Eq. (2.6) is

$$\sigma = \pm\sqrt{\frac{\Sigma\upsilon^2}{n-1}} = \pm\sqrt{\frac{1200}{7}}$$

$$= \pm\ \mathbf{13.1''}.$$

The most probable error of the mean from Eq. (2.11) is

$$e = \pm\ 0.6745\sigma_m$$

$$= \pm 0.6745\frac{\sigma}{\sqrt{n}}$$

$$= \pm\ 0.6745 \times \frac{13.1}{\sqrt{8}}$$

$$= \pm\ \mathbf{3.1''}$$

The maximum error

$$e_{max} = \pm\ 0.29\sigma$$
$$= \pm\ 3.29 \times 13.1$$
$$= \pm\ \mathbf{43.1''}.$$

2.7 PROPAGATION OF ERROR

In surveying the two basic quantities which are measured, are distances and angles. Often these basic field measurements are used to calculate other quantities such as horizontal distances from measured slope distances, elevations from measured difference in height, areas, volumes, etc. The calculation of other quantities using the measured quantities is done through mathematical relationship between them. Since the measured quantities have errors, it is inevitable that the quantities computed from them will not have errors. Evaluation of the errors in the computed quantities as functions of the errors in the measurements, is called *error propagation*.

Let y be a quantity to be computed using a measured quantity x which has error dx through the relationship

$$y = ax + b \qquad ...(2.16)$$

The coefficient a and the constant b are assumed to be free of errors.

Now if x_t and y_t are the true values of x and y, respectively, then

$$x = x_t + dx \qquad ...(2.17)$$
$$y_t = ax_t + b \qquad ...(2.18)$$

But from Eq. (2.16) and Eq. (2.17)

$$y = a\,(x_t + dx) + b$$
$$= ax_t + adx + b$$
$$= (ax_t + b) + adx$$
$$= y_t + adx$$

If dy is the error in y, then from Fig. 2.6, we get

$$\tan\theta = \frac{dy}{dx} = a$$

or $$dy = adx \qquad ...(2.19)$$

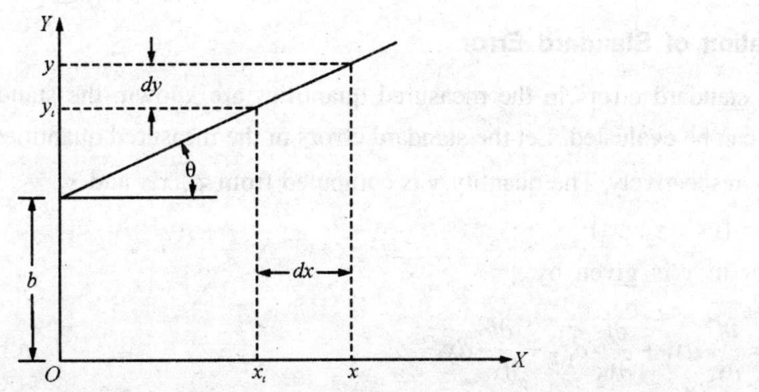

Fig. 2.6 Propagation of error in linear function

or $$dy = \left(\frac{dy}{dx}\right)dx \qquad ...(2.20)$$

The Eq. (2.19) or (2.20) gives the error dy in the computed quantity y. In Eq. (2.19), the error function $dy = adx$ is linear in error dx in identical manner to $y = ax + b$. This will not be true in case of nonlinear functions such as $y = x^2$.

Let us take an example of a nonlinear function.

$$y = x^2 \qquad ...(2.21)$$

$$y_t = x_t^2$$

or $$y = (y_t + dy) = (x_t + dx)^2$$

or $$y_t + dy = x_t^2 + 2x_t dx + (dx)^2$$

or $$dy = 2x_t dx + (dx)^2 \qquad ...(2.22)$$

Neglecting $(dx)^2$ as dx is a small quantity, we get

$$dy = 2x_t dx \qquad ...(2.23)$$

$$\frac{dy}{dx} = 2x_t$$

From Eq. (2.23), we find that $2x_t$ is the derivative of y with respect to x, evaluated at $x = x_t$.

$$\left(\frac{dy}{dx}\right)_{x=x_t} = 2x_t$$

Thus, from Eq. (2.22)

$$dy = \frac{dy}{dx}dx + (dx)^2 \qquad ...(2.24)$$

Again neglecting $(dx)^2$, we get

$$dy = \frac{dy}{dx}dx \qquad ...(2.25)$$

with the assumption that $(dx)^2$ is negligible.

Propagation of Standard Error

If the standard errors in the measured quantities are known, the standard error in the computed quantity can be evaluated. Let the standard errors in the measured quantities x_1, x_2, and x_3 be σ_{x_1}, σ_{x_2}, and σ_{x_3}, respectively. The quantity y is computed from x_1, x_2, and x_3.

Thus $y = f(x_1, x_2, x_3)$

The error in y is given by

$$dy = \frac{\partial f}{\partial x_1}dx_1 + \frac{\partial f}{\partial x_2}dx_2 + \frac{\partial f}{\partial x_3}dx_3 \qquad ...(2.26)$$

and the standard error in y is obtained from the following equation:

$$\sigma_y^2 = \left[\frac{\partial f}{\partial x_1}\sigma_{x_1}\right]^2 + \left[\frac{\partial f}{\partial x_2}\sigma_{x_2}\right]^2 + \left[\frac{\partial f}{\partial x_3}\sigma_{x_3}\right]^2 \qquad ...(2.27)$$

ILLUSTRATIVE EXAMPLES

Example 2.3

The dimensions of a trapezoidal land parcel is shown in Fig. 2.7. What is the ordinate y for a measured distance x = 37.325 m? If the error in the measured distance is 0.015 m, what would be the corresponding error in the calculated distance y ?

Solution:

Let us represent

$$y = ax + b$$

From Fig. 2.7, we have

$$a = \tan\theta = \frac{EC}{DE} = \frac{80-50}{100} = 0.3 \text{ (exact)}$$

and b = AD = 50 (exact)

As a and b have exact values, therefore, they are errorless.

$$y_{(x=37.325)} = 0.3 \times 37.325 + 50$$

$$= \mathbf{61.1975\ m}$$

and error in y for dx = 0.015 m is

$$dy = adx$$

$$= 0.3 \times 0.015$$

$$= \mathbf{0.0045\ m.}$$

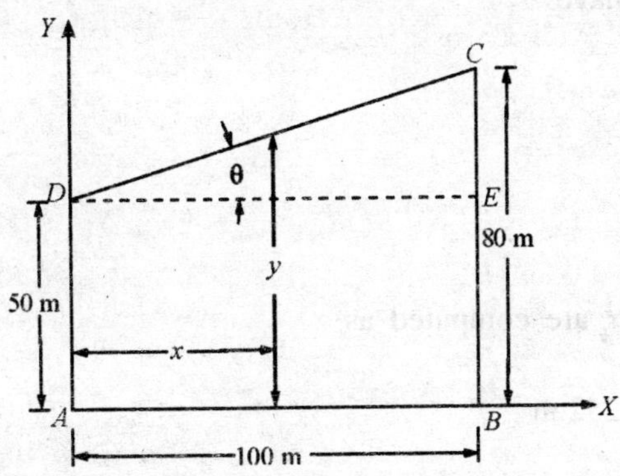

Fig. 2.7

Example 2.4

A measured side of a square piece of land is 140.140 m, and is in error by 0.030 m. What is the corresponding error in the computed area of the land?

Solution:

If x is the length of the side, the area is given by

$$y = x^2$$

$$\frac{dy}{dx} = 2x$$

$$\left(\frac{dy}{dx}\right)_{x=140.140} = 2 \times 140.140 = 280.28$$

Error in y will be

$$dy = \frac{dy}{dx} dx$$

$$= 280.28 \times 0.030 \text{ m}$$

$$= \mathbf{8.408 \ m^2.}$$

Example 2.5

The measured sides of a rectangular tract are 30.270 m and 56.070 m. The measurement was made using a 30 m metallic tape, too short by 0.025 m. What would be the error in the area of the tract.

Solution:

Let the two sides be x_1 = 30.270 m and x_2 = 56.070 m, then the area

$$y = x_1 x_2 \qquad \text{... }(a)$$

and the error in y

$$dy = \frac{\partial y}{\partial x_1} dx_1 + \frac{\partial y}{\partial x_2} dx_2 \qquad \text{... }(b)$$

Now from Eq. (a), we have

$$\frac{\partial y}{\partial x_1} = x_2 = 56.070 \text{ m}$$

$$\frac{\partial y}{\partial x_2} = x_1 = 30.270 \text{ m}$$

Errors dx_1 in x_1, and dx_2 in x_2 are computed as

$$dx_1 = \frac{0.025}{30} \times 30.270 = 0.0252 \text{ m}$$

and $dx_2 = \frac{0.025}{30} \times 56.070 = 0.0467 \text{ m}$.

Therefore, from Eq. (*b*), the error in the area is

$$dy = 56.070 \times 0.0252 + 30.270 \times 0.0467$$

$$= \mathbf{2.827\ m^2.}$$

Example 2.6

The angle α is related to the angles β and γ as below:

$$\alpha = 3\beta\gamma$$

The observed values of β and γ are 30″ and 18″, respectively. If $\sigma_\beta = \pm\ 0.02''$ and $\sigma_\gamma = \pm\ 0.04''$, determine σ_α.

Solution:

It is given that

$$\alpha = 3\beta\gamma$$

From Eq. (2.27), we have

$$\sigma_\alpha^2 = \left[\frac{\partial \alpha}{\partial \beta}\sigma_\beta\right]^2 + \left[\frac{\partial \alpha}{\partial \gamma}\sigma_\gamma\right]^2$$

$$= \left[\frac{\partial (3\beta\gamma)}{\partial \beta}\sigma_\beta\right]^2 + \left[\frac{\partial (3\beta\gamma)}{\partial \gamma}\sigma_\gamma\right]^2$$

$$= (3\gamma\sigma_\beta)^2 + (3\beta\sigma_\gamma)^2$$

$$\sigma_\alpha = \sqrt{(3 \times 18 \times 0.02)^2 + (3 \times 30 \times 0.04)^2}$$

$$= \mathbf{\pm\ 3.76''.}$$

QUESTIONS AND PROBLEMS

2.1 Write a brief note on the role of errors in survey measurements.

2.2 What do you understand by significant figures and rounding off numbers? How these affect the computations?

2.3 Write a short note on the classification of errors. Discuss each giving suitable examples.

2.4 Discuss the application of theory of probability to the random errors.

2.5 Write a note on the normal distribution.

2.6 Differentiate between precision and accuracy.

2.7 Explain the following terms:

(*a*) Survey Measurement, (*b*) True value, (*c*) True error, (*d*) Residual, (*e*) Standard deviation, (*f*) Variance, (*g*) Standard error of the mean, (*h*) Standard error of the single measurement, (*i*) Most probable error.

2.8 Write a brief note on propagation of errors.

2.9 The difference in elevation Δh between two fixed points was measured repeatedly for a total of 16 times with the following results:

n	Δh (m)	n	Δh (m)
1	7.8621	9	7.8631
2	7.8632	10	7.8641
3	7.8630	11	7.8630
4	7.8646	12	7.8640
5	7.8642	13	7.8630
6	7.8652	14	7.8637
7	7.8620	15	7.8633
8	7.8638	16	7.8630

Compute the mean and standard error of the mean of these observations.

2.10 The following independent readings in seconds, were taken in order to determine the precision of the setting of the micrometer of 1″ direction theodolite:

52.9	54.9	54.1	52.1	54.1
55.0	52.9	55.4	51.5	53.4
53.9	52.1	53.5	52.1	51.0
54.9	54.1	50.8	50.3	54.6
54.1	50.2	50.0	55.9	53.1
54.2	51.9	52.4	51.0	53.9
52.3	51.3	53.2	51.6	53.1
53.0	52.1	50.3	51.9	53.6
52.2	54.6	51.1	51.1	54.9
51.6	51.4	49.9	53.6	54.1
53.5	53.7	50.3	53.0	52.6
55.4	54.4	51.6	51.7	48.9
54.9	51.8	49.2	56.3	52.7
50.7	48.2	50.6	52.2	53.1
52.5	50.7	53.1	57.1	51.9
52.3	54.2	52.9	51.6	50.9
52.9	54.0	54.3	50.1	51.9
51.3	53.8	53.3	54.2	54.1
55.9	55.1	47.4	56.2	53.2
48.8	52.9	50.5	53.9	53.5

(*i*) Plot a histogram for these readings, with a class interval of 1″, beginning with 47″.

(*ii*) Compute the mean value of the readings, the standard error, and standard error of the mean.

(*iii*) Using the standard error of the set of readings, compute ordinates of the normal distribution curve representing the set.

(*iv*) Plot the curve on the histogram in (*i*).

(*v*) Locate the positions of $+\sigma$ and $-\sigma$ on the curve in (*iii*).

2.11 The volume of a pyramid is 1/3 b^2h. The base of the pyramid is a square of measured side b as 30.4 ± 0.8 cm. The height h of the pyramid is measured as 25.0 ± 0.05 cm. Compute the volume of the pyramid and the standard error of the computed volume.

2.12 Calculate the standard error of the volume of a cuboid whose sides x, y, and z have the values and standard errors as under:

$x = 60 \pm 0.03$ cm

$y = 50 \pm 0.02$ cm

$z = 40 \pm 0.01$ cm.

2.13 Calculate the area of the field shown in Fig. 2.8, and its standard error, if the measured values of a and b with their standard errors are as under:

$a = 102.10 \pm 0.02$ m

$b = 260.75 \pm 0.03$ m.

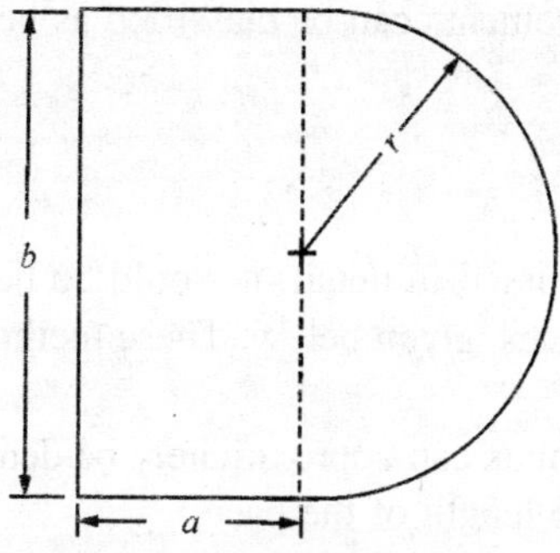

Fig. 2.8

2.14 Three sides of a triangle were measured as $a = 248.25 \pm 0.04$ m, $b = 107.10 \pm 0.02$ m, and $c = 336.65 \pm 0.05$ m. Compute the angles in the triangle with their standard errors.

2.15 Compute the area of the triangle in Problem 2.14 and its standard error.

2.16 The two sides and the included angle of a triangle are measured as under:
$a = 757.64 \pm 0.045$ m, $b = 946.70 \pm 0.055$ m, and $C = 54°18' \pm 25''$.
Compute the area of the triangle and its standard error.

3

MEASUREMENT OF HORIZONTAL DISTANCES

3.1 GENERAL

The determination of the distance between the given points on or above the surface of the earth, is one of the basic operations of surveying. For mapping purposes all the measured distances are finally reduced to their equivalent horizontal distances except those which are measured to determine the differences in level of the points. This may be achieved either by evolving measurement procedures to produce the horizontal distance or by computing the horizontal distance from a measured slope distance. The measurement of vertical distances is discussed in Chapter 6 on levelling.

3.2 METHODS OF DISTANCE MEASUREMENTS

The methods of making linear measurements can be classified as below:

1. Direct methods,
2. Indirect methods, and
3. E.D.M. methods.

Before the above methods are discussed in detail, it would be better to have some idea of approximate methods of measuring the distances, given below. These methods may be used in reconnaissance, or for detecting major mistakes.

Pacing: A distance between two points can approximately be determined by counting the number of paces, and multiplying it with average length of the pace.

Passometer: It is a small instrument which counts the number of paces.

Pedometer: This instrument directly gives the distance by multiplying the number of paces with the average pace length of the person carrying the instrument.

Odometer: It is a simple device which can be attached to the wheel of a bicycle or any such vehicle. It measures the distance by counting the number of revolutions made by the wheel to which it is attached, and multiplying the number of revolutions with the perimeter of the wheel.

Direct Methods of Distance Measurements

The direct distance measurement in the field is done using *chain* or *tape,* and the process of measuring the distance is known as *chaining* when a chain is used and *taping* when a tape is used. Formerly, for the survey of ordinary precision, the engineer's chain or Gunter's chain was used to measure the length of a line. For measurements of the highest precision special bars or tapes were used. The engineer's chain is 100 ft long, and has 100 links, each 1 ft long. At every 10 links brass tags are fastened. Notches on the tags indicate the number of 10 link segments between the tag and the end of the tape. The

Gunter's chain, also known as surveyor's chain, is 66 ft long, and divided into 100 links, each link of 0.66 ft. In chaining, the distances are recorded in chains and links.

The precision of distance measured with tapes depends upon the degree of refinement with which the measurements are taken. It is possible to get a relative precision better than 1/1,000,000 in distance measurements using tapes by taking extreme care to eliminate all possible errors.

Indirect Methods of Distance Measurements

In the indirect methods, the distances are not directly measured in the field. The distances are computed indirectly using other observed quantities. Such methods are discussed in Chapter 8 on tacheometry.

EDM Method of Distance Measurements

The electromagnetic or electronic distance measuring instruments referred to as EDM's are practically replacing the measurement of distances using tapes. There is a large variety of such instruments, and depending upon the precision required, a particular EDM instrument should be employed. The EDM instruments and their principles of working are discussed in Chapter 11 of *Higher Surveying* by the author.

3.3 EQUIPMENT FOR DISTANCE MEASUREMENTS

The direct distance measurements are made using measuring tapes. The tapes are made of a variety of material, length, and weight, and some of those which are commonly used in surveying, are briefly discussed below.

Linen tape: Linen tape is a painted and varnished strip of woven linen about 15 mm wide, attached to a spindle in a leather case into which it is wound when not in use (Fig. 3.1). These tapes are light and handy but not very accurate as they are subject to serious variations in length.

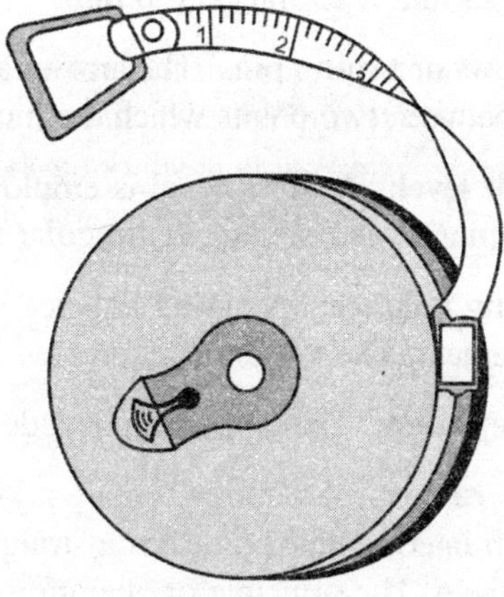

Fig. 3.1 Tape

Metallic tapes: These are woven ribbons of water proof fabric into which are woven thin brass or bronze wires to prevent stretching. Like linen tapes, these are also attached to a spindle in a leather, plastic, or metal case. The metallic tapes are 10, 20, 30, or 50 m long. Nonmetallic glass fibre tapes which are quite flexible, strong and nonconductive, are also available, and are used in the vicinity of power lines or electrical equipment.

Invar tapes: For high precision measurements such as those for base lines, the tapes made of the alloy *invar*, is used. It has a very low coefficient of thermal expansion, about 1.2×10^{-7} per degree centigrade.

Other Equipment for Distance Measurement

For direct measurement of long lines of more than a tape length, the following accessories are used (Fig. 3.2):

(*i*) Plumb bob

(*ii*) Ranging rods and poles

(*iii*) Pegs
(*iv*) Arrows or taping pins
(*v*) Spirit level
(*vi*) Spring balance
(*vii*) Tape clamp
(*viii*) Line ranger.

Plumb bob: The plumb bob is a pointed metal weight used to locate the horizontal position of a point above the ground.

Ranging rods and poles: These may be metallic, wooden, or of fibreglass. They are used as temporary signals to indicate the location of points or the direction of lines. The common length of the ranging rods is 2 or 3 m. Usually they are painted with alternate bands of white and red or black.

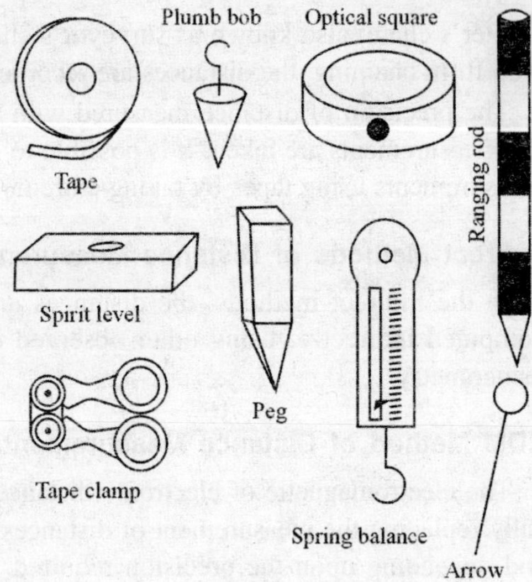

Fig. 3.2 Equipment for taping

Pegs: The wooden pegs are used to mark the end points of a survey line or positions of the survey stations. They are generally square in section, and tapered at one end. The common size of the wooden pegs is 25 mm × 25 mm × 150 mm.

Arrows or taping pins: The arrows are employed to mark the ends of the tape during the process of taping between two points which are more than a tape length apart. They are usually 25 to 35 cm long.

Spirit level: A Spirit level is employed to keep the two ends of the tape in same horizontal plane when taping over a sloping or irregular terrain. A hand level is also sometimes used.

Spring balance: A spring balance is used to apply desired pull or tension to the tape during the measurement. The tension is expressed in kilograms.

Tape clamp: The tape clamp is a device for holding a tape at any place other than at an end.

Line ranger: An optical square a kind of line ranger is an optical instrument, and is employed to establish intermediate points on a straight line joining two distant points without having to sight from one of them. The principle of operation can easily be understood from Fig. 3.3.

To range a point *P* on the line *AB*, two ranging rods are fixed at the two ends *A* and *B*, and the observer holds the line ranger at *P* very near to the line by eye judgement (Fig. 3.3a). If *P* is not on the line *AB*, the two images of the ranging rods at *A* and *B*, will not be seen in one vertical line as shown in Fig. 3.3b. The line ranger is moved back and forth along a line approximately at right angles to *AB*, until the images of *A* and *B* appear to be in one vertical line as shown in Fig. 3.3c. The point *P* is then transferred to the ground with the help of a plumb bob.

3.4 PROCEDURES FOR DISTANCE MEASUREMENTS

To measure the length of a survey line, the chain or tape has to be stretched from end to end. This is possible only when the length of the survey line is less than the tape length. However, if the length of the line is greater than the tape length, the length of the line cannot be measured accurately without establishing intermediate points on the line by the method of ranging.

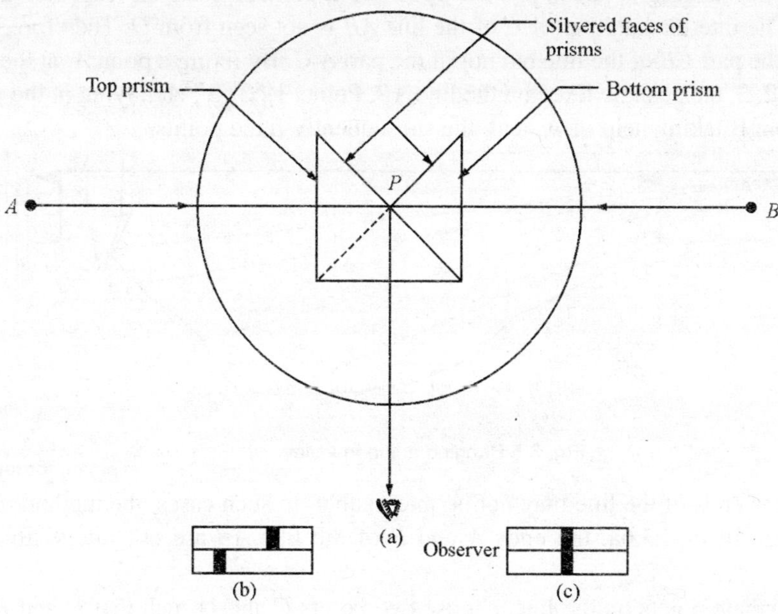

Fig. 3.3 Working principle of line ranger

Measuring a distance with chains was originally called chaining. The term is still in use and is often applied to the operation of measuring distances with tapes which is commonly termed as taping. The procedures discussed below are specific to chaining in chain surveying, and are equally applicable to taping.

Ranging

The term *ranging* is used to establish a set of intermediate points on a straight line whose two ends have already been fixed on the ground, whereas chaining means the measuring the length of a straight line with chain or tape. Chaining a long line necessarily involves ranging.

Let *A* and *B* are the two ends of a line *AB* as shown in Fig 3.4, and they are intervisible. On this line let three intermediate points *P*, *Q*, and *R* are to be established. To perform ranging for establishing the points *P*, *Q*, and *R*, the surveyor stands at a point *S*, close to the end *A* on the line *BA* produced. The assistant holds a ranging rod vertically, approximately near the line *AB*. By eye judgment the surveyor directs the assistant to move the ranging rod so that *A*, *P*, and *B* appear to be in one line. Similarly the other points *Q* and *R* are also fixed.

The procedure described above is also used to establish points 1 and 2 on either side of the ends *A* and *B* of the line.

Fig. 3.4 Ranging a line when its ends are intervisible

There may be a case when in a valley the whole length of the line is not visible from the ends of the line. In such cases, the ranging is accomplished by fixing a point A_1 near the edges of the valley as shown in Fig. 3.5. The intermediate part A_1C of the line AB is not seen from O. Therefore, the ranging is only possible for the part CB of the line but not of the part A_1C. By fixing a point A_1 at the edge of the valley, the points 1, 2, 3, etc., can be fixed on the line AB. Points 1′, 2′, 3′, etc., lying in the part A_1C are fixed by ranging from B taking help of A_1 and, the subsequently fixed points.

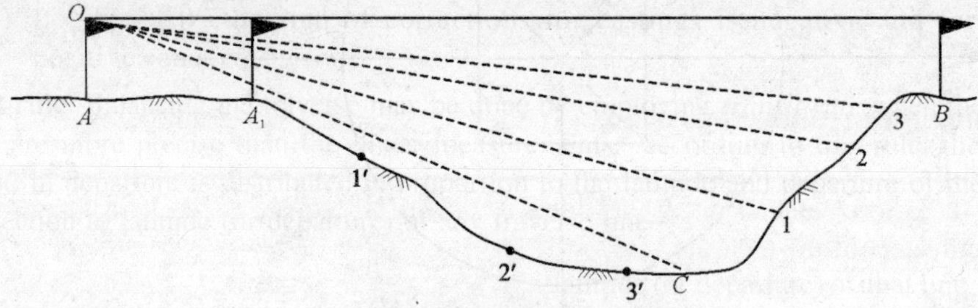

Fig. 3.5 Ranging a line in valley

In another case, the ends of the line may not be intervisible. In such cases, the method of *reciprocal ranging* is employed. In Fig. 3.6a, the ends A and B of the line AB are not intervisible due to an intervening hill.

To fix the intermediate points on the line, choose two points C and D such that D and B are visible from C and, C and A from D.

Let the initial selected position of C is C_1. Taking help of C_1 and B, range D at D_1. Then taking help of D_1 and A, range C_1 at C_2. By repeating this procedure the selected points move closer and closer to AB, and after a few repetitions, the points C and D are finally located on the line.

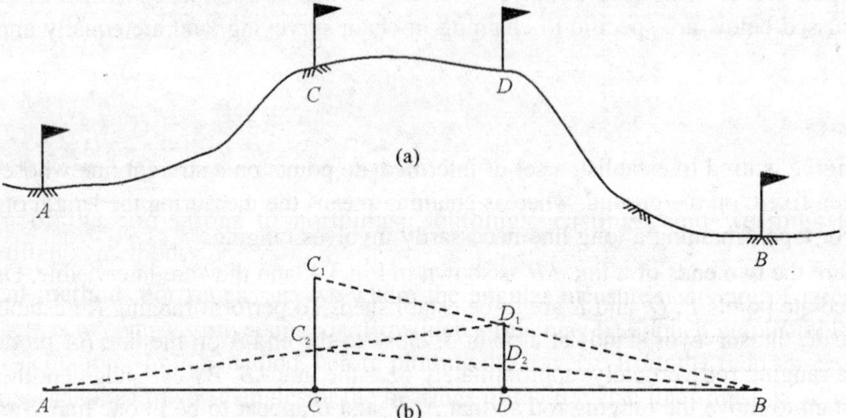

Fig. 3.6 Reciprocal ranging

Taping on a Flat Ground

The horizontal distance between the points can be measured with a tape directly when the length of the line is less than the length of the tape by laying straight the tape on the ground. If the length of the line is more than the length of the tape, the line is subdivided into parts of lengths less than the tape length. The intermediate points for the subdivision of the line, are fixed by ranging discussed in Sec. 3.4.1. In case of a moderately flat ground for obtaining better results, both the ends of the tape are kept at the same elevation using a hand level or by estimation, and transferring the ends of the tape on the ground by plumbing as shown in Fig. 3.7. The correction for sag discussed in Sec.3.5, is applied to the measured lengths for each span to get the final length of the line.

Fig. 3.7 Horizontal distance measurement on a moderately flat ground

Taping on a Sloping or Uneven Ground

If the slope of the ground is more than 3° or 1 in 20, there is considerable difference between the slope distance and the horizontal distance. One of the following procedures may be adopted to determine the horizontal equivalent of the measured slope distance in such cases:

1. Direct method
2. Indirect method.

Direct method: In the direct method, also known as *stepping method,* the horizontal equivalent of the slope distance is directly measured, as shown in Fig. 3.8a. It is more convenient to measure downhill than to measure uphill and, therefore, uphill measurement should be avoided as far as possible. In the case of downhill measurements, the horizontal distance is measured in steps as shown in Fig. 3.8a using the procedure explained for taping on the flat ground.

For taping uphill as shown in Fig. 3.8b, the rear end of the tape is held at A' above A and the other end at B on the line AE, and the measurement proceeds upwards in similar manner as above.

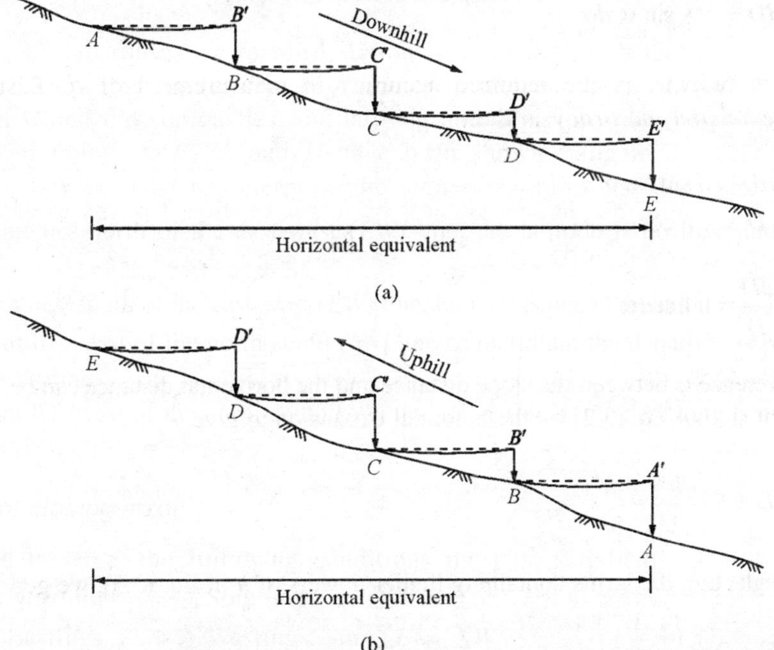

Fig. 3.8 Horizontal distance measurement on a sloping ground

Indirect method: In this method the slope distance S is measured directly with a tape, and the slope angle α shown in Fig. 3.9, is measured with some other instrument.

The horizontal equivalent is computed from

$$D = S \cos \alpha \quad \text{...(3.1)}$$

If any instrument for measuring the angle α is not available and the surveyor has hand level, the horizontal distance can be determined by measuring the difference in elevation h between the two ends of the line from the following expression:

$$D = \sqrt{S^2 - h^2} \quad \text{...(3.2)}$$

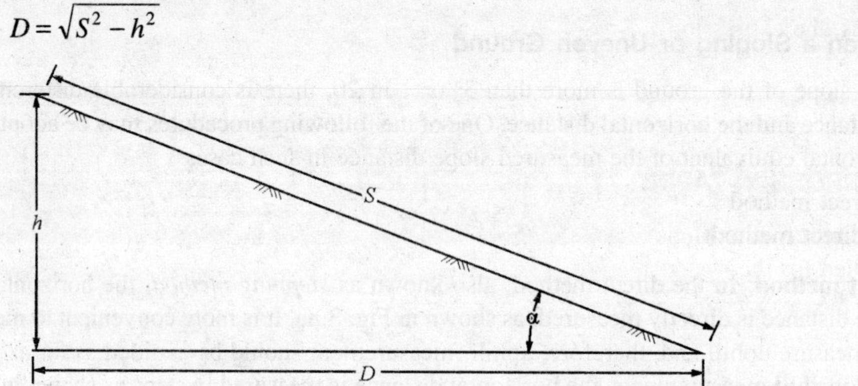

Fig. 3.9 Indirect measurement of horizontal distance

To determine the accuracy with which the vertical angle α must be measured in order to meet a given relative accuracy in the resulting horizontal distance, differentiate Eq. (3.1) with respect to α. Thus

$$dD = - S \sin \alpha \, d\alpha \quad \text{...(3.3)}$$

in which $d\alpha$ in radians, is the required accuracy in measurement of α. Disregarding the negative sign, the *relative accuracy* is then

$$\frac{dD}{D} = \frac{S \sin \alpha \, d\alpha}{S \cos \alpha}$$

or

$$\frac{dD}{D} = \tan \alpha \, d\alpha \quad \text{...(3.4)}$$

Further, the difference C between the slope distance and the horizontal distance can be determined by expanding the right side of Eq. (3.2) by the binomial expansion to give

$$D = S - \frac{h^2}{2S} - \frac{h^4}{8S^3} - \ldots.. \quad \text{...(3.5)}$$

Since $h << S$, neglecting the terms containing higher powers of h in Eq. (3.5), we get

$$S - D = \frac{h^2}{2S} \quad \text{...(3.6)}$$

or $$C = \frac{h^2}{2S} \qquad ...(3.7)$$

where $C = S - D$

Differentiating Eq. (3.7) with respect to h, we have

$$dC = \frac{hdh}{S}$$

Thus, the expression for relative accuracy is

$$\frac{dC}{S} = \frac{hdh}{S^2} \qquad ...(3.8)$$

3.5 ERRORS IN TAPING AND TAPE CORRECTIONS

The mistakes or blunders are the gross errors, and can easily be identified before any tape correction is applied for the systematic errors (*c.f.* Sec. 2.4). The gross errors in taping may be due to:

1. the displacement of arrows,
2. the omission of one or more units by miscounting,
3. reading numbers incorrectly,
4. calling numbers wrongly,
5. reading from the wrong end of the tape, and
6. wrong recording of readings, etc.

The systematic errors in taping and the respective tape corrections are discussed below. The tape corrections are required to be applied depending on the field conditions under which the measurements were carried out and the requirement of precision in measurements such as in the length of base line in triangulation system.

Correction for absolute length: If absolute (actual) length of the tape is different from the designated or nominal length of the tape, the difference between the two causes a systematic error. If a tape is in continuous use, due to wear and tear, stretch or shrink, the absolute length of the tape will become different from the designated length. The correction for this difference is also called as *correction for standardization,* and is determined from the following expression:

$$c_a = \frac{C}{l}L \qquad ...(3.9)$$

where

c_a = the correction for absolute length,
C = the correction per tape length,
l = the designated or nominal length of the tape, and
L = the measured length of the line.

If the absolute length is more than the nominal length, the sign of correction is positive and *vice versa.*

Correction for temperature: The tapes are standardized in the laboratory at a certain standard temperature. If the field temperature is different from the standard temperature, a correction known as correction for temperature has to be applied to the measured length of line. The temperature correction is given by:

$$c_t = \alpha\,(t_m - t_o)\,L \qquad \text{...(3.10)}$$

where

c_t = the correction for temperature,
α = the coefficient of linear expansion of tape material,
t_m = the mean temperature during the measurement, and
t_o = the standard temperature.

If t_m is more than t_o, the temperature correction is positive and *vice versa*. Thus, sign of c_t is same as that of $(T_m - t_o)$.

Correction for pull: The pull applied in the field during measurements, may be different from the standard pull at which the tape was standardized. This causes another correction known as correction for pull or tension, and is determined from the following expression:

$$c_p = \frac{(P - P_o)}{AE} L \qquad \text{...(3.11)}$$

where

c_p = the pull correction,
P = the pull applied in the field during measurement,
P_o = the standard pull,
A = the cross-section area of the tape, and
E = the modulus of elasticity of the tape material.

The sign of c_p will be same as that of $(P - P_o)$.

Correction for sag: When the measurement is made by stretching the tape above the ground, supports are needed at the ends of the tape. Consequently, the tape sags under its own weight, with the maximum dip occurring at the middle of the tape (Fig. 3.10), and the tape takes the shape of a catenary. This necessitates a correction known as correction for sag. It is given by

$$c_g = \frac{1}{24}\left[\frac{W}{P}\right]^2 L \qquad \text{...(3.12)}$$

where

c_g = the sag correction
W = the weight of the tape per span length, and
P = the pull applied during the measurement.

The sign of c_g is always negative.

If both the ends of the line are not at the same level, a further correction to c_g is required as below:

$$c_g' = c_g \cos^2\alpha \qquad \text{...(3.13)}$$

where α is the angle of slope between the end supports.

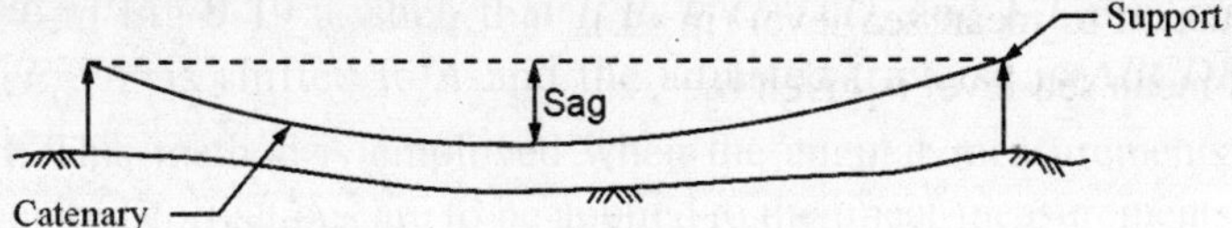

Fig. 3.10 Sagging of a tape

Correction for slope: If the two ends of the tape are at different elevations, the measured length needs a correction known as correction for slope. The expression given below is for the determination of this correction.

$$c_s = (1 - \cos\theta)\,L \quad (exact) \qquad ...(3.14)$$

$$c_s = \frac{h^2}{2L} \quad (approximate) \qquad ...(3.15)$$

where

c_s = the slope correction,

θ = the angle of the slope,

h = the difference in elevation of the two ends, and

L = the measured slope length.

c_g has always negative sign.

Correction for alignment: If the intermediate points are not in correct alignment with the ends of the line, or they are not on the line to be measured, a correction known as correction for alignment has to be applied to the measured length. It is computed from the following expression.

$$c_m = \frac{d^2}{2L} \quad (approximate) \qquad ...(3.16)$$

where

c_m = the correction for alignment, and

d = the distance by which the other end of the tape is out of alignment (Fig. 3.11).

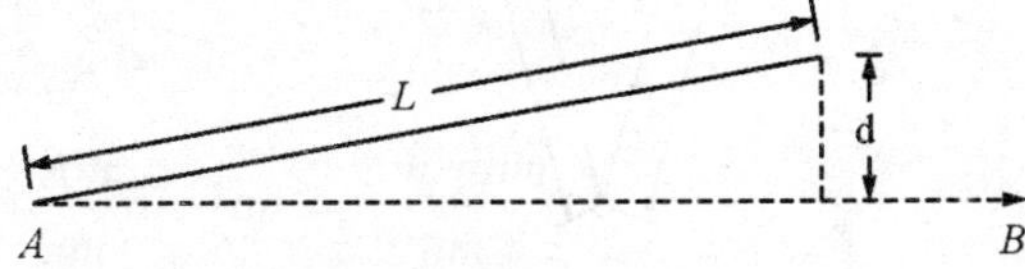

Fig. 3.11 Correction for alignment

The correction for alignment c_m is always negative.

Reduction to mean sea-level: For surveys of extensive areas, the geodetic surveys are carried out in which the base line is measured with highest precision. The measured linear distances of base lines (after applying necessary corrections discussed above) are reduced to their equivalent sea-level lengths. This is known as reduction to mean sea-level (m.s.l.).

The reduced length at mean sea-level is given by:

$$L' = \frac{R}{R + h_{av}} L \qquad \text{...(3.17)}$$

R = the mean radius of the earth (6370 km), and

h_{av} = the average elevation of the measured line (Fig. 3.12).

The correction to L which is $(L - L')$, is given by

$$c_l = \frac{h_{av} L}{R + h_{av}} \quad \textit{(exact)} \qquad \text{...(3.18)}$$

$$= \frac{h_{av} L}{R} \quad \textit{(approximate)} \qquad \text{...(3.19)}$$

where

$c_l = L - L'$.

The sign of the correction for reduction to mean sea-level is always negative.

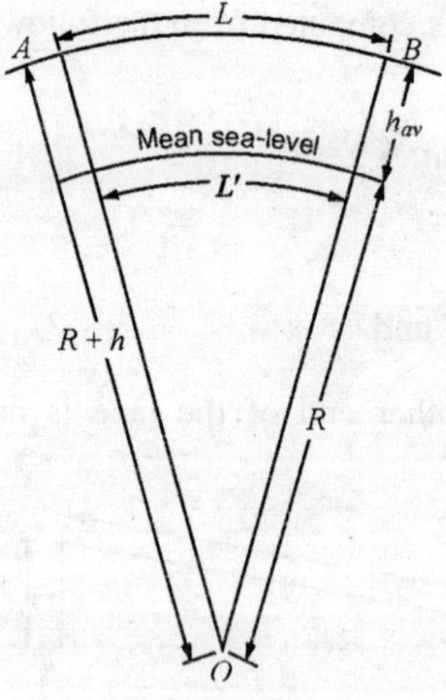

Fig. 3.12 Reduction to mean sea-level

Various tape corrections for systematic errors are summarised in Table 3.1.

Table 3.1 Corrections for systematic errors in taping

Correction	Sign	Formula
Standardisation	±	$\frac{C}{l}L$
Temperature	±	$\alpha(t_m - t_o)L$
Pull	±	$\frac{P - P_o}{AE}L$
Sag	–	$\frac{1}{24}\left(\frac{W}{P}\right)^2 L$
Slope	–	$(1 - \cos\alpha)\,L$ *(exact)* $\frac{h^2}{2L}$ *(approximate)*
Alignment	–	$\frac{d^2}{2L}$ *(approximate)*
Reduction to m.s.l	–	$\frac{hL}{R}$ *(approximate)*

After removal of gross errors and systematic errors, the errors which remain in the observations, are the random errors. These errors may be due to several causes. Some of these are

1. Error in determining temperature of tape,
2. Failure to apply the proper tension,
3. Wind deflecting the plumb bob,
4. Arrows not set exactly where the plumb bob touches the ground,
5. Inability of the observer to estimate the last place in reading between the graduations, etc.

Adjustment of random errors is discussed in Chapter 2 of *Higher Surveying.*

ILLUSTRATIVE EXAMPLES

Example 3.1

The measured slope distance between two points is 615 m. If the angle of slope between the points is 7°, what is the horizontal distance between the points?

Solution:

Slope distance $S = 615$ m

Angle of slope $\alpha = 7°$

The horizontal distance from Eq. (3.1) is

$$D = S\cos\alpha$$

$= 615 \times \cos 7^\circ$

$= \mathbf{610.4\ m.}$

Example 3.2

The distance between two points *A* and *B*, is measured along the slope as 435 m. The difference in elevation of these points is 49 m. Determine the horizontal distance between *A* and *B*.

Solution:

Slope distance $S = 435$ m

Difference in elevation $h = 49$ m

The horizontal distance from Eq. (3.2)

$$D = \sqrt{S^2 - h^2}$$

$$= \sqrt{435^2 - 49^2}$$

$$= \mathbf{432.23\ m.}$$

Example 3.3

If the slope of the ground is 1 in 5, and the measured distance between two points is 503 m, what is the horizontal equivalent of the measured distance?

Solution:

Slope distance S = 503 m

Slope = 1 in 5

For 1 unit of vertical distance, horizontal distance is 5 units,

$$\tan \alpha = \frac{1}{5}$$

or $\alpha = 11°18'36''$

Thus the horizontal equivalent

$$D = S \cos \alpha$$

$$= 503 \times \cos 11°18'36''$$

$$= \mathbf{493.23\ m.}$$

Example 3.4

What slope distance must be laid out along a line that rises 5 m /100 m in order to establish a horizontal distance of 830 m?

Solution:

For 100 m of horizontal distance the vertical rise is 5 m, therefore, the vertical rise for 830 m horizontal distance would be $5\times\frac{830}{100}=41.5$ m.

or $\quad h = 41.5$ m

We have

$$D = \sqrt{S^2 - h^2}$$

$$S = \sqrt{D^2 + h^2}$$

$$= \sqrt{830^2 + 41.5^2}$$

$$= \mathbf{831.04\ m.}$$

Example 3.5

A measurement is made along a line that is inclined by a vertical angle of 2° 26′. The measured slope distance is 4035.46 m. To what accuracy must the slope angle be measured if the relative accuracy of the horizontal distance is to be $\frac{1}{25000}$? Also compute the horizontal distance.

Solution:

The accuracy $d\alpha$ in measurement of slope angle α, is given by Eq. (3.4) as below:

$$\tan\alpha\ d\alpha = \frac{dD}{D}$$

or

$$d\alpha = \frac{dD}{D}\frac{1}{\tan\alpha}$$

$$= \frac{1}{25000}\times\frac{1}{\tan 2°26'}$$

$$= \frac{1}{1062.3808}$$

or

$$d\alpha = \frac{206265}{1062.3808}\ \text{seconds}$$

$$= 194''$$

$$= \mathbf{3'\ 14''}.$$

The horizontal distance

$$D = 4035.46 \times \cos 2°26'$$

$$= \mathbf{4031.82\ m.}$$

Example 3.6

To what accuracy must the slope angle of Example 3.5, be measured if the horizontal distance is to be accurate to 0.005 m?

Solution:

From Eq. (3.3), we have

$$S \sin \alpha \, d\alpha = dD \ (neglecting \ the \ sign)$$

$$d\alpha = \frac{dD}{S \sin \alpha}$$

or $$d\alpha = \frac{206265 \, dD}{S \sin \alpha} \text{ seconds}$$

$$= \frac{206265 \times 0.005}{4035.46 \times \sin 2°26'}$$

$$= \mathbf{6.0''}.$$

Example 3.7

What is the correct length of a line which is measured as 350 m with a 20 m tape, 10 cm too long?

Solution:

From Eq. (3.9), the correction required to the measured length is

$$c_a = \frac{C}{l} L$$

$$= \frac{0.10}{20} \times 350$$

$$= 1.75 \text{ m}$$

As the tape is too long by 10 cm, the sign of the correction is positive.

Thus the correct length will be

$$= 350 + 1.75$$

$$= \mathbf{351.75 \ m}.$$

Example 3.8

At the end of a survey of a parcel of land, a tape of 30 m length was found to be 10 cm short. The area of the plan drawn with the measurements taken with this tape is found to be 135 cm^2. If the scale of the plan is 1/1000, what is the true area of the field assuming that the chain was exact 30 m at commencement of the survey?

Solution:

Scale of the plan is $\frac{1}{1000}$

or 1 cm = 10 m

Measured area of the field = plan area × 10^2

$= 135 \times 10^2$

$= 13500\ m^2$

If the incorrect length of the tape is L', and the designated length is L then the true area A is given by

$$A = \left(\frac{L'}{L}\right)^2 \times \text{measured area}$$

The incorrect length L' is obtained by

$$= \frac{1}{2}\ \text{Length of the tape at the (commencement + end) of the survey}$$

$$= \frac{29.90 + 30.00}{2}$$

$$= 29.95\ m$$

$$A = \left(\frac{29.95}{30}\right)^2 \times 13500$$

$$= \mathbf{13455.04\ m^2}.$$

Example 3.9

A line was measured with a steel tape which was exactly 30 m at 25° C at a pull of 10 kg, the measured length being 1700.00 m. The temperature during measurement was 34°C and the pull applied was 18 kg. Compute the length of the line if the cross-sectional area of the tape is 0.025 cm². Take $\alpha = 3.5 \times 10^{-6}$ per 1°C and $E = 2.1 \times 10^6$ kg/cm² for the material of the tape.

Solution:

We have

$l = 30$ m $L = 1700$ m

$t_o = 25°$ C $t_m = 34°$ C

$P = 18$ kg $P_o = 10$ kg

$A = 0.025$ cm² $\alpha = 3.5 \times 10^{-6}$ per 1° C

$E = 2.1 \times 10^6$ kg/cm²

(*i*) From Eq. (3.10), the correction for temperature is

$$c_t = \alpha\,(t_m - t_o)\,L$$

$$= 3.5 \times 10^{-6} \times (34 - 25) \times 1700.00$$

$$= 0.0536\ \text{m (+ve)}$$

(*ii*) The correction for pull from Eq. (3.11) is

$$c_p = \frac{(P - P_o)}{AE} L$$

$$= \frac{(18 - 10)}{0.025 \times 2.1 \times 10^6} \times 1700.00$$

$$= 0.2591 \text{ m (+ve)}$$

The total correction $= 0.0536 + 0.2591$

$= 0.3127$ m

The corrected length of the line

$= c_t + c_p$

$= 1700.00 + 0.3127$

= 1700.31 m.

Example 3.10

A steel tape of nominal length 30 m was suspended between supports to measure the length of a line. The measured length of the line on a slope of angle 3° 50′ is 29.859 m. The mean temperature during the measurement was 12° C and the pull applied was 100 N. If standard length of the tape is 30.005 m at 20° C, and the standard pull is 45.0 N, calculate the corrected horizontal length. Take the weight of the tape = 0.15 N/m, its cross-sectional area = 2.5 mm², $\alpha = 1.15 \times 10^{-5}$ per °C, and $E = 2.0 \times 10^5$ N/mm².

Solution:

(*i*) Correction for standardization [from Eq. (3.9)]

$$c_a = \frac{C}{l} L$$

$$= \frac{(30.005 - 30)}{30} \times 29.859$$

= + 0.00498 m.

(*ii*) Correction for temperature [from Eq. (3.10)]

$$c_t = \alpha\ (t_m - t_o)\ L$$

$$= 1.15 \times 10^{-5}\ (12 - 20) \times 29.859$$

= – 0.00275 m.

(*iii*) Correction for pull [from Eq. (3.11)]

$$c_p = \frac{(P - P_o)}{AE} L$$

$$= \frac{(100-45)}{2.5 \times 2.0 \times 10^5} \times 29.859$$

$$= \mathbf{0.00328\ m.}$$

(*iv*) Correction for sag [from Eq. (3.12)]

$$c_g = \frac{1}{24}\left[\frac{W}{P}\right]^2 L$$

$$W = 0.15 \times 29.859$$

$$= 4.48 \text{ N}$$

$$c_g = \frac{1}{24}\left[\frac{4.48}{100}\right]^2 \times 29.859$$

$$= 0.0025 \text{ m}$$

$$= -\,0.0025 \text{ m (always –ve)}$$

Further, as the supports are not at the same level [from Eq. (3.13)]

$$c_g' = c_g \cos^2\alpha$$

$$= -\,0.0025 \times \cos^2 3°50'$$

$$= \mathbf{-\,0.00249\ m.}$$

(*v*) The correction for slope [from Eq. (3.14)]

$$c_s = (1 - \cos\alpha)\, L$$

$$= (1 - \cos 3°50') \times 29.859$$

$$= 0.0668 \text{ m}$$

$$= -\,0.0668 \text{ (always –ve)}$$

Total correction = 0.00498 – 0.00275 + 0.00328 – 0.00249 – 0.0668

= – 0.06378 m

Correct horizontal distance = 29.859 – 0.06378

= **29.795 m.**

QUESTIONS AND PROBLEMS

3.1 Explain why the distance measured on the surface of the earth is required to be reduced to equivalent horizontal distance.

3.2 Discuss the various methods of horizontal distance measurements.

3.3 Describe different kinds of tapes commonly used in surveying stating the advantages of each. Also discuss the equipment used for distance measurements.

3.4 Differentiate between Ranging and Taping.

3.5 Describe how you would range a survey line between two points which are not intervisible.

3.6 Discuss various sources of errors in linear measurements and identify that the resulting errors belong to which category of error.

3.7 What are different tape corrections and how are they applied?

3.8 A surveyor paces a 50 m length eight times with the following results: 57, $56\frac{1}{2}$, 56, 58, $56\frac{1}{3}$, 57, $56\frac{1}{2}$, and 56 paces. How many paces must he step off in order to lay off a distance of 400 m.

3.9 The distance measured between two points along a sloping ground with a slope angle of 5°15′ is 2023.47 m. What is the horizontal distance between the points?

3.10 If the measured slope distance between two points with difference in elevation of 11.326 m, is 256.74 m, what is the horizontal distance?

3.11 The measured slope distance between two points is 336.79 m, and the angle of slope is 8°28′. Compute the difference in elevation of the two points.

3.12 A horizontal distance of 950 m is to be laid out on the slope for which the slope angle is 4°58'. What slope distance should be laid out?

3.13 In Problem (3.9), if the vertical angle is in error by 3′30″ what error is produced in the computed horizontal distance?

3.14 In Problem (3.9), if it was desired that the error in the computed horizontal distance should not be more than 0.01 m, to what an accuracy the slope angle should be measured?

3.15 A line AB was measured in segments along sloping ground with a 30 m tape, and the following measurements were recorded:

Slope distance (m)	30.00	30.00	18.92	11.46	30.00	8.23
Difference in elevation (m)	1.58	0.95	0.90	0.56	3.01	0.69

Calculate the horizontal distance of the line *AB*.

3.16 A rectangular parcel of land of 315 m × 750 m is required to be established. A 30 m chain was calibrated and found to measure 30.03 m. What measurements must be laid off on the ground?

3.17 With what accuracy must a difference in elevation between two ends of 30 m tape be known if the difference in elevation is 3.150 m, and the accuracy ratio is to be at least 1:25000?

3.18 A base line was measured with a 30 m long steel tape at 15°C, and with a pull of 100 N (10 kgf). What is the correction per tape length if the temperature at the time of measurement was 22°C and the pull exerted was 150 N(15 kgf)? The weight of the steel is 0.0768 N per 1 cm^3, the weight of the tape is 8 N, the modulus of elasticity of the tape material is 2.1×10^7 N/cm^2 and its coefficient of linear expansion is 7.0×10^7 per °C.

3.19 The length of a steel tape was found exactly 30 m at a temperature of 30° C under pull of 5 kg when lying on the flat platform. The tape is stretched over two supports between which the measured distance is 30.000 m. There are two additional supports in between equally spaced. All the supports are at the same level, and the tape is allowed to sag freely between the supports.

Calculate the actual length between the two outer supports, and the reduced length at mean sea-level, if the mean temperature during the measurement was 37 °C, and the pull applied was 9 kg. The average elevation of the terrain is 945 m.

Weight of the tape = 1.50 kg

Area of cross-section of the tape = 6.5 mm^2

$\alpha = 1.2 \times 10^{-5}$ per °C

$E = 2.1 \times 10^6$ kg/cm^2

$R = 6372$ km

3.20 A base line *AB* was measured in two parts *AC* and *CB* of lengths 1540 m and 1919 m with a steel tape which was exactly 30 m at 20 °C at a pull of 10 kg. The applied pull during measurement of both parts was 25 kg whereas the respective temperatures were 40°C and 45°C. The slopes of the ground for the two parts were +2°40′ and +3°10′, and the deflection angle of *CB* was 11° right. Find the correct length of the base line. The cross-section area of the tape is 0.025 cm^2, the coefficient of linear expansion and modulus of elasticity of tape material are 2.5×10^{-6} per °C and 2.1×10^6 kg/cm^2, respectively.

4

MEASUREMENT OF ANGLES AND DIRECTIONS

4.1 GENERAL

The purpose of a survey is to determine the relative locations of points on, below or above the surface of the earth. Since the earth is three-dimensional, a three-dimensional rectangular coordinate system, $x'y'z'$, called the *geocentric coordinate system (right handed)* shown in Fig. 4.1, is required to locate the points. For geodetic surveys, points are located using spherical coordinates consisting of latitude ϕ, longitude λ, and the distance $(R + h)$ along the normal to the earth ellipsoid.

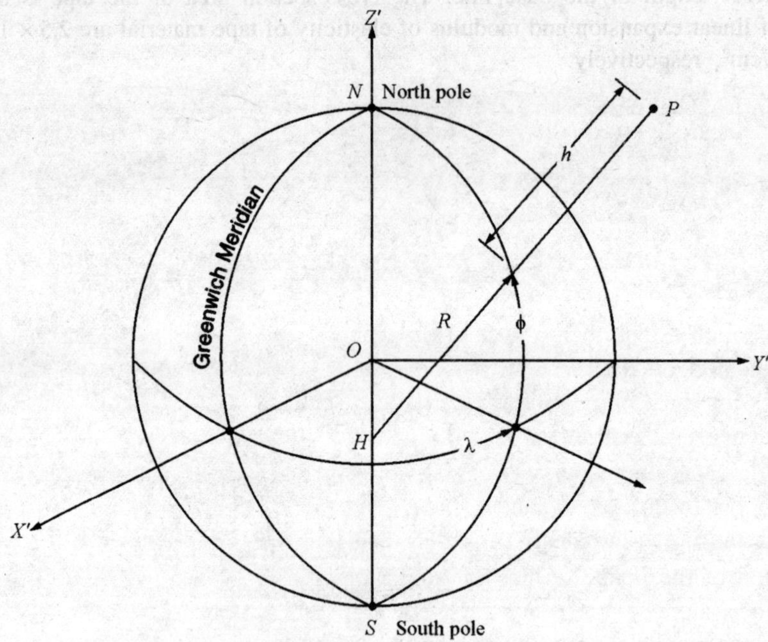

Fig. 4.1 Geocentric coordinate system

For plane surveying, a more convenient local *xyz* coordinate system as illustrated in Fig. 4.2, is adopted. The origin of such a system is usually taken near the centre of the area to be surveyed, *z*-axis coincides with the local vertical or the plumb line, and *xy*-plane is a horizontal plane (*i.e.*, *xy*-plane is tangent to the reference ellipsoid at the point of origin). The *y*-axis is generally taken towards the North pole. To locate any point P, either the coordinates (x,y,z) of the point or the two angles θ in horizontal plane known as horizontal angle, and α in vertical plane known as vertical angle, may be used, and the distance r of P from the origin O.

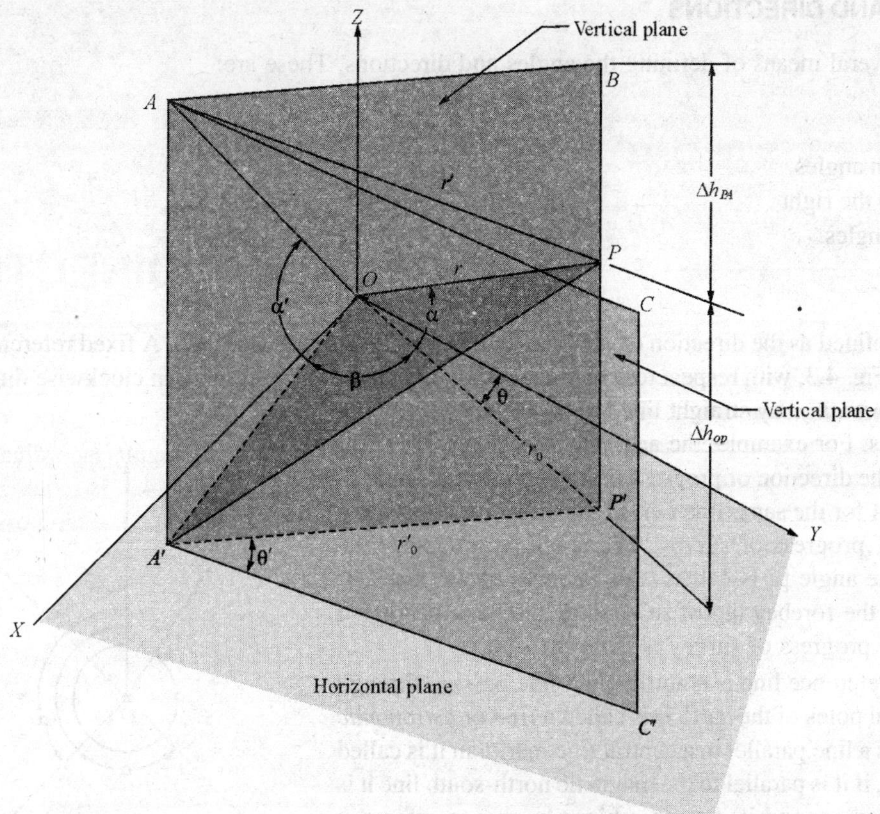

Fig. 4.2 Local coordinate system

In surveys of small extent, the position of the points P and A, and their slope distances r and r', are projected onto the horizontal plane xy as P', A', r_0, and r_0', respectively. Thus, any appropriate combination of the following measurements may be used to locate the point in space:

1. Horizontal angle measurements
2. Vertical angle measurements
3. Horizontal distance measurements
4. Vertical distance measurements.

The projection of the points on the horizontal plane may be defined by horizontal angles alone, horizontal distances alone, or horizontal angle and horizontal distance. For example, P' can be defined in the horizontal plane by one of the following:

1. Distance r_0 and direction θ from one known point O.
2. Directions θ and θ' from two known points O and A'.
3. Distances r_0 and r_0' from two known points O and A'.

For any two points P and A, the horizontal angle between them at O is the angle β, measured in the horizontal plane xy. The vertical angle to a point is the angle of elevation if the point is above the horizontal plane, or angle of depression if the point is below the horizontal plane, always measured from the horizontal plane. Thus the vertical angle to P at O is α and to point A is α'. The height difference between the points O and P is Δh_{OP}, and that of the points P and A is Δh_{PA} as shown in the figure.

4.2 ANGLES AND DIRECTIONS

There are several means of defining the angles and directions. These are:

1. Bearings
2. Azimuths
3. Deflection angles
4. Angles to the right
5. Interior angles.

Bearings

Bearing is defined as the direction of any line with respect to a given meridian. A fixed reference line *OM*, shown in Fig. 4.3, with respect to which the horizontal angles are measured in clockwise direction, is known as *meridian*. Any straight line has two diametrically opposite directions. For example, the angle α_1 is measured at *O* for the line *OA* in the direction of progress of survey, and the angle β_1 is measured at *A* for the same line *OA*, in the direction opposite to the direction of progress of survey. The angle α_1 is called *fore bearing*, and the angle β_1 is called *back bearing* of the line *OA*. Similarly, β_1 is the forebearing of *AO* and α_1 the back bearing if the direction of progress of survey is from *A* to *O*.

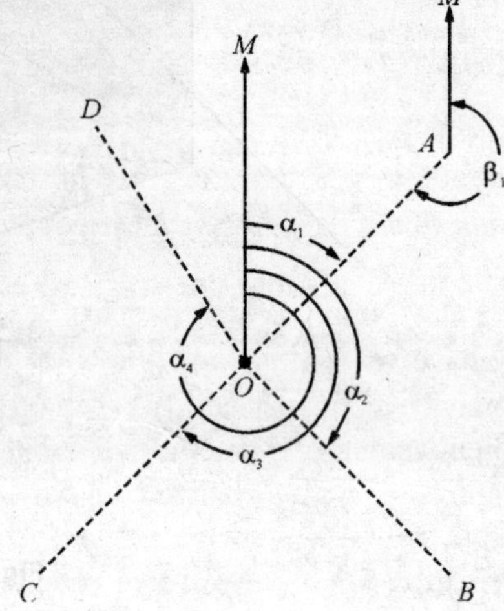

Fig. 4.3 Directions referred to a meridian

If the fixed reference line is a north-south line passing through the geographical poles of the earth it is called a *true* or *astronomic meridian*, if it is a line parallel to a central true meridian it is called a *grid meridian*, if it is parallel to the magnetic north-south line it is a *magnetic meridian*, and if it is an arbitrarily chosen reference line it is an *arbitrary* or *assumed meridian*.

As the bearings depend on the meridian chosen they may be *true bearings, magnetic bearings* or *assumed bearings.*

If the bearings θ_1, θ_2, θ_3, etc., are measured clockwise from north side of the meridian as shown in Fig. 4.4a, they are *whole-circle bearings*. The acute angle between the reference meridian and the line is known as the *reduced bearing* or *quadrantal bearing*. If the bearings are measured from north branch of the meridian in clockwise direction, and the line falls in the 0° to 90° quadrant as shown in Fig. 4.4b, it is written as NθE. If the line lies in the 270° to 360° quadrant, the bearing is measured from the north branch of meridian, and is written as NθW. Similarly, if the line lies in 90° to 180° quadrant and 180° to 270° quadrant, the bearings are measured from the south branch of the meridian, and are written as SθE and SθW, respectively. In Fig. 4.4b, the reduced bearings of the lines *OA*, *OB*, *OC*, and *OD* are Nθ_1E, Sθ_3E, Sθ_4W, and Nθ_2W, respectively.

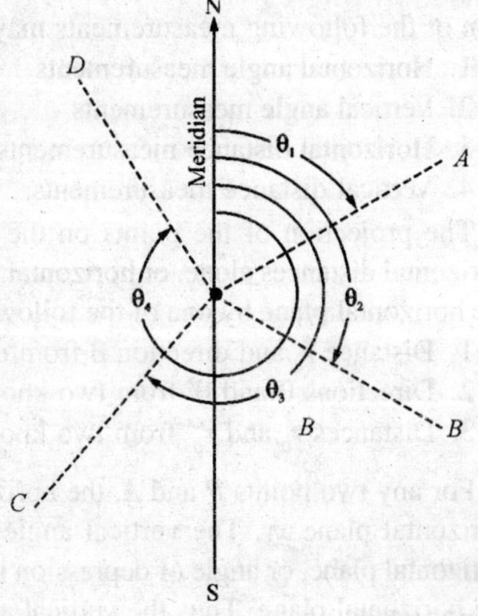

Fig. 4.4 (a)

Azimuths

The angle between a line and the meridian measured in clockwise direction usually from the north branch of the meridian is the

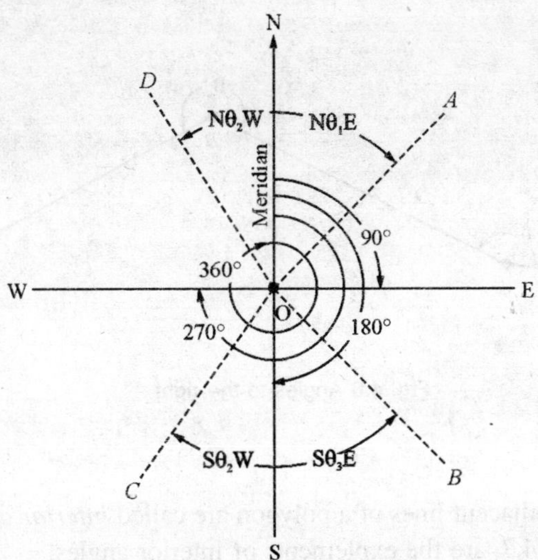

Fig. 4.4 (b) Whole-circle bearing and quadrantal or reduced bearing

azimuth of the line. Also, some surveyors reckon azimuths from the south branch of the meridian, and therefore, it becomes necessary to specify that the azimuth is from the north or from the south. Azimuths may be true (astronomic), magnetic, or assumed depending on the reference meridian adopted. They have values ranging from 0° to 360°. Thus, the azimuths are in fact whole-circle bearings.The two may be distinguished from each other when the convergence of meridians is considered in determination of azimuth. In practice the term azimuth is used in geodetic and astronomical surveying whereas the term bearing is used in plane surveying. If the direction of a line *OA* is defined from an origin *O* to the terminal point *A* as shown in Fig. 4.3, the azimuth is a *forward azimuth.* Conversely, the azimuth from *A* to *O* is the *back azimuth* of *OA*. The concept of forward and back azimuth of a line are only valid in plane surveying where there is no convergence of meridian.

Deflection Angles

The angle between a line and the prolongation of the preceding line is known as a *deflection angle.* The deflection angle may be on the right or left of the prolongation, and they are recorded as right or left depending on the angle measured on the right or left of the preceding line as shown in Fig. 4.5.

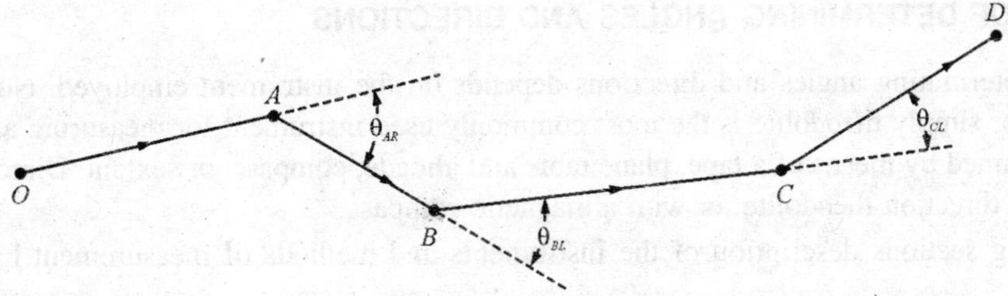

Fig. 4.5 Deflection angles

Angles to the Right

In a survey if the angles are measured clockwise from the preceding line to the following line, as illustrated in Fig. 4.6, the measured angles are called *angles to the right.*

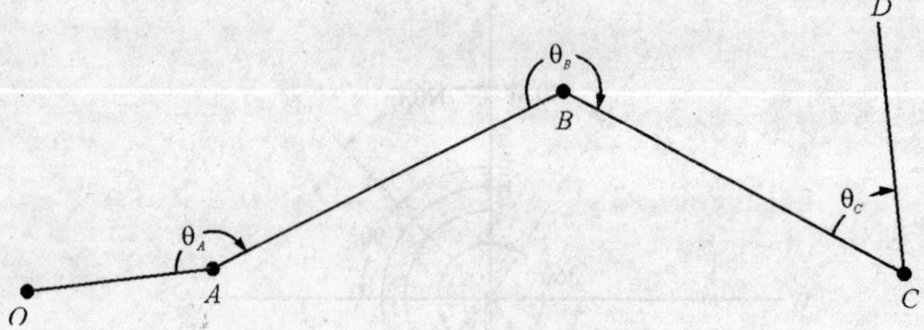

Fig. 4.6 Angles to the right

Interior Angles

The inside angles between adjacent lines of a polygon are called *interior angles*. The exterior angles, shown by dashed lines in Fig. 4.7, are the explements of interior angles.

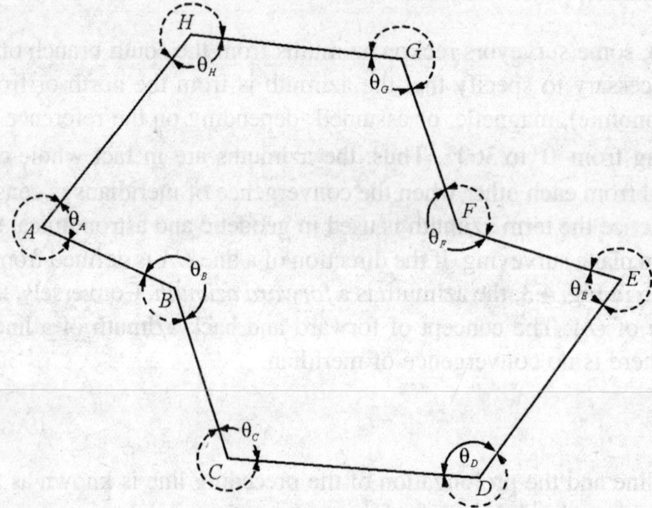

Fig. 4.7 Interior angles

4.3 METHODS OF DETERMINING ANGLES AND DIRECTIONS

The method of determining angles and directions depends on the instrument employed. Normally a transit theodolite or simply theodolite is the most commonly used instrument for measuring angles but can also be determined by means of a tape, plane table and alidade, compass, or sextant. Directions are determined with a direction theodolite, or with a magnetic compass.

In the following sections description of the instruments and methods of measurement have been discussed.

4.4 THEODOLITE

A theodolite shown in Fig. 4.8, is an instrument designed to measure horizontal and vertical angles. The sectional view of a theodolite given in Fig. 4.9 shows its main parts.

Parts of a Theodolite

A theodolite consists of the following essential parts.

Fig. 4.8 Theodolite

Levelling head: It consists of upper tribrach and lower tribrach. The upper tribrach has three arms, and each arm carries a levelling screw for supporting and levelling the instrument. The boss of the upper tribrach is pierced with a female axis in which the lower male vertical axis operates.

The lower tribrach has a circular hole through which a plumb bob may be suspended for centering the instrument over the ground mark.

The functions of a levelling head are to support the main part of the instrument, to attach the theodolite to the tripod, and to provide a means for levelling the theodolite.

Lower plate: The lower plate of the instrument, also known as vernier plate, is attached to the outer spindle and carries a graduated circle at its bevelled edge. The graduated circle is divided into 360° and each degree is further subdivided in 10′ or 20′ of arc intervals. The plate can be clamped at any desired position by a lower clamp screw, and a corresponding slow motion can be made with a tangential screw or slow motion screw.

Upper plate: The upper plate is attached to the inner spindle axis. Two diametrically opposite verniers, named as *A* and *B*, fitted with magnifiers, are fixed to the upper plate. The upper plate carries two standards to support a telescope, and one or two level tubes to level the instrument. It also carries an upper clamp screw and a corresponding tangent screw or slow motion screw. On clamping the upper clamp and unclamping the lower clamp, the instrument may be rotated on its outer spindle without any relative motion between the two plates, and thus causing no change in graduated circle reading. On the other hand, if the lower clamp is tightened and the upper clamp is unclamped, the instrument may be rotated on its inner spindle with a relative motion between the upper plate and lower plate. This property is utilized for measuring the angles between two settings of the instrument.

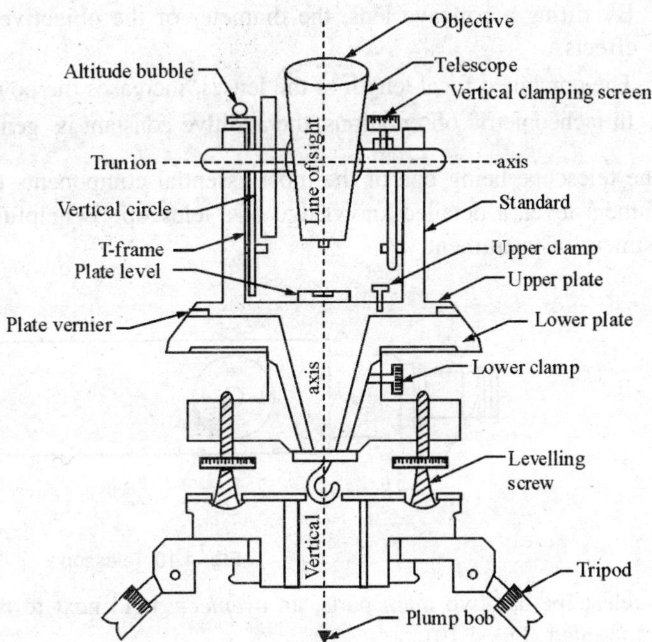

Fig. 4.9 Sectional view of a theodolite

Standards (or A Frame): Two standards resembling the English letter A, are firmly attached to the upper plate. The tops of these standards form the bearing of the pivots of the telescope allowing it to rotate on its trunion axis in vertical plane. The T–frame and arm of the vertical circle clamp are also attached to the standards.

T–frame or Index bar: T–frame resembles the English letter T, and is centered on the horizontal axis of the telescope in the frame of the vertical circle. The two verniers, named as *C* and *D*, are provided on it at the ends of the horizontal arm, called the index arm. A vertical leg known as clipping arm, is provided with a fork and two clipping screws at its lower extremity. At the top of this frame is attached a bubble tube called the *altitude bubble tube*.

Plate levels: The upper plate carries one or two plate levels. In the case of two plate levels, they are placed at right angles to each other. The plate level bubbles can be centered with the help of the foot screws.

Telescope: The telescope of a theodolite may be the internal focussing type or the external focussing type. The internal focussing telescopes are the most commonly used telescopes because of the following advantages:

1. The overall length of the telescope is not altered during focussing, and hence the balance of the telescope is not affected.
2. There is no risk of breaking the plate levels while transiting the telescope.
3. The line of collimation is least affected by focussing.
4. The telescope remains free from dust and moisture.
5. Wear of rack and pinion is less due to lesser movement of the concave lense.
6. By fitting a concave lens, the diameter of the objective can be increased without aberrative effects.
7. The combined focal length of the lenses, increases the power of the telescope.
8. In tacheometric observations, the additive constant is generally eliminated (*c.f.*, Chapter 8).

The telescope being one of the most essential components of a theodolite and another surveying instrument level, a detailed knowledge of a telescope is helpful not only to regular users but also in adjustment of instrument.

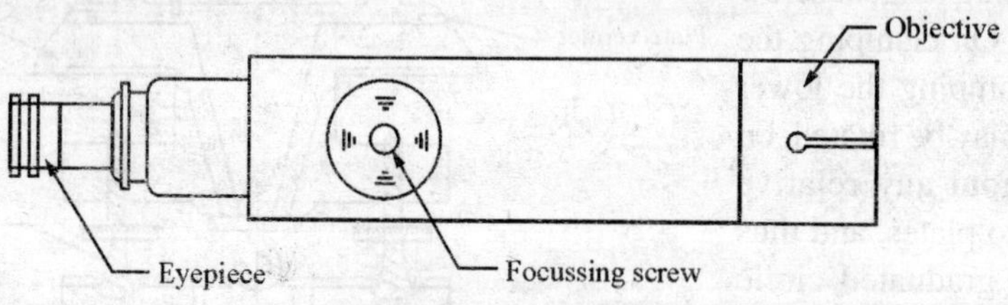

Fig. 4.10 Telescope

A telescope has two main parts, an *eyepiece*, held next to the eye and the *objective*, towards the object sighted (Fig. 4.10).

The objective or object glass of a surveying telescope consists of a compound lens, an outer double-convex lens and an inner convexo-concave lens, the two being cemented together at their common surface (Fig. 4.11)). The eyepiece used in a surveying telescope is of the Ramsden type shown in Fig. 4.12. It has two plano-convex lenses of equal focal length, mounted with their convex surfaces facing each other, and separated by a distance equal to two-thirds of the focal length of either lens.

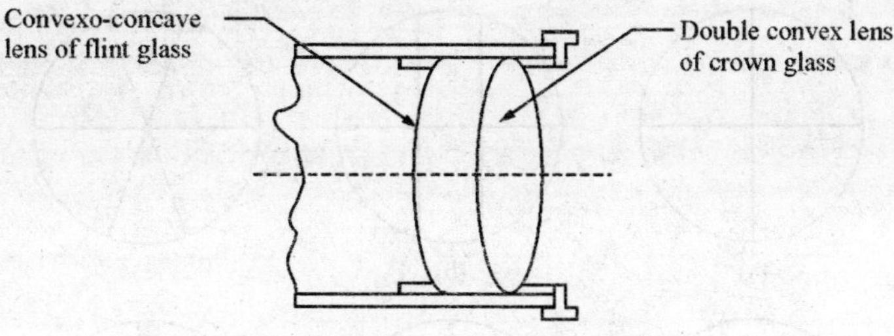

Fig. 4.11 Objective of a telescope

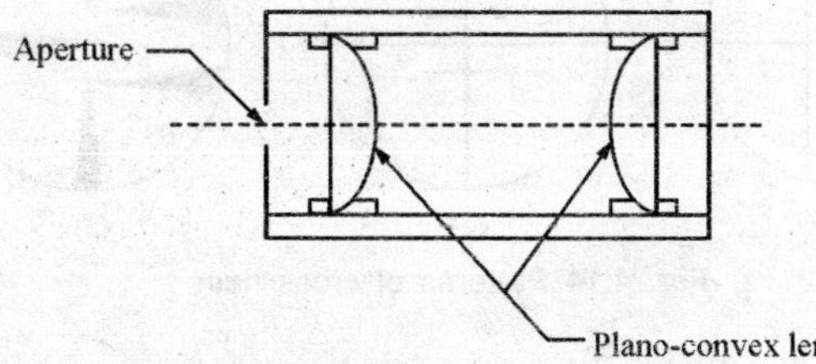

Fig. 4.12 Eyepiece of a telescope

Both the objective and the eyepiece are set in cylindrical metal cases of different sizes, that of the eyepiece being smaller, one sliding axially inside the other with a rack and pinion arrangement attached to a focussing screw. The focussing screw moves the objective relative to the eyepiece in order to bring the object into clear focus.

The *diaphragm* containing the cross hairs is another important part of the telescope. It is placed between the eyepiece and objective but nearer the former. This is held in place in the telescope tube by means of four capstan-headed screws as shown in Fig. 4.13. The capstan-headed screws allow the horizontal and vertical adjustments of the cross hairs.

Spider-web cross hairs are the simplest and commonly used with metal rings or glass diaphragms (Fig. 4.14 a). The cross hair patterns shown in Fig. 4.14a and b, are common in levels, and the other patterns are for theodolites and tacheometers.

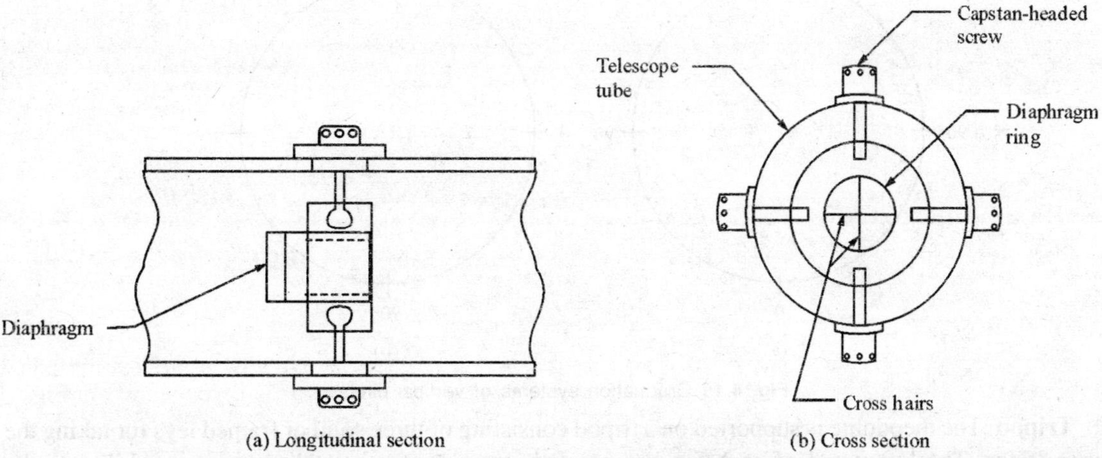

Fig. 4.13 Diaphragm of a telescope

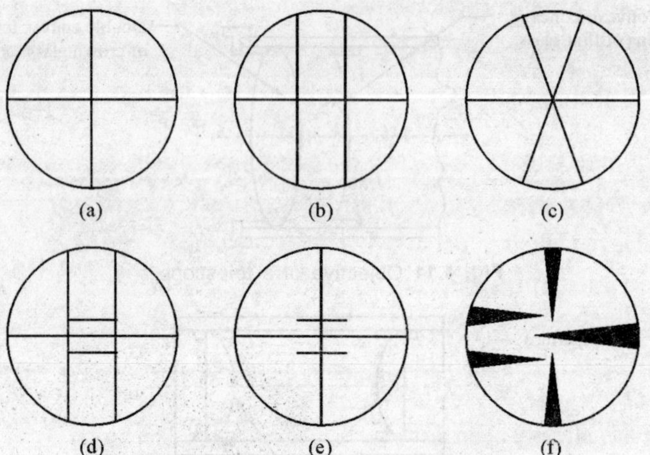

Fig. 4.14 Patterns of cross hairs

Since the primary purpose of a diaphragm is to facilitate sighting or striking an object, the image of the object must be brought into focus in the plane of the cross hairs. The line passing through the optical centre of the objective and entering the observer's eye through the eyepiece, is called the *line of sight*. The imaginary line joining the optical centre of the objective and the intersection of the cross hairs, is called the *line of collimation*.

Vertical circle: A vertical circle attached with the telescope is graduated in various ways by the manufacturers. The following graduations of vertical circles are in common use:

1. The vertical circle is divided into four quadrants each reading from 0° to 90°. The 0° - 0° line is a vertical line (Fig. 4.15a).
2. The vertical circle is divided into four quadrants from 0° to 90° in both the directions, 0° being at the eyepiece end and objective end (Fig. 4.15b). The 0° - 0° line is a horizontal line.

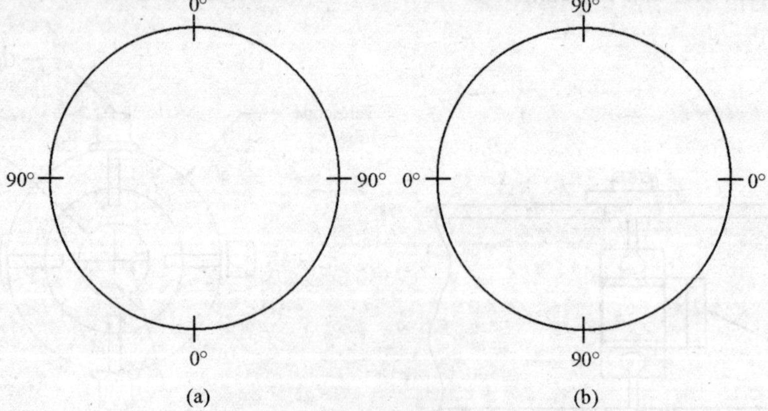

Fig. 4.15 Graduation systems of vertical circle

Tripod: The theodolite is supported on a tripod consisting of three solid or framed legs for taking the observations. The lower end of each leg has pointed iron shoe for providing greater stability to the instrument while working. The tripod head carries at its upper surface an external screw to which the foot plate of the levelling head is screwed.

Plumb bob: To centre the instrument exactly over the ground mark, a plumb bob is suspended from the hook fitted to the bottom of the main vertical axis.

Definitions and Other Technical Terms

The following terms are associated with the angle measurements with a theodolite (Fig. 4.16):

Vertical axis: The axis (*B*) about which a theodolite is rotated in a horizontal plane, is the vertical axis of the instrument. About this axis both upper and lower plates rotate.

Horizontal or trunnion axis: The axis (*C*) about which the telescope along with the vertical circle, rotates in a vertical plane, is called horizontal or trunnion axis.

Line of collimation: It has already been defined in Sec. 4.4. It is also known as line of sight (*D*).

Axis of the plate level bubble: The straight line (*A*) tangential to longitudinal curve of the level tube at its centre, is the axis of the plate level bubble (Fig. 4.17).

Instrumental centre: The point through which the vertical axis, horizontal axis, and the line of sight pass, is called the instrumental centre.

Centering: The process of setting up a theodolite over the ground station mark, is known as centering. When a theodolite is centered over the station mark, the vertical axis of the theodolite passes through the station mark.

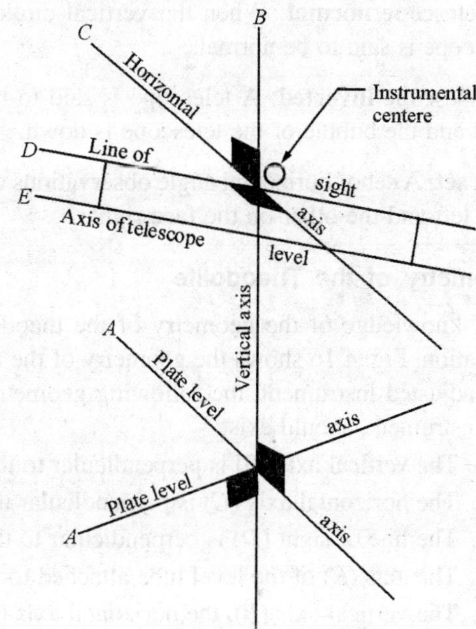

Fig. 4.16 Geometry of a theodolite

Leveling: The process of making the vertical axis of the instrument coinciding with the plumb line passing through the instrumental centre is called levelling. After centering and leveling the vertical axis of the instrument passes through the ground station mark.

Transiting: The process of turning the telescope in vertical plane through 180° about the horizontal axis is known as transiting. The terms *reversing* and *plunging* are also used sometimes for transiting.

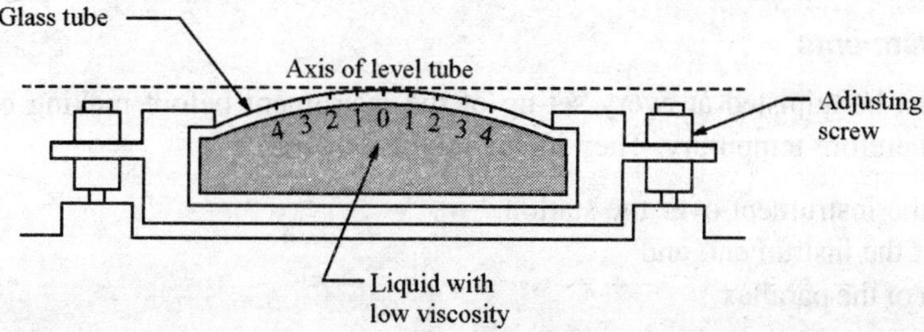

Fig. 4.17 Level tube

Swing: The continuous motion of the telescope about the vertical axis in horizontal plane is called swing. When the telescope is rotated clockwise, it is *right swing* and if anticlockwise it is *left swing.*

Face-left and right-observations: The observations made keeping the vertical circle on the left of the telescope are known as face left observations, and if the vertical circle is kept on the right of the telescope, the observations are called face right observations.

Changing face: When the face of the telescope is changed from left to right or *vice versa,* the process is known as changing face.

Telescope normal: When the vertical circle is on the left of the telescope and bubble is up, the telescope is said to be normal.

Telescope inverted: A telescope is said to be inverted or reversed when its vertical circle is to its right and the bubble of the telescope is down.

A set: A set of horizontal angle observations consists of two horizontal angle observations, one on the face left and the other on the face right.

Geometry of the Theodolite

A knowledge of the geometry of the theodolite is necessary for a thorough understanding of its operation. Fig. 4.16 shows the geometry of the theodolite in schematic form. In a perfectly constructed and adjusted instrument, the following geometrical requirements of relationships between the axes of the instrument, should exist:

1. The vertical axis (*B*) is perpendicular to the plane of the plate level bubble (*A*).
2. The horizontal axis (*C*) is perpendicular to the vertical axis (*B*).
3. The line of sight (*D*) is perpendicular to the horizontal axis (*C*).
4. The axis (*E*) of the level tube attached to the telescope is parallel to the line of sight (*D*).
5. The vertical axis (*B*), the horizontal axis (*C*) and the line of sight (*D*) pass through a single point (*O*) known as instrumental centre.

The above relationships are achieved by permanent adjustment procedures detailed in the following section.

Adjustments of a Theodolite

The adjustments of a theodolite are of two kinds:

1. Temporary adjustments, and
2. Permanent adjustments.

Temporary adjustments

Theodolite must be adjusted at every set-up of the instrument before making observations. These adjustments are therefore temporary. They include the following:

1. Setting up the instrument over the station,
2. Levelling of the instrument, and
3. Elimination of the parallax.

Setting up: The operation of setting up includes the centering of the theodolite over the ground station mark, and approximate levelling of the instrument.

The centering is carried out in following steps:

1. Suspend the plumb bob with a string attached to the hook fitted to the bottom of the vertical axis.
2. Place the theodolite over the station mark by spreading the legs of the tripod, well apart so that the telescope is at a convenient height for taking the observations.
3. Do approximate centering by moving the legs radially and circumferentially till the plumb bob hangs within 1 cm horizontally of the station mark.
4. Do finer centering by unclamping the centre-shifting arrangement.

Before centering the instrument over the station mark, it should be ensured that the level of the tripod head is approximately levelled. In case there is a considerable dislevelment, the centering will be disturbed when levelling is done. The approximate levelling may be done with reference to a small circular bubble attached to the tribrach, or by eye judgement.

Levelling of theodolite: The levelling operation is performed to make the vertical axis of the instrument truly vertical, and pass through the ground station mark. The following steps are involved in the levelling operation (Fig. 4.18):

1. Turn the horizontal plate until the longitudinal axis of the plate level becomes parallel to the line joining any two levelling screws (Fig. 4.18a).
2. By turning the levelling screws simultaneously in opposite directions either inwards or outwards, bring the bubble to the centre of its run.
3. Turn the instrument through 180° in azimuth.
4. If the bubble position is found different, move it by means of the same levelling screws to the approximate mean of the two positions.
5. Turn the instrument through 90° in azimuth so that the plate level becomes perpendicular to the previous position (Fig.4.18b).
6. Using the third levelling screw move the bubble to the approximate mean position already indicated.
7. Repeat the above steps until the bubble retains in the same position for every setting of the instrument in azimuth.

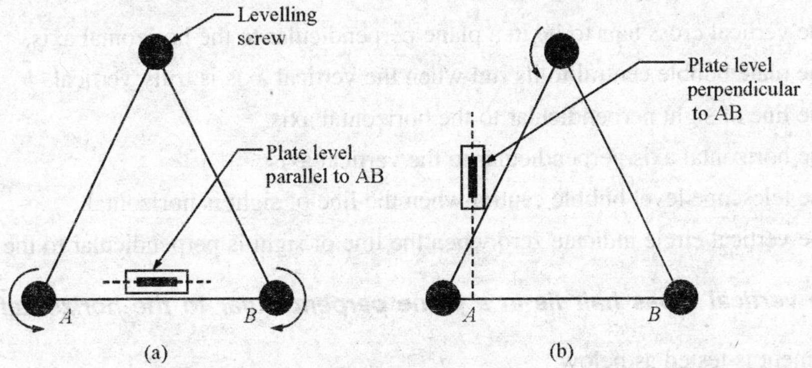

Fig. 4.18 Levelling a theodolite

Elimination of parallax: For making an observation first focus the eyepiece for the observer's eye. This is most easily done by holding a white paper about 15 cm in front of the objective and turning eyepiece in or out until the cross hairs are sharp and distinct. Then an object is selected and focused, and

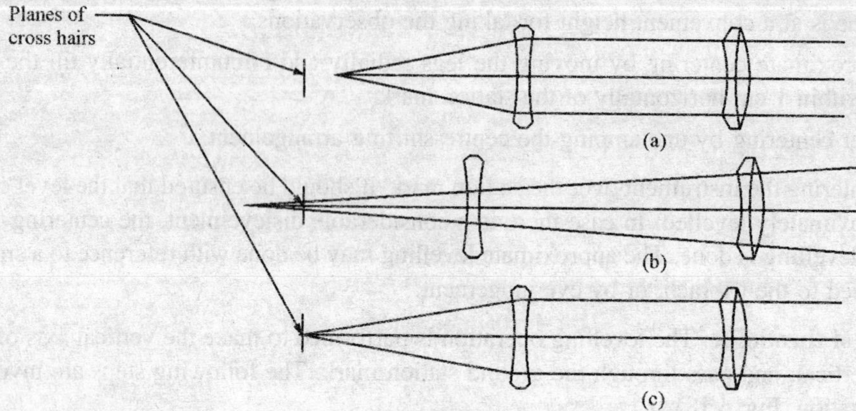

Fig. 4.19 Parallax

the image of the object is brought into the plane of the cross hairs. This can be checked by moving the eye up and down or sideways a small amount to detect whether or not the cross hairs appear to move with respect to the object sighted. If there is no relative movement, the focussing lens is in the proper position and the telescope is properly focused (Fig. 4.19c). If there is relative motion between the cross hairs and the object sighted, the condition called *parallax* exists between the image and the cross hairs. This condition arises when the focussing lens is not in its proper position as shown in Fig.4.19a and b, and the image is not formed in the plane of cross hairs. Refocussing brings the focussing lens in the proper position, and the parallax is eliminated.

Permanent adjustments

The permanent adjustments need to be made once in a while or before embarking on a precise job. They are based on the geometry of the theodolite discussed in Sec. 4.4.

It is possible that while carrying out some adjustments these may upset other adjustments. To avoid such possibility, the permanent adjustment should be made in the following order:

1. Make the vertical cross hair to lie in a plane perpendicular to the horizontal axis.
2. Make the plate bubble central to its run when the vertical axis is truly vertical.
3. Make the line of sight perpendicular to the horizontal axis.
4. Make the horizontal axis perpendicular to the vertical axis.
5. Make the telescope level bubble central when the line of sight is horizontal.
6. Make the vertical circle indicate zero when the line of sight is perpendicular to the vertical axis.

To make the vertical cross hair lie in a plane perpendicular to the horizontal axis

This adjustment is tested as below:

1. Sight the vertical cross hair on a well-defined point about 60 m away from the instrument.
2. Clamp both the horizontal motions of the instrument. Swing the telescope through a small vertical angle, so that the point traverses the length of the vertical cross hair.

3. If the point does not appear to move continuously on the hair and departs from the cross hair, adjust the vertical hair by the following procedure:

   (*a*) Loosen the two adjacent capstan-headed screws, and rotate the cross hair ring in the telescope tube until the point traverses the entire length of the hair.

   (*b*) Tighten the two capstan-headed screws.

The object of this adjustment is to bring the horizontal hair of the eyepiece into the horizontal plane through the optical axis.

The manufacturers generally take care that the vertical and horizontal cross hairs are perpendicular to each other. Therefore, if the vertical cross hair is set perpendicular to the horizontal axis, the horizontal cross hair is automatically made horizontal, and the horizontal hair of the eyepiece lies in the horizontal plane through the optical axis of the instrument and, therefore, no adjustment is required for the horizontal hair.

Adjustment of plate level

This adjustment makes the axis of the plate level perpendicular to the vertical axis of the instrument. When the plate level is in perfect adjustment, its bubble must remain at the centre of its run during complete revolution of the theodolite in azimuth.

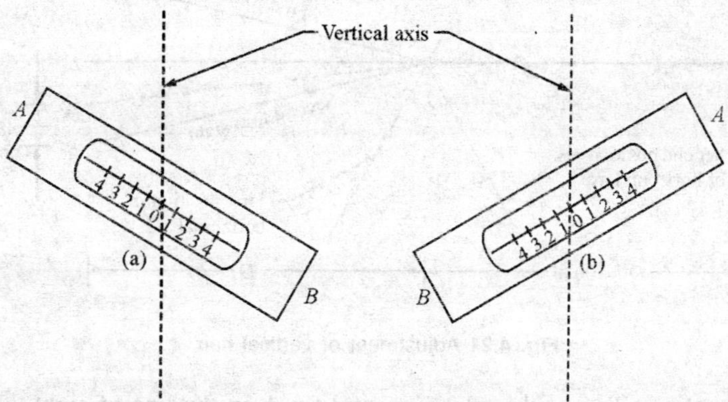

Fig. 4.20 Two positions of plate level

To test whether the plate bubble remains at its centre of run in all positions on a complete revolution of the instrument in azimuth or not, the following operations are required:

1. Set up the instrument on a firm ground. Clamp the lower plate, and turn the upper plate until plate level becomes parallel to any pair of levelling foot screws. Bring the bubble to the centre of its run by means of levelling screws as explained in Sec. 4.4.
2. Rotate the instrument about the vertical axis through 180°. The plate level is now again parallel to the same pair of levelling screws but the ends reversed in direction as shown in Fig. 4.20. If the bubble remains central, the vertical axis of the instrument is perpendicular to the plate level axis.

If the plate level bubble does not remain central, the adjustment of the plate level axis is done in the following steps:

1. Note down the reading of the bubble which is the apparent error and is twice the actual error of the axis of the plate level.

2. Correct half the error by means of the same pair of levelling screws.
3. Remaining half of the correction is made by means of the capstan-headed screw provided at the end of the level tube.

Repeat the test and adjustment until the bubble remains central at its run during full revolution of the instrument in azimuth.

Adjustment of vertical hair

This adjustment is to make the line of collimation perpendicular to the horizontal axis of the instrument. If this adjustment exists, the line of collimation will generate a plane when the telescope is revolved in vertical plane, otherwise a cone is generated with the horizontal axis as its axis.

To find out that whether the line of collimation is perpendicular to the horizontal axis, the following test is carried out:

1. Level the instrument, and sight a point *P* at about 100 m away from the instrument position *O*, with telescope normal. *P* should be nearly at same elevation as instrument axis (Fig. 4.21).

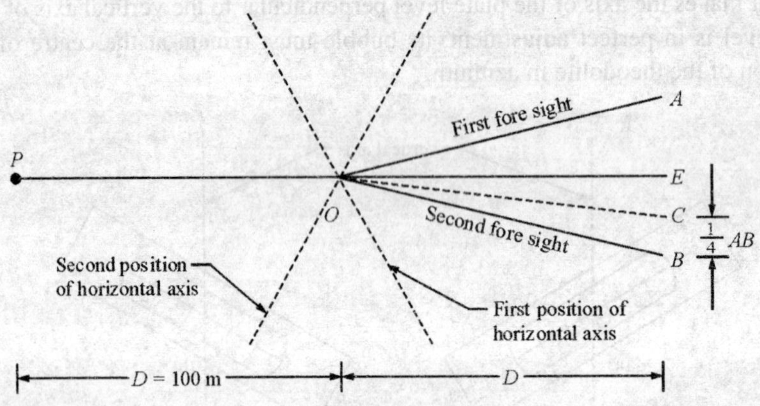

Fig. 4.21 Adjustment of vertical hair

2. Clamp both the plates. Transit the telescope, and fix *A* on the line of sight at the same distance away from *O* as *P*.
3. Unclamp the upper plate, swing the telescope and again sight *P*. The telescope is in inverted position.
4. Clamp the upper plate and transit the telescope. If the line of sight passes through *A*, the line of sight is perpendicular to the horizontal axis.

If the line of sight does not pass through *A* in step 4 above, the adjustment is done as follows:

1. Set a point *B* on the line of sight beside *A*.
2. Mark a point *C* at one-fourth distance of *AB* from *B*.
3. Adjust the vertical hair by means of two opposite capstan headed screws so that the line of sight passes through *C*.
4. Test the adjustment again and if needed, repeat the adjustment.

Adjustment of horizontal axis

With this adjustment the horizontal axis is made perpendicular to the vertical axis. This adjustment insures that the line of sight revolves in a vertical plane perpendicular to the horizontal axis when the instrument is levelled. This adjustment is very necessary for prolonging of straight lines by making observations on one face only.

The adjustment of the horizontal axis by the *spire test* is shown in Fig. 4.22. To test the adjustment the following steps are required:

1. Set up the instrument near any tall object on which a well-defined point *A* is available at about 60° to 70° vertical angle.
2. Level the instrument to make the vertical axis truly vertical.
3. Sight *A* keeping both upper and lower plates clamped, depress the telescope and fix a point *B* on the ground.
4. Transit the telescope and swing the telescope through 180° until positions of two standards are interchanged.
5. Bisect *A* again and depress the telescope and note that whether the line of sight passes through *B* or not. If it passes, the horizontal axis is perpendicular to the vertical axis and if not, the instrument needs adjustment.

To adjust the horizontal axis the procedure to be followed is as under:

1. When the line of sight does not pass through *B*, fix a point *C* on the line of sight beside *B*.
2. Locate *M* halfway between *B* and *C*. *M* will lie in the same vertical plane which contains *A*.
3. Sight on *M*, elevate the telescope until the line of sight is beside *A*.
4. Loosen the screws of the bearing cap, and raise or lower the adjustable end of the horizontal axis until the line of sight is in the same vertical plane with *A*.

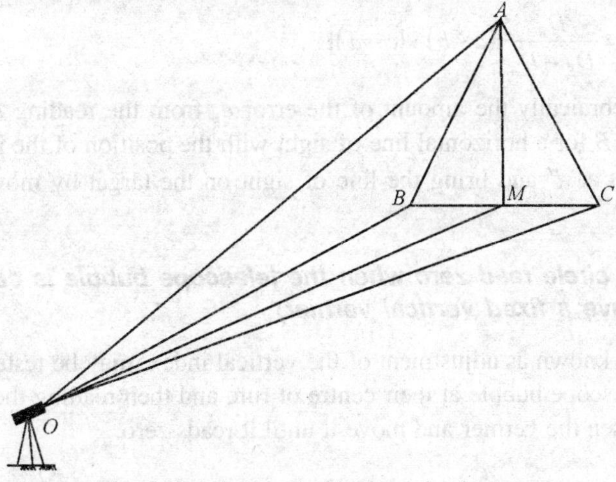

Fig. 4.22 Adjustment of horizontal axis

To make the axis of the telescope level parallel to the line of sight

This adjustment ensures that the line of collimation should remain horizontal when the bubble of the telescope level is at the centre of its run.

To test whether this adjustment exists, follow the steps as under (Fig. 4.23):

1. Set two pages *A* and *B* on fairly level ground about 100 m apart.
2. Set up the instrument at *M* on the line *AB*, and equally distant from *A* and *B*.

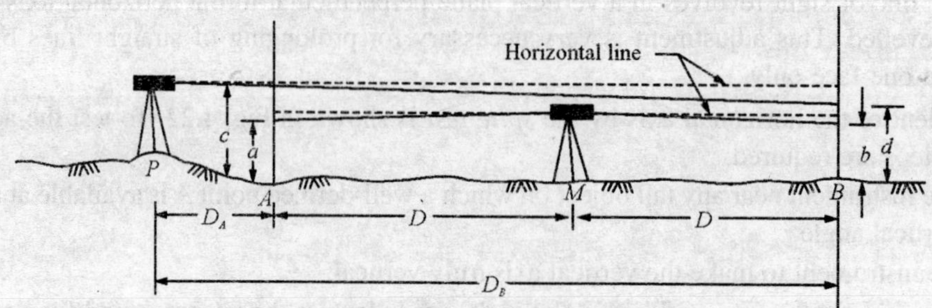

Fig. 4.23 Adjustment of the telescope level

3. Clamp the vertical circle, and bring the bubble central by means of vertical slow motion screw. Let the readings on the levelling staves at *A* and *B*, be *a* and *b*, respectively. The true difference in elevation Δh_1 for this set up is $(a - b)$.
4. Shift the instrument to *P*, on the prolonged line *BA*, about 25 m from *A*.
5. With the bubble central, read the levelling staff first on *A* and then on *B*. Let the readings on *A* and *B* be *c* and *d*, respectively. Now the difference in elevation Δh_2 will be $(c - d)$.
6. If Δh_2 is equal to Δh_1, the instrument is in adjustment.
   If Δh_2 is not equal to Δh_1, the instrument is adjusted in the following manner:
   (*i*) Calculate the inclination (error) of the line of sight in the net distance $(D_B - D_A)$ which is equal to $(a - b) - (c - d)$.
   (*ii*) Calculate the error e_B in the reading on the far staff on *B* as under

$$e_B = \frac{D_B}{D_B - D_A}[(a-b)-(c-d)]$$

   (*iii*) Subtract algebraically the amount of the error e_B from the reading *d* to obtain the correct reading *d′* at *B* for a horizontal line of sight with the position of the instrument at *P*.
   (*iv*) Set the target at *d′* and bring the line of sight on the target by moving the cross hair ring vertically.

To make the vertical circle read zero when the telescope bubble is central (only for those theodolites which have a fixed vertical vernier)

This adjustment also known as adjustment of the vertical index, may be tested by bringing the plate bubble and then the telescope bubble at their centre of run, and then reading the vertical vernier. If the reading is not zero, loosen the vernier and move it until it reads zero.

Types of Theodolite

The theodolites can be classified into the following categories:

1. Transit or engineer's transit
2. Repeating theodolites, optical transit or optical reading theodolite
3. Direction theodolite.
4. Electronic theodolite.

Transit or engineer's transit

Transit or engineer's transit, most commonly referred to as a theodolite, is an instrument of great versatility, and is sometimes called the universal surveying instrument. The instruments under this category have traditionally three or four levelling screws, metal graduated scales, verniers for direct reading of horizontal and vertical angles. Because of wide variety of its uses, it has been discussed in detail in Sec. 4.6.

Repeating theodolite or optical transit

The mechanical motions of optical transit are essentially the same as those of the engineer's transit. They are equipped with graduated scales etched on glass which are viewed by way of optical trains that contain optical micrometers for measuring horizontal and vertical angles. These instruments have three levelling screws and optical plummets which replace the plumb bob.

Direction theodolite

The direction theodolite does not provide for a lower motion as contained in a repeating instrument. When it is set over a station, the horizontal circle is essentially fixed in position. Both the back sight reading and the fore sight reading are taken by means of one motion, which is the movement of the reading device with respect to the graduated horizontal circle. The difference between the back sight and the fore sight readings is directly the value of the angle.

Electronic theodolite

Electronic theodolites contain circular encoders which sense the rotations of the spindles and the telescope, convert these rotations into horizontal and vertical (or zenith) angles electronically, and display the values of the angles on liquid crystal displays (LCD) or light emmitting diode displays (LED). Further details about these instruments are given in Chapter 11 of *Higher Surveying*.

4.5 ANGLE AND DIRECTION MEASUREMENTS WITH A THEODOLITE

A single set of measurement of horizontal angle between two points *P* and *Q* at a station *O* is made in the following steps (Fig. 4.24):

1. Fix two ranging poles or signals at *P* and *Q*.
2. Set up the instrument at *O* and perform the temporary adjustments.
3. Set the instrument for taking face left reading first by keeping the vertical circle to the left.
4. Release both the lower and upper clamp screws, and turn the upper plate to set the vernier *A* to 0° or 360° mark on the main scale. Tighten the upper clamp screw. Bring the index of vernier *A* exactly to the zero of the main scale using slow motion screw of the upper plate.
5. At this stage the reading of the vernier *B* will be 180°. If the difference in the two readings of verniers *A* and *B* is not equal to 180°, the instrument has error due to eccentricity of verniers, or due to eccentricity of centres of spindles or both. The mean of the two readings is taken to eliminate this error. For recording the readings, the degrees, minutes and seconds on the vernier *A*, and only minutes and seconds on vernier *B* are taken.

6. Swing the telescope in the horizontal plane, and point it at the left side station *P*. Tighten the lower clamp screw, and bisect exactly the ranging pole or signal at *P* using the lower slow motion screw. The vertical slow motion screw is also used to bring the vertical cross hair exactly on the target. To minimise the error in bisection due to non-verticality of the ranging pole, the vertical cross hair should be brought to the lowest visible point of the ranging pole.
7. Loosen the upper clamp screw, and turn the telescope clockwise until the line of sight is on the ranging pole at *Q*. Tighten the upper clamp screw, and bisect the ranging pole at *Q* exactly using the upper slow motion screw.
8. Read both the verniers *A* and *B* and record the reading in the Form-1 (Table 4.1), which is a page of the field book for recording the horizontal angles. The reading of the vernier *A* is the angle *POQ*. The vernier *B* gives the value of the angle *POQ* after deducting 180°. The mean of two values of the angles obtained from the verniers A and B, is the required angle *POQ*.
9. Change the face of the instrument to the face right by transiting the telescope, and swinging it by 180°.
10. Repeat steps 4 to 8, and determine another value of the angle *POQ*.
11. The mean of the face left and face right observations, is the final required angle *POQ*.

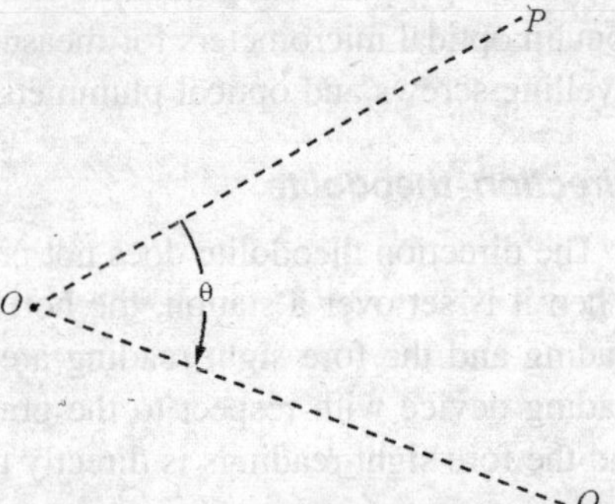

Fig. 4.24 Measurement of horizontal angle

Table 4.1 Measurement of horizontal angle

Form-1

		Face Left									Swing Right				Face Right									Swing Left					
Inst. at	Sighted to	*A*			*B*		Mean			No. of repetition	Horizontal angle			*A*			*B*		Mean			No. of repetition	Horizontal angle			Average horizontal angle		
		°	′	″	′	″	°	′	″		°	′	″	°	′	″	′	″	°	′	″		°	′	″	°	′	″

Common Mistakes

The mistakes often made in measuring horizontal angles are:

1. Turning the wrong slow motion screw.
2. Failing to tighten the clamps.

3. Reading the numbers on the horizontal scale in wrong direction.
4. Reading angles in the wrong direction.
5. Dropping 20′ or 30′ by failure to take the full-scale reading before reading the vernier (*e.g.*, with a circle graduated to 20′, calling an angle 35° 16′, the vernier reading being 16′ when the actual reading is 35°36′).
6. Reading the vernier in the wrong direction.
7. Reading the wrong vernier.

Horizontal Angle Measurement by Repetition Method

The method of repetition is used to measure a horizontal angle to a finer degree of accuracy than that obtainable with the least count of the vernier. By this method the value of the angle obtained is a closer value to the true value of the angle. The following example clearly explains the principle of repetition method.

Let the actual value of the angle *POQ* (Fig. 4.24) to be measured with a theodolite of 30″ least count, be 21°05′38″. For the first measurement as described in Sec. 4.5, the reading will be 21°5′30″. For the next measurement, loosen the lower clamp and bisect the ranging pole at *P* using the lower clamp and slow motion only. Loosen the upper plate and bisect the ranging pole at *Q*. The reading now will be 42°11′00″ whereas the exact reading should be 42°11′16″. The process after the third setting on the right ranging pole at *Q* should give the theodolite reading as 63°17′00″ whereas the exact reading should have been 63°16′54″. Dividing 63°17′00″ by 3, the number of repetitions, gives 21°05′40″ which is only 2″ in error.

In practice 6 to 10 repetitions with both faces readings are considered to be enough for measuring an angle to the highest degree of precision. When face left is kept, the instrument is rotated clockwise and for face right, the instrument is rotated anticlockwise. Mean of the face left and face right readings after dividing by the number of repetitions, is the final measured value of the angle.

Form-1 given in Table 4.1, may be used for recording the observations and deducing the angle by repetition method.

The following errors are eliminated by the method of repetition:

1. Taking reading on both the verniers eliminates the errors due to eccentricity of verniers and centres.
2. Taking reading at different parts of the circle, eliminates the errors due to inaccurate graduations.
3. Taking both faces readings, eliminates the errors due to inadjustment of line of collimation and the horizontal axis of the instrument.
4. Errors due to inaccurate bisection of the object, eccentric centering, etc., may be to some extent counter-balanced in different observations.

The errors due to the following are not eliminated as all these errors are of cumulative nature:

1. Slip
2. Displacement of station signal
3. Verticality of the vertical axis.

Horizontal Angle Measurement by Reiteration Method or Direction Method

When several angles are to be measured at one station, the reiteration method is used. The angle between the points *A, B, C,* and *D* shown in Fig. 4.25, are required to be measured at station *O*. Out of several stations *A, B, C, D,* etc., one may be chosen as an initial station from which the successive angles are measured. The angle between the last station and the initial station, is also measured, and this is known as *closing the horizon*. This provides a check that sum of all the angles measured at a station is 360°.

When the horizon is closed, the final reading of the vernier should be same as its initial reading. If there is any discrepancy within the permissible limits, it is distributed equally among all the angles measured. For example, if $\theta_1 + \theta_2 + \theta_3 + \theta_4 + \theta_5 = 360° + \delta\theta$, then the correction to each angle would be $\left(-\frac{1}{5}\delta\theta\right)$ for closing the horizon. In the case of a large discrepancy, the whole work is to be repeated.

For recording the measurements by reiteration method, Form-1 given in Table 4.1, may be used.

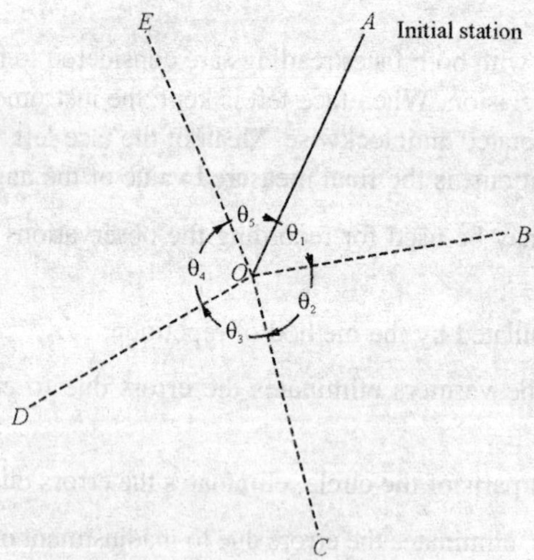

Fig. 4.25 Horizontal angle by reiteration method

When a direction theodolite is used, the instrument is set up over the selected station, and with telescope normal, the line of sight is directed at each adjacent station in turn. The telescope is rotated in a clockwise direction, and the verniers *A* and *B* are read. The telescope is then reversed, and another round of directions is observed. This entire set of readings constitutes one *position*. Depending on the precision required, number of positions may be decided. For example, for a first-order work a total of 8 to 32 positions, and for a second-order work, 4 to 16 positions are observed.

The circle reading should be advanced by 180°/n for each new position, n being the number of positions to be observed. This is done to distribute the readings over the entire circle to eliminate the errors of graduation of the circle.

Measurement of a Vertical Angle

The method for measuring vertical angles varies with the type of instrument used. The engineer's transit measures the vertical angle with reference to horizontal plane. Direction and repeating or optical transits measure the zenith angles. The electronic theodolites may have options for measuring the vertical angles from the horizontal or from the zenith.

Using the engineer's transit, the vertical angle to a point is its angle of elevation (+) or depression (–) from the horizontal as shown in Fig. 4.26a and b, respectively.

The procedure for measuring a vertical angle is as follows:

1. After setting up, centering, and levelling up the instrument, the object to which the vertical angle is required, is bisected using the telescope clamp and slow motion screw.
2. The reading device is now set to bring the altitude bubble to the centre of its run by means of the clip screw. If the theodolite is fitted with an optical split-bubble, it is set to have an apparently continuous edge.
3. The reading on the vertical circle is now read. The reading will be the vertical angle α, (180° – α), (90° + α), or a similar function of α, depending on the graduation system used for the vertical circle.

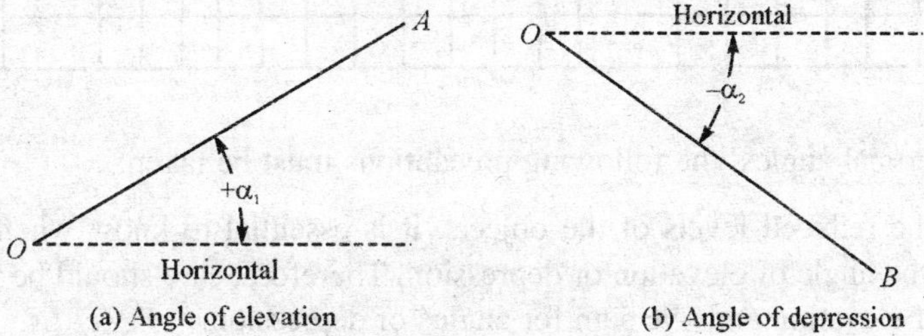

Fig. 4.26 Vertical angle

When several vertical angles are to be measured at one station, the altitude bubble is set to its centre of run for all pointings of the telescope in step 2 above. To achieve this, the procedure given below is followed:

1. Turn the instrument about the vertical axis so that the altitude level is parallel to the line joining any two levelling screws. Bring the bubble to its centre of run by turning the levelling screws either both inwards or both outwards.
2. Turn the telescope through 90° so that the altitude level is perpendicular to the line joining the same levelling screws. Bring the bubble of the altitude level again to the centre of its run by turning the third screw.

3. Turn back the telescope through 90° so that the altitude level is again parallel to the two levelling screws.
4. Repeat steps 2 and 3 until the bubble of the altitude level remains central in both the positions.
5. Now swing the telescope through 180° so that the altitude level is parallel to the two levelling screws but the eyepiece-end and the objective-end are reversed.The bubble will remain central if the instrument is in permanent adjustments, and it will remain central for all pointings of the telescope.

The vertical angle observations may be recorded in Form -2 given in Table 4.2.

Table 4.2 Measurement of vertical angle

Form-2

			Face Left												Face Right														
Inst. at	Sighted to	±	*C*			*D*		Mean			No. of repetition	Vertical angle			*C*			*D*		Mean			No. of repetition	Vertical angle			Average vertical angle		
			°	′	″	′	″	°	′	″		°	′	″	°	′	″	′	″	°	′	″		°	′	″	°	′	″

While measuring vertical angles, the following precautions must be taken:

1. For computing the reduced levels of the objects, it is essential to know whether the measured vertical angle is the angle of elevation or depression. Therefore, care should be taken to note +ve sign for angles of elevation and –ve sign for angles of depression.
2. Both the verniers must be read to obtain the mean vertical angle.
3. To eliminate or minimise the errors due to inadjustments of the instrument, both face readings should be taken.

4.6 FIELD OPERATIONS WITH A THEODOLITE

Theodolite is a versatile instrument, and several field operations other than the measurement of horizontal and vertical angles, are also carried out with it. Some of field operations which can be performed with theodolite, are discussed below. In fact, many other tasks can be performed by a theodolite, depending on the ingenuity of the surveyor. In all the measurements discussed below, it is a general practice to read both the verniers, repeat the work on both faces of the instrument, and take mean of all these values.

Measurement of Direct Angles

Direct angles are the angles to the right or azimuths from the preceding lines (*c.f.*, Sec. 4.2). They are commonly used in open traverses (*c.f.*, Sec. 4.7). These angles range between 0° to 360°.

The general procedure to measure the direct angles is to back sight on the preceding station with zero reading on one of the verniers, then turn it clockwise, sight the forward station and take the reading on the horizontal circles. This reading is the direct angle at the station.

Measurement of Deflection Angles

The measurement of deflection angles (*c.f.*, Sec. 4.2) is done by taking a back sight on the previous station with zero reading on one of the verniers. Then the telescope is transited and turned clockwise or anticlockwise as the case may be, the forward station is sighted and the horizontal circle is read. If the deflection angle is to the right, the reading itself is the measured value of the angle, otherwise the difference between 360° and the reading, gives the deflection angle to the left.

Measurement of Magnetic Bearing

Magnetic bearings (*c.f.*, Sec.4.2) may be measured with the aid of some form of compass fitted to the theodolite. The whole-circle bearing is measured by right swing, *i.e.*, turning the telescope clockwise. The following is the procedure to measure the whole-circle bearing of a line.

Set up the instrument, complete the temporary adjustments at the station and set one of verniers to zero. Loosen the lower clamp and the magnetic needle is released. Turn the telescope until the magnetic needle takes its normal position indicating the N–S direction. In this position of the instrument, the telescope points to the magnetic north while the reading is zero. Clamp the lower plate to loosen the upper clamp, and turn the telescope clockwise to sight the forward station. The reading on the horizontal circle now is the magnetic whole-circle bearing of the line.

Lining-in

Lining-in is the process of establishing intermediate points on a given line (Fig. 4.27), and is similar to ranging discussed in Sec. 3.4. It is assumed that the end points A and B are intervisible.

Set up the instrument over P, centre and level it accurately. Clamp the upper plate, and turn the telescope until Q is bisected. Clamp the lower plate, and bisect Q exactly using the slow motion screw. Ask the assistant to fix the station marks at 1, 2 and 3, such that they coincide exactly with the intersection of the cross hairs. The work should be repeated on the other face of the instrument to check the discrepancy which should then be set right by choosing the mean position for each of the intermediate points.

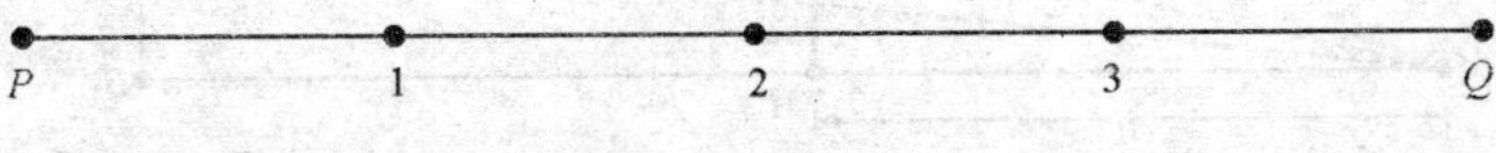

Fig. 4.27 Lining-in

Balancing-in

Method of establishing intermediate points on a line whose extremities are not intervisible but they are visible from some intermediate point, is known as *balancing-in*. It is also called *wiggling-in*.

In Fig. 4.28, the points A and B are the extremities of a line AB which are not intervisible due to intervening ground, but they are visible from the intermediate point M.

Set up the instrument at an intermediate point M_1 as close to the line AB as can be estimated. Take a backsight on A. Plunge the telescope and locate the point B_1 where the line of sight strikes near B. Measure the distance B_1B, and determine M_1M by which the instrument has to be shifted laterally. So that the point M is on the line AB.

$$M_1M = \frac{B_1B}{L}\, l \tag{4.1}$$

The distance L is found out from the known coordinates of A and B, or from an existing map. Since the problem is to locate M on the ground by measuring M_1M and M_2M, etc., on the existing map join AB and take point M at the estimated location and measure $AM = l$, for use in Eqs. (4.1 and 4.2).

Now set up the instrument at the estimated position M_2 which may not be at the required location M. Take a backsight again on A, plunge the telescope, and locate the point B_2. Shift the instrument laterally by a distance M_2M which is now computed from

$$M_2M = \frac{B_2B}{L}\, l \tag{4.2}$$

Repeat the above process until the line of sight strikes B when the telescope is plunged. The instrument station is then the required intermediate point M on the line AB. Locate the point M vertically beneath the centre of the instrument using the plumb bob or optical plumet.

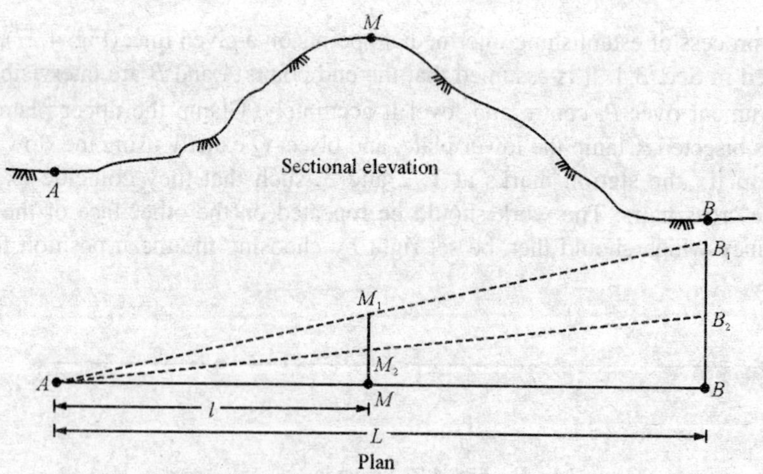

Fig. 4.28 Balancing-in

Double Sighting: If the intermediate point is to be established with high precision or when the instrument is not in perfect adjustment, the point M is obtained by the method of double sighting. In this method, two points M' and M'' are located by both face observations, *i.e.*, telescope normal and telescope inverted. The mean of the two positions is the required point M (Fig. 4.29).

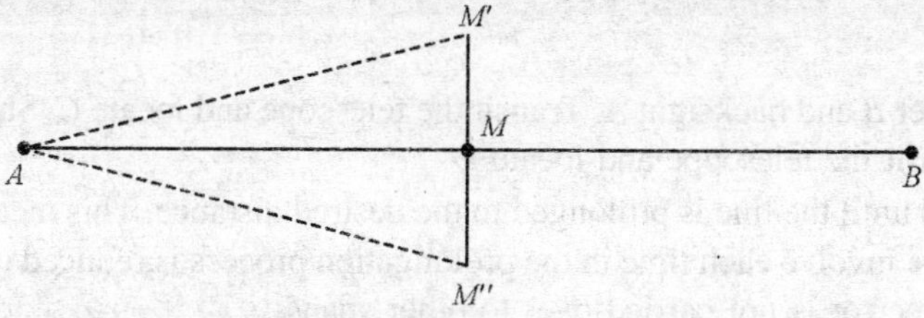

Fig. 4.29 Double sighting

Random Line Method of Running a Line

If the ends A and B of a line are neither intervisible nor are they visible from intermediate points, the random line method is used for running the line AB. These conditions arise when the area is thickly wooded or hilly. The line AC shown in Fig. 4.30, is called the *random line* or *a trial line*.

Locate a point C near to B from where both A and B are visible. Set up the instrument at C, and measure the angle ACB. Let this angle be θ. Measure the distances AC, and CB with a tape. Now locate a point p on the line AC, and set up the instrument over the point p. Lay off the angle ApP equal to θ. Measure the distance pP equal to $BC\dfrac{Ap}{AC}$. The point P is on the line AB. Other points Q, R, etc., are also located in the similar manner.

Check whether the line of sight strikes P, Q, and R exactly when the instrument is at A or B. If any point is found not to lie exactly on the line AB, it is shifted laterally to bring it on the line.

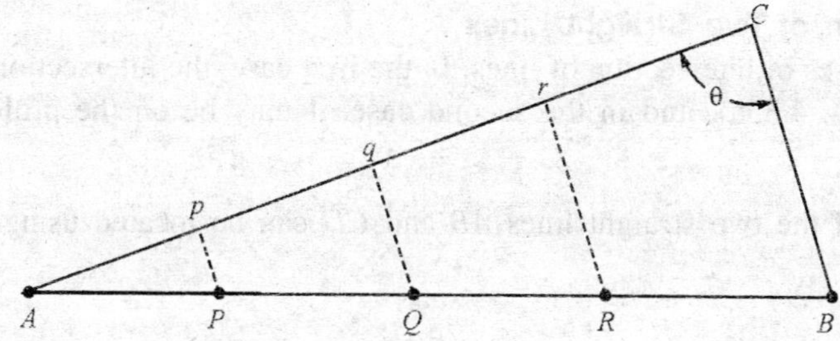

Fig. 4.30 Random line method of running a line

Prolonging a Straight Line

It is often necessary to prolong or extend a line for a significant distance by locating an adequate number of points along the line. There are three methods for prolonging a line, and they are illustrated below.

Method-I (Fig. 4.31)

Set up the instrument over the end A, and sight the end B of the line AB after the horizontal motion of the instrument has been fixed. Locate a point C at a reasonable distance. Shift the theodolite to B and locate another point D on the prolongation of BC. The process is repeated until the line is prolonged to the disired distance. This method will result in cumulative errors if the instrument is not in adjustment.

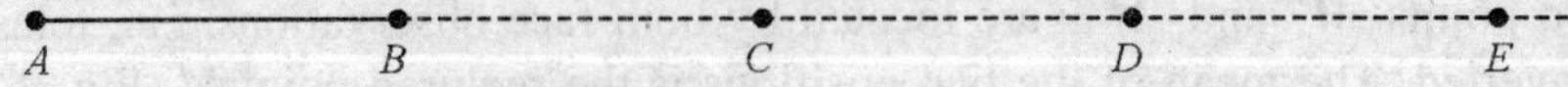

Fig. 4.31 Prolonging a line by first method

Method-II (Fig. 4.31)

Set up the instrument over B and backsight A. Transit the telescope and locate C. Shift the instrument to C and backsight B. Transit the telescope and locate D.

The process is continued until the line is prolonged to the desired distance. This method is superior to the first because the distance involve each time in the prolongation process is reduced to a uniform value of the order of AB, and the error is not carried over to other spans.

Method-III (Double Sighting) (Fig. 4.32)

Set up the instrument at B, backsight A with face left, plunge the telescope, and locate C_1. Change the face of the instrument to right, backsight A again, plunge the telescope and locate C_2. The point C_2 will be obtained only when the instrument is out of adjustments. The mean of the two locations C_1 and C_2 is the desired point C. The process is repeated and continued until the line is prolonged to the distance required. In this method, the error is doubled on reversal of the telescope, and the mean of two locations becomes the desired location of the point on the prolongation of the line. This method is used when high precision is required, and the instrument is suspect with regard to adjustment.

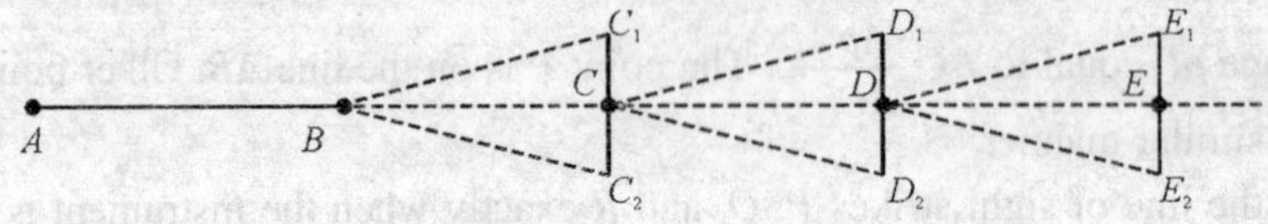

Fig. 4.32 Prolonging a line by double sighting

Location of Intersection of Two Straight Lines

There may be two cases of intersection of lines. In the first case, the intersection may fall on the junction of the lines (Fig. 4.33a), and in the second case, it may be on the prolongation of line (Fig. 4.33b).

The intersection X of the two straight lines AB and CD can be located using a theodolite, as explained below:

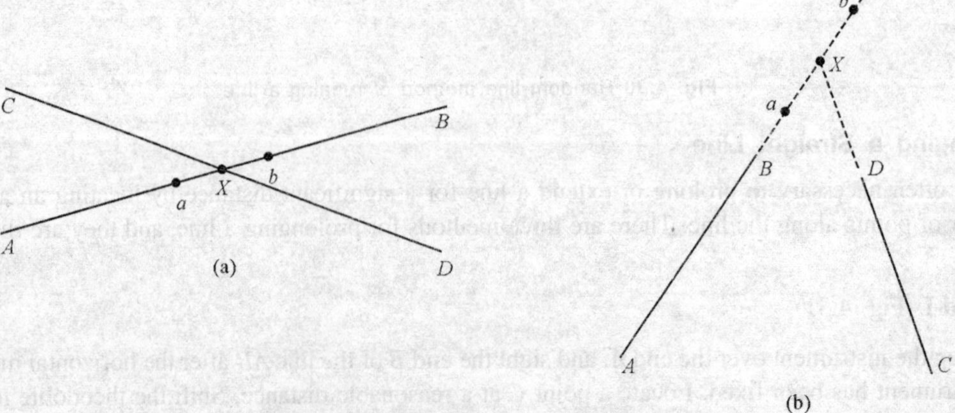

Fig. 4.33 The intersection of two lines

Case-I (Fig. 4.33a): Set up the instrument at one end of one of the lines, say at *A* on *AB*, and sight *B*. Clamp the horizontal motion and fix two points *a* and *b*, a small distance apart on either side of the estimated position of the intersection *X* with wire nails or tacks. Stretch a string between the points *a* and *b*. Now shift the instrument to the end *C* on the other line *CD*, and sight *D*. The point of intersection *X* is marked on the string where the line of sight cuts the string.

Case-II (Fig. 4.33b): Set up the instrument at *A*, and sight *B*. Fix the points *a* and *b* on the prolongation of *AB* on either side of the estimated position of the intersection *X*, and stretch a string between them. Now shift the instrument to *C*, the farther end of *CD*, and sight *D*. The prolongation of *CD* cuts the string at the intersection *X* of the two lines.

To achieve a better accuracy in locating the intersection, double sighting can be used in both the above cases.

4.7 THEODOLITE TRAVERSING

A traverse consists of a series of straight lines connecting successive established points along the route of a survey. The points defining the ends of the traverse lines are called *traverse stations*, and the processes of locating the traverse station is *traversing*. Traverse is required to be run in land surveys, city surveys, hydrographic surveys, and locations surveys in highways, railways, canals, etc.

When a traverse is run by using a theodolite, it is called theodolite traversing. Traverse can also be run by using a compass, a tacheometer or a plane table, and the process is known as compass traversing, stadia traversing, and plane-table traversing.

The traversing has been discussed in detail in Chapter 9.

4.8 TO LAY OFF A HORIZONTAL ANGLE

The laying off a horizontal angle is required sometimes in construction works, and the process is the reverse of process of that of measuring the angles.

To lay off an angle *AOB* equal to θ, as shown in Fig. 4.34, set up the instrument at *O*, and set the vernier *A* to read 0° or 360° using upper clamp and slow motion screw. Turn the telescope, and sight the station *A*. Clamp the lower plate, and bisect *A* accurately using the slow motion screw. Now loosen the upper clamp, and turn the upper plate until the vernier *A* reads the given angle θ. Use of slow motion screw is made to set the given angle accurately.

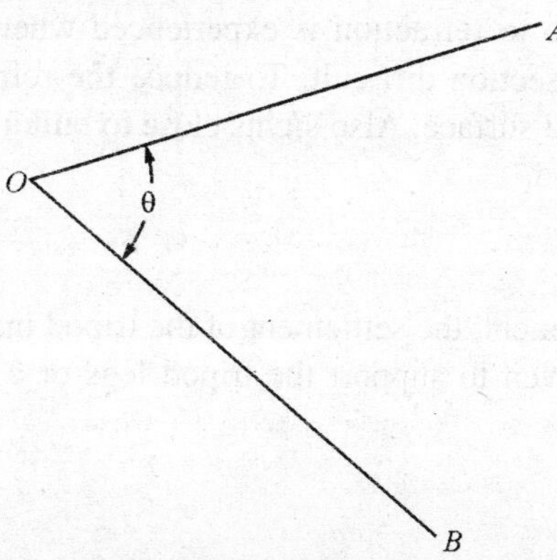

Fig. 4.34 Horizontal angle

The line of sight is now in the required direction OB. Depress the telescope and establish B on the ground along the line of sight. The angle AOB laid is equal to the angle θ.

When a horizontal angle is to be laid off with higher precision, the method of repetition should be used in similar manner as discussed above.

4.9 ERRORS IN THEODOLITE MEASUREMENTS

The sources which cause errors in the measurements made with the theodolites, may be classified as below:

1. Natural errors
2. Personal errors
3. Instrumental errors
4. Mistakes.

Natural Errors

Sources of natural errors are: (1) temperature, (2) wind, (3) refraction, and (4) settlement of tripod. In general, the natural errors are not very large enough to affect appreciably the measurements of ordinary precision. These errors are generally random, but under certain conditions they may be systematic in nature. For surveys of very high precision, special attempt is made to establish a procedure which will as nearly as possible minimise or eliminate systematic errors.

Temperature effect

Effect of temperature difference may be unequal expansion of various components of a theodolite leading to errors, It can be minimised by shielding the instrument from heat.

Wind effect

Effect of strong winds is to create vibrations in the instrument which makes it difficult to work. Also the plumb bob gets deflected making the accurate centering difficult. To reduce the wind effect, the instrument is shielded from the strong winds. Alternatively, the work can be suspended during the strong winds.

Refraction effect

Shimmering of the signals due to refraction is experienced when the line of sight is close to the ground. It makes the accurate bisection difficult. To reduce the refraction effect, the line of sight is always kept well above the ground surface. Also sights close to buildings, smoke stacks, and even large individual bushes are to be avoided.

Settlement of tripod

Due to the weight of the instrument, the settlement of the tripod may take place if the ground is soft. In such cases, stakes may be driven to support the tripod legs or a triangular frame may be used to support the tripod.

Personal Errors

Personal errors arise from the limitations of the human eye in setting up and levelling the instrument, and in making the observations. These errors are random and hence cannot be eliminated.

Errors due to inaccurate centering

If the instrument is not set up exactly over the station, it produces an error in all angles measured at the given station. The magnitude of the error varies directly with the direction of pointing and inversely with the length of sight. The error may be kept within negligible limits by taking reasonable care. When the sights are long, unnecessary time should not be wasted in setting up. Centering to within 6 to 9 mm is possible without difficulty using a plumb bob. When the instrument is provided with an optical plummet, centering errors less than 1 mm are possible.

Errors due to inaccurate levelling

This error is small when the sights are nearly level, but may be large for steeply inclined sights. This error may be minimised or eliminated by frequent checking of the position of the bubble centre, and if necessary it should be recentered. Relevelling should never be done between a back sight and fore sight.

Slip in screws

An error will occur if the clamp screws are not properly tightened. The magnitude of error will depend upon the slip. The error is avoided by properly tightening all the screws.

The slip may also occur when the shifting head is not properly tightened or when the instrument is not properly fixed to the tripod head.

Improper use of tangent screws

The error is introduced by improper use of the screws. While taking the back sights, the lower slow motion screw should be used and for the fore sights, upper slow motion screw. The slow motion screws should only be used after tightening the corresponding clamp screws. To avoid error due to backlash, the final bisection of the object should be achieved only by turning the slow motion screws in positive direction.

Errors in setting and reading the verniers

These functions are of the least count of the vernier, and of the legibility of scale and vernier lines. A magnifying glass can be used to enable closer reading. The vernier error may be reduced by using the method of repetition.

Inaccurate sighting

Inaccurate sighting is likely to be a source of rather large error in ordinary surveys when the sights are taken on the ranging pole of which often only the upper position is visible from the instrument.

The error can be minimised by accurately centering the vertical cross hair on the signal, and sighting the lowest portion of the ranging pole placed at the station mark. For short sights greater care is required than for long sights. If the station to be observed is quite close, the string of the plumb bob should be used in place of ranging pole for accurate sighting.

Parallax

The error due to imperfect focussing is always present to greater or lesser degree but can be reduced to a negligible quantity by taking reasonable care in focussing.

Instrumental errors

Instrumental errors are those errors which are due to instrumental imperfections and / or inadjustment. They are systematic errors, and can be either eliminated or reduced to a negligible amount.

Error due to imperfect adjustment of the plate level

This error causes the measurement of horizontal angles in an inclined plane instead of a horizontal plane, and cannot be eliminated by averaging the face left and face right readings. The permanent adjustment of the instrument has to be done to eliminate this error.

Error due to line of sight not being perpendicular to horizontal axis

If the line of sight is not exactly perpendicular to the horizontal axis of the instrument, the telescope does not revolve in vertical plane, instead it generates a cone.

The error in horizontal angle occurs if the angle of inclination of the back sight is not equal to that of the fore sight. The error is eliminated by averaging the face left and face right readings, *i.e.*, by double sighting.

Error due to horizontal axis not being perpendicular to the vertical axis

This error is similar to the error due to line of sight not being perpendicular to horizontal axis discussed above, and it is also eliminated by averaging the face left and face right readings.

Error due to eccentricity of inner and outer axes

This error is eliminated by averaging the readings taken on both the verniers.

Error due to eccentricity of verniers

The error due to zero marks of the verniers *A* and *B*, not being at the ends of the same diameter and not being exactly 180° apart, is also eliminated by taking mean of readings on verniers *A* and *B*.

It may be noted that eccentricity of verniers does not introduce any error in horizontal angles so long the same vernier is used for the initial and final readings.

Errors due to imperfect graduations

Errors of this source can be minimised to a negligible amount by taking the mean of several observations for which the readings are distributed over the circle and over the vernier.

Error due to non–adjustment of vertical vernier or vertical index error

Non-adjustment of vertical vernier introduces a constant error in the vertical angles. The error is eliminated by averaging the face left and face right readings.

Mistakes

The common mistakes or blunders which generally the surveyors make due to carelessness, are:

1. Misreading the vernier.
2. Reading the wrong vernier scale.
3. Turning wrong tangent screws.
4. Sighting on the wrong signal, or setting up the instrument over the wrong station.
5. Booking wrong values of the readings.
6. Missing sign (+ or –) for vertical angles.
7. Missing the word right or left for deflection angles.

The mistakes can only be avoided by adopting suitable field procedures.

4.10 ANGLE MEASUREMENT USING A TAPE

It is possible to make simple surveys by using just a tape. If the sides of a triangle are measured, sufficient data are obtained for computing the angles of a triangle. The error in the computed values of the angles depends on the care with which points are established, and the precision with which measurements are taken. The method is slow, and is generally employed as a check.

4.11 ANGLE MEASUREMENT USING PLANE TABLE AND ALIDADE

A plane table is a drawing board mounted on a tripod, and an alidade is a straight edge with some form of sighting device. Using a plane table and an alidade, angles can be determined graphically. The instrument and the method have been discussed in Chapter 10.

4.12 ANGLE MEASUREMENT USING A SEXTANT

Sextant is an instrument generally used for hydrographic surveys. An observer can measure the angles while he is moving, hence, angles can be read from a boat. The angles measured by a sextant are not

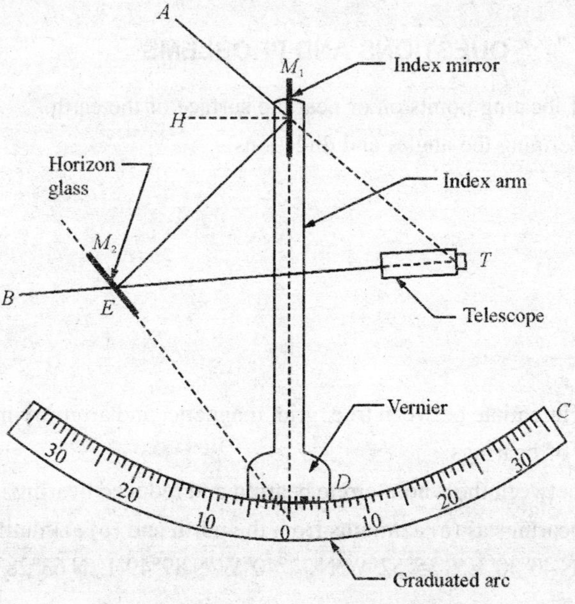

Fig. 4.35 Essential features of a sextant

generally in the horizontal plane, and, therefore, are not horizontal angles. Sextant is not an instrument of high accuracy for angles less than 15° and distances less than 300 m.

The essential features of a sextant are shown in Fig. 4.35. An index mirror M_1 is rigidly attached to a movable arm M_1D, which is fitted with a vernier, clamp, and a slow motion screw or tangent screw. The movable arm moves along the graduated arc shown in the figure. A second mirror, M_2, known as horizon glass, the lower portion of which is half silvered and the upper half clear. The mirror M_2 and a telescope T are rigidly attached to the frame. The telescope points towards M_2.

Let the angle to be measured is ATB. T is also the observer's position. The ray of light from signal at B passes through the clear portion of M_2 on through the telescope to the eye at T. The ray of light from signal at A strikes the index mirror at M_1, and is reflected to E and then through the telescope to T. Each set of rays forms its own image on its respective half of the objective. By moving the M_1D these images can be made to move over each other. There will be one position in which they coincide, and the vernier reading on the graduated arc C is the required angle ATB.

Measuring Angles with the Sextant

To measure the angle ATB (Fig. 4.35), hold the sextant in the right hand and adjust the index arm to read zero. Sight the left-hand object B through the telescope, and the clear portion of the horizon glass M_2. Move the index arm with the left hand until the image of second object A coincides with the image of B. The final setting is made with the tangent screw. The test for the exact coincidence is made by twisting the sextant slightly to make the reflected image move back and forth across the position of coincidence. Take the reading on the graduated arc using the vernier, which is the value of the desired angle between A and B at the instrument station T.

4.13 ANGLE MEASUREMENT USING A MAGNETIC COMPASS

The magnetic compass is useful for rough surveys and retracing early land surveys. The compass mounted on a theodolite helps in approximate checking of measured horizontal angles. A detailed discussion on compass and its uses are presented in Chapter 5.

QUESTIONS AND PROBLEMS

4.1 Describe the methods of locating points on or near the surface of the earth.

4.2 Describe the means of defining the angles and directions.

4.3 Define the following:

(*a*) Bearings
(*b*) Azimuths
(*c*) Deflection angles
(*d*) Angles to right
(*e*) Interior angles.

4.4 What is a meridian? Differentiate between true, grid, magnetic, and arbitrary meridians.

4.5 Describe various types of bearings.

4.6 Explain the difference between the whole-circle bearing and reduced bearing of a line.

4.7 Express the following bearings as (a) azimuths from the north and (b) azimuths from the south: N 43°20′ E, S 36°42′ E, N 40°30′ E, S 35°52′ W, N 77°40′ W, N 89°49′ E, N 63°28′ W, S 79°59′ W, N 8°15′ W, S 12°18′ E.

4.8 Following are the forward azimuths: A_{AB} = 185°30′, A_{AC} = 145°45′, A_{CD} = 205°40′, A_{DE} = 18°59′, A_{AF} = 98°15′.

Convert these directions to back azimuths.

4.9 The following azimuths of the lines are reckoned from the north:

AB = 162°19′, *BC* = 279°33′,

CD = 333°50′, *DE* = 5°35′.

What are the corresponding bearings? Also determine the deflection angles between the consecutive lines.

4.10 Draw a neat sketch of a transit, and explain the functions of its various components.

4.11 Differentiate between

(*a*) Transiting or plunging and swinging of the telescope.

(*b*) Face left and face right readings.

(*c*) Clamp screw and tangent screw.

(*d*) Telescope normal and telescope inverted.

4.12 What are the advantages of an internal focussing telescope?

4.13 Define the following terms associated with the angle measurements with a theodolite:

(*a*) Vertical axis; (*b*) Trunion axis; (*c*) Axis of the plate level; (*d*) Centering; (*e*) A set.

4.14 What do you understand by 'Temporary Adjustments'? Describe in brief the various temporary adjustments of a theodolite.

4.15 Discuss the relationships between the various axes of a transit.

4.16 What are the permanent adjustments in a theodolite? Discuss briefly their effects on the angle measurements.

4.17 Describe the various types of theodolite.

4.18 Discuss the procedure of measuring a horizontal angle by repetition. What are its advantages?

4.19 How would you measure horizontal angles by reiteration method?

4.20 Discuss the procedure of measuring a vertical angle using a transit.

4.21 Write briefly the procedures for the measurement of (*i*) Direct angles; (*ii*) Magnetic bearings; (*iii*) Deflection angles.

4.22 Write short notes on the following:

(*i*) Lining-in; (*ii*) Balancing-in; (*iii*) Random line; (*iv*) Prolonging; (*v*) Location of intersection; (*vi*) Double sighting.

4.23 How would you lay off a horizontal angle using a theodolite? If an angle is required to be laid off with higher precision, what method is to be used?

4.24 What are different types of errors in theodolite surveying? How are they eliminated or minimised?

4.25 Describe the various components of a sextant. Explain the method of measuring angles with a sextant. Why the angles measured with a sextant may not be true horizontal angles?

4.26 A theodolite having graduations 0° to 360° in clockwise direction on its circle, is used to measure an angle by 12 clockwise repetitions, 6 readings taken with telescope normal and 6 readings with telescope inverted. The observations are as under:

Telescope	Reading	Vernier	
		A	*B*
Direct	Initial	48°46′	228°46′
Direct	After first turning	161°9′	
Reversed	After twelfth turning	317°24′	137°25′

Compute the value of the angle.

4.27 A direction theodolite with a least count of 1″, is set over a station *S* to measure directions to station *R*, *Q*, and *P*. The observed directions are as given below:

Station	Telescope	Reading
R	*D* *R*	0° 10′16″ 180°10′26″
Q	*D* *R*	48°52′06″ 228°52′40″
P	*D* *R*	83°06′48″ 263°06′48″
D = Direct	R = Reverse	

Compute the average angles *RSQ* and *QSP*.

5

CHAIN AND COMPASS SURVEYING

5.1 GENERAL

The purpose of land surveying is to secure necessary data of a parcel of land for the purpose of defining or demarcating its boundaries, determining its area, preparing its plan or map, or execution of an engineering project. The collection of data can be done by any one or combination of surveying methods, *e.g.*, chain surveying, compass surveying, plane table surveying, tacheometric surveying, theodolite surveying, photogrammetry, or remote sensing, depending on accuracy required, extent and type of the area to be surveyed, time available for the survey work, and economic aspects. Once a work is assigned to the surveyor, he has to choose the best approach so that work can be completed within the given time-frame and available funds.

5.2 CHAIN SURVEYING

Chain surveying is the simplest method of surveying in which only linear measurements are made, and no angular measurements are taken. The area to be surveyed is divided into a number of triangles, and the sides of the triangles are directly measured in the field as shown in Fig. 5.1. Since a triangle is a simple plane geometrical figure, it can be plotted from the measured lengths of its sides alone. In chain surveying, a network of triangles is preferred.

Preferably, all the sides of a triangle should be nearly equal having each angle nearly 60° to ensure minimum distortion due to errors in measurement of sides and plotting. Generally, such an ideal condition is practically not possible always due to configuration of the terrain, and therefore, attempt should be made to have *well-conditioned triangles* in which no angle is smaller than 30° and no angle is greater than 120°. The arrangement of triangles to be adopted in the field depends on the shape, topography, and the natural or artificial obstacles met with.

Chain surveying is suitable in the following cases:

1. Ground fairly level and open with simple details
2. Large-scale plans
3. Extent of the area comparatively small.

Chain surveying is unsuitable in the following cases:

1. Area crowded with many details
2. Wooded countries

3. Undulating areas
4. Extent of area large.

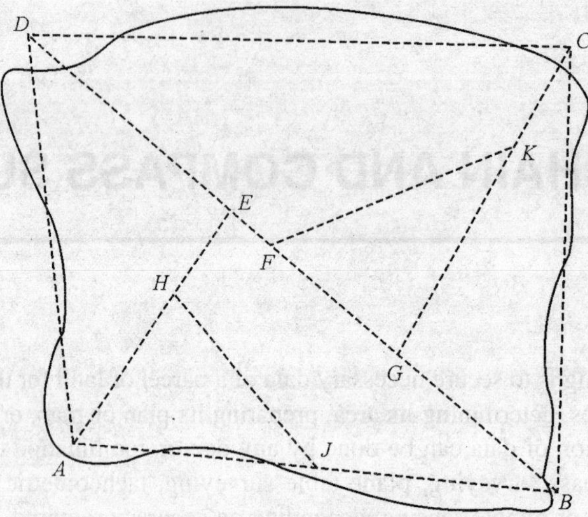

Fig. 5.1 Network of triangles in chain surveying

Definitions of Technical Terms Used in Chain Surveying

Main survey stations: A main survey station is a point where two sides of a triangle meet. These are the points at the beginning and at the end of a chain line.

Tie stations or subsidiary survey stations: These are the points selected on the main survey lines for running auxiliary lines.

Main survey lines: These are chain lines joining the main survey stations.

Tie or subsidiary lines: The chain lines joining the tie stations or subsidiary stations are tie or subsidiary lines. These lines help in locating the interior details which are far away from the main survey lines.

Base line: The longest of the main survey lines is known as the base line. Various survey stations are plotted with reference to this line.

Check lines: Those lines which are run to check the accuracy of the field work are called as check lines or proof lines. The length of a check line in the plan must agree with its measured length in the field. Each triangle must be provided with a check line.

Offsets: Offsets are lateral distances measured from the survey lines. Offsets are taken from the survey lines to determine the locations of details. These may be perpendicular offsets or oblique offsets.

The *perpendicular offset* or simply offset, is perpendicular to the survey line. It is the perpendicular distance of a detail from the survey line as shown in Fig. 5.2. The *oblique offset* or *tie* is a short measurement inclined to the survey line.

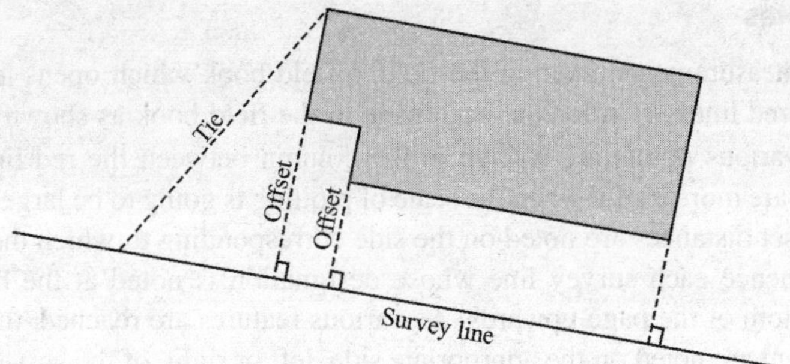

Fig. 5.2 Perpendicular and oblique offsets

In Fig. 5.1, the surveying stations, survey lines, etc., are as below:

Main survey stations	: *A, B, C, D*
Tie or subsidiary stations	: *E, F, G*
Main survey lines	: *AB, BC, CD, DA*
Tie or subsidiary lines	: *AE, CG*
Base line	: *BD*
Check lines	: *KF, HJ*

Planning and Carrying Out Chain Survey

In the field, chain surveys involve reconnaissance, selection of survey stations, and running the survey lines. These operations are described below.

Reconnaissance

Reconnaissance is the preliminary inspection of the area to be surveyed to collect preliminary information for planning and executing the survey work in the best possible manner. During reconnaissance, the surveyor prepares a rough sketch showing the arrangement of survey lines and other salient features of the network.

Selection of stations

Main survey stations at the ends of chain lines must be intervisible, and should be minimum possible in number to make the number of survey lines a minimum. Preferably these stations should be near the boundary of the area to be surveyed so that the principle of working from the whole to the part is observed. The base line should run through the centre of the area. The survey stations should form well-conditioned triangles, and every triangle should be provided with a check line. To avoid long offsets, tie lines should be run, and also the larger sides of the triangles should be laid parallel to boundaries, roads, buildings, etc. Tresspassing should be avoided by placing the main survey lines within the boundaries of the property to be surveyed. All survey lines should lie over level ground as far as possible, and obstacles to chaining or ranging, if any, should be avoided.

Running survey lines

The work of running a survey line comprises the chaining of the line, ranging, and the location of adjacent details from it by taking offsets. The distances along the survey line at which streams, roads, fences, and other salient features are intersected, are also noted down. The methods of measurement of horizontal distances have already been discussed in Chapter 3.

Recording Field Notes

For recording the measurements taken in the field, a field book which opens lengthwise is used. A single red line or two red lines are ruled on each page in the field book as shown in Fig. 5.3.

The chainages of various points are written in the column between the red lines. The field books containing single line, are more useful when the scale of plotting is going to be large and many details are to be entered. The offset distances are noted on the side corresponding to which they are taken. A fresh page is used to commence each survey line whose designation is noted at the bottom, and booking proceeds from the bottom of the page upwards. As various features are reached, they are sketched, and the offsets taken to them are noted on the appropriate side, left or right, of the survey line along with the chainage at which the offsets are taken. The surveyor should take extreme care while recording the various measurements, and should not leave anything to memory. To prevent the notes from being washed out by rains, recording should be done using a hard pencil (3H or 4H).

Plotting a Chain Survey

For plotting maps or plans of the area surveyed, the following are the steps:

1. Selection of scale
2. Plotting of framework
3. Plotting of offsets
4. Title, scale, legends, etc.
5. Inking in
6. Colouring.

Selection of scale of the map

Generally the scale of plotting is decided well before the commencement of the field work to maintain consistency in making the linear measurements and taking offsets.

Plotting of framework

The survey lines are first plotted to the scale on a tracing paper. A good quality drawing paper is taken, and the tracing paper is so oriented on the drawing paper that the framework of the triangles is centered and oriented properly. The ends of the base line are pricked through the tracing paper with a sharp pin, and then the tracing paper is removed. Join the ends of the base line obtained after pricking on the drawing paper.

The intermediate stations on the base line are marked, and the position of other stations is then located by drawing arcs from the ends of the base line. The triangles are checked by drawing check lines, and if any error is found, it is adjusted.

Plotting of offsets

After plotting the framework of triangles the details are plotted by taking offsets from the respective survey line using set square or offset scale. The details are shown in a map or plan using the conventional symbols. Some of the common conventional symbols are given in Fig. 5.4.

Title, scale, legend, etc.

The title of the plan, north direction, representative fraction (R.F.) of the scale of the plan, a graphical scale, and a legend giving the details of the conventional symbols should be given in the plan at appropriate places.

Inking in

After plotting the complete plan in pencil, the plan is sometimes inked in black. The chain lines are shown by dash and dot in red ink, and offsets and tie lines are not shown in the final drawing. The main stations are indicated by circles of about 6 mm diameter.

Colouring

If the plan is to be coloured, the drawing is cleaned with bread crumbs before commencing the colouring. The colours for various symbols/details are given in Fig. 5.4.

Obstacles in Chaining

While chaining a survey line, sometimes obstacles or obstructions are encountered making the direct chaining impossible.

There may be following situations in the field:

1. Chaining is possible but ranging obstructed
2. Ranging possible but chaining obstructed
3. Both ranging and chaining obstructed.

Obstacles to ranging but not to chaining

When the ends of a chain line are not intervisible generally due to an intervening hill, ranging is not possible. Ranging in such cases has been discussed in Sec. 3.4 (Fig. 3.6) and Sec. 4.6 (Fig. 4.28 and Fig. 4.30).

Obstacles to chaining but not to ranging

A typical obstacle of this class is a water body such as pond, wider than a tape or chain length. There may be two possibilities as below:

1. It is possible to chain round the obstacle.
2. It is not possible to chain round the obstacle.

When it is possible to chain round the obstacle: There are several methods available to determine the distance *AB* which cannot be measured directly due to the obstacle but only a few are discussed below.

(a) Fig. 5.5a

Set out two equal perpendiculars *AP* and *BQ*. Then *AB* is equal to *PQ*.

(b) Fig. 5.5b

Erect a perpendicular *AP* at *A*, and measure *AP* and *PB*. Then *AB* is equal to $\sqrt{(PB)^2 - (AP)^2}$.

(c) Fig. 5.5c

Locate A such that $\angle APB$ is 90°, and measure AP and PB. Then AB is equal to $\sqrt{(AP)^2 + (PB)^2}$.

(d) Fig. 5.5d

Set out a straight line PQ at A, and measure AP, AQ, BP, and BQ. Then AB is computed as follows:

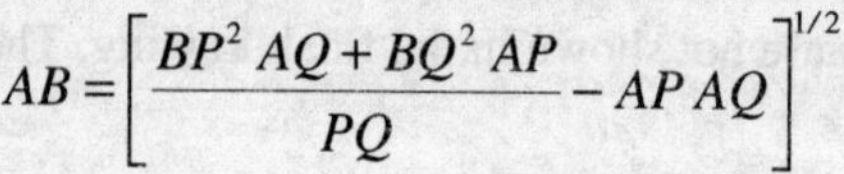

$$AB = \left[\frac{BP^2\,AQ + BQ^2\,AP}{PQ} - AP\,AQ\right]^{1/2}$$

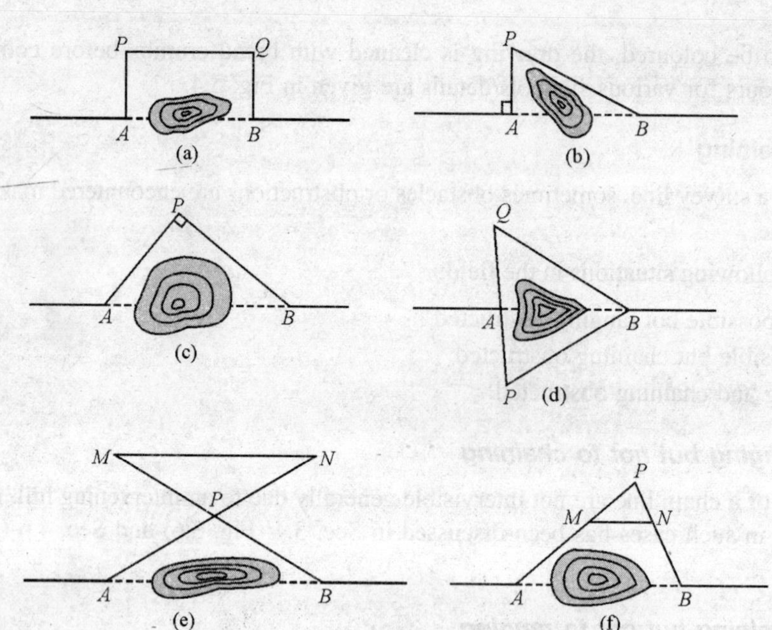

Fig. 5.5 Obstacle to chaining but not to ranging, and chaining possible round the obstacle

(e) Fig. 5.5e

Mark a point P clear of the obstacle, and a point N in line with A and P. Take $AP = PN$. Establish another point M by ranging so that it is in line with B and P. Take $BP = PM$. Measure MN which is equal to AB.

(f) Fig. 5.5f

Select a point P, and measure AP and BP. Mark M and N on the lines AP and BP, respectively, such that $PM = \dfrac{PA}{n}$ and $PN = \dfrac{PB}{n}$. Then $AB = nMN$.

In each of the above cases, the obstacle is surveyed taking offsets from the auxiliary lines.

When it is not possible to chain round the obstacle

A typical example of this case is a river. In such case, again there are several methods available to obtain the distance between two points across the river, but only a few shown in Fig. 5.6, are discussed below:

(a) Fig. 5.6a

Erect a perpendicular *AP* at *A*, and mark its midpoint *Q*. From *P* erect a perpendicular *PR* to *PA* such that *B*, *Q*, and *R* are in a straight line. Then $AB = PR$.

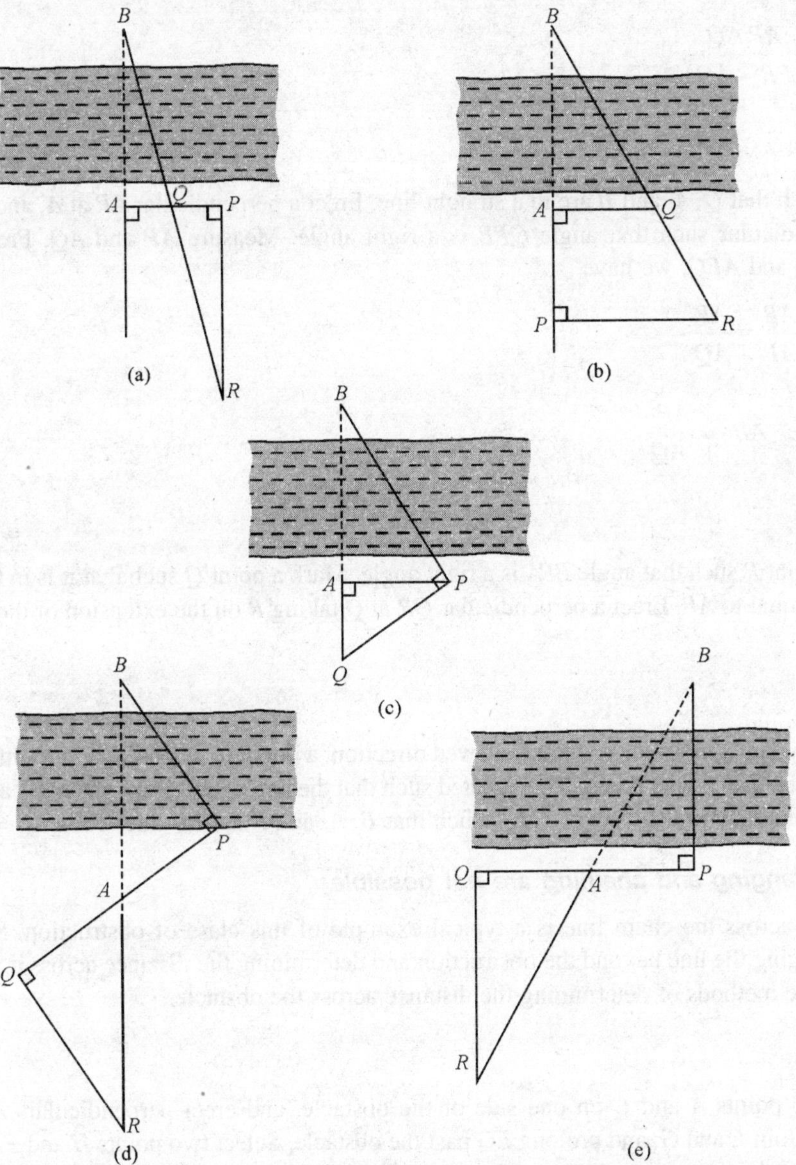

Fig. 5.6 Obstacle to chaining but not to ranging, and chaining not possible round the obstacle

(b) Fig. 5.6b

Mark a point P such that P, A, and B are in a straight line. Erect two perpendiculars AQ and PR at A and P, respectively, such that B, Q, and R are in a straight line. Measure AP, AQ, and PR. From two similar triangles ABQ and PBR, we have

$$\frac{AB}{PB} = \frac{AQ}{PR}$$

Taking $PB = AB + AP$, we get

$$AB = \frac{AP\,AQ}{(PR - AQ)}$$

(c) Fig. 5.6c

Mark Q such that Q, A, and B are in a straight line. Erect a perpendicular AP at A, and take a point P on the perpendicular such that angle QPB is a right angle. Measure AP and AQ. From two similar triangles BPQ and APQ, we have

$$\frac{AB}{AP} = \frac{AP}{AQ}$$

Therefore, $$AB = \frac{AP^2}{AQ}$$

(d) Fig. 5.6d

Locate a point P such that angle BPA is a right angle. Mark a point Q such that it is in line with A and P, and AQ is equal to AP. Erect a perpendicular QR at Q taking R on the extension of the line BA. Then $AB = AR$.

(e) Fig. 5.6e

If the survey line crosses the river in a skewed direction, a line PAQ is set out approximately along the bank of the river. The points P and Q are located such that the angle APB is a right angle and AQ is equal to AP. A perpendicular QR is erected at Q such that B, A, and R are in line. Then $AB = AR$.

When both ranging and chaining are not possible

A building across the chain line is a typical example of this class of obstruction. Such problems require prolonging the line beyond the obstruction and determining the distance across it. The following are some of the methods of determining the distance across the obstacle.

(a) Fig. 5.7a

Choose two points A and C on one side of the obstacle, and erect perpendiculars AE and CG of equal lengths. Join E and G, and prolong EG past the obstacle. Select two points H and F on the prolongation of EG, and erect perpendiculars HD and FB equal to AE. Join D and B, and prolong DB. Then $CD = GH$.

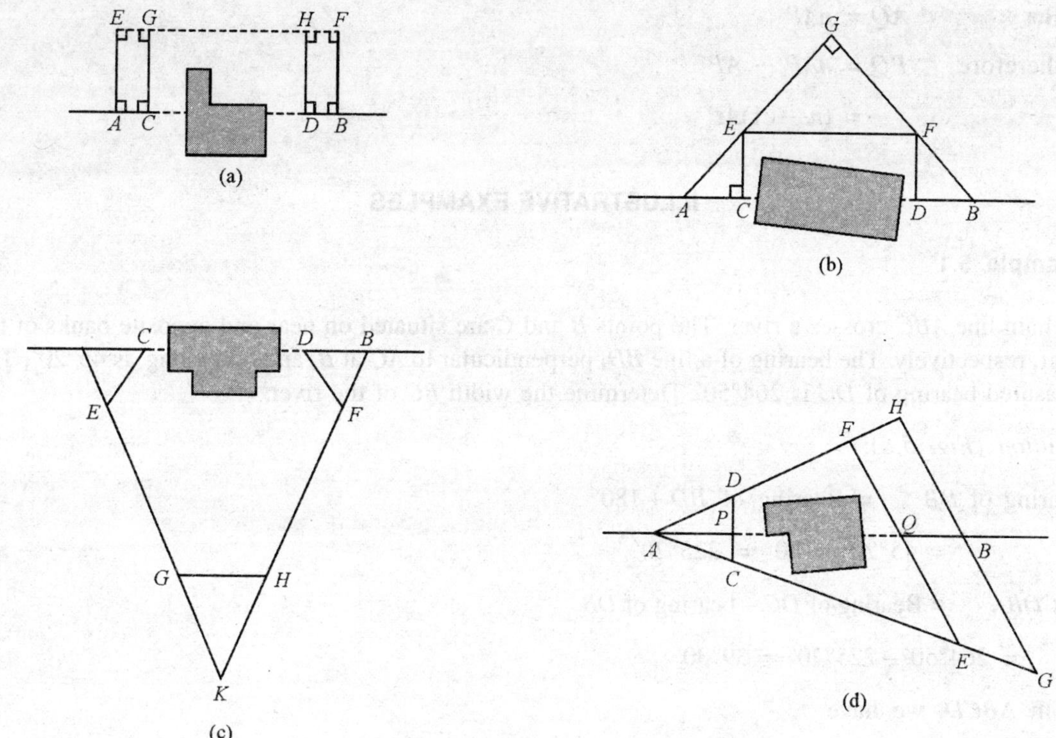

Fig. 5.7 Obstacle to both ranging and chaining

(b) Fig. 5.7b

Choose a point *C*, and erect a perpendicular *CE* of any convenient length on the chain line. Mark *A* such that *AC* equal to *CE*. Join *A* and *E* and prolong *AE* to any convenient point *G*. At *G*, set a right angle *AGB* such that *GB* = *GA*. Select a point *F* on *GB* taking *GF* = *GE*. From *F* and *B*, arcs of radii *AC* are swung, obtaining the intersection *D*. The line *BD* will be in range with the chain line, and *CD* will be equal to *EF*.

(c) Fig. 5.7c

Select the points *A* and *C* on the chain line, and construct an equilateral triangle *ACE* by swinging arcs. Join *A* and *E*, and prolong it to any point *K*. Select any point *G* on *AK*, and construct an equilateral triangle *GKH*. Join *K* and *H*, and produce *KH* to *B* such that *KB* = *KA*. Select *F* on *KB*, and construct an equilateral triangle *BDF*. The direction *DB* will be in range with the chain line.

The length *CD* will be equal to *AB* – *AC* – *DB*. As *AB* is equal to *AK*, *CD* = *AK* – *AC* – *DB*.

(d) Fig. 5.7d

Select the points *A* and *P* on the chain line and set a line *CPD* at any angle to *AP*. Join *A* and *C*, and produce *AC* to *E* such that *AE* = *nAC*. Similarly produce *AD* to *F* such that *AF* = *nAD*. Join *E* and *F* and select a point *Q* on EF such that *FQ* = *nPD*. Produce *AE* and *AF* to *G* and *H*, respectively, such that *AG* = *n′AC* and *AH* = *n′AD*. Join *G* and *H* and select *B* on *GH* such that *BH* = *n′PD*. Join *Q* and *B*. The line *QB* will be in range with the chain line. The distance *PQ* is

$$= AQ - AP$$

But $AQ = nAP$

therefore $PQ = nAP - AP$

$= (n - 1)AP$

ILLUSTRATIVE EXAMPLES

Example 5.1

A chain line *ABC* crosses a river. The points *B* and *C* are situated on near and opposite banks of the river, respectively. The bearing of a line *BD*, perpendicular to *AC* at *B*, and 50 m long, is 45°20'. The measured bearing of *DC* is 264°50′. Determine the width *BC* of the river.

Solution (Fig. 5.8):

Bearing of DB = Bearing of $BD + 180°$

$= 45°20' + 180° = 225°20'$

$\angle CDB$ = Bearing of DC – bearing of DB

$= 264°50' - 225°20' = 39°30'$

From ΔBCD, we have

$$\tan CDB = \frac{BC}{BD}$$

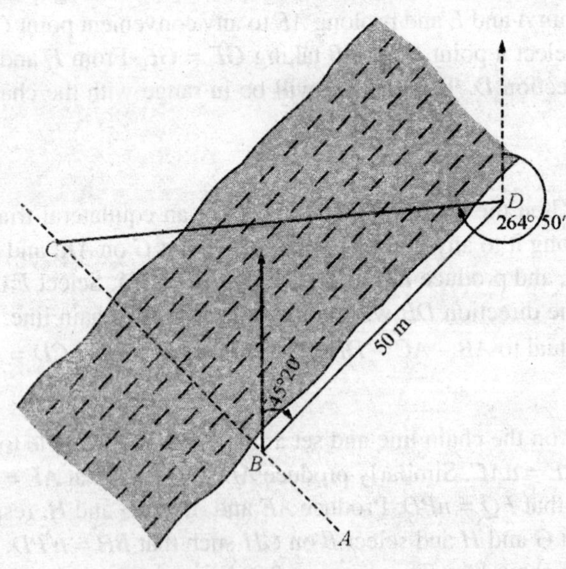

Fig. 5.8

or $BC = BD \tan CDB$

$= 50 \times \tan 39°30'$

$= \mathbf{41.22\ m.}$

Example 5.2

Two stations P and Q on the main survey line were taken on the opposite sides of a pond. On the right of PQ, a line PR, 210 m long was laid down and another line PS, 260 m long was laid down on the left of PQ. The points R, Q, and S are on the same straight line. The measured lengths of RQ and QS are 85 m and 75 m, respectively. What is the length of PQ?

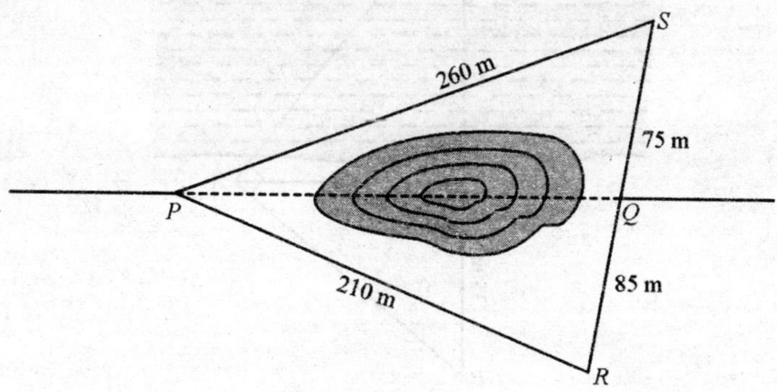

Fig. 5.9

Solution (Fig. 5.9):

It is given that

$RQ = 85$ m and $QS = 75$ m

$RS = RQ + QS$

$= 85 + 75 = 160$ m

Let $\angle PSR = \theta$

$$\text{Then } \cos\theta = \frac{SP^2 + SR^2 - PR^2}{2\,SP\,SR}$$

$$= \frac{260^2 + 160^2 - 210^2}{2 \times 260 \times 160}$$

$= 0.5901442$

Now considering ΔPQS, we have

$$\cos\theta = \frac{SP^2 + SQ^2 - PQ^2}{2\,SP\,SQ}$$

or $PQ = \sqrt{(SP^2 + SQ^2 - 2\,SP \times SQ \cos\theta)}$

$= \sqrt{(260^2 + 75^2 - 2 \times 260 \times 75 \times 0.5901442)}$

$= \mathbf{224.1\ m.}$

Example 5.3

The points P and Q were selected on the opposite banks of a river. To determine the length of PQ, a line PA was laid down perpendicular to PQ, and was measured to be 150 m. Another line AB, B on the line QP produced, was erected perpendicular to QA. The measured length of PB was found to be 35 m. Determine the length of PQ

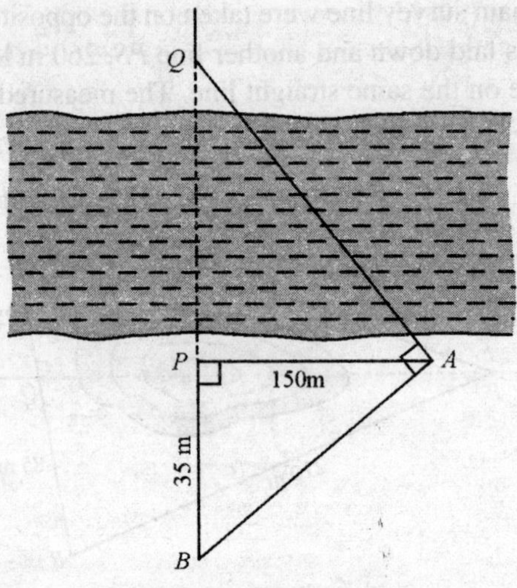

Fig. 5.10

Solution (Fig. 5.10):

It has already been proved (*c.f.*, Fig. 5.6c) that

$$PQ = \frac{PA^2}{PB} = \frac{150^2}{35} = \mathbf{642.9\ m.}$$

Example 5.4

While running a survey line AB, it was found that it is obstructed by a building. To overcome the problem of the obstruction, a perpendicular BC, 143.65 m long, was erected at B. From C two lines CD and CE were set out at angles 30° and 50°, respectively, from CB. Determine the length of BD and BE, if D and E are on the prolongation of AB. Also determine the lengths of CD and CE.

Solution (Fig. 5.11):

As D and E are on the line AB produced, we get

$$CD = BC \sec 30° = 143.65 \times \sec 30° = \mathbf{165.87\ m}$$

and

$$CE = BC \sec 50° = 143.65 \times \sec 50° = \mathbf{223.48\ m}$$

$$BD = BC \tan 30° = 143.65 \times \tan 30° = \mathbf{82.90\ m}$$

$$BE = BC \tan 50° = 143.65 \times \tan 50° = \mathbf{171.20\ m}$$

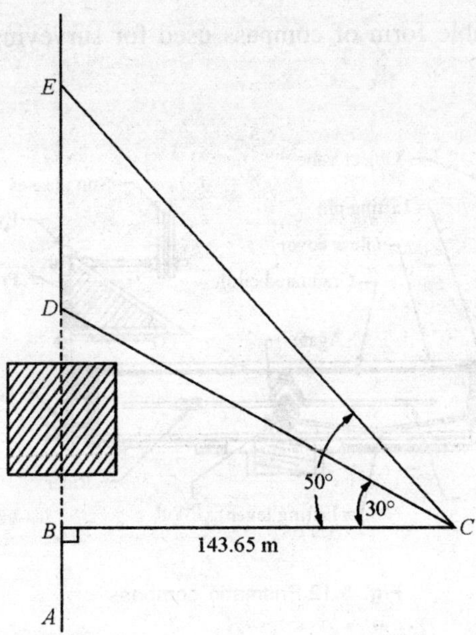

Fig. 5.11

5.3 COMPASS SURVEYING

Compass surveying is one of the methods of surveying in which a magnetic compass is employed to determine the directions of survey lines. Prior to the invention of theodolite and sextant, compass was the only means of measuring the directions and horizontal angles. The compass is still used for preliminary engineering surveys where the directions are measured using compass, and the lengths by chaining or taping. If the area to be surveyed is small in extent and higher accuracy is to be achieved, method of chain surveying is preferred. On the other hand, if the area is comparatively large with undulating terrain, compass surveying is adopted. The area in which compass surveying is to be employed, it should be ascertained that the area is not magnetically disturbed.

Magnetic Compass

The magnetic compasses used in surveying may be classified as:

1. Prismatic compass
2. Surveyor's compass
3. Trough compass
4. Tubular compass.

The general principle on which the compasses work is same for all types of compass. If a long and narrow magnetized iron or steel strip suspended on a pivot at its centre, is allowed to oscillate freely about its vertical axis passing through the pivot, it will always tend to assume a direction of the magnetic meridian at the place.

Prismatic compass

It is the most suitable portable form of compass used for surveying. Main parts of a prismatic compass are shown in Fig. 5.12.

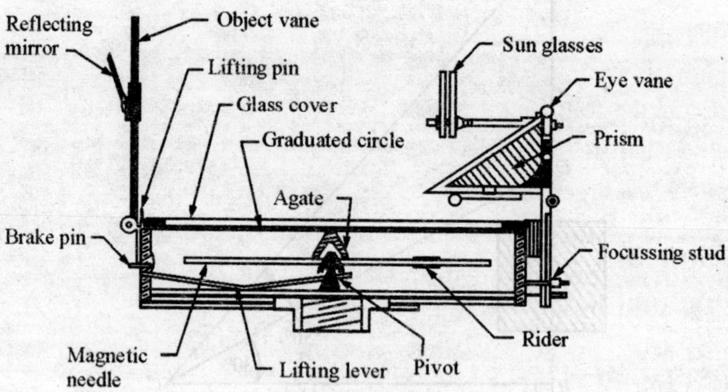

Fig. 5.12 Prismatic compass

A prismatic compass consists of a circular box of about 100 mm diameter. A magnetic needle is attached to a light circular aluminium ring balanced on a hard steel pointed pivot. The ring is graduated to degree and half degree with 0° mark at the south end of the needle, and 180° mark at its north end. The graduations run clockwise, therefore, 90° mark is towards west and 270° mark is towards east as shown in Fig. 5.13.

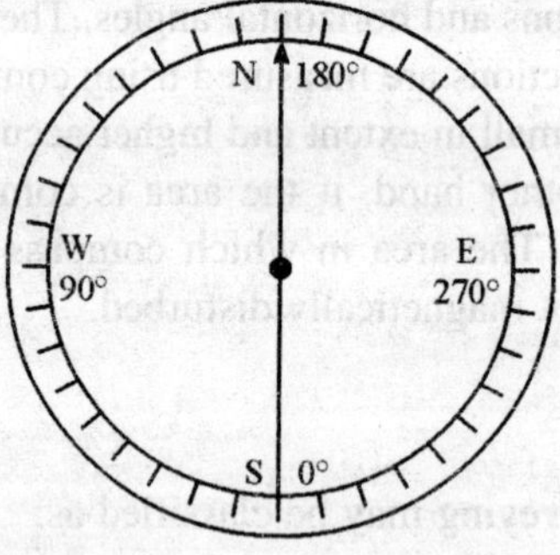

Fig. 5.13 Graduations on the ring

The figures on the ring are written inverted. When these are read using a prism, they are erected and magnified. The object vane carries a vertical hair attached to a suitable frame. Sight vane or eye vane consists of a vertical slit cut into the upper assembly of the prism. The object vane and sight vane are hinged to the box, diagonally opposite at the top.

To sight an object, the sight vane is rotated with respect to N-S ends of the ring through an angle which the line makes with the magnetic meridian. The angle read is the whole-circle bearing of the line at the compass station. Brake pin may be used to dampen the oscillations of the needle by pressing it. The sun glasses provided at the eye vane may be used to sight the bright objects. When the instrument is not in use, the object vane frame may be folded on the glass lid. It automatically presses against a bent lever, which lifts the needle off the pivot and holds it against the glass lid.

Surveyor's compass

Surveyor's compass is very much similar in construction to the prismatic compass. It is different to the prismatic compass in the following respect:

1. The magnetic needle is not attached to the graduated ring, and floats freely over the pivot.
2. The graduated ring is directly attached to the circular box.
3. No mirror is attached to the object vane for sighting the objects at higher elevation or depression.
4. The graduations on the ring are in quadrental system with 0° marks at north and south ends, 90° marks at east and west ends.
5. Readings are taken against the north end of the needle.

A surveyor's compass is shown in Fig. 5.14, and a comparison between a prismatic compass and a surveyor's compass is given in Table 5.1.

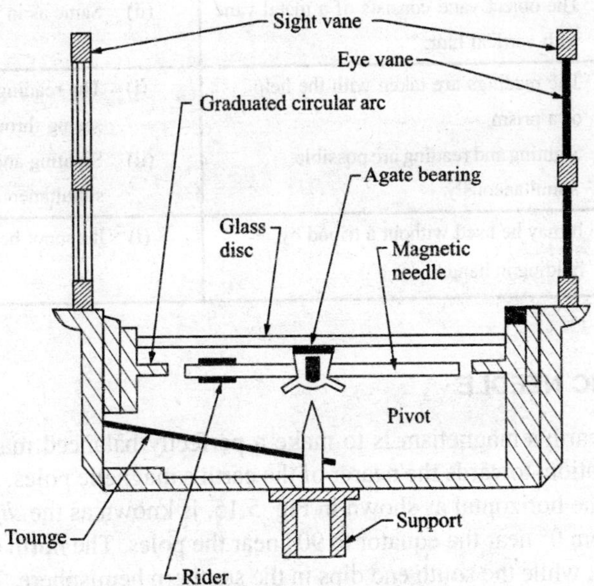

Fig. 5.14 Surveyor's compass

Trough and tubular compasses

Trough and tubular compasses are used as adjuncts to other instruments. They are not complete surveying instruments by themselves. They are used only to indicate magnetic meridian or to set the instrument in the magnetic meridian to measure the magnetic bearing of the lines.

A trough compass is generally used as an accessory to a plane table or theodolite, while a tubular compass is used only with a theodolite.

Table 5.1 Comparison between a prismatic compass and a Surveyor's compass

Item	Prismatic compass	Surveyor's compass
Magnetic needle	(i) The needle does not act as an index. (ii) The needle is of broad type.	(i) The needle acts as an index. (ii) The needle is of edge bar type.
Graduated ring	(i) The graduated ring is attached to the needle. (ii) The graduated ring does not rotate along with the line of sight. (iii) The graduations are in whole-circle bearing system. (iv) 0° at south, 90° at west 180° at north and 270° at east. (v) The graduations are engraved inverted.	(i) The graduated ring is attached to the circular box. (ii) The graduated ring rotates along with the line of sight. (iii) The graduations are in quadrental system (iv) 0° at north and south, and 90° at east and west. East and west are interchangeable. (v) The graduations are engraved erect.
Sighting vanes	(i) The eye vane consists of a metal vane with a slit. (ii) The object vane consists of a metal vane with vertical hair.	(i) The eye vane consists of a small vane with fine slit. (ii) Same as in prismatic compass.
Reading system	(i) The readings are taken with the help of a prism. (ii) Sighting and reading are possible simultaneously.	(i) The readings are taken directly by seeing through the top of glass. (ii) Sighting and reading are not possible simultaneously.
Tripod	(i) It may be used without a tripod by holding in hand.	(i) It cannot be used without a tripod.

5.4 DIP OF A MAGNETIC NEEDLE

One of the effects of the earth's magnetism is to make a perfectly balanced magnetic needle, incline downwards after magnetisation, towards the nearer of the earth's magnetic poles. The inclination (ω) of the magnetic needle with the horizontal as shown in Fig. 5.15, is known as the *dip* or *angle of dip*. It is not constant, and varies from 0° near the equator to 90° near the poles. The north end of the needle dips in the northern hemisphere, while the south end dips in the southern hemisphere. The dip may also vary at any place with time. The imaginary lines joining the points on the earth's surface with equal dip, are called the *isoclinic lines*.

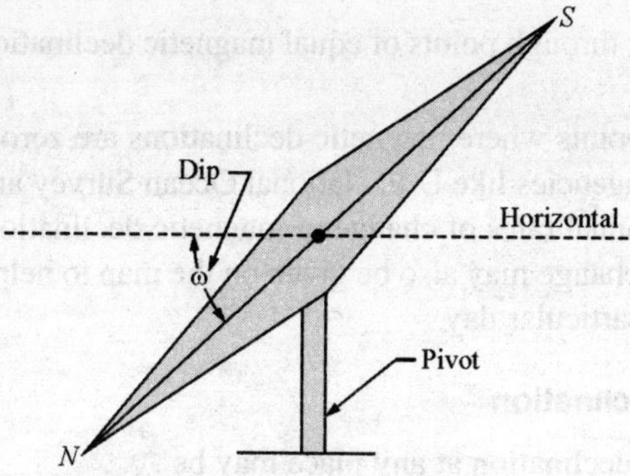

Fig. 5.15 Dip of a magnetic needle

To counteract the dip at any place to keep the magnetic needle in horizontal position, a sliding rider weight in the form of a brass or a silver wire coil, is provided towards the higher end of the needle at a suitable distance from the pivot.

5.5 MAGNETIC DECLINATION

The horizontal angle (δ) between the true or astronomic meridian and magnetic meridian is called the *magnetic declination*.

If the north end of the compass needle points to east of the true meridian as shown in Fig. 5.16, the declination is said to be east, and if it points to the west of the true meridian the declination is said to be west.

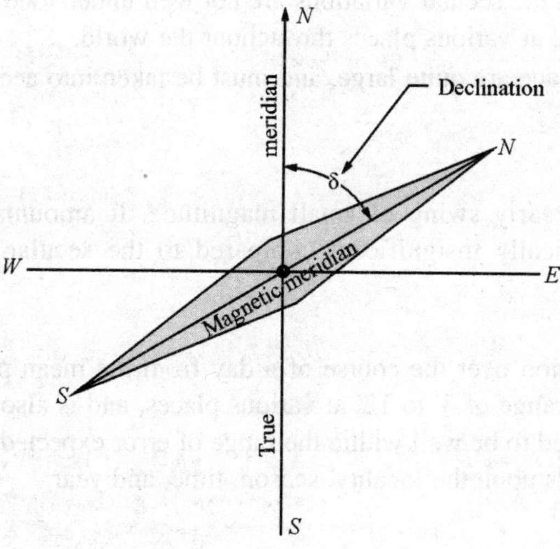

Fig. 5.16 Declination east

Isogonic Chart

The imaginary lines passing through points of equal magnetic declination are known as *isogonic lines* or *isogons*.

The lines passing through points where magnetic declinations are zero, are called *agonic lines*. Isogonic charts are published by agencies like U.S. National Ocean Survey and Survey of India. The charts also show the lines of equal annual rates of change of magnetic declination. The date on which the map was made and annual rates of change may also be given on the map to help in prediction of the magnetic declination at any place on a particular day.

Variations in Magnetic Declination

The variations in magnetic declination at any place may be

1. Regular or periodic, and
2. Irregular.

Regular or periodic variations

These variations are further classified as:

(a) Secular (with periods of about 300 yrs.),

(b) Annual, and

(c) Dirunal or daily.

Secular or periodic variation

Like a pendulum, the magnetic meridian swings in one direction for perhaps 150 yrs until it gradually comes to rest and then swings in the other direction for 150 yrs. Thus the cycle is completed in about 300 years. The variation follows approximately a sine curve. The rate of change per year, however, varies irregularly. The causes of the secular variations are not well understood. To estimate the secular variation, observations are made at various places throughout the world.

The secular variations at a place are quite large, and must be taken into account.

Annual variation

The annual variation is a yearly swing of small magnitude. It amounts to less than 01′ from the mean position. It is practically insignificant compared to the secular variation.

Dirunal or daily variation

The variation of the declination over the course of a day from the mean position is called dirunal variation. It is generally in the range of 3′ to 12′ at various places, and is also called the Solar-dirunal variation. The value is considered to be well within the range of error expected in compass survey. The dirunal variation mainly depends upon the locality, season, time, and year.

Irregular variation

Magnetic disturbances or magnetic storms usually associated with sunspots cause irregular variation. Such variations are random and uncertain, thus, unpredictable. They may amount to a degree or more, particularly at high latitudes.

Effect of Variation

The variation in magnetic declination changes the direction of magnetic meridian at a place, thus changing the magnetic bearings of the survey lines. Old survey records in which the directions of survey lines were determined with a magnetic compass can only be retraced accurately if the declination of the place at the time of survey and the present declination are known.

The date of survey, magnetic declination, and annual change of the secular variation should be noted on the plan prepared by compass survey for applying corrections for declination in future.

ILLUSTRATIVE EXAMPLES

Example 5.5

The magnetic bearing of a line is 62°30′. What is the true bearing of the line if the magnetic declination is (*a*) 3°45′ W, (*b*) 4°10′ E?

Solution:

(a) See Fig. 5.17a

True bearing = magnetic bearing – declination

= 62°30′ – 3°45′

= **58°45′**.

(b) See Fig. 5.17b

True bearing = magnetic bearing + declination

= 62°30′ + 4°10′

= **66°40′**.

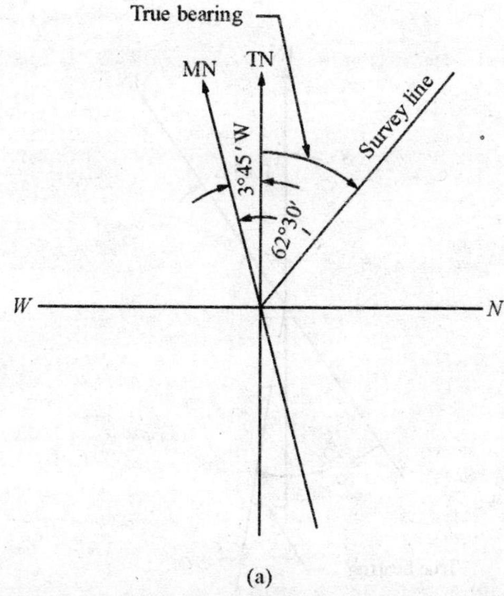

Fig. 5.17

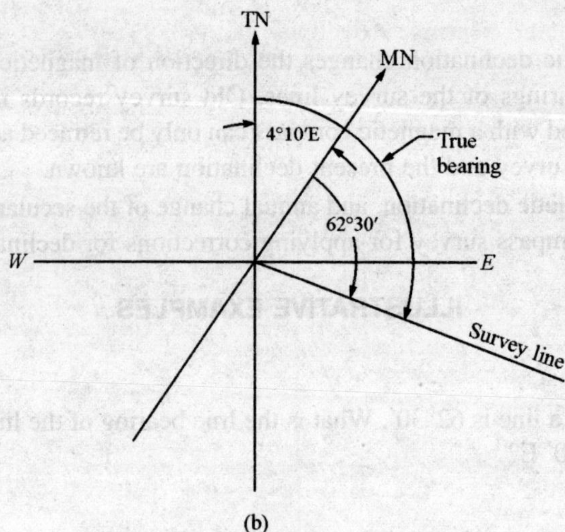

(b)

Fig. 5.17

Example 5.6

The magnetic bearing of a line *PQ* is S 46°15′ E. Calculate the true bearing of *PQ* if the magnetic declination is (*a*) 4°45′ E, (*b*) 3°15′ W.

Solution:

(a) See Fig. 5.18a

True bearing = magnetic bearing – declination
= S 46°15′ E – 4°45′
= S 41°30′ E.

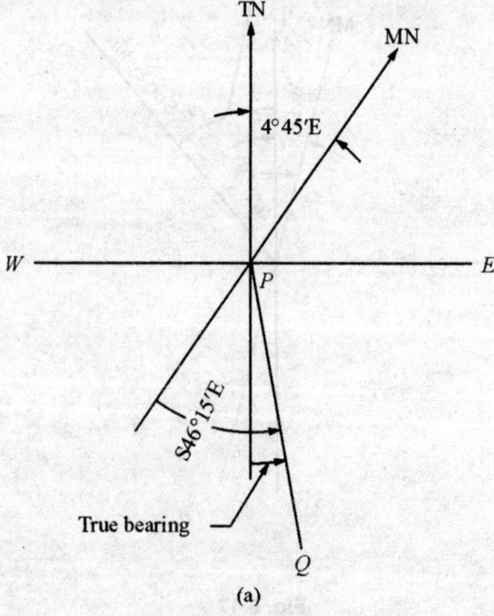

(a)

Fig. 5.18

(b) See Fig. 5.18b

True bearing = magnetic bearing + declination

= S 46°15′ E + 3°15′

= **S 49°30′ E.**

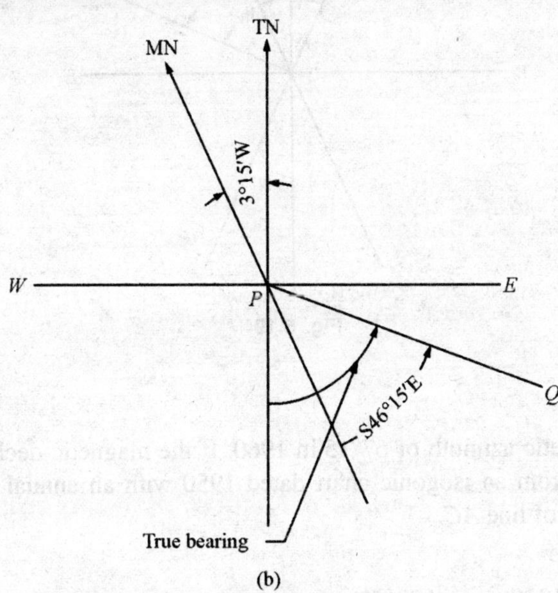

(b)

Fig. 5.18

Example 5.7

A line *AB* in an old map was having its magnetic bearing as 57°20′ when the magnetic declination was 1°50′ E. What is the magnetic bearing of *AB* now when the magnetic declination is 4°30′ W?

Solution (Fig. 5.19):

Let the magnetic bearing 57°20′ be θ_1 and the required magnetic bearing is θ_2.

If δ_1 = 1° 50′ E and δ_2 = 4° 30′ W,

we find that

$\theta_2 = \delta_1 + \delta_2 + \theta_1$

= 1°50′ + 4°30′ + 57°20′

= **63°40′**.

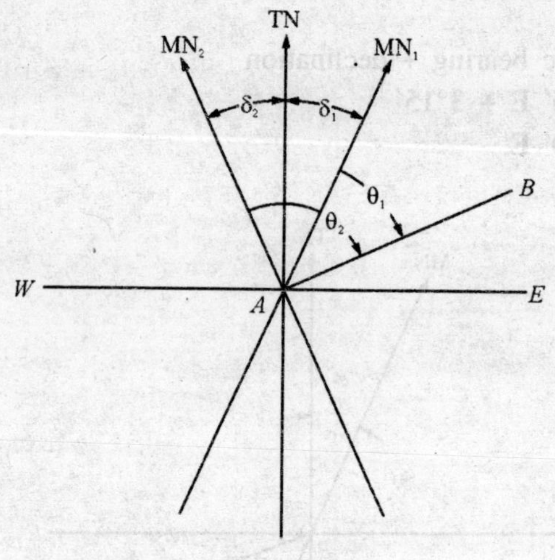

Fig. 5.19

Example 5.8

A line *AC* had the magnetic azimuth of 67°15′in 1960. If the magnetic declination was found to be 21°30′ E by interpolation from an isogonic chart dated 1950 with an annual change of 1′ westward. Determine the true azimuth of line *AC*.

Solution (Fig. 5.20):

Magnetic azimuth in 1960 = 67°15′

Declination in 1950 = 21°30′ E

Change in declination from 1950 to 1960, i.e., for 10 years = – 10′ @ 1′ per year westward

Magnetic declination in 1960 = (21°30′ – 10′) E

= 21°20′E

True azimuth = 67°15′ + 21°20′

= **88°35′**.

Example 5.9

A magnetic bearing of N 43° 45′ W is recorded on an old plan of 1940. It is desired to relocate this direction on the ground in 1975. An isogonic chart of 1960 shows a declination of 12° 00′ W for the survey site, with an annual change of 3′ eastward. Determine the magnetic bearing that is to be used to reestablish the direction of the line.

Solution (Fig. 5.21):

Magnetic declination in 1960 = 12°00′ W

Change in magnetic declination in 20 years @ 3′ per year eastward from 1940 to 1960 = 1°00′

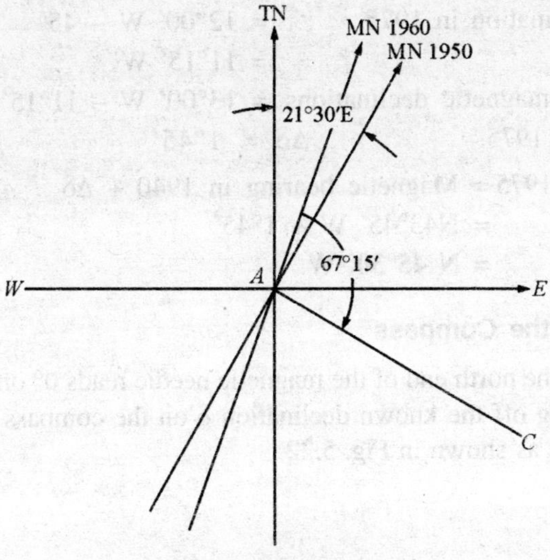

Fig. 5.20

Magnetic declination in 1940	= 12°00′ W + 1°00′
	= 13°00′ W
Magnetic bearing in 1940	= N43°45′ W
Change in magnetic declination	= 45′

in 15 years @ 3′ per year
eastward from 1960 to 1975

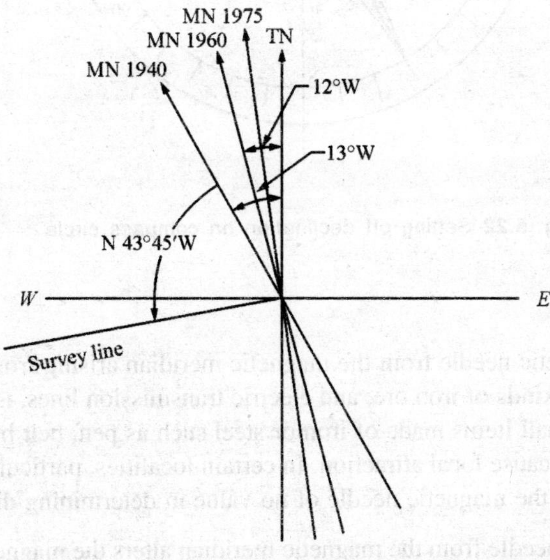

Fig. 5.21

Magnetic declination in 1975 = 12°00′ W – 45′

= 11°15′ W

Difference in magnetic declinations = 13°00′ W – 11°15′ W

from 1940 to 1975 $\Delta\delta$ = 1°45′

Magnetic bearing in 1975 = Magnetic bearing in 1940 + $\Delta\delta$

= N43°45′ W + 1°45′

= **N 45°30′ W.**

Setting off Declination on the Compass

Set up the compass so that the north end of the magnetic needle reads 0° on the graduated ring. Now take the line of sight by setting off the known declination δ on the compass circle from the direction shown by the magnetic needle as shown in Fig. 5.22.

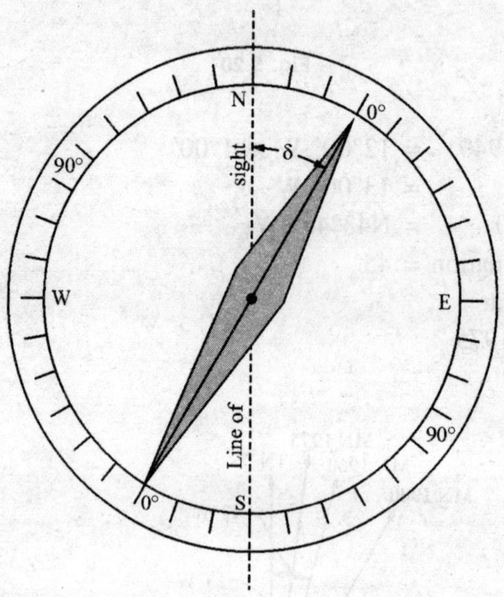

Fig. 5.22 Setting off declination on compass circle

5.6 LOCAL ATTRACTION

The deviation of the magnetic needle from the magnetic meridian arising from local sources such as objects of iron or steel, some kinds of iron ore, and electric transmission lines, is called *local attraction* or *local disturbance*. Even small items made of iron or steel such as pen, belt buckle, wristwatch case, taping arrows, and steel tapes cause local attraction. In certain localities, particularly in towns, its effect is so pronounced as to render the magnetic needle of no value in determining directions.

Deviation of the magnetic needle from the magnetic meridian alters the magnetic bearing, and consequently the observed magnetic bearings will be in error due to local attraction. To detect local attraction it is essential to take both the fore bearing and back bearing of each line. If the bearings differ by 180°, there is no local attraction in the area provided there are no instrumental and other errors.

Correction for Local Attraction

For applying correction for local attraction it assumed that all the bearings measured at a particular station, are affected equally. The measured bearing of the traverse lines (*c.f.,* Sec. 4.7 and Chapter 9) can be corrected for local attraction using either of the following methods.

Method-I: In this method, the line is found out whose fore bearing and back bearing differ exactly by 180°. For such lines, there is no local attraction at both the ends of the line and, therefore, all the bearings taken at these stations will be free from local attraction.

This helps in determining the corrections at the remaining traverse stations, and then in determination of corrected bearings of the traverse lines. The method is explained in Example 5.10.

Method-II: As all the bearings taken at a station are equally affected, the included angle between two lines at this station obtained from the magnetic bearings of the two lines, will be free from local attraction.

In this method, the included angles between different lines of a traverse are found out from the observed bearings, including for the line which is not affected by local attraction. The corrected bearings of all other lines are determined from the computed included angles. The method is explained in Example 5.11.

ILLUSTRATIVE EXAMPLES

Example 5.10

A closed compass traverse was conducted round a forest, and the following whole-circle bearings were observed. Determine which of the stations suffer from local attraction, and compute the values of the corrected bearings.

Line	Fore bearing	Back bearing
AB	74°20′	256°00′
BC	107°20′	286°20′
CD	224°50′	44°50′
DA	306°40′	126°00′

Solution [by Method-I (Fig. 5.23)]:

As the fore bearing and back bearing of *CD* differ exactly by 180°, stations *C* and *D* are free from local attraction. Hence, stations affected by local attraction are *A* and *B*. Further, all the bearings observed at *C* and *D* are also free from local attraction.

Therefore, the fore bearing 306°40′ of *DA* is correct.

Correct back bearing of *DA* = 306°40′ – 180° = **126°40′**

Error at A = 126°00′ – 126°40′ = – 40′

Correction at *A* = + 40′

Correct fore bearing of AB = 74°20′ + 40′ = **75°00′**
Correct back bearing of AB = 75°00′ + 180° = **255°00′**

Error at B = 256°00′ − 255°00′ = + 1°00′

Correction at B = − 1°00′
Correct fore bearing of BC = 107°20′ − 1°00′ = **106°20′**
Correct back bearing of BC = 106°20′ + 180° = **286°20′**.

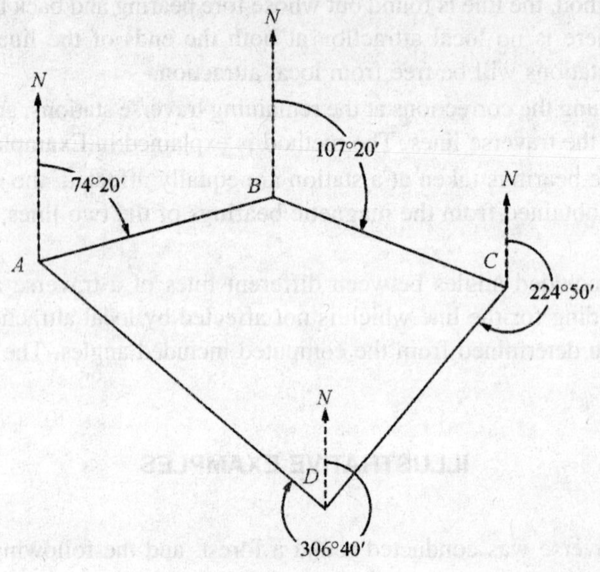

Fig. 5.23

Check: The computed back bearing of BC is same as the observed back bearing at C which is free from local attraction.

Line	Correct fore bearing	Correct back bearing
AB	75°00′	255°00′
BC	106°20′	286°20′
CD	224°50′	44°50′
DA	306°40′	126°40′

Example 5.11

Determine the corrected bearings of the traverse lines given in Example 5.10 by Method-II.

Solution [by Method-II (Fig. 5.23)]:

Interior angle at A = bearing of AD − bearing of AB
= 126°00′ − 74°20′ = 51°40′

Interior angle at B = bearing of BA – bearing of BC

= 256°00′ – 107°20′ = 148°40′

Interior angle at C = bearing of CB – bearing of CD

= 286°20′ – 224°50′ = 61°30′

Exterior angle at D = bearing of DA – bearing DC

= 306°40′ – 44°50′ = 261°50′

Interior angle at D = 360° – 261°50′ = 98°10′

Sum of interior angles = 51°40′ + 148°40′ + 61°30′ + 98°10′

= 360°00′

Theoretical sum = $(2n - 4) \times 90° = (2 \times 4 - 4) \times 90°$

= 360°

where n is number of lines in a traverse

Therefore, no correction is required for the included angles. If the computed sum minus the theoretical sum is dA, which is the error, the correction to each included angle will be $-\frac{dA}{n}$. After applying the correction, calculate the corrected bearings as below.

As the fore bearing and back bearing of CD differ exactly by 180°, stations C and D are free from local attractions. Hence the observed fore bearing of CD, back bearing of BC, back bearing of CD and fore bearing of DA are the correct bearings.

Correct fore bearing of DA = 306°40′ (given)

Correct back bearing of DA = 306°40′ – 180° = 126°40′

Correct fore bearing of AB = Correct back bearing of DA – included angle at A

= 126°40′ –51°40′ = **75°00′**

Correct back bearing of AB = 75°00′ + 180° = **255°00′**

Correct fore bearing of BC = Correct back bearing of AB – included angle at B

= 255°00′ – 148°40′ = **106°20′**

Correct back bearing of BC = 106°20′ + 180° = **286°20′**.

Check: The computed back bearing of BC is same as the observed back bearing at C which is free from local attraction.

Line	Correct fore bearing	Correct back bearing
AB	75°00′	255°00′
BC	106°20′	286°20′
CD	224°50′	44°50′
DA	306°40′	126°40′

5.7 CHAIN AND COMPASS SURVEY

An area bounded by a traverse may be surveyed with chain and compass in the following steps:

1. Reconnaissance of the area
2. Measurement of the directions
3. Measurement of lengths and taking offsets.

Reconnaissance

The entire area to be surveyed is inspected to collect the following information:

1. The adjacent traverse stations are intervisible.
2. Taping between the traverse stations is not obstructed.
3. Survey lines are as close to the details as possible.
4. Survey lines are minimum in number, and as long as possible.

Measurement of Directions

The directions of survey lines are measured with magnetic compass by free or loose-needle method (*c.f.,* Sec. 9.5). The fore and back bearings of each line are measured independently by setting up compass at each successive station to avoid accumulation of errors. If error between fore and back bearings of a line exceeds the limit of permissible error, i.e., 15′, the bearings of the line are observed again. Even if, on checking, the error remains, it may be due to local attraction at one or both the stations of the line. Before using the observed bearings in traverse plotting, they should be corrected for local attraction. The accuracy of field work mainly depends upon the accuracy with which bearings of survey lines are observed. Hence, to have less number of bearings, the survey lines of traverse legs should be as long as possible so that the number of lines are less.

A theodolite fitted with a magnetic compass is also used, to measure the directions. The following two methods are commonly used to measure the directions in compass surveying.

Loose-needle method

In this method, the direction of the magnetic meridian is established at each station of the traverse (*c.f.*, Sec. 9.3), and the directions of the line are determined with reference to the magnetic meridian. As the magnetic bearings are read directly with a compass, the accuracy of the loose-needle method is that of the compass, and not that of the theodolite. The loose-needle method is rarely used in a theodolite traverse.

Fast-needle method

In the fast-needle method, the magnetic meridian is established only at the starting station. The magnetic bearing of the first line is measured directly, and the magnetic bearings of the other lines are computed indirectly from the magnetic bearing of the first line and the included angles. Although the magnetic bearing of the first line has the accuracy of the compass, the difference of bearings of two adjacent lines has the accuracy of the theodolite. The method is more accurate than the loose-needle method, and is generally preferred.

Measurement of Length and Taking Offsets

The length of all the survey lines are measured by taping or chaining, and offsets are taken for the details on either side of the survey lines. The recording of the field notes is done in a field book as discussed in Sec. 5.2.

Plotting of Traverse Survey

Before plotting a traverse survey it should be ensured that all observed bearings are correct to have a perfect geometrical figure based on the field notes. To decide a proper layout of the plan on the drawing sheet, a rough sketch of the traverse should be drawn.

Plotting a compass traverse and its adjustment are given in Chapter 9.

5.8 ERRORS IN COMPASS SURVEY

The errors in compass survey may be classified as:

1. Instrumental errors
2. Observational or personal errors
3. Errors due to natural causes.

Instrumental Errors

These errors arise due to faulty adjustments and defective parts of the instruments, such as:

1. The needle not being perfectly straight
2. Pivot being bent
3. Sluggish needle
4. Blunt pivot points
5. Improper balancing weight
6. Sight vanes not being vertical
7. Line of sight not passing through the centre of the ring
8. Divisions of the graduated ring not being equal
9. Graduated ring not being horizontal.

Observational or Personal Errors

These errors include the following:

1. Inaccurate levelling of the compass box
2. Inaccurate centering
3. Inaccurate bisection of ranging rods
4. Inaccurate reading and recording.

Errors Due to Natural Causes

These errors may be due to the following reasons:

1. Presence of magnetic substances near or below the station of observation
2. Irregular variations due to magnetic storms, etc.

5.9 PRECAUTIONS IN COMPASS SURVEY

The following precautions should be taken during a compass survey to minimise the instrumental and observational errors:

1. Setting up and levelling of the compass should be done carefully.
2. If the needle is vibrating, use brake pin to stop the vibrations.
3. Avoid parallax in sighting by looking along the needle.
4. Always keep the needle off the pivot when compass is not in use to avoid unnecessary wear of the pivot.
5. Selected survey stations should be away from the sources causing local attraction.
6. Surveyor should not carry iron or steel articles with them at the time of making observations.
7. Object and eye vanes must be kept vertical at the time of reading.

QUESTIONS AND PROBLEMS

5.1 Explain the principle of chain surveying. What are the limitations of chain surveying? Write the conditions in which it is suitable and unsuitable.

5.2 Define the following terms used in chain surveying, and explain their use in chain surveying: (*i*) Main survey station; (*ii*) Tie station; (*iii*) Main survey lines; (*iv*) Tie lines; (*v*) Base line; (*vi*) Check line.

5.3 What are the instruments used in chain surveying? How is the chain survey executed in the field?

5.4 What do you understand by reconnaissance? State its importance in chain surveying.

5.5 What is a well-conditioned triangle? Why is it necessary to use well-conditioned triangles?

5.6 What factors should be considered in deciding the stations for chain survey?

5.7 Describe how you would range and chain a line between two points not intervisible because of an intervening hillock.

5.8 How would you chain a survey line if there is obstacle of the following type:

(*a*) Chaining possible but ranging obstructed.

(*b*) Ranging possible but chaining obstructed.

(*c*) Both ranging and chaining obstructed.

5.9 Discuss various methods for determining the width of a river.

5.10 Discuss briefly 'Recording Field Notes´ in chain surveying.

5.11 Discuss the steps for plotting a chain survey.

5.12 A river is flowing east-west, and a survey line *ABC* crosses the river perpendicular to the direction of flow. *B* is situated on the near bank and *C* on the far bank. A line *BD*, 60 m long, was laid at *B*, perpendicular to *AB*, and the bearing of *DC* and *DA* were measured and found to be 33°30′ and 131°20′, respectively. If *AB* is 42 m, calculate the length of *BC*.

5.13 A survey line *AB* if extended, intersects a pond at *P* and *Q*. Two lines *PC* and *PD* are laid on both sides of the pond, and measured as 900 m and 1150 m, respectively. *C*, *Q*, and *D* lie in a straight line. If the measured lengths of *CQ* and *DQ* are 580 m and 620 m, respectively, calculate the length of *PQ*.

5.14 Two points *A* and *B*, *A* being on the near bank and *B* on the far bank of a river, were located to measure the width of the river. Two perpendiculars *AQ* and *CP* were erected at *A* and *C*, *C* being on *BA* produced at a distance of 40 m from *A* so that *P*, *Q*, and *B* are colinear. If the measured lengths of *CP* and *AQ* are 135 m and 70 m, respectively, determine the width of the river.

5.15 For determining the width of a river, flowing east to west, two points *P* and *Q* are selected on the southern bank such that the distant *PQ* is equal to 60 m. Point *P* is westward. The bearings of a point *A* on the northern bank, are observed to be 40°00′ and 335°30′, respectively, from *P* and *Q*. Determine the width of the river.

5.16 Differentiate between chain survey and compass survey.

5.17 What are different types of compass? Discuss each briefly, and write their uses.

5.18 Explain with the help of neat sketches the graduations of a prismatic compass and Surveyor´s compass.

5.19 Give comparison between a prismatic compass and a Surveyor´s compass in a tabular form.

5.20 What do you understand by dip of a magnetic needle and isoclinic lines? Explain the method of counteracting the dip.

5.21 What is magnetic declination? What are different types of variation in declination. Discuss also the importance of isogonic lines.

5.22 Write a short note on the term "declination".

5.23 What is local attraction? How is it detected and eliminated?

5.24 Explain the methods of determination of the correct bearing of lines of a traverse if some stations are effected by local attraction.

5.25 Write a short note on survey of an area using chain and compass.

5.26 Discuss the sources of errors in compass survey. What are the precautions which a surveyor should take in compass survey?

5.27 Following are the observed magnetic bearings of the traverse legs:

Line	*PQ*	*QR*	*RS*	*SP*
F.B	124°30′	68°15′	310°30′	200°15′
B.B	304°30′	246°00′	135°15′	17°45′

At what stations local attraction is suspected ? Determine the correct bearings of the traverse legs, and also calculate the included angles.

5.28 The following fore and back bearings were observed in an open traverse:

Line	F.B.	B.B.
1 – 2	2°15′	182°15′
2 – 3	174°15′	354°00′
3 – 4	223°00′	42°45′
4 – 5	166°30′	346°45′

Which stations are affected by local attraction and how much? Determine the true bearings of the lines if the magnetic declination in the survey area is 2°10′E.

5.29 Determine the correct bearings of the lines of the traverse ABCDE from the following data taken from a compass survey:

Line	F.B.	B.B.
AB	N 55°00′E	S 54°00′W
BC	S 68°30′E	N 66°30′W
CD	S 24°00′W	N 24°00′E
DE	S 77°00′W	N 75°30′E
EA	N 64°00′W	S 63°30′E

5.30 A compass was set on the station *P*, and the bearing of *PQ* was observed as 312° 20′. Then the compass was shifted to station *Q* and the bearing of *QP* was observed as 132°20′.
Is there any local attraction at *P* or *Q* ? Give a precise answer supported by rational argument.

6

LEVELLING

6.1 GENERAL

For the execution of engineering projects, such as highways, railways, canals, tunnels, dams, irrigation and drainage works, the elevations (*c.f.,* Sec.1.5) of different points along the alignment of the project are required. *Levelling* is the operation in surveying performed to determine and establish elevations of points on the surface of the earth or beneath the surface of the earth, to determine differences in elevation between points, and to control grades in construction surveys. Success of the engineering projects such as above, depends upon accurate determination of elevations. Levelling is of prime importance to the engineers, both for design as well as for execution of a project.

Levelling is a branch of surveying which deals with measurements in vertical planes.

6.2 DEFINITIONS OF SOME BASIC TERMS

Some of the terms, *e.g.,* level surface, horizontal plane, elevation, vertical angle, etc., have already been defined in Sec.1.5. Definitions of some of the terms used in levelling are given below.

Datum or datum surface: It is a level surface with respect to which the levels of points are measured or referred to. It may be a standard surface like mean sea-level or an arbitrary surface.

Bench Mark (B.M.): A bench mark is a permanent or semi-permanent physical mark of known elevation. It is set as point of reference in order to provide a point of beginning for determining elevations of other points. A bench mark is a bronze plate either in the top of a concrete pillar or in the foundation of a structure. Other locations for bench mark may be the top of a culvert headwall, the top of an anchor bolt, or the top of a spike driven into the base of a tree. The bench marks are established by government agencies for the convenience of the surveyors and civil engineers. The surveyors or civil engineers may also establish temporary bench marks for their own use.

6.3 CURVATURE AND REFRACTION

Since levelling is measured in vertical plane, the effects of curvature of the earth and atmospheric refraction which occur in vertical direction, must be taken into account. The required correction to the observations are either determined by the appropriate calculations or else by the measurement techniques designed to eleminate these effects.

It is evident from the definitions that a horizontal line departs from a level surface because of the curvature of the earth as shown in Fig. 6.1.

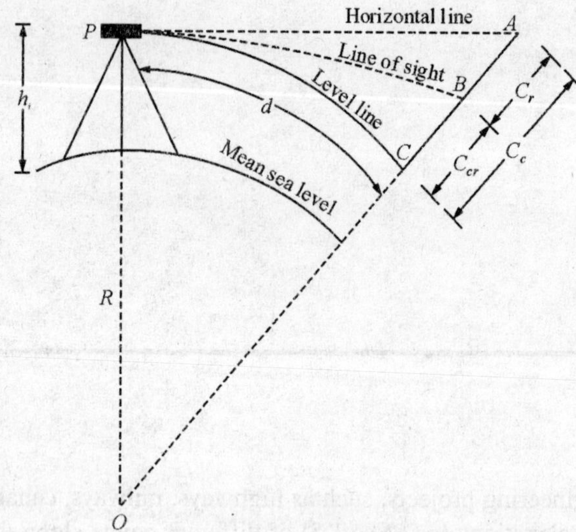

Fig. 6.1 Curvature and refraction

Since the line of sight cannot follow a curved line, an error is introduced, and objects appear lower than they really are. This causes increase in reading and, therefore, this correction is negative.

Similarly, the effect of atmospheric refraction is to bend light rays slightly downward as they pass through layers of air of different densities. Light rays reflected from objects and incident on the retina enable us to see them. But the eye perceives them only in the direction tangent to the line of sight at the point of incidence, so the effect of refraction is to make objects appear higher than they really are. Since due to the effect of refraction reading is decreased, the correction for refraction is positive.

In Fig. 6.1, *AB* is the correction for refraction (C_r), and *AC* is the correction for earth curvature (C_c). If the distance from the point of tangency *P* to the point in question in kilometres is *d*, and the mean earth's radius is *R* then from the right-angled triangle *OPA*, we have

$$(R + h_i)^2 + d^2 = (R + h_i + C_c)^2$$

where h_i is the height of the instrument axis above the mean sea level. Whilst the value of *R* is approximately 6370 km, the value of h_i will be of the order of 1.4 m, and therefore, can be neglected compared to the value of *R*.

Thus

$$(R + h_i)^2 + d^2 = (R + h_i)^2 + C_c^2 + 2(R + h_i)C_c$$

$$d^2 = C_c^2 + 2(RC_c + h_iC_c)$$

Since C_c is very small, the term C_c^2 and h_iC_c will be very small, and can be neglected. Therefore,

$$d^2 = 2RC_c$$

or $C_c = -\dfrac{d^2}{2R}$ (taking sign of the correction) ...(6.1)

Under the normal atmospheric conditions, C_r is one seventh of C_c but of opposite sign, *i.e.*,

$$C_r = +\frac{1}{7}C_c \qquad \text{...(6.2)}$$

Since the effects of curvature and refraction are in opposite directions to each other, the combined correction $BC = AC - AB$ will be

$$C_{cr} = C_c - \frac{1}{7}C_c$$

$$= \frac{6}{7}C_c = \frac{6}{7}\left(-\frac{d^2}{2R}\right) = -\frac{3}{7}\frac{d^2}{R} \qquad \text{...(6.3)}$$

Taking R as 6370 km, the combined correction is

$$\boxed{C_{cr} = -0.0673 d^2} \qquad \text{...(6.4)}$$

In Eq. (6.4), d is expressed in kilometre, and C_{cr} in metre.

In ordinary levelling work, the line of sight is seldom more than 100 m long and the corresponding value of C_{cr} is only 0.7 mm. Thus curvature and refraction are rarely significant except in precise levelling.

Distance to the Visible Horizon

In Fig. 6.2, let P be the point of observation at height h, and A be the point on the *horizon*, *i.e.*, a point where the tangent from P meets the level line. Taking value of R as 6370 km and the mean coefficient of refraction as 0.071 for sights over land, the distance to visible horizon is given by

$$d = 0.0483\sqrt{Rh} \text{ kilometres} \qquad \text{...(6.5)}$$

or $$d = \sqrt{\frac{h}{0.0673}} \text{ kilometres} \qquad \text{...(6.6)}$$

where h is in metres.

In Eqs. (6.5) and (6.6), both curvature and refraction corrections are taken into account.

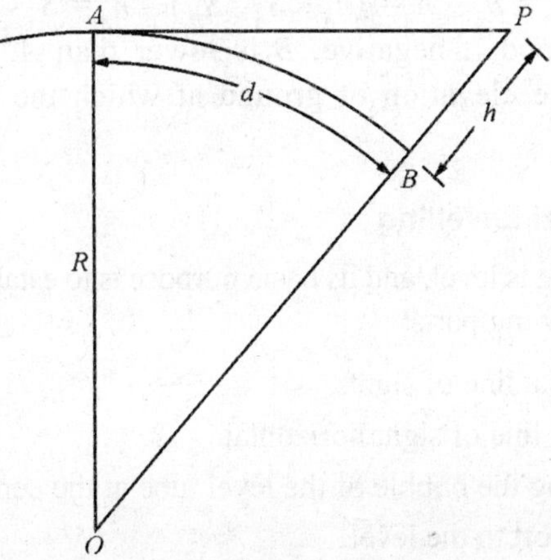

Fig. 6.2 Visible horizon

6.4 METHODS OF LEVELLING

Difference in elevations may be determined by the following methods:

1. Direct differential or spirit levelling
2. Indirect or trignometric levelling
3. Stadia levelling
4. Barometric levelling.

Direct Differential or Spirit Levelling

Differential levelling or spirit levelling is the most accurate and simple direct method for determining the difference of elevations between two points using an instrument known as *level* with a *levelling staff.* In Fig. 6.3, A is the point of known elevation, say h_A, with respect to which the elevation h_B of the point B is to be determined. The level is set up between the two points, and levelled with the help of a level tube attached to the level. When the instrument is levelled, the line of sight would be horizontal. The reading S_A is taken on the levelling staff by first putting it on A, and then S_B by putting on B.

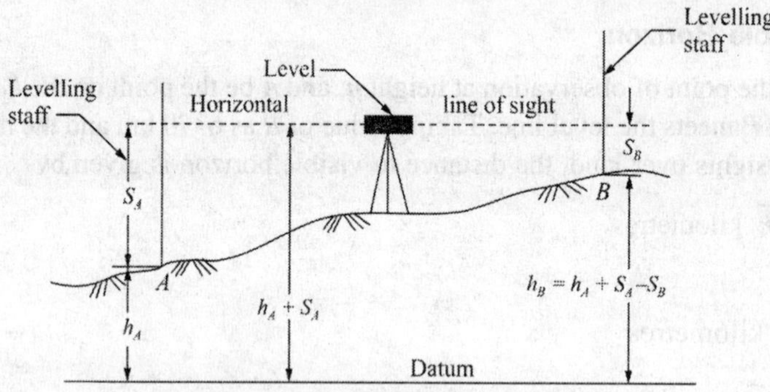

Fig. 6.3 Direct differential levelling

The elevation of the line of sight will be $h_A + S_A$, and the elevation of B will be $h_A + S_A - S_B$. Hence, the difference in elevation $\Delta h_{BA} = h_B - h_A = (h_A + S_A - S_B) - h_A = S_A - S_B$. If $(S_A - S_B)$ is positive, the point B is higher than A, and if negative, B is lower than A. It shows that to determine the difference in elevations, the elevation of ground at which the level is set up need not be considered.

Instrument Used in Differential Levelling

The instrument used in levelling is level, and its basic purpose is to establish a horizontal line of sight. It consists essentially of the following parts:

1. A telescope which provides a line of sight.
2. A level tube for making the line of sight horizontal.
3. A levelling head for bringing the bubble of the level tube at the centre of its run.
4. A tripod for providing support to the level.

The another instrument which is used with the level to determine amount by which a point is above or below the line of sight, is a levelling staff, straight rectangular rod having graduations and the foot of the staff representing zero reading. The vertical distance between the line of sight and the point over which the staff is held vertically, is the *staff reading*.

Types of levels

Of the various types of levels the following are the most common:

1. Dumpy level
2. Tilting level.

The modern levelling instruments used for precise works or geodetic surveys are:

1. Self-levelling or Automatic level
2. Geodetic level.

The instruments used in reconnaissance surveys to have an idea of change in levels are:

1. Hand level
2. Clinometer.

A brief description of the above levels is given below.

Dumpy level

The dumpy level shown in Fig. 6.4, consists of a telescope, generally the internal focussing type, fixed on a vertical spindle. The telescope tube and the vertical spindle are cast as one piece. The spindle revolves in the socket of the levelling head. The levelling head consists of two parallel plates held apart by three (or four) levelling screws. The upper plate is called tribrach and the lower one is called trivet stage. The telescope can be rotated in the horizontal plane about its vertical axis.

A sensitive bubble tube is fitted on the top of the telescope or on its side. An inclined mirror (not shown in the figure) is attached to the level tube to enable the observer to view the bubble from the eye end of the telescope without moving round the instrument.

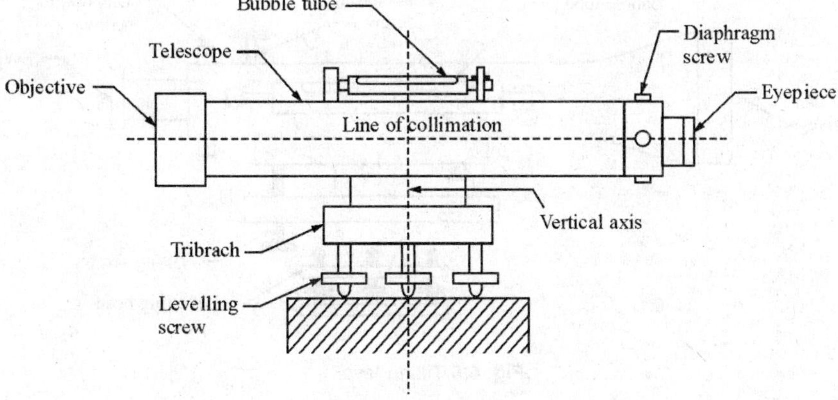

Fig. 6.4 Dumpy level

The cross hairs of the diaphragm normally have a vertical line and a horizontal line. When the instrument is in adjustment, the line of sight of the instrument is perpendicular to the vertical axis and parallel to the bubble tube axis as shown in Fig. 6.5.

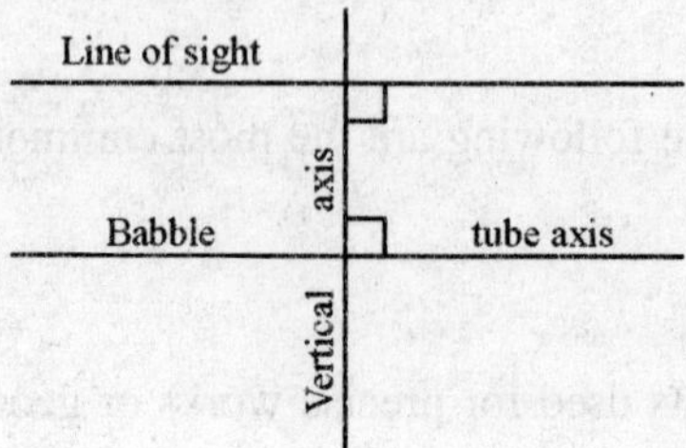

Fig. 6.5 Relationship of the line of sight with the vertical axis and bubble tube axis

The modern dumpy levels are provided with a clamp for clamping the telescope to the tribrach in any desired position. Also a graduated horizontal circle is provided to determine the direction of the telescope.

The dumpy level is simple in construction, and requires fewer permanent adjustments. Adjustments once carried out remain for a long period. Before taking reading, the instrument requires temporary adjustments. These are (a) setting up, (b) levelling up, and (c) elimination of parallax, discussed in Sec. 4.4. A dumpy level is most useful when from one setting of the instrument, levels of several points are to be determined.

Tilting level

The telescope of a tilting level is not rigidly fixed to the vertical spindle as in the case of dumpy level. The telescope can be tilted on a pivot about a horizontal axis in the vertical plane upwards or downward through a small angle by means of a tilting screw as shown in Fig. 6.6.

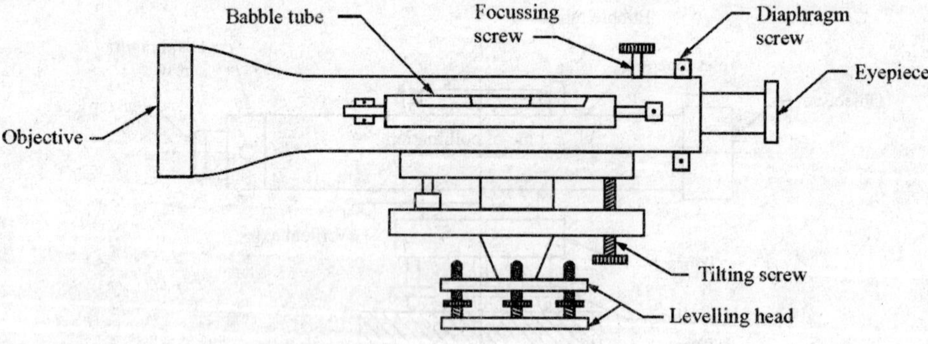

Fig. 6.6 Tilting level

The bull's eye or circular level is fixed to the upper plate of levelling head for approximate levelling by foot screws. The exact levelling of the instrument is done using the tilting screw before taking every reading. The tilting screw is usually graduated to set out gradient lines.

Tilting levels are more robust, compact and accurate than dumpy levels. These have shorter telescope and are lighter. The tilting arrangement saves time required for temporary adjustments. A tilting level is most useful when only a few readings are to be taken from one setting of the instrument.

Automatic level

The automatic level employs a gravity referenced prism or mirror compensator to automatically orient the line of sight (line of collimation). The instrument is quickly levelled when a circular spirit level is used. When the bubble has been centered or nearly so, the compensator takes over and maintains the horizontal line of sight, even if the telescope is slightly tilted. Fig. 6.7 shows the section through an automatic level.

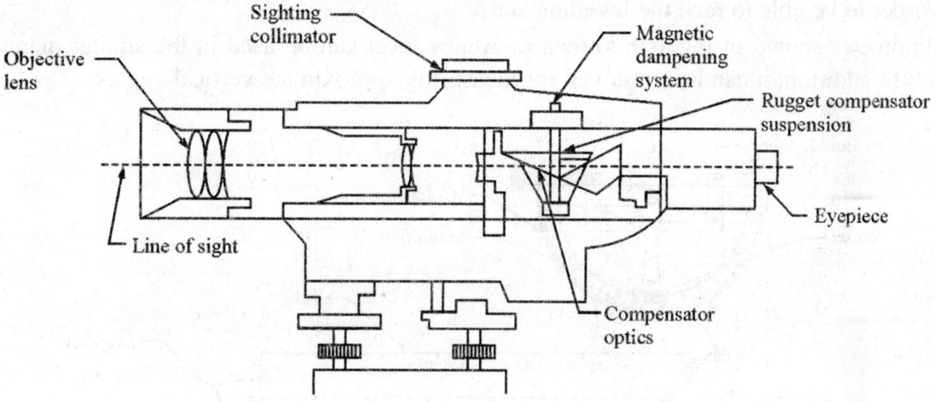

Fig. 6.7 Section through an automatic level

Automatic levels are extremely popular in present-day surveying operations. They are quick to set up, easy to use, and can be obtained for use at almost any required precision.

Geodetic level

The geodetic level is a tilting level used for extreme precision required in first-order levelling. It is made of invar to lessen the effect of temperature, and equipped with stadia hairs for determining three staff readings at one observation and for determining lengths of the sights.

Hand level and clinometer

The hand level, shown in Fig. 6.8, is a brass tube with a small level tube mounted on the top. A 45° mirror of half width, on the inside of the main tube, enables the user to view the bubble by reflection through the opening right beneath the bubble tube. As the staff viewed through the level is not magnified, the length of the sight is limited by the visibility of staff readings with the naked eye.

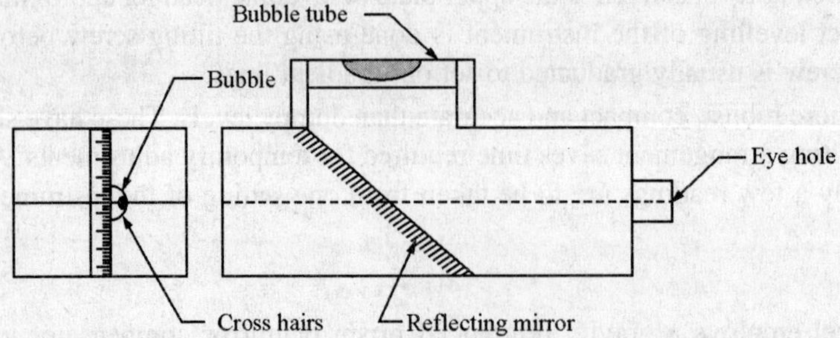

Fig. 6.8 Hand level

The hand level is used in reconnaissance surveys when the extreme accuracy is not required, and in taping to hold the tape horizontally. It is also used for estimating how high or low the dumpy level must be set in order to be able to read the levelling staff.

The clinometer shown in Fig. 6.9, known as Abney level can be used in the similar manner as the hand level. In addition, it can be employed for measuring approximate vertical angles.

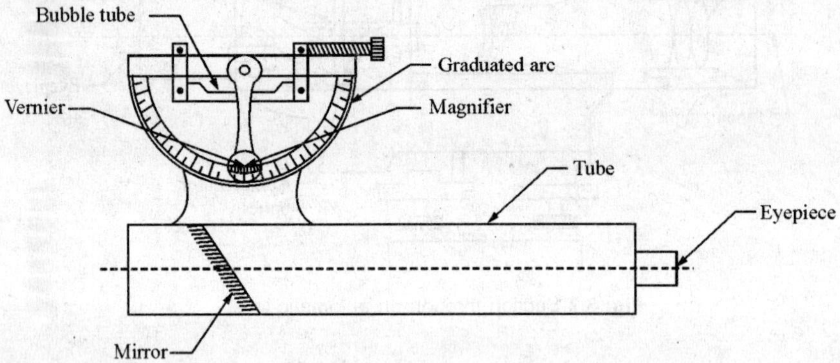

Fig. 6.9 Clinometer

Types of levelling staffs

The levelling staffs are classified as:

1. Self-reading staff, and
2. Target staff.

A self-reading staff is the one which can be read directly by the instrument man through the telescope. On the other hand, a target staff contains a moving target against which the reading is taken by staff man.

Self-reading staff

There are usually three types of self-reading staffs.

Solid staff or single-piece staff

The single-piece or solid staff shown in Fig. 6.10, is a single long flat rod of well-seasoned wood, about 75 mm wide and 25 mm thick, with a metal shoe at the bottom, and graduated on one face. The smallest division is of 5 mm in metric system. The length of the staff is generally 3 m.

Fig. 6.10 Self-reading or solid staff

Folding staff

A folding staff is hinged in the middle so that top half can be folded over to lie against the lower half. When fully extended, the upper part is held firmly in position by a metal pin passing through holes in plates at the side of the hinge. When the staff is not in use it can be folded about the hinge so that it becomes convenient to carry it from one place to the other.

Telescopic staff (sopwith pattern)

A telescopic staff consists of two hallow pieces and one solid top piece, each telescoping into the bottom one. The telescopic staff has advantage over the other types that greater lengths of staff are obtainable up to 4 m to 5 m. When the staff is folded up, it is only a little longer than the lowest piece. When the upper sections are pulled out for use, they are engaged and held by brass spring-catches.

Target staff

A target staff has a sliding target equipped with vernier which can be clamped at any point along the staff. If it is made in more than one piece, separate verniers are provided for each piece.

For taking the reading, the level man directs the staff man to raise or lower the target till it is bisected by the line of sight. The staff man then clamps the target and takes the reading.

Relative merits of self-reading and target staff

(*i*) With the self-reading staff, readings can be taken faster than with the target staff.

(*ii*) In target staff, adjusting the target is often tedius, and staff man must be a relatively trained person capable of coordinating with the instrument man. In the case of a self-reading type, on the other hand, ordinary man can hold the staff concentrating more on keeping the staff in plumb.

(*iii*) The refinement provided by the vernier is often lost when adjusting the target so that it is bisected by the line of sight. Thus the degree of precision finally attained is not significantly different in the two types. However, a target staff is valuable when very long sights are to be taken.

Classification of Direct Differential Levelling

The direct differential levelling can be further classified into the following methods.

Simple levelling

This is the easiest and straightforward type of direct levelling in which only one setting of the instrument is done to determine the difference in level between two points. It is only suitable when the distance involved is within the sighting range of the level. The instrument need not necessarily lie on the line joining the points.

Differential, compound or continuous levelling

When the two points whose difference in elevation is required are too far apart, or when there are intervening obstacles or the difference in elevation is too large, one setting of the instrument will be inadequate. In such cases, the method of simple levelling is used with as many intermediate level stations as required to reach the forward station maintaining a continuity.

Check levelling

It is employed for the purpose of checking of elevations which have already been determined. Generally check levelling is done at the end of each day's work from last station to the starting station for checking the day's work. Instead of returning to the starting station, sometimes, the day's work is checked by connecting the last station to a point of known elevation or a B.M.

Fly levelling

When a B.M. of known elevation is available, a series of levels may be run along a general direction to reach some other point whose level can be determined and fixed as a temporary B.M., if necessary, the method is called fly levelling. Fly levelling is also employed for the determination of approximate levels of different points. In such cases, the distances as long as possible between the level and staff are measured.

The fly levelling is done where rapidity but low precision is required. It is normally used for reconnaissance surveys or for approximate checking of the levels.

Profile or longitudinal levelling

It is used in route surveys such as a highway, railway, canal, sewer line. The elevations of points along the proposed centre line, at known (usually regular) distance apart, are obtained by differential or fly levelling. The object is to determine the profile of the ground in a vertical longitudinal section (*c.f.*, levelling practices).

Cross-section levelling

This type of direct differential levelling is employed to determine the difference of elevations of the gound surface along the lines perpendicular to the centre line of the proposed route. The cross-section levelling is required to determine the configuration across the alignment of the route. Generally, the profile levelling and cross-section levelling are done simultaneously to help in estimation of the earthwork involved in a route (*cf.*, levelling practices).

Reciprocal levelling

It is the accurate determination of the difference in level between two points by setting up the instrument near each of the points in succession and taking observations of staff readings on both. It is useful when it is not feasible to set up the level midway between the points (*cf.*, levelling practices).

Precise levelling

This is a very accurate method of differential levelling for establishing bench marks or where high precision is required. Refine instruments and procedures enhance the accuracy of the work. It is a specialised form of levelling, and is usually conducted by government agencies like Survey of India.

Booking and Reducing Levels

Before discussing the booking and reducing levels, the following terms associated with differential levelling must be understood.

Station

In levelling, a station is that point where the levelling staff is held and not where the level is set up. It is a point whose elevation is to be determined or the point that is to be established at a given elevation.

Height of instrument (H.I.)

For any set up of the level, the elevation of the line of sight is called height of instrument.

Back sight (B.S.)

When the forward calculations are made, generally, it is the first reading taken on the staff after setting up the instrument. Initially it is usually made to some form of bench mark or to the point whose elevation has already been determined.

The back sight is usually the first reading taken after setting up the instrument to determine the height of instrument. Thus, the height of instrument is equal to the elevation of the station where staff is held plus the reading on the staff.

Fore sight (F.S.)

It is the reading taken on the staff either held at the last point whose elevation is required or held at the turning point just before shifting the instrument. The fore sight is used to determine the elevation of the staff station. The elevation of the staff station is equal to the height of instrument minus the fore sight.

Change point (C.P.)

A change point or turning point (T.P.) is the point where staff is held and after taking fore sight to determine the elevation of the point where the staff is held, the instrument is shifted and back sight is taken at the same point to determine the new height of instrument. Therefore, at the change point both the back sight and fore sight are taken.

Intermediate station (I.S.)

It is the reading taken on a staff held at a point whose elevation is required, but is not a change point or the last point. Intermediate sites are taken at the intermediate stations.

In Fig. 6.3, S_A is the back sight and S_B is the fore sight. $h_A + S_A$ is the height of instrument. Fig. 6.11 shows the levelling operation between stations *A* to *C*. The elevations of the points *a, b, c,* and *C* are required to be determined. *A* is a bench mark whose elevation is known. The staff is held at *A* and the level is set up at 1. The first reading taken at *A* is the back sight. Then the staff is held at *a, b,* and *B*, the corresponding readings are the intermediate sights on *a* and *b*, and the fore sight on *B*. Then the instrument is shifted to the position 2, and the first reading taken on the staff at *B* is the back sight. As at *B* both the fore sight and back sight readings have been taken, it is the change point. After taking back sight at *B*, the staff is held at *c* and *C*, the corresponding readings being the intermediate sight on *c* and the fore sight on *C*.

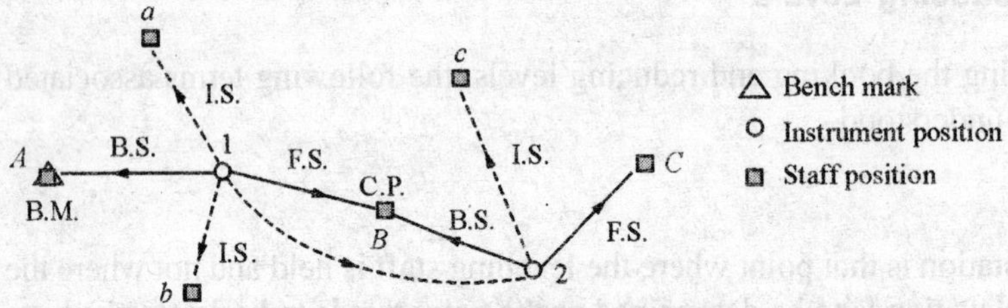

Fig. 6.11 Back sight, fore sight, and intermediate sight

Balancing of sights

When the distances of the points where back sight and fore sight are taken, kept approximately equal, it is known as balancing of sights. This is done to minimise the effect of instrumental and other errors.

Reduced level (R.L.)

In differential levelling, the elevations of the points are not directly observed. The elevations of points are reduced from the observed B.S., F.S., or I.S. This process of computing the levels is known as reducing the levels, and elevations so obtained are known as reduced levels. For booking and reducing the levels of points, there are two methods known as (1) Collimation or height of instrument method and (2) Rise and fall method.

Height of instrument method

In this method, height of instrument is calculated for each setting of the instrument by adding the back sight to the known elevation of the point at which back sight has been taken. The reduced level of the points are calculated by subtracting the intermediate sight or fore sight as the case may be, from the height of instrument. The specimen page of a level field book illustrating the method of booking staff readings and reducing the levels of the stations by height of instrument method is shown in Table 6.1.

The station 1 is a bench mark of known elevation of 100.00 m. The staff was held at this station and B.S. 0.685 was taken. Then the staff was held at station 2 and the F.S. 2.905 was taken. Now the instrument was shifted and the B.S. 1.800 was taken at station 2, therefore, this station is a change point. After this two I.S. 1.225 and 2.830 were taken at stations 3 and 4, respectively. The last reading 0.455 for this setting of the instrument is the F.S at station 5, and then the instrument is shifted to another position to take the B.S. 2.550 at station 5. Finally the last reading at station 8 is the F.S. 2.625. Between the stations 5 and 8, an I.S. was taken at station 6, and F.S. 1.555 and B.S. 2.590 on station 7.

Table 6.1 Height of instrument method of reduction of levels

Station (a)	B.S. (b)	I.S. (c)	F.S. (d)	H.I. (e)	R.L. (f)	Remarks
1	0.685			100.685	100.000	B.M.
2	1.800		2.905	99.580	97.780	C.P.
3		1.225			98.355	
4		2.830			96.750	
5	2.550		0.455	101.675	99.125	C.P.
6		2.745			98.930	
7	2.590		1.555	102.710	100.120	C.P.
8			2.625		100.085	

For the reduction of levels, the steps are given below:

R.L. 100.000 of St.1 + B.S. 0.685 at St. 1 = H.I. 100.685 in Col. (e)

H.I. 100.685 – F.S. 2.905 at St. 2 = R.L. 97.780 of St. 2 in Col. (f)

R.L. 97.780 of St. 2 + B.S. 1.800 at St. 2 (C.P.) = H.I. 99.580 in Col. (e)

H.I. 99.580 – I.S. 1.225 at St. 3 = R.L. 98.355 of St. 3 in Col. (f)

H.I. 99.580 – I.S. 2.830 at St. 4 = R.L. 96.750 of St. 4 in Col. (f)

H.I. 99.580 – F.S. 0.455 at St. 5 = R.L. 99.125 of St. 5 in Col. (f)

R.L. 99.125 of St. 5 + B.S. 2.550 at St. 5 (C.P.) = H.I. 101.675 in Col. (e)

H.I. 101.675 – I.S. 2.745 at St. 6 = R.L. 98.930 of St. 6 in Col. (f)

H.I. 101.675 – F.S. 1.555 at St. 7 = R.L. 100.120 of St. 7 in Col. (f)

R.L. 100.120 + B.S. 2.590 at St. 7 (C.P.) = H.I. 102.710 in Col. (e)

H.I. 102.710 – F.S. 2.625 at St. 8 = R.L. 100.085 of St. 8 in Col. (f)

The height of instrument method provides the following arithmetic check on the reduction of levels:

$$\Sigma B.S. - \Sigma F.S. = \text{Last R.L.} - \text{First R.L.}$$

$$7.625 - 7.540 = 100.085 - 100.000 = 0.085$$

Rise and fall method

In this method, the difference of level between two consecutive points for each setting of the instrument is obtained by comparing their staff readings. The difference indicates a rise if the back sight is more than the fore sight, and a fall if it is less than the fore sight. The two consecutive points may have readings as B.S. and F.S, B.S. and I.S., I.S. and I.S., or I.S. and F.S. The rise or fall worked out for all the points, give the difference in level of each point relative to the preceding one. Therefore, if the R.L. of the preceding point is known then the R.L. of the following point can be obtained by adding the rise or subtracting the fall as the case may be.

Table 6.2 shows a page of the level book illustrating the method of calculating the R.L.'s of stations by the rise and fall method. The booking of readings of B.S., I.S. and F.S. is same as in the height of instrument method.

Table 6.2 Rise and fall method of reduction of levels

Station (a)	B.S. (b)	I.S. (c)	F.S. (d)	Rise (e)	Fall (f)	R.L. (g)	Remarks
1	0.685					100.000	B.M.
2	1.800		2.905		2.220	97.780	C.P.
3		1.225		0.575		98.355	
4		2.830			1.605	96.750	
5	2.550		0.455	2.375		99.125	C.P.
6		2.745			0.195	98.930	
7	2.590		1.555	1.190		100.120	C.P.
8			2.625		0.035	100.085	

For the reduction of levels, let us first determine the rise and fall as below:

B.S. 0.685 at St. 1 – F.S. 2.905 at St. 2 = – 2.220 or fall 2.220 in Col. (f)

B.S. 1.800 at St. 2 – I.S. 1.225 at St. 3 = + 0.575 or rise 0.575 in Col. (e)

I.S. 1.225 at St. 3 – I.S. 2.830 at St. 4 = – 1.605 or fall 1.605 in Col. (f)

I.S. 2.830 at St. 4 – F.S. 0.455 at St. 5 = + 2.375 or rise 2.375 in Col. (e)

B.S. 2.550 at St. 5 – I.S. 2.745 at St. 6 = – 0.195 or fall 0.195 in Col. (f)

I.S. 2.745 at St. 6 – F.S. 1.555 at St. 7 = + 1.190 or rise 1.190 in Col. (e)

B.S. 2.590 at St. 7 – F.S. 2.625 at St. 8 = – 0.035 or fall 0.035 in Col. (f)

Now the R.L's of station are calculated as below:

R.L. of St. 1 = 100.000 m (known)

R.L. of St. 2 = R.L. 100.000 of St. 1 – (fall) 2.220 = 97.780 m

R.L. of St. 3 = R.L. 97.780 of St. 2 + (rise) 0.575 = 98.355 m

R.L. of St. 4 = R.L. 98.355 of St. 3 – (fall) 1.605 = 96.750 m

R.L. of St. 5 = R.L. 96.750 of St. 4 + (rise) 2.375 = 99.125 m

R.L. of St. 6 = R.L. 99.125 of St. 5 – (fall) 0.195 = 98.930 m

R.L. of St. 7 = R.L. 98.930 of St. 6 + (rise) 1.190 = 100.120 m

R.L. of St. 8 = R.L. 100.120 of St. 7 – (fall) 0.035 = 100.085 m.

The rise and fall method of reducing the levels, provides two arithmetic checks as below:

$$\Sigma B.S. - \Sigma F.S. = \Sigma Rise - \Sigma Fall = Last\ R.L. - First\ R.L.$$

i.e., $7.625 - 7.540 = 4.140 - 4.055 = 100.085 - 100.000 = 0.085$

Comparision of Height of Instrument Method with Rise and Fall Method

1. The height of instrument method is simple, quicker and less tedius.
2. In the height of instrument method, since the check on the calculations for intermediate sights is not available, the mistakes in their levels pass unnoticed.
3. The rise and fall method though more tedious, provides a full check in the calculations for all sights.
4. The height of instrument method is more suitable in case, where it is required to take a number of readings from the same instrument settings.
5. The rise and fall method should be used for a long run of differential levelling for important works.
6. The rise and fall method should be used when there are a number of important intermediate stations.

ILLUSTRATIVE EXAMPLES

Example 6.1

The following readings were taken with a level and a 4 m staff. Draw up a level book page and reduce the levels by

(a) the rise and fall method.

(b) the height of instrument method.

0.683 B.M.(51.362 m), 1.109, 1.838, 3.399, (3.877 and 0.451) C.P., 1.405, 1.896, 2.676, 3.478, (3.999 and 1.834) C.P., 0.649, 1.706.

Solution:

The first reading is on a B.M. of elevation 51.362 m, and, therefore, it is to be entered as back sight. As the fifth station is a change point 3.877 is to be entered as a fore sight and 0.451 as a back sight. The tenth station is also a change point, therefore, 3.999 is a fore sight and 1.834 is a back sight. The reading 1.706 being on the last station, is a fore sight. All remaining readings are the intermediate sights.

The readings and the reduced levels of the stations are tabulated below:

(a) By rise and fall method

Station	B.S.	I.S.	F.S.	Rise	Fall	R.L.	Remarks
1	0.683					51.362	B.M.
2		1.109			0.426	50.936	
3		1.838			0.729	50.207	
4		3.399			1.561	48.646	
5	0.451		3.877		0.478	48.168	C.P.
6		1.405			0.954	47.214	
7		1.896			0.491	46.723	
8		2.676			0.780	45.943	
9		3.478			0.802	45.141	
10	1.834		3.999		0.521	44.620	C.P.
11		0.649		1.185		45.805	
12			1.706		1.057	44.748	
Σ	2.968		9.582	1.185	7.799		

Arth. Check: 2.968 – 9.582 = 1.185 – 7.799 = 44.748 – 51.362 = – 6.614

(b) By height of instrument method

Station	B.S.	I.S.	F.S.	H.I.	R.L.	Remarks
1	0.683			52.045	51.362	B.M.
2		1.109			50.936	
3		1.838			50.207	
4		3.399			48.646	
5	0.451		3.877	48.619	48.168	C.P.
6		1.405			47.214	
7		1.896			46.723	
8		2.676			45.943	
9		3.478			45.141	
10	1.834		3.999	46.454	44.620	C.P.
11		0.649			45.805	
12			1.706		44.748	
Σ	2.968		9.582			

Arth. Check: 2.968 – 9.582 = 44.748 – 51.362 = – 6.614

Example 6.2

It was required to ascertain the elevations of two points *A* and *B* and a line of levels was run from *A* to *B*. The levelling was then continued to bench mark of 77.500 m elevation. The reading obtained being as shown below:

B.S.	I.S.	F.S.	R.L.	Remarks
1.525				*A*
1.776		0.304		
2.005		1.870		
	2.300			*B*
0.899		1.011		
1.913		2.784		
		2.113	77.500	B.M.

Solution:

Since in this problem the starting point *A* is not a station of known elevation, to find the R.L.'s of *A* and *B*, the computation are to be done from bottom to top. To find the height of instrument, the fore sight readings will be added to the R.L. of the known point and to determine the R.L. of the previous point, the back sight will be subtracted from the so obtained H.I. as shown in the table below:

Station	B.S.	I.S.	F.S.	H.I.	R.L.	Remarks
A	1.525			78.989	77.464	*A*
	1.776		0.304	80.461	78.685	
	2.005		1.870		78.591	
B		2.300		80.596	78.296	*B*
	0.899		1.011	80.484	79.585	
	1.913		2.784	79.613	77.700	
			2.113		77.500	B.M.
Σ	8.118		8.082			

Arth. Check : 8.118 – 8.082 = 77.500 – 77.464 = 0.036

Example 6.3

The following consecutive readings were taken with a dumpy level and 5 m levelling staff on continuously sloping ground at a common interval of 15 m. The first point is having an elevation of 185.275 m. Rule out a page of level field book and enter the readings. Calculate (a) the reduced levels of the points by rise and fall method, and (b) the gradient of the line joining the first and the last points.

0.415, 1.025, 2.085, 2.925, 3.620, 4.595, 0.715, 2.115, 3.090, 4.405

Solution:

Since the readings were taken on a continuously sloping ground, the readings are continuously increasing up to sixth reading and then suddenly the seventh reading is lesser than the sixth one showing that the sixth point is a change point. Therefore, the seventh reading is back sight. Again from the seventh reading, the readings are continuously increasing. Thus,

the 1st reading is B.S.,

the 2nd, 3rd, 4th and 5th readings are I.S.'S

the 6th reading is F.S.,

the 7th reading is B.S.,

the 8th and 9th readings are I.S.'S, and

the 10th reading is F.S.

The page of the level field book with tabulated readings and calculated R.L'S is given below:

(a)

Station	B.S.	I.S.	F.S.	Rise	Fall	R.L.	Remarks
1	0.415					185.275	Known elevation
2		1.025			0.610	184.665	
3		2.085			1.060	183.605	
4		2.925			0.840	182.765	
5		3.620			0.695	182.070	
6	0.715		4.595		0.975	181.095	C.P.
7		2.115			1.400	179.695	
8		3.090			0.975	178.720	
9			4.405		1.315	177.405	
Σ	1.130		9.000	0.000	7.870		

Arth. Check : 1.130 – 9.000 = 0.000 – 7.870 = 177.405 – 185.275 = – 7.870

(b) The gradient of the line

$$= \frac{\text{R.L. of the last point} - \text{R.L. of the first point}}{\text{The length of the line joining the first point to the last point}}$$

$$= \frac{177.405 - 185.275}{15 \times 8}$$

$$= -0.066$$

= **1 in 15.25** (*falling*).

Example 6.4

A page of level field book is reproduced below in which some readings are missing (marked by *). Complete the page with all arithmetical checks.

Station	B.S.	I.S.	F.S.	Rise	Fall	R.L.	Remarks
1	3.65						
2		*		2.75			
3		2.83					
4		3.64					
5	*		7.42				C.P.
6		12.41			7.32		
7		4.32					
8		3.00					
9		– 6.17					Staff held inverted against ceiling
10	*		*		*	108.26	C.P.
11			*		1.32		
Σ	17.66				25.93		

Solution:

(*i*) B.S. (3.65) at St. 1 – I.S.(*) at St. 2 = 2.75 (rise)

or I.S. at St. 2 = 3.65 – 2.75

= 0.90

(*ii*) B.S.(*) at St. 5 – I.S. (12.41) of St. 6 = 7.32 (fall)

or B.S. at St. 5 = 12.41 + 7.32 (fall)

= 12.41 – 7.32

= 5.09

(*iii*) ΣB.S. = B.S. at St. 1 + B.S. at St.5 + B.S. at St. 10

or 17.66 = 3.65 + 5.09 + B.S. (*) at St. 10

B.S. (*) at St. 10 = 17.66 – 3.65 – 5.09

= 8.92

(*iv*) Now calculate the rise or fall as the case may be, at the stations from 2 to 9 (*c.f.*, the tabulated values)

ΣFall = Fall at St. 10 + Σcomputed fall at remaining stations.

Fall (*) at St. 10 = 25.93 – (1.93 + 0.81 + 3.78 + 7.32+ 1.32)

= 10.77

(*v*) F.S. (*) at St. 10 = I.S. (– 6.17) at St. 9 – 10.77 (fall)

= – 6.17 – (–10.77)

= – 6.17 + 10.77

= 4.60

(*vi*) F.S. (*) at St. 11 = B.S. (8.92) at St. 10 – 1.32 (fall)

= 8.92 – (–1.32)

= 8.92 + 1.32

= 10.24

Now the R.L.'s can be computed in usual manner starting from station 10 upwards for calculating the R.L.'s of station 9 to 1 and downwards for the station 11.

Station	B.S.	I.S.	F.S.	Rise	Fall	R.L.	Remarks
1	3.65					111.54	
2		0.90		2.75		114.29	
3		2.83			1.93	112.36	
4		3.64			0.81	111.55	
5	5.09		7.42		3.78	107.77	C.P.
6		12.41			7.32	100.45	
7		4.32		8.09		108.54	
8		3.00		1.32		109.86	
9		– 6.17		9.17		119.03	Staff held inverted against ceiling
10	8.92		4.60		10.77	108.26	C.P.
11			10.24		1.32	106.94	
Σ	17.66		22.60	21.33	25.93		

Arth. Check : 17.66 – 22.26 = 21.33 – 25.93 = 106.94 – 111.54 = – 4.60

Example 6.5

The following readings were obtained in running fly levels from a bench mark of R.L. = 310.000 m.

1.285, (1.120, 2.100), (3.545, 1.890), (2.300, 2.635)

From the last setting of the instrument, five pegs at 20 m intervals are to be set out on a uniform rising gradient of 1 in 50. The R.L. of the first peg is 307.225 m. Work out the staff readings required for setting the tops of pegs on the required gradient.

Solution:

$$\text{Gradient} = \frac{\text{Difference in elevation between two consecutive points}}{\text{Distance between two consecutive points}}$$

or $\dfrac{1}{50} = \dfrac{\Delta h}{20}$

or $\Delta h = \dfrac{20}{50} = 0.4 \text{ m}$

Let us first determine the R.L. of the stations where staff readings have been taken.

R.L. of St. 1 = 310.000 m

H.I. = R.L. (310.000) of St. 1 + B.S. (1.285) at St. 1 = 311.285 m

R.L. of St. 2 = H.I. (311.285) – F.S. (1.120) at St. 2= 310.165m

H.I. = R.L. (310.165) of St. 2 + B.S. (2.100) at St. 2 = 312.265 m

R.L. of St. 3 = H.I. (312.265) – F.S. (3.545) at St. 3 = 308.72 m

H.I. = R.L. (308.72) of St. 3 + B.S. (1.890) at St. 3 = 310.610 m

R.L. of St. 4 = H.I. (310.610) – F.S. (2.300) at St. 4 = 308.310 m

H.I. = R.L. (308.310) of St. 4 + B.S. (2.635) at St. 4 = 310.945 m.

As the pegs are to be set out on a uniform rising gradient the R.L's of the pegs would be as below:

R.L. of the 1st peg = 307.225 (given)

R.L. of 2nd peg = R.L. 307.225 of 1st peg + 0.400 = 307.625 m

R.L. of 3rd peg = R.L. 307.625 of 2nd peg + 0.400 = 308.025 m

R.L. of 4th peg = R.L. 308.025 of 3rd peg + 0.400 = 308.425 m

R.L. of 5th peg = R.L. 308.425 of 4th peg + 0.400 = 308.825 m.

Therefore the I.S. readings for the four pegs and F.S. for the last peg would be as below:

I.S. for Ist peg= H.I. (310.945) – R.L.(307.225) of 1st peg= 3.720

I.S. for 2nd peg = H.I. (310.945) – R.L.(307.625) of 2nd peg = 3.320

I.S. for 3rd peg = H.I. (310.945) – R.L.(308.025) of 3rd peg= 2.920

I.S. for 4th peg = H.I. (310.945) – R.L.(308.425) of 4th peg= 2.520

I.S. for 5th peg = H.I. (310.945) – R.L.(308.825) of 5th peg= 2.120

The readings and the computed values are given below in a page of level field book.

Station	B.S.	I.S.	F.S.	H.I.	R.L.	Remarks
1	1.285			311.285	310.000	B.M.
2	2.100		1.120	312.265	310.165	C.P.
3	1.890		3.545	310.610	308.720	C.P.
4	2.635		2.300	310.945	308.310	C.P.
		3.720			307.225	Peg.1
		3.320			307.625	Peg.2
		2.920			308.025	Peg.3
		2.520			308.425	Peg.4
			2.120		308.825	Peg.5
Σ	7.910		9.085			

Arth. Check : 7.910 – 9.085 = 308.825 – 310.000 = – 1.175

Example 6.6

A gradient of 1 in 400 falling from elevation 67.45 m was set out by driving pegs at 100 m intervals with the top of pegs on the required gradient. After a time it was suspected that some of the pegs had been disturbed and the following observations were taken for checking their elevations. List the errors in the levels of the pegs if any.

Station	B.S.	I.S.	F.S.	R.L.	Remarks
1	1.76			64.13	B.M.
2	2.64		0.720		
3	1.96		1.420		
4		0.93			Peg.1
5		1.20			Peg.2
6		1.50			Peg.3
7		1.76			Peg.4
8		2.03			Peg.5
9		2.30			Peg.6
10	0.69		2.59		Peg.7
11		0.95			Peg.8
12		1.23			Peg.9
13		1.52			Peg.10
14	0.61		1.21		
15			1.72	64.13	B.M.

Solution:

Rule out a page of level field book and enter the given data. Calculate the R.L.'s of the points from the given data and also for the given gradient. Compare the two R.L.'s and enter them as errors of the pegs.

Station	B.S.	I.S	F.S.	Rise	Fall	R.L.	Gradient level	Error	Remarks
1	1.76					64.13			B.M.
2	2.64		0.72	1.04		65.17			
3	1.96		1.42	1.22		66.39			
4		0.93		1.03		67.42	67.45	0.03	Peg.1
5		1.20			0.27	67.15	67.20	0.05	Peg.2
6		1.50			0.30	66.85	66.95	0.10	Peg.3
7		1.76			0.26	66.59	66.70	0.11	Peg.4
8		2.03			0.27	66.32	66.45	0.13	Peg.5
9		2.30			0.27	66.05	66.20	0.15	Peg.6
10	0.69		2.59		0.29	65.76	65.95	0.19	Peg.7
11		0.95			0.26	65.50	65.70	0.20	Peg.8
12		1.23			0.28	65.22	65.45	0.23	Peg.9
13		1.52			0.29	64.93	65.20	0.27	Peg.10
14	0.61		1.21	0.31		65.24			
15			1.72		1.11	64.13			B.M.
Σ	7.66		7.66	3.60	3.60				

Arth. Check : 7.66 – 7.66 = 3.60 – 3.60 = 64.13 – 64.13 = 0.00

Precautions in Levelling

While levelling, the following precautions should be taken.

1. The staff should be held vertical while taking the reading. To ensure the verticality, the staff man should stand behind the staff and hold the staff between his palms. The bottom of the staff should be held between the toes. To get the reading when the staff is truly vertical, the following process, known as *rocking of the staff*, is used. The staff is first waved slightly, towards the instrument and then slightly away from the instrument as shown in Fig. 6.12. The instrument man should take the reading which is minimum. As clear from the figure, the reading would be minimum only when the staff is in vertical position *A* and not for any other positions *B* and *B′* of the staff. The verticality can also be checked with a circular level, if attached to the staff.

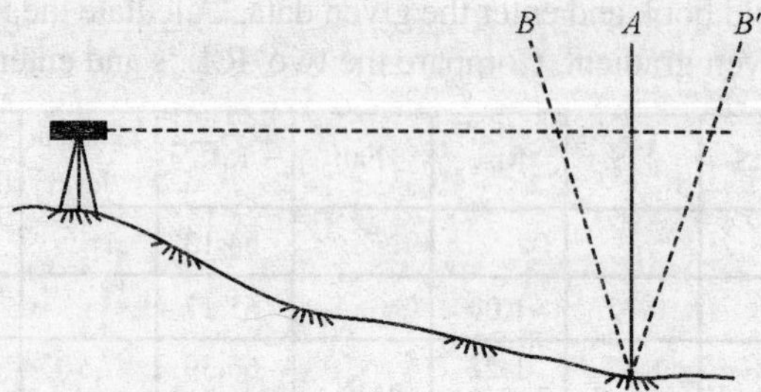

Fig. 6.12 Getting the reading when staff is vertical

2. Always make sure that the bubble of the level tube is central before taking the reading.
3. When the graduations on the staff are erect, the readings should be taken in the downward direction in which the reading increases.
4. To reduce the effect of the instrumental errors, the length of B.S. and F.S. should be kept nearly equal.
5. Do not drag the staff on the ground.
6. The instrument man should not grip the tripod or rest his hands on it while taking readings.
7. Read the staff correctly.
8. Avoid error in booking by reading back the recorded observation.
9. Avoid readings less than 0.5 m as intensive sunshine causes the air close to the ground to shimmer.

Errors in Levelling

Errors in levelling may be classified as below:

1. Personal errors
2. Errors due to natural causes
3. Instrumental errors.

Personal errors

Errors in sighting: Long sights, coarseness of the cross hairs, and staff graduations or sometimes, the atmospheric conditions make it difficult to see the exact coincidence of the cross hairs and the staff graduations. This error is accidental in nature.

Errors in manipulation: These errors are due to carelessly setting up the level, imperfect focussing of eyepiece and objective, the bubble not being central at the time of reading, and non-verticality of the staff.

Errors in reading the staff: These errors are generally committed by a beginner while reading the staff upwards, instead of downwards, reading against the top or bottom hair instead of the central hair, cocentrating the attention on the decimal part of the reading, and reading the whole metre wrongly, and reading the inverted staff as a vertically held staff.

Errors in recording and computing: The common errors in recording are entering a reading in wrong column, *e.g.*, B.S. as I.S., recording the reading with digits interchanged, omitting an entry, mistaking the numerical value of a reading called by the level man, entering the inverted staff reading without a minus sign, and adding the fore sight reading instead of subtracting it and or subtracting a back sight reading instead of adding.

Errors due to natural causes

Errors due to curvature and refraction: The effects of earth's curvature and atmospheric refraction have already been discussed in Sec. 6.3. In the case of ordinary levelling, the errors due to the curvature and refraction are negligible.

Errors due to wind and sun: In strong wind it is always difficult to hold the staff vertical. The strong wind also causes vibrations in the instrument and the bubble of the level tube does not remain central. It is always advisable to suspend the work in such conditions.

The sun causes considerable trouble in taking the readings if it shines on the objective. In such a condition, it is always recommended to protect the objective by an umbrella.

Instrumental Errors

Imperfect adjustment of the level: If the level is in imperfect adjustment, the line of sight will not be horizontal when the bubble of the level tube is central. It causes collimation error which can be compensated by balancing of sights. It may be noted that the error due to imperfect adjustment of the instrument is very common and serious, and hence, the instrument must always be carefully tested and adjusted before its use.

Defective level tube: If the bubble of the level tube is sluggish, it will remain central even though the bubble axis is not horizontal. On the other hand, if it is too sensitive, considerable time is spent to make the bubble central. Irregularity of curvature of the tube is also a serious defect. This effect gets neutralized if the sights are equal.

Shaky tripod: A shaky tripod causes instability to the instrument, and considerable time is wasted to make accurate observations.

Imperfect graduations of the staff: Imperfect graduations of a staff will cause errors in staff readings. In an ordinary levelling, the error may be negligible, because the readings are generally made correct to 0.005 m. In the case of precise levelling, the graduations must be compared against invar tape.

Sensitivity of a Level Tube

The sensitivity of a level tube is expressed in terms of the angle in seconds subtended at the centre by an arc of the level tube equal to one division of the tube. For example, if the divisions are 2 mm apart and the bubble is off the centre by one division when the axis of the level tube is inclined to the horizontal by $20''$, the sensitivity is $20''$ per 2 mm. The radius of curvature of the inner surface of the upper portion of the level tube is also a measure of the sensitivity.

The sensitiveness of a level tube depends upon the following:

(*i*) The radius of curvature of inner surface of the level tube. Larger is the radius, greater is the sensitivity.

(*ii*) The diameter of the level tube. Larger is the diameter, greater is the sensitivity.

(*iii*) The length of the vapour bubble. Greater is the length, greater is the sensitivity.

(*iv*) The viscosity and surface tension of the liquid. More is the viscosity, less is the sensitivity.

(*v*) Smoothness of inner surface of the tube. Smoothness increases the sensitivity of the level tube.

Determination of sensitivity

There are following two methods for determination of sensitivity.

Method-I

Set the instrument at *O*, and level it accurately, sight a staff at *P* and take the reading *PE* as shown in Fig. 6.13. Let the distance of the staff from the instrument be *D*. Now, using a foot screw, deviate the bubble over *n* number of divisions and again take the reading *PC* on the staff.

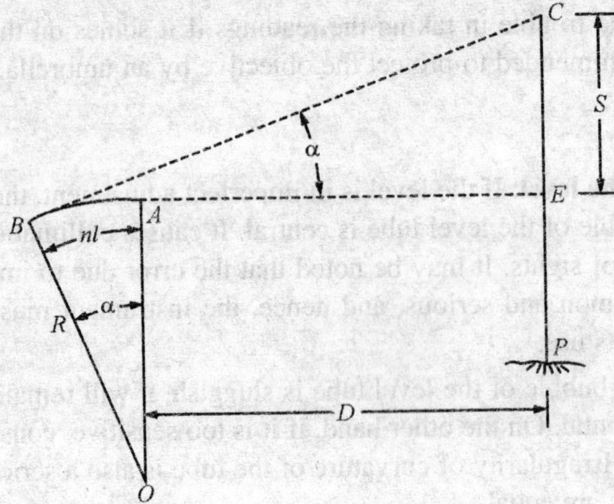

Fig. 6.13 Method-I of determining the sensitivity of a level tube

Let $s = PC - PE$

From ΔBCE, we have

$$\tan\alpha = \alpha = \frac{s}{D} \quad \textit{(approximately)} \qquad \text{...(6.7)}$$

Similarly from ΔAOB

$$\alpha = \frac{AB}{R} = \frac{nl}{R} \qquad \text{...(6.8)}$$

where R = radius of carvature of the bubble tube

l = length of one division of the bubble tube

n = number of divisions by which the bubble is moved,

Equating Eq. (6.7) to Eq. (6.8), we get

$$\frac{s}{D} = \frac{nl}{R}$$

or $$R = \frac{nlD}{s} \quad ...(6.9)$$

Eq. (6.9) is an expression for the radius of curvature of the bubble tube which is a measure of sensitivity.

If α' is the sensitivity of the bubble tube, it is the angular value of one division, *i.e.*,

$$\alpha' = \frac{\alpha}{n}$$

From Eq. (6.8), we have

$$\frac{\alpha}{n} = \frac{l}{R}$$

or $$\alpha' = \frac{l}{R} \quad ...(6.10)$$

Substituting the value of R from Eq. (6.9), we have

$$\alpha' = \frac{l}{\frac{nlD}{s}}$$

or $$\alpha' = \frac{s}{nD} \text{ radians} \quad ...(6.11)$$

$$= 206265 \frac{s}{nD} \text{ seconds} \quad ...(6.12)$$

or $$\alpha' = \frac{s}{nD \sin 1''} \text{ seconds} \quad ...(6.13)$$

Eqs. (6.11), (6.12), and (6.13), are the expressions for the sensitivity of the bubble tube.

Method-II

Set up the instrument at O and the staff at P at a distance D from O as shown in Fig. 6.14. Observe the staff reading PF with bubble near one end of its run by means of levelling screw beneath the telescope. Again observe the staff reading PE with the bubble near the other end of its run by means of the same levelling screw. Let the total run of the bubble be AB.

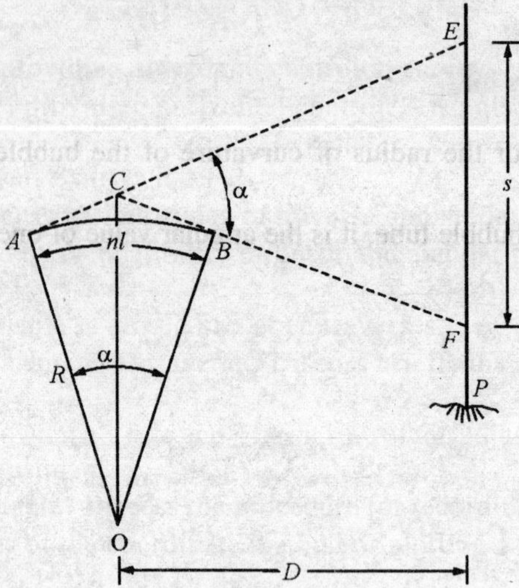

Fig. 6.14 Method-II for determining the sensitivity of a level tube

Let $s = PE - PF$, and n = the total number of divisions through which the bubble is moved. If the length of one division of the graduations is l then

$$AB = nl \qquad ...(6.14)$$

Considering the similar Δ's AOB and ECF, we get

$$\alpha = \frac{AB}{R} = \frac{EF}{D}$$

or
$$\frac{nl}{R} = \frac{s}{D}$$

or
$$R = \frac{nlD}{s} \qquad ...(6.15)$$

where R is the radius of curvature of the bubble tube.

Now putting the value of R from Eq. (6.15) into Eq. (6.10), we get

$$\alpha' = \frac{s}{nD} \text{ radians.}$$

The above expression is same as Eq. (6.11).

ILLUSTRATIVE EXAMPLES

Example 6.7

To determine the sensitivity of a bubble tube, the reading taken on a staff 200 m from the instrument bringing the bubble central, was 2.816 m. The bubble was then moved 5 divisions out of the centre and the staff reading observed was 2.875 m.

Taking the length of one division of the bubble tube as 2 mm, calculate the sensitivity in terms of radius of curvature and angular value.

Solution:

Given that $n = 5$

$l = 2$ mm

$D = 200$ m

$s = 2.875 - 2.816 = 0.059$ m

The radius of curvature R from Eq. (6.19) is

$$R = \frac{nlD}{s}$$

$$= \frac{5 \times 2 \times 200}{0.059}$$

$$= \mathbf{33.90\ m.}$$

The angular value α' is given by Eq. (6.13), *i.e.*,

$$\alpha' = 206265 \frac{s}{nD}$$

$$= 206265 \times \frac{0.059}{5 \times 200} \text{ seconds}$$

$$= \mathbf{12.17''}.$$

Example 6.8

Determine the radius of curvature of the bubble tube if length of one division is 2 mm and the angular value of one division is

(*a*) 30″, and
(*b*) 1′.

Solution:

From Eq. (6.10), we have

$$\alpha' = \frac{l}{R}$$

or $$R = \frac{l}{\alpha'}$$

Taking α' in seconds, we have

(*i*) $R = 206265 \times \dfrac{2}{30}$ mm

$= \mathbf{13.75\ m}$

(*ii*) $R = 206265 \times \dfrac{2}{1 \times 60}$ mm

$= \mathbf{6.88\ m.}$

Example 6.9

If the sensitivity of a bubble tube is 30″ per 2 mm division, what would be the error in staff reading on a vertically held staff at a distance of 200 m when the bubble is out of centre by 2.5 divisions?

Solution:

From Eq. (6.12), we have

$$\alpha' = 206265 \frac{s}{nD} \text{ seconds}$$

where s can be taken as the error in the staff reading. Therefore,

$$s = \frac{nD\alpha'}{206265}$$

Given that $n = 2.5$

$D = 200$ m

$\alpha' = 30''$

$$s = \frac{2.5 \times 200 \times 30}{206265}$$

$= \mathbf{0.073\ m.}$

Example 6.10

To the measure of the sensitivity of a bubble tube the following data were obtained:

Sl. No.	Bubble reading		Staff reading
	L.H.	R.H.	
1.	13	5	1.618
2.	8	12	1.767

Distance of the instrument from the staff = 75 m

Length of one division of the bubble tube = 2 mm

Determine the angular value of one division of the bubble tube.

Solution:

The deviation of the bubble from the centre

(1) $n_1 = \frac{1}{2} \times (13 - 5) = 4$ div.

(2) $n_2 = \frac{1}{2} \times (12 - 8) = 2$ div.

The total number of divisions n through which the bubble has moved is

$$n = n_1 + n_2 = 4 + 2 = 6$$

The staff intercept is

$$s = 1.767 - 1.618 = 0.149 \text{ m}$$

From Eq. (6.12), we have

$$\alpha' = 206265 \frac{s}{nD}$$

$$= 206265 \times \frac{0.149}{6 \times 75} \text{ seconds}$$

$$= \mathbf{1'8.3''}.$$

Degree of Precision

The quality of levelling is judged by line or loop of closures, or by the maximum allowable difference between the forward and backward runnings of a section of a line of levels.

A *line closure* is the discrepancy between the measured difference of elevations between two points of fixed elevations and the difference of the established elevations of those points. Another interpretation is that it is the amount by which the observed elevation of a terminal bench mark fails to equal the known or published value. A *loop closure* is the amount by which a level circuit fails to close. The degree of precision depends upon (i) the type of instrument, (ii) skill of observer (iii) character of country, and (iv) atmospheric conditions, and therefore, practically all the errors in levelling are accidental or random in nature. For a given instrument and atmospheric conditions, the precision depends upon the number of set-ups and also upon the length of the sights. Thus precision on plains can be expected to be more than that on hills. There is no hard and fast rule by which the desired precision in levelling can be maintained. However, assuming that number of set-ups per kilometer will generally be about the same, maximum permissible error in levelling work is expressed as some coefficient times the square root of the distance in kilometres. If E is the maximum permissible error in millimetres, then

$$E = C\sqrt{K} \quad \text{...(6.16)}$$

where C is the coefficient, and K is the distance in kilometre.

The standards for quality of levelling work for loops or lines are given in Table 6.3.

Table 6.3 Maximum permissible errors in levelling

Order	Class	Permissble error (mm)
First	I	$\pm 4\sqrt{K}$
	II	$\pm 5\sqrt{K}$
Second	I	$\pm 6\sqrt{K}$
	II	$\pm 8\sqrt{K}$
Third		$\pm 12\sqrt{K}$

In Table 6.4, the permissible errors in levelling for different types of surveys are given.

Table 6.4 Maximum permissible errors in levelling for different types of surveys

Types of survey	Purpose	Permissible error (mm)
Rough levelling	Reconnaissance and preliminary surveys	$\pm 100\sqrt{K}$
Ordinary levelling	Location and construction surveys	$\pm 24\sqrt{K}$
Accurate levelling	Principal bench marks and for extensive surveys	$\pm 12\sqrt{K}$
Precise levelling	Geodetic levelling and bench marks of widely distributed points	$\pm 4\sqrt{K}$

Adjustment of a simple level loop

In a loop or closed circuit, the loop closure or *misclosure* is given by

e = Computed value of R.L. – known value of the R.L.

If the total length of the loop or circuit is L, and the distance of the station A from the starting point of known elevation be l_A, then the correction in elevation at A is given by

$$C_A = -\frac{l_A}{L} e \qquad \text{...(6.17)}$$

Alternatively, the correction is applied to the elevations of each change point and the closing point B.M., generally equally. For example, if the levelling starts from a B.M. of R.L. 100.000 m, and after completing the observations at various points, the work is closed at the same B.M., the computed value of the R.L. of the B.M. is 100.018 m, then the misclosure e is equal to 100.018 – 100.000 = 0.018 m.

If there are 5 change points, then total number n of points at which the corrections are to be applied will be

n = number of change points + closing point.

= 5 + 1 = 6

The correction at each station $= -\dfrac{0.018}{6}$ m

$= -\ 0.003$ m.

The correction is applied cumulatively to the R.L.'s of the change points. Thus correction in R.L. of

C.P. 1 = – 0.003 m
C.P. 2 = – 0.006 m
C.P. 3 = – 0.009 m
C.P. 4 = – 0.012 m
C.P. 5= – 0.015 m
Closing point (B.M.)= – 0.018 m.

The intermediate sights, have the corrections as the change points to which they are related. For example, if an intermediate sight is taken after C.P.3, the correction to the R.L. of the intermediate sight will be – 0.009 m.

Levelling practices

The fundamentals of levelling have been discussed in Sec. 6.4. In practice, differential levelling is used for profile levelling, cross-section levelling, reciprocal levelling, countouring, etc. While the profile levelling, cross-section levelling and reciprocal levelling have already been defined in Sec. 6.4 and are discussed below, the contouring is discussed in Chapter 7.

Profile levelling

The profile levelling being differential levelling is for determining the reduced levels of the points at measured intervals along a line, generally, the centre line, of a route such as highway, railway, canal, sewer, or any other such utility. Stakes or pegs are placed at regular intervals along the proposed centre line, and the levels of the ground at these points are determined. The peg interval depends upon the topography, nature of the work, and scale. Generally, it is 10 m, 15 m, 20 m or 30 m. In addition, levels are taken at points where a change in direction occurs, at breaks in the slope of the ground, and at critical points like culverts, bridges, and other features crossing the alignment.

When plotted, these levels show a profile which depicts elevations of ground points on a longitudinal vertical section along the alignment. Since distances and bearings are required, they are also be measured. Therefore, additional columns shown in Table 6.5 are made in the level field book to record them. The reduction of levels can be done either by height of instrument method or rise and fall method.

Table 6.5 Recording of observations and reducing levels in profile levelling

Station	Distance or chainage	Bearing	B.S	I.S	F.S	H.I.	R.L.	Remarks

After reducing the levels, the profile is plotted. The datum line is drawn, the chainage of the points plotted on it, and heights are marked corresponding to the reduced levels. A continuous line joining all these points represents the profile of the ground. Since the horizontal distances are usually far greater than variations in level, the vertical scale is generally kept larger than the horizontal one to help in assessing the relationship between the formation level of the highway, railway or other work, and the original ground surface.

Figure 6.15 shows a typical profile or longitudinal section. In the profile, the datum and ground lines are drawn in black, and the ordinates in blue. The value of the datum line should be given, reduced levels written against the ordinates, and necessary explanatory notes given. Plotted profiles are used for the purposes such as determining the depth of cutting or filling on proposed highway or railway, studying grade crossing problems, and selecting the most economical grade, location and depth of sewers, tunnels, and similar projects.

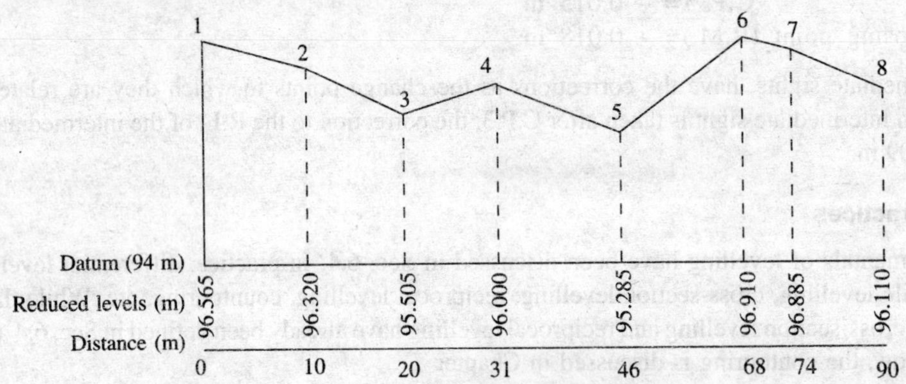

Fig. 6.15 A typical profile of longitudinal section

The grade or gradient is expressed as a percentage, and the rise and fall in metres per 100 metres. Ascending grades are considered positive, and descending ones negative (*c.f.*, Sec. 1.5).

A *working section* or *working profile* is prepared after deciding a formation line. It consists of the original ground features, formation level, the depth of cut and heights of fill, proposed gradients, and other relevant information.

Cross-section levelling

For highways, railways, embankments, etc., information regarding ground levels in the direction transverse to the alignment are obtained by taking cross-sections at right angles to the longitudinal direction or centre line, generally at regular intervals. If, for any reason, a cross-section is run in any other direction, the angle with the centre line or bearing must be measured to show it in a line plan. The observation must be recorded as being to the left (L) or the right (R) of the centre line. The distance along the longitudinal section at which the cross-section is taken, is noted right at the beginning of the levels corresponding to a section.

Cross-sections are plotted in the manner as the longitudinal sections or profiles are plotted, but the horizontal and vertical scales are generally kept equal. Usually the scale for cross-sections ranges from 1:100 to 1:500, depending on need. In plotting different cross-sections, the datum level can be chosen differently to keep the ordinates within limits (Fig. 6.16).

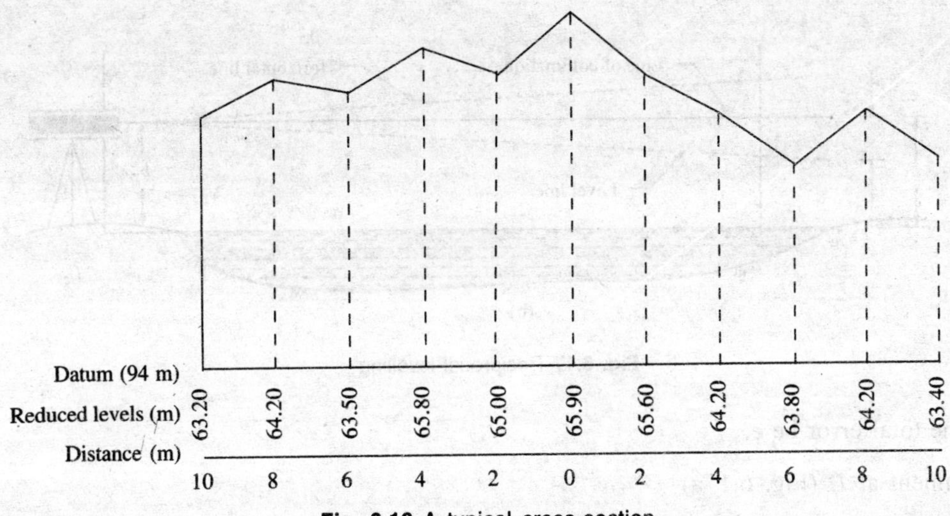

Fig. 6.16 A typical cross-section

Reciprocal levelling

Reciprocal levelling is employed to determine the correct difference of elevations between two points which are quite apart and where it is not possible to set up the instrument midway between the points to balance the back sight and fore sight. Reciprocal levelling is generally employed to determine difference in elevations between two intervisible points situated:

(a) on the opposite banks of a large water stream or river,

(b) on either side of a deep gorge or valley, and

(c) between which the instrument cannot be set up for balancing the sights.

Reciprocal levelling eliminates the errors due to the curvature of the earth, atmospheric refraction, and collimation.

The procedure is illustrated in Fig. 6.17. Let *A* and *B* be the two points on the opposite banks of a river. Drive pegs at *A* and *B*. Set up the instrument at L_1 near the peg *A*. Take readings a_1 and b_1 on the staffs held at *A* and *B*, respectively. Shift the instrument to L_2 near the peg *B*, and take the readings a_2 and b_2 on the staffs held at *A* and *B*, respectively. Assuming that the point *B* is at higher elevation than *A*, the correct difference in elevations between *A* and *B*, is determined as explained below.

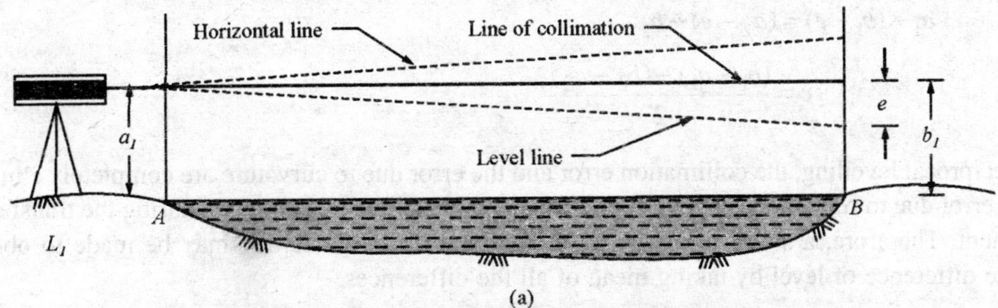

(a)

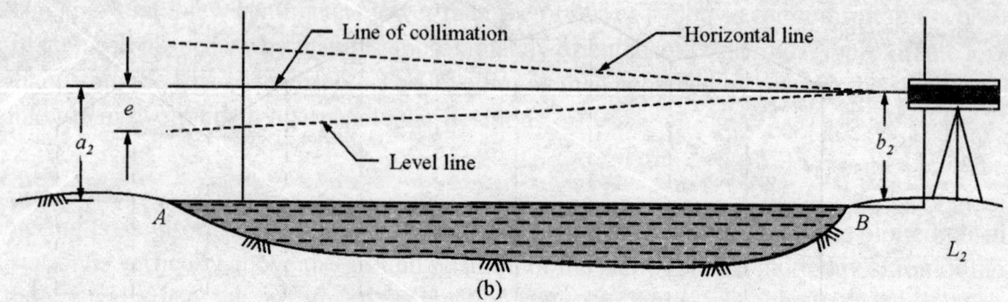

Fig. 6.17 Reciprocal levelling

Let the total error be e.

(*i*) Instrument at L_1 (Fig. 6.17a)

The correct staff reading at $A = a_1$

The correct staff reading at $B = b_1 - e$

The correct difference of level $\Delta h = a_1 - (b_1 - e)$ ...(6.18)

(*ii*) Instrument at L_2 (Fig. 6.17b)

The correct staff reading at $A = a_2 - e$

The correct staff reading at $B = b_2$

The correct difference of level $\Delta h = (a_2 - e) - b_2$ ...(6.19)

Adding Eqs. (6.18) and (6.19), we get

$$2\Delta h = a_1 - (b_1 - e) + (a_2 - e) - b_2$$

or
$$\Delta h = \frac{(a_1 - b_1) + (a_2 - b_2)}{2} \quad ...(6.20)$$

The true difference in elevation, therefore, is equal to the mean of the two apparent differences in elevations obtained by reciprocal observations.

The combined error e can be obtained by equating the Eqs. (6.18) and (6.19), *i.e.*,

$$a_1 - (b_1 - e) = (a_2 - e) - b_2$$

or
$$e = \frac{(b_1 - a_1) - (b_2 - a_2)}{2} \quad ...(6.21)$$

In reciprocal levelling, the collimation error and the error due to curvature are completely eliminated, but the error due to refractions depends upon change in the climatic conditions during the transfer of the instrument. Therefore, a set of observations at different times of the day may be made to obtain the accurate difference of level by taking mean of all the differences.

Eq. (6.21) gives the total error e which is expressed as

$$e = e_l + e_c - e_r$$

where e_l = collimation error, assumed positive when the line of sight is inclined upwards

e_c = error due to earth's curvature

e_r = error due to atmospheric refraction

$e_c - e_r$ = combined curvature and refraction error

or $C_{cr} = 0.0673\, d^2$

The collimation error e_l is thus given by

$$e_l = e - 0.0673\, d^2 \qquad ...(6.22)$$

ILLUSTRATIVE EXAMPLES

Example 6.11

Two points P and Q are on the opposite banks of a river. The following observations were obtained in reciprocal levelling:

Instrument near	Staff reading at	
	P	Q
P	2.000	3.720
Q	0.810	2.420

If the R.L. of P is 100.000 m, determine the R.L. of Q.

Solution:

From Eq. (6.20), the difference in elevation is

$$\Delta h = \frac{(a_1 - b_1) + (a_2 - b_2)}{2}$$

$$= \frac{(2.000 - 3.720) + (0.810 - 2.420)}{2}$$

$$= -1.665 \text{ m}$$

Δh being negative, Q is lower than P

R.L. of Q = 100.000 − 1.665

= 98.335 m.

Example 6.12

The following readings refer to reciprocal levels taken with one level:

Instrument near	A	B
Staff readings on A	1.824	0.929
Staff readings on B	2.748	1.606

The distance AB is 1110 m, and the reduced level of A is 130.815 m. Determine the following:

(*a*) True R.L. of B.

(*b*) Combined correction for curvature and refraction.

(*c*) Angular error in the collimation adjustment of the instrument.

Solution:

(*a*) From Eq. (6.20), we get

$$\Delta h = \frac{(1.824 - 2.748) + (0.929 - 1.606)}{2}$$

$$= -\ 0.801\text{m}. \qquad \dots (a)$$

As the difference in elevation from A to B is negative, A is higher than B. Therefore, elevation of B

= 130.815 – 0.801

= 130.014 m.

(*b*) From Eq. (6.22), the combined correction is

$$C_{cr} = 0.0673\ d^2$$

We have d = 1110 m

= 1.110 km

$$C_{cr} = 0.0673 \times 1.110^2$$

= 0.083 m.

(*c*) When the instrument is at A, the apparent difference in elevation

= 1.824 – 2.748

= – 0.924 m

The correct difference in elevation from (a)

= – 0.801 m

Neglecting the sign, the error in observation = 0.924 – 0.801 = + 0.123 m

This error consists of (*i*) the error due to curvature and refraction, and (*ii*) collimation error.

Collimation error, e_l = 0.123 – 0.083

= 0.040 m.

If the angular error in collimation adjustment is ε, then it is given by

$$\varepsilon = \frac{e_l}{d}$$

$$= \frac{0.040}{1110} \text{ radians}$$

$$\varepsilon = \mathbf{8''}.$$

Example 6.13

The following reciprocal levels were taken with one level on two points *A* and *B*, 1645 m apart:

Level near	Staff reading on	
	A	*B*
A	2.165	3.810
B	0.910	2.355

Calculate the true difference in elevation between *A* and *B*, and the error due to refraction when the collimation error is – 0.003 m per 100 m.

Solution:

(*i*) From Eq. (6.23) the difference in elevation is given by

$$\Delta h = \frac{(a_1 - b_1) + (a_2 - b_2)}{2}$$

$$= \frac{(2.165 - 3.810) + (0.910 - 2.355)}{2}$$

$$= -\ \mathbf{1.545\ m}.$$

As Δh is negative, *A* is higher than *B*.

(*ii*) From Eq. (6.1), taking $R = 6371$ km, the error due to curvature will be

$$C_c = 0.07848\ d^2$$

$$= 0.07848 \times 1.645^2$$

$$= 0.212 \text{ m}.$$

When the instrument is at *A*, the corrected staff reading on *B* would be

$$b = 3.810 - [(C_c - C_r) + C_l]$$

where C_l = collimation error

$$= \frac{(-0.003)}{100} \times 1645$$

$$= -\ 0.049 \text{ m}$$

Therefore, $b = 3.810_l - [(0.212 - C_r) - 0.049]$

$$= 3.647 + C_r$$

Thus the true difference in elevation between A and B

$$= (3.647 + C_r) - 2.165$$

The computed difference in elevation between A and B is 1.545 m.

Thus, $3.647 + C_r - 2.165 = 1.545$

or $\quad C_r = 1.545 - 3.647 + 2.165$

$\quad = \mathbf{0.063\ m.}$

Levelling Problems

The following are some of the difficulties commonly found in the field while doing levelling.

Taking level of an overhead point or staff station above the line of sight

When the point under observation is higher than the line of sight, staff should be kept inverted on the overhead point keeping the foot of the staff touching the point. The reading taken in this manner will show height of that point above the line of sight, and should be added to the H.I. to obtain the R.L. of the point.

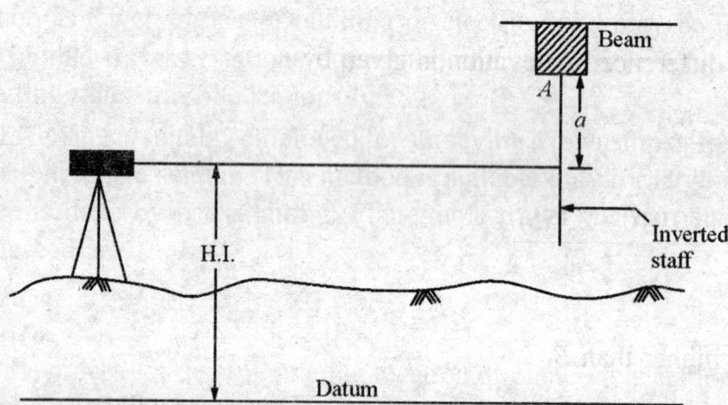

Fig. 6.18 Determination of R.L. of an overhead point

In Fig. 6.18, the R.L. of A = H.I. + a where a is the reading on the inverted staff. In case, such point happens to be a bench mark, the back sight reading on the point should be subtracted from the elevation of the bench mark to get the H.I.

Taking level of a point much below the line of sight

When the staff station is much below the line of sight, it is not possible to take reading as the line of sight will not cut the staff. In such cases, the staff is raised until it can be read. Measure the vertical height by which the staff has been raised, and add to the staff reading. In Fig. 6.19, the staff reading after raising the staff by amount d, is given by

$$s = a + d$$

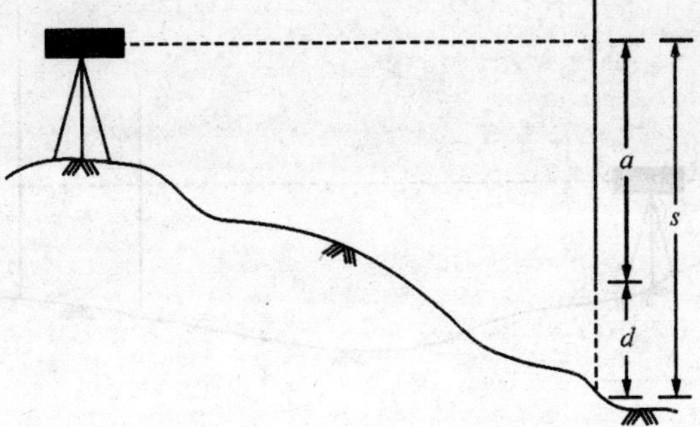

Fig. 6.19 Determination of R.L. of a point much below the line of sight

Staff too near to the instrument

If the staff is too near to the instrument, the graduations will not be distinctly visible. Such situations should always be avoided as far as possible. If it is not possible to avoid, one of the following methods may be adopted:

(*i*) Move a white paper sheet up or down the staff until its one of the horizontal edges is bisected by the line of sight. Take the corresponding staff reading with naked eyes. As the edge of the paper is out of focus, the reading corresponding to the edge cannot be taken through the telescope.

(*ii*) Turn the telescope by 180° and take the reading through the objective of the telescope. Move a pencil point on the staff untill it is bisected by the line of sight. Take the staff reading corresponding to the pencil point.

Levelling on summits and hallows

In levelling over summit or hill, the level should be kept sufficiently high so that the summit can be sighted without extra setting (Fig. 6.20). Similarly in levelling across a hallow, level should be set sufficiently low to enable the levels of all the required points to be observed (Fig. 6.21).

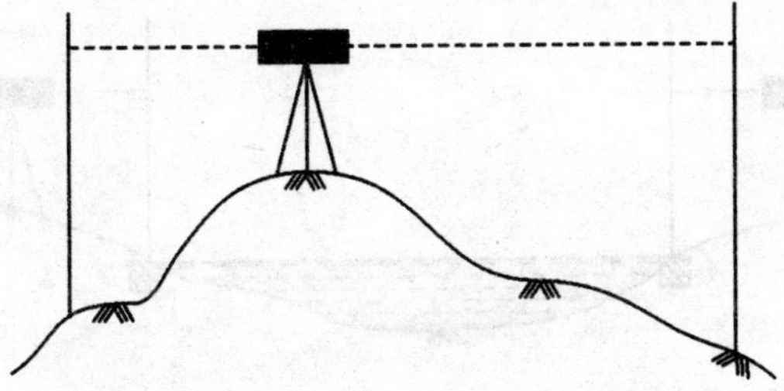

Fig. 6.20 Levelling over summit

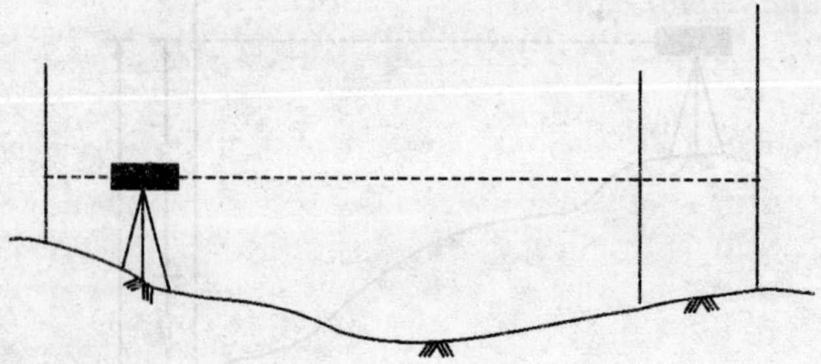

Fig. 6.21 Levelling across hallow

Levelling on steep slopes

When levelling is done on steep slopes, back sights and fore sights may not be equal unless short lengths are adopted. It is, therefore, recommended that the instrument should be set up away from the line joining the staff positions in zig-zag manner so that the back sight and fore sight distances can be kept equal to eliminate the effects of curvature, refraction, and non-adjustment of the instrument.

Levelling across a pond or lake

When the ponds or lakes are too wide, it becomes difficult to sight the staff on the other side of the pond or lake. Advantage may be taken of the fact that the surface of still water is a level surface. Two pegs *A* and *B* are driven on either sides of the pond keeping their tops flush with the water surface as shown in Fig. 6.22. Reduced level of the top of peg *A* is determined by usual method. As the tops of pegs *A* and *B* are on the same level surface, their levels will be same. The levelling proceeds after taking the back sight on *B* as its elevation is same as that of *A*. In this case, the two pegs *A* and *B* together have been considered as a single change point for the purpose of running down the level.

Levelling across river

The above method is not suitable in case of a wide river as water flows in rivers with appreciable velocity. This difficulty is overcome by the method of reciprocal levelling.

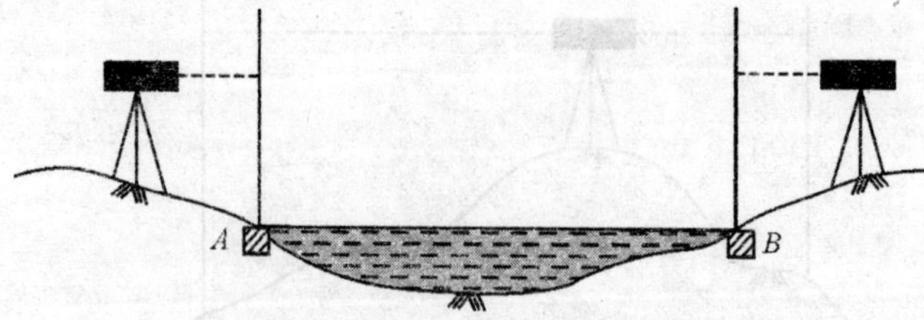

Fig. 6.22 Levelling across lake

In case the river is too wide to adopt even reciprocal levelling, transfer of level is done by driving two pegs on opposite banks as in the case of levelling across the pond or lake but separated by the shortest distance at right angles to the flow of water.

Levelling across an intervening high wall

There can be two cases as follows:

Case-I The height of the top of the wall above the line of sight is less than the staff length.

Take the reading on the staff inverted with its foot touching the top of the wall and determine the R.L. of the top of the wall. Shift the instrument to the other side of the wall and take another reading on the staff inverted with its foot touching the top of the wall. If the two readings are a_1 and a_2 as shown in Fig. 6.23a, then

R.L. of the top of the wall $= (\text{H.I.})_1 + a_1$

$(\text{H.I.})_2$ of the instrument on the other side of the wall $= (\text{H.I.})_1 + a_1 - a_2$

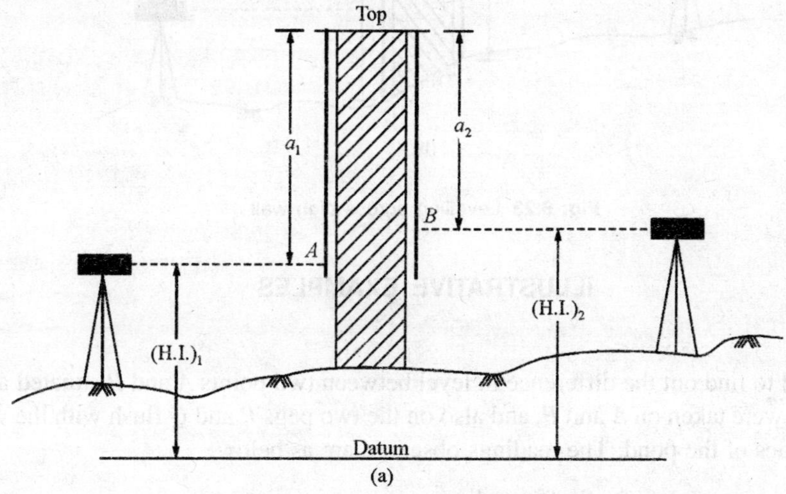

Fig. 6.23 Levelling across high wall

Case-II The height of the top of the wall above the line of sight is more than the staff length.

There are two methods of levelling in this case and either of the following method can be adopted.

(*a*) Mark a point *A* on the wall where the line of sight strikes the wall (Fig. 6.23a), and measure the vertical distance a_1 from *A* to the top with a tape. The R.L. of the top is

$$= (\text{H.I.})_1 + a_1$$

Shift the instrument to the other side of the wall and locate the point *B* where the line of sight strikes the wall. Measure the vertical distance a_2 between the top of the wall and *B*. The new height of instrument will be

$$(\text{H.I.})_2 = (\text{H.I.})_1 + a_1 - a_2$$

In this case, instead of putting the inverted staff as in the case-I, the points are marked on the wall, and the measurement is done using tape. Theoretically, this method is same as the method described in the case-I.

(*b*) In the second method, two pegs *P* and *Q* are driven on either side of the wall (Fig. 6.23b). Determine the R.L. of *P* by taking the fore sight on the staff held at *P*. Measure the height h_1 of the wall and get the R.L. of the top of the wall by adding h_1 to the R.L. of *P*. Measure the height h_2 of the wall on the other side, and determine the R.L. of *Q* by subtracting h_2 from the R.L. of the top of the wall. Continue the levelling with instrument on the other side of the wall after taking a back sight on the peg *Q*.

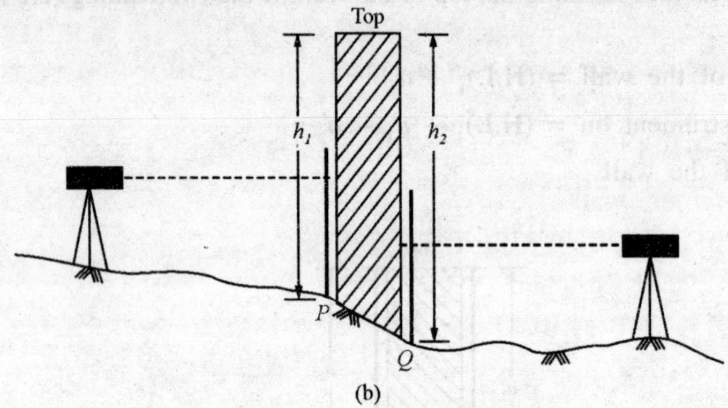

Fig. 6.23 Levelling across high wall

ILLUSTRATIVE EXAMPLES

Example 6.14

It was proposed to find out the difference in level between two points *A* and *B* situated across a lake. The staff readings were taken on *A* and *B*, and also on the two pegs *P* and *Q* flush with the water surface on the opposite sides of the pond. The readings observed are as below:

Staff at	Staff reading
A	1.850
P	1.375
Q	1.860
B	1.450

A and *P* are on one side of the pond, and *Q* and *B* on the other side. Determine the difference in level between *A* and *B*.

Solution:

Let us assume the R.L. of *A* as 100.00 m.

H.I.= R.L. (100.00) of *A* + B.S. (1.850) on *A* = 101.850 m

R.L. of *P* = H.I. (101.850) – F.S. (1.375) on *P* = 100.475 m

As *P* and *Q* are at same level, R.L. of *Q* is 100.475 m. Therefore, the new

H.I. = R.L. (100.475) of *Q* + B.S. (1.860) on *Q* = 102.335 m

R.L. of *B* = H.I. (102.335) – F.S. (1.450) on *B* = 100.885 m

Thus, difference in level between A and B is

= R.L. of B – R.L. of A

= 100.885 – 100.00

= **0.885 m.**

Example 6.15

While performing levelling, a low boundary wall was found on the route. The height of instrument on the one side of the wall as calculated was 121.705 m, and the fore sight taken putting the staff on the wall, was 0.330. After shifting the instrument on the other side of the wall the back sight reading taken was 0.600. What is the height of instrument after shifting the instrument?

Solution:

R.L. of the top of the wall

= H.I. (121.705) – F.S. (0.330) = 121.375 m

H.I. after shifting the instrument

= R.L. (121.375) + B.S. (0.600) = **121.975 m.**

Example 6.16

R.L. of a floor in an industrial complex is 64.500 m. Staff reading on the floor is 1.715 and staff reading when it is held inverted with bottom touching the ceiling of the room is 2.970. Find the height of the ceiling above the floor.

Solution:

H.I. = R.L. (64.500) of the floor + B.S. (1.715) = 66.215 m

R.L. of the ceiling = H.I. (66.215) – F.S. (– 2.970) = 69.185 m

Height of the ceiling above the floor

= 69.185 – 64.500 = **4.685 m.**

Alternatively, the height of the ceiling above the floor is

= *B.S.* + *F.S.*

= 1.715 + 2.970 = **4.685 m.**

Permanent adjustments of a dumpy level

For a dumpy level to be in a proper adjustment the following conditions should be satisfied:

1. The axis of the bubble tube should be perpendicular to the vertical axis of the instrument.

   This adjustment is done in the same manner as the adjustment of plate level of a theodolite. (*c.f.*, Sec. 4.4).

2. The horizontal cross hair should lie in a plane perpendicular to the vertical axis.
   To test this adjustment, sight some well-defined point P as shown in Fig. 6.24 so that it appears on the horizontal cross hair on one side of the field of view. Rotate the instrument slowly about its vertical axis. If the point P appears to travel along the horizontal cross hair, the instrument in

adjustment. If the point does not appear to travel along the horizontal cross hair, adjust the instrument as under.

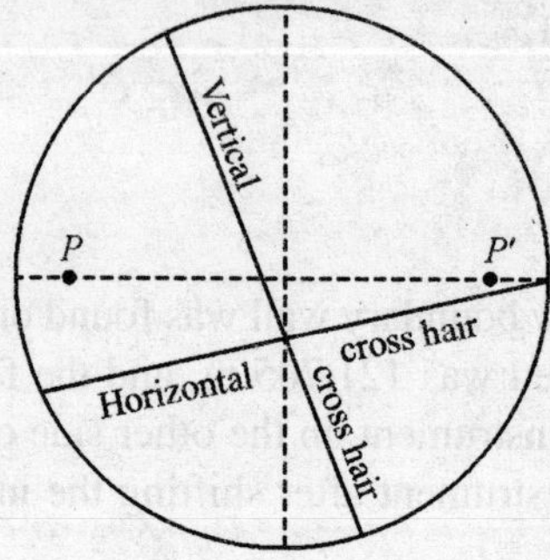

Fig. 6.24 Adjustment of horizontal cross hair

Find the position P' taken by P on the opposite side of the field of view. Loosen the two adjacent capstan screws on the diaphragm ring, and rotate the ring by the required amount to make P' lie on the horizontal cross hair. Again sight P and repeat the test till P appears to travel along the horizontal cross hair.

3. The line of sight should be parallel to the axis of the level tube. This adjustment is done in the same manner as the axis of the telescope level of a theodolite is made the parallel to the line of sight (*c.f.*, Sec. 4.4).

6.5 INDIRECT OR TRIGONOMETRIC LEVELLING

Trigonometric levelling involves observing the vertical angle and either the horizontal or slope distance between two points. The vertical angles are generally measured by a theodolite and the horizontal distances are either measured or computed. The difference in elevation can then be computed.

In Fig. 6.25, A represents a point of known elevation, and B is the point whose elevation is to be determined. Within the limits of ordinary practice, triangle ECK can be assumed to be a right triangle, and the distance EK can be taken equal to EF. If the horizontal distance $EK = D$, is known then

$$KC = D \tan \alpha \qquad \text{...(6.26)}$$

where α is the measured vertical angle.

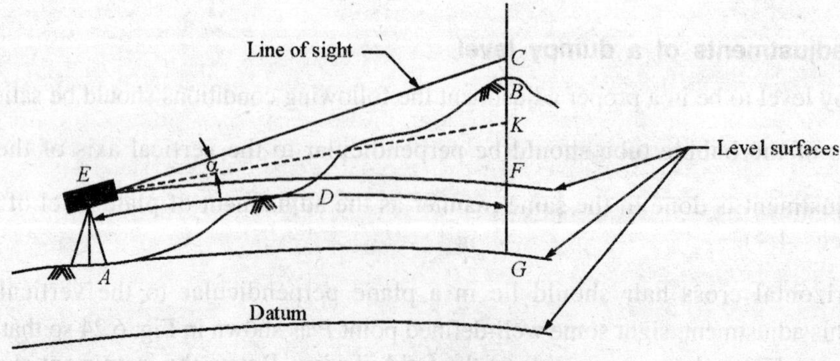

Fig. 6.25 Trigonometric levelling

The correction *FK* for earth curvature and refraction (C_c and C_r) can be calculated using Eq. (6.1), (6.2), or (6.4). The difference in elevation, between *A* and *B* is

$$\Delta h_{AB} = AE + FK + KC - BC \qquad ...(6.24)$$

where *AE* is the instrument height at *A* and *BC* is the target height above *B*.

If the slope distance *EC* is measured very accurately by using electronic distance measuring (*EDM*) equipment then

$$KC = EC \sin \alpha \qquad ...(6.25)$$

Depending upon the situation in the field there may be three cases as discussed below. The effect of earth's curvature and refraction has not been considered for ordinary levelling in the following cases.

Base of the object accessible

In this case, the horizontal distanced *D* between the instrument station *A* and the object *B* can be measured accurately (Fig. 6.26). The elevation of *B* is given by

$$h_B = h_A + h \qquad ...(6.26)$$

where $h = D \tan \alpha$

h_A = instrument height at *A*

α = vertical angle of *B*

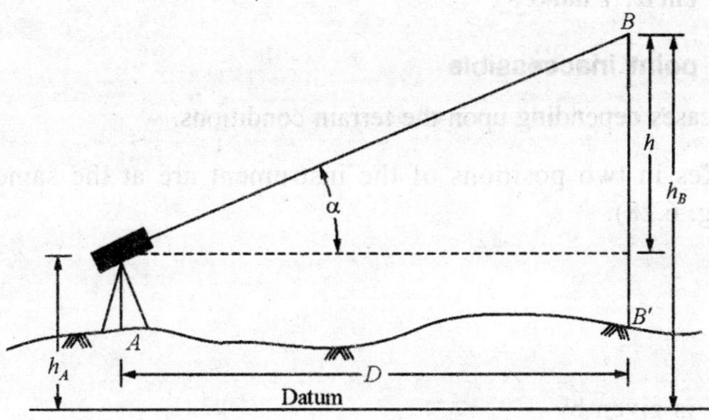

Fig. 6.26 Base accessible

This method is usually employed when the distance between the instrument station *A* and the foot *B'* of the elevated point *B* can be measured accurately.

Base of an inclined object accessible

In this case, the horizontal distances D_1 and D_2 between the foot of the inclined object *PQ*, and the instrument stations *A* and *B*, respectively, as shown in Fig. 6.27, can be measured.

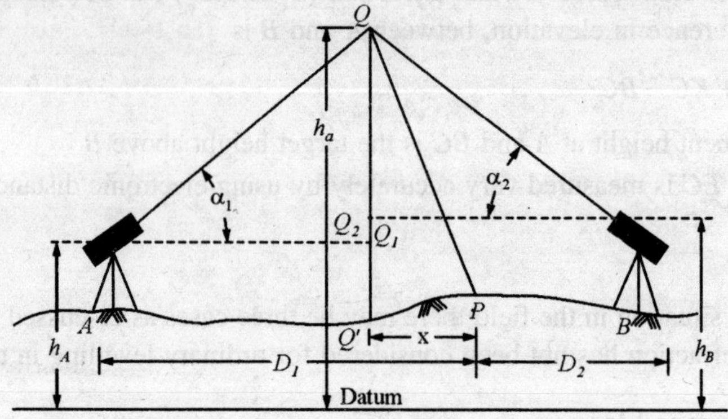

Fig. 6.27 Object inclined and base accessible

If the height of instrument at A and B are h_A and h_B, respectively, and Q' be the projected point of the top of the object then taking PQ' equal to x, the elevation of Q will be

$$h_Q = h_A + (D_1 - x)\tan\alpha_1 \qquad \text{...(6.27)}$$

where $$x = \frac{(h_A - h_B) + D_1 \tan\alpha_1 - D_2 \tan\alpha_2}{\tan\alpha_1 + \tan\alpha_2}$$

Base of an elevated point inaccessible

There may be three cases depending upon the terrain conditions.

(*a*) The instrument axes in two positions of the instrument are at the same level in the same vertical plane. (Fig. 6.28).

We have

$$h_A = h_B$$

The elevation of F is given by

$$h_F = h_A + h \qquad \text{...(6.28)}$$

where $$h = \frac{d \sin\alpha_1 \sin\alpha_2}{\sin(\alpha_1 - \alpha_2)}$$

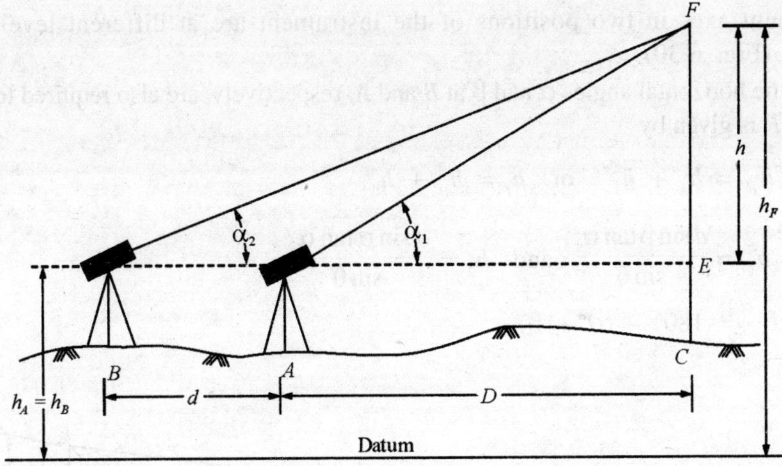

Fig. 6.28 Instrument axes at the same level and in the vertical plane containing the object

(*b*) The instrument axes in two positions of the instrument are at different levels in the same vertical plane. (Fig. 6.29).

In this case, let the staff reading from *A* and *B* on the staff at the B.M., be S_1 and S_2, then

$$S = S_2 - S_1$$

The elevation of *F* is given by

$$h_F = h_A + h_1 \qquad ...(6.29)$$

or

$$= h_B + h_2 \qquad ...(6.30)$$

where $$h_1 = \frac{(d + S\cot\alpha_2)\sin\alpha_1\sin\alpha_2}{\sin(\alpha_1 - \alpha_2)}$$

and $$h_2 = \frac{(d + S\cot\alpha_2)\sin\alpha_1\sin\alpha_2}{\sin(\alpha_2 - \alpha_1)}$$

d = the distance between the two instrument stations *A* and *B*, and

h_A = R.L. of B.M. + S_1

and h_B = R.L. of B.M. + S_2

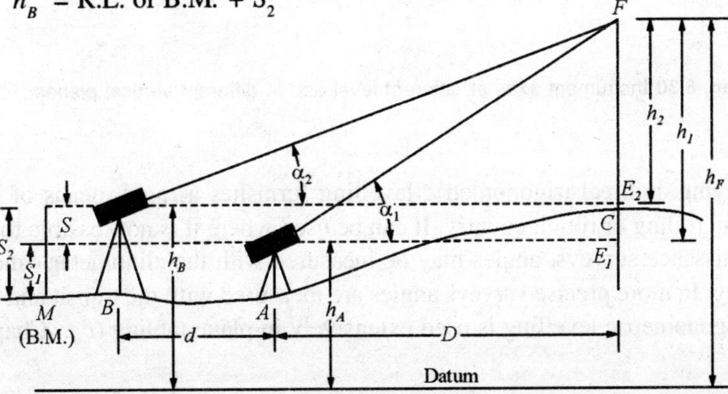

Fig. 6.29 Instrument axes at the different level and in the vertical plane containing the object

(*c*) The instrument axes in two positions of the instrument are at different levels in different vertical planes. (Fig. 6.30).

In this case, the horizontal angles α and β at *B* and *A*, respectively, are also required to be measured. The elevation of *F* is given by

$$h_F = h_A + h_1 \quad \text{or} \quad h_F = h_B + h_2 \qquad \text{...(6.31)}$$

where $$h_1 = \frac{d \sin\beta \tan\alpha_1}{\sin\theta} \quad \text{and} \quad h_2 = \frac{d \sin\alpha \tan\alpha_2}{\sin\theta}$$

$$\theta = 180^\circ - (\alpha + \beta)$$

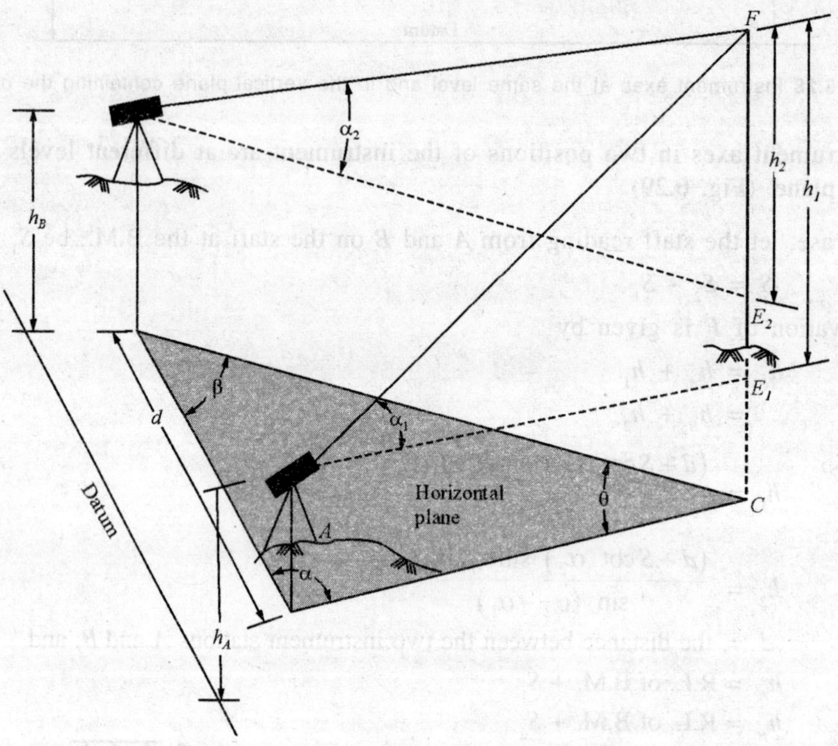

Fig. 6.30 Instrument axes at different level and in different vertical planes

Uses

In ordinary surveying, indirect trigonometric levelling furnishes a rapid means of determining the elevations of points in rolling or rough country. It can be used where it is not feasible to use a level. For example, on reconnaissance surveys, angles may be measured with the clinometer, and distances may be obtained by pacing. In more precise surveys angles are measured with the transit and distances by the stadia. Indirect or trigonometric levelling is used extensively in plane tabling (*c.f.*, Chapter 10).

ILLUSTRATIVE EXAMPLES

Example 6.17

A theodolite was set up at a point *P* and a staff was kept at a station *Q*. The distance *PQ* was 3010 m. If the angle of elevation to a vane 3.5 m above the foot of the staff, was 7°59′, determine the reduced level of the station *Q*. The elevation of the instrument axis was 120.80 m.

Solution (Fig. 6.31):

Height of the vane above the instrument axis is given by

$$h = D \tan \alpha = 3010 \times \tan 7°59' = 422.135 \text{ m}$$

and combined correction for earth curvature and atmospheric refraction by

$$C_{cr} = 0.06735D^2 = 0.06735 \times 3.010^2 = 0.610 \text{ m}$$

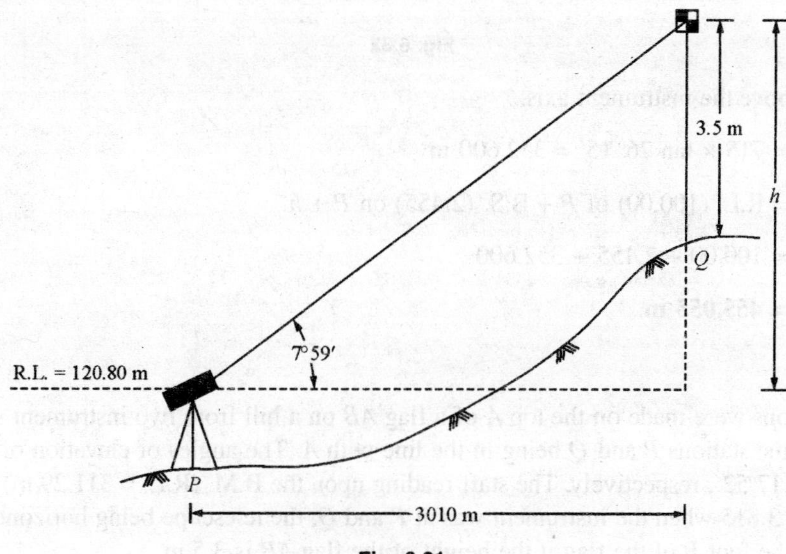

Fig. 6.31

The correct difference in elevation between the vane and the instrument axis,

$$H = h + C_{cr} = 422.135 + 0.610 = 422.745 \text{ m}$$

R.L. of the vane = R.L. (120.80) of inst. axis + *H*

= 120.80 + 422.745 = 543.545 m

R.L. of *Q* = R.L. (543.545) of vane − 3.5

= 543.545 − 3.5 = **540.045 m.**

Example 6.18

An instrument was set up at *A* and the angle of elevation of the top *C* of a tower *BC* was 26°15′. The horizontal distance *AB*, *B* being the foot of the tower, was 715 m. Determine the R.L. of the top of the tower if the staff reading held on a station *P* of R.L. 100.00 m was 2.455 with the telescope horizontal.

Solution (Fig. 6.32):

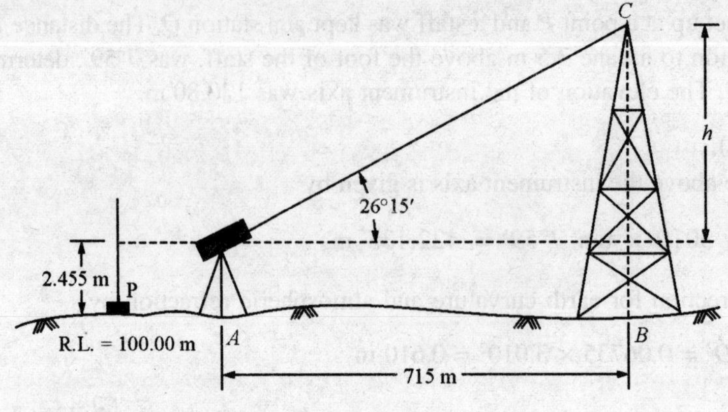

Fig. 6.32

Height of C above the instrument axis,

$$h = 715 \times \tan 26^{o} 15' = 352.600 \text{ m}$$

R.L. of C = R.L. (100.00) of P + B.S. (2.455) on $P + h$

= 100.00 + 2.455 + 352.600

= **455.055 m.**

Example 6.19

The observations were made on the top A of a flag AB on a hill from two instrument stations P and Q, 100 m apart, the stations P and Q being in the line with A. The angles of elevation of A at P and Q were 30° 05′ and 17°52′, respectively. The staff reading upon the B.M. (R.L. = 311.29 m) were, respectively, 2.690 and 3.815 when the instrument was at P and Q, the telescope being horizontal. Determine the elevation of the foot B of the flag if the height of the flag AB is 3.5 m.

Solution (Fig. 6.33):

R.L. of instrument axis at P

= R.L. (311.29) of BM + B.S. (2.690) on B.M.

= 313.980 m

R.L. of instrument axis at Q

= R.L. (311.29) of B.M. + B.S. (3.815) on B.M.

= 315.105 m

Difference in level of the instrument axes

S = 315.105 – 313.980

= 1.125 m.

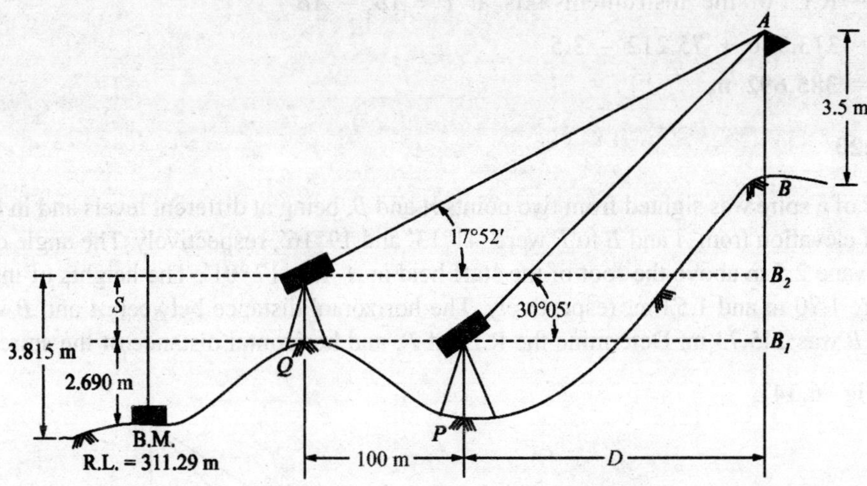

Fig. 6.33

If D is the horizontal distance between P and B then

$$AB_1 = D \times \tan 30°05'$$

$$AB_2 = (100 + D) \times \tan 17°52'$$

But we have

$$B_1B_2 = AB_1 - AB_2 = S$$

$$D \times \tan 30°05' - (100 + D) \times \tan 17°52' = S = 1.125$$

or $D \times [\tan 30°05' - \tan 17°52'] = 1.125 + 100 \times \tan 17°52$

$$\text{or } D = \frac{1.125 + 100 \times \tan 17°52'}{\tan 30°05' - \tan 17°52'}$$

$$= \frac{1.125 + 32.349}{(0.57929 - 0.32235)}$$

$$= 129.834 \text{ m.}$$

We have

$$AB_1 = D \times \tan 30°05''$$

$$= 129.834 \times \tan 30°05'$$

$$= 75.212 \text{ m.}$$

R.L. of B = R.L. of the instrument axis at $P + AB_1 - AB$

= 313.980 + 75.212 − 3.5

= **385.692 m.**

Example 6.20

The top P of a spire was sighted from two points A and B, being at different levels and in line with P. The angle of elevation from A and B to P were 41°13′ and 19°16′, respectively. The angle of elevation from B to a vane 2.5 m above the foot of the staff held at A, was 17°01′. The heights of instrument at A and B were 1.70 m and 1.53 m, respectively. The horizontal distance between A and B was 133 m. The R.L. of B was 245.73 m. Determine the R.L. of P, and horizontal distance of the spire from A.

Solution (Fig. 6.34):

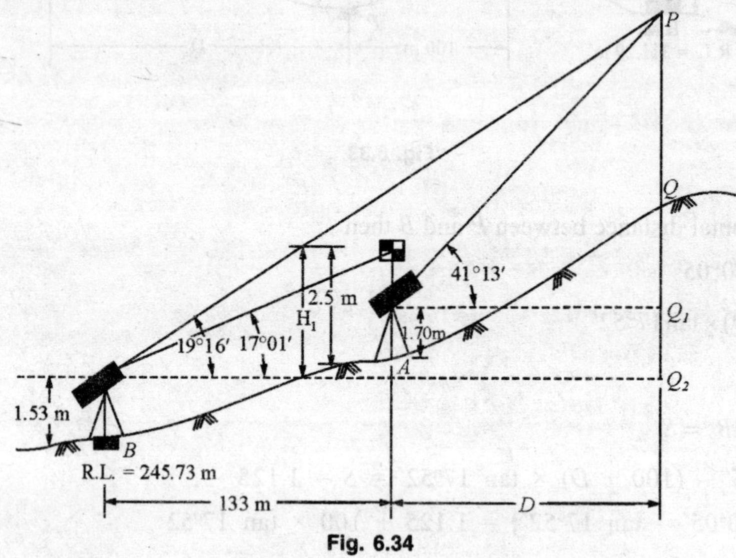

Fig. 6.34

R.L. of B = 245.73 m

R.L. of A = R.L. (245.73) of B + 1.53 + H_1 − 2.5

$H_1 = 133 \times \tan 17°01' = 40.704$ m

R.L. of A = 245.73 + 1.53 + 40.704 − 2.5 = 285.464 m

R.L. of instrument axis at A = 285.464 + 1.70 = 287.164 m

R.L. of instrument axis at B = 245.73 + 1.53 = 247.260 m

Difference in level Q_1Q_2 between the two instrument axes

= 287.164 − 247.260 = 39.904 m.

Now, $PQ_1 = D \times \tan 41°13'$

and $PQ_2 = (133 + D) \times \tan 19°16'$

But, $Q_1Q_2 = PQ_2 - PQ_1$

or $39.904 = (133 + D) \times \tan 19°16' - D \times \tan 41°13'$

or $$D = \frac{133 \times \tan 19°16' - 39.904}{\tan 41°13' - \tan 19°16'}$$

$= \mathbf{12.510\ m.}$

Thus

$PQ_1 = 12.510 \times \tan 41°13' = 10.958$

R.L. of P = Height of instrument axis at $A + PQ_1$

= 287.164 + 10.958 m

= **298.122 m.**

Example 6.21

To determine the elevation of a point *A* on the top of a hill, a flag staff *AB* of 3 m height, was erected, and the observations from two stations *M* and *N*, 50 m apart, were made as given below:

Horizontal angle between *B* and *N* at *M* = 65°25′

Horizontal angle between *B* and *M* at *N* = 72°30′

Angle of elevation of *B* from *M* = 12°24′29″

Angle of elevation of *B* from *N* = 12°34′32″

Staff reading on B.M. when instrument at *M* = 1.785 m

Staff reading on the same B.M. when instrument at *N* = 2.305 m

If the R.L. of the B.M. is 200.00 m, what is the R.L. of *A*?

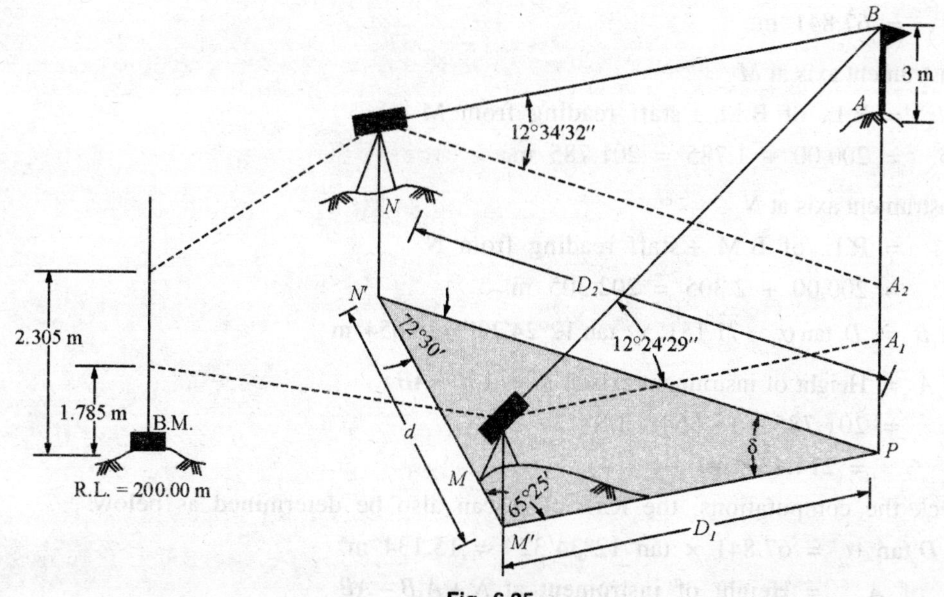

Fig. 6.35

Solution (Fig. 6.35):

Considering the Δ M′N′P in horizontal plane in which $\theta_1 = 65°25'$, $\theta_2 = 72°30'$, and $d = 50$ m we get

$$\theta_1 + \theta_2 + \delta = 180°$$

$$\delta = 180° - \theta_1 - \theta_2$$

$$= 180° - 65°25' - 72°30'$$

$$= 42°05'$$

From the sine rule, we have

$$\frac{M'P}{\sin\theta_2} = \frac{M'N'}{\sin\delta} = \frac{N'P}{\sin\theta_1}$$

or
$$\frac{D_1}{\sin\theta_2} = \frac{d}{\sin\delta} = \frac{D_2}{\sin\theta_1}$$

or
$$D_1 = d\,\frac{\sin\theta_2}{\sin\delta}$$

$$= 50 \times \frac{\sin 72°30'}{\sin 42°05'}$$

$$= 71.151 \text{ m.}$$

and
$$D_2 = d\,\frac{\sin\theta_1}{\sin\delta}$$

$$= 50 \times \frac{\sin 65°25'}{\sin 42°05'}$$

$$= 67.841 \text{ m.}$$

Height of instrument axis at M

= R.L. of B.M. + staff reading from M

= 200.00 + 1.785 = 201.785 m.

Height of instrument axis at N

= R.L. of B.M. + staff reading from N

= 200.00 + 2.305 = 202.305 m.

$$A_1B = D_1 \tan\alpha_1 = 71.151 \times \tan 12°24'29'' = 15.654 \text{ m}$$

R.L. of A = Height of instrument axis at $M + A_1B - AB$

= 201.785 + 15.654 − 3.0

= **214.439 m.**

To check the computations, the R.L. of A can also be determined as below.

$$A_2B = D_2 \tan\alpha_2 = 67.841 \times \tan 12°34'32'' = 15.134 \text{ m.}$$

R.L. of A = Height of instrument at $N + A_2B - AB$

= 202.305 + 15.134 − 3.0

= 214.439 m.

6.6 STADIA LEVELLING

Levelling can also be performed using the method of tacheometry. In this method the vertical distances are determined using engineer's transit and levelling staff; plane table and telescopic alidade and levelling staff; or self-reducing tacheometer and levelling staff. Details for levelling procedure by tacheometry are given in Chapter 8.

6.7 BAROMETRIC LEVELLING

Barometric levelling is the method of determining elevation by measurement of atmospheric pressure. The pressure caused by the weight of the column of air above the observer's station, decreases with rise in altitude. Assuming isothermal condition, *i.e.*, the atmosphere has a constant temperature between points of different altitudes, the following relationship exists between the atmospheric pressure and the altitude:

$$H_B - H_A = \left[18402.6 \log_{10}\left(\frac{p_A}{p_B}\right)\right]\left(1+\frac{t_m}{273}\right) \qquad ...(6.32)$$

where

H_A, H_B = the altitudes of points *A* and *B*,

p_A, p_B = the pressure at *A* and *B*, expressed in millimetres of mercury, and

t_m = the mean absolute temperature of atmosphere at *A* and *B* in degree Celsius.

The above relationship between altitude and pressure is not constant because air is compressible. Additional factors, although not quite as important, which influence the density of air, are temperature and humidity. This method of levelling is, therefore, very rough, and is generally used in reconnaissance survey and surveys in rough country where a high order of accuracy is not necessary.

Surveying altimeter is an improved version of the old aneroid barometer used in surveying primarily to determine differences in elevation between points, one of which has to be a bench mark or station of known elevation.

Altimeter surveys can be conducted in several ways. The two methods discussed below, are most common.

Single instrument method

The altimeter reading and temperature are taken under shade at the point of known elevation. The instrument is shifted to the point whose elevation is to be determined, and the altimeter reading and temperature are observed under shade. If the points are situated on a circular route, it is better to again observe the readings of the starting point at regular interval to find out the rate of change of atmospheric pressure and to correct the intermediate readings against atmospheric variations.

This method is an approximate method since the readings involve all atmospheric errors due to changes in the atmosphere which take place during the observations.

Simultaneous observations method

In this method, where a single base is taken, it is known as *single-base method* and where two bases are considered it is *two-base method.* The readings at the base stations, which are bench marks or points of known elevations and other points whose elevations are required to be determined, are observed simultaneously to minimise the errors due to changes in atmospheric conditions.

Single-base method: This method requires two altimeters. One altimeter remains at the base station where readings of the altimeter and a thermometer are made at regular intervals. The other altimeter called the roving altimeter, is transported to those points whose elevations are desired. Readings are of the altimeter and a thermometer are taken. The difference of elevation is computed using Eq. (6.32).

Two-base method: Two altimeters are placed at two base stations, one at the lowest point and one at the highest point. Simultaneous observations are made at these base stations throughout the period. A third altimeter which is roving, is employed to make observations at the points whose elevations are desired. The roving altimeter is started from one of the bases and finished at the other. All the three altimeters are compared before and after the work, in order to determine the *index correction*. The index correction is given by the following expression.

Index correction = Roving altimeter reading – base altimeter reading

Because the readings of all the three altimeters are taken at the same time, calculation of heights becomes simple. From Fig. 6.36, the following expression can be derived by simple proportion:

$$\frac{H_R - H_B}{H_T - H_B} = \frac{R_R - R_B}{R_T - R_B} \qquad \text{...(6.33)}$$

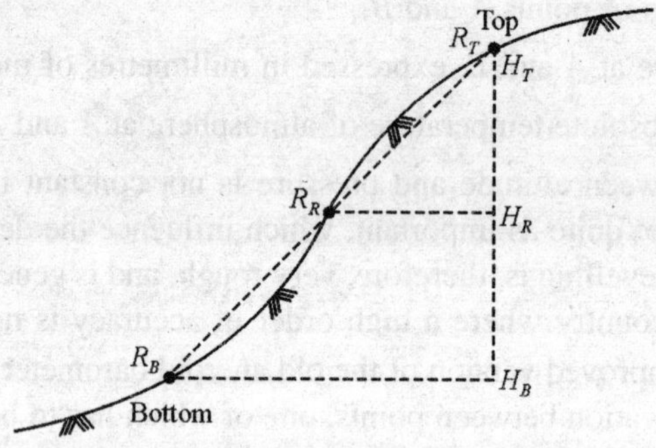

Fig. 6.36 Two-base method of barometric levelling

where H_B, H_T, H_R = the elevations of bottom base station, top base station, and roving altimeter station, in metres

R_B, R_T, R_R = the altimeter readings at the bottom base station, top base station, and roving altimeter station.

With proper techniques and good equipment, barometric levelling in a stable atmospheric conditions, may be expected to yield differences of elevation with errors not in excess of ± 1 m.

ILLUSTRATIVE EXAMPLES

Example 6.22

To determine the elevation of a station *B*, the barometer and thermometer readings were taken at stations *A* and *B* as below:

Stations	Barometer reading (mm)	Thermometer reading (°C)	Remarks
A	693.00	15	R.L. = 313.5 m
B	650.00	25	

What is the elevation of *B*?

Solution:

From Eq. (6.32), we have

$$H_B - H_A = \left[18402.6 \log_{10}\left(\frac{h_A}{h_B}\right)\right]\left(1 + \frac{t_m}{273}\right)$$

We have

$$H_A = 313.5 \text{ m}$$

$$h_A = 693.00 \text{ mm}$$

$$h_B = 650.00 \text{ mm}$$

$$t_A = 15°\text{C}$$

$$t_B = 25°\text{C}$$

From the given data, we have

$$t_m = \frac{15+25}{2} = 20°\text{C}$$

$$H_B = 313.5 + \left[18402.6 \log_{10}\left(\frac{693}{650}\right)\right] \times \left(1 + \frac{20}{273}\right)$$

$= 313.5 + 549.5$

$= \mathbf{863.0 \text{ m}}$

Example 6.23

Find the elevation of the station *B* from the following data:

(*i*) Barometer reading at *A* = 620.4 mm at 8 A.M, temperature of air = 32°C
= 620.8 mm at 12 noon, temperature of air = 36°C

(*ii*) Barometer reading at *B* = 614.0 mm at 10A.M., temperature of air = 10°C

(*iii*) Elevation of *A* = 286.5 m.

Solution:

The probable reading of *A* at 10 A.M.

$$h_A = \frac{620.4 + 620.8}{2} = 620.6 \text{ mm}$$

The probable temperature at A at 10 a.m.

$$t_A = \frac{32+36}{2} = 34°C$$

$$t_m = \frac{34+10}{2} = 22°C$$

From Eq. (6.31)

$$H_B = H_A + \left[18402.6 \log_{10}\left(\frac{h_A}{h_B}\right)\right]\left(1+\frac{t_m}{273}\right)$$

$$= 286.5 + \left[18402.6 \log_{10}\left(\frac{620.6}{614.0}\right)\right] \times \left(1+\frac{22}{273}\right)$$

$$= 286.5 + 92.3$$

$$= \mathbf{378.8\ m.}$$

Example 6.24

Find the elevation of the station P where the altimeter reading is 130 mm. The altimeter reading at upper base of R.L. = 406.6 m, is 355 mm and at the lower base of R.L. = 109.5 m, is 110 mm.

Solution:

From Eq. (6.33), we have

$$\frac{H_P - H_B}{H_T - H_B} = \frac{R_P - R_B}{R_T - R_B}$$

Putting the value of H and R, we get

$$\frac{H_P - 109.5}{406.6 - 109.5} = \frac{130-110}{355-110}$$

$$H_P = \frac{20}{245} \times 297.1 + 109.5$$

$$= 24.3 + 109.5$$

$$= \mathbf{133.8\ m.}$$

QUESTIONS AND PROBLEMS

6.1 (a) Define the following terms:

(1) Datum; (2) Bench mark; (3) Reduced level.

(b) How a horizontal surface is different from a level surface?

6.2 Describe briefly the various methods of levelling.

6.3 Describe in brief the various methods of direct differential levelling.

6.4 (a) Explain the working of a dumpy level and a tilting level. Also write under what conditions they are most useful.

(b) In what respect a dumpy level differs from a tilting level.

6.5 What are the essential features of an automatic level?

6.7 With the help of neat sketches, explain the working of hand level and clinometer.

6.8 Describe briefly the various types of levelling staffs. State the merits and demerits of each.

6.9 What are the relative merits of self-reading staff and target staff?

6.10 Define the following terms used in levelling:

(1) Station

(2) Height of instrument

(3) Back sight, fore sight and intermediate sights

(4) Change point.

6.11 What do you understand by balancing of sights? How it helps in reducing the errors in levelling?

6.12 Describe the methods of reducing the levels, and their relative advantages and disadvantages.

6.13 Discuss the effect of curvature and refraction in levelling. Find the correction due to each and the combined correction. Why are these effects ignored in ordinary levelling?

6.14 What are the sources of errors in levelling? What precautions are necessary to avoid them?

6.15 (a) What is sensitivity of a level tube? On what factors does it depend?

(b) Describe methods of determining the sensitivity of a level tube.

6.16 Define degree of precision in levelling. Discuss the method of adjustment of a simple level loop.

6.17 Explain why it is necessary to keep the level midway between back sight and fore sight readings.

6.18 Explain in detail how profile levelling is conducted for route alignment. Draw a typical longitudinal section.

6.19 What do you understand by cross-section levelling? Explain how it is conducted. Draw a typical cross-section.

6.20 (a) Explain fully the process of reciprocal levelling, and state its advantages.

(b) Explain how reciprocal levelling eliminates the effect of earth's curvature, atmospheric refraction, and non-adjustment of the line of collimation.

6.21 What are the common difficulties generally faced in levelling? How would you overcome them?

6.22 What is trigonometric levelling? What are its advantages and disadvantages over direct levelling?

6.23 How would you determine the difference in elevation of the instrument station and top of a chimney in the following cases:

(*a*) The base of the chimney is accessible.

(*b*) The base of the chimney is inaccessible.

6.24 What is barometric levelling? Derive an expression for the difference of the levels of two points.

6.25 How the difference of levels is determined by simultaneous observation in barometric levelling?

6.26 Compute and tabulate the combined effect of curvature and refraction on level sights of 20 m, 30 m, 50 m, 100 m, 150 m, 200 m, 300 m and 500 m. Draw also a curve level sight verses distance.

6.27 What error in elevation results from the combined effects of curvature and refraction on a downhill of differential levels having back sight and fore sight distances in metre given below:

(*a*) 30, 60; 45, 75; 40, 45; 65, 75

(*b*) 50, 55; 50, 60; 67, 73; 25, 45

(*c*) 24, 36; 42, 55; 36, 49; 24, 46

6.28 A back sight of 3.105 m is taken on a point 50 m from a level. A foresight of 2.055 m is then taken on a point 220 m from the level. Compute the correct difference in elevation between the two points, taking into account the effect of earth´s curvature and neglecting the effect of refraction on the line of sight.

6.29 On a large lake without waves, how far from the shore will a boat with a 6 m mast disappear from view of a man lying on the beach at the edge of the water?

6.30 Find the distance of visible horizon from the top of a lighthouse 50 m high. Take $R = 6336$ km.

6.31 An observer at a height of 30 m above mean sea level just sees a luminous object on the top of a hill situated at a distance of 85 km from him. What is the height of the hill above sea level?

6.32 The back sight reading at *A* is 2.457 m and the fore sight reading at *B* is 3.762 m.What is the difference in level of *A* and *B*?

6.33 The back sight reading on a staff held vertical on a bench mark of R.L. 600.00 m is 1.394 m, and the fore sight on a staff held vertically inverted against a beam is 3.665 m. Determine the reduced level of the beam.

6.34 Staff readings on the floor of a factory is 1.320 m and on a beam at the roof of truss when the bottom of the staff touching the beam, is 3.905 m. Reduced level of the beam is 475.000 m. What is the reduced level of the floor.

6.35 To ascertain the level difference between *A* and *B*, differential levelling was performed from *A* to *B*, and extended to *C* which is a bench mark having R.L. of 95.75 m. The observations were recorded in level field book given below. Fill the remaining columns of the level field book.

Point	B.S.	I.S.	F.S.	Rise	Fall	R.L.	Remarks
1	1.195						*A*
2	0.445		2.375				
3	2.150		1.000				
4		0.720					*B*
5	1.465		0.260				
6	2.630		0.905				
7	2.140		0.975				
			1.305			95.75	*C*

6.36 The following readings were observed successively with a levelling instrument. The instrument was shifted after 5th and 11th readings.

0.485, 1.020, 1.785, 3.395, 3.875, 0.360, 1.305, 1.785, 2.675, 3.385, 3.885, 1.835, 0.435, 1.705

Draw up a page of level book, and determine the R.L. of various points by rise and fall method if the R.L. of the point on which the first reading was taken is 264.350 m.

6.37 The following is the page of a level book. Fill in the missing readings, and calculate the reduced levels of all the points. Apply the usual checks.

Point	B.S.	I.S.	F.S.	Rise	Fall	R.L.	Remarks
1	3.150					***	
2	1.770		***		0.700	***	
3		2.200			***	***	
4	***		1.850	***		***	
5		2.440			0.010	***	
6	***		***	1.100		***	
7	1.185		2.010	***		222.200	
8		1.735			***	***	
9	***		1.685	0.050		***	
10			1.525		0.805	***	
Sum	12.055						

6.38 Given the following data, determine the R.L. of the points 1, 2, 3, 4, 5, and 6. If an uniform upward gradient of 1 in 20 starts at point 1, having elevation of 150 m, calculate the height of embankment and depth of cutting at the points 1, 2, 3, 4, 5 and 6.

Chainage	Station	B.S.	I.S.	F.S.	R.L.	Remarks
-	B.M.	10.11				153.46 m
0	1		3.25			
100	2		1.10			
200	3	6.89		0.35		
300	4		3.14			
400	5	11.87		3.65		
500	6			5.98		

6.39 A 20 km closed levelling traverse reveals a closing error of 38.37 cm on the starting B.M. Would you consider the work acceptable? Give reasons in support of your answer.

6.40 Two kilometre stones *A* and *B* are separated by 10 km. A line of levels is run from *A* to *B*, and then from *B* to *A*. The differences of levels are found as below:

A to *B*	+ 55.272 m
B to A	– 55.114 m

Would you accept the levelling job for an engineering project?

6.41 Find the radius of curvature of bubble tube whose length of one division is 2 mm and if the angular value of its one division is
(a) 15 seconds, and (b) 25 seconds.

6.42 The reading taken on a staff held 100 m from the instrument with bubble central is 1.655 m. The bubble is then moved 3 divisions out of centre, and the staff reading observed is 1.675 m. Find the angular value of one division of bubble, and radius of curvature of the bubble tube. The length of one division is 2 mm.

6.43 If the sensitivity of the bubble tube of a level is 20" per 2 mm division, find the error in the staff reading on a staff held at a distance of 100 m caused by the bubble being 3 divisions out of the centre.

6.44 Determine the radius of curvature and the sensitivity of the bubble tube from the data given below:

Staff reading (m)	1.452	1.370
Eyepiece end of bubble reading	20	11
Objective end of bubble reading	11	20

The distance of the staff from the instrument station was 100 m, and one division on the bubble tube measures 2 mm.

6.45 The following reciprocal levels were taken with one level:

Instrument at	Staff reading on		Remarks
	A	*B*	
A	1.564	2.787	*AB* = 900 m
B	0.436	1.695	R.L. of *A* = 200.00 m

Determine (a) the true difference in elevation between A and B, (b) the R.L. of B, and (c) the collimation error.

6.46 Two peg method of testing was conducted on a dumpy level, and the following results were obtained:

Instrument near *P*
Staff reading at *P* = 3.145 m
Staff reading at *Q* = 1.500 m

Instrument near *Q*
Staff reading at *P* = 2.740 m
Staff reading at *Q* = 1.105 m

Calculate the staff reading at *Q* to give a horizontal line of sight. What was the error of collimation?

6.47 The following observations were taken in reciprocal levelling using one instrument:

Instrument near	Staff reading at	
	A	*B*
A	1.625	2.545
B	0.725	1.405

Determine the R.L. of B if the R.L. of *A* is 100.000 m. Also calculate the angular error in collimation if the distance between *A* and *B* is 1100 m.

6.48 While carrying out the permanent adjustments of a dumpy level by two-peg method, the follwing observations were made:

Instrument at *C* midway between *A* and *B*, 100 m apart.

Reading at $A = 2.000$ m

Reading at $B = 3.000$ m

Instrument at *D* in line of *AB* such that $AD = 120$ m and $BD = 20$ m

Reading at $A = 1.500$ m

Reading at $B = 2.750$ m

Check whether the instrument needs permanent adjustments or not, and whether the line of sight is inclined upwards. What should be the correct reading at *A* if the instrument is to be adjusted?

6.49 The angle of elevation from station *A* to a vane 3 m above the foot of the staff held at *B*, was 9°35′. What is the R.L. of *B* if the distance *AB* is equal to 3000 m, and R.L. of the instrument axis at *A* was 120.35 m.

6.50 In order to determine the elevation of the top *P* of a signal *PQ* of height 5 m, observations were made from two instrument stations *A* and *B* which are in line with the signal. *A* and *B* are 75 m apart. The vertical angles of *P* as observed at *A* and *B* were, respectively, 31°40′ and15°12′.

The staff reading on the bench mark of elevation 200.00 m was 2.950 m when the instrument was at *A*, and 3.665 m when at B. Determine the elevations of the top *P* and foot *Q* of the signal.

6.51 To find the elevation of the top of a hill, a flag staff of 4 m height was erected with its top at *Q*. Observations were made from two stations *M* and *N*, 60 m apart and not in line with *Q*. The angles of elevation to the top of the flag staff from stations *M* and *N* were measured as 10°50′ and 11°28′, respectively. The horizontal angle measured at *M* betwen *N* and the top of the flag staff was 56°30′, and that measured at *N* between *A* and the top of the flag was 62°10′.

If the staff reading on B.M. with an elevation of 335.550 m when the instrument was at *M* and the line of sight was horizontal, was 1.785 m, determine the elevation of the top of the hill. If the staff reading on the B.M. when the instrument was at *N*, was 1.794 m, determine the elevation of the top of the hill, and compare with the earlier computed value.

6.52 Deduce the R.L. of a point *Q* in metres from the following simultaneous observations:

Barometer reading at $P = 70.32$ cm at 25.10°C

Barometer reading at $Q = 65.19$ cm at 26.15°C

R.L. of $P = 1502.75$ m.

6.53 Find the elevation of the station B from the following observations if the reduced level of A is 250.50 m :

Station	A	B
(1) Barometer reading	75.42 cm	71.98 cm
Time	8 A.M.	10 A.M.
Temperature	32°C	27°C
(2) Barometer reading	75.57 cm	
Time	12 Noon	
Temperature	35°C	

7

CONTOURING

7.1 GENERAL

The process of determining the positions of the natural and man-made features of a given area on the earth's surface, and the configuration of terrain, is called *topographic surveying*. The purpose of survey is to gather data necessary for the construction of a graphical portrayal of planimetric and topographic features. This graphical portrayal is a *topographic map*. The location of the features is referred to as *planimetry*, and the configuration of the terrain is referred to as *topography*. The utility of a plan or map is highly enhanced if the relative position of the points is represented both horizontally and vertically. On a map, the relative vertical position of the points can be represented by shading, hachure, spot heights, or contour lines. Out of these, contour lines or contours are most widely used for direct representation of the configuration of the ground and the elevation of the points.

7.2 CONTOURS AND CONTOUR LINES

A *contour* is an imaginary line of constant elevation on the ground surface. It may be thought of as the trace formed by the intersection of a level surface with the ground surface. Fig. 7.1a shows a pond with water level at elevations 110 m, 100 m, 90 m, 80 m, 70 m, 60 m, 50 m, 40 m, etc. If the locations of the several ground points on the same water surface having elevations 110 m, 100 m, 90 m, 80 m, 70 m, 60 m, 50 m, 40 m, *etc*., are plotted on a drawing (Fig. 7.1b), a line joining the points having the same elevation, is called a *contour line*.

Thus, contours on the ground are represented by contour lines on the map.

7.3 CONTOUR INTERVAL AND HORIZONTAL EQUIVALENT

On a given map the successive contour lines represent elevations differring by a fixed vertical distance called the *contour interval* (C.I.). The horizontal distance between two points on the consecutive contour lines for a given slope, is the *horizontal equivalent*. In Fig.7.2, the vertical distance between the successive contours, is 10 m, thus the contour interval is 10 m. If the given slope is 1 in 5, for 10 m vertical distance, the horizontal distance would be 50 m.

In other words, let the points *a*, *b*, and *c* representing the ground points *A*, *B*, and *C*, respectively, be situated on the contours of 130 m, 140 m and 150 m, respectively, on a map at centain scale. If the length's *ab* and *bc* are equal to 50 m on ground, then the slope of the lines *AB* and *BC* is 1 in 5. While the horizontal equivalent depends upon the slope of the ground or required grade for construction of a road, canal, etc., the choice of suitable contour interval depends upon four principal considerations discussed below.

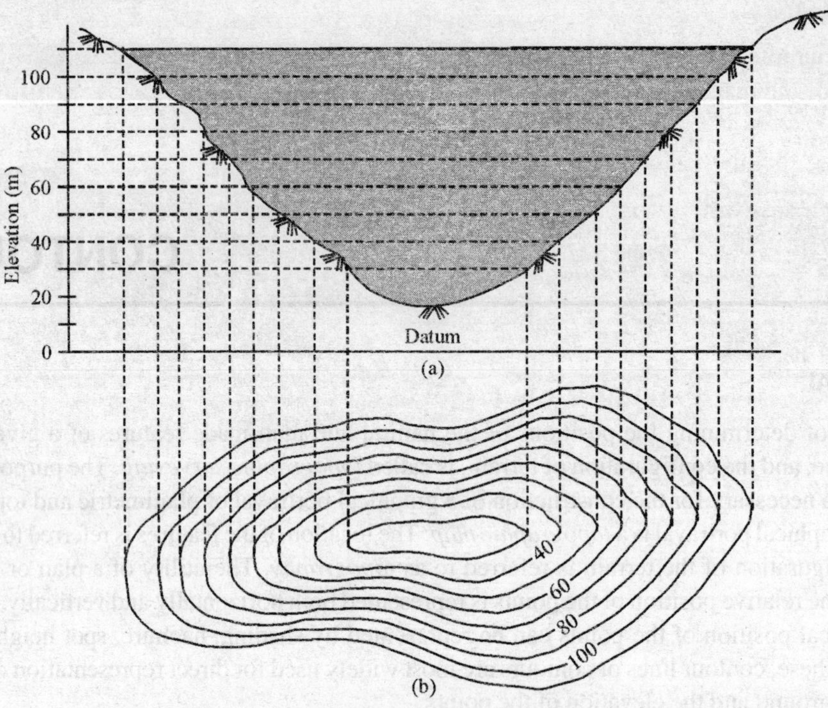

Fig. 7.1 Contour lines for a pond

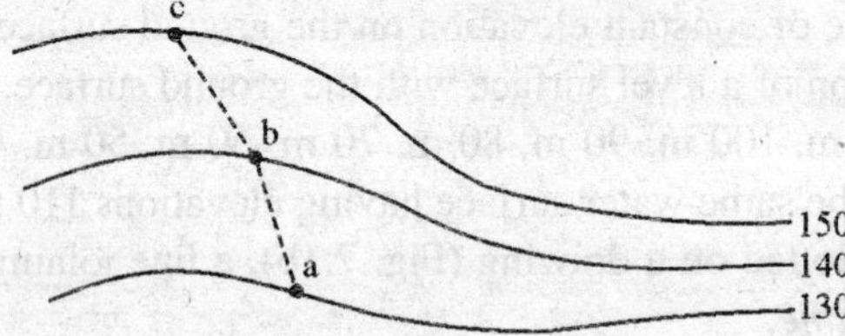

Fig. 7.2 Horizontal equivalent

Nature of terrain

The contour interval depends upon the nature of the terrain. A contour interval chosen for a flat ground will be highly unsuitable for undulating ground. For flat ground, a small contour interval is chosen whereas for undulating and broken ground, larger contour interval should be adopted.

Scale of the map

The contour interval is normally inversely proportional to the scale of the map. If the scale is large, the contour interval should be small. If the scale is small, the contour interval should be large.

Purpose and extent of the survey

The purpose and the extent of the survey also decide the contour interval. If the survey is intended for detailed design work or for accurate earthwork calculations, a small contour interval will be required. The extent of survey in such cases will generally be small. In the case of location surveys, for lines of communications, and for reservoir and drainage areas, where the extent of survey is large, a large contour interval should be used.

Time and expense

If the contour interval is small, greater time and funds will be required in the field survey, in reduction and plotting of the map. If the time and funds available are limited, the contour interval may be kept large.

Considering the above aspects, Table 7.1 suggests the contour interval for specific purposes and Table 7.2 suggests the contour interval for various scales of the map and type of ground.

Table 7.1 Contour interval for different types of survey

Survey	Scale	Contour interval (m)
Building site	1/1000 or less	0.2 to 0.5
Town planning, reservoir, etc.	1/50,00 to 1/100,00	0.5 to 2
Location survey, earthwork, etc.	1/100,00 to 1/200,00	1 to 3

Table 7.2 Contour interval for different scales and typest of ground

Map Scale	Type of ground	Contour interval (m)
Large (1/1000 or less)	Flat Rolling Hilly	0.2 to 0.5 0.5 to 1 1 to 2
Intermediate (1/1000 to1/10000)	Flat Rolling Hilly	0.5 to 1.5 1.5 to 2 2 to 3
Small (1/10000 or more)	Flat Rolling Hilly Mountainous	1 to 3 3 to 5 5 to 10 10, 25 or 50

Contour interval for topographical surveys is decided from the following general rule:

$$\text{C.I.} = \frac{20}{\text{Number of centimetres per kilometre}} \text{ (metres)}$$

7.4 CHARACTERISTICS OF CONTOURS

In the topographic maps, the configuration of the terrain is represented by drawing contours at constant vertical distance. A knowledge of contour characteristics helps in identifying the natural features of the area from the given map and in avoiding mistakes in plotting the contours correctly.

The following characteristics help in plotting or reading a contour map (Fig. 7.3):

(1) The ground slope between contour lines is assumed to be uniform.

(2) The direction of the steepest slope at a point on the contour is at right angles to the contour (Fig.7.3a).

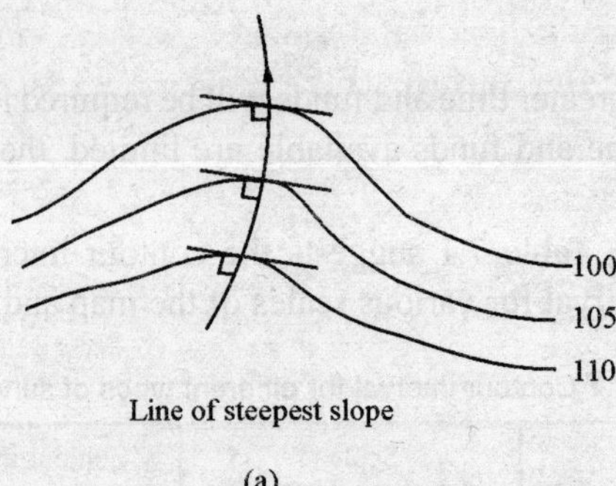

Line of steepest slope

(a)

(3) Closely spaced contours indicate steep slope (Fig. 7.3b).

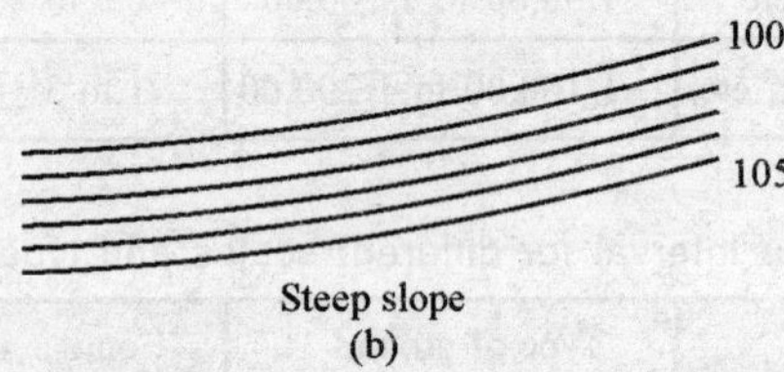

Steep slope
(b)

(4) Widely spaced contours indicate moderate slope (Fig. 7.3c).

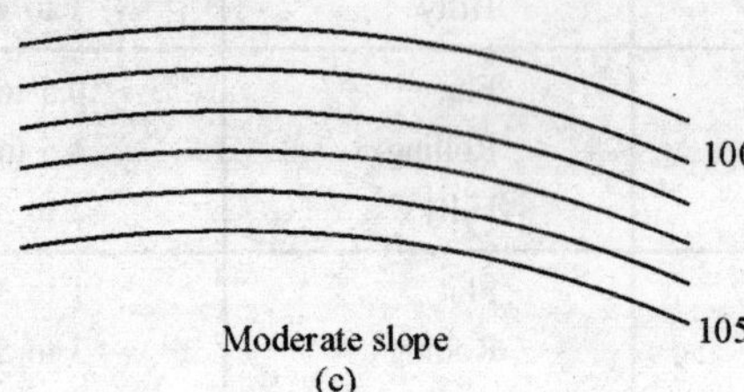

Moderate slope
(c)

(5) Equally spaced contours depict a uniform slope (Fig. 7.3d).

Uniform slope
(d)

(6) Contours are not shown going through buildings (Fig. 7.3e).

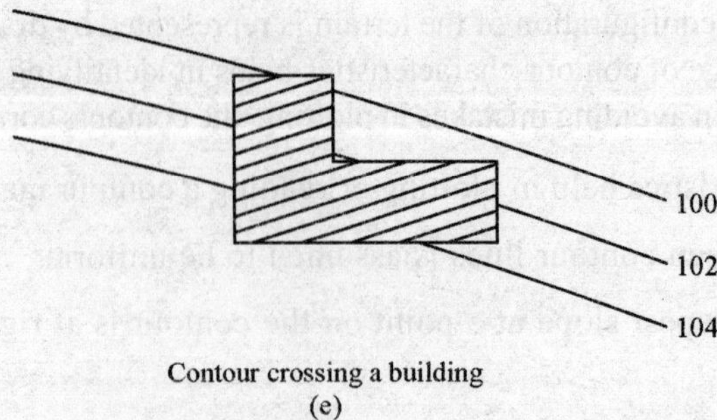

Contour crossing a building
(e)

(7) Contours crossing a man-made horizontal surface (roads, railway track) will be straight parallel lines as they cross the surface (Fig. 7.3f).

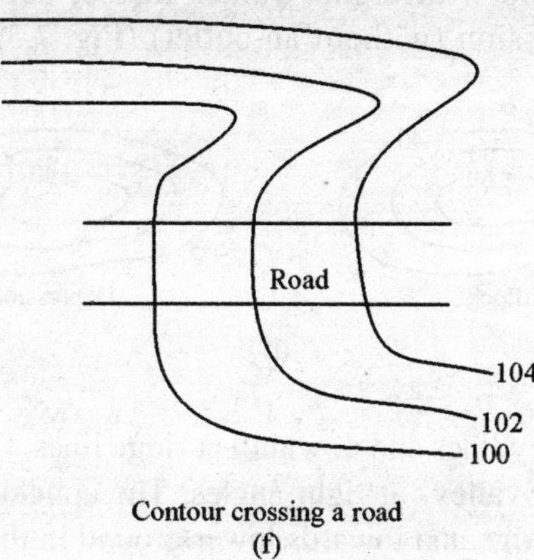

Contour crossing a road
(f)

(8) Contours of different elevations cannot cross each other since contours join points of equal elevation (caves and overhanging cliffs are the exceptions) (Fig. 7.3g).

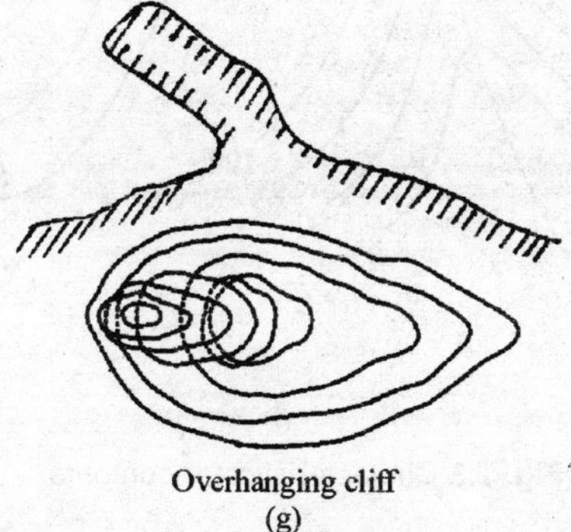

Overhanging cliff
(g)

(9) Contours of different elevations cannot unite to form one contour (vertical cliff is an exception) (Fig. 7.3h).

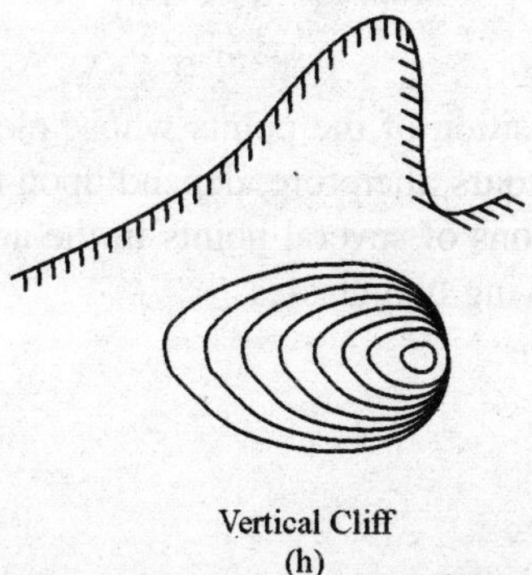

Vertical Cliff
(h)

(10) Contour lines cannot begin or end on the plan.

(11) A contour line must close itself but need not be necessarily within the limits of the map.

(12) Depressions and hills look the same. One must note the contour values to distinguish the terrain. A set of ring contours with higher values inside, depicts a hill whereas the lower value inside, depicts a depression (without an outlet) (Fig. 7.3i).

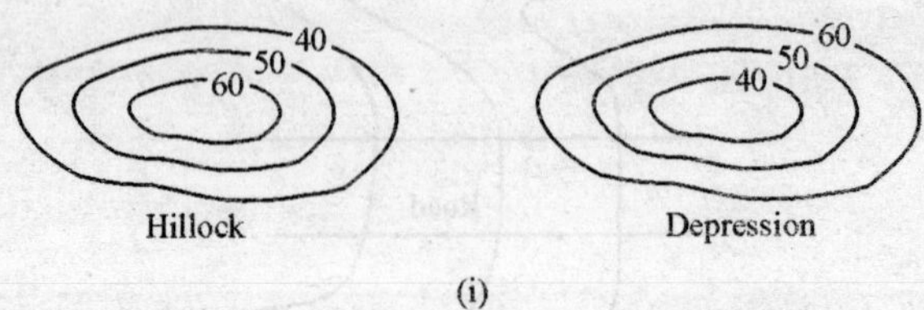

(i)

(13) Contours deflect uphill at valley lines and downhill at ridge lines. Contour lines in U-shape cross a ridge, and in V-shape cross a valley at right angles. The concavity in contour lines is towards higher ground in the case of ridge and towards lower ground in the case of valley (Fig. 7.3j).

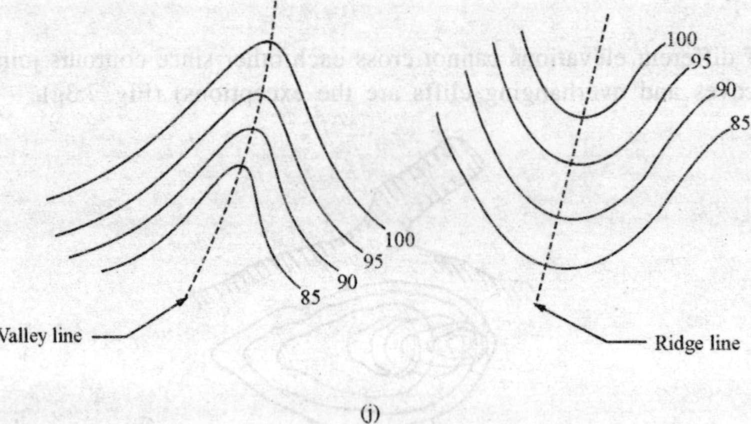

(j)

Fig. 7.3 Characteristics of contours

(14) The same contour must appear on both sides of a ridge or valley.

(15) Contours do not have sharp turnings.

(16) A single contour line cannot lie between two contour lines of higher or lower elevation.

7.5 METHODS OF CONTOURING

Contouring requires the planimetric position of the points whose elevations have been determined by levelling. The methods of locating contours, therefore, depend upon the instruments used to determine the horizontal as well as vertical positions of several points in the area. In general, however, the field methods may be divided into the following two classes:

(1) Direct methods

(2) Indirect methods.

Direct methods

In the direct method, the contour to be plotted is actually traced on the ground. Only those points are surveyed which happen to fall on a particular contour. After having surveyed such points, they are plotted and joined. The method is slow and tedious. This method is employed only for small areas where superior accuracy is demanded.

The method of locating contours directly consists of providing vertical control for location of points on the contours and horizontal control for plotting the located points.

Direct method of contouring can be employed in the following two ways.

Method-I

Vertical control: For providing the vertical control the instruments most commonly employed are level, levelling staff, and plane table with accessories.

A bench mark of known elevation is established in the project area. The level is set up on any commanding position *A* (Fig. 7.4), and back sight is taken on the bench mark. Let the back sight reading on the bench mark be 1.320 m. If the reduced level of the bench mark is 200 m, the height of instrument would be 200 + 1.320 = 201.320 m.

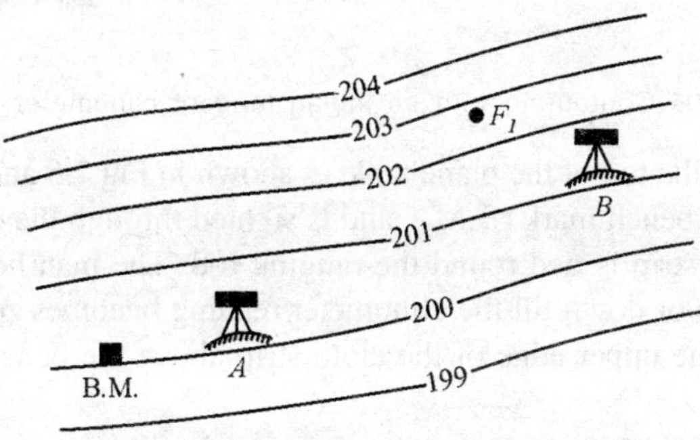

Fig. 7.4 Locating contours directly with a level

Now, to locate the contour of 200 m value, the staff man is directed to occupy the position on the ground where the staff reading is 201.320 – 200 = 1.320 m. Mark all such positions on the ground where the staff reading would be 1.320 m by inserting wooden pegs. Similarly locate the points where the staff reading would be 201.320 – 201 = 0.321 m for 201 m contour. The contour of 202 m cannot be set from this setting of the instrument because the height of instrument for this setting of the instrument is only 201.320 m. Therefore, locating the contours of higher value the instrument has to be shifted to some other suitable position.

Establish a forward station F_1 on a firm ground, and take fore sight on it. This point acts as a point of known elevation for shifting the position of the instrument to a new position *B* from where the work proceeds in the similar manner till the entire area is contoured.

Horizontal control: The horizontal control is generally provided using a plane table with accessories, tape, ranging rods, etc. In case of small areas, the locations of the points on each contour, are plotted on the plane table section by radiation method. If the extent of the area is large, one has to take many plane table positions to cover the entire area.

Method-II

In this method, Indian tangent clinometer, ranging rod, plane table with accessories, and tape are used. In Sec. 10.13 the Indian tangent clinometer and its use have been discussed. The clinometer, instead of a level, is used for providing vertical control, and the horizontal distances are measured directly with a tape.

A number of bench marks are established in the area by method of levelling. The plane table is set upon a commanding position. The plane table position is found out by the methods of plane tabling, and plotted on the plane table section. If the points are already plotted, the plane table should be set over such points.

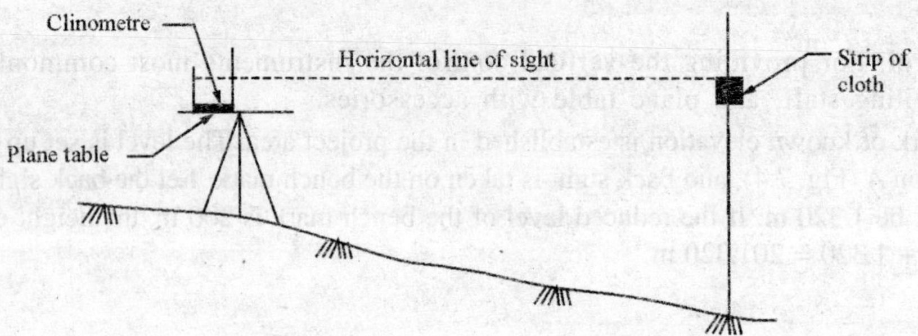

Fig. 7.5 Contouring with an Indian tangent clinometer

The clinometer is placed on the top of the plane table as shown in Fig.7.5 and levelled. A ranging rod is held vertically on the nearby bench mark (B.M.), and is sighted through the eye whole of the clinometer. A 5 cm wide white cloth strip is tied round the ranging rod. The man holding the ranging rod is asked to slide the cloth strip up or down till the clinometer reading becomes zero for the upper edge of the cloth strip. The height of the upper edge of the cloth strip above the bench mark is measured. Let this height be 1.655 m.

If the R.L. of the bench mark is 500 m, the height of the eye hole above the datum is 500 + 1.655 = 501.655 m. Now to locate the point on 500 m contour, tie the cloth strip at height of 501.655 – 500 = 1.655 m.

Now the ranging rod man is asked to hold the rod on the points where the clinometer reading is zero. The horizontal distance of the points are measured directly with a tape, and the points are plotted by radiation method of plane tabling.

Other contours of 501 m, 502 m, 503 m, etc. can be located in similar manner by tying the cloth strips at appropriate heights.

Indirect methods

In this method, sufficient number of points are located and given spot levels. The locations of all such points are easily plotted on a plane table section as the points are generally the corners of well-shaped geometrical figures such as squares, rectangles, and triangles. The selection of points for giving spot levels is done taking cognizance of salient topographic features, for example, hilltops, ridge lines, beds of streams, and lowest points of depressions, to depict their correct features while drawing contour lines. The contours in between spot levels are interpolated and drawn.

Indirect methods are less expensive, less time consuming, and less tedious as compared with the direct methods. These methods are commonly employed in small scale surveys of large areas.

There are three different ways of employing the indirect method of contouring.

1. Grid method
2. Cross-section method
3. Radial line method or tacheometric method.

Grid method

If the area is not large, it is divided into a grid or series of squares. The grid size may vary from 5 m × 5 m to 25 m × 25 m depending upon the nature of the ground, the contour interval, and the scale of the map. Also, the grids may not be of the same size throughout but may vary depending upon the requirement and field conditions. The grid corners are marked on the ground, and spot levels of these corners are given by normal method of levelling using a level.

The grid is plotted to the scale of the map, and the spot levels of the grid corners are entered. The contours of desired values are then located by interpolation as shown in Fig. 7.6. Special care should be taken to give the spot levels to the salient features of the ground such as hilltops, deepest points of the depressions, and their measurements from respective corners of the grids, for correct depiction of the features.

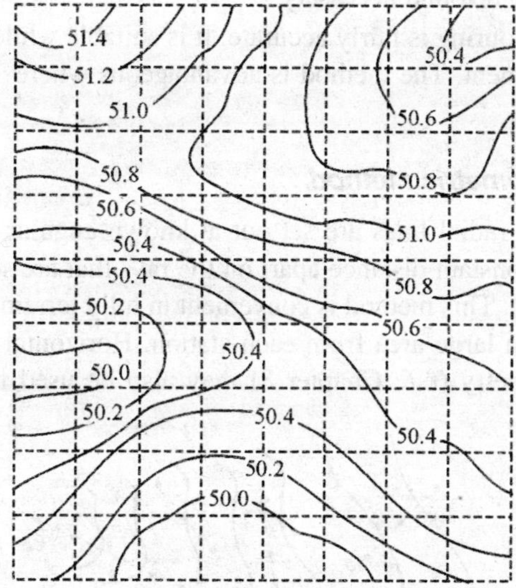

Fig. 7.6 Contouring by grid method

Cross-section method

In this method, suitably spaced cross-sections are projected on either side of the centre line of the area. Several points are chosen at reasonable distances on either sides. The spot levels are given to these points by normal levelling methods. The cross-section lines are plotted to the scale, the points on these lines are marked, and spot levels are entered. The points on the chosen contours are interpolated assuming uniform slope between adjacent points, and joined by a smooth curve (Fig.7.7).

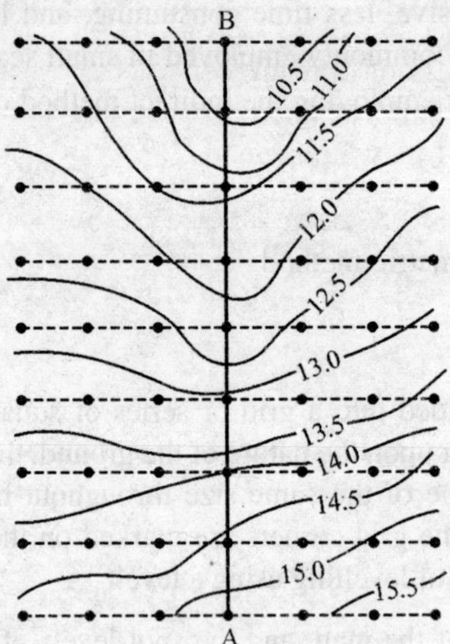

Fig. 7.7 Contouring by cross-section method

The spacing of cross-sections depends upon the contour interval, the scale of the plan, and nature of the ground. In general, the spacing may vary from 20 m in hills to 100 m in flat country. The layout of the cross-sections need not necessarily be at right angles to the centre line, and these may be inclined at suitable angles to the centre line if found necessary.

Cross-section method of contouring is fairly accurate. It is suitable while preparing a contour plan of a road, railways, or canal alignment. The method is advantageous where the sections can be used for both estimates and construction.

Radial line method or tacheometric method

In this method, a number of radial lines are set out at known angular interval at each station, and points are fixed at convenient constant distance apart on the rays that are set by compass or, for greater accuracy by theodolite (Fig. 7.8). This method is convenient in hilly terrain with level stations chosen at high points so as to command a large area from each station. Horizontal control may be obtained by taping. The method of tacheometry (*c.f.*, Chapter 8) may also be used for providing horizontal and vertical controls.

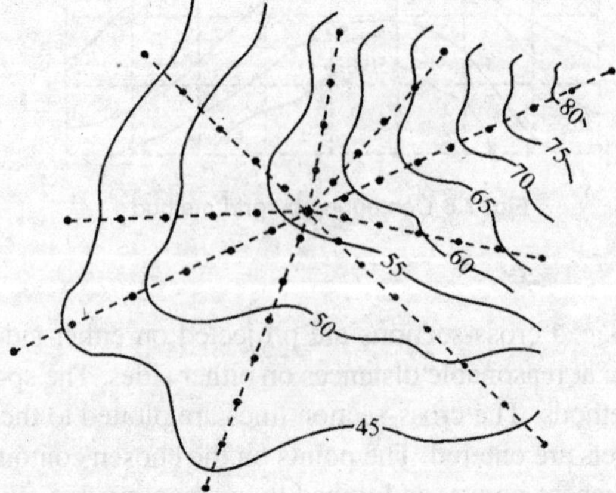

Fig. 7.8 Contouring by radial line method

7.6 INTERPOLATION OF CONTOURS

Interpolation of contours is a process of drawing contours between plotted ground points of known elevations by proportion assuming uniform slope between any two points or in between plotted contours. It may be done by one of the following methods:

1. Estimation
2. Arithmetical calculation
3. Mechanical or graphical method.

Estimation

The points on the required contour are located by eye judgement or estimation between points whose elevations are already known. This method is good for small-scale maps and for locating the contours between two already plotted contours.

Arithmetical Calculation

The position of point on the required contour between two points of known elevation is determined by linear interpolation on the basis of assumption of uniform slope between the two points.

Let *A*, *B*, *C*, and *D* be the four points (Fig. 7.9) of known elevations 82.3 m, 87.5 m, 92.4 m, and 84.7 m, respectively, already plotted on the plane table section. These points lie on the corner of a grid of size 2 cm × 2 cm and the contours are to be drawn at contour interval of 2 m.

The point of minimum elevation is *A* having elevation 82.3 m, and the point of maximum elevation is *C* having elevation 92.4 m. Therefore, the contours which will pass over the grid are 84 m, 86 m, 88 m, 90 m, and 92 m. The points are located on the lines *AB*, *BC*, *CD*, and *DA* as explained below.

(a) Interpolation along *AB*

Difference of elevation between *A* and *B* in a distance of 20 mm
= 87.5 – 82.3 = 5.2 m.

(*i*) Difference of level between *A* and 84 m contour point

= 84 – 82.3 = 1.7 m.

$$\text{The distance of 84 m contour from } A = 20 \times \frac{1.7}{5.2} = 6.5 \text{ mm}$$

The 84 m contour will lie on *AB* at 1_{AB}, 6.5 mm from *A*.

(*ii*) Difference of level between *A* and 86 m contour point

= 86 – 82.3 = 3.7 m.

$$\text{The distance of 86 m contour from } A = 20 \times \frac{3.7}{5.2} = 14.2 \text{ mm.}$$

The 86 m contour will lie on *AB* at 2_{AB}, 14.2 mm from *A*.

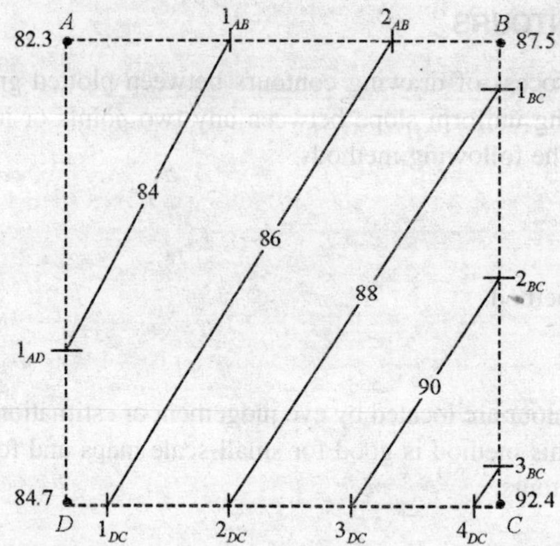

Fig. 7.9 Interpolation by arithmetical calculation

(b) Interpolation along *BC*

Difference of elevation between *B* and *C* in a distance of 20 mm

$= 92.4 - 87.5 = 4.9$ m.

(*i*) Difference of level between *B* and 88 m contour point

$= 88 - 87.5 = 0.5$ m

The distance of 88 m contour from $B = 20 \times \dfrac{0.5}{4.9} = 2.0$ mm.

The 88 m contour will lie on *BC* at 1_{BC}, 2.0 mm from *B*.

(*ii*) Difference of level between *B* and 90 m contour point

$= 90 - 87.5 = 2.5$ m

The distance of 90 m contour from $B = 20 \times \dfrac{2.5}{4.9} = 10.2$ mm.

The 90 m contour will lie in *BC* at 2_{BC}, 10.2 mm from *B*.

(*iii*) Difference of level between *B* and 92 m contour point

$= 92 - 87.5 = 4.5$ m

The distance of 92 m contour from $B = 20 \times \dfrac{4.5}{4.9} = 18.4$ mm.

The 92 m contour will lie on *BC* at 3_{BC}, 18.4 mm from *B*.

Locate points 1_{AD} for 84 m contour on *AD*, 1_{DC} for 86 m contour, 2_{DC} for 88 m contour, 3_{DC} for 90 m contour, and 4_{DC} for 92 m contour on *DC*, in similar manner as above. Join the points of equal elevation by smooth curves to get the contours of 84 m, 86 m, 88 m, 90 m, and 92 m elevations.

To achieve better accuracy interpolation along the diagonals *AC* and *BD* can also be done.

Mechanical or Graphical Method

There could be various approaches to interpolate the contours by mechanical or graphical method. One of such methods consists of drawing several parallel lines on a tracing paper or cloth. (Fig. 7.10) Every fifth or tenth line may be made thicker to facilitate easy counting.

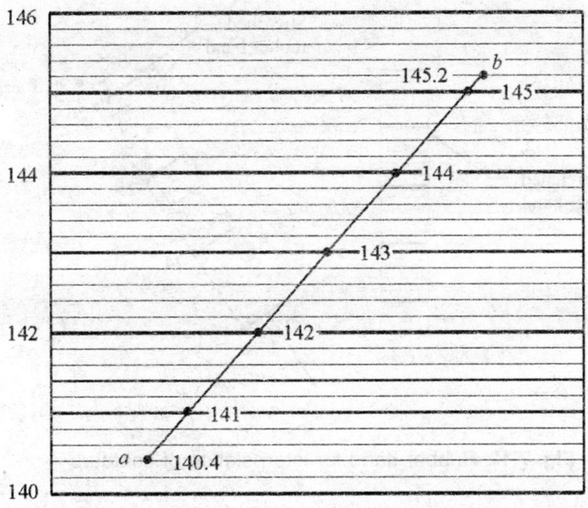

Fig. 7.10 Parallel lines for interpolation of contours

The tracing paper is adjusted so that the extremities *a* and *b* of the line of known reduced levels occupy a proportionate length. The required points are then the intersections with the corresponding horizontal lines.

Another method consists of drawing radial lines with boundaries and equally spaced guidelines on a tracing paper or cloth (Fig. 7.11). The tracing paper is so turned that the guide lines become parallel to the line *ab* and the line gets adjusted till the difference of levels matches. The required points on chosen contours are easily located now on the radial lines and pricked.

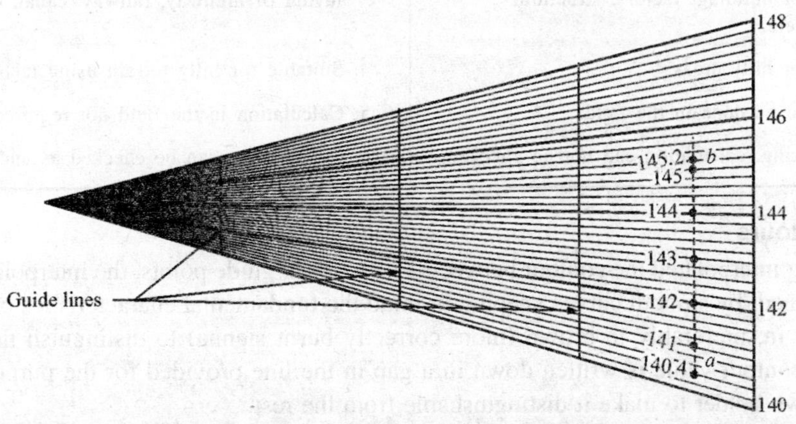

Fig. 7.11 Radial lines for interpolation of contours

A rubber band with a number of equal divisions marked on it, may also be used (Fig. 7.12). The band is stretched on the drawing sheet so that the appropriate number of divisions are intercepted between the points. Now the intermediate points can easily be located.

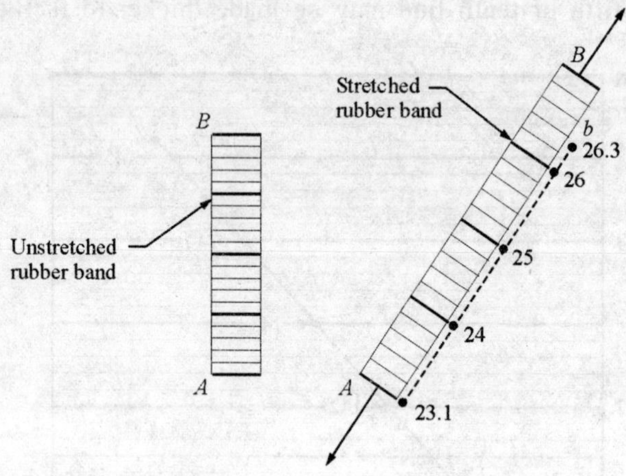

Fig. 7.12 Rubber band for interpolation of contours

Comparison of Direct and Indirect Methods of Contouring

Table 7.3 gives a comparison of direct and indirect methods of contouring.

Table 7.3 Comparison of direct and indirect methods of contouring

Direct Method	Indirect Method
1. Most accurate but slow and tedious.	1. Not very accurate but quicker and less tedious.
2. Expensive.	2. Very cheap.
3. Used for small projects requiring higher accuracy, *e.g.*, layout of building, factory, structural foundations, etc.	3. Used for large projects requiring lower accuracy, *e.g.*, layout of highway, railway, canal, etc.
4. Unsuitable for hilly areas.	4. Suitable for hilly terrain using tacheometry.
5. Calculation to be done in the field.	5. Calculation in the field not required.
6. After contouring, calculation can not be checked.	6. Calculations can be checked as and when needed.

Drawing contours

After having interpolated the contour between a network of guide points, the interpolated points on a contour are joined by smooth curves keeping in mind the fundamental characteristics of contour. They are then inked in, preferably in brown (more correctly burnt sienna) to distinguish them from other features. The contour value is written down in a gap in the line provided for the purpose. Every fifth contour is drawn bolder to make it distinguishable from the rest.

7.7 CONTOUR GRADIENT

An imaginary line on the surface of the earth having a constant inclination (slope) to the horizontal, is referred to as *contour gradient.* The inclination of a contour gradient is generally given either as rising gradient or falling gradient, and is expressed as ratio of the vertical height to a specified horizontal distance. If the inclination of a contour gradient is 1 in 50, it means that for every 50 m horizontal distance there is rise (or fall) of 1 m.

When the inclination of a contour gradient is given its direction from a point may be easily located either on the map or on the ground by the methods discussed below.

Locating Contour Gradient on a Map

With the aid of a contour plan, it is easy to trace a contour gradient of desired inclination on a paper, and even transfer it later to the ground.

To locate a rising gradient of 1 in 20 from a point *a* situated on 100 m contour (Fig. 7.13) on the map at a scale of 1:1000 with contour interval of 5 m, draw an arc of radius

$$= \frac{20 \times 5}{1000} = 10 \text{ cm}$$

with centre at *a*. The arc cuts the 105 m contour at *b*. Locate *c*, *d*, and *e* on 110 m, 115 m, and 120 m contours taking arcs of radius of 10 cm with centres at *b*, *c* and *d*, respectively. Join *a*, *b*, *c*, *d*, and *e*. The line *a* to *e* represents the contour gradient on the ground having constant slope of 1 in 20.

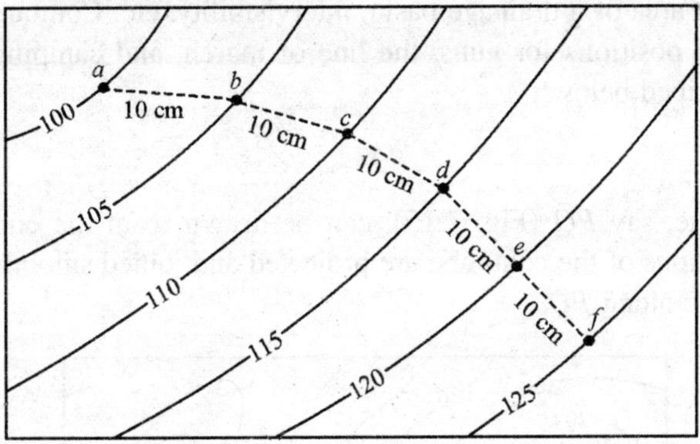

Fig. 7.13 Locating contour gradient on a map

Locating Contour Gradient on the Ground

To locate a rising gradient of 1 in 100 from the station *A* (Fig. 7.14), a level is set up at a commanding position, and back sight is taken at *A*. Let the back sight reading be 1.50 m. The staff reading at any point *p* on the contour gradient can be calculated using its distance from *A*. For the distance *Ap* of 50 m, the required staff reading would be

$$1.50 - \frac{50}{100} = 1.00 \text{ m}$$

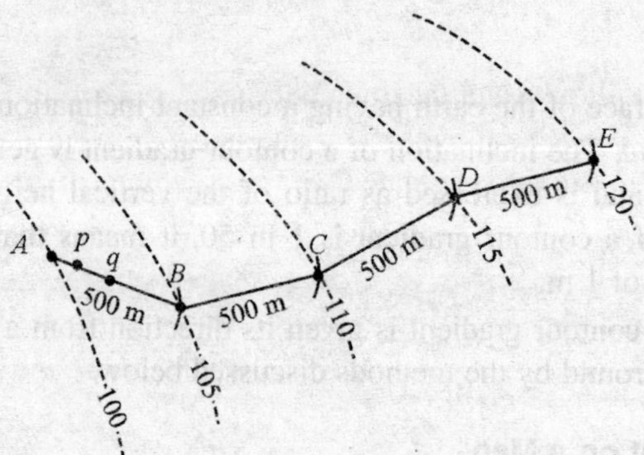

Fig. 7.14 Locating contour gradient on the ground

To locate the point *p* on the ground, the staffman holds the 50 m-mark of the tape, keeping the zero-mark at *A*, and moves till the staff reading of 1.00 m is obtained. Likewise, the staff readings for other points at known distance from *A*, are calculated and the points are located. If the point *B* is on the contour of 105 m, its distance from *A* would be 500 m in this case.

The instruments such as Indian clinometer, theodolite, and Ghat tracer (*c.f.*, Sec.7.9) may also be used for tracing the contour gradient on the ground.

7.8 USES OF CONTOUR MAPS

Contour maps provide valuable information about the character of the country, whether it is flat, undulating or mountainous. These information are used in civil engineering projects for selection of sites, determination of catchment area of a drainage basin, intervisibility, etc. Contour maps are also used in army for deciding the best positions for guns, the line of march, and camping grounds during War. Some of the uses are described below.

Cross-section

A section along any line, say *PQ* (Fig. 7.15), can be drawn from the contours. The horizontal locations at different elevations of the contours, are projected and joined smoothly to give the configuration of the ground surface along *PQ*.

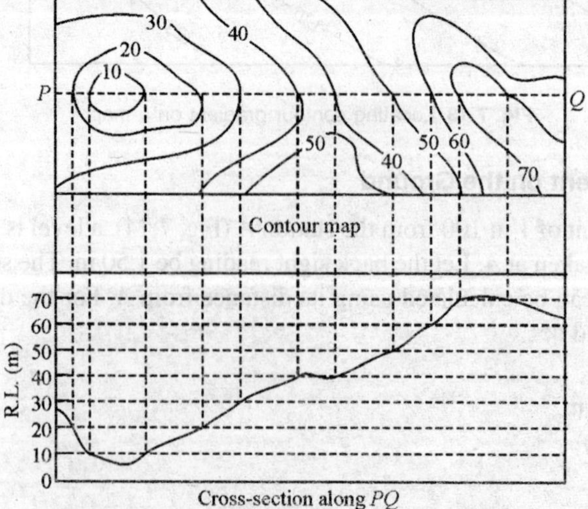

Fig. 7.15 Drawing a section from a contour map

Canal Alignment

Canals have down slope to allow water to flow under gravity. Therefore, the canal alignment should be below the reservoir level. Let *R* be the reservoir site at an elevation of 195 m approximately (Fig. 7.16), and the villages *M* and *N* are to be irrigated by constructing canals.

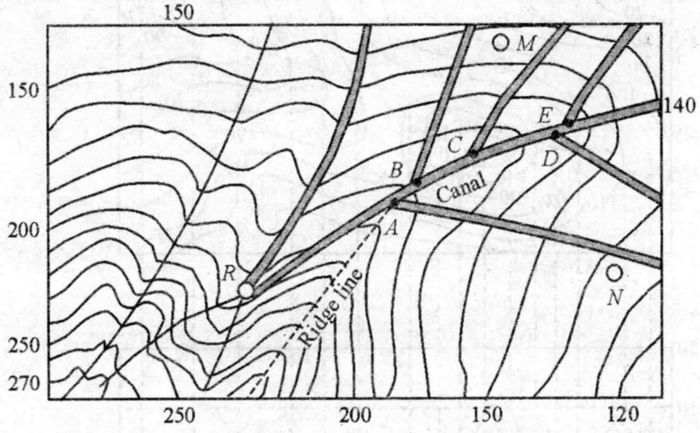

Fig. 7.16 Alignment of canals on a map

Mark the watershed or ridge line by dotted line. From *R*, the canal is taken along *R–A–B–C–D–E*, where *A, B, C, D,* and *E* are located on the watershed. Branch canals may also be located to cover the areas of both the villages. The canal alignment may be chosen by considering the other factors also to avoid construction of aquaducts over the intercepting drainages enroute.

Contour Gradients

On a contour map, the alignment of a proposed road or railway for a given contour gradient can easily be marked as explained in Sec. 7.7.

Intervisibility of Points

Sometimes the intervisibility between two points can be ascertained by inspection of the area on the map. When the intervening ground does not have contours of higher value than elevations of the two points, the points will be intervisible (Fig. 7.17).

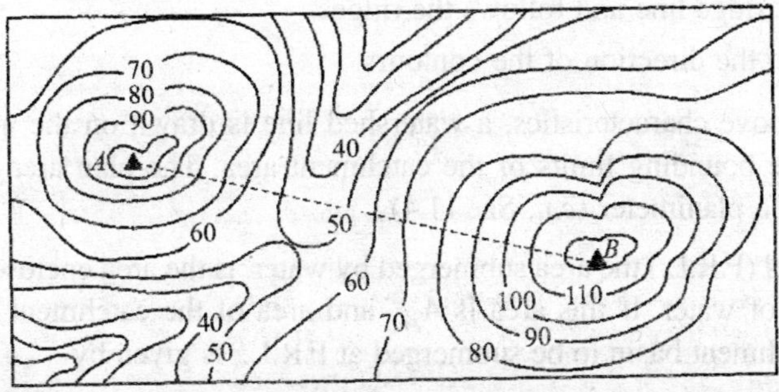

Fig. 7.17 Checking intervisibility by inspection

If the intervisibility is not evident from the inspection of the map, draw a line AB joining the points, and plot the elevations of the points on the contours where AB intersects the contours as shown in Fig. 7.18. If the intervening ground is found to be above $A'B'$ line, the intervisibility is obstructed, and if below, A and B are intervisible. In the present case, the ground is obstructing the line of sight.

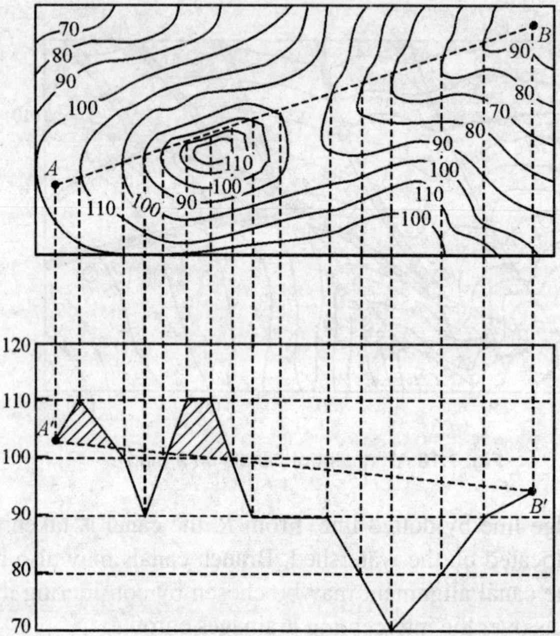

Fig. 7.18 Checking intervisibility by drawing a section

Catchment Area or Drainage Area

The tract of land which contributes water flow over the surface of the ground into river or stream at any point, is called *catchment* or *drainage area.*

The limits of the catchment area can be delineated sufficiently accurate on a contour map. The line forming the limit, separating the catchment area of a river from the rest of the area is called the *watershed line.* It possesses the following characteristics:

1. It follows the highest ridge line and follows the ridges.
2. It is at right angles to the direction of the contours.

Keeping in mind the above characteristics, a watershed line is drawn on the map (Fig. 7.19) with dashes or dots to mark the bounding limits of the catchment area. The plan area of the catchment is measured with the help of a planimeter (*c.f.,* See 11.4)

At the full reservoir level (F.R.L.) the area submerged by water, is the area enclosed by the water level when the reservoir is full of water. If this area is A_{FRL} and area of the catchment basin is A, then the percentage area of the catchment basin to be submerged at F.R.L., is given by

$$\frac{A_{FRL}}{A} \times 100\ \% \qquad \ldots(7.1)$$

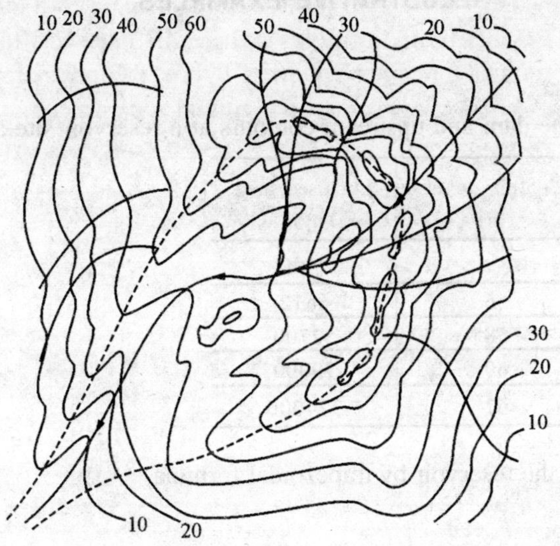

Fig. 7.19 A catchment area

Storage Capacity of a Reservoir

The contour line indicating the F.R.L. (Full Reservoir Level) is drawn on the contour map. The F.R.L. begins and ends at the dam. The volume of water between this line and the river bed is estimated by measuring the area enclosed by all contours lying between the river bed and F.R.L. contour using the following formulae:

1. Trapezoidal formula

$$V = h\left[\frac{A_1 + A_n}{2} + A_2 + A_3 ...... + A_{n-1}\right] \quad ...(7.2)$$

2. Prismoidal formula

$$V = \frac{h}{3}\left[A_1 + A_n + 4\left(A_2 + A_4 + ...\right) + 2\left(A_3 + A_5 + ...\right)\right] \quad ...(7.3)$$

where V = the volume or capacity of the reservoir

A_1 = the area enclosed by F.R.L. contour

$A_2, A_3, ..., A_n$ = the area enclosed by other successive contours, and

h = the contour interval.

ILLUSTRATIVE EXAMPLES

Example 7.1

Areas enclosed between the dam and upstream contours at a reservoir site are as follows:

Contour level (m)	Enclosed area (sq.m)
54	714
56	6512
58	52700
60	79000
62	374000

Determine the capacity of the reservoir by trapezoidal formula.

Solution:

Volume of the reservoir by trapezoidal formula is

$$V = h\left[\frac{A_1 + A_5}{2} + A_2 + A_3 + A_4\right]$$

Contour interval $h = 2$ m

$$V = 2\times\left[\frac{0.714+374.0}{2} + 6.512 + 52.7 + 79.0\right]\times 1000$$

$= \mathbf{65113.8\ m^3}$.

Example 7.2

Using a topographical map, the areas enclosed within contour lines and along the face of a proposed dam, are as given as follows :

Contour (m)	Area (sq.m.)
200	305500
190	257000
180	200000
170	160500
160	135400
150	96500
140	55500
130	8000
120	500

It is proposed that the storage capacity of the reservoir between the lowest draw down (L.D.D.) and top water level (T.W.L.) should be 80 million cu.m. If L.D.D. is to be 124 m what would be the T.W.L. for full storage capacity?

Solution:

(*i*) Area contained in 124 m contour

Contour interval = 10 m

Difference in areas of contours of 120 m and 130 m

= 8000 – 500 = 7500 sq.m

The height of 124 m contour from 120 m contour is 4 m.

For a 10 m height, the difference in area = 7500 sq.m

For a 4 m height the difference in area

$$= \frac{4}{10} \times 7500 = 3000 \text{ sq.m}$$

The area contained in 124 m contour

= area contained in 120 m contour + 3000

= 500 + 3000

= 3500 sq.m.

(*ii*) Volume of water between 124 m and 130 m contours

$$V_1 = (130 - 124)\left[\frac{3500 + 8000}{2}\right]$$

= 34500 cu.m.

(*iii*) Let the T.W.L. for full capacity be above 190 m.

Volume of water contained between 130 m and 190 m contours

$$V_2 = 10 \times \left[\frac{8.0 + 257.0}{2} + 55.5 + 96.5 + 135.4 + 160.5 + 200.0\right] \times 1000$$

= 7804000 cu.m

Total volume between 124 m and 190 m

= V_1 + V_2 = 34500 + 7804000

= 7838500 cu.m

Volume short of target

= 8000000 – 7838500

= 161500 cu.m.

(*iv*) If the height of water level above 190 m contour be y to meet the shortage of 161500 cu.m then y is determined as below.

Difference in areas of 200 m and 190 m contours

$$= 305500 - 257000$$

$$= 48500 \text{ sq.m}$$

Difference in area of (190 + y) m and 190 m contours

$$= \frac{y}{10} \times 48500 \text{ sq.m}$$

Area contained in (190 + y) m contour

$$= \left[257000 + \frac{y}{10} 48500\right] \text{ sq.m}$$

Volume of water between (190 + y) m and 190 m contours

$$V = \frac{y}{2}\left[\left(257000 + \frac{y}{10} 48500\right) + 257000\right]$$

This additional volume V of the water is equal to 161500 cu.m.

Therefore $$\frac{y}{2}\left[\left(257000 + \frac{y}{10} 48500\right) + 257000\right] = 161500$$

or $$257y + 2.425y^2 = 161.5$$

or $$24.25y^2 + 257y - 161.5 = 0$$

or $$y = \frac{-257 \pm \sqrt{257^2 - 4 \times 2.425 \times 161.5}}{2 \times 24.25}$$

$$= 0.63 \text{ m.}$$

Water level for full capacity = 190 + 0.67 = **190.67 m.**

7.9 GHAT TRACER

The instrument is also known as Cylon Ghat Tracer. It is a simple instrument and extensively used for locating a number of points on a given gradient, *i.e.*, on a contour gradient during preliminary route surveys. It is also used for measuring grades or angles of slopes.

The instrument essentially consists of a long circular tube having an eye hole on one end and a cross-wires at the other end (Fig. 7.20). The tube is supported by a A-frame having a hole at its top to suspend the instrument from a straight rod or stand. With a suitable rack and pinion arrangement, a heavy weight slides along the tube. The weight at its top contains one bevelled edge which slides along the graduations of the scale attached to the tube and serves as an index. The line of sight of the instrument is defined by the line joining the eye-hole to the intersection of the cross-wires. The line of sight will be horizontal when the instrument reads zero. The weight is slided towards the observer for having rising gradient, and away from the observer for falling gradient.

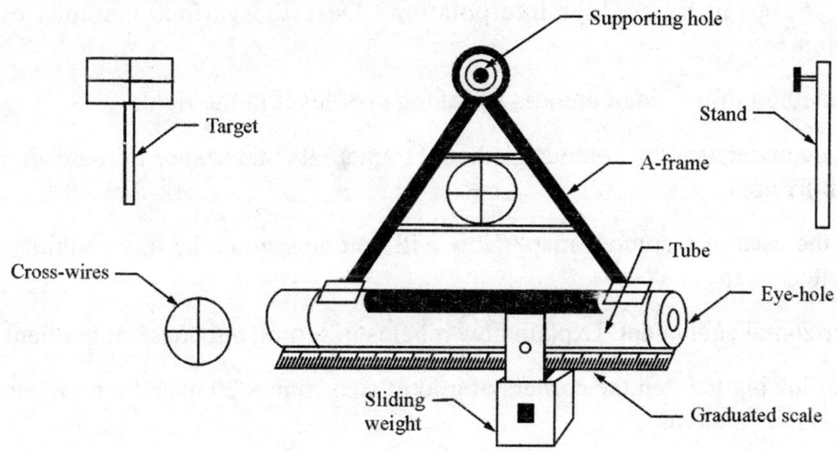

Fig. 7.20 Ghat tracer

Measuring a Gradient

To measure a gradient or slope, fix the instrument on the stand, and hold it at one end of the line whose gradient is to be measured. Keep the target at the other end of the line. Looking through the eye hole, the sliding weight is moved till the target is bisected by the line of sight. The reading against the bevelled edge of the weight, is the gradient of the line.

Setting out a Gradient

To set out a gradient or to trace a contour gradient on the ground, the instrument is held at one end of the line, and the assistant moves to the other end of the line with the target. The weight is set to the given gradient say 1 in n, and the assistant is directed to raise or lower the target till it is bisected. The foot of the target is pegged. The instrument is shifted to the peg, and repeat the above process to fix another points on the given gradient.

QUESTIONS AND PROBLEMS

7.1 Define contour. What do you understand by contour interval and on what factors does it depend?

7.2 Draw neat sketches of the pattern of contours that show
(*i*) An overhanging cliff, (*ii*) a depression, (*iii*) a pond, (*iv*) area having flat slope, (*v*) area having uniform steep slope, (*vi*) a ridge line, (*vii*) a saddle, (*viii*) a valley, (*ix*) a plateau, (*x*) a vertical cliff, (*xi*) a hillock.

7.3 Define contour and discuss characteristics of contours giving suitable sketches.

7.4 What is meant by contouring? Describe various methods of contouring, and discuss their merits and demerits.

7.5 Differentiate between direct and indirect methods of contouring.

7.6 What do you mean by contour interpolation? Describe various methods of contour interpolation.

7.7 Describe method of plotting contours by taking spot level in the field.

7.8 What do you understand by contour gradient? Explain its importance in route alignment for a road in hilly area.

7.9 What are the uses of a contour map? How will you determine the intervisibility of points from a contour map.

7.10 Define horizontal equivalent. Explain how it helps in setting out constant gradient of a line.

7.11 Take the following R.L. on the corners of grid of size 20 m × 20 m and interpolate contours with 5m contour interval:

11.0	16.0	25.0	33.0	41.0	48.0
20.0	17.0	24.0	35.0	45.0	46.0
30.0	31.0	26.0	28.0	35.0	35.0
36.0	41.0	31.0	19.0	29.0	28.0
44.0	40.0	30.0	13.0	20.0	21.0
42.0	33.0	25.0	13.0	08.0	11.0

7.12 The areas enclosed by contours at the site of a reservoir and the face of the proposed dam, are as given below.

Contour (m)	Area (sq.m)
800	450
805	1680
810	2900
815	9500
820	17000
825	27400
830	45500

If bottom level of the reservoir is 800 m and highest level acheivable is 830 m, compute the storage capacity of the reservoir by (*a*) trapezoidal formula and (*b*) prismoidal formula.

7.13 The areas enclosed by contours on the upstream face of a dam in a proposed hydro-electric project, are tabulated below:

Contour value (m)	Area enclosed (sq.m)
1000	314100
990	267400
980	248900
970	222300
960	193700
950	177400
940	129100
930	53500

Considering the lowest draw down level to be 933 m, compute the total volume at 1000 m.

7.14 In a proposed hydro-electric project a storage reservoir was required to provide a storage of 5.9 million cu.m between lowest draw down and top water level. The areas contained within the stated contours and upstream face of the dam, were as follows:

Contour (m)	200	195	190	185	180	175	170	165
Area (hectare)	44	34	28	23	20	16	11	8

If the lowest draw down was to be 167 m, calculate the top water level in the following cases:

(i) Full storage capacity of reservoir

(ii) 70% storage capacity of reservoir.

7.15 Mark the following topographic features on a contour map shown in Fig. 7.21.

(i) Valley, (ii) Saddle points, (iii) Stream, (iv) Ridge line, (v) Watershed.

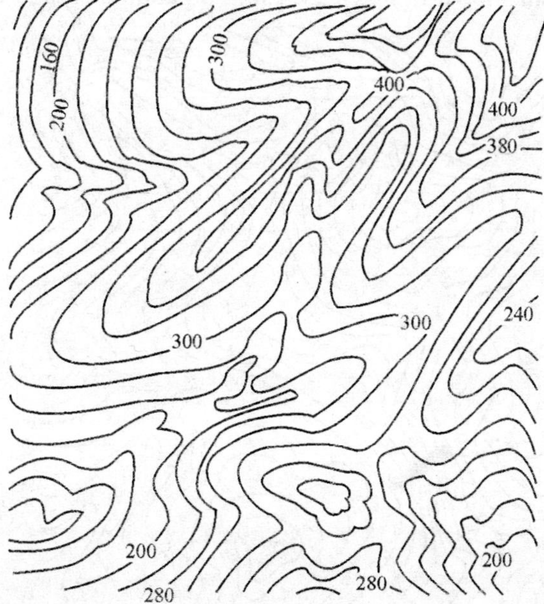

Fig. 7.21

7.16 Draw sections A_1A_2, B_1B_2, and C_1C_2 from the contour map shown in Fig.7.22.

Fig. 7.22

7.17 Measure the areas contained within the contours having elevation of 150 m to 120 m on the upstream of the dam shown in Fig.7.23, using a planimeter, and calculate the reservoir capacity.

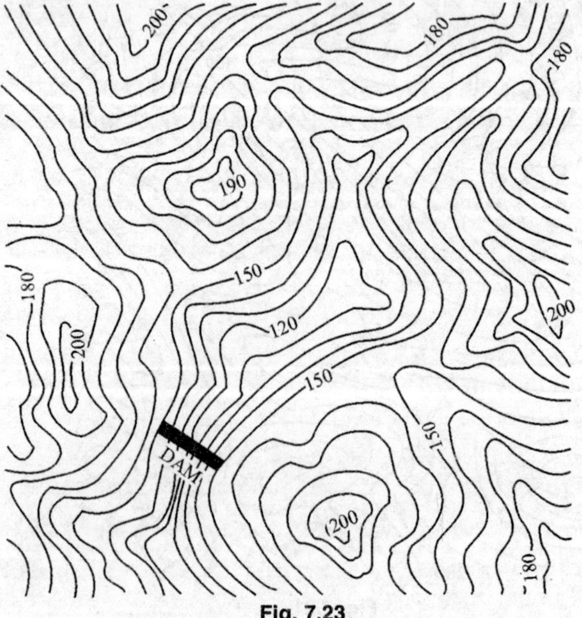

Fig. 7.23

8

TACHEOMETRY

8.1 GENERAL

Tacheometry is an indirect method by which horizontal distances and differences in elevation are determined using subtended intervals and angles observed with a transit or theodolite on a graduated scale. The word tacheometry is derived from the Greek words ταχυs (tachus) meaning swift, and μετρον (metron) meaning measure. As the name implies, the methods of tacheometric surveying are very rapid but are usually of a lower order of accuracy than is possible by conventional methods such as taping, differential levelling, etc. However, the results are very adequate for many purposes where taping is difficult. Tacheometry eliminates operation of taping, therefore, it is very useful for rough terrains such as ravines, river, valleys, steep slopes, broken grounds, stretches of water or swamps.

Stadia is a tacheometric form of distance measurement that relies on fixed angle intercept.

8.2 USES OF TACHEOMETRY

The tacheometric methods of surveying are used with advantage over the direct methods of measurement of horizontal distances and differences in elevations. Some of the uses are:

1. Preparation of topographic maps which require both elevations and horizontal distances.
2. Survey work in difficult terrain where direct methods are inconvenient.
3. Detail filling.
4. Reconnaissance surveys for highways, railways, etc.
5. Checking of already measured distances.
6. Hydrographic surveys, and
7. Establishing secondary control.

8.3 PRINCIPLE OF STADIA MEASUREMENTS

For the measurement of stadia distances, the reticle or diaphragm in the telescope of the theodolite (some levels) is equipped with two additional horizontal hairs (Fig. 8.1a) in addition to the normal cross-hairs, one above and the other below the main horizontal hair. These additional horizontal hairs are known as *stadia hairs*. Let us assume that the telescope is external focussing type and the line of sight is horizontal. In Fig. 8.1b, *a* and *b* represent the two stadia hairs, and *A* and *B* the corresponding points on the staff and *c*, is the middle horizontal hair having its corresponding point *C* on the staff.

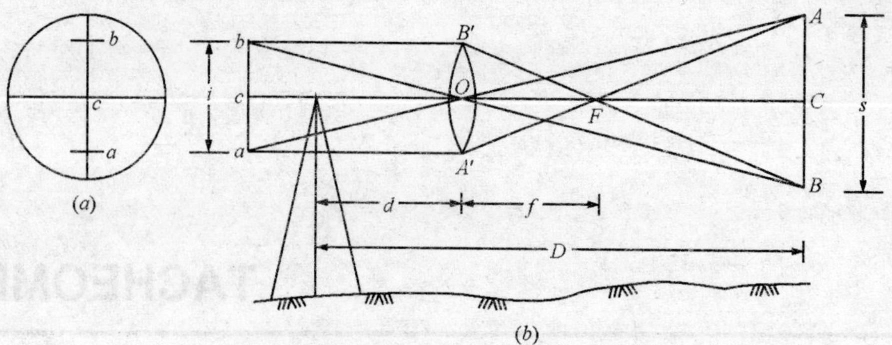

Fig. 8.1 Principle of transit stadia measurement

Let f = focal length OF of the object length

i = stadia hair interval ab

s = staff interval AB

D = horizontal distance of the staff from the instrument axis

d = distance of the optical centre of the object glass from the instrument axis.

From similar $\Delta^s A'B'F$ and ABF, we get

$$\frac{CF}{OF} = \frac{AB}{A'B'}$$

or $$CF = OF\frac{AB}{A'B'}$$

We have $A'B' = ab$

$$CF = OF\frac{AB}{ab}$$

Substituting the value of AB, OF, and ab, we have

$$CF = \frac{f}{i}s$$

But $D = CF + f + d$

or $$= \frac{f}{i}s + (f + d) \qquad ...(8.1)$$

Substituting k for $\frac{f}{i}$ and c for $(f + d)$, the Eq. (8.1) becomes

$$D = ks + c \qquad ...(8.2)$$

In Eq. (8.2), k and c are known as the *tacheometric constants*.

To make the computations simple, the stadia hairs are positioned in the reticle so that if a levelling staff or rod is held 100 m away from the theodolite, the difference between the upper and lower stadia hair readings on the staff, would be exactly 1.00 m for an internal focussing instruments. Figure 8.2 shows reticles with different patterns of stadia hairs used in theodolite.

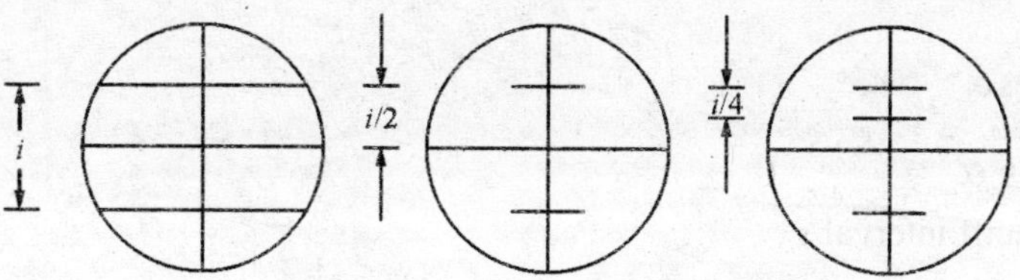

Fig. 8.2 Reticles with different patterns of stadia hairs

Generally, the values of the multiplying constant k and the additive constant c are kept equal to 100 and 0 (zero), respectively. With these values of k and c, the distance can be determined simply by sighting a staff with the telescope horizontal and determining the staff interval (Fig 8.3). The staff interval is then multiplied by 100 to get the horizontal distance, i.e.,

$$D = 100\ s \qquad \text{...(8.3)}$$

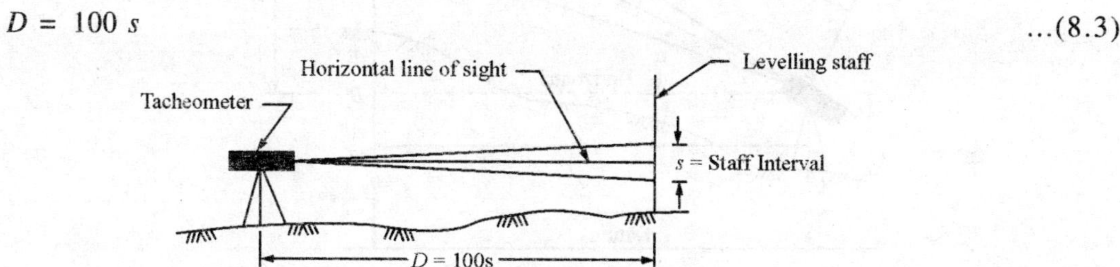

Fig. 8.3 Horizontal distance by stadia method

Elevations are obtained by stadia by determining the height of the instrument (H.I.) and middle hair reading on the staff. The computation of the elevation of B, if the elevation of the instrument station A is known, is illustrated in (Fig. 8.4).

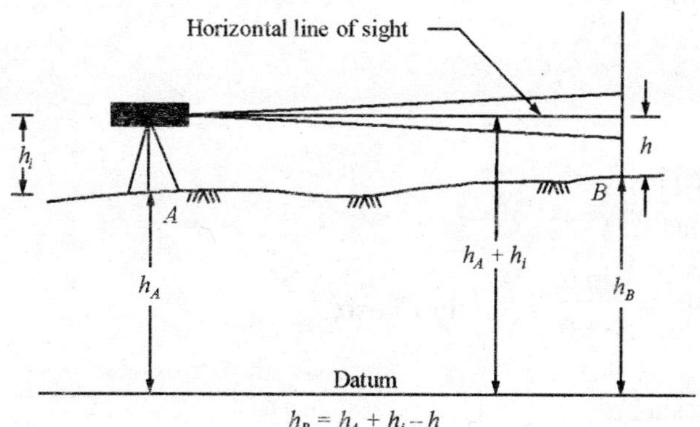

Fig. 8.4 Elevation by stadia method

Inclined Stadia Measurements

The stadia method is particularly well suited for the inclined sights required by rolling topography.

When the telescope is inclined up or down (Fig. 8.5) the computations must account for the inclined sights. For an internal focussing telescope having $c = 0$, and considering the angles $CM'M$ and $CN'N$ as right angles,

$$CM' = CM \cos\alpha$$

or $$\frac{s'}{2} = \frac{s}{2}\cos\alpha$$

or $$s' = s \cos \alpha \qquad ...(8.4)$$

Where $M'N'$ is the staff interval s'.

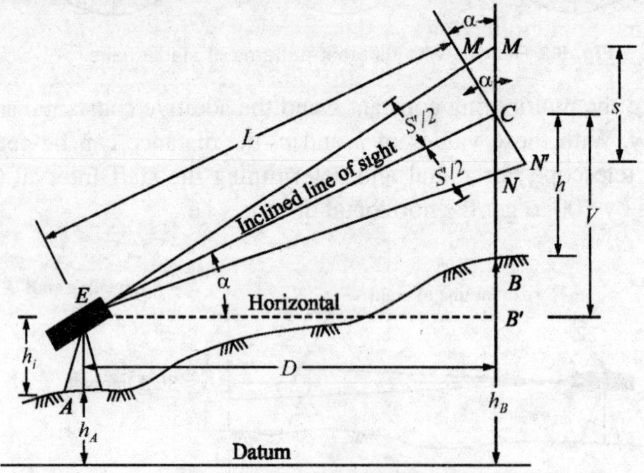

Fig. 8.5 Inclined stadia measurement (c = 0)

The slope distance L from Eq. (8.2) taking $c = 0$ is given by

$$L = ks'$$

or $$= ks \cos\alpha \qquad ...(8.5)$$

and the horizontal distance by

$$D = L \cos\alpha$$

From Eq. (8.5), we have

$$D = ks \cos^2\alpha \qquad ...(8.6)$$

The vertical distance is given by

$$CB' = V = D \tan\alpha$$

$$= ks \cos^2 \alpha \frac{\sin \alpha}{\cos \alpha} = ks \sin\alpha \cos\alpha$$

$$= \frac{1}{2} ks \sin 2\alpha \qquad ...(8.7)$$

The elevation h_B of B is equal to the elevation of instrument axis + V – middle-hair reading, *i.e.*,

$$h_B = h_A + h_i + V - h \qquad ...(8.8)$$

8.4 TACHEOMETER AND STADIA RODS

A *tacheometer* is a theodolite or transit, fitted with a stadia reticle or diaphragm discussed in Sec.8.3.

For short distances, say upto 100 m or so, an ordinary vernier theodolite with stadia diaphragm may be used. For long sights, tacheometers with high magnifying power are used for accurate readings. The aperture of the objective of such tacheometers is quite large so as to have a bright image. The multiplying constant k of a tacheometer is mostly 100. The additive constant is either zero or negligible. The tacheometers having external focussing telescopes, are provided with an anallactic lens to make the additive constant equal to zero.

Stadia rods are the levelling staffs having uniform graduations. For short distances ordinary levelling staff with 5 mm graduations can be used. For long distances a stadia rod, 3 to 5 m long, 50 to 150 mm wide having simple and bold graduations as shown in Fig. 8.6, for taking readings from long distances is used.

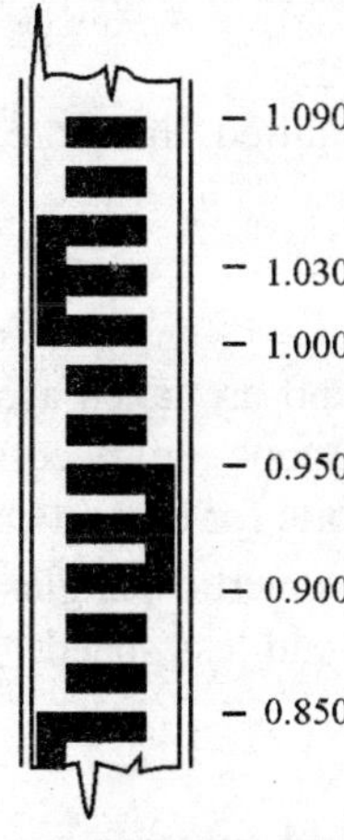

Fig. 8.6 Stadia rod

8.5 BASIC SYSTEMS OF TACHEOMETRIC MEASUREMENTS

There are two following basic systems of tacheometric measurements:

1. Stadia systems
   (a) Fixed-hair method
   (b) Movable-hair method.
2. Non-stadia systems
   (a) Tangential system
   (b) Subtense bar system.

Stadia Systems

The principle of stadia system has already been discussed in Sec. 8.3.

The two methods of stadia system are discussed below.

Fixed-hair method

In this method, stadia hairs are kept at fixed interval, and the staff interval or intercept on the levelling staff varies, depending upon the horizontal distance between the instrument station and the staff. This is the most common method in tacheometry, and the name stadia-hair method generally refers to this method, unless mentioned otherwise.

Movable-hair method

In this method, the staff interval is kept constant by changing the distance between the stadia hairs. Targets on the staff at a known fixed distance apart are fixed and the stadia hairs are adjusted such that the upper hair bisects the upper target and the lower hair bisects the lower one. Instruments used for this system of tacheometry, have provision for the measurement of the variable interval between the stadia hairs.

As it is inconvenient to measure the stadia interval accurately, the movable-hair method is rarely used.

Non-stadia Systems

In this system, the stadia hairs are not required, therefore, the telescopes not provided with a stadia diaphragm can be used.

Tangential system

In the tangential system, readings on a staff are taken against the horizontal cross hair. To measure the staff intercept, two pointings of the telescope are necessary. Readings to full metre values on the staff are generally taken to avoid decimal parts for ease in computations.

The method is generally not adopted as two vertical angles are required to be measured for one single observation. It involves more computations and less speed.

Subtense bar system

In this system, a bar of fixed length, called a subtense bar is used (*c.f.*, Sec 8.9). The bar is placed in horizontal position, and the angle subtended at the instrument station by the two targets of the subtense bar is measured. The horizontal distance between the subtense bar and the instrument is computed from the known distance between the targets and the measured subtended horizontal angle.

ILLUSTRATIVE EXAMPLES

Example 8.1

The following readings were taken with a transit fitted with stadia hairs. The line of sight was horizontal and the staff was held vertical.

	Reading on staff (m)
Top hair	0.875
Middle hair	1.340
Bottom hair	1.805

If the tacheometric constants k and c have the value as 100 and 0.20 m, respectively, what is the horizontal distance between the staff and the instrument?

Solution:

From Eq. (8.2), we get

$$D = ks + c$$

$$s = 1.805 - 0.875 = 0.930 \text{ m}$$

$$D = 100 \times 0.930 + 0.20 = \mathbf{93.200 \text{ m}}.$$

Example 8.2

Taking the data from Example 8.1, determine the R.L. of the staff station if the R.L. of the instrument station is 201.20 m and the height of the instrument above the ground is 1.51 m.

Solution:

From Fig. 8.4, we have

$$h_B = h_A + h_i - h$$

$$= 201.20 + 1.51 - 1.340 = \mathbf{201.37\ m.}$$

Example 8.3

To determine the distance between two points P and Q, and the R.L. of Q, the following observations were made:

Height of tacheometer at P = 1.480 m
Vertical angle at P = + 5°20′
Staff readings (with staff vertical) = 0.545, 0.905, 1.265
R.L. of P = 150.000 m
k = 100.00
c = 0.00 m.

Solution (Fig. 8.7):

From Eq. (8.6), we have

$$D = ks \cos^2\alpha$$

We have

$$s = 1.265 - 0.545 = 0.720 \text{ m}$$

$$\alpha = +\ 5°20'$$

$$D = 100 \times 0.720 \times \cos^2 5°20' = \mathbf{71.378\ m.}$$

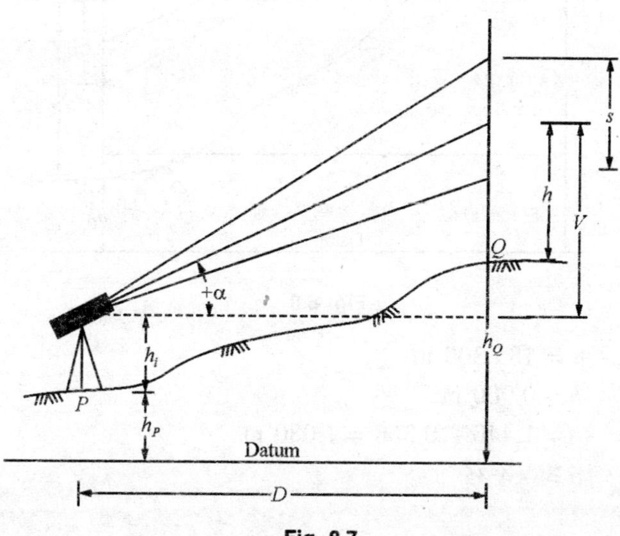

Fig. 8.7

From Eq. (8.8), we have

R.L. of $Q = h_p + h_i + V - h$

We have $h_i = 1.480$ m

$h = 0.905$ m

From Eq. (8.7), we get

$$V = \frac{1}{2} ks \sin 2\alpha$$

$$= \frac{1}{2} \times 100 \times 0.720 \times \sin (2 \times 5°20') = 6.663 \text{ m}$$

R.L. of $Q = 150.000 + 1.480 + 6.663 - 0.905 =$ **157.238 m.**

Example 8.4

Determine the distance between the points P and Q from the following data:

R.L. of the tacheometer axis at $P = 185.300$ m.

Vertical angle at $P = -4°35'$

Staff readings at $Q = 1.440, 0.900, 0.360$

Also determine the R.L.of Q if the staff at Q was held vertical, and $k = 100$ and $c = 0.00$ m.

Solution (Fig. 8.8):

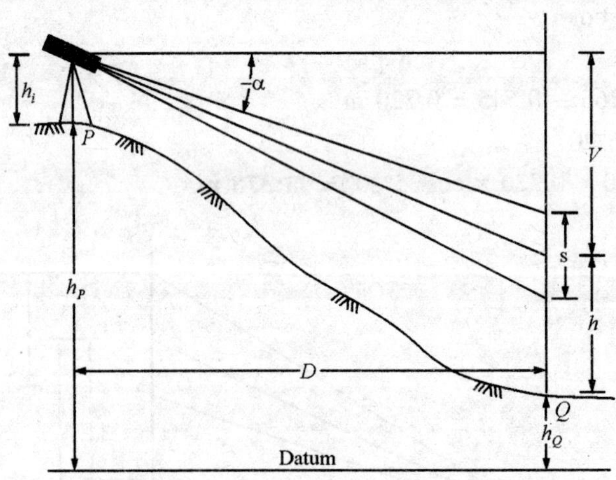

Fig. 8.8

We have $h_p + h_i = 185.300$ m

$h = 0.900$ m

$s = 1.440 - 0.360 = 1.080$ m

$\alpha = -4°35'$

From Eq. (8.6), we get

$$D = 100 \times 1.080 \times \cos^2 4°35' = 107.310 \text{ m}$$

From Eq. (8.7), we get

$$V = \frac{1}{2} \times 100 \times 1.080 \times \sin(2 \times (-4°35'))$$

$$= -8.603 \text{ m}$$

R.L. of Q $\quad h_Q = h_P + h_i + V - h$

$$= 185.300 - 8.603 - 0.900$$

$$= \mathbf{175.797 \text{ m}}.$$

Example 8.5

To determine the distance between two stations A and B, a tacheometer was set up at a point P on the line AB and the following observations were made:

(*a*) When the staff was held at A

Staff readings = 2.225, 2.605, 2.985

Vertical angle = + 8°24′

(*b*) When the staff was held at B

Staff readings = 1.640, 1.920, 2.200

Vertical angle = – 1°06′

Also determine the R.L. of B if the R.L. of A is 315.673 m (k = 100.00 and c = 0.00).

Solution (Fig. 8.9):

We have $\quad s_1 = 2.985 - 2.225 = 0.760$ m

$s_2 = 2.200 - 1.640 = 0.560$ m

$h_1 = 2.605$ m

$h_2 = 1.920$ m

$\alpha_1 = +8°24'$

$\alpha_2 = -1°06'$

$D_1 = 100 \times 0.760 \times \cos^2 8°24' = 74.378$ m

$D_2 = 100 \times 0.560 \times \cos^2 1°06' = 55.979$ m

Distance $\quad AB = D_1 + D_2 = 74.378 + 55.979 =$ **130.357 m.**

also $\quad V_1 = 1/2 \times 100 \times 0.760 \times \sin(2 \times 8°24') = 10.983$ m

$V_2 = 1/2 \times 100 \times 0.560 \times \sin(2 \times 1°06') = 1.075$ m

The R.L. of the instrument axis is

$$= h_A + h_1 - V_1$$

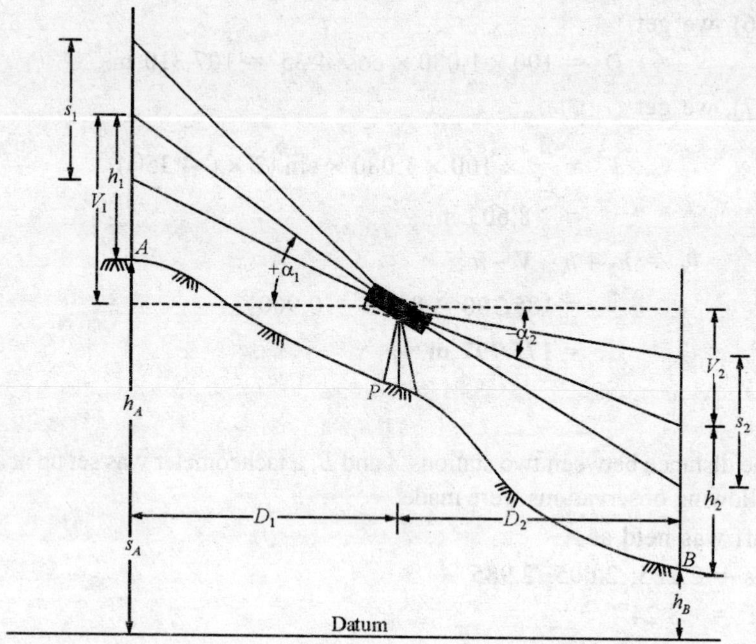

Fig. 8.9

The R.L. of B is

$$h_B = \text{R.L. of the instrument axis} - V_2 - h_2$$
$$= h_A + h_1 - V_1 - V_2 - h_2$$
$$= 315.673 + 2.605 - 10.983 - 1.075 - 1.920$$
$$= \mathbf{304.300\ m.}$$

Example 8.6

The vertical angles to vanes fixed at 1 m and 3 m above the foot of the staff held vertically at a station A, were + 2°15′ and + 5°50′, respectively. Determine the horizontal distance and reduced level of A if the height of the instrument axis is 235.665 m above datum.

Solution (Fig. 8.10):

We have $h_1 = 1$ m

$h_2 = 3$ m

$\alpha_1 = +\,2°15'$

$\alpha_2 = +\,5°50'$

$V_1 = D \tan \alpha_1$

$V_2 = D \tan \alpha_2$

but $V_2 - V_1 = h_2 - h_1 = 3 - 1 = 2$ m

$D\,(\tan \alpha_2 - \tan \alpha_1) = 2$

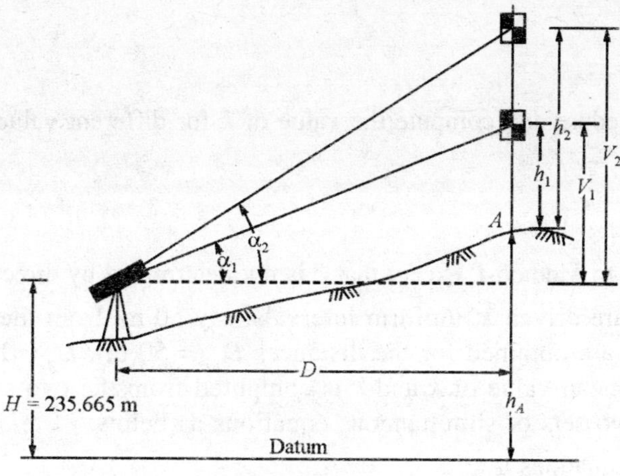

Fig. 8.10

or $D = \dfrac{2}{\tan 5°50' - \tan\ 2°15'} = 31.810 \text{ m}$

Thus,

$V_1 = 31.810 \times \tan 2°\ 15'$

$= 1.250$ m

The R.L. of A, $h_A = H + V_1 - h_1$

$= 235.665 + 1.250 - 1.000$

$=$ **235.915 m.**

8.6 DETERMINATION OF TACHEOMETRIC CONSTANTS

The following two field methods are most common for determining the values of the tacheometric constants k and c.

Method-I

In this method, c is determined by directly measuring f and d (Fig. 8.1), and k by field observations.

(*a*) Measure the distance between the object glass and the plane of the cross-hairs with an accurate scale. This distance is approximately equal to f. Then measure accurately the distance between the object glass and the vertical axis of the instrument. This is equal to d. The value $(f + d)$ is equal to c.

(*b*) Set up the instrument at any point P and level it. Sight any distant object Q and focus the instrument using focussing screw. Measure the distance PQ. Read the staff interval s for top and bottom stadia hairs for horizontal line of sight.

Let PQ is equal to D. From Eq. (8.2), we get

$$D = ks + c$$

or $$k = \frac{D - c}{s} \quad \text{...(8.9)}$$

Repeat the above procedure and compute the value of k for different values of D. Determine the mean value of k.

Method-II

This method is similar to Method-I, except that c is not determined by direct measurements.

In this method pegs are driven at uniform intervals, say 50 m, from the instrument, and staff reading s_1, s_2, s_3, and s_4 are obtained for the distances D_1 (= 50 m), D_2 (=100 m), D_3 (= 150 m), and D_4 (= 200 m). The mean value of k and c is computed from the two sets of values of k and c obtained by solving two sets of simultaneous equations as below.

Set-I of simultaneous equations is

$$D_1 = k_1 s_1 + c_1$$

$$D_2 = k_1 s_2 + c_1$$

Set-II of simultaneous equations is

$$D_3 = k_2 s_3 + c_2$$

$$D_4 = k_2 s_4 + c_2$$

The mean values of k and c are

$$k = \frac{k_1 + k_2}{2}$$

and $$c = \frac{c_1 + c_2}{2}.$$

ILLUSTRATIVE EXAMPLES

Example 8.7

To determine the tacheometric constants of a transit fitted with stadia hairs, the following observations were taken on a staff held vertically at distances measured from the instrument:

Horizontal distance (m)	50	100	150
Staff interval (m)	0.495	0.998	1.500

The line of sight was kept horizontal. The focal length of the object glass is 20 cm and the distance of the objective glass from the trunion axis of the instrument is 11 cm. Determine the values of k and c.

Solution:

We know that

$$c = f + d$$
$$= 20 + 11 = \mathbf{0.31\ m}.$$

and $D = ks + c$

$$\text{or } k = \frac{D-c}{s}$$

(i) For D = 50 m and s = 0.495 m

$$k = \frac{50-0.31}{0.495} = 100.383$$

(ii) For D = 100 m and s = 0.998 m

$$k = \frac{100-0.31}{0.998} = 99.890$$

(iii) For D = 150 m and s = 1.500

$$k = \frac{150-0.31}{1.500} = 99.793$$

$$\text{Mean value of } k = \frac{1}{3} \times (100.383 + 99.890 + 99.793)$$

$$= \mathbf{100.022}.$$

Example 8.8

The following are the distances of the staff positions from the instrument and the corresponding staff intervals. Calculate the tacheometric constants.

D (m)	20	50	100	120
s (m)	0.195	0.495	0.997	1.197

Solution:

$$D = ks + c$$

Taking first set of equations as

$$20 = k \times 0.195 + c$$

$$50 = k \times 0.495 + c$$

and solving them we get

$$k = 100 \text{ and } c = 0.5$$

Taking second set of equations as

$$100 = k \times 0.997 + c$$

$$120 = k \times 1.197 + c$$

and solving them, we get

$$k = 100 \text{ and } c = 0.3$$

The mean values of k and c are

$$k = \mathbf{100}$$

$$c = \frac{0.5+0.3}{2} = \mathbf{0.4 \text{ m}}.$$

8.7 BEAMAN STADIA ARC

The Beaman stadia arc is a mechanical attachment (Fig. 8.11) which is fitted to the vertical circle of transits and telescopic alidades (*cf.*, Sec 10.3). It is used to determine horizontal distances and differences in elevation by stadia without reading the vertical angles and without use of tables. The stadia arc has no vernier but settings are read by an index mark.

Principle of Beaman stadia arc

The *V*-scale of the Beaman stadia arc gives the vertical component between the staff position and the instrument station, *i.e.*, $V = \frac{1}{2}ks\sin(2\alpha)$ from Eq. (8.7). For $k = 100$ and $c = 0.00$, *V* is equal to ($50s$ ($\sin 2\alpha$)). The *V*-scale is so graduated that the vertical distance is obtained by multiplying the staff interval *s* with the ($R_V - 50$) where R_V is the vertical scale reading which gives the value of ($50 \sin 2\alpha$). It is so, because the *V*-scale reading for telescope horizontal is 50 instead of 0. When the telescope is elevated the reading is greater than 50 and when depressed, less than 50. Therfore, in all cases, 50 is subtracted from the reading of the stadia arc.

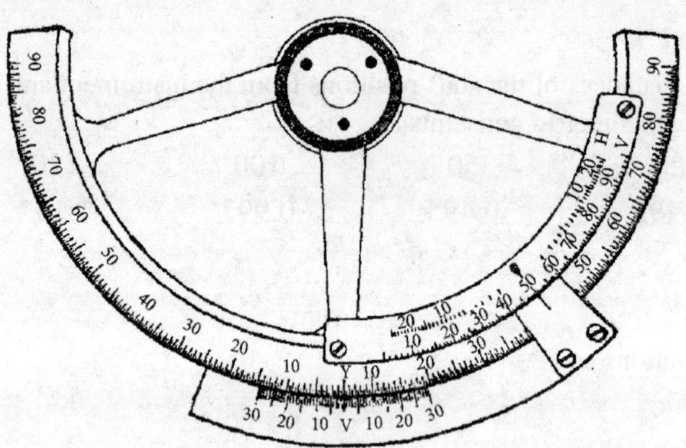

Fig. 8.11 Beaman stadia arc

For example, if the *V*-Scale reading is 52, and *s* is 2.50 m, the vertical distance *V* is given by

$$V = 2.50 \times (52 - 50)$$
$$= 5.00 \text{ m.}$$

The *H*-scale gives the value of $k \cos^2 \alpha$, and it is multiplied by *s*, and subtracted from *ks* to get the horizontal distance, *i.e.*,

$$D = ks - sk\cos^2\alpha$$
$$= ks - sR_H$$
$$= s(k - R_H)$$

where R_H is the horizontal scale reading, *i.e.*, $k \cos^2 \alpha$.

For $k = 100$, we have

$$D = s\ (100 - R_H) \qquad \text{... (8.10)}$$

If we write

$$D = 100s - s\ (100 \cos^2 \alpha\ ) \qquad \text{...(8.11)}$$

the second term in Eq. (8.11) can be said to be a percentage correction to 100*s*.

For example, if the *H*-scale reading is 0.54 and *s* is 2.00, the horizontal distance will be

$$D = 100 \times 2.00 - 2.00 \times 0.54$$

$$= 198.92 \text{ m.}$$

While using the Beaman stadia arc, if the index is not against a division of *V*-scale, the exact coincidence of the index mark with the nearest division may be made with the help of the tangent screw of the vertical circle of the instrument. This causes a slight tilt in the line of sight without changing the value of staff interval significantly.

ILLUSTRATIVE EXAMPLES

Example 8.9

The following observations were made on Beaman stadia arc fitted on the vertical circle of a transit:

Staff reading (m) = 1.772, 2.565, 3.358

V-scale reading = 56

H-scale reading = 0.46

R.L. of the instrument axis = 300.00 m

Calculate the horizontal distance and elevation of the staff station.

Solution:

We have $D = s\ (100 - H\text{-scale reading})$

$V = s\ (V\text{-scale reading} - 50)$

$s = 3.358 - 1.772 = 1.586 \text{ m}$

$D = 1.586 \times (100 - 0.46)$

$= \mathbf{157.870\ m.}$

and $V = 1.586 \times (56 - 50)$

$= 9.516 \text{ m.}$

As *V*-scale reading is more than 50, *V* is + ve, indicating the angle of elevation.

R.L. of the staff station

$= \text{R.L. the instrument axis} + V - \text{central hair reading}$

$= 300.00 + 9.516 - 2.565$

$= \mathbf{306.95\ m.}$

Example 8.10

Calculate the horizontal distance and vertical component between two stations from where the following observations were made on Beaman stadia arc fitted to a tacheometer. Also determine the R.L. of the staff station.

Central hair reading = 2.465 m
Staff interval = 1.540 m
Reading on V-scale = 44
Reading on H-scale = 0.55
Height of trunion axis of the instrument = 1.455 m
R.L. of the instrument station = 600.00 m

Solution:

We know that

$D = s$ (100 – H-scale reading)

$V = s$ (V-scale reading – 50)

$D = 1.540 \times (100 - 0.55) =$ **153.153 m.**

$V = 1.540\ (44 - 50) = -$ **9.240 m.**

As V-scale reading is less than 50, V is –ve. It indicates that the line of sight is depressed.

R.L. of the staff station = R.L. of instrument station + height of trunion axis – V – central hair reading

= 600.00 + 1.455 – 9.240 – 2.465 = **589.750 m.**

8.8 SELF-REDUCING TACHEOMETER

The self-reducing tacheometer is a theodolite designed specifically for stadia observations. The reticle of such an instrument is equipped with three curved lines of varying radius instead of two stadia hairs and a main horizontal hair. These curved lines, also called curved stadia, appear to move apart or closer together as the telescope is moved up or down. The interval between the main (lower) hair, also called *base line*, and the upper hair moves in such a way that 100 times the rod interval automatically gives the horizontal distance, regardless of the vertical angle. The middle hair also moves such that the interval between the middle hair (elevation curve) and the main hair, when multiplied by some factor, it gives the difference in elevation. In some instruments the elevation factor is 100. In some other instruments it is shown in the field of view of the telescope (Fig. 8.12). The algebraic sign and magnitude of the elevation factor as seen in the field of view, change as the telescope is revolved.

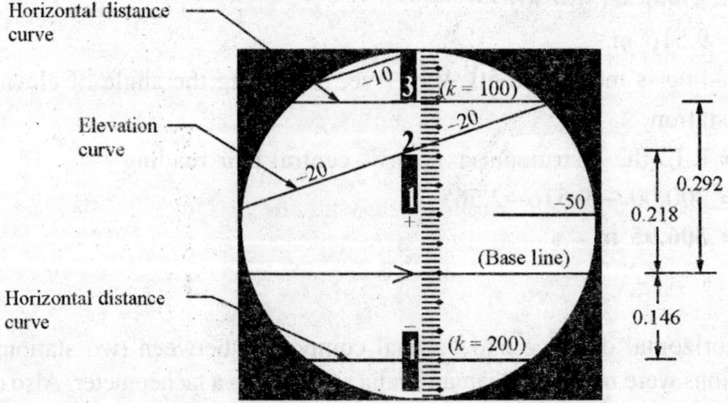

Fig. 8.12 Reticle of a self-reducing tacheometer

In Fig. 8.12, the interval between the base line and the horizontal distance curve having k equal to 100, is 0.292. Therefore, the horizontal distance is

$$= 100 \times 0.292 = 29.2 \text{ m.}$$

The interval between the base line and the other horizontal distance curve with $k = 200$, is 0.146. In this case, the horizontal distance is

$$= 200 \times 0.146 = 29.2 \text{ m.}$$

To determine the difference in elevation or the vertical component, the interval between the base line and the elevation curve is read and multiplied by the factor appearing on the elevation curve. In the figure, the interval is 0.218 and the factor is –20, therefore the difference in elevation is

$$= 0.218 \times (-20)$$

$$= -4.36 \text{ m.}$$

Essentially, a self-reducing tacheometer eliminates the time consumed in computations.

8.9 SUBTENSE BAR

Subtense method is an indirect method of distance determination. This method essentially consists of measuring the angle subtended by two ends of a horizontal rod of fixed length, called a *subtense bar*.

If the length of the subtense bar is s (Fig. 8.13) and the angle subtended by the two targets at the end of the bar at O be θ, then the horizontal distance

$$D = \frac{1}{2} s \cot \frac{\theta}{2} \qquad \text{...(8.12)}$$

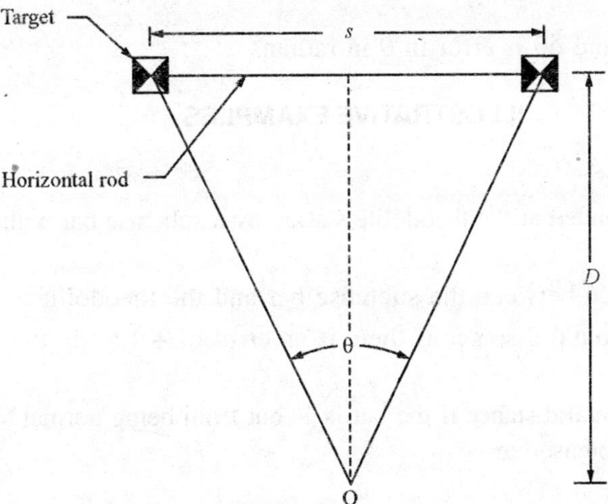

Fig. 8.13 Principle of subtense bar method

The subtense bar has two targets at its ends which are connected by invar wires that are under a slight but constant tension to minimize the effect of variations in temperature. The subtense bar is mounted on tripod and can be centered over the desired station. The bar is levelled by centering a circular level bubble using three levelling screws. The bar can then be oriented perpendicular to the line to be measured by sighting through a small telescope attached to the midpoint of the bar.

Determination of horizontal distances using subtense bar is advantageous in rough terrain where direct taping is very difficult or where accuracy requirement is not high.

Effect of Angular Error

From Fig. 8.13, we can write approximately

$$\theta = \frac{s}{D} \quad \text{...(8.13)}$$

or

$$D = \frac{s}{\theta} \quad \text{...(8.14)}$$

Differentiating Eq. (8.14), we get

$$\delta D = -\frac{s}{\theta^2}\delta\theta \quad \text{...(8.15)}$$

The negative sign indicates that a positive error in θ results into a negative error in D, and *vice versa*.

Putting the value of θ from Eq. (8.13) in Eq. (8.15), and neglecting the sign we get

$$\delta D = \frac{D^2}{s}\delta\,\theta \quad \text{...(8.16)}$$

Putting the value of s from Eq. (8.13), Eq. (8.16) can also be written as

$$\delta D = D\frac{\delta\theta}{\theta} \quad \text{...(8.17)}$$

where δD is error in D and $\delta\theta$ is error in θ in radians.

ILLUSTRATIVE EXAMPLES

Example 8.11

The horizontal angle subtended at the theodolite station by a subtense bar with targets 2 m apart, is 17′30″. Compute

(a) the horizontal distance between the subtense bar and the theodolite,

(b) the error in the horizontal distance if there is an error of + 1.5″ in the measurement of the horizontal angle, and

(c) the error in the horizontal distance if the bar is 1° out from being normal to the line joining the instrument and the subtense bar.

Solution:

It is given that

s = 2 m

θ = 17′ 30″

$\delta\theta$ = + 1.5″

(a) From Eq. (8.12)

$$D = \frac{1}{2} s \cot \frac{\theta}{2}$$

$$= \frac{1}{2} \times 2 \times \cot \frac{17'30''}{2}$$

$$= \mathbf{392.88\ m.}$$

(b) From Eq. (8.16)

$$\delta D = \frac{D^2}{s} \delta\theta$$

$$= \frac{392.88^2}{2} \times \frac{1.5}{206265}$$

$$= \mathbf{0.561\ m.}$$

Also from Eq. (8.17)

$$\delta D = D \frac{\delta\theta}{\theta}$$

$$= 392.88 \times \frac{1.5}{17 \times 60 + 30}$$

$$= \frac{392.88 \times 1.5}{1050}$$

$$= \mathbf{0.561\ m.}$$

(c) In Fig. 8.14, let the angle $A'CA$ = 1° then

$$OC' = D' = A'C' \cot \frac{\theta}{2}$$

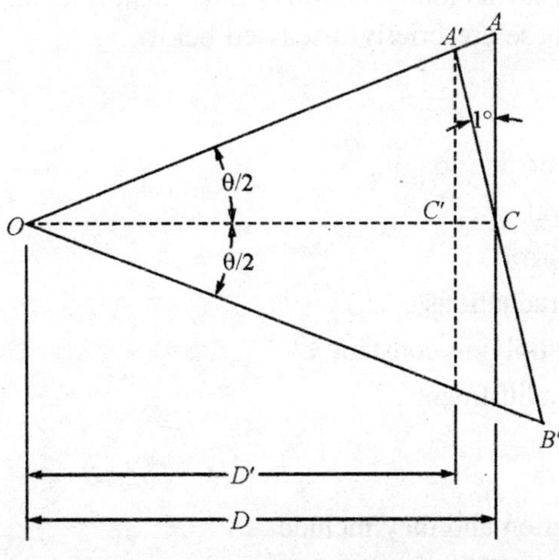

Fig. 8.14

But $A'C' = A'C \cos 1°$

$$D' = A'C \cos 1° \cot\frac{\theta}{2}$$

We have $A'B' = 2$ m

$A'C = 1$ m

Thus

$$D' = 1 \times \cos 1° \cot\frac{17'30''}{2}$$

$$= 392.82 \text{ m}$$

Error in horizontal distance $= D - D'$

$= 392.88 - 392.82 =$ **0.06 m.**

Example 8.12

A distance of approximately 400 m is to be measured with a 3 metre subtense bar and a theodolite. Find the uncertainty in the length associated with an angular error of 1″.

Solution:

From Eq. (8.16)

$$\delta D = \frac{D^2}{s}\delta\theta$$

$$= \frac{400^2}{3} \times \frac{1''}{206265} = \mathbf{0.259\ m.}$$

8.10 ERRORS IN TACHEOMETRY

Like in other survey methods, tacheometry can also have instrumental errors, personal errors, and errors due to natural causes. These are briefly discussed below.

Instrumental errors

Instrumental errors may occur due to

1. Improper stadia interval
2. Vertical circle index error
3. Incorrect stadia rod graduations
4. Incorrect value of multiplying constant k
5. Imperfect permanent adjustments.

Personal errors

These are errors of manipulation and they include

1. Inaccurate centering and levelling of the instrument

2. Non-verticality of the staff or stadia rod
3. Careless levelling of the altitude bubble
4. Inaccurate sighting
5. Angle of elevation noted as angle of depression, and *vice-versa*
6. Incorrect staff readings.

Errors due to natural causes

These errors are due to

1. High wind making it difficult to keep the staff vertical
2. Unequal atmospheric refraction
3. Change in atmospheric temperature
4. Poor visibility.

Higher degree of accuracy in tacheometric observations can be achieved by

1. Taking proper care in manipulating the instrument
2. Limiting the length of sights
3. Using instruments of good quality
4. Averaging the forward and backward readings
5. Working in favourable atmospheric conditions.

In stadia traversing the obtainable degree of precision ranges from 1/300 to 1/500. A much lower accuracy is acceptable in topographic and military surveys. The linear error of closure in traversing can be computed from $c\sqrt{P}$ metres, where c varies from 0.03 to 0.06 and p is the perimeter of the traverse. The closing error in levelling circuits in bench marks is given by $n\sqrt{l}$ metres, where n is from 0.003 to 0.005, and l is the total length traversed.

ILLUSTRATIVE EXAMPLES

Example 8.13

What is the permissible closing error in a traverse of total length of 3500 m. Also determine the permissible closing error in levelling in a bench mark at distances of (*i*) 1500 m, (*ii*) 2500 m, and (*iii*) 3500 m.

Solution:

Taking the closing error in traversing as

$$e_t = \pm\, 0.03\sqrt{p}$$

$$= \pm\, 0.03\sqrt{3500} = \mathbf{1.77\ m}$$

and the closing error in levelling as

$$e_l = \pm\, 0.003\sqrt{l}$$

(*i*) $= \pm\ 0.003\sqrt{1500} = \pm$ **0.116 m**

(*ii*) $= \pm\ 0.003\sqrt{2500} = \pm$ **0.150 m**

(*iii*) $= \pm\ 0.003\sqrt{3500} \pm$ **0.177 m.**

8.11 STADIA FIELD PRACTICE

In stadia work, the transit is set on a point for which the horizontal location and elevation are known. If necessary, the elevation of the instrument station can be determined by back sighting on a point of known elevation.

The horizontal circle is set to read zero and a sight is taken on another control point. All stadia pointings are accomplished by working on the circle using the upper clamp and upper slow motion screw (tangent screw). It is a good practice to periodically check the zero setting by sighting back on the original back sight to ensure that the setting is not being disturbed by inadvertent use of the lower clamp or lower tangent screw. At a bare minimum, a zero check must be made before shifting the instrument to other station.

Before taking any observation, the height of instrument above the instrument station is measured with a steel tape. The levelling staff or stadia rod is held at the points of observation and the horizontal angles, vertical angles, stadia hair readings, and central hair readings are recorded in the field book. Usually, the calculations for horizontal distance and elevation are performed after the field work is over.

In practice, the lower stadia hair is made to read the closest even decimetre mark by moving the telescope slightly up or down. The upper stadia hair is then read, and the staff interval is determined mentally by simply subtracting the lower hair reading from the upper hair reading. After booking the staff interval, instead of stadia hair readings, the central hair is then moved to its original position and reading for the central hair is noted. This technique of temporarily moving the lower stadia hair to an even value introduces errors in the readings which are not large enough to significantly affect the results.

Sometimes it may not be possible to see the entire staff interval due to tree branches, intervening ground, etc., obstructing the full view. In such cases, half the staff interval can be read and doubled. Reading only half the staff interval reduces the precision considerably, so extra care should be taken when half-interval is being taken.

ADDITIONAL ILLUSTRATIVE EXAMPLES

Example 8.14

The following observations were made for two stations *A* and *B* to determine the gradient of the line *AB*. A tacheometer was set up at station *C*, and the staff at *A* and *B* was held vertically.

Staff station	Vertical angle	Staff reading (m)
A	+ 3°50′	1.250 1.720 2.190
B	+ 0°12′	1.095 1.520 1.945

Horizontal angle $ACB = 40°50'$

Tacheomeric contants $k = 100$ and $c = 0.0$ m.

Solution (Fig. 8.15):

From the given data, we have

$s_1 = (2.190 - 1.250) = 0.940$ m

$s_2 = (1.945 - 1.095) = 0.850$ m

$h_1 = 1.720$ m

$h_2 = 1.520$ m

$\alpha_1 = +\,3°50'$

$\alpha_2 = +\,0°12'$

From Eq. (8.6)

$AC \quad = ks_1 \cos^2\alpha_1 = 100 \times 0.940 \times \cos^2 3°50' = 93.580$ m

$BC \quad = ks_2 \cos^2\alpha_2 = 100 \times 0.850 \times \cos^2 0°12' = 85.000$ m

The vertical components from Eq. (8.7), are

$$V_1 = \frac{1}{2} ks_1 \sin 2\,\alpha_1 = \frac{1}{2} \times 100 \times 0.940 \times \sin\left(2 \times 3°50'\right) = 6.270 \text{ m}$$

$$V_2 = \frac{1}{2} ks_2 \sin 2\alpha_2 = \frac{1}{2} \times 100 \times 0.850 \times \sin\left(2 \times 0°12'\right) = 0.297 \text{ m.}$$

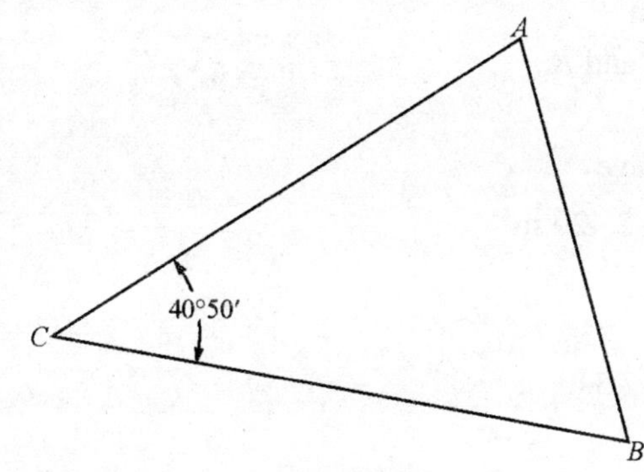

Fig. 8.15

Assuming R.L. of the instrument axis as h, we have

R.L. of $A = h + V_1 - h_1$

and R.L. of $B = h + V_2 - h_2$

Difference of R.L.'s of A and B

$\Delta h \quad = (h + V_1 - h_1) - (h + V_2 - h_2)$

$= (V_1 - V_2) - (h_1 - h_2)$

$= (6.270 - 0.297) - (1.720 - 1.520)$

$= 5.773$ m.

The distance AB can be determined from

$$\cos ACB = \frac{AC^2 + BC^2 - AB^2}{2 AC\, BC}$$

$$\cos\ 40°50' = \frac{93.580^2 + 85.000^2 - AB^2}{2 \times 93.580 \times 85.000}$$

or $$AB = 62.813\ \text{m}.$$

Therefore, the gradient of AB $\frac{\Delta h}{AB} = \frac{5.773}{62.813} = 0.092 = \mathbf{1\ in\ 10.88}.$

Example 8.15

A line was levelled tacheometrically with tacheometer fitted with an anallactic lens, the value of the multiplying constant being 100. The following observations were made, the staff having been held vertically:

Instrument station	Height of instrument axis (m)	Staff held at	Vertical angle	Staff reading (m)		
				Bottom	Center	Top
P	1.40	B.M.	−1°35′	1.120	2.330	3.540
P	1.40	Q	+2°54′	1.210	2.380	3.550
Q	1.38	R	+3°12′	0.865	2.425	3.985

R.L.of B.M. = 583.66 m.

Compute the R.L.'s of P, Q and R.

Solution (Fig. 8.16):

From the given data, we have

$s_1 = 3.540 - 1.120 = 2.420$ m

$h_1 = 2.330$ m

$\alpha_1 = -1°35'$

$s_2 = 3.550 - 1.210 = 2.340$ m

$h_2 = 2.380$ m

$\alpha_2 = 2°54'$

$s_3 = 3.985 - 0.865 = 3.120$ m

$h_3 = 2.425$ m

$\alpha_3 = 3°12'$

$h'_p = 1.40$ m

$h'_Q = 1.38$ m

From Eq. (8.6), we get

$D = ks\cos^2\alpha$

$D_1 = 100 \times 2.420 \cos^2 1°35' = 241.815$ m

$D_2 = 100 \times 2.340 \cos^2 2°54' = 233.401$ m

$D_3 = 100 \times 3.120 \cos^2 3°12' = 311.028$ m.

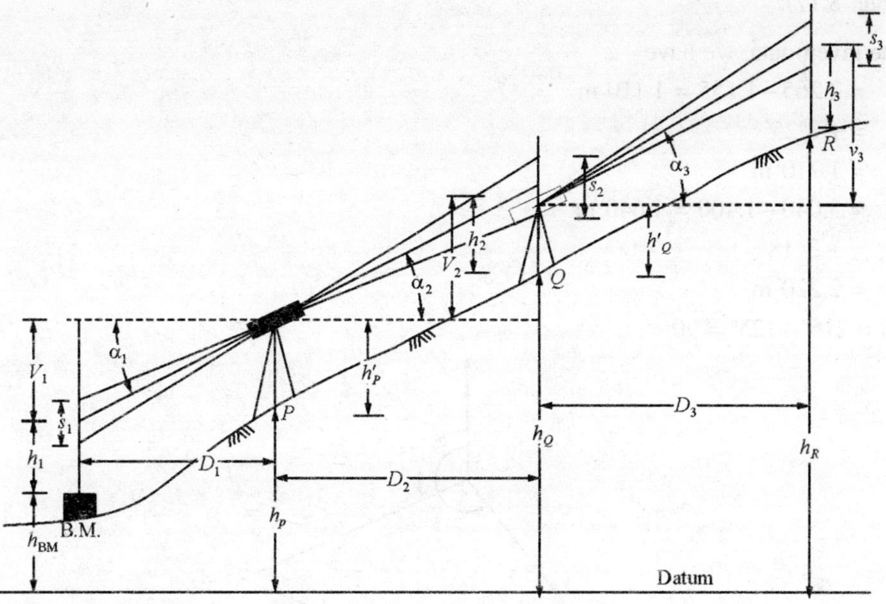

Fig. 8.16

From Eq. (8.7)

$$V = 1/2\ ks \sin 2\alpha$$

$$V_1 = 1/2 \times 100 \times 2.420 \sin (2 \times 1°35') = 6.684 \text{ m}$$

$$V_2 = 1/2 \times 100 \times 2.340 \sin (2 \times 2°54') = 11.824 \text{ m}$$

$$V_3 = 1/2 \times 100 \times 3.120 \sin (2 \times 3°12') = 17.389 \text{ m.}$$

The R.L. of instrument axis at P

$$\text{H.I.} = h_{BM} + h_1 + V_1 = 583.66 + 2.330 + 6.684 = 592.674 \text{ m}$$

$$\text{R.L. of } P = h_p = H.I. - h'_p = 592.674 - 1.40 = \mathbf{591.274\ m}$$

$$\text{R.L. of } Q = h_Q = H.I. + V_2 - h_2 = 592.674 + 11.824 - 2.380 = \mathbf{602.118\ m}$$

$$\text{R.L. of } R = h_R = h_Q + h'_Q + V_3 - h_3 = 602.128 + 1.38 + 17.389 - 2.425 = \mathbf{618.462\ m.}$$

Example 8.16

Determine the gradient from a point A to another point B from the following observations made with a tacheometer having k = 100 and c = 0.0 m. The staff was held vertically.

Inst.stn.	Staff stn.	Bearing	Vert. angle	Staff reading (m)
P	*A*	125°	+ 8°25′	1.155, 1.710, 2.265
	B	215°	+ 3°18′	1.400, 2.220, 3.040

Solution (Fig. 8.17):

From the given data, we have

$s_1 = 2.265 - 1.155 = 1.110$ m

$\alpha_1 = +8°25'$

$h_1 = 1.710$ m

$s_2 = 3.040 - 1.400 = 1.640$ m

$\alpha_2 = +3°18'$

$h_2 = 2.220$ m

$\angle APB = 215° - 125° = 90°$

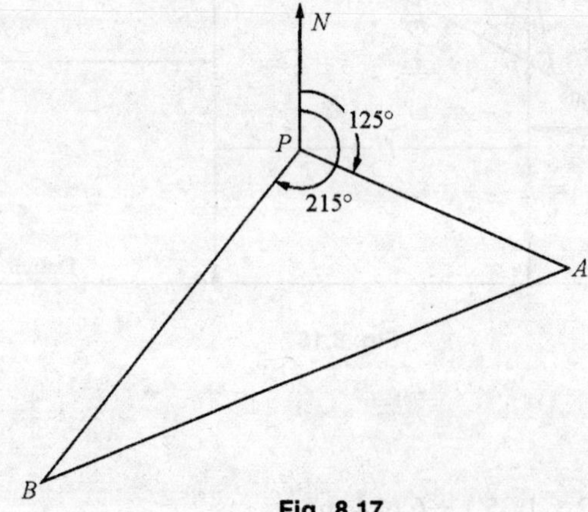

Fig. 8.17

From Eq. (8.6), the horizontal distance is given by

$$D = ks \cos^2 \alpha$$

$$AP = D_1 = 100 \times 1.110 \cos^2 8°25' = 108.622 \text{ m}$$

$$BP = D_2 = 100 \times 1.640 \cos^2 3°18' = 163.457 \text{ m.}$$

From Eq. (8.7), the vertical components is given by

$$V = 1/2\ ks \sin (2\alpha)$$

$$V_1 = 1/2 \times 100 \times 1.110 \times \sin (2 \times 8°25') = 16.072 \text{ m}$$

$$V_2 = 1/2 \times 100 \times 1.640 \times \sin (2 \times 3°18') = 9.425 \text{ m.}$$

Let us assume that R.L. of the instrument axis be h, then

R.L. of $A = h + V_1 - h_1$

R.L. of $B = h + V_2 - h_2$

Difference in R.L.'s of A and B

$$\Delta h = (h + V_1 - h_1) - (h + V_2 - h_2)$$

$$= (V_1 - V_2) - (h_1 - h_2)$$

$$= (16.072 - 9.425) - (1.710 - 2.220)$$

$$= 7.157 \text{ m.}$$

Since $\angle APB = 90°$, the distance A is given by

$$= \sqrt{AP^2 + BP^2}$$

$$= \sqrt{108.622^2 + 163.457^2}$$

$$= 196.257 \text{ m.}$$

$$\text{Gradient of } AB = \frac{\Delta h}{AB} = \frac{7.157}{196.257} = 0.036$$

$$= \mathbf{1 \text{ in } 27.42.}$$

QUESTIONS AND PROBLEMS

8.1 What is tacheometry? Describe its uses.

8.2 Explain the principle of stadia measurements, and derive expressions for horizontal and vertical distances by tacheometry.

8.3 Discuss briefly various systems of tacheometry.

8.4 Differentiate between the fixed-hair method and movable-hair method. Discuss advantages and disadvantages of each method.

8.5 Differentiate between the stadia and non-stadia systems of tacheometry. Discuss their merits and demerits.

8.6 What is tangential system of tacheometry? What are its advantages and disadvantages over the stadia method?

8.7 Derive an expression for the horizontal distance of a vertical staff from a tacheometer, if the line of sight is horizontal.

8.8 What do you understand by tacheometry? What is the utility of an anallactic lens in a tacheometer?

8.9 Derive an expression for the horizontal distance of a vertical staff from a tacheometer, if the line of sight is inclined.

8.10 Discuss the field methods of determination of tacheometric constants.

8.11 Explain different systems of tacheometry, and discuss their relative merits.

8.12 What is Beaman stadia arc? Explain its principle.

8.13 Discuss the principle of a self-reducing tacheometer and its relative merits.

8.14 Discuss the subtense bar method of tacheometric surveying. What are its advantages?

8.15 What are different errors in tacheometry? What precautions are to be taken to minimize them?

8.16 Describe the conditions under which tacheometric surveying is advantageous.

8.17 Describe the field practice of stadia measurements.

8.18 Calculate the tacheometric constants from the following readings taken with a tacheometer on to a vertical staff:

Horizontal distance between instrument and staff (m)	Staff reading (m)		
66.3	0.770	1.100	1.430
75.3	1.680	2.055	2.430

8.19 Two distances of 50 m and 80 m were accurately measured on a fairly level ground. The interval on the staff held vertical were 0.495 m and 0.795 m, respectively. Determine the constants of the instrument.

8.20 A tacheometer reads 1.274 m and 1.770 m corresponding to the stadia hairs on a vertical staff 50 m away. The measured distance between the object glass and the trunion axis was found to be 140 mm. If the focal length of the object glass is 356 mm compute the value of the multiplying constant.

8.21 Compute the difference in height between two points *A* and *B* from the following observations:

Point	Vertical angle	Staff readings (m)
A	+08′	0.825 1.300 1.775
B	−22′	0.802 1.850 2.898

($k = 100$; $c = 0.0$ m)

8.22 A staff held vertically at a distance of 50 m and 100 m from a transit fitted with stadia hairs, the staff intervals with the telescope normal were 0.494 m and 0.994 m, respectively. The instrument was then set up near a B.M. of R.L. 1500.00 m, and the readings on the staff held on the B.M. was 1.495 m. The staff readings at the station *A*, with staff held vertically, and the line of sight horizontal, were 1.00, 1.85, 2.70. What is the horizontal distance between the B.M. and *A*, and R.L. of *A*.

8.23 A level with stadia hairs was set up on the line joining two points *A* and *B*, and the staff readings for points *A* and *B* were, respectively, as 1.000, 1.160, 1.320 and 1.630, 1.750, 1.870. Compute the distance between *A* and *B* and the gradient from *A* to *B*. Take the multiplying constant as 100 and the additive constant as 0.0 m.

8.24 A tacheometer was set up at an intermediate point on a line *AB*, and the following observations were made on a vertically held staff:

Staff at	Vertical angle	Central hair reading (m)	Staff interval (m)
A	+9°45′	1.910	2.300
B	+5°30′	1.750	2.105

The instrument is fitted with an anallactic lens and the multiplying costant is 100. Determine the length *AB* and the R.L. of *B* if the R.L. of *A* is 150.50 m.

8.25 The following readings were taken on a vertical staff with a tacheometer fitted with an anallactic lens:

Staff station	Bearing	Vertical angle	Staff readings		
A	34°20′	+11°	0.850	1.410	1.970
B	202°50′	−4°	0.755	1.885	3.015

If the values of *k* and *c* for the instrument are 100 and 0, respectively, calculate the difference of level between *A* and *B*, and the distance *AB*.

8.26 A tacheometer is set up on a bench mark of R.L. 60.00 m. The horizontal axis of the instrument is 1.240 m above the bench mark.The following observations were made with staff held vertically:

Staff stn.	Vertical angle	Stadia hair reading		Central hair reading
A	+3°30′	0.400	1.660	1.030
B	−8°20′	0.900	1.640	1.270
C	+9°50′	1.00	2.320	1.660

If the instrument constants k and c are 100 and 0.0 m, respectively, determine the R.L. of the staff stations.

8.27 Two observations are taken upon a vertical staff by means of a theodolite. In the first case, the line of sight is directed to give a staff reading of 0.880 m and an angle of elevation of 4°08′. In the second case, the staff reading is 3.340 m and the angle of elevation is 5°30′. If the elevation of the trunion axis of the instrument is 195.60 m, compute the R.L. of the staff station and its horizontal distance from the instrument.

8.28 During the course of tacheometric traversing from A to D, the following observations were made with a theodolite fitted with an anallactic lens:

Line	Bearing	Vertical angle	Staff readings (m)		
AB	33°35′	+5°45′	1.050	1.950	2.850
BC	115°50′	+6°30′	1.300	2.165	3.030
CD	202°32′	– 2°55′	1.385	2.250	3.115

Assuming the staff was held vertical and the multiplying constant of the instrument as 100, calculate the distance of D from A along the traverse line. Also determine the R.L. of B, C, and D if the R.L. of A is 215.50 m and heights of instrument axis at A, B, and C are, respectively, 1.45 m, 1.50 m, and 1.55 m.

8.29 The horizontal angle subtended at the theodolite by a subtense bar of 3 m length is 9°50″. Calculate the horizontal distance of the theodolite station from the subtense bar.

8.30 The horizontal angle subtended at a theodolite station by a subtense bar with vanes 2.60 m apart, is 0°40′. What is the horizontal distance of the subtense bar station from the instrument station? What will be the error in horizontal distance if the bar were 0.4° away from the normal direction to the line of sight.

8.31 In a subtense measurement, two targets were set up at right angles to the line of sight from the instrument station. The following observations were made using a theodolite at station P:

Distance between the vanes of subtense bar	=	2.4 m
Angle subtended at P by the subtense bar at A	=	10′40″
Angle subtended at P by the subtense bar at B	=	6′20″
Angle of elevation to target A	=	15′20″
Angle of elevation to target B	=	50′30″
Horizontal angle APB	=	2°02′15″
Height of target at A above ground	=	1.5 m
Height of target at B above ground	=	1.6 m
Height of instrument P	=	1.45 m
R.L. of P	=	120.000 m

Compute the R.L.'s of A and B, the horizontal distance AB, and slope distance AB. What is the inclination of AB with the horizontal?

9

TRAVERSE SURVEYING

9.1 GENERAL

In order to provide a framework of survey points whose horizontal and vertical positions are accurately known, basic horizontal and vertical control surveys are executed. The results of such surveys are the horizontal coordinates (x, y) and the elevations (z) of the points. These position data are initially necessary for detailed surveys and for all kinds of comprehensive mapping. The fundamental network of points whose horizontal positions have been accurately determined, is called the *horizontal control*.

Horizontal control is generally established either by traversing, triangulation, or trilateration (*c.f.*, Chapter 1 of *Higher Surveying*). Traversing is most frequently employed especially for surveys of limited extent and where the points whose positions are desired, lie along a devious route. Triangulation or trilateration is generally preferred in hilly country where numerous intervisible points are available to set up the instrument and signals at elevated ground.

9.2 USES OF TRAVERSE SURVEYING

Traverse surveying is most widely employed operation in the execution of local horizontal control surveys. It is used for many purposes and types of projects, some of which are:

1. To determine the positions of existing boundary markers.
2. To establish the position of boundary lines.
3. To determine the area encompassed within the confines of a boundary.
4. To determine the positions of arbitrary points from which data may be obtained for preparing various types of maps, *i.e.*, to establish control for mapping.
5. To establish ground control for photogrammetric mapping.
6. To establish control for gathering data regarding earthwork quantities in railways, highways, utility and other construction works.
7. To establish control for locating railways, highways, and other construction works.

9.3 TRAVERSE

A traverse consists of a series of straight lines of known length related to one another by known angles. The lines connect successive established points along the route of a survey. The points defining the ends of the traverse line, are called *traverse stations* or *traverse points.* The length of the lines are determined either by direct measurement using a tape or Electronic Distance Measuring (EDM) equipment, or by indirect measurement using the methods of technometry. The angles at the traverse stations between the traverse lines, are measured with a transit or theodolite. When the extent or survey is not large and desired accuracy is not high, other methods of traversing where the angle is not measured (*c.f.*, Sec. 9.4) may be employed or the angle can be determined with compass.

Types of Traverse

The two general classes of traverse are

1. Open traverse, and
2. Closed traverse.

Open traverse

The open traverse originates at a point of known position and terminates at a point of unknown position. Open traverses may extend for long distances without the opportunity for checking the accuracy of the ongoing work. Accordingly, all survey measurements are carefully repeated at the time of work, and every opportunity for checking the position and direction, is utilized.

In Fig. 9.1, the traverse *PABCDE* originates at known point *P* with a back sight along line *PQ* of known azimuth but does not terminate at point of known position. Such traverses are called open traverses.

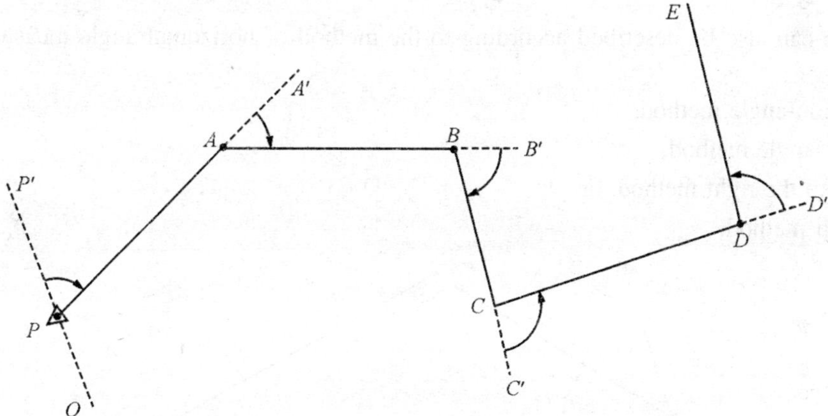

Fig. 9.1 Open traverse

An open traverse is particularly useful for providing control in preliminary and construction surveys for roads, pipelines, electricity transmission lines, and the like. These should never be run for any permanent project because it does not reveal mistakes or errors, and the results are always open to doubt.

The open traverses may be from a few hundred metres to many kilometres. The distances are normally measured by using tape or EDM equipment and directions, generally the deflection angles, with theodolites.

Closed traverse

Closed traverses originate at a point of known position and close on another point of known position. In Fig. 9.2, the traverse *PABCDR* originates at known point *P* with a back sight along line *PQ* of known azimuth and closes on another known point *R*, with a fore sight along line *RS* also of known azimuth. This type of traverse provides computational checks allowing detection of systematic errors in both distance and direction, and therefore, preferred to open traverses.

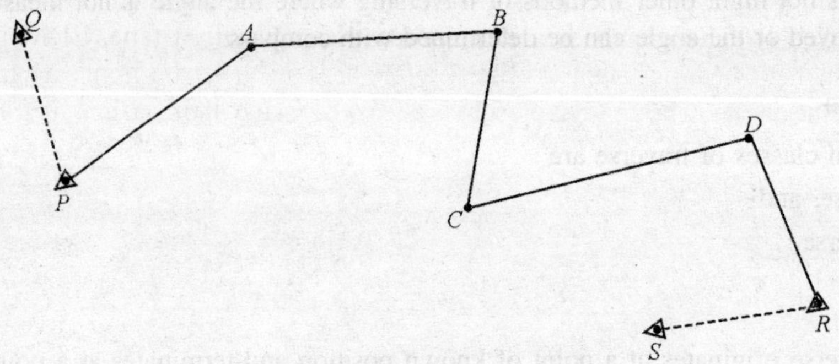

Fig. 9.2 Closed traverse

Another type of a closed traverse *PABCDEP* is *closed-loop traverse* (Fig. 9.3), which originates and terminates on a single point *P* of known horizontal position. This type of traverse permits an internal check on the angular measurements, but detection of systematic errors in linear measurement or errors in the orientation of the traverse, is not possible, and therefore, not recommended for use in major projects.

A traverse can also be described according to the method of horizontal angle measurement. Thus, they are by

1. deflection-angle method,
2. interior-angle method,
3. angles to the right method, or
4. azimuth method.

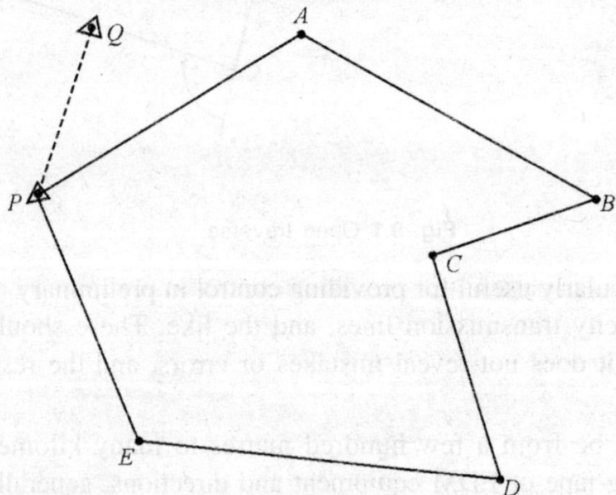

Fig. 9.3 Closed-loop traverse

Deflection-angle traverse

This is probably the most commonly employed method of traversing for open traverses where only a few details are located as the traverse is run. It is most useful for the location surveys for highways, railways, canals, and pipelines.

Successive stations are occupied, and at each station the deflection angle is measured (*cf.*, Sec. 4.2) using a transit (Fig. 9.4). The distances are measured directly with a tape, EDM instrument or tacheometrically. Magnetic bearings are also observed forward and backward from each traverse station as a rough check on the angles. The angular closure is checked by calculating azimuths from known line *PQ* to known line *RS*.

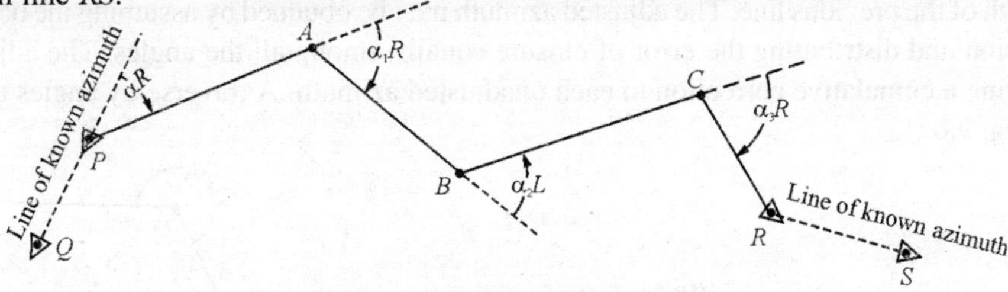

Fig. 9.4 Deflection-angle traverse

The arithmetical check of the sum of the angles should be performed immediately on completing the traverse in order to detect blunders or excessively large errors. The angular error of closure should not exceed the estimated standard deviation for observing an angle from a single setup times the square root of the number of instrument stations. In practice, this estimated standard deviation in angular measurement is usually taken equal to 0.5 to 1.0 times the least count of the instrument used in measuring the angles.

Interior-angle traverse

A closed-loop traverse run by the method of interior angles (*cf.*, Sec. 4.2) is illustrated in Fig. 9.5. Field operations for this method of traversing are not much different from those used for the deflection-angle. Except, for surveys of very low order of accuracy, all interior angles should be observed twice, once with telescope direct and once with the telescope reversed. The most rapid and simple field check of observed interior angles is to calculate the sum of the observations and compare with $(n-2)180°$. The sum of the interior angles should not deviate from $(n-2)180°$ by more than the square root of the number of instrument setups times the estimated standard deviation in observing the angles.

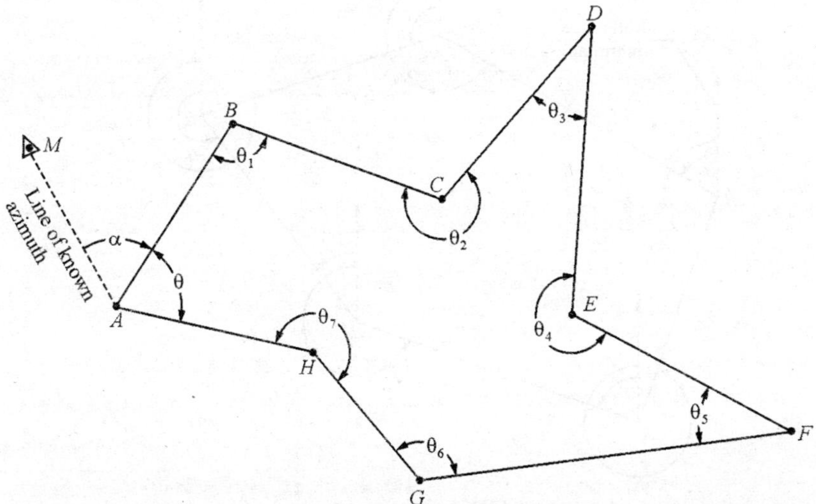

Fig. 9.5 Interior-angle traverse

Traverse by angle to the right

The angle to the right has been defined in Sec.4.2. The method using angles to the right may be used for open, closed or closed-loop traverse. A repeating transit or a direction theodolite may be employed to measure the angles. The azimuths of the traverse lines are calculated by adding the angles to the right to the back azimuth of the previous line. The adjusted azimuth may be obtained by assuming the observations of equal precision and distributing the error of closure equally among all the angles. The adjustment is made by applying a cumulative correction to each unadjusted azimuth. A traverse by angles to the right is shown in Fig. 9.6.

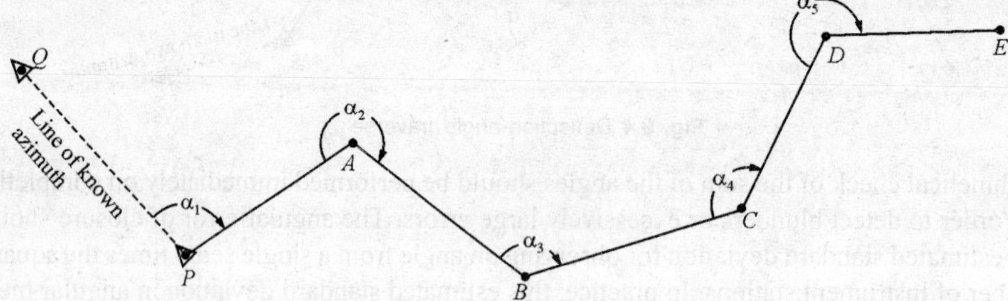

Fig. 9.6 Traverse by angles to the right

Azimuth traverse

In this method, at each traverse station the back azimuth of the preceding line and the azimuth of the forward line are measured using a transit. The reference meridian may be either true or assumed. The method is used extensively for topographic and other surveys where a large number of details are located by angular and linear measurements from the traverse stations. Fig. 9.7 illustrates an azimuth traverse.

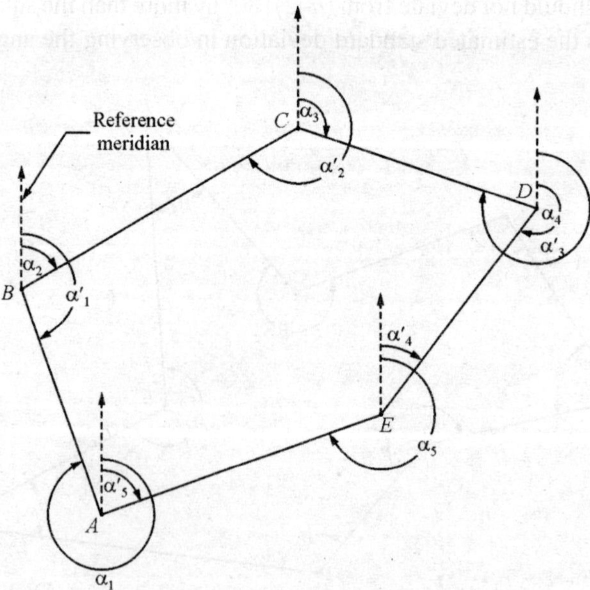

Fig. 9.7 Azimuth traverse

Another classification of traverse given below, is based upon the instruments employed:

1. Chain traverse
2. Compass traverse
3. Theodolite traverse
4. Plane-table traverse
5. Stadia traverse or tacheometric traverse.

The various types of traverses discussed above, can be run by employing an appropriate instrument. The following section explains the use of instrument and method for running the traverse.

9.4 METHODS OF TRAVERSING

A traverse can be run by several methods depending upon the instrument employed for determining the relative position of the traverse stations. The classification of traverses based upon the instrument employed and the methods of running the traverses, are explained in the following sections.

Chain Traversing

In this method, the entire work is done with a chain or tape and no angle measuring instrument is employed. The directions of lines are fixed by linear measurements only. Angles fixed by linear or tie measurement, are known as *chain angles*.

Let the chain angle *QPR* in Fig.9.8, be α. With *P* as centre and radius equal to a chain length, *i.e.*, 20 m or 30 m, draw an arc intersecting *PQ* and *PR* in *q* and *r*, respectively. Locate *p* on *qr* such that *pq* is equal to *pr*.

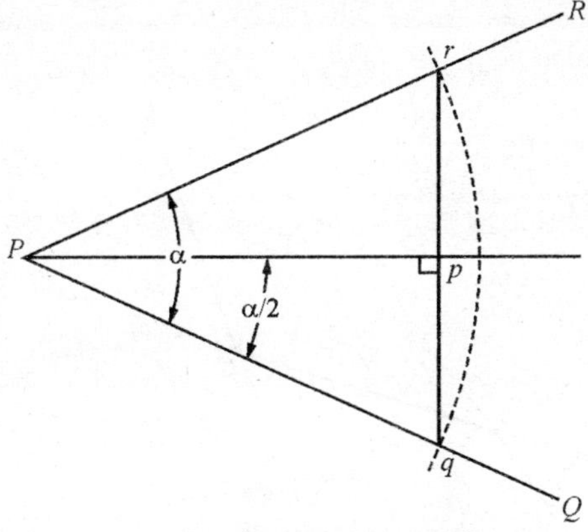

Fig. 9.8 Chain angle

Now we have

$$\sin\frac{\alpha}{2} = \frac{pq}{Pq} = \frac{qr}{2Pq} \tag{9.1}$$

For a 20 m chain, $Pq = 20$ m

$$\alpha = 2\sin^{-1}\left(\frac{qr}{40}\right) \tag{9.2}$$

and for a 30 m chain, $pq = 30$ m

$$\alpha = 2\sin^{-1}\left(\frac{qr}{60}\right) \tag{9.3}$$

Fig. 9.9a shows a closed traverse. At A, the directions of AB and AD are fixed by measuring Aa_1, Aa_2 and a_1a_2. However, the external measurements such as at station B, are also used to fix the directions. Fig.9.9b shows fixing of diredction in an open traverse.

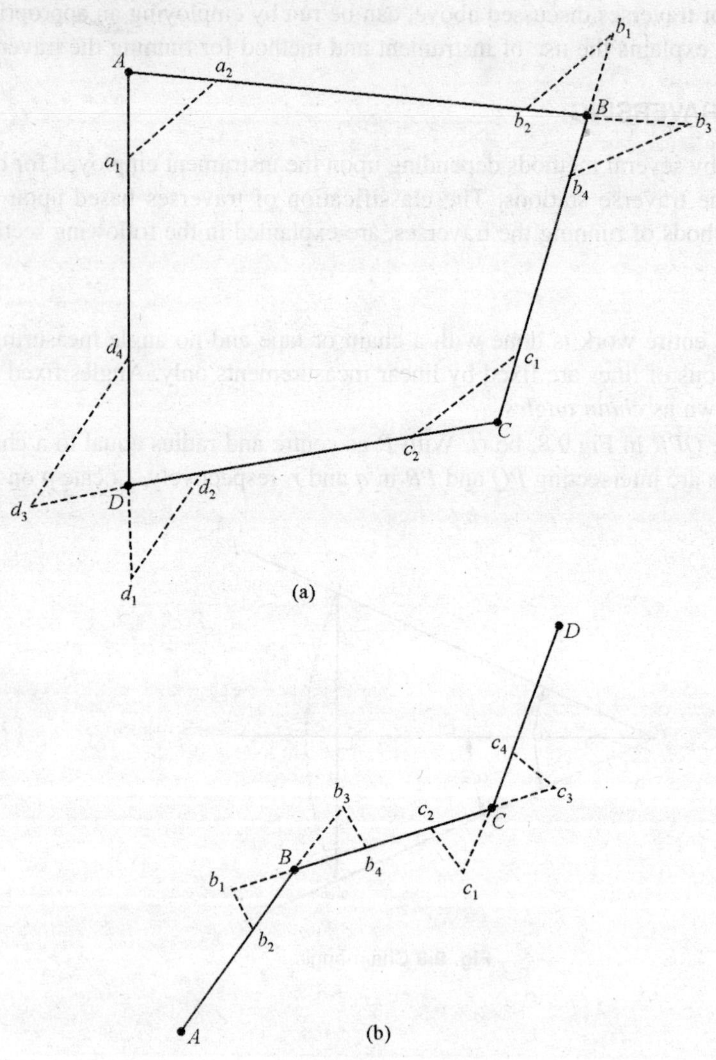

Fig. 9.9 Chain traverse

Chain angles are generally liable to errors as the principle of surveying, *i.e.*, working from the whole to the part, is not adopted. The accuracy in the measurement of the angles, is proportional to the accuracy achieved in measuring the distances Pq, Pr and qr, etc., (Fig. 9.8).

Compass Traversing

Use of compass is described in Sec.5.3. When a compass traverse is performed, forward and back bearings are observed from each traverse station, and distances are measured with a tape. The offsets to the objects (details) on either side of the traverse lines are taken as in chain surveying. The interior angles are computed from the observed bearings. The included angles are not affected by local attraction as the forward and backward bearings at a station are equally affected. The sum of the interior angles provides a legitimate indication of the angular error in the traverse, and it is used to check accuracy of a compass traverse. If the error in the sum of interior angles exceeds 10′ to 15′ times the square root of the number of angles, it is likely that a blunder in reading the compass has occurred, and the measurements should be repeated.

Theodolite Traversing

In theodolite traversing the directions are measured in the form of bearings, deflection angles, angles to the right, interior angles, or azimuths using a theodolite, and distances with a tape, EDM equipment, or by tacheometry. The bearings are measured with a theodolite fitted with a magnetic compass by loose-needle method or fast-needle method (*cf.*, Sec.5.7). As discussed in Sec. 9.3, the name of a traverse depends upon the type of angle measured.

A theodolite traverse is commonly used for providing a horizontal control system to determine the relative positions of various points on the surface of the earth. It is specially used for providing control for site surveys in urban areas where the triangulation is not feasible.

Plane-table Traversing

Plane table is an instrument which is widely used for direct plotting of details and contouring. Use of plane table is discussed in Chapter 10. Traversing with the plane table involves the same principle as running a traverse with a transit or theodolite, and has been described in Sec.10.7.

A plane-table traverse is used for providing the control for small surveys and extension of control for larger surveys in order to locate points from which map details can be plotted advantageously.

Stadia Traversing

When the distances between traverse stations are determined by the stadia method (*cf.*, Chapter 8), the method of traversing is termed as stadia traversing. Stadia traversing is useful for certain types of preliminary and reconnaissance surveys, rough surveys for boundary locations, and topographic surveys. When only horizontal controls are required, this method of traversing provides an excellent means for establishing control points on surveys of low precision. An advantage of the stadia traverse is that, if desired, elevations may be determined concurrently with horizontal positions.

9.5 TRAVERSING PROCEDURE

The following steps are required to establish a traverse:

1. Reconnaissance
2. Selection of traverse stations
3. Marking of stations
4. Making linear and angular measurements
5. Locating details.

Reconnaissance

Preliminary field inspection of the entire area to be covered is known as *reconnaissance*. During the reconnaissance, the surveyor goes to the entire area and decides the best plan of working. If a map of the area is available, it would be of great help in planning the survey work. Reconnaissance includes the following:

1. Examination of the area to be surveyed
2. Selection of suitable positions for traverse stations
3. Insuring the intervisibility of the traverse stations
4. Deciding method of traversing and instruments to be employed
5. Collection of miscellaneous information related to traversing such as
   (*i*) Transport facilities
   (*ii*) Availability of food and water for the survey party
   (*iii*) Camping ground or stay arrangements
   (*iv*) Availability of labour.

Selection of Traverse Stations

While selecting the traverse stations, the following points must be taken into account:

1. As far as possible the survey work should be based upon the basic principle of surveying, i.e., working from the whole to the part.
2. Number of stations is a minimum.
3. Length of the traverse lines is as long as possible to reduce the effect of centering errors.
4. Stations are according to the requirement of the work, and they are also useful for picking up details.
5. Stations are intervisible.
6. Stations are selected on firm and level ground.
7. The ground conditions between the stations are suitable for linear measurements.
8. The line of sights should be at least 1 m above the ground surface to reduce the effect of shimmering due to refraction.

Marking of Stations

After finalizing the locations of traverse stations, their positions are marked on the ground. The station mark should be of permanent nature as far as possible so that the stations can be used in future, if required.

For ordinary traverse survey, a peg with a tack on its top, is driven almost flush with ground (Fig. 9.10a)

If the traverse stations are to be permanently fixed, the station mark of concrete block with steel bolt indicating the centre of the block, should be used (Fig. 9.10b). The station mark is etched on the bolt.

In mountainous areas, the station marks are usually cut in the natural solid rocks.

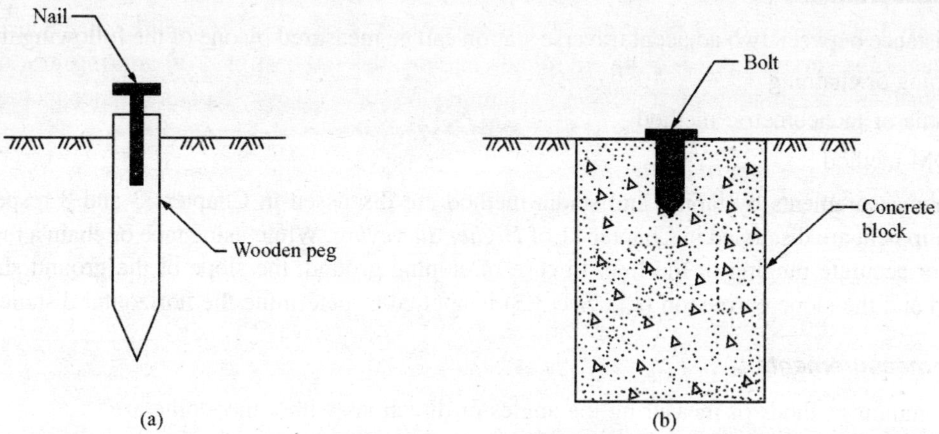

Fig. 9.10 Station marks

After marking the stations, their distances from at least three permanent reference points around the station should be measured and recorded making sketch (Fig. 9.11) to relocate the stations at a later stage.

In some cases, the station marks may not be visible directly from the adjacent stations for taking the observations. In such cases, it is necessary to provide signals at the traverse stations. Signals usually consist of ranging poles or plumb bob with string depending upon the length of the traverse line between the stations. Signals should be perfectly vertical, and should be centered exactly over the station to avoid centering error.

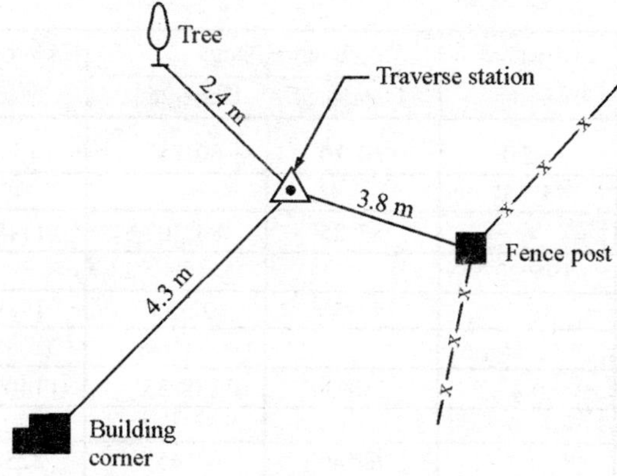

Fig. 9.11 Reference sketch for a traverse station

Linear and Angular Measurements

After fixing the traverse stations, the measurement of length of the traverse lines and angles or directions proceeds simultaneously. The choice of instrument for making measurements depends upon the traversing method employed.

Linear measurements

The distance between two adjacent traverse station can be measured by one of the following methods:

1. Taping or chaining
2. Stadia or tacheometric method
3. EDM method.

Linear measurements by taping and stadia method are discussed in Chapters 3 and 8 respectively. EDM equipment are discussed in Chapter 11 of *Higher Surveying*. While using tape or chain a theodolite is used for accurate ranging of the line. In case of sloping ground, the slope of the ground should be measured and the slope correction (*c.f.*, Sec 3.5) is applied to determine the horizontal distance.

Angular measurements

The common methods of measuring the angles or directions with a theodolite are

1. Loose needle method of bearings
2. Fast needle method of bearings
3. Method of deflection angles
4. Method of angles to the right
5. Method of interior angles
6. Azimuth method.

Loose-needle method of bearings: In this method a theodolite fitted with a magnetic compass is used to determine the bearings of the lines with reference to the magnetic meridian at each traverse station. Figure 9.12, illustrates the measurements of the angles by loose needle method in a closed-loop traverse. The figure also illustrates the method of recording the observed bearing and computation of adjusted bearings.

Station		Distance	Observed	Interior angle		Corrected
At	To	(m)	bearing	Computed	Corrected	bearing
A	B		15°20′	60°10′	60°15′	15°20′
	E		75°35′			
B	C			83°25′	83°30′	111°50′
	A		195°20′			
C	D			92°50′	92°55′	198°55′
	B					
D	E			238°30′	238°35′	140°20′
	C					
E	A			64°40′	64°45′	225°35′
	D					
				539°35′	540° 00′	

Fig. 9.12 Loose-needle method of angular measurements

At any station the included angle is difference of the forebearing of the forward line and back bearing of the preceding line. For example, in (Fig. 9.7) at station *D* the interior angle is $(\alpha_4 - \alpha'_3)$. The sum of the computed interior angles is compared with $(n-2)180°$, where n is the number of lines in a traverse. The difference, if any between the two values, is the amount of the error of closure. The correction is applied equally to all the interior angles, and the corrected bearings are computed. Loose needle method is rarely used because of the reasons given in Sec. 5.7.

Fast-needle method of bearings: In this method the magnetic bearing of the first line is only measured with reference to the magnetic meridian. The magnetic bearing of all other lines are determined indirectly from the magnetic bearing of the first line and the interior angles. This method is more accurate than the loose needle method, and is generally preferred.

The following three methods of traversing by fast-needle method are usually employed.

(a) Direct method with transiting: In this method the instrument is set up at the starting station *A* (Fig. 9.7), and the reading is set to zero. By releasing the magnetic needle, the telescope is brought in magnetic meridian with upper plate clamped. Now the lower plate is clamped and the telescope is directed towards *B*, and the reading is taken. This reading is the magnetic bearing of the *AB*. Now the instrument is shifted to *B* with both the plates clamped and after setting up the instrument, the telescope is directed towards *A* by releasing the lower clamp. Transit (plunge) the telescope. In this position the telescope has the line of sight of *AB* and the instrument still reads the bearing of *AB*. Hence the instrument is oriented at *B* with reference to the magnetic bearing. The upper clamp is released and the telescope is directed towards *C*. The reading now is the bearing of the line *BC*.

Shift the instrument to the next station, and repeat the process of orientation and measure the bearing of other lines.

The direct method with transiting is preferred for an open traverse.

(b) Direct method without transiting: In this method after shifting the instrument to *B* (Fig. 9.7) as in the direct method with transiting, the telescope is not plunged, and the telescope is directed towards *C* to take the reading. In this case the bearing of *BC* will be out by 180° on the alternate stations. Therefore, a correction has to be applied to the readings at alternate stations to obtain the magnetic bearing. Add 180° if the reading is less than 180°, and subtract 180° in case the reading is more than 180°.

It may be noted that the telescope is always rotated clockwise in the horizontal plane while taking fore sights.

(c) Back bearing method or azimuth method: In back bearing method, after shifting the instrument to *B* (Fig. 9.7) and the telescope sighting at *A* as in the direct method with transiting, calculate the back bearing of *AB* from its fore bearing measured at *A*. By releasing the upper clamp, the vernier *A* is set to read the back bearing of *AB* and by releasing the lower clamp, *A* is again bisected. Now the instrument is oriented as the vernier *A* reads the back bearing of *AB*. Rotate the telescope in clockwise direction after unclamping the upper plate and bisect the station *C*. The reading now is the fore bearing of *BC*. The process is repeated at other stations to obtain the bearings of other lines.

Table 9.1 presents a brief comparison between the above three methods of traversing by fast-needle method.

Method of deflection angle: In this method, the instrument is set up at the starting station *A* (Fig. 9.4) and directly the magnetic bearing of *AB* is measured at *A* or computed from the known azimuth of the line *PQ* by setting up the instrument at *P*.

Table 9.1 Relative merits and demerits of the three methods

Transiting	Without transiting	Back bearing
1. A mechanical and quite convenient method.	1. Gives the best results.	1. Inconvenient as at each station bearing is to be calculated and the reading is to be set to read back bearing.
2. Can not be used if the instrument is not adjusted.	2. Can be used even when the instrument is not in perfect adjustment.	2. Seldom used.
3. All the methods require almost same time, and produce the results of same accuracy if the instrument is in adjustment.		

If the azimuth of *PQ* is known, the following procedure is used to determine the bearing of the traverse lines from observed deflection angles (*cf.*, Sec. 4.6.).

Set up the instrument at *P* with the vernier *A* set to zero. Unclamp the lower plate and rotate the telescope to take a back sight on *Q*. Plunge the telescope. Now the line of sight is along *QP*. Unclamp the upper plate and turn the telescope clockwise to take a fore sight on *A*. The reading (mean of vernier *A* and *B*) is the deflection angle α_{1R}. When the instrument is set at *B*, the telescope is turned anti-clockwise and the deflection angle will be α_{2L}. At each station the angles are observed with face left as well as face right.

Method of angles to the right: For measuring the angles to the right, the instrument is set up at the starting station *P* (Fig. 9.6), when the azimuth of the line *PQ* is known. The vernier *A* is set to zero. The lower plate is unclamped and a back sight is taken on *Q*. Loosen the upper plate and turn the telescope clockwise to take a fore sight on *A*. Take mean of the vernier *A* and *B* readings. The readings are taken with face left and face right of the instrument at each station. The required angle to the right is the average of the values obtained with face left and face right.

Method of Interior angles: For the measurement of the interior angles Sec. 4.5 may be referred to. The angles measured clockwise are included angles or interior angles if the traverse is run counter clockwise from the starting point. When the traverse is run clockwise from the starting station, the angles measured clockwise, are the exterior angles.

Locating Details

In traversing, the details can be located by any method discussed in Sec. 1.4, depending on the field conditions. The angles and distances should preferably be measured from the traverse stations to avoid the errors in measurement of distances along the traverse lines. But when a detail is located by taking offsets from the traverse line, the distances along the traverse lines have to be measured.

9.6 COMPATIBILITY OF LINEAR AND ANGULAR MEASUREMENTS

The precision achieved in a measurement depends upon the instruments used and method employed. Therefore, the instruments and method to be employed should be so chosen that the precision in linear and angular measurements should be consistent with each other. This can be achieved by making the error in linear measurement equal to the error in angular measurement.

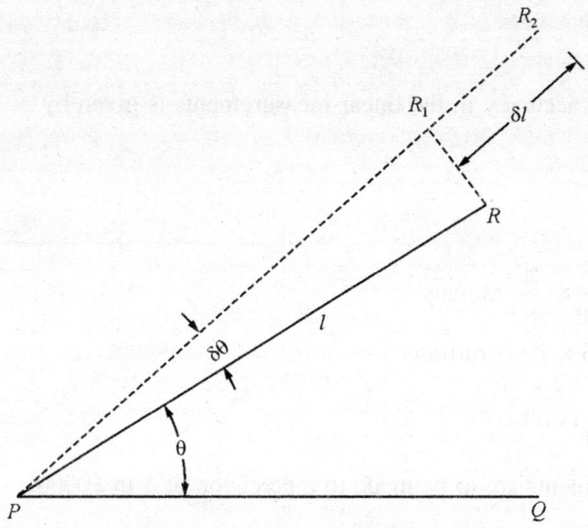

Fig. 9.13 Error in linear and angular measurements

In Fig. 9.13, PQ is the traverse line, and the point R is located with reference to PQ by taking angular measurement θ and linear measurement l. But, assuming the errors in θ as $\delta\theta$ and in l as δl, the point is located at R_2 instead of at R.

The displacement due to angular error

$$RR_1 = l \tan\delta\theta$$

The displacement due to linear error

$$R_1R_2 = \delta l$$

For consistency in linear and angular errors

$$RR_1 = R_1R_2$$

or $l \tan \delta\theta = \delta l$

$$\tan \delta\theta = \frac{\delta l}{l}$$

As $\delta\theta$ is small, $\tan \delta\theta = \delta\theta$

$$\delta\theta = \frac{\delta l}{l} \qquad \text{...(9.4)}$$

Eq. (9.4) is the required relationship which expresses the consistency in precision in the linear and angular measurements.

ILLUSTRATIVE EXAMPLES

Example 9.1

In a traverse survey, the angular measurements were made with an error of 20″. What is the relative accuracy in the linear measurements?

Solution:

We have $\delta\theta = 20''$

From Eq. (9.4), the relative accuracy in the linear measurements is given by

$$\frac{\delta l}{l} = \delta\theta$$
$$= 20''$$
$$= \frac{20}{60 \times 60} \times \frac{\pi}{180} \text{ radians}$$
$$= 9.6963 \times 10^{-5} \text{ radians}$$
$$= \frac{1}{10000} \text{ (say).}$$

Thus the linear measurements are to be made to a precision of 1 in 10000.

Example 9.2

In a theodolite traversing, the distances are to be measured to a precision of 1 in 15000. Determine the accuracy in the angular measurements.

Solution:

From Eq. (9.4), we have

$$\delta\theta = \frac{\delta l}{l}$$

or
$$= \frac{1}{15000}$$
$$= \frac{60 \times 60}{15000} \times \frac{180}{\pi} \text{ seconds}$$
$$= 13.75''$$
$$= 13'' \text{ (say)}$$

9.7 CHECKS IN CLOSED AND OPEN TRAVERSES

The checking of the linear measurements consists in taping each traverse line a second time, preferably in the reverse direction on different dates and by different parties.

The checks for the angular measurements in a closed traverse and in an open traverse are given below.

Closed Traverse

In the case of an closed traverse the different checks are available for included angles, deflection angles and bearings.

Included angles: The sum of all included or interior angles in a closed traverse is compared to the theoretical sum, *i.e.*, $(n - 2)180°$ for determining the misclosure in the field. If the misclosure is within the permissible limits, it is adjusted. However, if it is large, the error should be located and corrected before leaving the field. If necessary the whole work should be repeated. The permissible closing error can be computed from the formula

$$E = K\sqrt{n} \qquad \ldots(9.5)$$

where $K = 20''$ for ordinary theodolite traverse. However, it depends upon the least count of the theodolite, the number of repetitions and the accuracy desired.

n = number of sides (or angle) in a traverse.

Deflection angles: The algebraic sum of the deflection angles should be equal to 360°, taking the right deflection angles as positive and left deflection angles as negative. This rule applies to a loop traverse if the traverse lines do not criss-cross one another. The rule also applies if they cross an even number of times. However, if they cross an odd number of times, the algebraic sum is equal to zero.

Bearings: In a traverse run by bearings, the closing error is determined by setting up the theodolite again on the starting station after occupying the last station completing the loop. The bearing of the initial line is again measured and compared with the previously observed value. The difference between the two values is the closing error. Alternatively, the fore bearing of the last line measured at the last station should be compared with its back bearing ± 180° measured at the starting station.

Open Traverse

In the case of open traverse, no direct check of angular measurements is available. However, some indirect checks can be applied as illustrated in Fig. 9.14.

As shown in Fig. 9.14a, in addition to the bearings of the traverse lines, if the traverse stations *A* and *E* are intervisible, the fore bearing of the line *AE* known as *cut off line*, is observed from *A*, and its back bearing is observed from *E*. If the bearing differ by 180°, the work up to the station *E* may be taken as correct. If a small discrepancy is found, it can be adjusted before proceeding further.

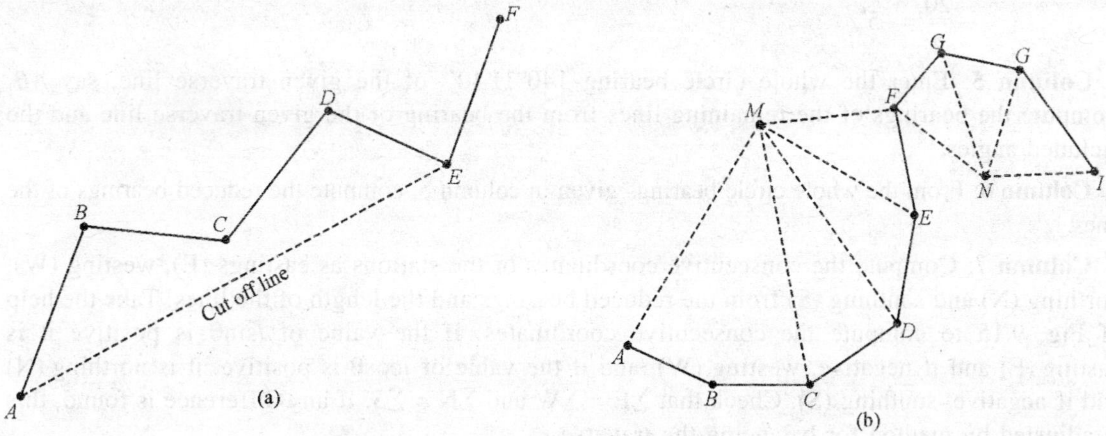

Fig. 9.14 Checks for angular measurements in open traverse

Another way of checking the work in open traverses is to check the work at the time of plotting. If any prominent point *M* (Fig. 9.14b) such as a church spire or a chimney is found, its bearings are also read from as many stations as possible. At the time of plotting the traverse, the lines *AM*, *CM*, *DM*, etc., are laid off. If these lines pass through same point, the work may be accepted to be correct.

In the case of long and precise traverse, astronomical observations are taken to determine the angular errors.

9.8 TRAVERSE COMPUTATION

The objective of the traverse computation is to determine the adjusted independent coordinates of the traverse stations so that they can be plotted on the drawing sheet. Once the traverse stations are plotted, the details can be plotted with reference to the traverse lines or traverse stations themselves, depending upon the type of measurements taken for locating the details.

The computations can be performed systematically, if the observations are recorded in a tabular form as suggested by Gale. Such table is known as *Gale's traverse table* (Table 9.2). The columns of Gale's table are filled as illustrated below:

Column 1: Enter the names *A*, *B*, *C*, etc., of the stations at which the instrument is set up and the names *B*, *C*, *D*, etc., of the forward stations to which the observations have been made.

Column 2: Enter the lengths of the lines *AB*, *BC*, *CD*, etc., between the instrument station and the forward station.

Column 3: Enter the observed included or interior angles. Determine the sum of all the included angles and compare with $(n-2)180°$.

Column 4: If the sum of all the included angles is equal to $(n-2)180°$, the corrections to the included angles are zero. If difference is found, apply the corrections equally to all the angles. For the values entered in Table 9.2, sum is 360°00′20″. The value of $(n-2)180° = (4-2)180° = 360°$. The difference of +20″ is the error. Therefore, to apply the correction of −20″, it is distributed equally among all the angles, *i.e.*, the correction to each angle is

$$-\frac{20}{4} = -5''$$

Column 5: Enter the whole circle bearing 140°11′40″ of the given traverse line, say *AB*. Compute the bearings of the remaining lines from the bearing of the given traverse line and the included angles.

Column 6: From the whole circle bearings given in column 5, compute the reduced bearings of the lines.

Column 7: Compute the consecutive coordinates of the stations as eastings (E), westing (W), northing (N) and southing (S) from the reduced bearings and the length of the lines. Take the help of Fig. 9.15 to compute the consecutive coordinates. If the value of $l\sin\theta$ is positive it is easting (E) and if negative, westing (W), and if the value of $l\cos\theta$ is positive, it is northing (N) and if negative, southing (S). Check that $\Sigma E = \Sigma W$ and $\Sigma N = \Sigma S$. If any difference is found, this is adjusted by method for balancing the traverse.

Column 8: Enter the independent coordinates of the starting station *A* (say 1000, 1000). Compute the independent coordinates of other stations by adding or subtracting the consecutive coordinates of the forward stations, as the case may be.

Table 9.2 Gale's traverse table

(1)		(2)	(3)	(4)	(5)	(6)	(7)				(8)		
Station		Length	Included	Corr-	W.C.B.	R.B.	Consecutive coordinate				Independent coordinate		Remarks
At	to	(m)	angle	ection			E (+)	W (–)	N (+)	S (–)	E	N	
A	B	156.2	86° 30′ 02″	– 5″	140° 11′ 40″	S 39° 48′ 20″ E	100.0	–	–	120.0	1000.0*	1000.0*	A
B	C	318.9	80° 59′ 34″	– 5″	41° 11′ 09″	N 41° 11′ 09″ E	210.0	–	240.0	–	1100.0	880.0	B
C	D	88.4	91° 31′ 29″	– 5″	312° 42′ 33″	N 47° 17′ 27″ W	–	65.0	60.0	–	1310.0	1120.0	C
D	A	304.0	100° 59′ 15″	– 5″	233° 41′ 43″	S 53° 41′ 43″ W	–	245.0	–	180.0	1245.0	1180.0	D
Sum			360° 00′ 20″	– 20″			310.0	310.0	300.0	300.0	1000.0	1000.0	A

* Assumed values

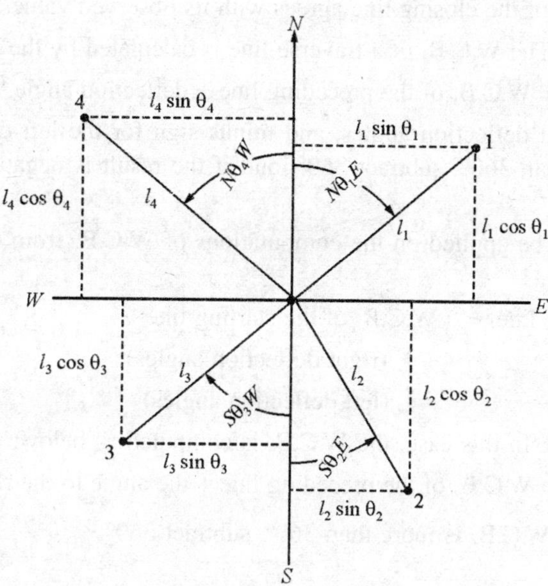

Fig. 9.15 Consecutive coordinate (Easting/Westing and Northing/Southing)

Computation of Bearings, Consecutive Coordinates, and Independent Coordinates

The following computations are required to determine the adjusted independent coordinates of the traverse stations:

1. Ascertaining the bearing of one of the traverse lines.
2. Running down the bearings of remaining traverse lines.
3. Computation of reduced bearings of traverse lines.
4. Calculation of consecutive coordinates of traverse stations.
5. Calculation of closing error.

6. Balancing of consecutive coordinates.
7. Calculation of independent coordinates.

Ascertaining the bearing of the first traverse line

The bearing of one of the traverse lines, say *AB*, may be determined by connecting the traverse to a line *PQ* of known azimuth (Fig. 9.2). It requires the measurement of the angles *QPA* and *PAB*. If a line of known azimuth is not available in the vicinity of the starting station, the bearing of the starting line *AB* can directly be observed with a magnetic compass. When the true bearings are required, the astronomical observations are also required to be made.

Running down the bearings of remaining traverse lines

The method of computation of the whole-circle bearings (W.C.B) of remaining lines depends upon the kind of angular observations made.

From included angles: The corrected included angle is added to the W.C.B. of the preceding line. If the sum is more than 180°, subtract 180°, if less than 180°, add 180° and if more than 360°, subtract 360°. Check that the bearing of the closing line agrees with its observed value.

From deflection angles: The W.C.B. of a traverse line is calculated by the following rule:

W.C.B. of a traverse line = W.C.B. of the preceding line ± deflection angle.

Use plus sign for the right deflection angles, and minus sign for the left deflection angles. If the computed W.C.B. is more than 360°, subtract 360°, and if the result is negative add 360° to get the W.C.B.

The following check may be applied on the computations of W.C.B. from the observed deflection angles:

W.C.B. of the last traverse line = W.C.B. of the starting line
+ Σ (right deflection angles)
− Σ (left deflection angles)

From angles to the right: In this case, the W.C.B. is computed as below:

W.C.B. of a traverse line = W.C.B. of the preceding line + the angle to the right.

If the computed value of W.C.B. is more than 360°, subtract 360°.

Computation of reduced bearings

The reduced bearings (R.B.) of the traverse lines, help in the computation of the consecutive coordinates of the traverse stations. Thus, the whole-circle bearings of the lines must be converted into reduced bearings. Table 9.3 helps in obtaining the R.B. from W.C.B. (*c.f.*, Fig. 4.4).

Table 9.3 R.B. from W.C.B.

W.C.B.	Quadrant	R.B.
0° to 90°	*NE*	= W.C.B.
90° to 180°	*SE*	= 180° − W.C.B.
180° to 270°	*SW*	= W.C.B. − 180°
270° to 360°	*NW*	= 360° − W.C.B.

Calculation of consecutive coordinates

The coordinates of points are defined as *latitude* and *departure*. The latitude is always measured parallel to the assumed meridian or true meridian and the departure perpendicular to the meridian. In Fig. 9.16, the NS line is the meridian. The latitude and departure of a point Q are given by:

$$\text{Latitude } (L) = AQ = l\cos\theta$$

$$\text{Departure } (D) = BQ = l\sin\theta \qquad \text{...(9.6)}$$

where l is the length of the traverse line PQ and θ is its reduced bearing.

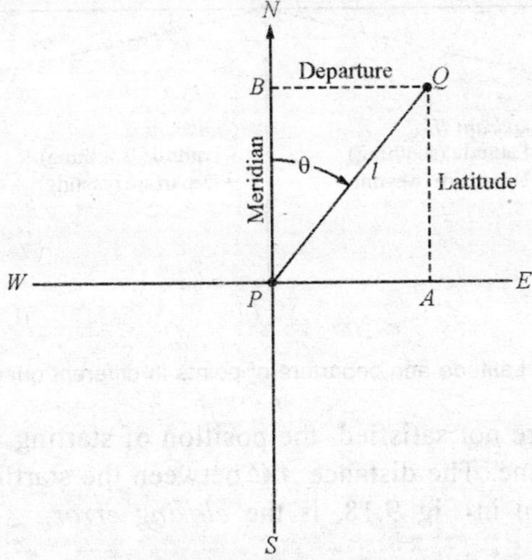

Fig. 9.16 Latitude and departure

If the latitude and departure of a forward station is computed with reference to the preceding station, they are known as *consecutive coordinates* or *dependent coordinates.* Depending upon the quadrant in which the station lies, the latitude and departure may be positive or negative. In Fig. 9.17, four points A, B, C, and D have been shown lying in different quadrants. The following rules may be used to determine the sign of latitude and departure of the points.

(*i*) If the point lies north of the east-west (*EW*) line, the latitude is positive and it is known as *northing*.

(*ii*) If the point lies south of the east-west (*EW*) line, latitude is negative, and it is known as *southing*.

(*iii*) If the point lies east of the north-south (*NS*) line or meridian, the departure is positive, and it is known as *easting*.

(*iv*) If the point lies west of the north-south (*NS*) line or meridian, the departure is negative, and it is known as *westing*.

Computation of closing error

In a closed traverse, the following conditions must be satisfied:

$$\Sigma\,\text{Northings} = \Sigma\,\text{Southings} \quad \text{or } \Sigma N = \Sigma S$$

$$\text{and} \quad \Sigma\,\text{Eastings} = \Sigma\,\text{Westings} \quad \text{or } \Sigma E = \Sigma W \qquad \text{...(9.7)}$$

$$\text{or} \quad \Sigma\,\text{Latitude} = 0$$

$$\text{and} \quad \Sigma\,\text{Departure} = 0 \qquad \text{...(9.8)}$$

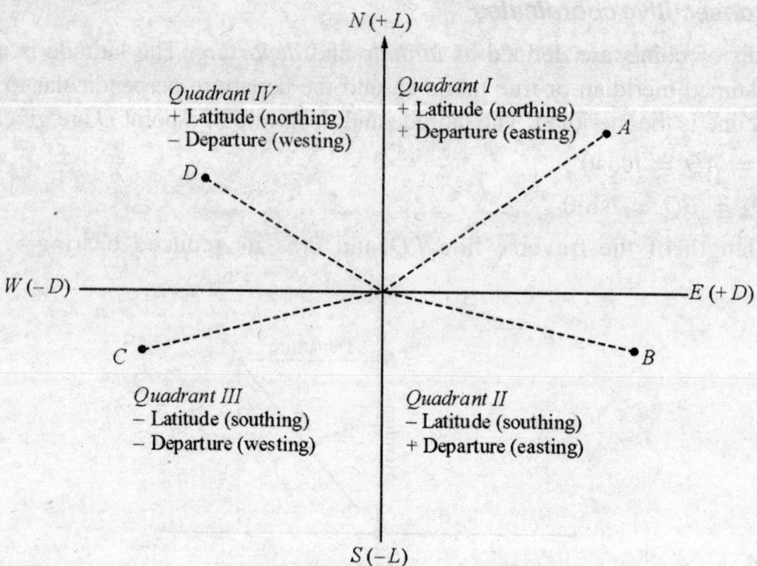

Fig. 9.17 Latitude and departure of points in different quadrants

If the above conditions are not satisfied, the position of starting station A and its computed position A' will not be the same. The distance AA' between the starting and computed positions A and A', respectively, shown in Fig. 9.18, is the *closing error*.

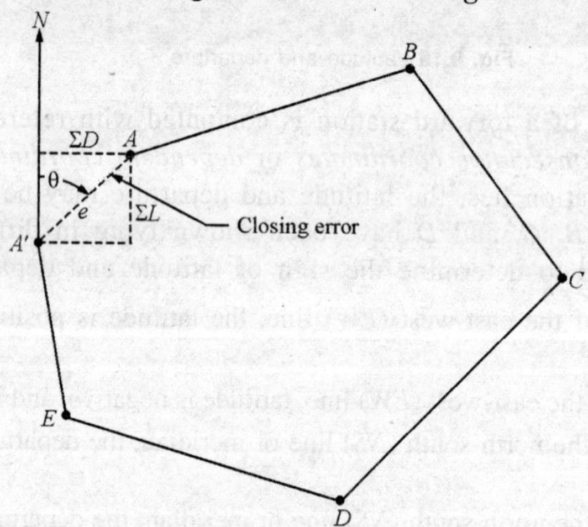

Fig. 9.18 Closing error

The closing error may be computed from the following formula:

$$\text{Closing error} = AA' = e = \sqrt{\left(\sum L\right)^2 + \left(\sum D\right)^2} \tag{9.9}$$

and its direction or reduced bearing θ is given by

$$\tan\theta = \frac{\sum D}{\sum L} \tag{9.10}$$

The sign of $\sum D$ and $\sum L$, thus define the quadrant in which the closing error lies. Sometimes, the term relative error of closure is also used. It is given by

$$\text{Relative error of closure} = \frac{\text{Closing error}}{\text{Total length of traverse}}$$

$$= \frac{e}{p}$$

$$\text{or} \quad = \frac{1}{(p/e)} \qquad (9.11)$$

where p is the total length or perimeter of the traverse.

Balancing the traverse

The term *balancing* is generally applied to the operation of applying corrections to latitudes and departures to satisfy the conditions given by Eq. (9.8), if $\sum L \neq 0$ and $\sum D \neq 0$ for a closed traverse.

The following are common methods of balancing a traverse:

1. Bowditch's method
2. Transit method
3. Graphical method
4. Axis method.

Bowditch's method: The basis of the method suggested by C.F. Bowditch, is on the assumption that the errors in linear measurements are proportional to $\sqrt{l}$ and that the errors in angular measurements are inversely proportional to $\sqrt{l}$, where l is the length of the line. The *Bowditch's rule* also known as *compass rule*, is used when linear and angular measurements are compatible, i.e., they are of equal precision.

In this method, the total error in the latitude and departure is distributed in proportion to the lengths of the traverse lines. Therefore,

correction to latitude (or departure) of any traverse line

$$= \text{Total error in latitude (or departure)} \; \frac{\text{length of that traverse line}}{\text{total length of traverse}} \qquad ...(9.12)$$

Thus, if C_L = correction to latitude of any line

C_D = correction to departure of any line

$\sum L$ = total error in latitude

$\sum D$ = total error in departure

$\sum l$ = total length of traverse or perimeter p

l = length of that line for which the correction is being computed.

Then we have

$$C_L = \sum L \times \frac{l}{\sum l} \qquad ...(9.13)$$

and $$C_D = \Sigma D \times \frac{l}{\Sigma l} \qquad ...(9.14)$$

The sign of the above corrections C_L and C_D are decided as follows:

(i) If $\Sigma N > \Sigma S$, the sign of corrections for northings is negative and for the southings positive, and *vice versa*.

(ii) If $\Sigma E > \Sigma W$, the sign of corrections for eastings is negative and for the westings positive, and *vice versa*.

Transit rule: Balancing the traverse may be done by employing *transit rule* when the angular measurements are more precise than the linear measurements. According to this rule, the total error in latitude and in departure is distributed in proportion to the latitude and departure of the traverse line. Thus, correction to latitude (or departure) of any traverse line

$$= \text{Total error in latitude (or departure)} \; \frac{\text{latitude (or departure) of that line}}{\text{arithmetic sum of latitudes (or departures)}}$$

Thus, if L = latitude of any line

D = departure of any line

L_T = arithmetic sum of latitudes (ignoring the signs)

D_T = arithmetic sum of departures (ignoring the signs)

ΣL = total error (algebraic sum) in latitude

ΣD = total error (algebraic sum) in departure.

Then we have

$$C_L = \Sigma L \times \frac{L}{L_T} \qquad ...(9.15)$$

$$C_D = \Sigma D \times \frac{D}{D_T} \qquad ...(9.16)$$

The sign of the corrections to northings, southings, eastings, and westings are decided as in Bowditch's method.

Graphical method: For rough surveys where the angular measurements are of inferior degree of accuracy, such as in compass traversing, the Bowditch's rule may be applied graphically without doing theoretical calculations. In this method, before plotting the traverse from the field observations on sufficiently large scale, the traverse angles or the bearings of the traverse lines must be adjusted to satisfy the geometric conditions of the traverse.

Let $AB'C'D'E'A'$ be an unbalanced traverse having a closing error equal to AA' (Fig. 9.19a). The total closing error AA' is distributed linearly to all the sides of the traverse in proportion to their lengths. Draw a line A_0A_0' equal to the sum of lengths of all the sides to some suitable scale, and mark B_0, C_0, D_0, E_0, etc., on this line such that A_0B_0, B_0C_0, C_0D_0, D_0E_0, and E_0A_0' represent the lengths of sides AB', $B'C'$, $C'D'$, $D'E'$, and $E'A'$, respectively (Fig. 9.19b). Draw $A_0'a$ parallel and equal to the closing error AA' (e) shown in Fig.9.19a. Draw lines B_0b, C_0c, D_0d, and E_0e, parallel to $A_0'a$, then B_0b, C_0c, D_0d, E_0e, and $A_0'a$ are the required amount of corrections to be applied at B', C', D', E', and A', respectively. The direction of error at station is shown by arrow. Mark *B, C, D,* and *E* in Fig 9.19 a, such that $B'B$, $C'C$, $D'D$, and $E'E$ are, respectively, equal to bB_0, cC_0, dD_0, and eE_0. A' is shifted to *A* and the adjusted traverse is *ABCDEA*.

The axis method: This method is employed when the angular measurements are very accurately measured, and the required corrections are to be applied to the linear measurements. Thus the directions of the lines are unchanged and the general shape of the figure of the traverse remains the same.

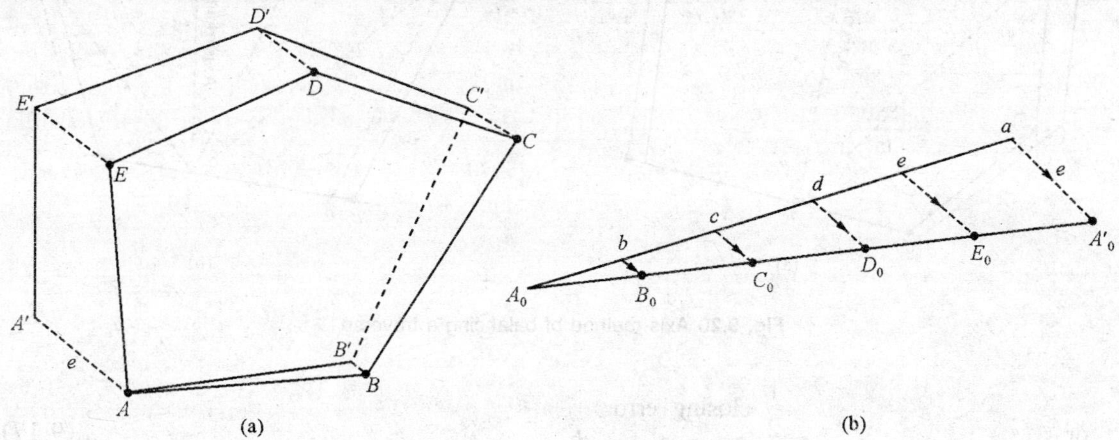

Fig. 9.19 Graphical method of balancing a traverse

Fig. 9.20a shows an unadjusted traverse *abcdefa'*. Join *a'a* and produce it to intersect *cd* at *m*. The line *a'm* is known as the *axis of adjustment*. Join *b, e,* and *f* with *m* by drawing lines *bm, em* and *fm,* respectively. Locate point *A* such that *a'A* is equal to *Aa*. Through *A* draw a line *AB* parallel to *ab* cutting *mb* produced in *B*. Through *B* draw a line *BC* parallel to *bc* cutting *mc* produced at *C*. Similarly, locate *F* and *E* by drawing *AF*, through *A* parallel to *a'f* cutting *mf* in *F*, and by drawing *FE* through *F* parallel to *fe* cutting *me* in *E*. *D* is also located in the similar manner. Join *A, B, C, D, E, F,* and *A* to get the adjusted traverse *ABCDEFA*.

The principle of this method is explained below.

We have

$$\frac{AB}{ab} = \frac{Am}{am}$$

The correction to the line *ab*

$$= AB - ab = \frac{Am}{am}ab - ab = \frac{Am - am}{am}ab$$

We have $Am - am = Aa = \frac{1}{2}a'a$

$$\text{Thus the correction to } ab = \frac{\frac{1}{2}a'a}{am}ab$$

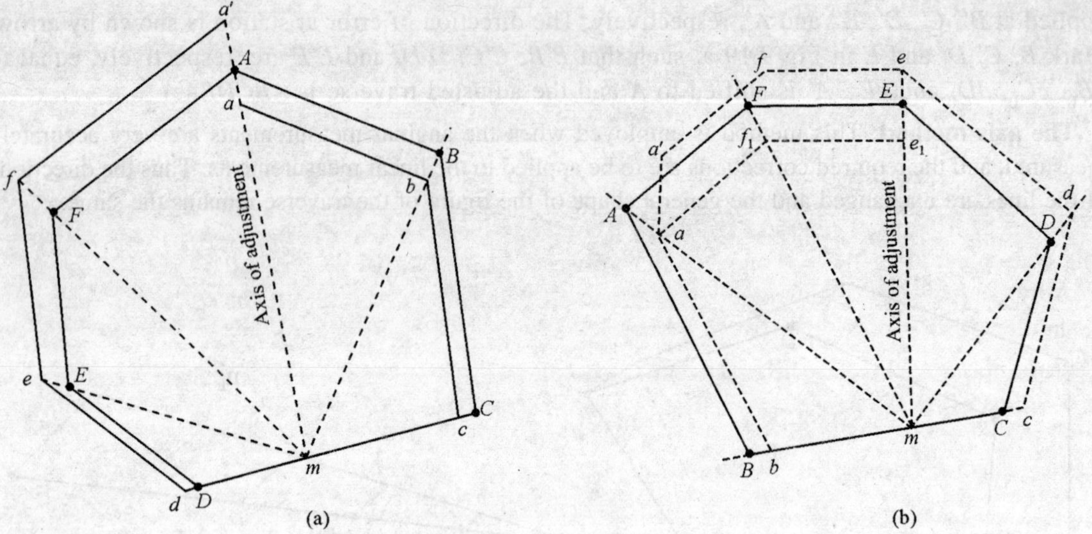

Fig. 9.20 Axis method of balancing a traverse

$$\text{or} \qquad = \frac{\frac{1}{2}\text{ closing error}}{am}\, ab \qquad \ldots(9.17)$$

In general, we can write

$$\text{Correction to any side} = \frac{\frac{1}{2}\text{closing error}}{\text{length of axis}} \text{ length of the side} \qquad \ldots(9.18)$$

From Eq. (9.18), we can write

$$\text{Correction to } a'f = \frac{\frac{1}{2}a'a}{am}\, a'f$$

$$\text{and correction to } fe = \frac{\frac{1}{2}a'a}{am}\, fe$$

Accuracy of the adjustment by the axis method depends upon the location of the axis of adjustment. The method is more accurate if the axis of adjustment divides the figure approximately into two equal parts. However, in some cases this may not happen as shown in Fig.9.20b. In such cases, the error is transferred to some other point say *e*, by drawing af_1 parallel and equal to $a'f$ and f_1e_1 parallel and equal to *fe*. Now the unadjusted traverse is $edcbaf_1e_1$ having the closing error ee_1. The line ee_1 when produced roughly divides the figure into two equal parts.

Use of Gale's Traverse Table for Balancing a Traverse

When the conditions $\sum L = 0$ and $\sum D = 0$ are not satisfied, the traverse needs adjustment by any method of balancing a traverse depending upon the precision maintained in the linear and angular observations. If Gale's traverse table (Table 9.2) is being used for recording the observations and computations of the coordinates, it is modified to accommodate the corrections in latitudes and departures.

In Table 9.2, after column 7, two columns are added. Thus, the independent coordinates will be entered in column 10. After calculating $\sum L$ and $\sum D$ in column 7 the entries of column 8 and 9 will be as given below.

Column 8: Enter necessary corrections in the latitude (E and W) and the departure (N and S) of the stations so that $\sum L = 0$ and $\sum D = 0$. The correc-tions may be computed either by transit rule or by compass rule (Bowditch's rule) depending upon the precision maintained in the linear and angular observations.

Column 9: Enter the corrected consecutive coordinates of the stations for computing the independent coordinates for column 10.

9.9 PLOTTING A TRAVERSE SURVEY

The accuracy of a survey depends upon the accuracy with which its control points are plotted. The traverse stations, which are the control points, can be plotted by either (1) the angle and distance method or (2) the coordinate method.

In angle and distance method, the traverse stations are plotted with reference to the previous station and, therefore, the accuracy of the location of each station on the plan evidently depends upon the accuracy with which previous points have been plotted. Even if there is a slight error in plotting, the error gets accummulated and the position of the last station may be displaced to a considerable distance from its true position. This difficulty is not faced in plotting by the coordinate (independent) system.

The angle and distance method may be used for the small surveys of low accuracy.

Angle and Distance Method

In this method, distances between the stations are laid off to scale and angles or bearings are plotted by one of the methods given below:

(a) Protractor method

(b) Tangent method

(c) Chord method.

As the angle and distance method is of very inferior accuracy it is not preferred compared to the coordinate method, which is generally used for traverse plotting, and therefore not being discussed.

Coordinate Method

In this method, traverse stations are plotted by calculating the independent coordinates. This method is by far the most practical and accurate one for plotting traverses or any other extensive system of horizontal control. The advantage of this method of plotting is that the closing error can be adjusted prior to plotting.

Before starting the plotting by coordinates, it is essential to draw the grid very accurately using a graticule or by the following procedure (Fig. 9.21).

Draw two diagonals from the corners of the drawing sheet and locate its intersection *m*. From *m*, scale off equal distance on the diagonals using a beam compass, and locate the points *A*, *B*, *C*, and *O*.

Join these points using a steel straight edge. Mark points at equal distance on *AB*, *BC*, *CO*, and *OA*. Join the points with the corresponding points on the opposite side to make the grid.

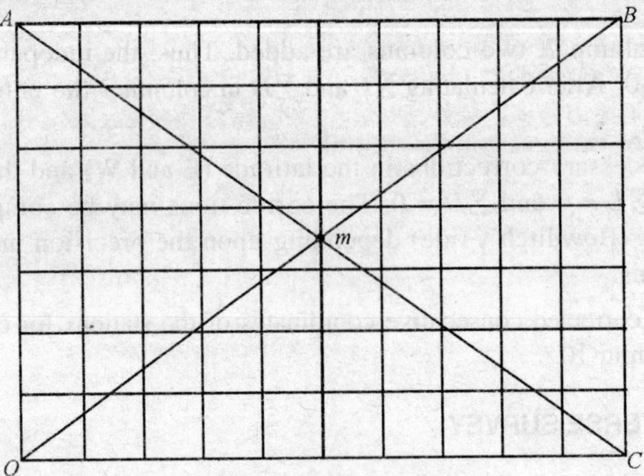

Fig. 9.21 Drawing the grid

9.10 OMITTED MEASUREMENTS

In a closed traverse, lengths and bearings of all the traverse lines are measured. However, sometimes it may not be possible to take all the measurements due to obstacles or oversights. Such omitted measurements or missing quantities can be computed provided the number of such quantities is not more than two. In such cases, there can be no check on the accuracy of the field work nor can the traverse be balanced. It is because of the fact that all the errors propagated throughout the survey work are thrown into the computed values of the omitted quantities.

For a closed traverse from Eq. (9.8), we have

$$\Sigma L = l_1 \cos \theta_1 + l_2 \cos \theta_2 + \ldots\ldots\ldots + l_n \cos \theta_n = 0 \quad \ldots(9.19)$$

$$\Sigma D = l_1 \sin \theta_1 + l_2 \sin \theta_2 + \ldots\ldots\ldots + l_n \sin \theta_n = 0 \quad \ldots(9.20)$$

where $l_1, l_2, l_3, \ldots$ = length of the traverse lines

$\theta_1, \theta_2, \theta_3, \ldots$ = reduced bearings of the traverse lines

n = total number of traverse lines or stations.

Solving Eqs. (9.19) and (9.20), any two missing quantities may be calculated. The quantities may be:

(*i*) Length of a traverse line, l $= \sqrt{L^2 + D^2}$

(*ii*) Latitude of stations, L $= l \cos \theta$

(*iii*) Departure of station, D $= l \sin \theta$

(*iv*) Reduced bearing of a traverse line, θ $= \tan^{-1} \dfrac{D}{L}$

The omitted measurements may be classified in the following cases:

1. (*a*) Length of a line not measured

   (*b*) Bearing of a line not measured

   (*c*) Length and bearing of a line not measured.

2. Length of a line and bearing of adjacent line not measured
3. Length of two lines not measured
4. Bearing of two lines not measured.

In all other cases except in case (1), the two traverse lines may or may not be adjacent.

(*i*) Length or bearing or both of a line omitted

In Fig. 9.22, BC is the affected traverse line. Let $\sum L'$ and $\sum D'$ be the sum of latitudes and departures, respectively, of the observed lines, and L_{BC} and D_{BC} be the latitude and departure of BC, respectively,

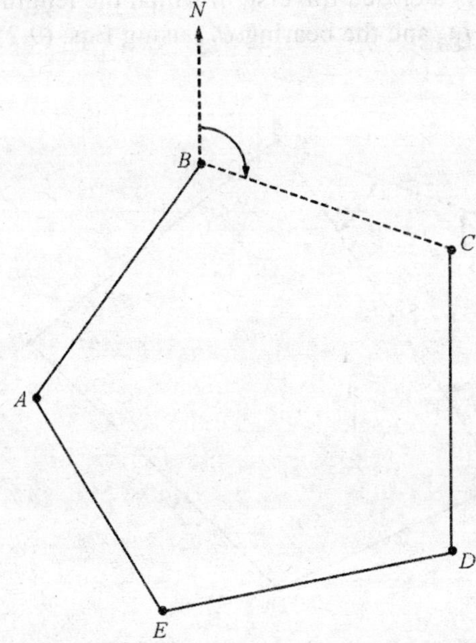

Fig. 9.22 Length or bearing or both of a line omitted

then we have

$$\sum L' + L_{BC} = 0 \qquad \text{...(9.21)}$$

$$\sum D' + D_{BC} = 0 \qquad \text{...(9.22)}$$

or

$$L_{BC} = l_{BC} \cos \theta_{BC} = -\sum L' \qquad \text{...(9.23)}$$

$$D_{BC} = l_{BC} \sin \theta_{BC} = -\sum D' \qquad \text{...(9.24)}$$

From Eqs. (9.23) and (9.24), we get

$$l_{BC} = \sqrt{L_{BC}^{\ 2} + D_{BC}^{\ 2}}$$

$$= \sqrt{(\sum L')^2 + (\sum D')^2} \qquad \text{...(9.25)}$$

and

$$\tan \theta_{BC} = \frac{l_{BC} \sin \theta_{BC}}{l_{BC} \cos\theta_{BC}}$$

$$= \frac{\Sigma D'}{\Sigma L'} \quad ...(9.26)$$

The quadrant of the reduced bearing of the line is determined from the signs of the latitude and departure by inspection.

(*ii*) Length of one line and bearing of an adjacent line omitted

In Fig. 9.23, the length of *AB* and the bearing of *EA* could not be measured.

If *B* and *E* are joined, *BCDE* is a closed traverse in which the length and the bearing of *EB* are not known. Compute the length l_{EB} and the bearing θ_{EB} using Eqs. (9.25) and (9.26), as discussed is the case (*i*).

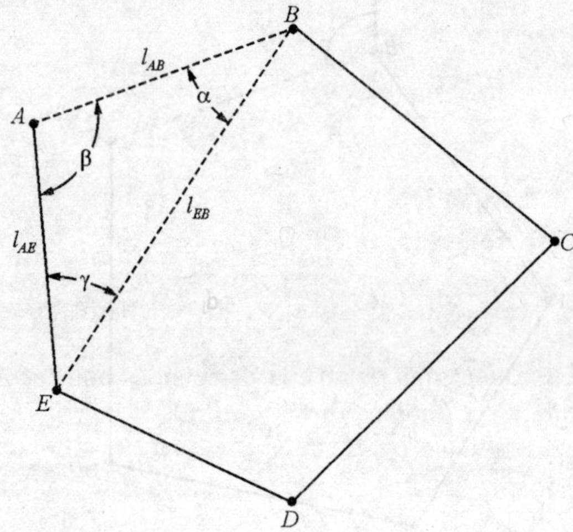

Fig. 9.23 Length of a line and bearing of an adjustment line omitted

From the bearing of *AB* and *EB*, compute the angle *ABE*. In triangle *ABE*, l_{AE}, l_{EB}, and the angle *ABE* are known. Therefore, from sine rule,

$$\frac{AB}{\sin AEB} = \frac{BE}{\sin BAE} = \frac{AE}{\sin ABE}$$

or $$\frac{l_{AB}}{\sin \gamma} = \frac{l_{BE}}{\sin \beta} = \frac{l_{AE}}{\sin \alpha}$$

Therefore $$\beta = \sin^{-1}\left[\frac{l_{BE} \sin \alpha}{l_{AE}}\right] \quad ...(9.27)$$

$$l_{AB} = l_{AE}\frac{\sin \gamma}{\sin \alpha} \quad ...(9.28)$$

where $\gamma = 180° - (\alpha + \beta)$. ...(9.29)

Knowing the bearing of *AB* and the angle β, the bearing of *AE* can be computed. Also, the bearing of *EA* can be computed from the bearing of *EB* and the angle γ.

It may be noted that as the value of sine near 90° changes very slowly, a small error in calculated values may cause a large error in the angle β, and therefore, as far as possible, the value of β close to 90° should be avoided.

(*iii*) Length of two adjacent lines omitted

In Fig 9.24, let us consider that the lengths *AB* and *EA* could not be measured.

If we consider *BCDE* as a closed traverse, the unknown bearing and length of *EB* can be determined by the method, given in the case (*i*).

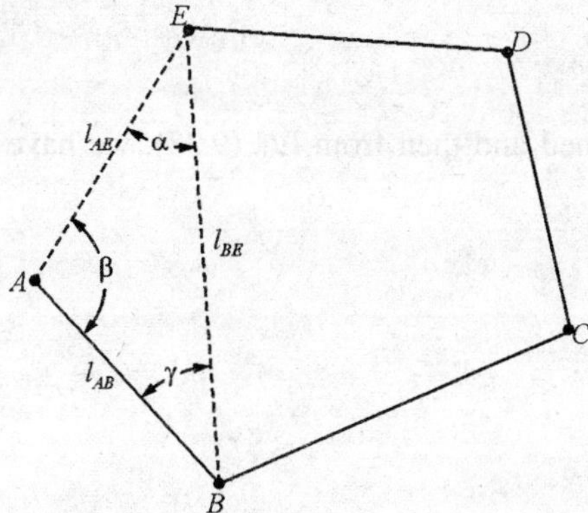

Fig. 9.24 Length or bearing of two adjacent lines omitted

Now in the triangle *ABE*, the bearings of all the three sides and length of *BE* are known, and therefore, the angles α, β and γ are known. From sine rule we have

$$\frac{AE}{\sin\gamma} = \frac{AB}{\sin\alpha} = \frac{BE}{\sin\beta}$$

or
$$\frac{l_{AE}}{\sin\gamma} = \frac{l_{AB}}{\sin\alpha} = \frac{l_{BE}}{\sin\beta}$$

Therefore, $$l_{AE} = l_{BE}\frac{\sin\gamma}{\sin\beta} \qquad ...(9.30)$$

and $$l_{AB} = l_{BE}\frac{\sin\alpha}{\sin\beta} \qquad ...(9.31)$$

(*iv*) Bearing of two adjacent lines omitted

Let us consider that the bearings of the lines *AB* and *EA* (Fig. 9.24) could not be measured. Let the bearing and length of *BE* have been determined by the method discussed in the case (*i*).

Now in the triangle *ABE*, the lengths of all the sides and bearing of *BE* are known. If the lengths of *AB*, *BE*, and *EA* are l_{AB}, l_{BE}, and l_{AE}, respectively, then the area *A* of the triangle is given by

$$A = \sqrt{s(s-l_{BE})(s-l_{AE})(s-l_{AB})} \qquad ...(9.32)$$

where $s = \dfrac{l_{AB} + l_{BE} + l_{AE}}{2}$

The area A can also be determined from the following formulae:

$$A = \frac{1}{2} l_{AB}\, l_{AE} \sin\beta$$

$$\text{or} \quad = \frac{1}{2} l_{AB}\, l_{BE} \sin\gamma \qquad \text{...(9.33)}$$

$$\text{or} \quad = \frac{1}{2} l_{AE}\, l_{BE} \sin\alpha$$

From Eq. (9.32), A is determined and then from Eq. (9.33), we have

$$\beta = \sin^{-1}\left[\frac{2A}{l_{AB}\, l_{AE}}\right] \text{ radians}$$

$$\gamma = \sin^{-1}\left[\frac{2A}{l_{AB}\, l_{AE}}\right] \text{ radians} \qquad \text{...(9.34)}$$

$$\alpha = \sin^{-1}\left[\frac{2A}{l_{AE}\, l_{BE}}\right] \text{ radians.}$$

Now knowing the bearing of BE, bearings of EA and AB can be computed.

(v) When affected lines are not adjacent

If the lines of a traverse whose measurements could not be made, are not adjacent, then they can be made adjacent by shifting and bringing one of them adjacent to the other one.

In Fig. 9.25a, let $ABCDEFA$ be a closed traverse in which either the length or the bearing of lines BC and DE are omitted.

To bring the affected sides adjacent to each other, draw CD' parallel and equal to DE, and join D' and E. The line $D'E$ will be parallel and equal to CD. Now in the new closed traverse $ABCD'EFA$, the lines BC and CD' are the affected lines and they are adjacent to each other. The bearing and length of the line BD' in the traverse $ABD'EFA$ are unknown and can be determined. After knowing the bearing and length of the line BD', the omitted measurements of BC and CD' considering the triangle BCD', may be computed as explained in earlier cases.

Two other examples of this case are shown in Fig. 9.25b and c.

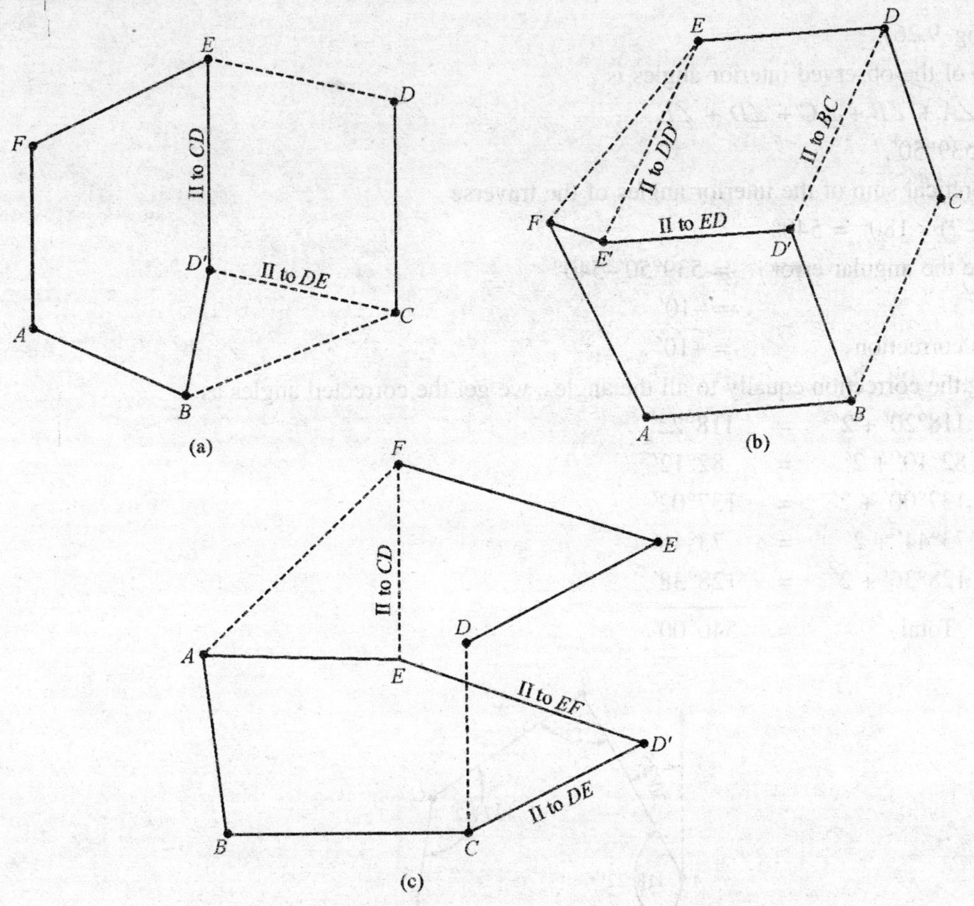

Fig. 9.25 Affected lines are not adjacent

ILLUSTRATIVE EXAMPLES

Example 9.3

The following data were obtained for a closed traverse *ABCDEA* which was run in the clockwise direction:

Line	Length (m)	Bearing	Included Angle
AB	186	30°25′	∠*A* = 118°20′
BC	164		∠*B* = 82°10′
CD	303		∠*C* = 137°00′
DE	162		∠*D* = 73°44′
EA	240		∠*E* = 128°36′

Determine the closing error and adjust the traverse. Also compute the corrected consecutive coordinates of the traverse stations.

Solution (Fig. 9.26):

The sum of the observed interior angles is

$= \angle A + \angle B + \angle C + \angle D + \angle E$

$= 539°50'$.

The theoretical sum of the interior angles of the traverse

$= (5-2) \times 180° = 540°$

Therefore the angular error $= 539°50' - 540°$

$= -10'$

and the correction $= +10'$

Applying the correction equally to all the angles, we get the corrected angles as

$\angle A = 118°20' + 2' = 118°22'$

$\angle B = 82°10' + 2' = 82°12'$

$\angle C = 137°00' + 2' = 137°02'$

$\angle D = 73°44' + 2' = 73°46'$

$\angle E = 128°36' + 2' = 128°38'$

Total $= 540°00'$

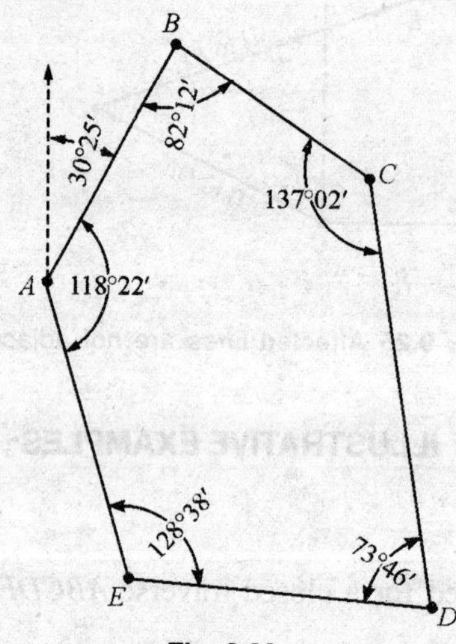

Fig. 9.26

The bearing of *AB* is 30°25′

Back bearing of *AB* = 180° + 30°25′ = 210°25′

Fore bearing of the *BC* = 210°25′ – 82°12′ = 128°13′

Back bearing of *BC* = 180° + 128°13′ = 308°13′

Fore bearing of *CD* = 308°13′ – 137°02′ = 171°11′

Back bearing of *CD* = 180° + 171°11′ = 351°11′

Fore bearing of *DE* = 351°11′ – 73°46′ = 277°25′

Back bearing of *DE* = 360° – (180° + 277°25′) = 97°25′

Fore bearing of *EA* = (97°25′ – 128°38′) + 360° = 328°47′

To compute the consecutive coordinates, the above fore bearings are to be converted into reduced bearings. Table 9.4 gives the corresponding reduced bearings and the consecutive coordinates of the traverse stations.

We have $\Sigma L = 386.563 - 400.876 = -14.313$ m

and $\Sigma D = 269.462 - 285.031 = -15.569$ m

Therefore, the closing error = $\sqrt{(\Sigma L)^2 + (\Sigma D)^2} = 21.148$ m

Assuming the linear and angular measurements of equal precision, the corrections to the latitude and departure are computed as below by applying the Bowditch's rule.

Corrections to latitude (or departure) of a line

$$= \text{Total error in latitude (or departure)} \; \frac{\text{length of the lines}}{\text{total length of the traverse}}$$

From Table 9.4 we find that, $\Sigma N < \Sigma S$ and $\Sigma E < \Sigma W$, therefore, the corrections to the northings will be positive and to the southings negative. Similarly the corrections to the eastings will be positive and to the westings negative.

Taking $\Sigma L = 14.313$ m, $\Sigma D = 15.569$ m, and $\Sigma l = 1055$ m, the corrections have been computed and tabulated. The corrected consecutive coordinates have also been tabulated. It may be noted that for the corrected consecutive coordinates $\Sigma N = \Sigma S$ and $\Sigma E = \Sigma W$, *i.e.*, $\Sigma L = 0$ and $\Sigma D = 0$.

Example 9.4

To locate a point *M* midway between the two stations *A* and *E*, the following traverse was run:

Line	Length (m)	Bearing	Angles to right
AB	350	80°10′	∠*B* = 165°30′
BC	400		∠*C* = 225°15′
CD	375		∠*D* = 152°40′
DE	425		

If the coordinates of *A* are (500, 500), compute the following:

(*i*) Independent coordinates of *B, C, D, E* and *M*.

(*ii*) Length of *AE*.

(*iii*) Distance of *M* from *B, C* and *D*.

(*iv*) Bearing of the line *CM*.

Solution (Fig. 9.27):

Fore bearing of *AB* = 80°10′

Back bearing of *AB* = 180° + 80°10′ = 260°10′

Fore bearing of *BC* = 165°30′ – (360° – 260°10′) = 65°40′

Back bearing of *BC* = 180° + 65°40′ = 245°40′

Fore bearing of *CD* = 225°15′ – (360° – 245°40′) = 110°55′

Back bearing of *CD* = 180° + 110°55′ = 290°55′

Fore bearing of *DE* = 152°40′ – (360° – 290°55′) = 83°35′

Table 9.4

Line	W.C.B.	R.B. (θ)	Length (l) m	Consecutive coordinate Lat. (l cos θ)		Dep. (l sin θ)		Corrections				Corrected consecutive coordinates			
				N	S	E	W	N	S	E	W	N	S	E	W
AB	30°25′	N 30°25′ E	186	160.400	–	94.169	–	+2.523	–	+2.745	–	162.923	–	96.914	–
BC	128°13′	S 51°47′ E	164	–	101.456	128.851	–	–	–2.225	+2.420	–	–	99.231	131.271	–
CD	171°11′	S 08°49′ E	303	–	299.420	46.442	–	–	–4.111	+4.471	–	–	295.309	50.913	–
DE	277°25′	N 82°35′ W	162	20.912	–	–	160.645	+2.198	–	–	–2.391	23.110	–	–	158.254
EA	328°47′	N 31°13′ W	240	205.251	–	–	124.386	+3.256	–	–	–3.542	208.507	–	–	120.844
Total			1055	386.563	400.876	269.462	285.031					394.54	394.54	279.098	279.098

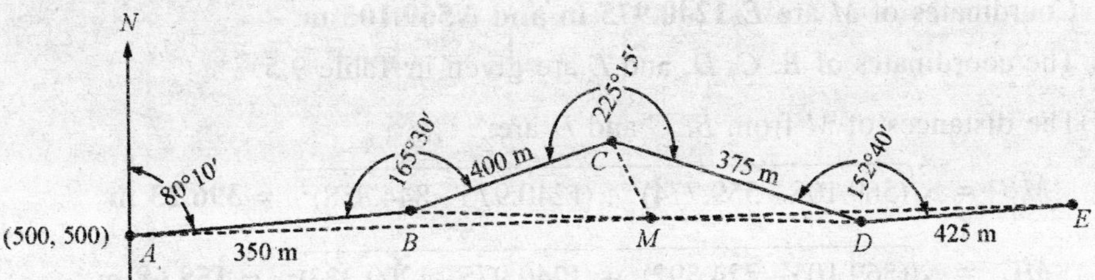

Fig. 9.27

(*i*) The reduced bearings of the lines and the independent coordinates of the traverse stations are given in Table 9.5.

Table 9.5

Line	Length (m)	R.B.	Latitude		Departure		Ind. coordinates		St.
			N	*S*	*E*	*W*	*N*	*E*	
AB	350	N 80° 10′ E	59.774	–	344.858	–	500.000	500.000	*A*
BC	400	N 65° 40′ E	164.818	–	364.465	–	559.774	844.858	*B*
CD	375	S 69° 05′ E	–	133.879	350.288	–	724.592	1209.323	*C*
DE	425	N 83° 35′ E	47.497		422.338	–	590.713	1559.611	*D*
–	–	–	–	–	–	–	638.210	1981.949	*E*
Total			272.089	133.879	1481.949	0.000			

$\Sigma L = 272.089 - 133.879 = 138.210$ m

$\Sigma D = 1481.949 - 0.000 = 1481.949$ m

(*ii*) The length *AE* is given by

$$AE = \sqrt{(\Sigma L)^2 + (\Sigma D)^2}$$

$$= \sqrt{(138.210)^2 + (1481.949)^2} = \mathbf{1488.38\ m.}$$

The coordinates of *M* are as below.

$$\text{Easting of } M = \frac{1}{2} \text{(Sum of eastings of } A \text{ and } E)$$

$$= \frac{1}{2}(500 + 1981.949) = 1240.975 \text{ m.}$$

$$\text{Northing of } M = \frac{1}{2} \text{(Sum of northings of } A \text{ and } E)$$

$$= \frac{1}{2} \times (500 + 638.210) = 569.105 \text{ m.}$$

Coordinates of M are **E 1240.975 m and N569.105 m.**

The coordinates of B, C, D, and E are given in Table 9.5.

(*iii*) The distances of M from B, C and D are:

$$MB = \sqrt{(569.105 - 559.774)^2 + (1240.975 - 844.858)^2} = \mathbf{396.23\ m}$$

$$MC = \sqrt{(569.105 - 724.592)^2 + (1240.975 - 1209.323)^2} = \mathbf{158.68\ m}$$

$$MD = \sqrt{(569.105 - 590.713)^2 + (1240.975 - 1559.611)^2} = \mathbf{319.37\ m.}$$

(*iv*) The reduced bearing of CM

$$\tan\theta = \frac{D_{CM}}{L_{CM}} = \frac{1209.323 - 1240.975}{724.592 - 569.105} = \frac{-31.652}{155.487}$$

$$\theta = \tan^{-1}\left(\frac{31.652}{155.487}\right) = \mathbf{11°30''\ (S\text{-}E\ quadrant).}$$

Example 9.5

A traverse $ABCD$ was to be run but due to an obstruction between the stations A and B, it was not possible to measure the length and direction of the line AB. The following data could only be obtained:

Line	Length (m)	R.B.
AD	44.5	*N* 50° 20′ *E*
DC	67.0	*S* 69° 45′ *E*
CB	61.3	*S* 30° 10′ *E*

Determine the length and directions of BA. Also determine the perpendicular distance of C from AB, and the distance of the foot of perpendicular from C on AB from B.

Solution (Fig. 9.28):

The latitude and departure of the lines are as below:

Table 9.6

Line	Latitude		Departure	
	N	*S*	*E*	*W*
AD	28.405	–	34.255	–
DC	–	23.190	62.859	–
CB	–	52.998	30.804	–
BA	–	–	–	–
Total	28.405	76.188	127.918	0.000

From Table 9.6, we get

$$\Sigma L = L_{BA} + 28.405 - 76.188 = 0$$

$$L_{BA} = 76.188 - 28.405 = 47.783 \text{ m.}$$

and $\Sigma D = D_{BA} + 127.918 - 0.000 = 0$

$$D_{BA} = -127.918 \text{ m}$$

The length of *BA* is

$$BA = \sqrt{47.783^2 + 127.918^2} = \mathbf{136.551 \text{ m.}}$$

and the bearing

$$\theta = \tan^{-1} \frac{127.917}{47.783} = 69°31' \; (\textit{N-W} \textbf{ quadrant}).$$

As the line is in the fourth quadrant, its reduced bearing in N 69°31′ W.

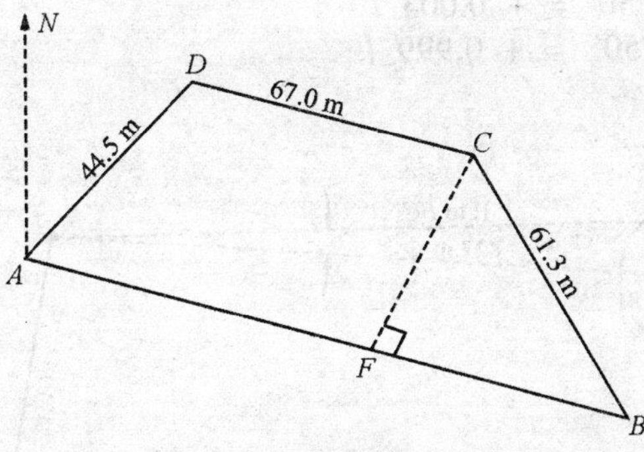

Fig. 9.28

In ΔCBF

$$\angle CBF = 69°31' - 30°10' = 39°21'$$

The perpendicular distance of *C* from *AB* is

$$CF = BC \sin CBF$$

$$= 61.3 \sin 39°21' = \mathbf{38.87 \text{ m}}$$

$$BF = BC \cos CBF$$

$$= 61.3 \cos 39°21' = \mathbf{47.40 \text{ m.}}$$

Example 9.6

The following data were collected while running a closed traverse *ABCDA*. Determine the missing data.

Line	Length (m)	Bearing
AB	330	181°25′
BC	?	89°50′
CD	411	355°00′
DA	827	?

Solution (Fig. 9.29):

The reduced bearing of the traverse lines are as below:
Reduced bearing of AB = $S\,1°25'\,W$
Reduced bearing of BC = $N\,89°50'\,E$
Reduced bearing of CD = $N\,5°00'\,W$
Let the length of BC be l and the bearing of DA be θ.
Consecutive coordinates of B

Latitude = 330 cos 1°25′ = – 329.899 m
Departure = 330 sin 1°25′ = – 8.159 m

Consecutive of coordinates of C

Latitude = l cos 89°50′ = + 0.003 l
Departure = l sin 89°50′ = + 0.999 l

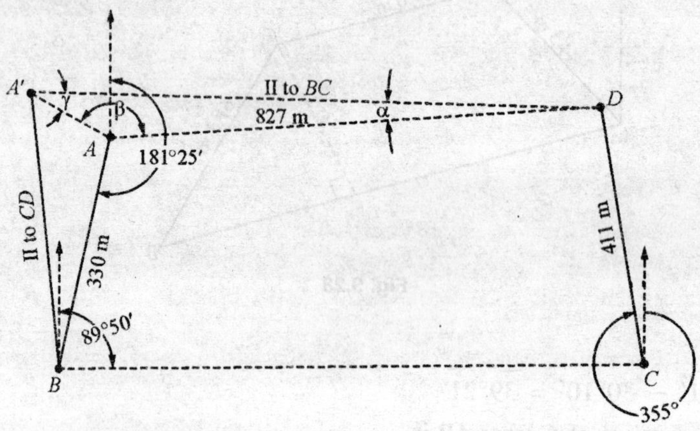

Fig. 9.29

Consecutive of coordinates of D

Latitude = 411 cos 5°00′ = + 409.436 m
Departure = 411 sin 5°00′ = – 35.821 m

Consecutive of coordinates of A

Latitude = 827 cos θ
Departure = 827 sin θ

$\Sigma L = -329.899 + 0.003\,l + 409.436 - 827\cos\theta = 0$

$\Sigma D = -8.159 + 0.999\,l - 35.821 - 827\sin\theta = 0$

$827\cos\theta - 0.003\,l = 79.537$ ...(9.35)

$827\sin\theta - 0.999\,l = -43.980$ ...(9.36)

Taking $0.003\,l = 0$ in Eq. (9.35), we get

$$\cos\theta = \frac{79.537}{827}$$

or $\theta = 84°28'52''$

Putting the value of θ in Eq. (9.36), we have

$$l = \frac{43.980 + 827 \quad \sin 84°28'52''}{0.999}$$

$$= 868.018 \text{ m.}$$

Now substituting the value of l as 868.018 m in Eq. (9.35), we again find out the value of θ, which comes out to be 84°17′59″. Taking this value of θ in Eq. (9.36), we get l as 867.76. In the third iteration, the values of θ and l remain same, therefore,

θ = **84°18′** (in third quadrant)

and l = **867.76 m.**

Alternate Solution II

The problem can be solved be drawing *DA′* from *D*, parallel and equal to *BC* and *BA′* from *B*, parallel and equal to *CD*. By doing this the two lines with omitted measurements, become adjacent.

As the traverse *AA′B* is closed,

$\Sigma L = 0$ and $\Sigma D = 0$

Let the length and bearing of *AA′* be l and θ, then

$$330 \cos 181°25' + 41 \cos 355° + l \cos \theta = 0$$

$$330 \sin 181°25' + 41 \sin 355° + l \sin \theta = 0$$

or

$$l \cos \theta = -\ 79.537$$

$$l \sin \theta = 43.980$$

$$\tan \theta = \frac{43.98}{79.53}$$

or θ = 28°56′ 26″ (in second quadrant)

or W.C.B. of *A′A* = 180° − 28°56′26″

= 151°03′34″

and

$$l = \sqrt{(l \cos \theta)^2 + (l \sin \theta)^2} = \sqrt{79.537^2 + 43.98^2}$$

$$= 90.887 \text{ m}$$

In Δ *ADA′* from sine rule, we have

$$\frac{A'D}{\sin \beta} = \frac{AD}{\sin \gamma} = \frac{AA'}{\sin \alpha}$$

γ = W.C.B. of *AA′* − W.C.B of *A′D*

As *A′D* is parallel to *BC*, the bearing of *A′D* is equal to that of *BC*. Also *A′D* is equal to *BC*.

$$\gamma = 151°03'34'' - 89°50' = 61°13'34''$$

$$\sin \alpha = \frac{AA' \sin \gamma}{AD} = \frac{90.887 \sin 61°13'34''}{827}$$

$$\sin \alpha = 0.0963299$$

$$\alpha = 5°31'40''$$

In Δ ADA'

$$\beta = 180° - (\alpha + \gamma) = 180° - (5°31'40'' + 61°31'34'')$$
$$= 113°14'46''$$

Also, we have

$$A'D = \frac{AD \sin \beta}{\sin \gamma} = \frac{827 \sin 113°14'54'}{\sin 61°13'34''}$$

$$= \mathbf{866.90 \ m.}$$

and bearing of DA = bearing of $DA' - \alpha$

$$= (180° + 89°50') - 5°31'40''$$

$$= \mathbf{264°18'20''}.$$

Example 9.7

In a closed traverse *ABCDEA*, the lengths of the lines *DE* and *EA* could not be measured due to an obstruction. Determine the lengths from the following data.

Line	Length (m)	Bearing
AB	480	99°00′
BC	625	31°05′
CD	470	301°20′
DE	?	235°00′
EA	?	153°25

Solution (Fig. 9.30):

The reduced bearings of the traverse lines are as below:

AB = *S* 81°00′*E*

BC = *N* 31°05′*E*

CD = *N* 58°40′*W*

DE = *S* 55°00′*W*

EA = *S* 44°35′*E*

The closing line for the traverse *ABCD* is *DA*.

Let the reduced bearing and length of *DA* be θ and l, respectively.

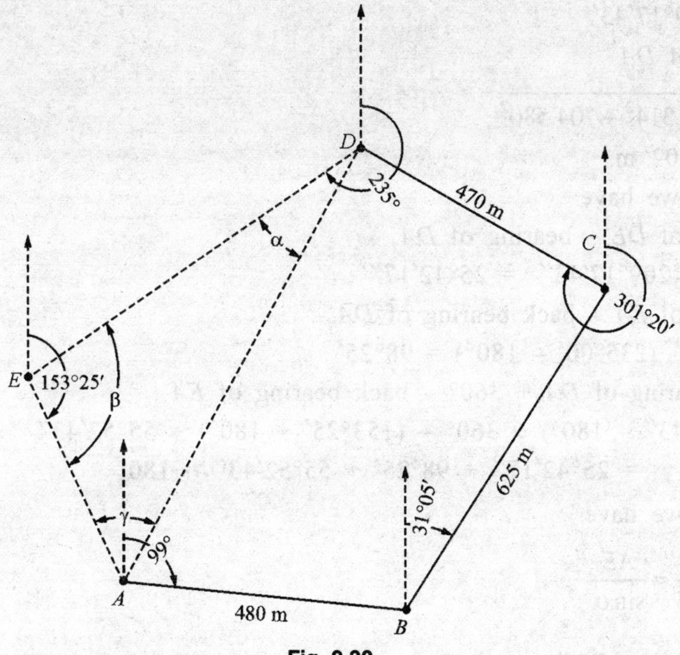

Fig. 9.30

Consecutive coordinates of B

Latitude = 480 cos 81°00′. = – 75.089 m.

Departure = 480 sin 81°00′ = + 474.090 m.

Consecutive coordinates of C

Latitude = 625 cos 31°05′ = + 535.261 m.

Departure = 625 sin 31°05′ = + 322.678 m.

Consecutive coordinates of D

Latitude = 470 cos 58°40′ = + 244.408

Departure = 470 sin 58°40′ = – 401.454

Let the consecutive coordinates of A be $l \cos \theta$ and $l \sin \theta$ then

$$\sum L = -75.089 + 535.261 + 244.408 + l \cos \theta = 0$$

$$\sum D = 474.090 + 322.678 - 401.454 + l \sin \theta = 0$$

or $704.580 + l \cos \theta = 0$

$395.314 + l \sin \theta = 0$

or $l \cos \theta = -704.580$

$l \sin \theta = -395.314$

Thus the reduced bearing of DA

$$\theta = \tan^{-1} \frac{395.314}{704.580}$$

$$= 29°17'43'' \text{ (S-W quadrant)}$$

or W.C.B. = 209°17′43″

and the length of DA

$$l = \sqrt{395.314^2 + 704.580^2}$$

$$= 807.902 \text{ m.}$$

Now in ΔADE, we have

α = Bearing of DE – bearing of DA

= 235°00′ – 209°17′43″ = 25°42′17″

β = Bearing of EA – back bearing of DA

= 153°25′ – (235°00′ – 180°) = 98°25′

γ = Back bearing of DA + 360° – back bearing of EA

= (209°17′43″ – 180°) + 360° – (153°25′ + 180°) = 55°52′43″

Check: $\alpha + \beta + \gamma$ = 25°42′17″ + 98°25′ + 55°52′43″ = 180°

From ΔADE, we have

$$\frac{DE}{\sin\gamma} = \frac{AD}{\sin\beta} = \frac{AE}{\sin\alpha}$$

Therefore $$DE = AD\frac{\sin\gamma}{\sin\beta}$$

$$= 807.902 \times \frac{\sin 55°52'43''}{\sin 98°25'} = \mathbf{676.10 \text{ m}}$$

and $$AE = AD\,\frac{\sin\ \alpha}{\sin\ \beta}$$

$$= 807.902 \times \frac{\sin\ 25°42'17''}{\sin\ 98°25'} = \mathbf{354.23 \text{ m.}}$$

Example 9.8

Two traverses were run from a common point A and the following data were collected:

Traverse	Line	Length (m)	Bearing
1	*AB*	200	85°26′20″
	BC	100	125°10′40″
2	*AD*	225	175°50′00″
	DE	500	85°06′40″

Calculate the distance from C to a point F on DE due south of C and the distance EF.

Solution (Fig. 9.31):

Let us consider a closed traverse *ABCFDA*, and let *DF* and *CF* be *x* and *y*, respectively. The lengths and bearings of the sides of the traverse are as below:

Side	Length (m)	W.C.B.	R.B.
AB	200	85°26′20″	*N*85°26′20″*E*
BC	100	125°10′40″	*S*54°49′20″*E*
CF	*y*	180°00′00″	*S*
FD	*x*	265°06′40″	*S*85°06′40″*W*
DA	225	355°50′00″	*N*4°10′00″*W*

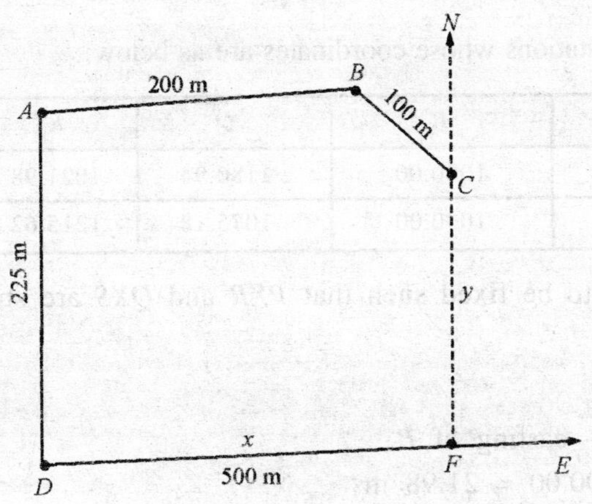

Fig. 9.31

Consecutive coordinates of *B*

Latitude of *B* = 200 cos 85°26′20″ = + 15.904 m

Departure of *B* = 200 sin 85°26′20″ = + 199.367 m

Consecutive coordinates of *C*

Latitude of *C* = 100 cos 54°49′20″ = – 57.612 m

Departure of *C* = 100 sin 54°49′20″ = + 81.737 m

Consecutive coordinates of *F*

Latitude of *F* = *y* cos 0° = – *y*

Departure of *F* = *y* sin 0° = 0.00 m

Consecutive coordinates of *D*

Latitude of *D* = – *x* cos 85°06′40″

Departure of D = – *x* sin 85°06′40″

Consecutive coordinates of *A*

Latitude of *A* = 225 cos 4°10′00″ = + 224.405 m

Departure of *A* = 225 sin 4°10′00″ = – 16.348 m

For a closed, we have

$$\Sigma L = 15.904 - 57.612 - y - x \cos 85°06'40'' + 224.405 = 0$$

$$\Sigma D = 199.367 + 81.737 + 0.00 - x \sin 85°06'40'' - 16.348 = 0$$

From the above two equations we have

$$x = \frac{264.756}{\sin 85° 06' 40''} = 265.723$$

$$y = 160.051 \text{ m}$$

Therefore the distance CF = **160.051 m.**

and the distance EF = 500 − 265.723 = **234.277 m.**

Example 9.9

P, Q, R, and S are four stations whose coordinates are as below:

Stations	P	Q	R	S
Easting (m)	1000.00	1180.94	1021.98	939.70
Northing(m)	1000.00	1075.18	1215.62	1102.36

Another station X is to be fixed such that PXR and QXS are straight lines. Calculate the coordinates of station X.

Solution (Fig. 9.32):

RR' = Easting of R − easting of P
= 1021.98 − 1000.00 = 21.98 m

PR' = Northing of R − northing of P
= 1215.62 − 1000.00 = 215.62 m

$$PR = \sqrt{RR'^2 + PR'^2} = \sqrt{21.98^2 + 215.62^2}$$

= 216.74 m

SS' = Northing of S − northing of Q
= 1102.36 − 1075.18 = 27.18 m

QS' = Easting of Q − easting of S
= 1180.94 − 939.70 = 241.24 m

$$QS = \sqrt{QS'^2 + SS'^2} = \sqrt{241.24^2 + 27.18^2}$$

= 242.766 m.

QP' = Easting of Q − easting of P
= 1180.94 − 1000.00 = 180.94 m

PP' = Northing of Q − northing of P
= 1075.18 − 1000.00 = 75.18 m

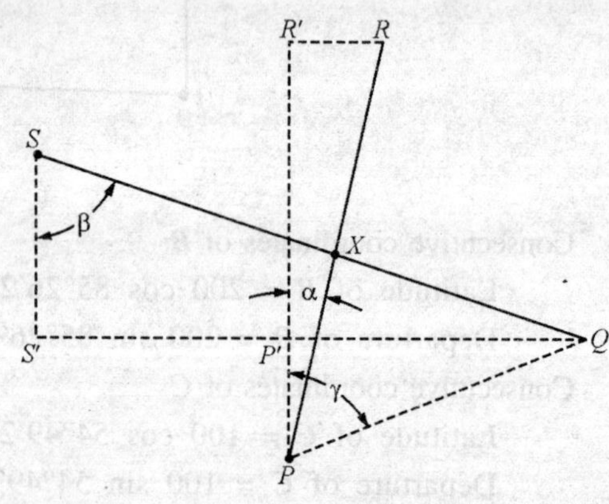

Fig. 9.32

$PQ \quad = \sqrt{QP'^2 + PP'^2} = \sqrt{180.94^2 + 75.18^2}$

$= 195.937$ m.

If α, β, and γ be the reduced bearings of *PR*, *SQ* and *PQ*, respectively, then

$$\tan\alpha = \frac{RR'}{PR'} = \frac{21.98}{215.62} = 0.101938595$$

$\alpha = N5°49'14''E$

$$\tan\beta = \frac{QS'}{SS'} = \frac{241.24}{27.18} = 8.875643856$$

$\beta = S83°34°18''E$

$$\tan\gamma = \frac{QP'}{PP'} = \frac{180.94}{75.18} = 2.406757116$$

$\therefore \quad \gamma = N67°26'14''E$

W.C.B. of *PR* = 5°49′14″

W.C.B. of *SQ* = 96°25′42″

W.C.B. of *PQ* = 67°26′14″

In Δ*PQX*,

Angle *XPQ* = 67°26′14″ – 5°49′14″ = 61°37′00″

Angle *PQX* = (96°25′42″ + 180°) – (67°26′14″ + 180°) = 28°59′28″

Angle *PXQ* = Bearing of *RP* – bearing of *SQ*

= 180° + 5°49′14″ – 96°25′42″ = 89°23′32″

By applying sine rule in Δ*PQX*, we get

$$\frac{PX}{\sin PQX} = \frac{PQ}{\sin QP}$$

or $$PX = \frac{195.937 \sin 28°59'28''}{\sin 89°23'32''} = 94.971 \text{ m}$$

The reduced bearing of *PX* is *N*5°49′14″*E*

Therefore,

Latitude of *PX* = 94.971 cos 5°49′14″ = 94.48 m

Departure of *PX* = 94.971 sin 5°49′14″ = 9.63 m.

Therefore

Easting of *X* = Easting of *P* + departure of *PX*

= 1000.00 + 9.63

= **1009.63 m.**

Northing of *X* = Northing of *P* + latitude of *PX*

= 1000.00 + 94.48

= **1094.48 m.**

Alternate Solution II (Fig. 9.33):

Let the coordinates of X be (X, Y)

$$XD = m, \; DQ = n$$

$$XB = x, \; RB = y$$

From the similar Δs RBX and RAP

$$\frac{y}{x} = \frac{RA}{PA}$$

$$\frac{1215.62 - Y}{1021.98 - X} = \frac{1215.62 - 1000}{1021.98 - 1000} = \frac{215.62}{21.98}$$

$$(1215 \cdot 62 - Y) \times 21.98 = (1021.98 - X) \times 215.62$$

$$1215.62 \times 21.98 - Y\,21.98 = 1021.98 \times 215.62 - 215.62\,X$$

$$26719.328 - 220359.328 = 21.98\,Y - 215.62\,X$$

$$21.98\,Y = -\,193640 + 215.62\,X$$

$$Y = -\,8809.827 + 9.810\,X \qquad \ldots(a)$$

Fig. 9.33

From the similar Δs SQC and XQD, we have

$$\frac{m}{n} = \frac{SC}{CQ}$$

$$\frac{Y - 1075.18}{1180.94 - X} = \frac{1102.36 - 1075.18}{1180.94 - 939.70} = \frac{27.18}{241.24}$$

$$241.24\,Y - 1075.18 \times 241.24 = 1180.94 \times 27.18 - 27.18\,X$$

$$241.24\,Y = 291474.372 - 27.18\,X$$

$$Y = 1208.234 - 0.113\,X \qquad \ldots(b)$$

Equating (a) and (b), we get

$$-\,8809.827 + 9.810\,X = 1208.234 - 0.113\,X$$

$$9.923\,X = 10018.061$$

$$X = \mathbf{1009.58\ m.}$$

Substituting the value of X in (b), we get

$$Y = \mathbf{1094.15\ m}$$

Alternate Solution III (Fig. 9.34):

$$PQ = \sqrt{[(1075.18 - 1000)^2 + (1180.94 - 1000)^2]}$$

$$= 195.937 \text{ m}$$

$$RQ = \sqrt{[(1215.62 - 1075.18)^2 + (1180.94 - 1021.98)^2]}$$

$$= 212.112 \text{ m}$$

$$PR = \sqrt{[(1021.98 - 1000)^2 + (1215.62 - 1000)^2]}$$

$$= 216.737 \text{ m}$$

$$SQ = \sqrt{[(1075.18 - 1102.36)^2 + (1180.94 - 939.70)^2]}$$

$$= 242.766 \text{ m}$$

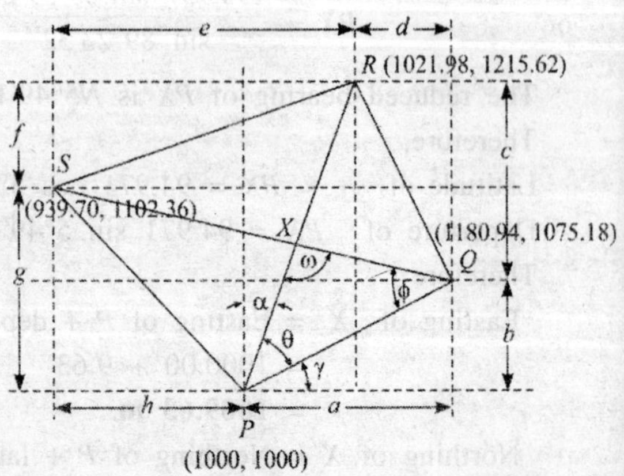

Fig. 9.34

$SP = \sqrt{[(1102.36 - 1000)^2 + (939.70 - 1000)^2]}$

$= 118.801$ m

From Δ *RPQ*, we get

$$\cos\theta = \frac{PR^2 + PQ^2 - RQ^2}{2 \cdot PR \cdot PQ}$$

$$= \frac{216.737^2 + 195.937^2 - 212.112^2}{2 \times 216.737 \times 195.937}$$

$$\theta = 61° \, 37' \, 00''$$

From Δ *SQP*, we get

$$\cos\phi = \frac{SQ^2 + PQ^2 - SP^2}{2 \times SQ \cdot PQ}$$

$$= \frac{242.766^2 + 195.937^2 - 118.88^2}{2 \times 242.766 \times 195.937}$$

$$\phi = 28° \, 59' \, 28''$$

$$\gamma = \tan^{-1}\frac{b}{a} = \tan^{-1}\left(\frac{75.18}{180.94}\right) = 22° \, 33' \, 46''$$

$$\omega = 180° - (\theta + \phi) = 89° \, 23' \, 32''$$

From the sine law in Δ *PQX*, we get

$$\frac{PX}{\sin\phi} = \frac{PQ}{\sin\omega}$$

$$PX = l = \frac{PQ \times \sin\phi}{\sin\omega} = \frac{195.937 \sin(28°59'28'')}{\sin(89°23'32'')} = 94.9710 \text{ m}$$

Bearing of *PX* $\quad \alpha = 90° - \theta + \gamma = 5° \, 49' \, 14''$

Latitude of *PX* $\quad = l \cos\alpha = 94.971 \cos(5° \, 49' \, 14'') = 94.48$ m

Departure of *PX* $\quad = l \sin\alpha = 94.971 \sin(5° \, 49' \, 14'') = 9.63$ m

Easting of *X* $\quad = 1000 + 9.63 =$ **1009.93 m**

Northing of *X* $\quad = 1000 + 94.48 =$ **1094.48 m.**

Alternate Solution IV (Fig. 9.34):

Since *PR* and *QS* are the straight lines, knowing the equations of these straight lines, the intersection *X* of these lines can be determined.

Equation of a straight line $\quad Y = ax + b$

For the line *PR*

$$a_1 = \frac{1215.62 - 1000}{1021.98 - 1000} = \frac{215.62}{21.98} = 9.801$$

$$y_1 = 9.801 \, x_1 + b_1$$

or at *P* $\quad 1000 = 9.801 \times 1000 + b_1$

$$b_1 = -8801$$

For the line QS

$$a_2 = \frac{1075.18 - 1102.36}{1180.94 - 939.70} = \frac{-27.180}{241.24} - 0.113$$

$$y_2 = -0.113\, x_2 + b_2$$

or at Q $$1075.18 = -0.113 \times 1180.94 + b_2$$

$$b_2 = 1208.63$$

Line PR $\quad y_1 = 9.801\, x_1 - 8801$ ...(*a*)

Line QS $\quad y_2 = -\,0.113\, x_2 + 1208.63$ ...(*b*)

At X, $\quad y_1 = y_2 = y$ and $x_1 = x_2 = x$

Therefore, from (*a*) and (*b*)

$$9.801\, x - 8801 = -\,0.113\, x + 1208.63$$

or $$x = \mathbf{1009.65\ m}$$

$$y = \mathbf{1094.54\ m.}$$

Example 9.10

The bearings of two stations A and B were observed from station C as 225°00′ and 153°26′, respectively. If the coordinates of A and B are as under, calculate the independent coordinates of C.

Station	Easting (m)	Northing (m)
A	300	200
B	400	150

Solution (Fig. 9.35):

MB = Easting of B – easting of A

= 400 – 300 = 100 m

MA = Northing of A – northing of B

= 200 – 150 = 50 m

Therefore $AB = \sqrt{MB^2 + MA^2} = \sqrt{100^2 + 50^2} = 111.80$ m

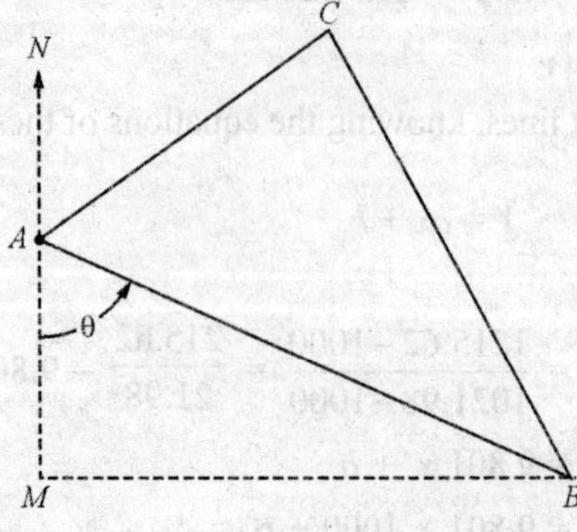

Fig. 9.35

If reduced bearing of AB is θ, then

$$\tan\theta = \frac{MB}{MA} = \frac{100}{50} = 2$$

or $\theta = S63°26'06''E$

W.C.B $= 116°33'54''$

In ΔABC we have

ABC = Bearing of BC − bearing of BA

$= (180° + 153°26') - (180° + 116°33'54'')$

$= 36°52'06''$

BCA = Bearing of CA − bearing of CB

$= 225°00' - 153°26'$

$= 71°34'00''$

CAB = Bearing of AB − bearing of AC

$= 116°33'54'' - (225°00' - 180°)$

$= 71°33'54''$

By sine rule in ΔABC, we have

$$\frac{AC}{\sin ABC} = \frac{AB}{\sin ACB}$$

or $$AC = AB\frac{\sin ABC}{\sin ACB}$$

$$= \frac{111.80 \sin 36°52'06''}{\sin 71°34'00''}$$

$= 70.71$ m

Latitude of AC $= AC \cos(225° - 180°)$

$= 70.71 \cos 45° = 50.00$ m

Departure of AC $= AC \sin(225° - 180°)$

$= 70.71 \sin 45° = 50.00$ m

The independent coordinates of C are

Easting = Easting of A + departure of AC

= 300 + 50

= **350.00 m.**

Northing = Northing of A + latitude of AC

= 200 + 50

= **250.00 m.**

QUESTIONS AND PROBLEMS

9.1 What is the purpose of providing horizontal control in surveys?

9.2 What are the methods of providing horizontal control? Also discuss the conditions under which they are most suited.

9.3 Discuss the uses of traverse surveying.

9.4 What is a traverse? Discuss various types of traverse and method of traversing.

9.5 What do you understand by compatibility of linear and angular measurements in traversing, and why it is necessary?

9.6 Discuss the checks available in closed and open traverses.

9.7 What do you mean by balancing of traverse? Discuss briefly the common methods of balancing a traverse.

9.8 Differentiate between Bowditch's rule and Transit rule of the adjustment of a traverse. Also discuss both the methods of adjustment.

9.9 What is Gale's traverse table? Discuss the procedure for recording the various entries in the table.

9.10 What are the advantages of the coordinate method of plotting a traverse over other methods?

9.11 Differentiate between:

(*i*) Open traverse and Closed traverse.

(*ii*) Bowditch's rule and Transit rule.

(*iii*) Latitude and Departure.

(*iv*) Consecutive coordinates and Independent coordinates.

9.12 What do you understand by omitted measurement? Discuss the various cases in brief.

9.13 Discuss how the omitted measurements are determined in case the affected sides are not adjacent.

9.14 Coordinates of *A* and *B* are as (*N*15 m, *E*200 m) and (*N*1500 m, *E*1300 m), respectively. A third point *C* was chosen such that the bearing of line *AC* and *CB* are 29°30′ and 45°45′, respectively. Calculate the lengths of *AC* and *CB*.

9.15 From a point *C* it is required to set out a line *CD* parallel to a given line *AB*, such that the angle *ABD* is a right angle. The points *C* and *D* are not visible from *A* and *B*, and traversing is performed as follows:

Line	Length (m)	W.C.B.
BA	—	360°
BE	50.8	291°
EF	63.5	350°
FC	38.0	265°

Determine the required length and bearing of the line *CD*.

9.16 In order to fix a point *M* exactly between *A* and *E*, the following traverse was run:

Line	Length (m)	Bearing
AB	450	325°
BC	350	0°
CD	370	32°
DE	390	320°

If the coordinates of A are (1000 m, 1000 m), calculate

(a) the independent coordinates of B, C, D, E, and M and

(b) the length and bearing of CM.

9.17 Calculate the missing data in the following table:

Line	Length (m)	R.B.
AB	?	?
BC	450.00	*N* 22° 30′ *E*
DC	535.40	*N* 78° 35′ *W*
DA	587.00	*S* 75° 10′ *W*

9.18 The following data pertains to a theodolite traverse:

Line	Length (m)	Latitude (m)	Departure (m)
AB	129.64	+ 129.56	+ 4.52
BC	300.08	+ 17.27	+ 299.58
CD	147.61	– 147.53	+ 4.94
DA	307.20	0	– 307.20

Balance the traverse by Transit rule, and compute the independent coordinates of the stations, given the coordinates of the station A as (N 400 m, E 200 m).

9.19 **(a)** A man travels from a point A to due west and reaches the point B. The distance between A and B is 139.6 m. Calculate the latitude and departure of the line AB.

(b) In a closed traverse, latitudes and departures of the sides were calculated, and it was observed that

Σ Latitude = 1.39 m

Σ Departure = – 2.17 m.

Calculate the length and bearing of the closing error.

(c) What is a closing error in a theodolite traverse? How would you distribute the closing error graphically?

9.20 Part of data and calculations in respect of a closed traverse *ABCDA* are as under:

Line	Length	R.B.	Northing	Southing	Easting	Westing
AB	?	*S* 560°*E*	–	30.00	?	–
BC	?	*N* 45°*E*	?	–	45.50	–
CD	?	?	?	–	–	?
DA	?	–	–	51.65	–	63.15

Calculate the missing data.

10

PLANE-TABLE SURVEYING

10.1 GENERAL

Plane-table surveying or simply plane tabling is a graphical method of survey in which the field observations and plotting proceed simultaneously. Primary use of this method of survey is in compilation of maps. It is a means of making a manuscript map in the field without intermediate steps of recording and transcribing field notes.

By means of the plane table, points on the ground to which the observations are made, can be plotted immediately in their correct relative positions on the drawing. The plane-table method is especially adopted for securing the details of the map. On extensive surveys the primary points of horizontal and vertical controls are generally established by other more precise methods. It is a valuable and commonly used means of completing the compilation of maps from aerial photographs, especially where the ground is hidden by overgrowth. Plane tabling is particularly suitable for small scale surveys where high degree of precision is not required for plotting details.

10.2 PRINCIPLE OF PLANE TABLING

The principle of plane tabling is based on the fact that all the lines drawn on the drawing are parallel to the corresponding lines on the ground, if the plane table is in properly oriented position. A plane table is said to be *oriented* if all the plotted lines on the drawing are parallel to the corresponding lines on the ground.

In Fig. 10.1, the triangle *ABC* joining the ground stations *A*, *B*, and *C* has been graphically reduced to the triangle *abc* at some scale on the drawing sheet attached to the plane table. If the base *AB* is plotted as *ab*, on a desired scale and *ab* is parallel to *AB*, the base angles *cab* and *cba* are plotted directly, and the intersection *c* of rays *ac* and *bc* is the location of the vertex *C*. The lines *ab*, *bc*, and *ca* are parallel to the corresponding lines *AB*, *BC*, and *CA*. The intersection of lines *Aa*, *Bb*, *Cc* is the point *p* in the drawing which represents the plane-table station *P* on the ground over which the plane table is centered.

To plot any other point *D* from the plane table position *P*, one has to simply draw the ray *pD* and measure the distance *PD*, and locate the point *d* on the drawing sheet by measuring the distance *pd* to the given scale on the ray *pD*.

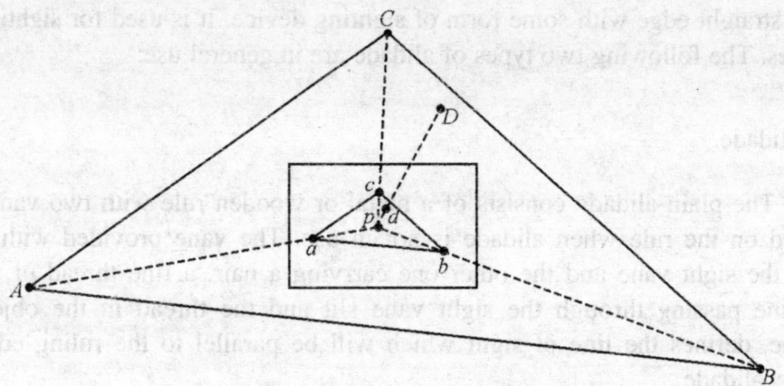

Fig. 10.1 Principle of plane tabling

Thus, the plane tabling can be defined as graphical construction of straight lines, angles and triangles for securing the details for plotting maps.

10.3 PLANE TABLE AND ITS ACCESSORIES

There are three different types of plane table but the simplest and the most commonly used is the traverse table shown in Fig. 10.2. It consists of a well seasoned wooden table mounted on a light wooden tripod. The table top (board) can be rotated about its vertical axis and can be clamped in any position. The table top is levelled by adjusting the legs of the tripod.

While using a plane table, the following accessories are required:

1. Alidade or sight rule
2. Spirit level
3. Magnetic compass
4. Plumbing fork and plumb bob (for large scale surveys only)
5. Miscellaneous accessories.

Fig. 10.2 Plane table

Alidade

An alidade is a straight edge with some form of sighting device. It is used for sighting the objects and drawing the lines. The following two types of alidade are in general use:

(*i*) Plain alidade

(*ii*) Telescopic alidade.

Plain alidade: The plain alidade consists of a metal or wooden rule with two vanes at the ends which can be folded on the rule when alidade is not in use. The vane provided with a narrow slit with three holes is the sight vane and the other one carrying a hair, a fine thread or thin wires the object vane. The line passing through the sight vane slit and the thread in the object vane both contained in a plane, defines the line of sight which will be parallel to the ruling edge, known as *fiducial edge* of the alidade.

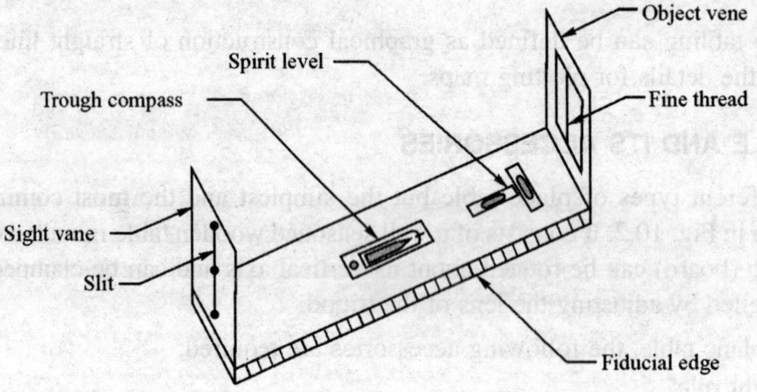

Fig. 10.3 Plain alidade

The alidade can be rotated about the points which represent the plane table station on the sheet, so that the line of sight passes through the station sighted.

The length of the ruling edge of the alidade should not be less than the longest side of the plane table. The two vanes should be perpendicular to the surface of the table. In case the elevations or depressions of the objects are more than what can be accommodated by the line of sight, a thin thread is stretched between the tops of the two vanes to sight such objects (Fig. 10.4).

Telescopic alidade: A telescopic alidade shown in Fig. 10.5, essentially consists of small telescope with a level tube and graduated arc mounted on horizontal axis resting on a A-frame fitted with verniers as in a transit. The telescope is mounted on a column that is fixed to a straight edge ruler. The telescope can be clamped in any position with a clamp screw. Small movements are possible with the tangent screw. The line of sight of the telescope is aligned along the fiducial edge of the ruler.

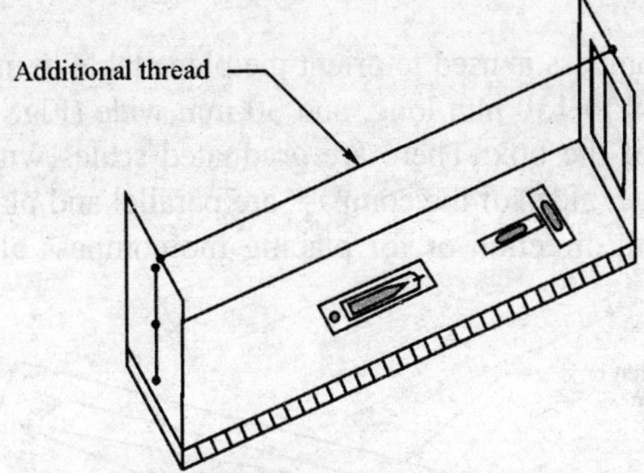

Fig. 10.4 Plain alidade with thin thread stretched between the vane

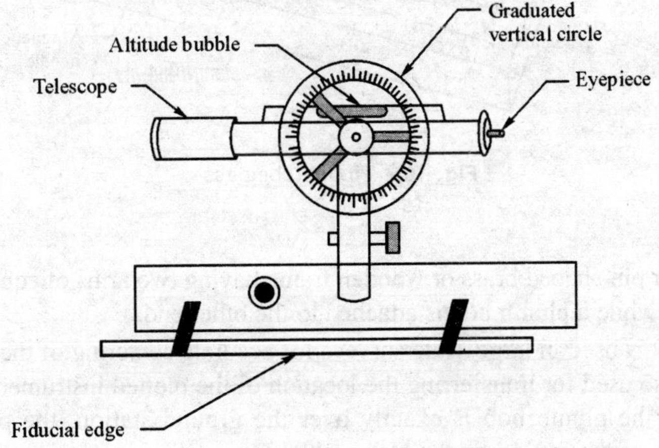

Fig. 10.5 Telescopic alidade

The telescopic alidade is used for inclined sights. It is designed for greater accuracy and increased range of sights. Moreover, the telescope fitted with a stadia diaphragm directly helps in determination of horizontal distances and elevations. It is extremely useful for contouring and topographic surveys. For small scale surveys, the professional surveyors prefer the plain alidade as it is convenient and faster to use.

Spirit Level

It consists of a small metal tube which contains a small bubble (Fig. 10.6). It may be circular or tubular but its base must be flat so that it can be laid on the plane table.

A spirit level is used to check that the plane table is properly levelled. Levelling is checked by placing the spirit level on the board in two positions at right angles to each other. The table is truly levelled when the bubble remains central all over the table.

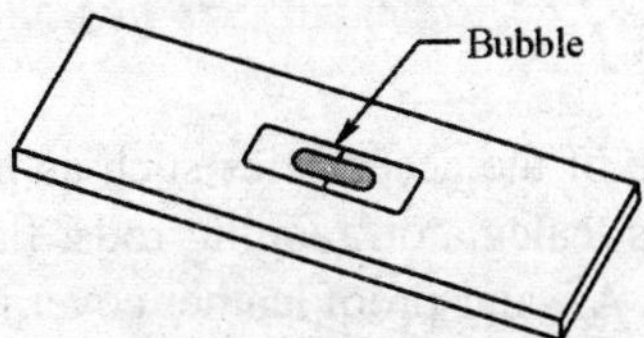

Fig. 10.6 Spirit level

Magnetic Compass

In plane tabling a trough compass is used to orient the plane table to magnetic north. It consists of long, narrow rectangular box 80 to 150 mm long, and 30 mm wide (Fig. 10.7). The magnetic needle rests on a pivot at the centre of the box. There are graduated scales with zero at the centre of the extremities of the box. The longer sides of the compass are parallel and plane so that they can be used as a ruler for drawing the north direction or for placing the compass along an already drawn line indicating the magnetic north.

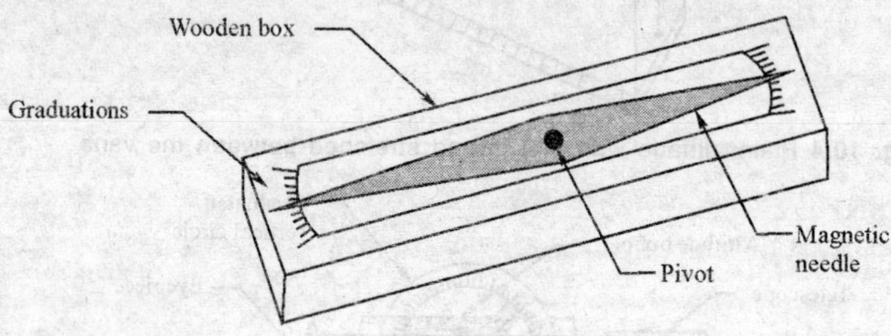

Fig. 10.7 Trough compass

Plumbing Fork

It consists of a hair pin-shaped brass or wooden frame having two arms of equal length (Fig. 10.8). One end has a pointer while a plumb bob is attached to the other end.

The plumbing fork is used in large-scale surveys for accurate centering of the plane table over the ground station. It is also used for transferring the location of the plotted instrument station position on to the ground. When the plumb bob is exactly over the ground station, the pointer indicates the corresponding position of the station on the plane table. On small-scale survey exact centering of the point is not required.

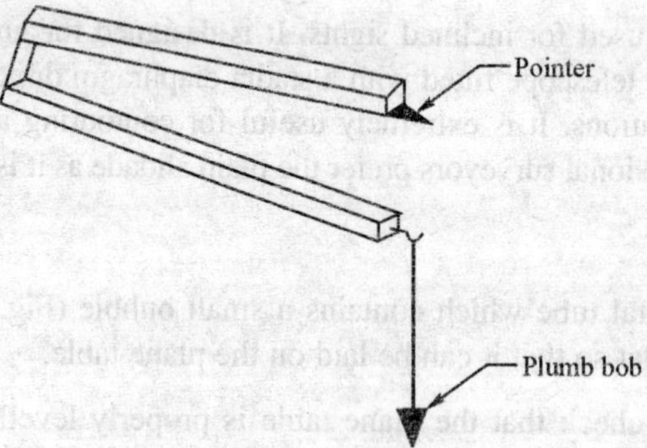

Fig. 10.8 Plumbing fork

Miscellaneous Accessories

While using the plane table some of the accessories such as pencil, eraser, protractor, set-square, scale, French curve, magnifying glass, calculator, ranging rods, flag poles, metallic tape, and tangent clinometer and clinopole are required. A water-proof leather cover is also carried to protect the drawing and table from sun and rains, when not in use. While working, an umbrella is also carried to protect the plane-table from sun working.

10.4 DRAWING PAPER

The drawing paper used for plane table work must be of high quality, must be well seasoned to prevent undue expansion and contraction, must contain a surface with a reasonable amount of tooth or roughness to take pencil lines without under grooving of the paper, and must be tough enough to stand erasers. For high accuracy works, plane table sheets containing thin aluminium sheets laminated with paper are used.

If a single ordinary sheet is used it should be seasoned for atleast one week by exposing it alternately to damp and dry conditions. Celluloid sheets are also used in damp climates.

10.5 BASIC DEFINITIONS

The following terms are commonly used in plane tabling.

Centering: The process of setting up the plane table on the plotted position of the ground station exactly over the station, is known as centering.

Orientation: This process involves positioning the plane table in such a manner that all lines on the paper are parallel to the corresponding lines on the ground.

Back sight: It is a sight taken from a plane table station to another station whose position has already been plotted on the drawing paper. Back sighting is one of the methods of orienting the plane table.

Fore sight: The sight taken from a plane table station to another station whose position has not been plotted, is known as fore sight. The fore sight is taken to locate the forward station.

Radiation: Radiation is a method of locating the points by drawing radial lines from the plane-table station to those points.

Intersection: The points can also be plotted by method of intersection. In this method rays are drawn for the points to be plotted from two different stations whose positions are already plotted, and the intersection of the respective rays is the position of the points on the plane-table sheet. The condition for plotting by intersection is that the plance table should be oriented before drawing the rays to various points from a station.

Resection: This is a method of locating the plane table station on the plane table by drawing the resectors through other stations and their plotted positions.

10.6 SETTING UP THE PLANE TABLE

The setting up of a plane table over a station is done in the following steps:

1. Levelling
2. Centering
3. Orienting.

Levelling

This operation makes the top of the plane table horizontal. Levelling can be done by eye estimation for rough and small-scale works. For accurate and large-scale works, spirit level is used to achieve the levelling.

The table is kept a few centimeters lower than the observer's elbows for comfortable working. The table is first placed in such a way that it is approximately oriented and centered. Approximate levelling is done by adjusting the legs of the tripod. The levelling is then achieved by placing the spirit level on the plane-table top in two mutually perpendicular positions.

Centering

Centering is the process of setting up the plane table in such a manner that the plotted position of a ground station is vertically above the ground position of the station. If the plotted position of the station lies on the vertical axis of the instrument, its position does not change when the table is turned about this axis during the orienting operation.

The centering is achieved by using the plumbing fork. The tip of the pointer of the plumbing fork is placed over the plotted position of the station, and then table is so adjusted that the plumb bob is over the ground station.

However, accurate centering is a rare requirement in plane tabling as the error due to inaccurate centering is insignificant in small-scale surveys.

Orienting

This operation involves positioning the table in such a manner that all lines on the plane-table sheet are parallel to the corresponding lines on the ground. This is essential when more than one station is occupied for plotting the details.

The plane table may be oriented by

1. A compass
2. Backsighting
3. Resection.

Orienting by a compass: At the first plane-table station, a trough compass is placed on the table, preferably outside the limits of the area to be plotted, and a line is drawn adjacent to it showing the direction of magnetic north. Then the compass is placed against this line at the subsequent stations, and the table is turned till the magnetic needle points towards north.

This method is not preferred if one of the other two methods can be used due to the effect of local attraction on the accuracy of orientation.

However, this method is generally used for rapid and approximate orientation before final orientation by other methods.

Orienting by backsighting: In this method, a ray is drawn from the plotted position of the instrument station to the next forward station. The plane table is shifted to the forward station, the alidade is laid along the ray drawn from the previous station and the table is turned until the line of sight intersects the previous station. In this position table is oriented (*c.f.*, Sec. 10.7 Intersection).

This method is independent of magnetic compass and thus, not affected by local attraction. It is essential that the same edge of the alidade is used for drawing lines. It may be ensured that the back ray remains vertically above the ground position of the forward station.

Orienting by resection: Resection being an important operation in plane tabling, is dealt with separately under the method of plane tabling in Sec. 10.7 (Resection).

10.7 PLANE TABLING METHODS

Plane-table surveying may be carried out by one of the following methods:

1. Radiation
2. Intersection
3. Traversing
4. Resection.

The first two methods are generally employed for locating the details while the third method is a method of traverse survey, and the fourth one is a method of simultaneously orienting the table and locating the plane-table station.

In the following discussions, the points on the ground have been designated by upper-case letters and the corresponding points on paper by the lower-case letters.

Radiation

An instrument station *P* is chosen in the centre of the area to be surveyed such that all the points to be plotted are visible and within measuring range. The plane table is set up over it, levelled and the horizontal movement is clamped. A point *p* on the paper, representing the ground station *P* approximately vertically above *P*, is selected (Fig. 10.9). With the alidade touching *p*, radial lines are drawn to the points *A*, *B*, *C*, *D*, etc., to be plotted. The corresponding ground distances *PA*, *PB*, *PC*, *PD*, etc., are measured and set off to scale from *p* on the respective radial lines, thus plotting the points *a*, *b*, *c*, *d*, etc. The points are then joined as required.

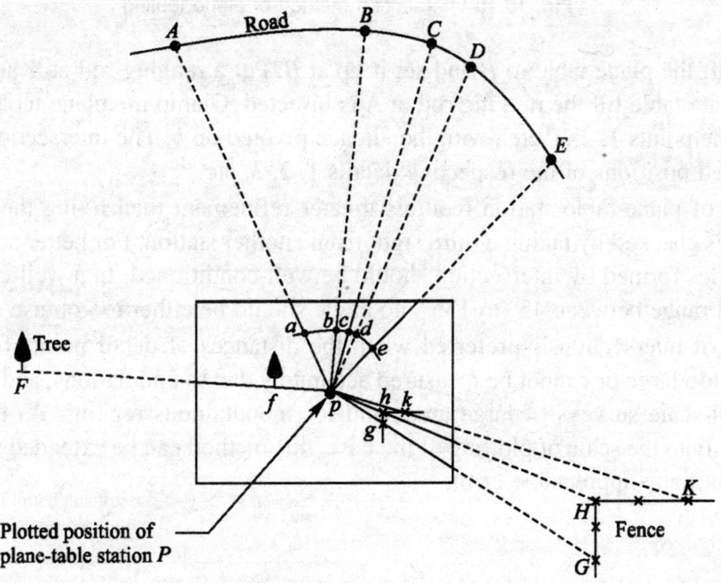

Fig. 10.9 Radiation method of plane tabling

The method is more suitable for large-scale surveys where the distances are small and one single setting of the instrument can control the points to be detailed. The method has wider scope if the distances are obtained tacheometrically using telescopic alidade.

Intersection

This method is also known as graphic triangulation. In this method, sights are taken to a particular object from two different stations whose positions are known on the plane-table sheet. The line joining such two stations is called *base*.

The plane table is set up at station *A*, and a ranging rod is put on the other station *B* (Fig. 10.10). A ray *ab* is drawn from *a* towards *B* sighting the ranging rod, and the distance *AB* is measured and plotted as *ab* at the chosen scale of plotting. Draw the rays to the selected points 1, 2, 3, etc., from the alidade

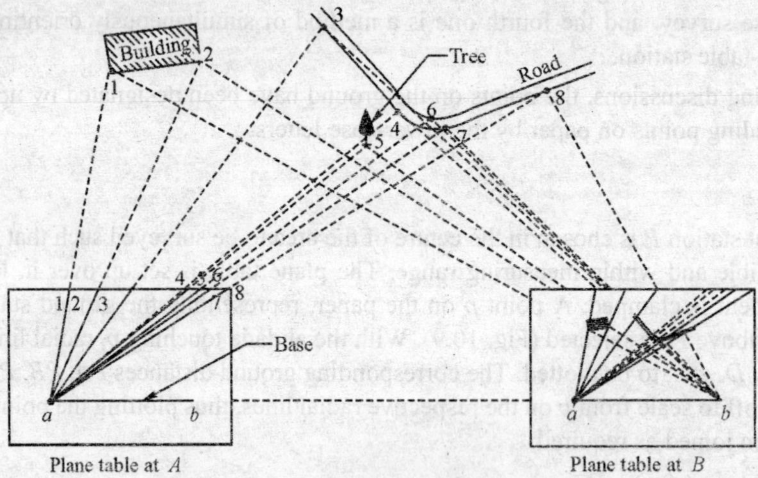

Fig. 10.10 Intersection method of plane tabling

pivoted on *a.* Shift the plane table to *B* and set it up at *B*. Put a ranging rod at *A* and place the alidade along *ba*, and rotate table till the ranging rod at *A* is bisected. Clamp the plane table and draw the rays again from *b* to the points 1, 2, 3, etc., with the alidade pivoted on *b*. The intersections of the respective rays are the plotted positions of the respective details 1, 2, 3, etc.

The plotting of plane-table station requires greater refinement than fixing the details. Plotting of important points is checked by taking a third sight from another station. For better accuracy in fixing the details, the triangles formed by intersection should be well-conditioned. In a well-conditioned triangle, the angles should range between 45° to 135°, no angle should be either too obtuse or too acute.

The method of intersection is preferred when the distances of detail points from the plane-table station are either too large or cannot be measured accurately due to undulations, and therefore, it is most suitable for small-scale surveys of large areas and for mountainous regions. As the accumulation of error is limited only to the scale of plotting of the base, this method can be extended to cover a large area without introducing any appreciable error.

Traversing

Traversing with the plane table involves the same principle as running a traverse with a theodolite. In this method, each successive station is occupied and the table is oriented usually taking a back sight on the preceding station. A fore sight is then taken to the next station and its location is plotted on the plane-table sheet. Horizontal distances and differences in elevations are determined by stadia using a conventional or self-reducing alidade.

In Fig. 10.11, *A*, *B*, *C*, *D*, and *E* are the traverse stations which are to be plotted by plane-table traversing. Let the initial setup of the plane table is on station *A* from which *B* and *E* are visible. The plane table is set up at *A*, levelled, and *A* is plotted as *a* on the plane-table sheet in such a location so that all other stations will fall within the limits of the sheet. With the alidade pivoted on *a*, draw rays to *B* and *E*. The distances *AB* and *AE* are measured and plotted to the scale on the respective rays as *ab* and *ae*. The location of *B* and *E* have been plotted as *b* and *e*, respectively.

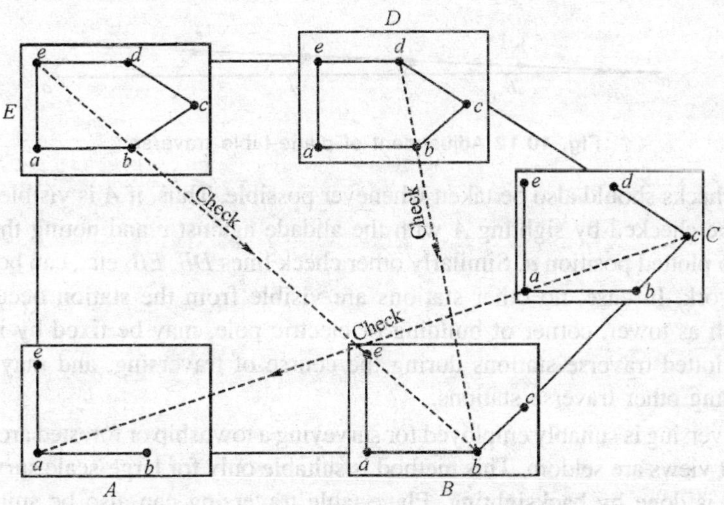

Fig. 10.11 Plane-table traversing

The plane table is then shifted to *B* and levelled. The alidade is aligned with *ba*, and the plane table is rotated until the station *A* is bisected. Clamp the horizontal motion of the plane table and draw a ray on the plane-table sheet for station *C*. The distance *BC* is measured and plotted to the scale as *bc*. The point *c* thus plotted, represents the ground station *C*.

The procedure of plotting the stations discussed above, is repeated for each station in the traverse. When the last station *E* is occupied and plotted, finally, a foresight is made on station *A*. For improved accuracy each distance is measured twice and average distance is considered. For example, when at *A*, the distance *AB* is measured and when at *B*, the distance *BA* is measured. The average of these two distances is taken to plot *b* when at *B*. Similarly when at *E*, the distance *EA* is also measured. When the average of the distance *AE* and *EA* is plotted to scale along the line *EA* from *e* to establish a final position for *a*, it may not necessarily coincide with its original position plotted at the beginning of the work. Let this new position be a_1 as shown in Fig. 10.12. The difference in the initial location *a* and the final location a_1 is the error of closure or closing error aa_1 (*e*). The closing error is adjusted by graphical method of adjusting a traverse discussed in Sec. 9.8.

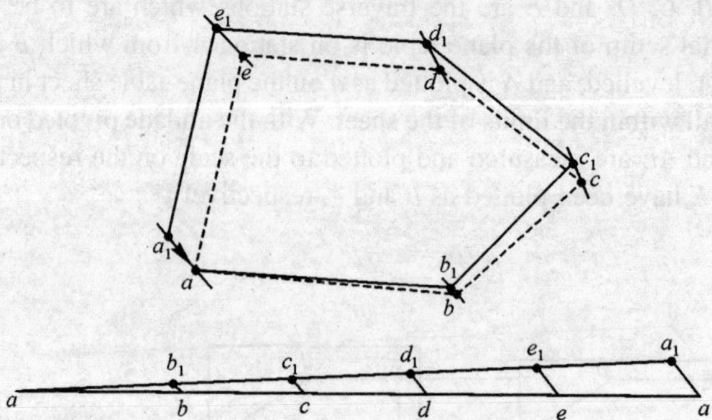

Fig. 10.12 Adjustment of plane-table traverse

Intermediate checks should also be taken whenever possible. Thus, if *A* is visible from *C*, the work done upto *C* can be checked by sighting *A* with the alidade against *c* and noting that the edge of the alidade touches the plotted position *a*. Similarly other check lines *DB*, *EB*, etc., can be used to check the accuracy of the work. In case, no other stations are visible from the station occupied, some well-defined object such as tower, corner of building or electric pole, may be fixed by intersection taking sights from two plotted traverse stations during the course of traversing, and may be used later for checks when plotting other traverse stations.

Plane-table traversing is suitably employed for surveying a township or forested areas where clearings are rare and distant views are seldom. This method is suitable only for large-scale surveys as orientation of the plane table is done by backsighting. Plane-table traversing can also be suitably employed in magnetically disturbed area.

Resection

Resection is the process of determining the location of plane-table station by means of drawing rays from stations whose locations have already been plotted. It requires that before drawing the rays, the plane table is oriented. The method of resection is used for locating the station points only and is never employed for detail plotting.

There are four methods of locating the plane-table station by the method of resection, and these are:

1. Resection after orientation by back ray
2. Resection after orientation by a compass
3. Resection after orientation by two points
4. Resection after orientation by three points.

Resection after orientation by back-ray method

In Fig. 10.13, the plotted positions of stations *A* and *B* are shown as *a* and *b*, respectively. Let the plane table be set up initially at *A*. The plane table is oriented by back sighting on *B*, and a ray is drawn to *P* which is going to be occupied by the plane table and its location is not known on the plane-table sheet.

Set up the plane table over the estimated position of *P*. Orient the plane table by back sighting on *A*, placing the alidade along the ray drawn to *P* from *A* and clamp it. Place the alidade on *b*, pivot it around this point and rotate until the station B is sighted. Draw a ray intersecting the previously drawn ray to P from A, at p. This point p is the required location of P obtained by resection. The line bp is called the *resector* or *resection line*.

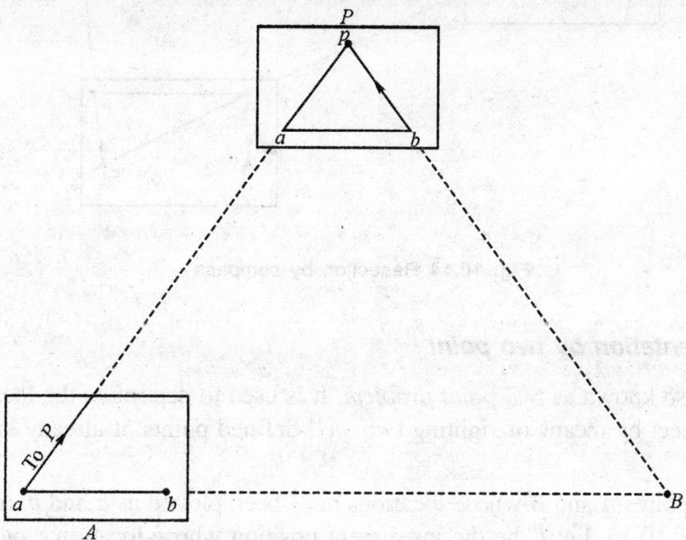

Fig. 10.13 Resection by back-ray method

In orienting the plane table by back ray method the following precautions must be taken.

1. The plane table should be centered such that the estimated location of the plane-table station is over the ground station whose location is to be determined and not the centre of the table as the error in centering is accumulative.
2. The forward and back stations must be carefully located and marked by the wooden pegs to avoid error in sighting.
3. The same side of the alidade should always be used for drawing rays.

This method is suitable for plane-table survey when a prominent point such as chimney, temple or church spire is available in the centre of the area. This method is also suitable for large-scale surveys where long rays are possible.

Resection after orientation by compass

In this method a base AB is selected, measured and plotted as ab on the sheet in a convenient position (Fig. 10.14). The plane table is set up at A and levelled. The plane table is oriented by placing the alidade along ab and sighting B. The plane table is clamped and a magnetic compass is placed on the table in a position that the magnetic needle rests in north-south direction. Draw a line and mark the north direction. The table is then shifted to the station C, levelled, oriented with the help of the magnetic compass and clamped. Two resectors are drawn by pivoting the alidade about the points a and b and the point of intersection c of these resectors is the required location of the ground station C.

This method is only suitable in those areas which are not magnetically disturbed and when the scale of survey is comparatively small.

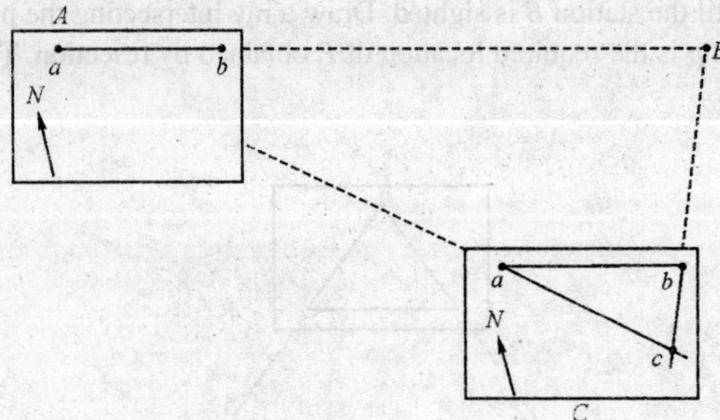

Fig. 10.14 Resection by compass

Resection after orientation by two point

This method is also known as *two-point problem.* It is used to determine the location of the plane-table station on the sheet by means of sighting two well-defined points of already known locations on the sheet.

Let there be two points *A* and *B* whose locations have been plotted as *a* and *b*, respectively, on the sheet as shown in Fig. 10.15. Let *C* be the instrument position whose location *c* on the sheet is to be determined.

The solution of the problem consists in correctly orienting the plane table, *i.e.*, placing *ab* exactly parallel to *AB* when the table is set at *C*, and then finding *c* on the sheet.

Select a suitable fourth point *P* as an auxiliary point such that the angles *CAP* and *CBP* are not too small for good intersections at *A* and *B*. Set up the table at *P* and level it. Orient the table approximately using a compass or by placing *ab* parallel to *AB* by judgement and clamp it.

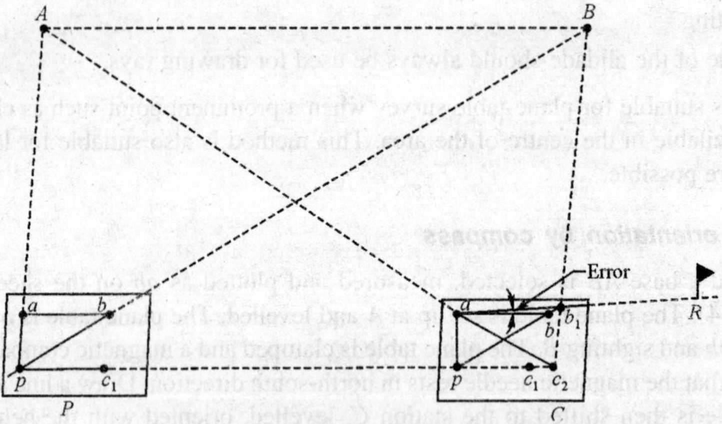

Fig. 10.15 Resection by two-point problem

With the alidade pivoted on *a*, *A* is sighted and a ray is drawn through *a*. Similarly with the alidade pivoted on *b*, *B* is sighted and another ray is drawn through *b*. The intersection *p* of these two rays is the approximate location of *P* as the orientation of the plane table at *P* is only approximate. Draw a ray to *C* by pivoting the alidade on *p*. By estimating the distance *PC*, cut off pc_1 to scale and c_1 so obtained is the approximate position of *C*.

Now shift the plane table to *C*, set it up with c_1 over *C* and level it. Orient the table by back sighting at *P* and clamp it. With the alidade against *a*, *A* is bisected. Draw a ray through *a* intersecting the line pc_1 in c_2. With the alidade centered on c_2, *B* is sighted and a ray is drawn through c_2. This ray will pass through *b*, provided the initial orientation at *P* was correct. But since the orientation at *P* as well as at *C* is only approximate, the ray will not pass through *b*. Let the rays c_2B and *pb* intersect at b_1. Thus apc_2b_1 represents *APCB*. But since *ab* is the true representation of *AB*, on the sheet, the error in orientation of the table is the angle bab_1. To eliminate this error, the plane table is required to be rotated through this angle. This will make the line *ab* parallel to *AB*. To achieve this, align the alidade along ab_1 and fix a ranging rod *R* on the line ab_1 produced at some convenient distance. Place the alidade along *ab* and turn the table until the ranging rod *R* is bisected and clamp the table. In this position table is correctly oriented. Now place the alidade against *a*, draw a ray sighting to *A* and then place the alidade against *b*, draw another ray sighting to *B*. The intersection of these two rays is the point *c*, which is the correct location of *C* on the sheet.

This method of resection by two-point problem is not very accurate. Also it requires more labour and time to set the plane table at two stations to achieve the orientation.

Resection after orientation by three points

This method is also known as *three-point problem.* It is finding the location of the station occupied by a plane table on the sheet, by means of sighting to three well-defined points of known locations on the sheet.

The principle of this method lies in the fact that if the plane table is correctly oriented, the three resectors through *a*, *b*, and *c*, shown in Fig. 10.16, meet at a point *p* which is the location of the plane-table station on the sheet, provided the points *A*, *B*, *C*, and *P* do not lie on the circumference of a circle. By solving three-point problem, thus, the orientation and resection are accomplished simultaneously.

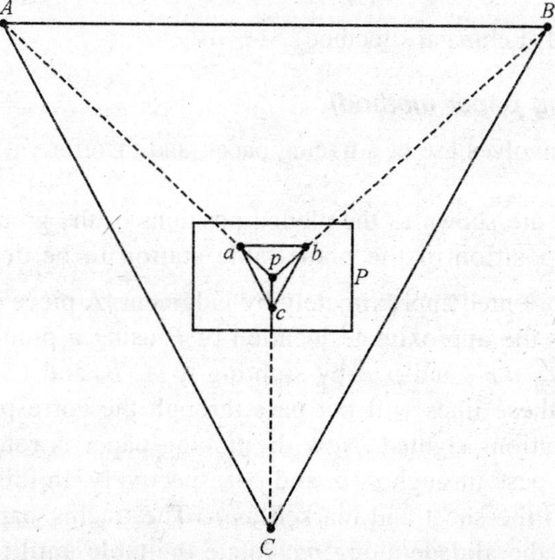

Fig. 10.16 Principle of three-point problem solution

The solution of three-point problem is further illustrated graphically in Fig. 10.17. The stations *A*, *B*, and *C* are of known positions, and *P* is of unknown position. If the angle α is observed between *PB* and *PA*, the position of *P* is indeterminate, because *P* can be anywhere on the circle circumscribing the triangle *PAB*. Additional information is needed to make the problem determinate. If the angle β, which is the angle subtended by *AC* at *P*, is also observed then the solution is unique since *P*, *A*, and *C* lie on the circle that circumscribe triangle *PAC*, and *P* is one of the two intersection points of the circles and *A* is the other intersection point. This solution becomes indeterminate if *A*, *B*, *C*, and *P* fall on the circumference of one circle.

If the two circles tend to merge into one circle, the problem will be less stable, and finally becomes indeterminate again when the two circles coincide. Points should be selected in the field so as to avoid this situation.

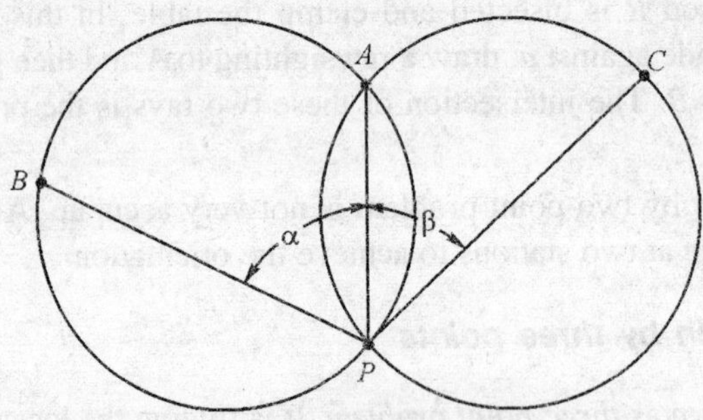

Fig. 10.17 Three-point resection

There are a number of solutions of three-point problem but only the following methods applicable to the plane table, have been discussed.

1. Mechanical method (Tracing paper method)
2. Graphical method
3 Trial and error method (Lehmann's method).

Mechanical method (Tracing paper method)

The mechanical method involves use of a tracing paper, and therefore, it is also known as tracing paper method.

In Fig. 10.18, *a*, *b*, and *c* are shown as the plotted positions of the ground stations *A*, *B*, and *C*, respectively. Let *P* be the position of the plane-table station to be determined on the sheet.

The table is set on *P* and oriented approximately by judgment. A piece of tracing paper is fixed on the sheet, and mark *p*′ as the approximate location of *P* using a plumbing fork. Pivoting the alidade at *p*′, draw lines *p*′*a*′, *p*′*b*′, and *p*′*c*′ by sighting to *A*, *B*, and *C*, respectively. Since the orientation is approximate, these lines will not pass through the corresponding plotted position *a*, *b*, and *c* of the ground stations sighted. Now the tracing paper is rotated in such a way that the lines *p*′*a*′, *p*′*b*′, and *p*′*c*′ pass through *a*, *b*, and *c*, respectively. In this position of the tracing paper, *p*′ is transferred on to the sheet and marked as *p*. The tracing paper is removed and join *p* with *a*, *b*, and *c*. Keeping the alidade along *pa*, rotate the table until the station *A* is bisected and clamp the table. Now the table is in correct orientation. Check the orientation by placing the alidade along *pb* and *pc*, and seeing that the stations *B* and *C* are bisected, respectively.

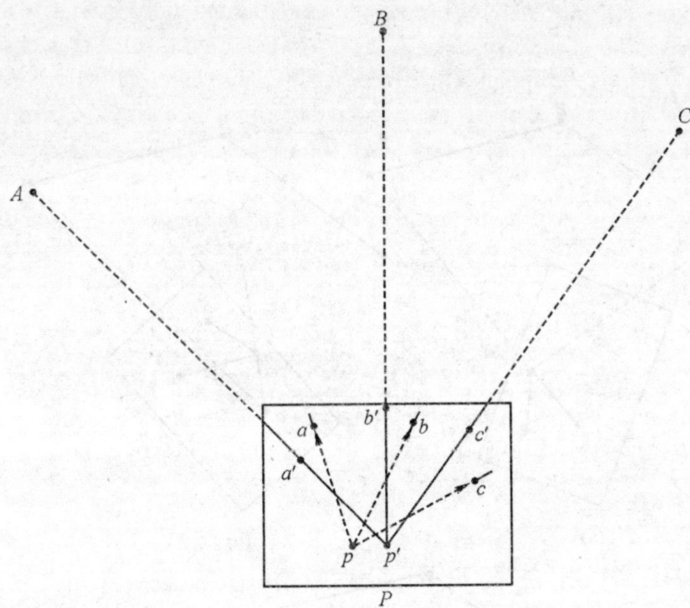

Fig. 10.18 Solution of three-point problem by mechanical method

The accuracy of the method depends upon the accuracy with which lines are drawn from the assumed position of the plane-table station on the tracing paper. This method may be used only to orient the table and to determine the plane-table station when plotting the detail points, and should not be used for providing controls.

Graphical method

Three-point problem can be solved graphically in many ways but only the important ones have been described below:

(*i*) Bessel's method

(*ii*) Perpendicular method.

Bessel's method

In Bessel's graphical method, the plane table is set up on the station *P* whose location is to be determined on the sheet (Fig. 10.19). The plotted positions of the stations *A*, *B*, and *C* are *a*, *b*, and *c*, respectively. The alidade is aligned along *ba* and the table is rotated until the point *A* is sighted. The table is clamped, and a ray *be* is drawn pivoting the alidade on *b* and sighting the station *C*. Then the alidade is aligned at *ab* and the table is rotated until the point *B* is sighted. The table is clamped and a ray is drawn by pivoting the alidade on *a* and sighting the station *C*. Let this ray intersects the previously drawn ray *be* at *d*. The points *d* and *c* are joined, and placing the alidade along *dc*, the table is rotated until *C* is sighted. The table is now in correct orientation. The table is clamped and rays are drawn to *A* and *B* by pivoting the alidade on *a* and *b*, respectively. These rays will intersect at *p*, which will lie on the line *cd* produced. *p* is the required location of *P* on the plane-table sheet.

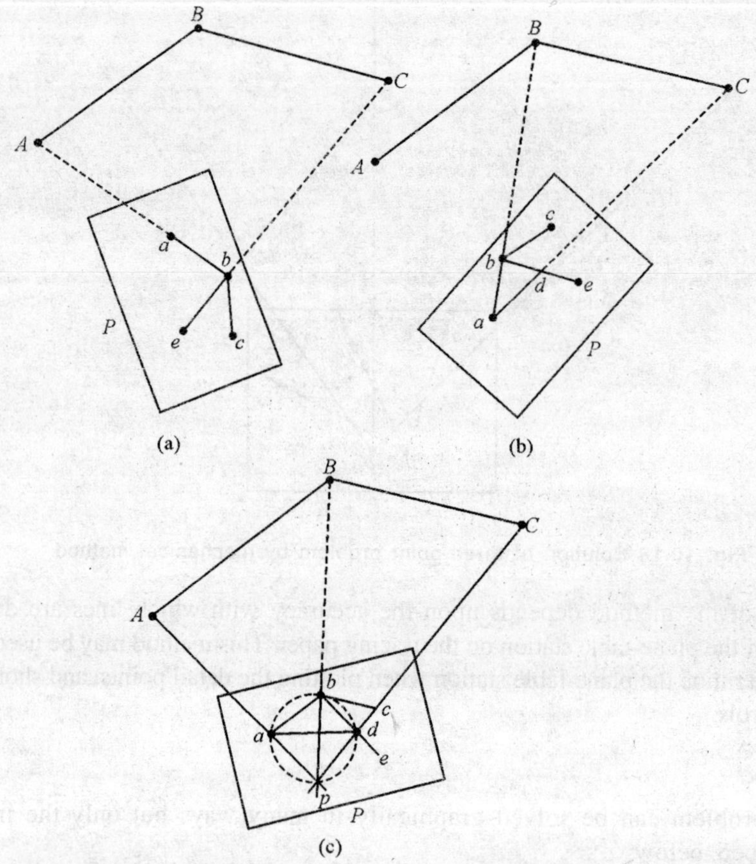

Fig. 10.19 Solution of three-point problem by Bessel's method

Perpendicular method

In this method two lines *ad* and *ce* as shown in Fig.10.20, are drawn at *a* and *c*, perpendicular to *ab* and *cb*, respectively. The alidade is aligned along *da* and the table is rotated until *A* is sighted. The table is clamped and pivoting the alidade on *b*, *B* is sighted and a ray is drawn through *b*, intersecting *ad* at *d*. Similarly the alidade is aligned along *ec* and the table is rotated until *C* is sighted. The table is clamped, and pivoting the alidade on *b*, *B* is sighted again and a ray is drawn through *b*, intersecting *ce* at *e*. Then *d* and *e* are joined and a perpendicular to *de* is drawn from *b* to intersect *de* at *p*. *p* is the required location of the plane-table station *P*. Now the alidade is aligned along *pa* (assuming *A* is the farthest station to minimise the error in bisection), the table is rotated until *A* is sighted and the table is clamped. The table is now in correct orientation. This can be checked by aligning the alidade along *pb* and *pc* and seeing that *B* and *C* are sighted, respectively.

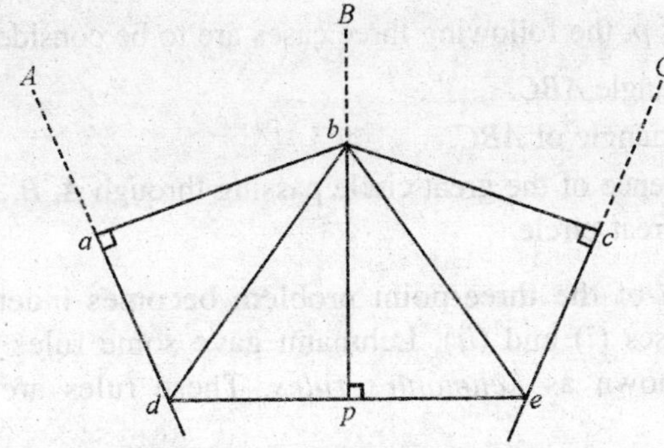

Fig. 10.20 Solution of three-point problem by perpendicular method

Trial and error method

In this method, the location of the station occupied is determined by trial and error. This method was given by a well known mathematician, Lehmann, and hence this method is also known as *Lehmann's method*. It is quick and accurate method.

This method is based upon the principle discussed in the beginning of this section (Fig. 10.16) that if the plane table is oriented, the resectors through *a*, *b*, and *c* will meet at point *p* which is the location of the plane-table station. If the table is out of orientation, then the resectors will not meet at a point, and they will form a triangle which is known as *triangle of error*, shown in Fig. 10.21.

The size of the triangle of error depends upon the angular error in the orientation. In this method, the location *p* of the plane-table station on the sheet is estimated by trial. If the estimated position of *p* is close to the correct position then the size of the triangle will reduce for the next trial, and like this we try to reach to the correct position of *p*, in which case, the triangle of error will reduce to zero and all the resectors will pass through *p*.

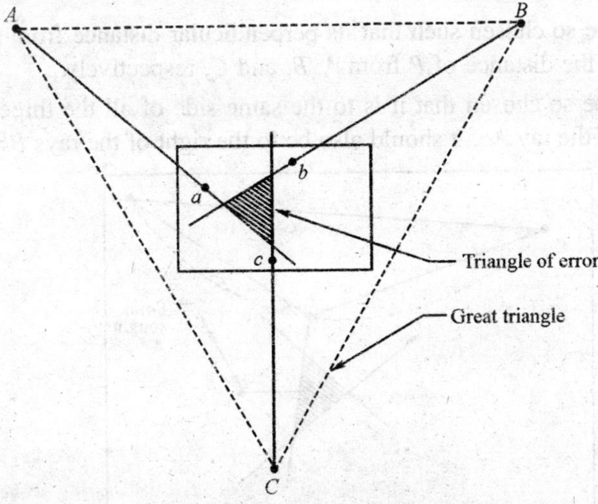

Fig. 10.21 Triangle of error

To estimate the location of *p*, the following three cases are to be considered:

(*i*) *P* is inside the great triangle *ABC*.

(*ii*) *P* is outside the great triangle of *ABC*.

(*iii*) *P* lies on the circumference of the great circle passing through *A*, *B*, and *C* or it is close to the circumference of the great circle.

In the case (*iii*), the solution of the three-point problem becomes indeterminate or unstable as stated earlier. But for the cases (*i*) and (*ii*), Lehmann gave some rules to estimate the location of *p*, and these rules are known as *Lehmann's rules*. These rules are given below.

Lehmann's rules

1. If the station *P* is inside the great triangle *ABC*, the point *p* should be chosen inside the triangle of error (Fig. 10.22).

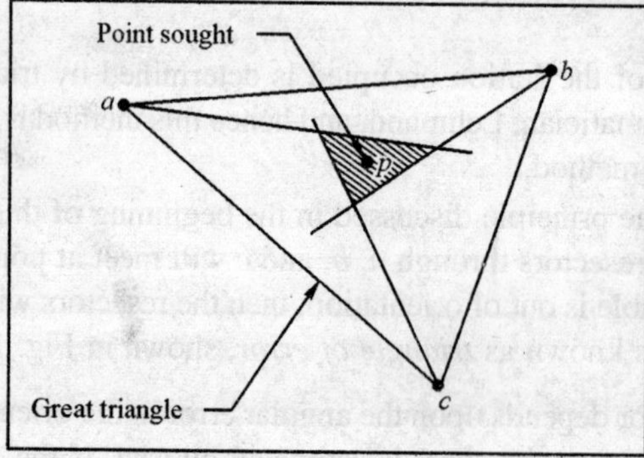

Fig. 10.22 Estimated location of plane table when the table inside the great triangle

2. If the station *P* is outside the great triangle *ABC*, the point *p* should be chosen outside the triangle of error.
3. The point *p* should be so chosen such that its perpendicular distance from the rays *Aa*, *Bb*, and *Cc* is proportional to the distance of *P* from *A*, *B*, and *C*, respectively.
4. The point *p* should be so chosen that it is to the same side of all the three rays. That is, if *p* is chosen to the right of the ray *Aa*, it should also be to the right of the rays *Bb* and *Cc* (Fig. 10.23).

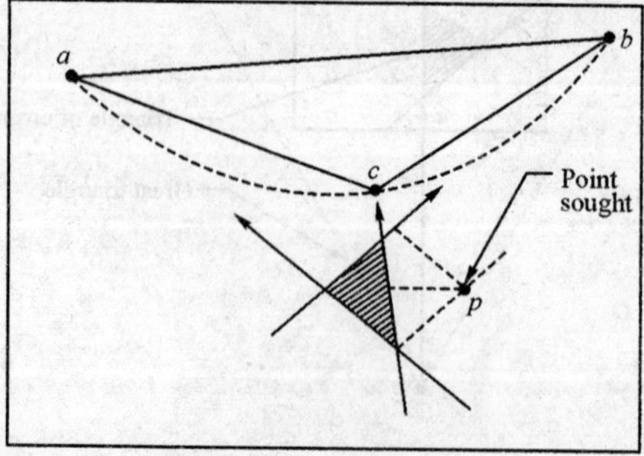

Fig. 10.23 Estimated location of instrument station always on the same side of all the rays

The following sub-rules of rule (4) are useful in estimating the location of *p*.

Rule 4a: If the station *P* is outside the great circle, the point *p* is so chosen that

(*a*) It lies on the same side of ray to the most distant point as the intersection *k* of the other two rays (Fig. 10.24).

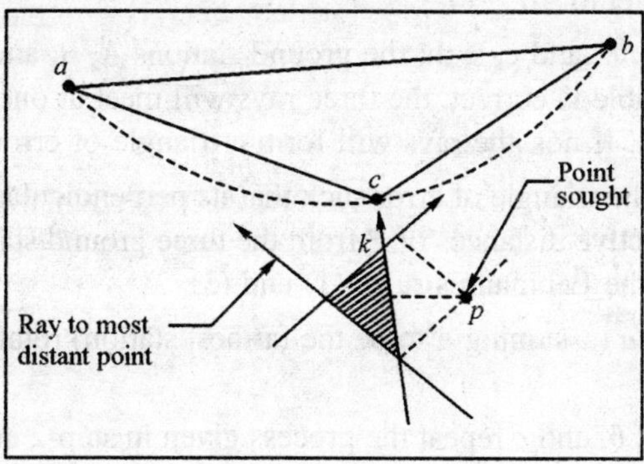

Fig. 10.24 Rule 4a

(*b*) The intersection *k* of two rays to the nearer points, is midway between the point *p* and the ray to the most distant point (Fig. 10.24).

Rule 4b: If the station *P* is outside the great triangle but inside the great circle, the point *p* is so chosen that the ray to the middle point lies between *p* and the intersection *k* of the rays to the two extreme points.

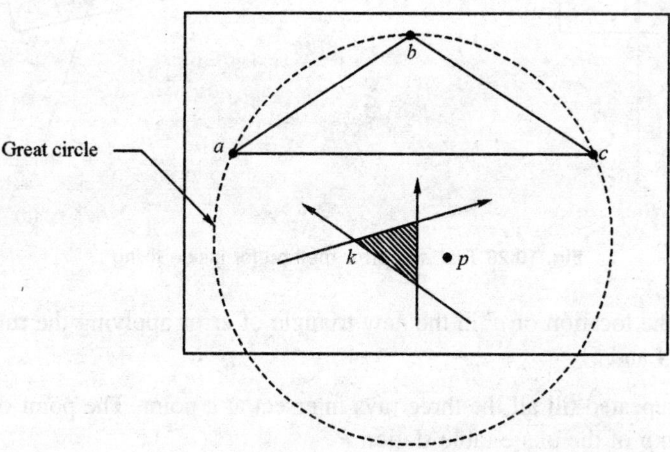

Fig. 10.25 Rule 4b

In practice, it is preferred to occupy a position of the plane table is inside the great triangle. Hence, the observer simply applies the rule (1) and (3) only, and avoids other complicated positions. This also avoids any possibilities of the case (*iii*) arising without being noticed by the observer.

Procedure for solving three-point problem (Fig. 10.26)

Let *A*, *B*, and *C* represent the ground stations and their corresponding plotted locations on the sheet be *a*, *b*, and *c*, respectively. Let *P* be the plane-table station whose location *p* on the sheet is to be determined.

1. Set up the table over *P* selecting *P* inside the great triangle *ABC*, and orient it by judgment so that *ab* is approximately parallel to *AB*.
2. Pivoting the alidade on *a*, *b*, and *c*, sight the ground stations *A*, *B*, and *C* in turn, and draw rays. If the orientation of the table is correct, the three rays will meet at one point which is the desired location of *p* on the sheet. If not, the rays will form a triangle of error (Fig. 10.26a).
3. Choose a point *p′* inside the triangle of error such that its perpendicular distances from each ray is in proportion to the respective distances of *P* from the three ground stations. Selection of location of *p′* here is based upon the Lehmann's rules (1) and (3).
4. Align the alidade along *p′a* (assuming *A* to be the farthest station) rotate the table till *A* is sighted, and clamp the table.
5. Pivoting the alidade on *a*, *b*, and *c* repeat the process given in step-2 above. If the estimation of *p* as *p′* was correct, the three rays will intersect at a point (Fig. 10.26b) otherwise again a triangle of error will be formed but of smaller size.

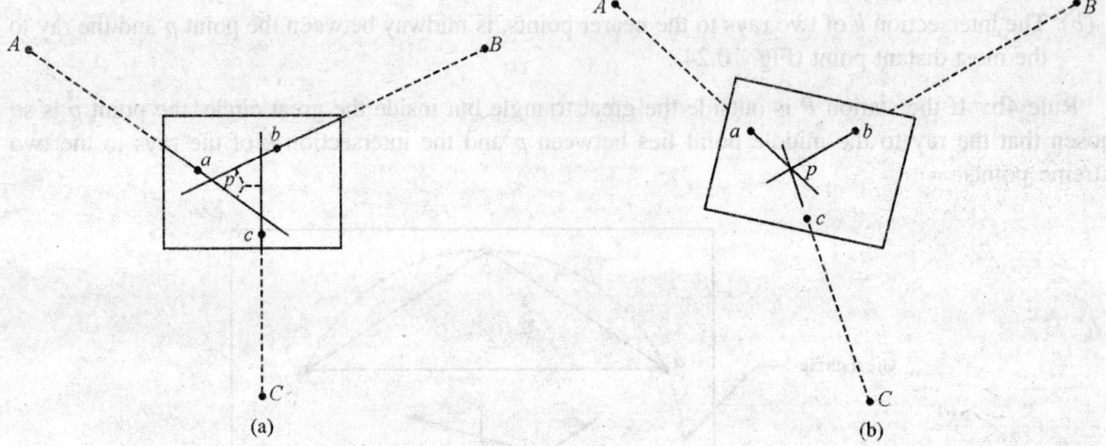

Fig. 10.26 Trial and error method for inside fixing

6. Estimate again the location of *p′* in the new triangle of error applying the rules, (1) and (3), and repeat the steps 4 and 5.
7. The method is repeated till all the three rays intersect at a point. The point of intersection is the required location *p* of the plane-table station *P*.

Strength of fix

The relative position of *A*, *B*, *C*, and *P* has an important influence on the accuracy with which the position of *P* can be fixed on the sheet as *p*. It has already been shown that the solution becomes less stable if *P* lies close to the circumference of great circle passing through *A*, *B*, and *C*, and becomes indeterminate if *P* lies on the circumference of the great circle. For other positions of *P*, if the table is not oriented, the resectors will not pass through a point, and they will either form a triangle of error or two of them may be parallel and intersected by the third. In such cases the accuracy with which the position of *P* is fixed varies with position of *P* relative to *A*, *B*, and *C*. The accuracy of fix is also termed as *strength of fix*.

The strength of fix is good if

(*i*) *P* is within the great triangle *ABC*,

(*ii*) the middle station is much nearer than others, and

(*iii*) of the two angles subtended at *P*, one is small and the other is large, provided the points subtending the small angle are not too close to each other.

The strength of fix is bad if

(*i*) both angles subtended at *P* are small, and

(*ii*) *P* is near the circumference of the great circle.

Practical utility of three-point resection

Resection by three-point problem provides a great advantage of saving the necessity of selecting and plotting the forward instrument station in advance. The observer may choose stations best suited to him for plotting the detail. In doing so he has to only insure the visibility of three well-defined points already plotted on the sheet from the station to be occupied. The observer is not dependent upon the previous instrument station as in other resection methods.

10.8 ERRORS IN PLANE TABLING

The following are the common sources of errors in plane-table surveying:

1. Instrumental errors
2. Errors of manipulation and sighting
3. Errors due to other causes.

Instrumental Errors

These errors occur when the plane table and alidade are not in perfect adjustment. The instrumental errors occur due to the following causes:

(*i*) The top surface of the plane table is not perfectly plane.

(*ii*) The fittings of the table and the tripod are loose. This will make the table unstable during the course of work.

(*iii*) The fiducial edge of the alidade is not straight.

(*iv*) The sight vanes are not perpendicular to the base of the alidade. It will cause error in sighting.

(*v*) The magnetic compass is sluggish. This will cause error in orientation done with the magnetic compass.

(*vi*) The level tube is defective. If the level tube has been used for levelling the plane table in large-scale surveys, the table will not be horizontal, and the resulting plan will be inaccurate. In small-scale surveys, perfect levelling using level tube is not required.

Errors of Manipulation and Sighting

(*i*) If the plane table is not properly levelled, the sight vanes will be inclined to the vertical and the plotted positions of points will be in error.

(*ii*) If the plane table is not accurately centered, it will cause error in plotting. The error is more important in large-scale surveys.

(*iii*) Inaccurate orientation of the plane table causes inaccurate plotting of detail, and the resulting map will be in error.

(*iv*) If the plane table is not properly clamped after orientation, the plane table may rotate between sights causing errors.

(*v*) Inaccurate sighting or bisection causes error in plotting.

(*vi*) If the alidade is not pivoted properly on the point, the rays drawn will be in error.

(*vii*) If the tripod is not firmly planted into the ground, it will be unstable and may cause error in plotting. The plane table should always be set up on a firm and unyielding ground.

(*viii*) Undue pressure on the plane table of leaning against it while working, may disturb the table which will cause error.

Errors due to Other Causes

(*i*) If a good quality drawing sheet is not used, the change in temperature may cause contraction or expansion of the sheet which will result into plotting errors.

(*ii*) The drawing sheet should be properly stretched on the table to avoid plotting errors.

(*iii*) Care should be taken in drawing the rays and in the use of scale during plotting the details to avoid any error in drawing the rays or in reducing the distances to scale.

10.9 ERRORS DUE TO INACCURATE CENTERING

Inaccurate centering introduces error in the plotted positions of the points. It is very essential to have a proper conception of error introduced due to inaccurate centering to avoid unnecessary waste of time in achieving accurate centering of the plane table at every station. This problem is avoided when the plane-table position on the sheet is determined by three-point problem and details are plotted by the method of intersection. The change in temperature may cause contraction or expansion of the sheet which will result into plotting errors.

Let A, B, and C be the positions of the ground stations and a, b, and c be their plotted positions on the sheet, respectively, as shown in Fig. 10.27. The point a' on the table is exactly over the ground station A (not shown in the figure), where the plotted position a should have been for correct centering. If the linear error in centering is e $(= aa')$, and the angles aBa' and aCa' are α and β, respectively, the angular error in centering can be obtained as below.

Draw ab_1 parallel to $a'B$, and ac parallel to $a'c$, then

$$\angle b_1aB = \alpha \text{ and } \angle c_1aC = \beta$$

Taking $\angle Ba'C = b_1ac_1 = \phi$ and $\angle BaC = \gamma$, we have

$$\phi = \alpha + \gamma + \beta$$

or

$$\phi - \gamma = (\angle Ba'C - \angle BaC)$$

$$= (\angle BAC - \angle BaC) = \alpha + \beta$$

Thus the angular error in centering is $(\alpha + \beta)$.

Angular error

From a' drop $a'D$ and $a'E$ perpendiculars to aB and aC, respectively. From triangles $a'DB$ and $a'EC$, we have

$$\alpha = \sin^{-1}\frac{a'D}{a'B}$$

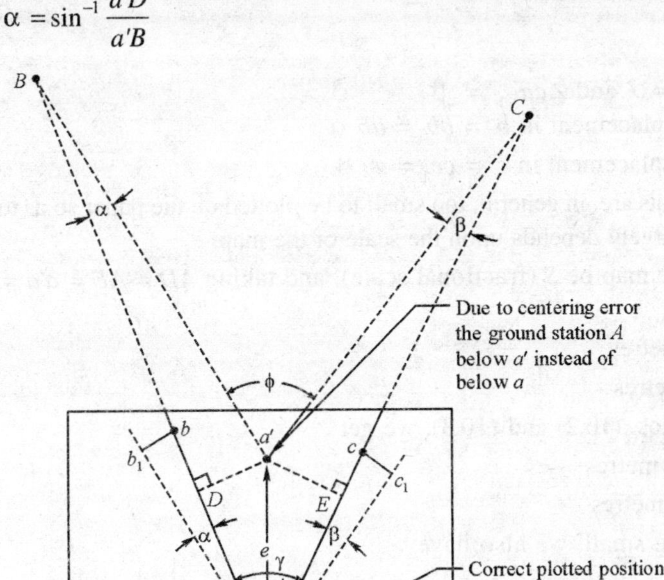

Fig. 10.27 Inaccurate centering

and $$\beta = \sin^{-1}\frac{a'E}{a'C}$$

$$\text{Angular error} = \alpha + \beta$$

$$= \sin^{-1}\frac{a'D}{a'B} + \sin^{-1}\frac{a'E}{a'C} \qquad ...(10.1)$$

In practice, for plane table of size 750 mm × 600 mm the maximum values of $a'D$ and $a'E$, do not exceed 300 mm. Assuming the length of sights $a'B$ and $a'C$ equal, the extent of the resulting angular error for different sights may be judged from the following:

Distance (m) ($a'B$ and $a'C$)	Angular error
10	3°26′18″
30	1°08′46″
50	0°41′15″
100	0°20′40″
500	0°04′08″
1000	0°02′04″

Positional error

But, the more significant is the positional errors of b and c. To determine these errors, draw rays ab_1 and ac_1 parallel to $a'B$ and $a'C$, respectively. Evidently, the true positions b will be at b_1 to the left of b and that of c at c_1 to the right of c.

Thus,

$$\angle bab_1 = \alpha \text{ and } \angle cac_1 = \beta$$

$$\text{Displacement in } b = bb_1 = ab\ \alpha \qquad \text{...(10.2)}$$

and

$$\text{displacement in } c = cc_1 = ac\ \beta \qquad \text{...(10.3)}$$

These displacements are, in general, too small to be plotted on the paper so as to affect the accuracy of the map, and this largely depends upon the scale of the map.

Let the scale of the map be S (fractional scale), and taking $AD = AE = d'a = e$ metres, we have the plotted lengths

$$ab = AB\ S \text{ metres} \qquad \text{...(10.4)}$$

and

$$ac = AC\ S \text{ metres} \qquad \text{...(10.5)}$$

Therefore, from Eqs. (10.2) and (10.3), we get

$$bb_1 = AB\ S\alpha \text{ metres} \qquad \text{...(10.6)}$$

$$ce_1 = AC\ S\alpha \text{ metres} \qquad \text{...(10.7)}$$

α and β being small, we also have

$$\alpha = \frac{e}{AB} \text{ and } \beta = \frac{e}{AC} \qquad \text{...(10.8)}$$

Putting the values of α and β in Eqs. (10.6) and (10.7), we have

$$bb_1 = AB\ S\frac{e}{AB} = eS \text{ metres} \qquad \text{...(10.9)}$$

$$cc_1 = AC\ S\frac{e}{AC} = eS \text{ metres} \qquad \text{...(10.10)}$$

Hence the displacement of the point = eS metres.

Now if we take 0.25 mm as the limit of precision in plotting on paper,

$$eS = 0.00025 \text{ metres}$$

or

$$e = \frac{1}{4000S} \text{ metres} \qquad \text{...(10.11)}$$

or

$$= \frac{1}{40S} \text{ centimetres} \qquad \text{...(10.12)}$$

Thus, the above expression shows that the error in centering should always be less than $\frac{1}{40S}$ cm so that there is no error in plotting of the detail points. Further, we find that very accurate centering is required only in the case of large-scale surveys where the sights are short. In case of small-scale surveys where sights are generally longer, accurate centering is not necessary, and the centre of the table may be centered over the ground station. For very small-scale surveys, even the table may be set up within a radius of reasonable distance. For example, on a scale of 1:25000, the plotting error is $\frac{1}{4000 \times (1/25000)} = 6.25$ m, therefore, setting up the table within a distance of 5 m from the ground station will not cause plotting error, and thus will not affect the accuracy of the map.

ILLUSTRATIVE EXAMPLES

Example 10.1

In plane table survey at one plane table station it was found that the table was not accurately centered over the ground station. If the displacement was 25 cm in a direction at right angles to the ray, calculate the displacement of the point from its true position on the plane table sheet if the scale of plotting is

$$(i)\ \frac{1}{50};\quad (ii)\ \frac{1}{500};\quad (iii)\ \frac{1}{5000}$$

Solution:

From Eq. (10.9), we have

displacement = eS

S being a dimensionless quantity, the unit of the displacement will be same as that of e.

It is given that $e = 25$ cm = 250 mm.

(*i*) Displacement $= 250 \times \frac{1}{50} = \mathbf{5.0\,mm}$

(*ii*) Displacement $= 250 \times \frac{1}{500} = \mathbf{0.5\,mm}$

(*iii*) Displacement $= 250 \times \frac{1}{5000} = \mathbf{0.05\,mm}$.

Example 10.2

In setting up the plane table at a station A, the corresponding point on the plan was not accurately centered above A. If the displacement of A was 30 cm in a direction perpendicular to the ray, how much on the plan would be the consequent displacement of a point from its true position if scale is (*i*) 1 cm = 100 m, and (*ii*) 1 cm = 1 m.

Solution:

From eq. (10.9) the displacement = eS

(*i*) $S = \frac{1}{100 \times 100} = \frac{1}{10000}$

and $e = 300$ mm

Thus displacement $= 300 \times \frac{1}{10000}$

$= \mathbf{0.03\,mm}$.

(*ii*) $S = \frac{1}{1 \times 100} = \frac{1}{100}$

and $e = 300$ mm

Thus displacement $= 300 \times \frac{1}{100}$

$= \mathbf{3.00\ mm}$.

Example 10.3

On a map at a scale of 1 cm = 10 m three points *A*, *B*, and *C* were selected. The distance *AB* and *BC* are known to be 125 m and 80 m, respectively, and the angle *ABC* = 135°. Further on the ground a station *P* was established and the angles *APB* and *BPC* were measured as 40° and 60°, respectively. Plot the point *P* on the map graphically and scale off the distances *PA*, *PB*, and *PC*.

Solution (Fig. 10.28):

The graphical solution of the problem requires the following steps:

1. Join the points *A* and *B*, and *B* and *C* on the map.
2. Errect perpendiculars *AD* and *CE* at *A* and *C* to the lines *AB* and *CB*, respectively.
3. Draw line *BD* at 50° (= 90° – 40°) to *BA* to intersect *AD* at *D*, and another line *BE* at 30° (= 90° – 60°) to *BC* to intersect *CE* at *E*.

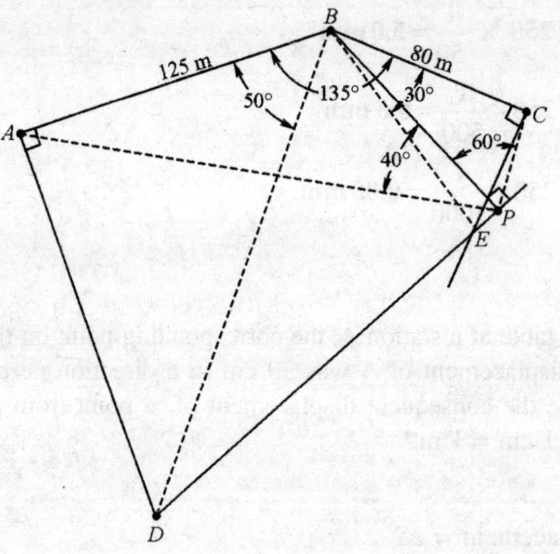

Fig. 10.28

4. Join *D* and *E*.
5. Drop a perpendicular from *B* on *DE* to meet at *P*.
6. Join *P* to *A*, *B*, and *C*.

7. *PA*, *PB* and *PC* are the desired distances as given below:

$PA = 197.0$ m

$PB = 93.5$ m

$PC = 37.3$ m.

It may be noted that the quadrilaterals *PBAD* and *PEBC* being concyclic, angle *BPA* = angle *ADB* and angle *BPC* = angle *CEB*. In step 3, the angle *ABD* is taken equal to 50° which comes from the triangle *BAD* where angles *BAD* = 90° and angle *ADB* = 40°. Similarly the angle *CBE* is taken as 30°, which comes from the triangle *BCE* where angle *BCE* = 90° and *CEB* = 60°.

10.10 PLANE TABLE TESTING AND ADJUSTMENT

To obtain good results it is very essential that the plane table and its accessories are in perfect adjustment. The conditions to be satisfied for, testing and adjustments for plane table and plain alidade are briefly discussed below.

1. The surface of the plane-table board should be a plane surface.

Test: Place a straight edge in different directions and see that if there is any gap between the straight edge and the surface of the board. If there are gaps, remove them as under.

Adjustment: The high spots should be removed by plaining or by sand papering.

2. The surface of the plane table should be perpendicular to the vertical axis.

Test: Place a spirit level on the plane table and centre the bubble by adjusting the legs of the tripod. Turn the table through 180°. If the bubble remains centered, the surface of the plane table is perpendicular to the vertical axis. If the bubble deviates from its central position, the table needs adjustment.

Adjustment: Correct half the apparent error by inserting a packing or a washer between the underside of the board and its support. Level the tube and place the spirit level in a direction at right angles to the previous direction. Repeat the test and adjustment till the bubble remains central in all directions and on reversals through 180°.

3. The fiducial edge of the alidade should be straight.

Test: Draw a fine line on a paper along the fiducial edge of the alidade. Reverse the alidade, end for end, and place it against the ends of the line already drawn. Draw again a line along the fiducial edge. If two lines coincide the fiducial edge is straight. If not, make the edge straight as under.

Adjustment: Fill the fiducial edge of the alidade to make it straight and repeat the test till the condition given above is satisfied.

4. The sight vanes should be perpendicular to the base of the alidade when pulled out in full.

Test: Level the plane table. Suspend a plumb bob at a point about 10 m away from the plane table. Direct the sight vane on the plumb bob string. If the vanes are perpendicular to the base, the sighting slit, object vane hair and the plumb bob string will be in the same vertical line. If not, do the adjustment as below.

Adjustment: Fix some packing under the base of the sight vane or fill the base. Repeat the test and adjustment till the vanes become vertical to the base of the alidade.

5. The spirit levels fixed to the alidade, should have their axes parallel to the base of the alidade.

Test: Place the alidade on the plane table and make the bubble central to one of the spirit levels. Draw a line against the edge of the ruler. Reverse the alidade, end for end and place it against the same line. If the bubble is found central, the axis of the spirit level is parallel to the base of the alidade. If not, do the adjustment as under:

Adjustment: Bring the bubble half way back by inserting some packing below the spirit level and remaining half by levelling the plane table. Repeat the test and adjustment for the second spirit level in similar manner.

Testing and Adjustment for the Telescopic Alidade

For a telescope alidade the following conditions must be satisfied. The testing and adjustment is similar to the methods discussed for theodolites and levels in Chapters 4 and 6.

1. The line of collimation should be perpendicular to the horizontal axis of the telescope.
2. The horizontal axis should be parallel to the base of the alidade.
3. The axis of the telescope level should be parallel to the line of collimation.
4. The vertical circle should read zero when the line of collimation is horizontal.

10.11 PRACTICAL SUGGESTIONS AND PRECAUTIONS FOR GOOD WORK

For good work in plane-table surveying, the following points should be kept in mind:

1. To reduce glare, buff paper should be used.
2. To avoid smudging, always a hard pencil should be used.
3. Cover the portion of the sheet that is not being used.
4. To keep drawing clean, ensure that the underside of the alidade ruler stays unsoiled by lifting, rather than sliding the alidade into position.
5. The blade of the alidade should be cleaned frequently to remove graphite.
6. The drawing sheet must be kept free from moisture and dust.
7. The lines should be drawn as fine as possible.
8. The lines should be drawn close to the fiducial edge of the alidade.
9. Rays should be drawn short, just enough to serve the purpose. They must be properly referenced for easy identification after shifting the alidade to a new position.
10. Rays and reference marks must be erased as soon as they are no longer needed.
11. Set up the plane table at a level slightly lower than your elbow height.
12. The table should be turned only when it is to be oriented, and after performing the orientation, it must be kept clamped in position.
13. While sights are being taken, the fiducial edge of the alidade must be set touching the plotted station-point on the sheet and not the other edge.
14. Do not spend much time on very accurate centering. In most of the cases even very rough centering would be good enough.
15. Check the locations of the stations by resection and by sighting on some prominent objects in the area.
16. Always carry a waterproof cloth to cover the paper.

10.12 ADVANTAGES AND DISADVANTAGES

The plane-table surveying has the following advantages and disadvantages over other types of surveying.

Advantages

1. It is quite suitable for small scale surveys.
2. All the plotting work including contouring is done in the field.
3. As the surveyor has full view of the details while plotting, the chances of omission of any detail is avoided.
4. The accuracy of the plot can be ascertained as the work progresses in the field.
5. Less number of control points are required as the extension of control can be done by plane tabling itself while the survey proceeds.
6. Depiction of irregular details and contours can be done accurately as the entire area remains in view during work.
7. Relevant and irrelevant details can be distinguished and only those which are required, can be plotted.
8. As the numerical values of angular as well as linear measurements are not observed and are obtained graphically, errors and mistakes in reading and recording are eliminated.
9. It is particularly useful in areas affected by magnetism where compass surveying is not possible.
10. No great skill is required to produce a satisfactory map, and the work may be entrusted to a subordinate.
11. The amount of office work is practically reduced to nil. Subsequent office work involves only finishing up the drawing.
12. It is less costly as compared to other methods of surveying.
13. The method is rapid when the details can be sketched by estimation.

Disadvantages

1. The plane table and its accessories are heavy and awkward to carry.
2. The various accessories being loose, are likely to be lost in the field.
3. It is unsuitable for work in wet climate and in high wind.
4. It is not useful for large-scale surveys and accurate works.
5. It is unsuitable for surveying in a densely wooded area. It can only be used in open country with clear visibility.
6. The absence of field notes is sometimes inconvenient if the survey has to be replotted to a different scale.
7. Considerable time is required for a surveyor to gain proficiency in plane tabling.

10.13 CONTOURING IN PLANE-TABLE SURVEYING

Plane table is generally useful for preparing small-scale contoured map. The details are plotted by radiation or intersection in large-scale survey and by intersection in small-scale survey. When a telescopic alidade is used, the horizontal distances and elevations of various points are determined by tacheometry discussed in Chapter 8. The points are selected whose elevations will help in contouring. These are plotted, and their elevations are determined and marked on the plan. The contours are then drawn by interpolation by the methods discussed in Chapter 7.

For a small-scale survey, it is very convenient to use plain alidade for sighting and drawing rays, and a tangent clinometer for determining the horizontal and vertical distances. The Indian pattern clinometer also known as tangent clino-meter, is sometimes used along with a clinopole. These are discussed below.

Indian Pattern Clinometer and Clinopole

The clinometer shown in Fig.10.29, consists of three parts: a base plate supported on three buttons, a brass bar that supports two vanes; an eye vane, and an object vane. The eye and object vanes may be folded down when not in use. The object vane is graduated in degrees on the left side of the slit and in natural tangents on the right side. The zero of both the scales is exactly opposite the eye-hole in the eye vane. The angle of elevations are read above the zero and the angles of depression, below the zero. Clamps or struts are provided to maintain the perpendicularity of the vanes with the bar when in use. A spirit level is attached to the brass bar. The bubble is centered by means of a milled-head tangent screw. When the bubble is in centre, the line joining the eyehole and the zero of the scale on the object vane, is horizontal. The line joining the eye-hole and the horizontal wire is the line of sight. The object vane carries a rider having a small frame with a horizontal wire, which may be moved up or down by rack and pinion arrangement for taking readings.

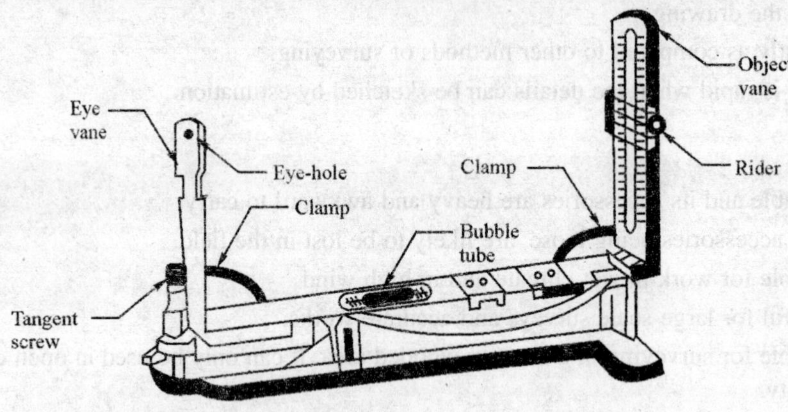

Fig. 10.29 Tangent clinometer

A clinopole is shown in Fig. 10.30. It is a wooden pole painted alternately in red and white or black and white colours at fixed known distances. The pole carries two targets painted in such a manner that centres can be bisected clearly at the time of sighting. These targets are placed at a known distance apart and at known height from the bottom of the pole.

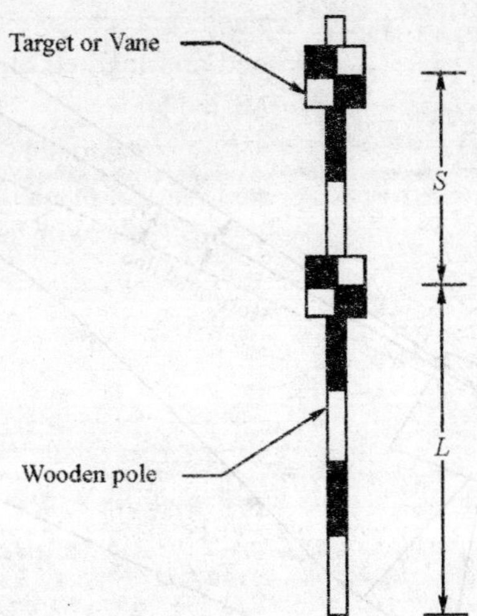

Fig. 10.30 Clinopole

Observations with a tangent clinometer

The tangent clinometer may be used with a clinopole or without a clinopole, depending upon the field conditions as discussed under.

Using tangent clinometer with a clinopole

When the points to be plotted are accessible, a clinopole may be used to determine the horizontal and vertical distances by the principles of tacheometry.

Let P be the point whose position p on the plane table sheet is already plotted, and A be the point which is to be plotted and also its elevation is to be determined (Fig. 10.31). The elevation h_p of P is known.

Set up the plane table over P, perform centering, levelling, and orientation if required. Place the tangent clinometer on the board and make the bubble central by means of milled-head screw. Place the clinopole on A. Pivoting the alidade on p, draw a ray for A. Measure the height h_i of the eye-hole accurately above the ground. Now look through the eye-hole and slide the frame containing the rider along the scale until the horizontal wire bisects one of the targets of the pole. Let the target bisected is the lower one. Read the angle α_1 or its tangent value ($\tan \alpha_1$) directly. Similarly take $\tan \alpha_2$ for the upper target.

From the figure, we have

$$\tan \alpha_1 = \frac{V}{D} \qquad \text{...(10.13)}$$

and

$$\tan \alpha_2 = \frac{V+S}{D} \qquad \text{...(10.14)}$$

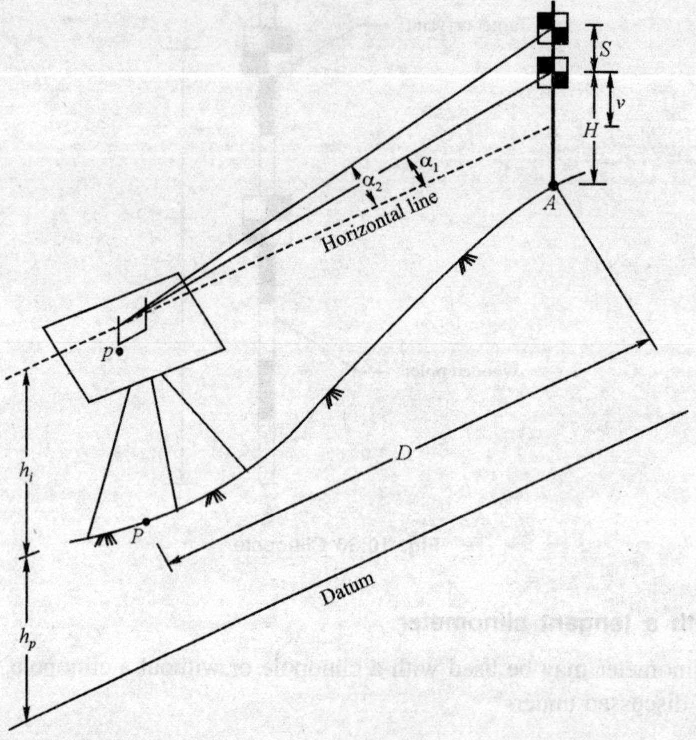

Fig. 10.31 Using tangent clinometer with a clinopole

In Eqs. (10.13) and (10.14), V and D are the two unknown quantities and $\tan\alpha_1$, $\tan\alpha_2$ and S are the known quantities. Solving these two equations we get

$$D = \frac{S}{\tan\alpha_2 - \tan\alpha_1} \quad \text{...(10.15)}$$

and $$V = \frac{S\tan\alpha_1}{\tan\alpha_2 - \tan\alpha_1} \quad \text{...(10.16)}$$

$$\text{Elevation of } A = h_P + h_i + V - H \quad \text{...(10.17)}$$

In the case of angle of depression, elevation of A

$$= h_P + h_i - V - H \quad \text{...(10.18)}$$

Using tangent clinometer without a clinopole

When a point is inaccessible then a clinopole cannot be used. In such cases, the point A is plotted by the method of intersection. For the determination of elevation, the tangent values of angles are read from both the plane-table stations P and Q (Fig. 10.32), if accuracy desired in the determination of elevation is more, otherwise it may be read from one of the plane-table stations only. Once A is plotted as a on the sheet by intersection, the distances pa and qa can be measured on the sheet and knowing the scale of the map, PA and QA can be computed.

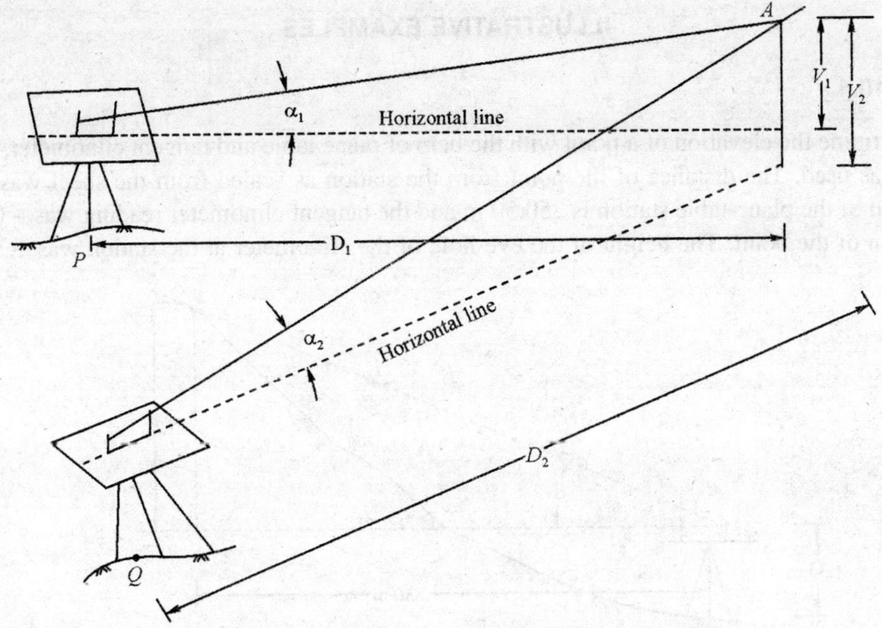

Fig. 10.32 Using tangent clinometer without a clinopole

Let PA and QA be D_1 and D_2, and $\tan\alpha_1$ and $\tan\alpha_2$ be the clinometer readings taken on A from P and Q, respectively. Let the elevations of P and Q be h_P and h_Q, and the heights of the eye-hole at these stations be h_{iP} and h_{iQ}, respectively.

From the figure, we have

$$V_1 = D_1 \tan \alpha_1 \quad \text{...(10.19)}$$

and $$V_2 = D_2 \tan \alpha_2 \quad \text{...(10.20)}$$

The elevation of A is computed from the observations made from P and Q, and the mean of the two values are accepted as elevation of A.

From P, $$h_{AP} = h_P + h_{iP} + V_1 \quad \text{...(10.21)}$$

From Q, $$h_{AQ} = h_Q + h_{iQ} + V_2 \quad \text{...(10.22)}$$

Thus average elevation $$h_A = \frac{h_{AP} + h_{AQ}}{2}. \quad \text{...(10.23)}$$

When more accuracy is not required in elevation, determination either of the value h_{AP} and h_{AQ} is good enough.

If the sights are long then the combined curvature and refraction correction C_{cr}, discussed in Sec. 6.3, is added to the vertical distance V in the case of angle of elevation and subtracted when angle of depression.

ILLUSTRATIVE EXAMPLES

Example 10.4

To determine the elevation of a point with the help of plane table and tangent clinometer, method of resection was used. The distance of the point from the station as scaled from the sheet was 830 m. If the elevation of the plane-table station is 250.50 m and the tangent clinometer reading was + 0.045, find the elevation of the point. The height of the eye-hole of the clinometer at the station was 1.35 m.

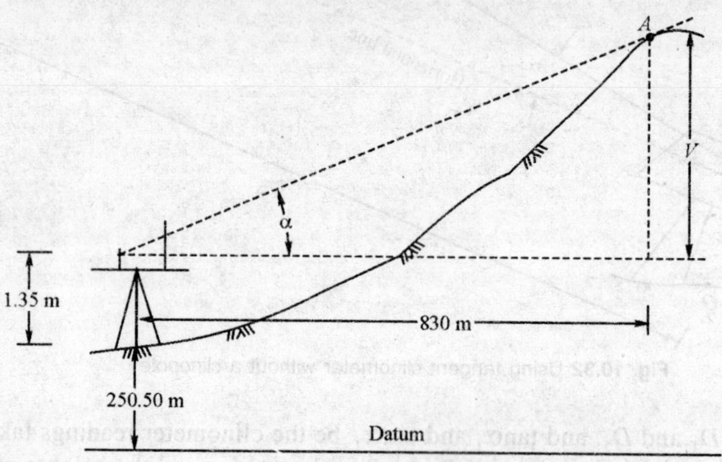

Solution (Fig. 10.33):

From the figure, we have

$V = 830 \times \tan\ \alpha$

$= 830 \times 0.045$

$= 37.35$ m

Elevation of the point A

$= 250.50 + 1.35 + 37.35 = \mathbf{289.20}$ **m.**

Example 10.5

The R.L. of plane-table station is 50 m and the height of the eye-hole of the clinometer above the ground is 1.5 m. Calculate the R.L. of clinopole station *A*, when the reading upon the tangent clinometer scale is + 0.035. The distance to *A* scaled from the plan is 3500 m and the clinopole target 3 m above the ground at *A*, was sighted.

Solution:

From Eq. (10.19), we get

$V = D \tan\ \alpha$

$= 3500 \times 0.035$

$= 122.5$ m.

Correction for curvature and refraction

$= 0.067 \times 3.5^2$

$= 0.821$ m.

$\therefore$ R.L. of $A = 50.00 + 1.5 + (122.5 + 0.821) - 3.0$

$= \mathbf{171.82\ m.}$

QUESTIONS AND PROBLEMS

10.1 What do you understand by the term plane tabling? When is it recommended?

10.2 Describe briefly the various accessories of a plane-table. What are their functions?

10.3 Briefly explain advantages of telescopic alidade in plane-table surveying.

10.4 Explain the principle of plane tabling.

10.5 Define the following terms used in plane-table surveying:

(*i*) Orientation

(*ii*) Back sighting

(*iii*) Radiation

(*iv*) Resection.

10.6 What do you mean by setting up the plane table? Discuss the steps required in setting up a plane table.

10.7 What do you understand by the term orientation of plane table? Discuss the various methods of orientation with their merits and demerits.

10.8 Enumerate the different methods of plane-table surveying. Describe one of them in detail with sketches.

10.9 Explain the procedure for plane-table traversing.

10.10 What is resection? Describe any two methods of resection.

10.11 What is two-point problem? Describe the procedure in detail.

10.12 What is three-point problem? Discuss the trial and error method of solution of the problem.

10.13 State three-point problem in plane tabling. Describe its solution by trial and error method. Briefly indicate the rules which may be followed in estimating the point sought.

10.14 Explain the mechanical method and graphical method for the solution of three-point problem.

10.15 Describe Lehmann's rules using sketches.

10.16 What do you mean by strength of fix. Explain the following with the help of neat sketches:

(*i*) Good fix

(*ii*) Bad fix

(*iii*) Failure of fix

10.17 Write a short note on practical utility of three-point resection.

10.18 What are the sources of errors in plane-table survey. Explain in detail.

10.19 Derive an expression to determine the positional error in plotting detail due to inaccurate centering.

10.20 What are the different types of errors in plane-table surveying? How are they minimised?

10.21 Write a short note on plane table testing and adjustments. Also discuss the testing and adjustments of an alidade.

10.22 What are the points which must be kept in view for good plane table work?

10.23 Discuss the advantages and disadvantages of plane tabling.

10.24 Describe the method of drawing contours in plane-table survey.

10.25 Describe the various parts of a tangent clinometer and their functions.

10.26 Explain the uses of tangent clinometer in plane tabling. Also discuss the conditions when a clinometer is used and when it is not used.

10.27 Prove that the centering error depends upon the scale of plan. Hence show that if the scale is 1 cm = 10 m, the centering error would not affect the accuracy of the plotting.

10.28 A plane table was set inaccurately over a ground station *M*. A ray was taken to an object *Z*, and the centering error was found to be 200 mm in a direction perpendicular to the ray *MZ*. The scale of plotting was 1/1000. If the distances to *Z* from *M* was 1000 m, what is the displacement of *z* from its correct plotted position, and state whether it is significant?

10.29 The error in centering at a station *P* led to an error of 120 mm, at right angle to a ray *PR*. If the approximate distance *PR* is 160 m, determine the limiting value of the scale of plotting so that the centering error does not affect the accuracy of plotting of *R* assuming the minimum distance which can be plotted as 0.25 mm.

10.30 A plane-table survey is to be carried out at a scale of 1 : 5000. Show that at this scale, accurate centering of the plane table over the ground station is not required. What error would be caused on a map if the point is out by 45 cm from the vertical through the station.

10.31 An observation was made from station *A* to another station *B* by means of a tangent clinometer and the reading on tangent scale was + 0.035. The distances *AB* as scaled from the map was 1826.305 m. The R.L. of the plane-table station was 75.000 m. and height of the eye-hole was 1.495 m from the ground.

Compute the R.L. of station *A*

(*a*) without considering the effect of earth's curvature and refraction.

(*b*) considering the effect of earth's curvature and refraction.

11

AREAS AND VOLUMES

11.1 GENERAL

One of the primary objects of land surveys is to determine the area of tract. The area is required for the title documents of the land. In civil engineering works such as designing of bridges, dams, reservoirs, etc., the area of the catchment of a river is required. The areas of fields are also required for planning and management of a project.

In many civil engineering projects, earthwork involves the excavation, removal, and dumping of earth, therefore it is required to make good estimates of volumes of earthwork. Volume computations are also needed to determine the capacity of bins, tanks, and reservoirs, and to check the stockpiles of coal, gravel, and other material.

Computing areas and volumes is an important part of the office work involved in surveying.

11.2 AREAS

In plane surveying the term 'areas' refers to the orthographic projection of a tract of land on a horizontal plane and not the actual area of the tract. For steep tracts, the actual area is much more than the projected area. However, for flat tract the difference between the actual and the projected area may not be much and the area of the tract of the land is computed from its plan.

The method of computation of area depends upon the shape of the boundary of the tract and the accuracy required. If the plan is enclosed by straight boundaries, it can be subdivided into simple geometrical shapes, such as triangles, rectangles, trapezoid, etc., and areas of these figures are determined from the dimensions obtained from the plan. When the boundaries are irregular they are replaced by short straight boundaries, and the area is computed using approximate methods. In case boundaries being very irregular, the area can be determined by means of a planimeter.

The degree of accuracy of the computed area depends on the following:

1. The accuracy of the field measurements.
2. The accuracy of plotting when the calculations are made from a plan.
3. The method adopted for the computation.

Needless refinements in the values employed for computations will not result in increased accuracy of the final results. One must try to estimate the probable accuracy of the field and office works, and express the final result with just as many significant figures as can be relied upon.

The area is expressed in the following S.I. units:

1 are (a) = $(10 \text{ m})^2 = 10^2 \text{ m}^2$

1 hectare (ha) = $(100 \text{ m})^2 = 10^4 \text{ m}^2$

1 square kilometre $(\text{km})^2 = (1000 \text{ m})^2 = 10^6 \text{ m}^2$.

11.3 AREA FROM FIELD MEASUREMENTS

If the area is to be obtained directly from field measurements, the survey should be planned to include the whole area. The whole area within survey, may be divided as below:

1. The area consisting of regular boundary
2. The area consisting of irregular boundary.

Area Consisting of Regular Boundary

The area of the part A_1 consisting of regular boundary shown in Fig. 11.1, can be determined either by further dividing it into triangles, trapezoids, etc., or from the coordinates of the traverse stations *A*, *B*, *C*, etc.

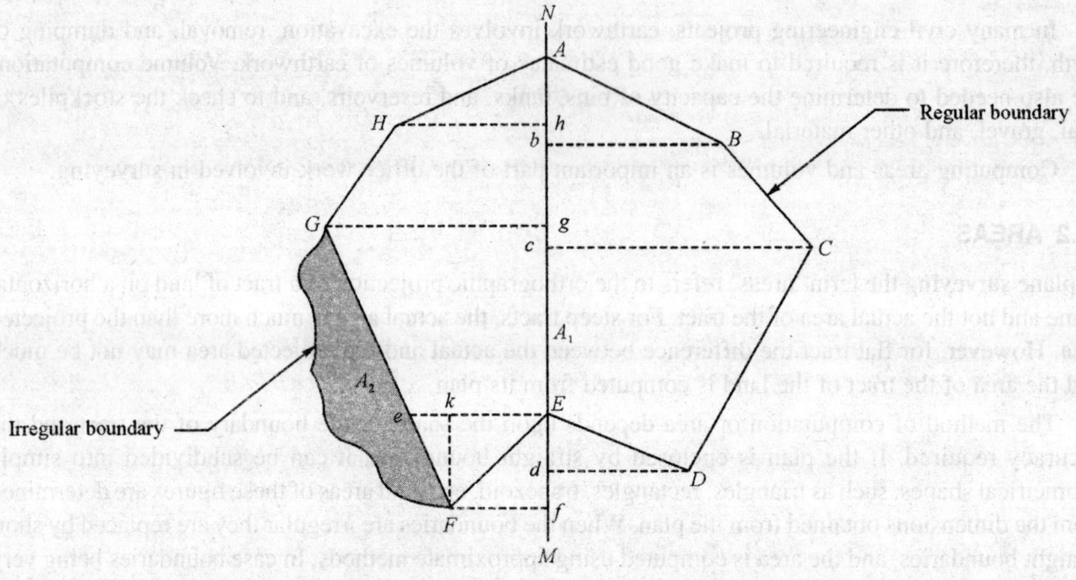

Fig. 11.1 Area comprising of regular and irregular boundaries

Area by geometric figures

A fairly long base line *MN* is so chosen that it approximately passes through the middle of the area, and the perpendicular distances of the salient points from the base line, are measured.

The area of a triangle (Fig. 11.2) is calculated from the following well known formulae.

$$A_\Delta = \sqrt{s(s-a)(s-b)(s-c)} \qquad \text{...(11.1)}$$

$$= \frac{1}{2}bh \qquad \text{...(11.2)}$$

$$= \frac{1}{2} ab \sin C \qquad \text{...(11.3)}$$

where A_Δ = area of triangle

$s = \frac{1}{2}(a+b+c)$

a, b, c = three sides of a triangle

h = altitude when b is the base

C = the angle ACB.

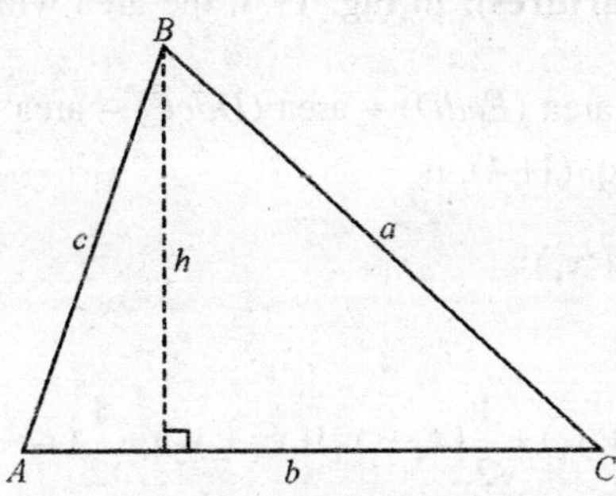

Fig. 11.2 Triangle

For a trapezoid shown in Fig. 11.3, the area is given by

$$A_{\square} = \frac{1}{2} h(a+b) \qquad \text{...(11.4)}$$

where $A_{\square}$ = area of a trapezoid

a, b = the two parallel sides

h = the perpendicular distance between the parallel sides.

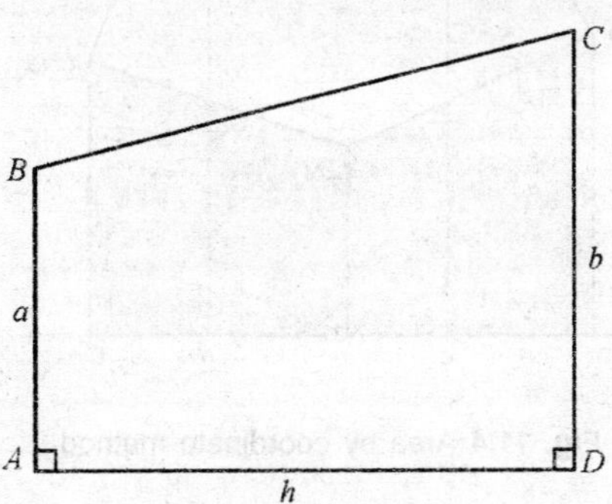

Fig. 11.3 Trapezoid

Area determination by running a base line and measuring the perpendicular offsets to salient points, is very common method employed in rural and municipal surveys to measure the extent of a tract for civil purposes for transferring the property from one person to another.

Area from coordinates

If the coordinates of the points *A*, *B*, *C*, etc., shown in Fig. 11.1, can be obtained by running a closed traverse the area within the traverse can be computed from the coordinates obtained after balancing the closing error, if any.

The area from the coordinates can be computed by any one of the following approaches.

Coordinates (latitudes and departures): In Fig. 11.4, the area within the closed traverse *ABCDE* is given by

$$A = \text{Area } (AaeE) + \text{area } (EedD) + \text{area } (DdcC) - \text{area } (AabB) - \text{area } (BbcC)$$

Area of a trapezoid *AaeE* from Eq. (11.4), is

$$\frac{1}{2}(x_5 - x_1)(y_5 + y_1)$$

Thus,

$$A = \frac{1}{2}(x_5 - x_1)(y_5 + y_1) + \frac{1}{2}(x_4 - x_5)(y_4 + y_5) + \frac{1}{2}(x_3 - x_4)(y_3 + y_4) - \frac{1}{2}(x_2 - x_1)(y_2 + y_1) - \frac{1}{2}(x_3 - x_2)(y_3 + y_2)$$

$$= \frac{1}{2}[x_1(y_2 - y_5) + x_2(y_3 - y_1) + x_3(y_4 - y_2) + x_4(y_5 - y_3) + x_5(y_1 - y_4)]$$

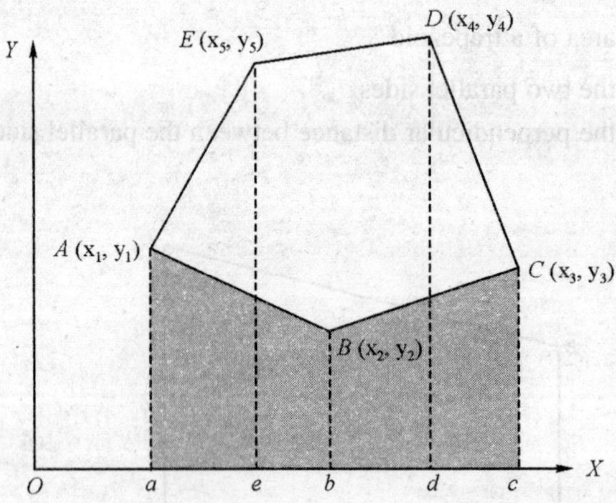

Fig. 11.4 Area by coordinate method

If a traverse has *n* sides, then

$$A = \frac{1}{2}[x_1(y_2 - y_n) + x_2(y_3 - y_1) + ... + x_{n-1}(y_n - y_{n-2}) + x_n(y_1 - y_{n-1})] \qquad ...(11.5)$$

A similar formula is obtained by interchanging x and y, if the projection on the y-axis is considered:

$$A = \frac{1}{2}\left[y_1(x_n - x_2) + y_2(x_1 - x_3) + \ldots + y_{n-1}(x_{n-2} - x_n) + y_n(x_{n-1} - x_1)\right] \quad \ldots(11.6)$$

Area can be computed from any one of the above equations, and the other one can be used as a check on the computation. Eqs. (11.5) and (11.6) give positive or negative values depending upon the suffix numbering the coordinates goes clockwise or counterclockwise.

The area can also be computed by arranging the coordinates in the determinant form given below:

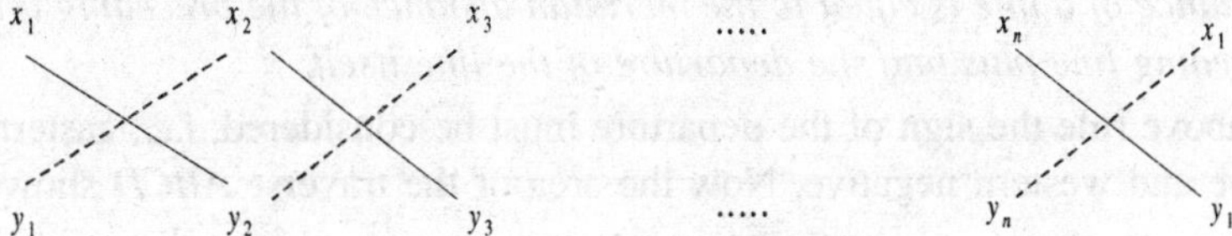

Take the product of the coordinates along full lines positive and along dashed lines negative. Half of the sum of the products is the required area.

For example,

$$A = \frac{1}{2}\left[x_1 y_2 - y_1 x_2 + x_2 y_3 - y_2 x_3 + \ldots + x_n y_1 - y_n x_1\right]$$

Meridian distance method: The *meridian distance* of any point is the perpendicular distance of the point from the reference meridian. In Fig. 11.5, the meridian distance of the points 1, 2, 3, and 4, are m_1, m_2, m_3, and m_4, respectively, measured at right angles from the reference meridian AN. To ease the problem of signs, the reference meridian is usually taken such that all meridian distances are positive.

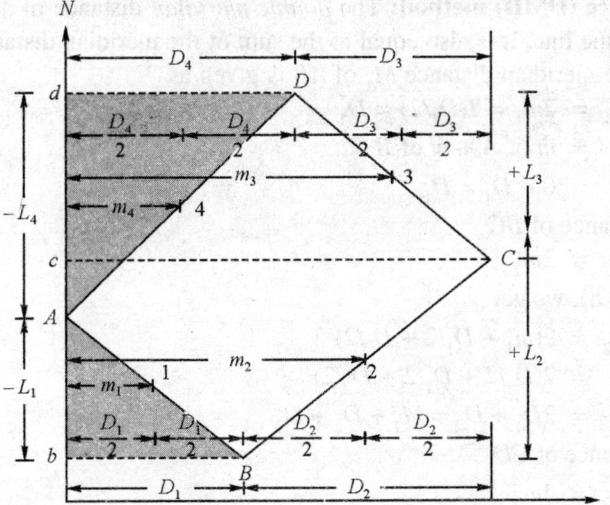

Fig. 11.5 Area by meridian distance method

The meridian distance of a line is equal to the meridian distance of its midpoint. Thus, if the point 1 is the midpoint of the line AB, the meridian distance of AB will be m_1. Obviously, the meridian distance of the line AB will be half its departure. Therefore, if the departures of the lines AB, BC, CD, and DA are D_1, D_2, D_3, and D_4, respectively, then we have

$$m_1 = D_1/2 \qquad \text{...(11.7)}$$

$$m_2 = m_1 + D_1/2 + D_2/2 \qquad \text{...(11.8)}$$

$$m_3 = m_2 + D_2/2 + (-D_3/2) \qquad \text{...(11.9)}$$

$$m_4 = m_3 + (-D_3/2) + (-D_4/2) \qquad \text{...(11.10)}$$

From the above equations the following general rule can be derived for the determination of the meridian distance:

The meridian distance of a line is equal to the meridian distance of the preceding line plus half the departure of the preceding line plus half the departure of the line itself.

In applying the above rule the sign of the departure must be considered, *i.e.*, eastern departures to be considered positive and western negative. Now the area of the traverse $ABCD$ shown in Fig. 11.5, can be written as

$$\begin{aligned} A &= \text{Area } (CcbB) + \text{area } (CcdD) - \text{area } (DAd) - \text{area } (BAb) \qquad \text{...(11.11)} \\ &= m_2L_2 + m_3L_3 - m_4L_4 - m_1L_1 \\ &= -m_1L_1 + m_2L_2 + m_3L_3 - m_4L_4 \\ &= \Sigma\,(mL) \end{aligned}$$

If there are n sides in a traverse then

$$A = \sum_{i=1}^{n} (m_i L_i) \qquad \text{...(11.12)}$$

In Eq. (11.12) the symbol Σ indicates the algebraic summation of the products of the meridian distances and the latitudes of various lines.

Double meridian distance (DMD) method: The *double meridian* distance of a line is equal to twice the meridian distance of the line. It is also equal to the sum of the meridian distance of the two ends of the line. Thus, the double meridian distance M_1 of AB is given as

$$\begin{aligned} M_1 &= 2m_1 = 2(D_1/2) = D_1 \\ &= m \text{ of } A + m \text{ of } B \\ &= 0 + D_1 = D_1 \qquad \text{...(11.13)} \end{aligned}$$

The double meridian distance of BC

$$M_2 = 2m_2$$

From Eqs. (11.7) and (11.8), we get

$$\begin{aligned} M_2 &= 2(m_1 + D_1/2 + D_2/2) \\ &= 2(D_1/2 + D_1/2 + D_2/2) \\ &= 2D_1 + D_2 = M_1 + D_1 + D_2 \qquad \text{...(11.14)} \end{aligned}$$

The double meridian distance of CD

$$M_3 = 2m_3$$

From Eqs. (11.7) to (11.9), we get

$$M_3 = 2(m_2 + D_2/2 - D_3/2)$$

$$= 2(m_1 + D_1/2 + D_2/2 + D_2/2 - D_3/2)$$
$$= 2(D_1/2 + D_1/2 + D_2/2 + D_2/2 - D_3/2)$$
$$= (2D_1 + D_2) + D_2 - D_3$$
$$= M_2 + D_2 + (-D_3) \qquad ...(11.15)$$

The double meridian distance of DA

$$M_4 = 2m_4$$

From Eqs. (11.7) to (11.10), we get

$$M_4 = 2(m_3 - D_3/2 - D_4/2)$$
$$= 2(m_2 + D_2/2 - D_3/2 - D_3/2 - D_4/2)$$
$$= 2(m_1 + D_1/2 + D_2/2 + D_2/2 - D_3/2 - D_3/2 - D_4/2)$$
$$= 2(D_1/2 + D_1/2 + D_2/2 + D_2/2 - D_3/2 - D_3/2 - D_4/2)$$
$$= (2D_1 + D_2) + D_2 - D_3 - D_3 - D_4$$
$$= M_3 + (-D_3) + (-D_4) \qquad ...(11.16)$$

From the above the following rule can be stated:

The double meridian distance of any line is equal to the double meridian distance of the preceding line plus the departure of the preceding line plus the departure of the line itself.

Proper sign of the departures, must be considered while applying the above rule.

Now the area of the traverse $ABCD$ (Fig. 11.5) from Eq. (11.11) can be expressed in terms of double meridian distances as under.

$$A = \frac{1}{2}(Bb + Cc)bc + \frac{1}{2}(Cc + Dd)cd - \frac{1}{2}(0 + Dd)Ad - \frac{1}{2}(0 + Bb)Ab$$

Now $\quad Bb + Cc = D_1 + D_1 + D_2$

$$= M_1 + D_1 + D_2$$
$$= M_2$$

Similarly, $\quad Cc + Dd = M_3$

$$0 + Dd = M_4$$
$$0 + Bb = M_1$$

Therefore,

$$A = \frac{1}{2}M_2L_2 + \frac{1}{2}M_3L_3 - \frac{1}{2}M_4(-L_4) - \frac{1}{2}M_1(-L_1)$$
$$= \frac{1}{2}(M_1L_1 + M_2L_2 + M_3L_3 + M_4L_4)$$
$$= \frac{1}{2}\sum(ML)$$

In general for a traverse of n sides

$$A = \frac{1}{2}\sum_{i=1}^{n}(M_iL_i) \qquad ...(11.17)$$

Departure and total latitude method: The *total latitude* of a point is its distance from the reference station measured parallel to the reference meridian. In Fig. 11.6, the reference station chosen is *A*, through which the reference meridian *AN* is passing. The total latitudes of the stations *A*, *B*, *C*, and *D* are L_0', $-L_1'$, $-L_2'$, and $+L_3'$. Since the reference station is *A* its total latitude L_0' will be zero. The total latitude of a point can be computed froom the following rule:

Total latitude of a point is equal to the algebraic sum of the latitude of the preceding station and latitude of the preceding line.

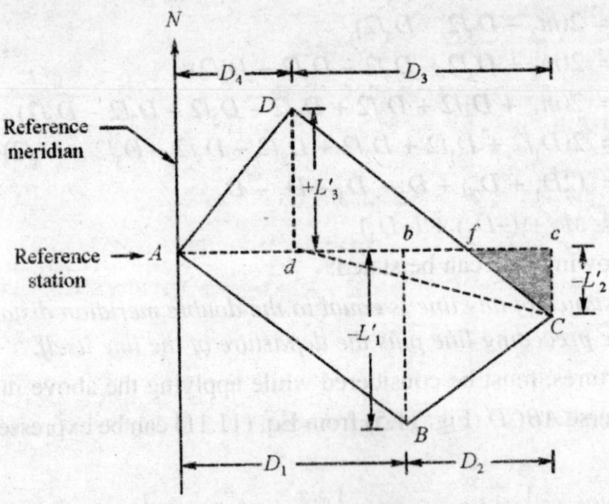

Fig. 11.6. Departure and total latitude method

In Fig. 11.6, the area of the traverse *ABCD* can be written as

$$A = \text{Area } ABb + \text{area } BbcC + \text{area } DdCc + \text{area } DdA$$

It may be noted that the area *Ccf* appears twice in the areas of *BbcC* and *DdCc*, and gets cancelled being positive in one and negative in the other.

In terms of the departures and total latitudes, the area *A* can be written as

$$A = \frac{1}{2}D_1(0-L_1')+\frac{1}{2}D_2(-L_1'-L_2')+\frac{1}{2}(-D_3)(-L_2'+L_3')+\frac{1}{2}(-D_4)(L_3'-0)$$

$$= \frac{1}{2}[(-L_1')(D_1+D_2)+(-L_2')(D_2-D_3)(-L_3')(D_3+D_4)] \qquad \text{...(11.18)}$$

$$= \frac{1}{2}\Sigma[\text{Total latitude of point} \times \text{algebraic sum of two adjacent departures}]$$

Double parallel distance (DPD) method: The *parallel distance* of a line is the distance of its midpoint from a reference parallel measured at right angles to the reference parallel. The reference parallel is taken at right angles to the reference meridian and passing through the most southernly corner of the traverse.

The double parallel distance (*DPD*) is twice the parallel distance of the line. It is represented by the letter *P*, and it is similar to the double meridian distance. The area of a traverse can be obtained in terms of *DPD* by replacing *M* and *L* by *P* and *D*, respectively, in Eq. (11.17). Thus,

$$A = \frac{1}{2}\sum_{i=1}^{n}(P_i D_i) \qquad ...(11.19)$$

where *D* is the departure of the lines.

Area Consisting of Irregular Boundary

If the boundary of a tract is irregular, as shown for the tract A_2 in Fig. 11.1, the determination of area by the above methods is not possible. In such cases, the area is computed using the offsets taken at a regular interval as shown in Fig. 11.7.

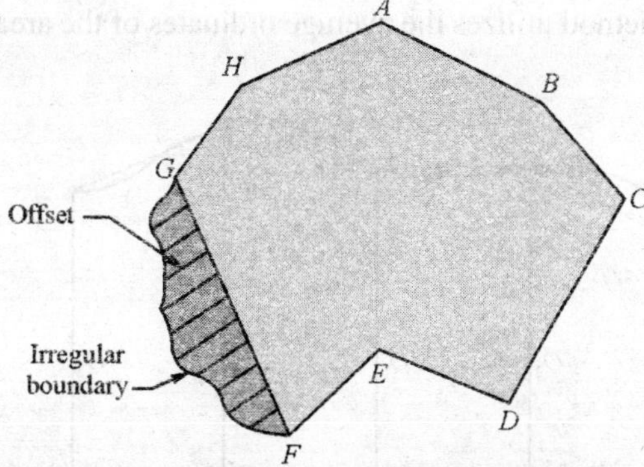

Fig. 11.7. Offsets to irregular boundary

The area between the traverse line and irregular boundary may be determined by any one of the following methods depending upon the accuracy desired.

Mid-Ordinate rule: In this method, the tract is divided into segments, and the offsets, M_1, M_2, M_3, etc., at the midpoint of each interval are taken as shown in Fig. 11.8. The measured offsets are the mid-ordinates. The area of the tract can be written as

$$A = d\,(M_1 + M_2 + M_3 + M_4)$$

$$= \frac{L}{4}(M_1 + M_2 + M_3 + M_4)$$

$$A = \frac{L}{n}\sum_{i=1}^{n} M_i \qquad ...(11.20)$$

where L = length of the base line

n = number of segments

$d = \frac{L}{n}$.

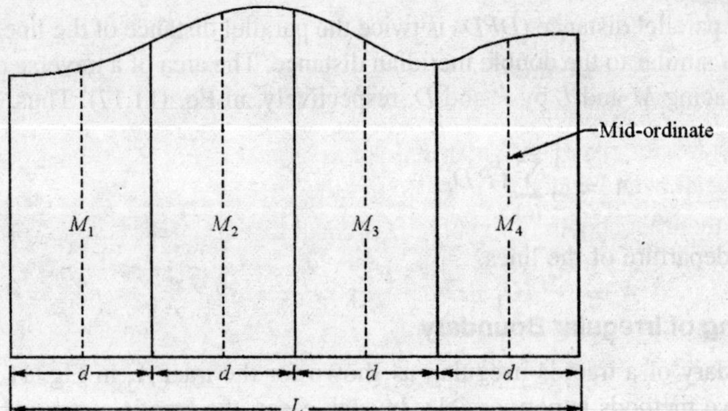

Fig. 11.8 The mid-ordinates rule

Average-ordinate rule: This method utilizes the average ordinates of the area. In Fig. 11.9, the average-ordinate is

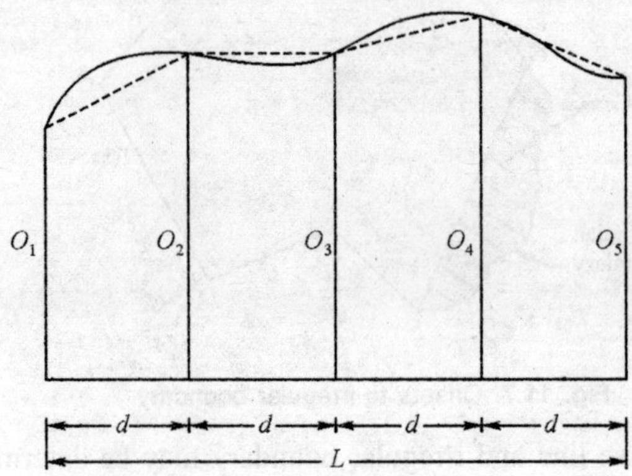

Fig. 11.9 The average-ordinates rule

$$O_m = \frac{O_1 + O_2 + O_3 + O_4 + O_5}{5}$$

In general,

$$O_m = \frac{O_1 + O_2 + ... + O_{n+1}}{n+1}$$

$$= \frac{1}{n+1}\sum_{i=1}^{n+1} O_i$$

Therefore,

$$A = LO_m = \frac{L}{n+1}\sum_{i=1}^{n+1} O_i \qquad ...(11.21)$$

where L = length of the base line

n = number of segments

If the offsets are not taken at regular interval as shown in Fig. 11.9, then the area of each trapezoid is computed separately and added together to get the total area.

The area of the tract shown in Fig. 11.10 is equal to

$$A = \frac{d_1}{2}(O_1 + O_2) + \frac{d_2}{2}(O_2 + O_3) + \frac{d_3}{2}(O_3 + O_4)\frac{d_4}{2}(O_4 + O_5) \qquad ...(11.22)$$

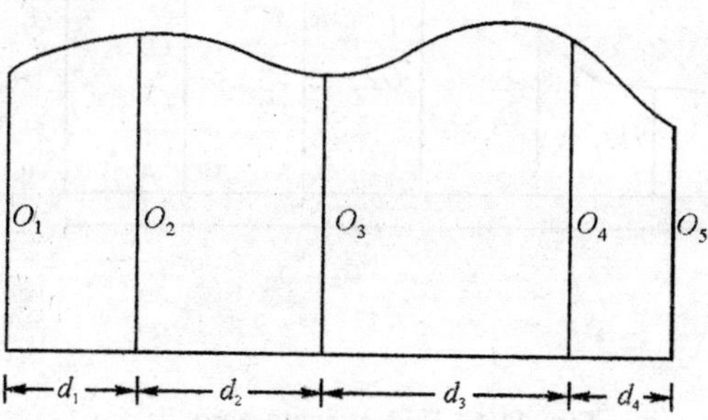

Fig. 11.10 Offsets at irregular interval

Trapezoidal rule: In this method, the area is divided into a number of trapezoids assuming that the short lengths between the offsets are straight lines as shown in Fig. 11.9 by dashed lines. The area of each trapezoid is determined and added to get the total area of the tract. Thus the area of the tract shown in Fig. 11.9, is

$$A = \left[\frac{O_1 + O_2}{2}\right]d + \left[\frac{O_2 + O_3}{2}\right]d + \left[\frac{O_3 + O_4}{2}\right]d + \left[\frac{O_4 + O_5}{2}\right]d$$

$$= d\left[\frac{O_1 + O_5}{2} + O_2 + O_3 + O_4\right]$$

In general,

$$A = \frac{L}{n}\left[\frac{O_1 + O_{(n+1)}}{2} + O_2 + O_3 + ... + O_n\right] \qquad ...(11.23)$$

$$= \frac{L}{n}\left[\frac{\text{First ordinate + last ordinate}}{2} + \Sigma(\text{intermedia te ordinates})\right]$$

$$= \frac{L}{n} \text{ [Average of the two end ordinates + } \Sigma \text{ (intermediate ordinates)]}$$

where L = length of the base line.

n = number of segments.

While using the trapezoidal rule, the end ordinates must be considered even if they happen to be zero. For example, the area for the tract shown in Fig. 11.11, is computed as below.

$$A = \frac{L}{6}\left[\frac{0+O_7}{2} + O_2 + O_4 + O_5 + O_6\right]$$

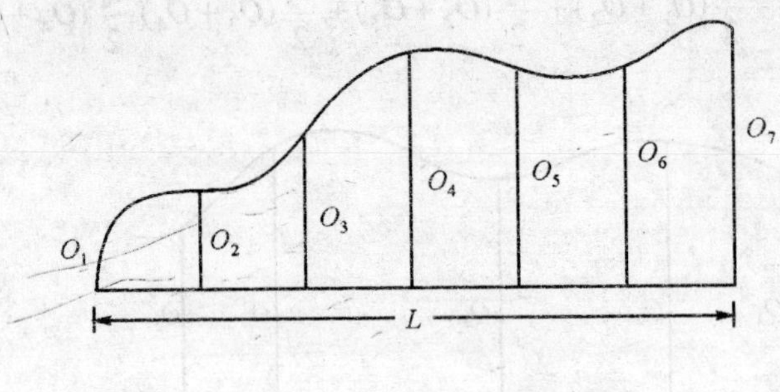

Fig. 11.11 End ordinate zero

The trapezoidal rule is more accurate than mid-ordinate rule and the average ordinate rule.

Simpson's rule: In *Simpson's rule*, the irregular boundary assumed to be made up of parabolic arcs; this is, therefore, also called the *parabolic rule.* This method should be preferred to the trapezoidal rule when the boundary line is curved and departs considerably from the straight line as shown in Fig. 11.12.

The area between the line *AC* and the curve boundary *abc* is equal to

$$A_1 = \text{Area } (AacC) + \text{area } (abcb'a)$$

The line *a'c'* is drawn parallel to *AC* and passing through *b.*

$$A_1 = \left[\frac{O_1+O_3}{2}\right]\times(2d) + \frac{2}{3}\times(2d)\times(b'b)$$

$$= \left[\frac{O_1+O_3}{2}\right]\times(2d) + \frac{2}{3}\times(2d)\times\left[O_2 - \frac{O_1+O_3}{2}\right]$$

$$= \frac{d}{3}[O_1 + 4O_2 + O_3]$$

Similarly, the area between the line *CE* and the curved boundary *cde* is equal to

$$A_2 = \frac{d}{3}[O_3 + 4O_4 + O_5]$$

and the area between the line *EG* and the curved boundary *efg* is equal to

$$A_3 = \frac{d}{3}[O_5 + 4O_6 + O_7]$$

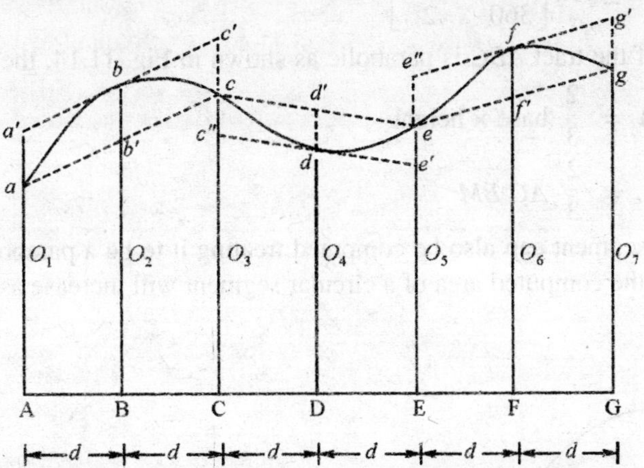

Fig. 11.12 Simpson's rule

Therefore, the total area will be

$$A = A_1 + A_2 + A_3$$

$$= \frac{d}{3}[(O_1 + O_7) + 4(O_2 + O_4 + O_6) + 2(O_3 + O_5)]$$

In general,

$$A = \frac{d}{3}[(O_1 + O_{n+1}) + 4(O_2 + O_4 + ... + O_n) + 2(O_3 + O_5 + ... + O_{n-1})] \quad ...(11.24)$$

$$= \frac{d}{3}\Big[\sum(\text{End ordinates}) + 4\sum(\text{intermediate even ordinates})$$

$$+ 2\sum(\text{intermediate odd ordinates})\Big]$$

where $d = \frac{L}{n}$

L = length of the base line

n = number of segments.

Since pair of intercepts are taken in Simpson's rules it will be evident that an even number of intercepts is required to determine an area. If an odd number of intercepts is present then the first or last intercept is treated as a trapezoid.

Area of a Circular Segment and Parabolic Segment

If a tract of land is a circular segment ABC, shown in Fig. 11.13, its area can be computed as below.

$$A = \text{Area of sector } ABC - \text{area of triangle } AOC$$

$$= \frac{\pi R^2}{360}\theta - \frac{1}{2}R^2 \sin\theta$$

$$= R^2\left[\frac{\pi\theta}{360} - \frac{\sin\theta}{2}\right] \qquad ...(11.25)$$

When the segment of the tract *ABC* is parabolic as shown in Fig. 11.14, the area is equal to

$$A = \frac{2}{3}\text{ base} \times \text{height}$$

$$= \frac{2}{3}\ AC\ BM \qquad ...(11.26)$$

The area of circular segment can also be computed treating it to be a parabolic segment and using Eq. (11.26). The error in the computed area of a circular segment will increase as the angle θ increases.

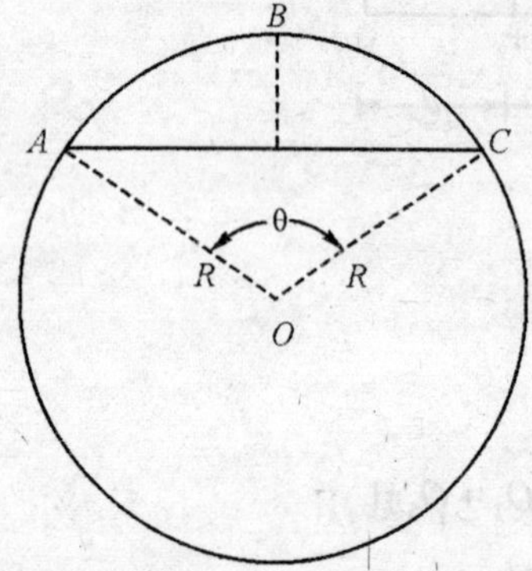

Fig. 11.13. Segment of a circle

Fig. 11.14. Segment of parabola

ILLUSTRATIVE EXAMPLES

Example 11.1

The latitudes and departures of the lines of a closed traverse *ABCD* are given below. Calculate the area of the traverse by

1. Coordinate method,
2. Meridian distance method,
3. DMD method, and
4. Departure and total latitude method.

Solution:

Line	Northing (m)	Southing (m)	Easting (m)	Westing (m)
AB	.....	164.5	162.1	.....
BC	217.8	.....	59.8	.....
CD	168.1	.....	.....	105.6
DA	.....	221.4	.....	116.3

1. By coordinate method

Let the independent coordinates of the station *A* be (0, 0). The independent coordinates of other points are as below:

Line	Latitude (m)	Departure (m)	Station	Independent coordinates x (m)	y (m)
AB	– 164.5	162.1	*A*	0.0	0.0
BC	217.8	59.8	*B*	– 164.5	162.1
CD	168.1	– 105.6	*C*	53.3	221.9
DA	– 221.4	– 116.3	*D*	221.4	116.3
			A	0.0	0.0

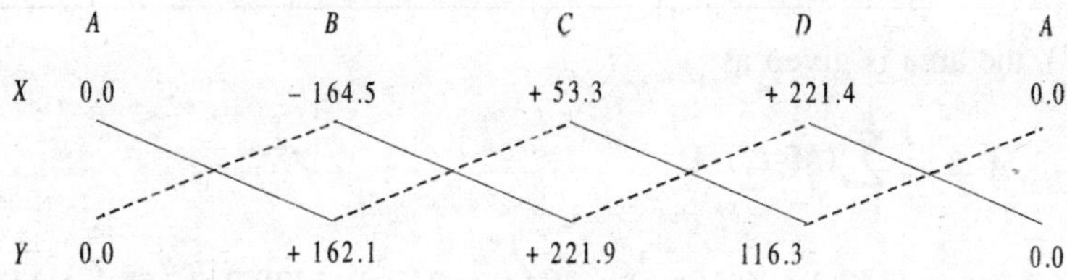

Thus, the area of traverse

$$A = \frac{1}{2}[0.0 \times 162.1 - 0.0 \times (-164.5) + (-164.5) \times 221.9 - 162.1 \times 53.3$$

$$+ 53.3 \times 116.3 - 221.9 \times 221.4 + 221.4 \times 0.0 - 116.3 \times 0.0]$$

$$= \frac{1}{2}[-88072.350]$$

$$= -44036.2 \text{ m}^2$$

$$= \mathbf{44036.2 \ m^2} \textit{ (neglecting the sign).}$$

2. By meridian distance method

From the definition of the meridian distance, the meridian distance of the lines are as below:

Line	Latitude (L) (*m*)	Meridian distance of the Preceding line (m)	Half departure of the preceding line (m)	Half departure of the line (m)	Meridian distance (m)
AB	– 164.5	0.0	0.0	81.05	81.05
BC	+ 217.8	81.05	81.05	29.90	192.00
CD	+ 168.1	192.00	29.90	– 52.80	169.10
DA	– 221.4	169.10	– 52.80	– 58.15	58.15

From Eq. (11.12), we have

$$A = \sum_{i=1}^{n}(m_i L_i)$$

$= 81.05 \times (-164.5) + 192.00 \times 217.8 + 169.10 \times 168.1 + 58.15 \times (-221.4)$

$= \mathbf{44036.2\ m^2}$

3. By DMD distance method

From the definition of the DMD, the DMD of the lines are as below:

Line	Latitude (L) (m)	DMD of the preceding line (m)	Departure of the preceding line (m)	Departure of the line (m)	DMD (M) (m)
AB	– 164.5	0.0	0.0	162.1	162.1
BC	+ 217.8	162.1	162.1	59.8	384.0
CD	+ 168.1	384.0	59.8	– 105.6	338.2
DA	– 221.4	338.2	– 105.6	– 116.3	116.3

From Eq. (11.17), the area is given as

$$A = \frac{1}{2}\sum_{i=1}^{n}(M_i L_i)$$

$$= \frac{1}{2}[162.1 \times (-164.5) + 384.0 \times 217.8 + 338.2 \times 168.1 + 116.3 \times (-221.4)]$$

$$= \frac{1}{2}[88072.350]$$

$= \mathbf{44036.2\ m^2}$.

4. By departure and total latitude method

Considering the station *A* as the reference station, the total latitudes of the stations will be as under:

Station	Departure (m)	Total latitude (m)
A	0.0	0.0
B	162.1	– 164.5
C	59.8	53.3
D	– 105.6	221.4
A	– 116.3	0.0

From Eq. (11.18), the area is given as

$$A = \frac{1}{2}[(-164.5) \times 162.1 + 59.8) + 53.3 \times (59.8 - 105.6) + 221.4 \times (-105.6 - 116.3)]$$

$$= \frac{1}{2}[-88072.350]$$

$= \mathbf{44036.2\ m^2}$ *(neglecting the sign)*.

Example 11.2

A tract of land has three straight sides *AB*, *BC*, and *CD*. The fourth side *DA*, is irregular. The dimensions of the sides are as below:

AB = 168 m, BC = 255 m, CD = 180 m, DA = 240 m, AC = 340 m

To determine the area of the tract with irregular boundary, the offsets measured outside from the side *AD* to the irregular boundary, are as below:

Chainge from *A* (m)	0	60	120	180	240
Offset (m)	0.0	5.8	1.5	4.8	0.0

Calculate the area of the tract in hectares.

Solution (Fig. 11.15):

From Eq. (11.1), the area of a triangle is

$$A = \sqrt{[s(s-a)(s-b)(s-c)]}$$

For ΔABC

$$s = \frac{1}{2}(255 + 340 + 168) = 381.5 \text{ m}$$

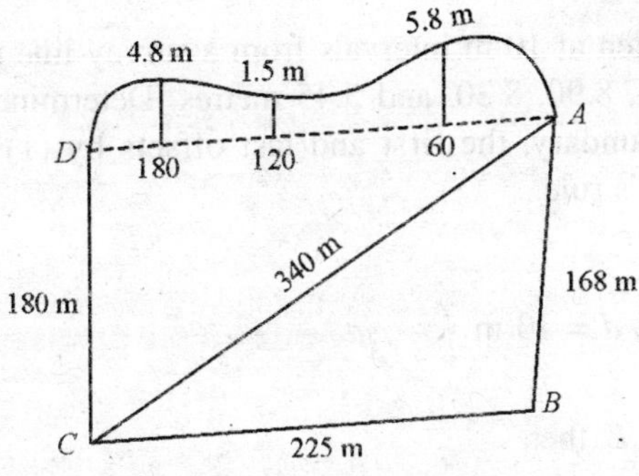

Fig. 11.15

The area of the Δ *ABC*

$$A_1 = \sqrt{38.5 \times (381.5 - 255) \times (381.5 - 340) \times (381.5 - 168)}$$

$$= 20678.3 \text{ m}^2$$

For Δ *ACD*

$$s = \frac{1}{2}(180 + 240 + 340) = 380.0$$

The area of the Δ *ACD*

$$A_2 = \sqrt{380 \times (380 - 180) \times (380 - 240) \times (380 - 340)}$$

$$= 20630.1 \text{ m}^2$$

The area of the tract with irregular boundary has the offsets at regular interval of 60 m. Thus, from Eq. (11.21) its area is

$$A_3 = \frac{L}{n+1}\sum_{i=1}^{n+1} O_i$$

$$= \frac{240}{4+1} \times (0.0 + 5.8 + 1.5 + 4.8 + 0.0)$$

$$= \frac{240}{5} \times 12.1$$

$$= 580.8 \text{ m}^2.$$

Hence the total area of the tract is

$$A = A_1 + A_2 + A_3$$

$$= 20678.3 + 20630.1 + 580.8$$

$$= 41889.2 \text{ m}^2$$

$$= \mathbf{4.2 \text{ hectares.}}$$

Example 11.3

The perpendicular offsets taken at 10 m intervals from a survey line to an irregular boundary are 2.25, 3.85, 4.50, 6.80, 5.20, 7.35, 8.90, 8.30, and 5.45 metres. Determine the area enclosed between the survey line, the irregular boundary, the first and last offsets by (1) average-ordinates rule, (2) trapezoidal rule, and (3) Simpson's rule.

Solution:

Distance between the offsets, $d = 10$ m

Number of segments $n = 8$

If the length of survey line is L, then

$$d = \frac{L}{n}$$

or $$L = n\,d = 8 \times 10 = 80 \text{ m.}$$

(1) By average-ordinate rule

From Eq. (11.21), we have

$$A = \frac{L}{n+1}[O_1 + O_2 + O_3 + ... + O_9]$$

$$= \frac{80}{9}\ [2.25 + 3.85 + 4.50 + 6.80 + 5.20 + 7.35 + 8.90 + 8.30 + 5.45]$$

$$= \frac{80}{9} \times 52.6$$

$$= \mathbf{467.6 \text{ m}^2.}$$

(2) By trapezoidal rule

From Eq. (11.23), we have

$$A = d\left[\frac{O_1+O_9}{2}+O_2+O_3+\ldots+O_8\right]$$

$$= 10\times\left[\frac{2.25+5.45}{2}+3.85+4.50+6.80+5.20+7.35+8.90+8.30\right]$$

$$= 10 \times 48.75$$

$$= \mathbf{487.5\ m^2.}$$

(3) By Simpson's rule

From Eq. (11.24), we have

$$A = \frac{d}{3}[(O_1+O_9)+4(O_2+O_4+O_6+O_8)+2(O_3+O_5+O_7)]$$

$$= \frac{10}{3} \times [(2.25 + 5.45) + 4 \times (3.85 + 6.80 + 7.35 + 8.30) + 2 \times (4.50 + 5.20 + 8.90)]$$

$$= \frac{10}{3}\times 150.1$$

$$= \mathbf{500.3\ m^2.}$$

11.4 AREA FROM PLAN

The methods for the determination of area using a plan, can be either (1) graphical, or (2) mechanical or instrumental. The measured area from the plan is multiplied by the scale of the plan to convert the area to its ground equivalent. The methods of area determination for irregular boundaries discussed in Sec. 11.3, are also applicable when using a plan. The offsets, called ordinate in this context, are scaled off from the plan at convenient equal intervals, and generally, the trapezoidal or Simpson's rule is applied to compute the area.

Graphical Method

There are two methods to determine the area by graphical method. These methods are also known as approximate methods.

Subdivision into geometric figures

The area of the plan is subdivided into triangles, trapezoids, or a combination of both either by pencil lines on the plan or on superimposed tracing paper. The required dimensions of the geometric figures to compute their areas are scaled, the area of each is obtained and summed up. For irregular boundaries, *equalizing* or *give-and-take* lines are drawn as shown in Fig. 11.16, so that the area contained between them and the irregular boundary are equally disposed on either sides of the straight line. The position of these lines is estimated by eye-judgement.

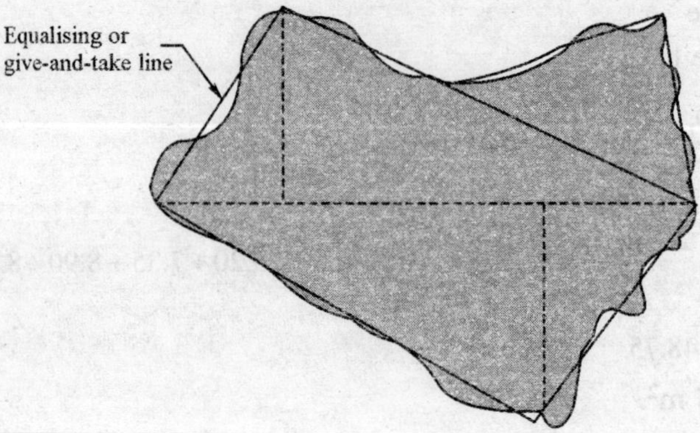

Fig. 11.16. Division of the area into simple geometric figures.

Subdivision into squares

The plan is covered with a transparent sheet on which the lines are drawn forming a pattern of squares, each representing some definite number of square metres on some scale related to the scale of the plan (Fig. 11.17).

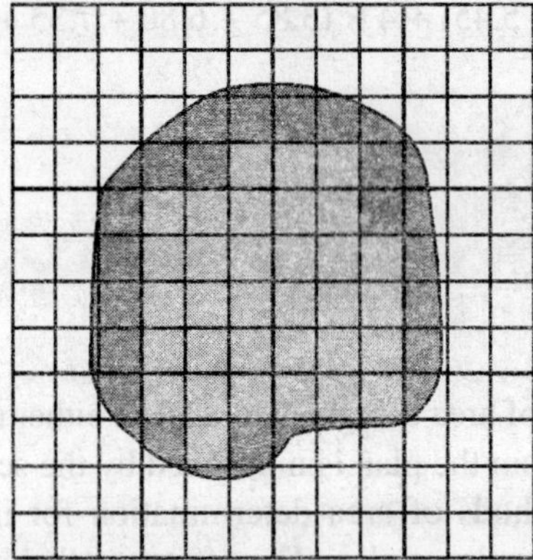

Fig. 11.17 Division into squares

The number of full squares is counted and the part squares are added up as fractional squares, by eye estimation. Usually, part squares less than half are ignored, and those more than half taken as full. The accuracy of the method depends upon this estimation.

Division into trapezoids or strips

In this method, a number of parallel lines, at regular interval are drawn on a tracing paper. The distance between the lines is related to the scale of the plan. Midway between each pair of lines, lines in different colour or dashed lines are drawn as shown in Fig. 11.18.

The tracing paper is placed on the plan, and the length of plan covered by each strip is then measured. The total area is obtained by adding the lengths of the strips considered and multiplying by the constant distance between the strips. Apply the scale factor to both these dimensions to get the equivalent area on the ground.

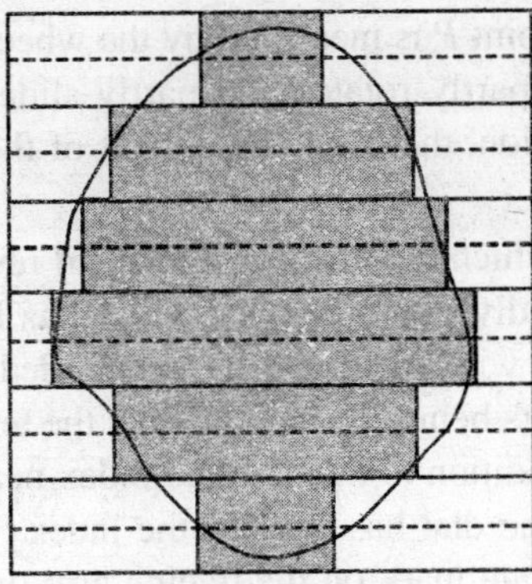

Fig. 11.18 Division into trapezoids or strips

Mechanical Method

The mechanical method is also known as instrumental method since it uses an instrument planimeter to measure the area. This instrument gives more accurate results than those obtained by the methods discussed in Sec. 11.3 and 11.4.

11.5 PLANIMETER

There are two types of planimeter:

1. The rolling planimeter
2. Amsler polar planimeter.

The Amsler planimeter is most commonly employed and will be discussed in detail.

Amsler Polar Planimeter

Figure 11.19 shows a Amsler polar planimeter. It consists of two bars PQ and QR hinged at Q. A tracing point P is guided around the boundary of the area to be measured. The QR terminates at R which is a stationary point and it is fixed on the paper by a needle point and a weight.

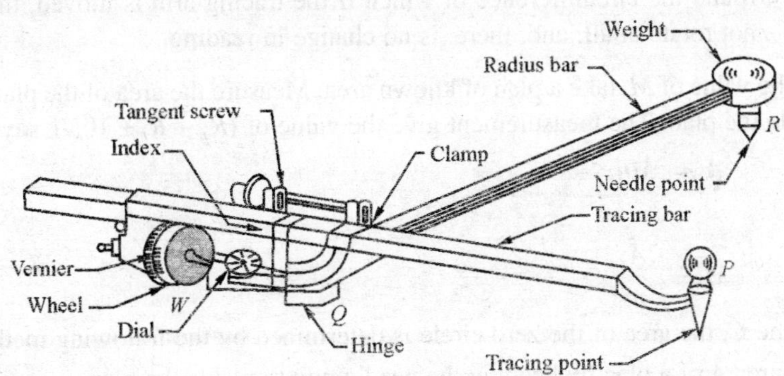

Fig. 11.19 Amsler polar planimeter.

The displacement of the tracing point P is measured by the wheel W fixed in a plane perpendicular to PQ. While PQ moves, the wheel partly rotates and partly slides on the paper. The total normal displacement is measured by the rotation, the axial component of the motion causes slip and does not affect the measurement.

The wheel W is geared to a dial which records the number of revolutions made by the wheel. One revolution of the wheel is equal to one division of the dial which has 10 equal divisions on its periphery. The wheel is graduated on its periphery with 100 divisions, subdivided into tenths by a vernier. Thus each reading consists of four digits. The units being read on the dial, the tenths and hundredths on the wheel, and the thousands on the vernier. In addition to this, a fixed index near the dial can be utilized to know the number of the times the zero of the dial has crossed the index. The distance between P and Q is adjustable, and on setting the appropriate mark on the tracing arm opposite the index by means of the clamp and tangent screw, the readings are directly obtainable in square centimetres, etc.

Measurement of area by Planimeter

To obtain the area in the desired unit, adjust the tracing arm. Fix the needle point on the paper outside the area to be measured in such a manner that the tracing point can reach all parts of the boundary of the area. Select any arbitrary point on the boundary and move the tracing point from this point all around the boundary in a clockwise direction till the tracing point reaches the starting point.

The area of the plan is calculated from the following formula:

$$A = M(R_F - R_I \pm 10N + C) \qquad \text{...(11.27)}$$

where M = multiplying constant whose value is marked on the tracing arm,

R_I and R_F = initial and final readings,

N = number of complete revolutions of the dial. It is taken as positive when the zero mark passes the index mark in a clockwise direction and as negative when in counter clockwise direction, and

C = constant of the instrument marked on the tracing arm just above the scale divisions and considered only when the needle point is kept inside the boundary of the plan. For the needle point outside the area, $C = 0$.

C multiplied by M is equal to the area of zero circle (A_0). The *zero circle* is the circle round the circumference of which if the tracing arm is moved, the wheel W does not rotate at all, and, there, is no change in reading.

To determine the value of M, take a plan of known area. Measure the area of the plan by keeping the needle point outside the plan. The measurement give the value of $(R_F - R_I \pm 10N)$, say it is equal to n,

then $A = Mn$

Therefore,

$$M = \frac{A}{n} \qquad \text{...(11.28)}$$

To determine the C, the area of the zero circle is determined by the following method.

Determine the area A of a plan by keeping the needle point outside the plan.

Thus $A = M(R_F - R_I \pm 10\,N)$

$= Mn_1$ ...(11.29)

where $n_1 = R_F - R_I \pm 10\,N$

Now keep the needle point inside the plan, and determine the area A of the plan again.

Thus $A = M(n_2 + C)$ ...(11.30)

where $n_2 = R_F - R_I \pm 10\,N$ for needle point inside the plan.

From Eq. (11.29) and (11.30), we get

$$Mn_1 = M(n_2 + C)$$

Therefore, $C = n_1 - n_2$ ...(11.31)

The area of the zero circle is equal to

$A_0 = MC$ ...(11.32)

$= M(n_1 - n_2).$ ...(11.33)

ILLUSTRATIVE EXAMPLES

Example 11.4

A planimeter was used to determine the area of a plan with an irregular boundary. The initial and final reading were 8.348 and 1.435, respectively. It was observed that the zero mark of the dial passed the fixed index mark twice. The tracing point was moved in the clockwise direction and the needle point was outside the plan. Calculate the area of the plan if $M = 100\text{ cm}^2$.

Solution:

From Eq. (11.27), the area of the plan is given by

$$A = M(R_F - R_I \pm 10N + C)$$

Since the needle point was outside the plan, $C = 0$ and the tracing point was moved in clockwise direction, $N = +2$. Thus,

$$A = 100 \times (1.435 - 8.348 + 10 \times 2)$$

$$= \mathbf{1308.7\ cm^2}.$$

Example 11.5

Calculate the area of a plan from the following planimeter readings.

Initial reading = 6.480

Final reading = 8.460

When the needle point was inside the plan and the tracing point was moved clockwise. It was noted that the zero of the dial passed the fixed index twice in the reverse direction, *i.e.*, counter clockwise direction. Take $M = 100\text{ cm}^2$ and $C = 20$.

Solution:

From Eq. (11.27), the area is equal to

$$A = M(R_F - R_I \pm 10\,N + C)$$

Since the needle point was inside the plan, C will not be equal to zero. Hence C is to be retained in the above formula. The sign of N will be negative, since the zero of the dial passed the fixed index in the reverse direction. Thus,

$$A = 100 \times (8.460 - 6.840 - 10 \times 2 + 20)$$
$$= \mathbf{198\ cm^2}.$$

Example 11.6

Determine the area of the zero circle from the following data:

(*a*) Needle point outside the plan
Initial reading = 8.364
Final reading = 4.234

The zero of the dial passed the index mark once in the clockwise direction.

(*b*) Needle point inside the plan
Initial Reading = 2.484
Final Reading = 5.443

The zero of the dial passed the fixed index mark twice in the counter clockwise direction. Take $M = 100$ cm².

Solution:

From Eq. (11.27), the area of the plan is given as

$$A = M(R_F - R_I \pm 10N + C)$$

(*a*) $N = +1, C = 0$

Therefore, $A = 100 \times (4.234 - 8.364 + 10)$
$= 587.0$ cm².

(*b*) $N = -2, C \neq 0$

Therefore, $A = 100 \times (5.443 - 2.484 - 20 + C)$
$= -1704.1 + 100 \times C$

Substituting the value of A, we get

$$100 \times C = 587.0 + 1704.1$$
$$= 2291.1$$

Therefore, $C = 22.911$

From Eq. (11.32), we have

$$A_0 = MC$$
$$= 100 \times 22.911$$
$$= \mathbf{2291.1\ cm^2}.$$

Precautions in using a planimeter

The following precautions must be observed in using a planimeter:

1. The plan of the area should be kept on a horizontal table.

2. The needle point should be kept outside the plan to avoid the additive constant.
3. If the area of the plan is too large, it may be divided into parts of convenient sizes.
4. The area should be found twice with diferent positions of the needle point, and the mean value should be accepted.
5. The surface of the paper on which the wheel rolls, should be smooth. If the paper of the plan is rough, a kodatrace may be placed over it.
6. The folds in the paper of the plan should be avoided as they affect the results.
7. The tracing point should be guided by a straight edge or a French curve in order to keep it exactly on the outline of the plan.
8. The measured area should also be checked roughly by calculations to provide a check against any gross error.
9. Time should not be wasted in setting the vernier to read zero. Whatever reading it indicates, may be accepted as the initial reading.

11.6 SOURCES OF ERRORS IN COMPUTATION OF AREA

The following are some common sources of errors in computation of area:

1. Use of unadjusted coordinates of traverse sections.
2. Poor selection of intervals for offsets.
3. Use of large size of squares or strips.
4. Improper setting of the tracing arm of the planimeter.
5. The planimeter wheel running off the edge of the plan.
6. Improper calibration of the planimeter.
7. Confusion in the signs of the coordinates, or the values derived from them.
8. Poor selection of the origin when using traverse notes.

11.7 AREA OF CROSS-SECTIONS

Cross-sections are invariably employed in route surveys for road, railways, and canal works. For estimation of volume of earthwork, cross-sections are taken at right angles to a fixed line, generally, the centre-line, which runs longitudinally through the earthwork. The spacing of the cross-sections depends upon the accuracy required and the character of the ground. The earthwork involved may be excavation (cutting) or in embankment (filling), depending on the relative values of the formation level and natural ground level at the centre-line of the route, and on the configuration of the ground surface. Other values which are of relevance are breadth or width of formation and side slopes of the cut or fill.

The cross-sections generally occurring in practice, are of the following types:

1. Level section
2. Two-level section
3. Three-level section
4. Side hill two-level section
5. Multi-level section.

The following notation has been employed in deriving various formulae related to this section:

b = width or breadth of formation

h = depth of cut or height of fill, at the midpoint of the formation

s = side slope (S horizontal to 1 vertical)

n = lateral or transverse slope of the natural ground (n horizontal to 1 vertical; for a two-level section)

n_1, n_2 = transverse slopes of the natural ground; n_1 on the upward side of the slope, and n_2 on the downward side for a cutting, and *vice versa* for an embankment (for a three-level section)

w = half-breadth, *i.e.*, the horizontal distance from the centre line to the intersections of the side slopes with the natural ground surface (for a level section)

w_1, w_2 = side-width, *i.e.*, horizontal distances from the centre-line to the intersections of the side slopes with the natural ground surface (w_1 on the upward side of the slope, and w_2 on the downward side for a cutting, and *vice versa* for an embankment)

A = area of the cross-section (A_c : area of cutting, A_e : area of embankment)

The various formulae given in the following sections, can be easily derived from the geometry of the figures, and hence, the derivation of the formulae has not been given.

Level Section

A level section is that section in which the ground AB is level transversely, *i.e.*, the value of n approaches to infinity (Fig. 11.20). For a level section the cross-sectional area is given by

$$A = h(b + sh) \quad \text{...(11.34)}$$

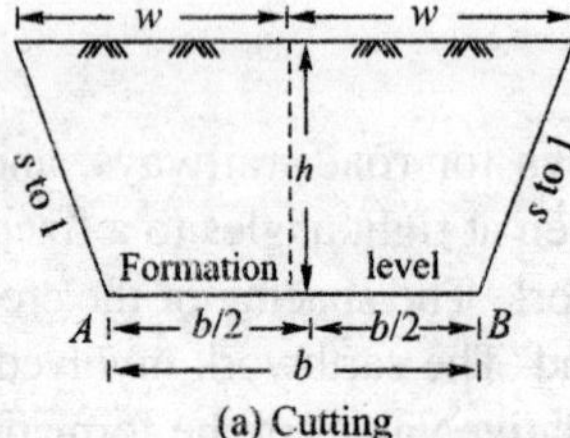

(a) Cutting

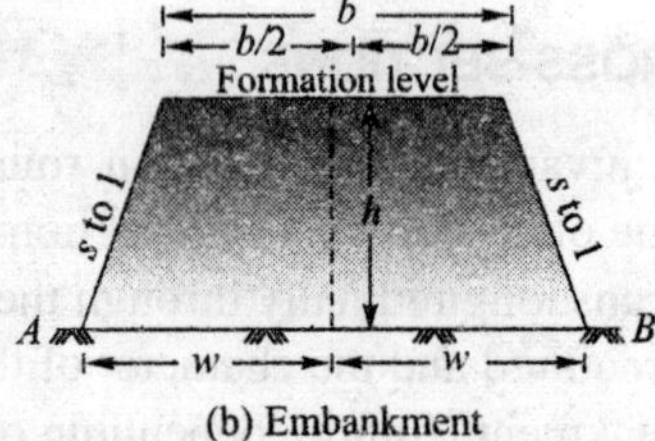

(b) Embankment

Fig. 11.20 Level section

Two-level section

Fig. 11.21 shows the two-level sections in embankment and cutting. The two-level section has a crossfall of the ground surface relative to the centre-line. It has two levels of the ground surface at points A and B, which are required to establish the crossfall.

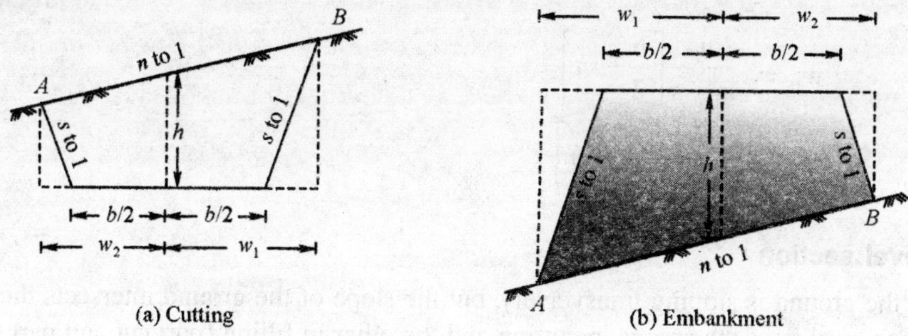

Fig. 11.21 Two-level section

For a two-level section, the area is given by the following formulae:

$$A = \frac{n^2 s}{n^2 - s^2}\left[h + \frac{b}{2s}\right]^2 - \frac{b^2}{4s}$$

$$A = \frac{w_1 w_2}{s} - \frac{b^2}{4s} \qquad \text{...(11.35)}$$

where
$$w_1 = \frac{b}{2} + \frac{ns}{n-s}\left[h + \frac{b}{2n}\right] \qquad \text{...(11.36)}$$

$$w_2 = \frac{b}{2} + \frac{ns}{n+s}\left[h - \frac{b}{2n}\right]$$

Three-level section

In the case of a three-level section, the transverse slope of the ground is not uniform. At least three levels at *A*, *B* and *C*, as shown in Fig. 11.22, are required to define the ground slopes $n_1 : 1$ and $n_2 : 1$ on the two sides of the centre-line.

The area of cross-section of a three-level section is given by the following expressions:

$$A = \frac{1}{2}(w_1 + w_2)\left[h + \frac{b}{2s}\right] - \frac{b^2}{4s} \qquad \text{...(11.37)}$$

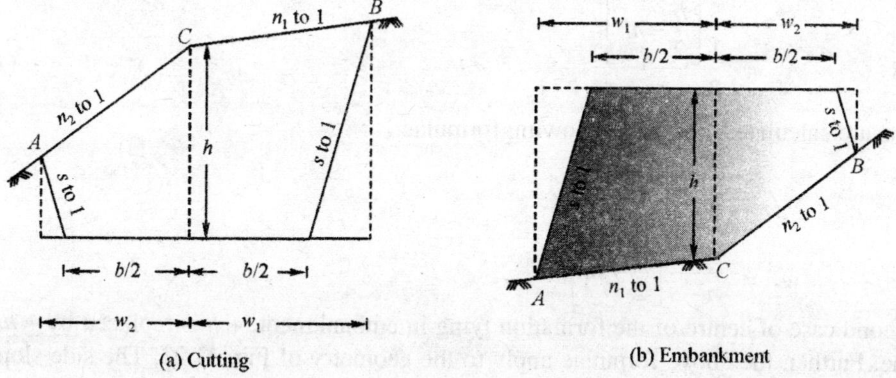

Fig. 11.22 Three-level section

where $$w_1 = \frac{n_1}{n_1 - s}\left[\frac{b}{2} + sh\right]$$

$$w_2 = \frac{n_2}{n_2 - s}\left[\frac{b}{2} + sh\right]$$

Sidehill two-level section

In this case the ground is sloping transversely, but the slope of the ground intersects the formation level such that one portion of the area is in cutting and the other in filling (part cut and part fill).

In field, the following cases may exist:

(*i*) Centre of the formation in cutting (Fig. 11.23a).

(*ii*) Centre of the formation in embankment (Fig. 11.23b).

When the centre of the formation is in cutting, the areas of cut and fill are determined using the following formulae.

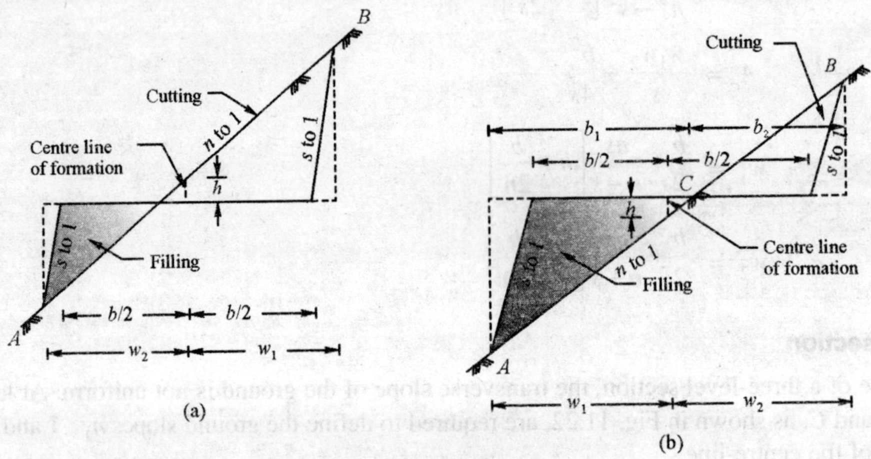

Fig. 11.23 Side hill two-level section

Area of cut $$A_c = \frac{1}{2}\frac{\left[\frac{b}{2} + nh\right]^2}{n - s} \quad ...(11.38)$$

Area of fill $$A_e = \frac{1}{2}\frac{\left[\frac{b}{2} - nh\right]^2}{n - s} \quad ...(11.39)$$

The side widths are calculated from the following formulae.

$$w_1 = \frac{n}{n - s}\left[\frac{b}{2} + sh\right]$$

$$w_2 = \frac{n}{n - s}\left[\frac{b}{2} - sh\right]$$

For the second case of centre of the formation lying in embankment, + h is replaced by – h in the above formulae. Further, the above formulae apply to the geometry of Fig. 11.23. The side slopes are usually steeper in cutting than in filling or embankment, and in such cases the corresponding value of s should be used in the formulae.

Multi-level section

A multi-level section is that section in which the natural ground has more than two different transverse slopes in the width covered by the cross-section (Fig. 11.24).

In this case, spot levels and their distances from the central-line are usually recorded in the following tabular form (Fig. 11.24a).

Left		Centre	Right	
$\pm\dfrac{h_2}{w_2}$	$\pm\dfrac{h_4}{w_4}$	$\pm\dfrac{h}{0}$	$\pm\dfrac{h_3}{w_3}$	$\pm\dfrac{h_1}{w_1}$

(a) Cutting (b) Embankment

Fig. 11.24 Multi-level section

Heights are recorded as numerators and distances from the centre are recorded as denominators. Conventionally, a cut is denoted by a positive sign and fill by a negative sign. With the origin at the midpoint of the formation width, these notes provide the coordinates for each point of break in slope or the intersection of the side slopes with the natural ground.

The area of the cross-section may be computed by the method of coordinates. Taking the heights as y-coordinates and the distances as x-coordinates. For a cutting shown in Fig. 11.24a taking the origin at O, the coordinates of the points A, B, C, D, E, F, and G are $\left(\frac{-b}{2}, 0\right)$, $(-w_2, h_2)$, $(-w_4, h_4)$, $(0, h)$, (w_3, h_3), (w_1, h_1) and $\left(\frac{b}{2}, 0\right)$ respectively. They are written in the form of determinant as below. Preparation of the determinant starts from the centre and proceeds to the right and to the left.

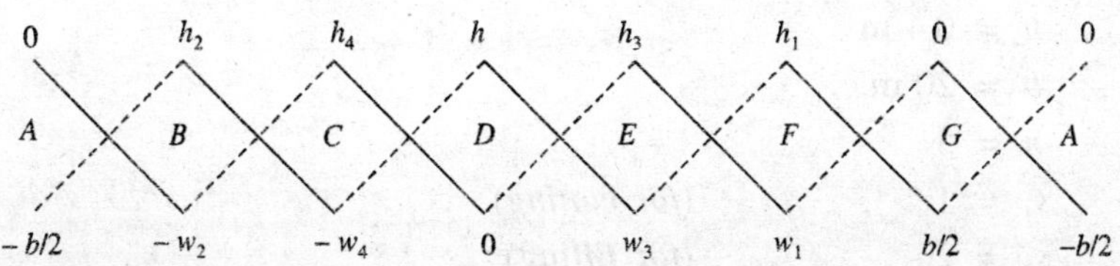

If ΣP is the algebraic sum of products taken along the full lines in the above diagram, and ΣQ is that taken along the dashed lines then the area is given by

$$A = \frac{1}{2}(\Sigma P - \Sigma Q) \qquad ...(11.40)$$

Alternatively, the area can be determined by dividing the cross-section into triangles, trapezoids, and their individual areas are summed up.

ILLUSTRATIVE EXAMPLES

Example 11.7

Compute the area of the cross-section if the formation width is 10 m, side slope is 1 to 1, average height along the centre-line is 5 m, and transverse slope of the ground is 10 to 1.

Solution (Fig. 11.21):

From the given data, we have

$$h = 5 \text{ m}$$
$$b = 10 \text{ m}$$
$$s = 1$$
$$n = 10$$

From Eq. (11.35), we have

$$A = \frac{n^2 s}{n^2 - s^2}\left[h + \frac{b}{2s}\right]^2 - \frac{b^2}{4s}$$

$$= \frac{10^2 \times 1}{10^2 - 1^2} \times \left(5 + \frac{10}{2 \times 1}\right)^2 - \frac{10^2}{4 \times 1}$$

$$= \frac{100}{99} \times 100 - \frac{100}{4}$$

$$= \mathbf{76\ m^2}.$$

Example 11.8

The width of a certain road at formation level is 20 m, side slopes 1 in 1 for cutting and 1 in 2 for filling. The ground transverse to the centre-line of the road is 1 in 5. If the depth of the excavation at the centre-line of the section is 0.4 m, calculate the areas of the cross-section in cutting and filling.

Solution (Fig. 11.23):

From the given data, we have

$$h = 0.4 \text{ m}$$
$$b = 20 \text{ m}$$
$$n = 5$$
$$s_1 = 1 \qquad \textit{(for cutting)}$$
$$s_2 = 2 \qquad \textit{(for filling)}$$

(*i*) Cutting

From Eq. (11.38), we have

$$A_c = \frac{1}{2}\frac{\left[\frac{b}{2}+nh\right]^2}{n-s}$$

$$= \frac{1}{2}\times\frac{\left[\frac{20}{5}+5\times 0.4\right]^2}{5-1}$$

$$= \mathbf{18\ m^2}.$$

(*ii*) Embankment

From Eq. (11.39), we have

$$A_e = \frac{1}{2}\frac{\left[\frac{b}{2}-nh\right]^2}{(n-s)}$$

$$= \frac{1}{2}\times\frac{\left[\frac{20}{2}-5\times 0.4\right]^2}{5-2}$$

$$= \mathbf{10.7\ m^2}.$$

Example 11.9

Compute the area of a cross-section from the following data:

Width of the formation	= 20 m
Depth of cut at the midpoint of the formation	= 3.5 m
Transverse slope on the right side of the midpoint of the formation	= 10 to 1
Transverse slope on the left side of the midpoint of the formation	= 7 to 1
Side slope	= 2 to 1

Solution (Fig. 11.22a):

From the given data, we have

$$b = 20\text{ m}$$
$$h = 3.5\text{ m}$$
$$n_1 = 10$$
$$n_2 = 7$$
$$s = 2$$

From Eq. (11.37), we have

$$A = \frac{1}{2}(w_1+w_2)\left[h+\frac{b}{2s}\right]-\frac{b^2}{4s}$$

$$w_1 = \frac{n_1}{n_1 - s}\left[\frac{b}{2} + sh\right]$$

$$= \frac{10}{10-2} \times \left[\frac{20}{2} + 2 \times 3.5\right]$$

$$= 21.25 \text{ m}$$

$$w_2 = \frac{n_2}{n_2 + s}\left[\frac{b}{2} + sh\right]$$

$$= \frac{7}{7+2} \times \left[\frac{20}{2} + 2 \times 3.5\right]$$

$$= 13.22 \text{ m}$$

Thus,

$$A = \frac{1}{2} \times (21.25 + 13.22) \times \left(3.5 + \frac{20}{2 \times 2}\right) - \frac{20^2}{4 \times 2}$$

$$= \mathbf{96.50 \ m^2}.$$

11.8 PARTITION OF LAND

Sometimes a surveyor may be required to assist in the partition of land. Some of the simpler cases frequently encountered in the subdivision of irregular tracts of land are discussed below. The principles discussed here can also be applied to other cases of partitioning of land.

Whenever a given tract is to be divided, a resurvey is done, the departures and latitudes are computed, the survey is adjusted, and the area of the entire tract is determined. The corrected departures and latitudes are further employed in the computations of subdivision.

Area Cut off by a Line Joining Two Points (Case-I)

In Fig. 11.25, let *ABCDEF* represents a tract of land to be divided by a line joining the points *A* and *D*. The adjusted departures and latitudes of the corners have been determined after doing a resurvey of the tract.

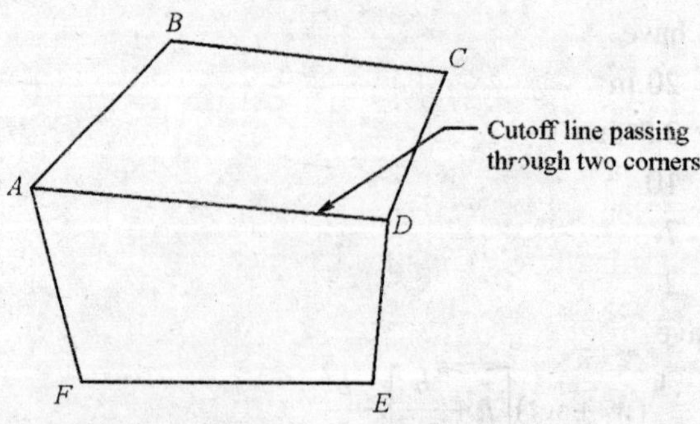

Fig. 11.25 Partition of area by a line joining two corners

It is desired to determine the length and direction of the cutoff line *AD* without additional field measurements, and to calculate the area of each of the two parts into which the tract is divided.

If the coordinates of *A* and *D* are (D_A, L_A) and (D_D, L_D), respectively, the length *L* and bearing θ of *AD* are given by

$$L = \sqrt{(D_A - D_D)^2 + (L_A - L_D)^2} \quad \text{... (11.41)}$$

and

$$\theta = \tan^{-1}\left[\frac{D_D - D_A}{L_D - L_A}\right] \quad \text{... (11.42)}$$

The areas of the two parts can be computed from the coordinates of the corners by the coordinate method (Eq. 11.5).

Area Cut off by a Line Running in a Given Direction (Case-II)

In Fig. 11.26, the line *AG* is the cutoff line of known direction. From the adjusted coordinates of the traverse stations *A, B, C,* and *D* in the traverse *ABCDA*, the length and the bearing of *AD* are determined as explained in Case-I. From the known directions of *AD, AG,* and *CD*, the three angles of the triangle *ADG*, are computed. Using these angles and the length of *AD*, the lengths of *AG* and *GD* are computed by sine law, and then the coordinates of the point *G* are computed.

The areas of the two parts *ABCG* and *AGDEF* are computed from the coordinates using Eq. (11.5).

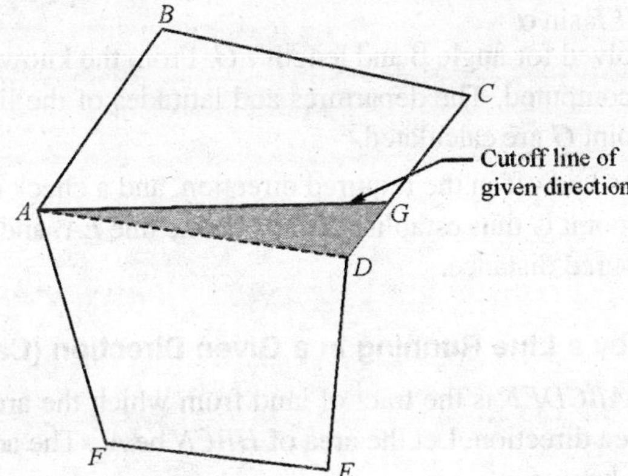

Fig. 11.26 Partition of area by a line running in a given direction

To Cut off a Required Area by a Line Through a Given Point (Case-III)

In Fig. 11.27, the required area A_1 is *ABCFG*. The line *FG* is passing through the given point *F*. From inspection, find out the station *E* on the traverse which is nearest to the cutoff line. Join *E* and *F*.

Determine the length and bearing of *EF* from the adjusted coordinates of *A, B, C, F,* and *E*. Also compute the area *A'* of *ABCFE* by coordinate method (Eq. 11.5). The area of the triangular part *FEG* is given by

$$A_2 = A' - A_1 \quad \text{...(11.43)}$$

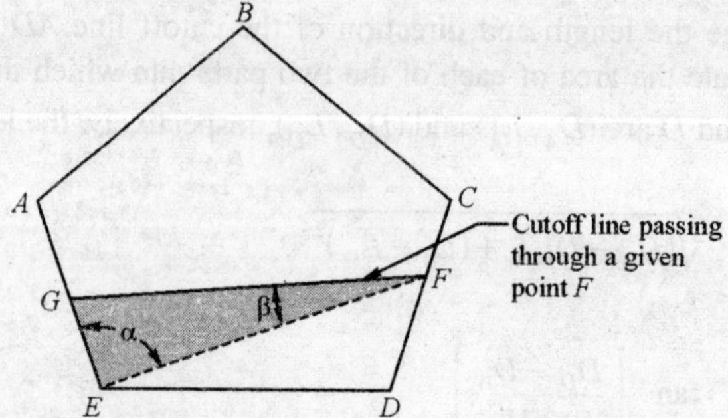

Fig. 11.27 Cutting off a required area by a line passing through a given point

For Eq. (11.43), it is assumed that the area A' of *ABCFE*, is greater than the desired area A_1 of *ABCFG*.

In triangle *FEG*, the angle α is computed from the bearings of the lines *FE* and *EA*. The length of the line *GE* is determined from the known area A_2 of the triangle *FEG*, the length of *FE*, and the angle α from the following formula:

$$A_2 = \frac{1}{2} GE\, EF \sin \alpha$$

Thus,

$$GE = \frac{2A_2}{EF \sin \alpha} \quad \text{...(11.44)}$$

The triangle *EFG* is then solved for angle β and length *FG*. From the known direction of *FE* and the angle β, the azimuth of *FG* is computed. The departures and latitudes of the lines *FG*, *EG*, and *GA* are computed and coordinates of point *G* are calculated.

In the field, the length *FG* is laid off in the required direction, and a check on the field work and the computations is obtained if the point *G* thus established falls on the line *EA*, and if the computed distance *EG* or *GA* agrees with the measured distance.

To Cut off a Required Area by a Line Running in a Given Direction (Case-IV)

In Fig. 11.28, the traverse *ABCDEF* is the tract of land from which the area *HBCN* is to be cut off by the line *NH* running in a given direction. Let the area of *HBCN* be A_2. The adjusted coordinates of all the corners of the traverse are known.

From inspection, find out the corner (*D*) which seems to be nearest the line *NH*, cutting off the required area A_2. Draw the line *DG* in the given direction. Then in the closed traverse *GBCDG*, the coordinates (D_G, L_G) of *G* are determined by the method discussed in Case-II, and the area A_1 of *GBCDG* is computed.

The difference between the two areas A_1 and A_2 is equal to the area A_3 of the trapezoid *GHND*. Let the perpendicular distance between the two parallel sides *DG* and *NH* of the trapezoid be *d*. The angles θ and ϕ can be computed from the known directions of the adjacent sides. The values of tan θ and tan ϕ are positive if the angles fall inside the trapezoid, and negative if they fall outside. The area of the trapezoid shown in Fig. 11.28 will be

$$A_3 = \text{Area of } GKMD - \text{area } GKH - \text{area } DMN$$

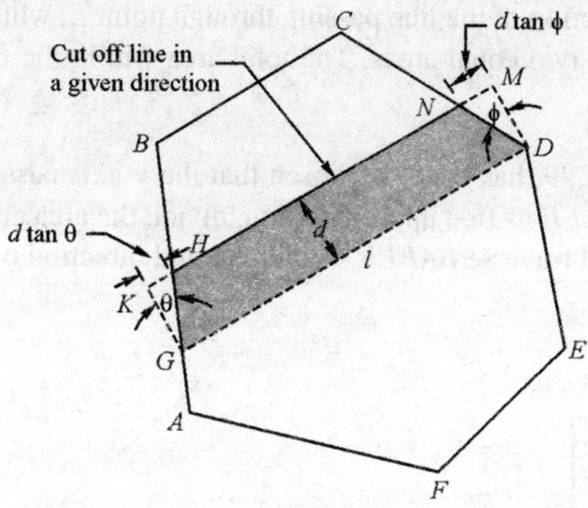

Fig. 11.28 Cutting off a required area by a line running in a given direction

or $$= dDC + \frac{1}{2}dd\,(-\tan\theta) + \frac{1}{2}dd\,(-\tan\phi)$$

or $$= dDG - \frac{1}{2}d^2\,(\tan\theta + \tan\phi)$$

or $$= \frac{1}{2}(\tan\theta + \tan\phi)\,d^2 - DGd + A_3 = 0 \qquad \text{...(11.45)}$$

Eq. (11.45) is a quadratic equation in which θ, ϕ, DG and A_3 are known quantities. Solution of this equation will give the value of d.

The distances of the points H and N from G and D, respectively, are computed as below:

$$GH = d \sec\theta$$

$$DN = d \sec\phi.$$

In the field, points H and N are established on the lines AB and CD, at the calculated distances GH and DN from G and D. The side HN is then measured. If this measured value agrees with the computed value, the field work and computations are verified. A further check on the computations can be applied by calculating the area $BCNH$ and comparing it with the required area of this figure.

ILLUSTRATIVE EXAMPLES

Example 11.10

The adjusted departures and latitudes of the sides of a closed traverse *ABCDEF* are as follows:

Side	*AB*	*BC*	*CD*	*DE*	*EF*	*FA*
Departure (m)	+ 388.84	+ 285.13	– 134.96	– 135.41	– 251.85	– 151.75
Latitude (m)	– 113.92	+ 178.86	+ 295.85	– 164.31	– 13.53	– 182.95

Determine the length and direction of the line passing through point *E*, which divides the area of the tract enclosed by the traverse into two equal areas. The total area within the tract is 157250 m^2.

Solution (Fig. 11.29):

The traverse shown in Fig. 11.29, has been so chosen that the y-axis passes through *A*, and let the coordinates of *A* be (0, 0). Let line *EB* as first approximation, divide the area enclosed by the traverse in two halves. Considering the closed traverse *BAFEB*, the length and direction of *EB* are found as below:

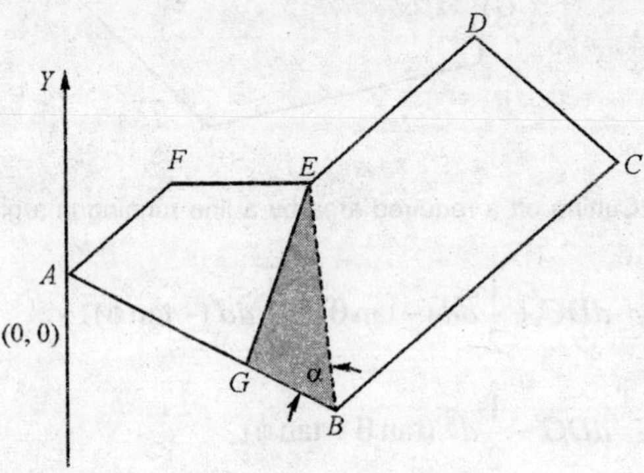

Fig. 11.29

$$\Sigma D = 388.84 + D_{BE} - 251.85 - 151.75 = 0$$

$$D_{BE} = 14.76 \text{ m}$$

$$\Sigma L = -113.92 + L_{BE} - 13.53 - 182.95 = 0$$

$$L_{BE} = 310.40 \text{ m.}$$

Therefore,

$$BE = \sqrt{D_{BE}^2 + L_{BE}^2}$$

$$= \sqrt{14.76^2 + 310.40^2}$$

$$= 310.75 \text{ m.}$$

Azimuth of *BE* is

$$A_{BE} = \tan^{-1} \frac{D_{BE}}{L_{BE}}$$

$$= \tan^{-1} \frac{14.74}{310.40}$$

$$= 2°43'21''.$$

Bearing of $BE = 2°43'21''$

Bearing of $EB = 180° + 2°43'21''$

$= 182°43'21''.$

Azimuth of *AB* is

$$A_{AB} = \tan^{-1}\frac{D_{AB}}{L_{AB}}$$

$$= \tan^{-1}\frac{388.84}{113.92}$$

$$= 73°40'15''.$$

Bearing of $AB = 180° - 73°40'15''$
$= 106°19'45''.$

Bearing of $BA = 180° + 106°19'45''$
$= 286°19'45''$

Angle *ABE* is given by

$$\alpha = 360° - (\text{bearing of } BA - \text{bearing of } BE)$$
$$= 360° - (286°19'45'' - 2°43'21'')$$
$$= 76°23'36''.$$

The area enclosed by stations *A*, *B*, *E*, and *F* is equal to the half of the total area. If the area of *ABEF* is A_1, then

$$A_1 = \frac{157250}{2} = 78625 \text{ m}^2.$$

Writing the coordinates of *A*, *B*, *E*, and *F* in determinant form, we have

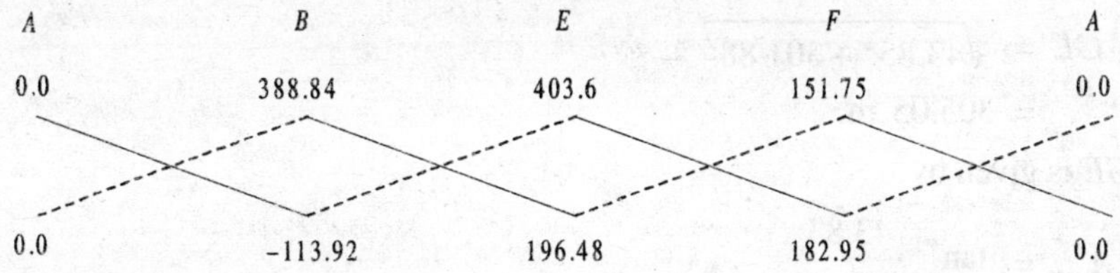

A	B	E	F	A
0.0	388.84	403.6	151.75	0.0
0.0	-113.92	196.48	182.95	0.0

From Eq. (11.5), The area is equal to

$$A = \frac{1}{2}\times[\,0.0\times(-113.92) - 0.0\times 388.84 + 388.84\times 196.48 - (-113.92)\times 403.60$$
$$+ 403.60\times 182.95 - 196.48\times 151.75 + 151.75\times 0.0 - 182.95\times 0.0]$$
$$= 83200 \text{ m}^2.$$

Excess area $A_2 = A - A_1$
$= 83200 - 78625$
$= 4575 \text{ m}^2.$

From Eq. (11.44), the distance *BG* is given by

$$BG = \frac{2A_2}{BE\sin\alpha}$$

$$= \frac{2\times4575}{310.75\times\sin 76°23'36''}$$

$$= 30.2952 \text{ m.}$$

Departure of $BG = D_{BG} = -BG \sin A_{AB}$

$$= -30.2952 \times \sin 73°40'15''$$

$$= -29.07 \text{ m}$$

Latitude of $BG = L_{BG} = +BG \cos A_{AB}$

$$= +30.2952 \times \cos 73°40'15''$$

$$= +8.52 \text{ m.}$$

Departure and latitude of G

$$D_G = D_B + D_{BG} = 388.84 - 29.07 = +359.77 \text{ m}$$

$$L_G = L_B + L_{BG} = -113.92 + 8.52 = -105.40 \text{ m}$$

If the departure and latitude of GE are D_{GE} are L_{GE}, respectively, then in the closed traverse $AGEFA$, we have

$$\Sigma D = 359.77 + D_{GE} - 251.85 - 151.75 = 0$$

or $$D_{GE} = 43.83 \text{ m}$$

$$\Sigma L = -105.40 + L_{GE} - 13.53 - 182.95 = 0$$

or $$L_{GE} = 301.88 \text{ m.}$$

The length of GE is given by

$$GE = \sqrt{43.83^2 + 301.88^2}$$

$$= 305.05 \text{ m.}$$

Azimuth of GE is given by

$$A_{GE} = \tan^{-1}\frac{43.83}{301.88}$$

$$= 8°15'40''$$

or $$A_{EG} = 188°15'40''.$$

Writing the coordinates of A, G, E, and F in determinant form , we have

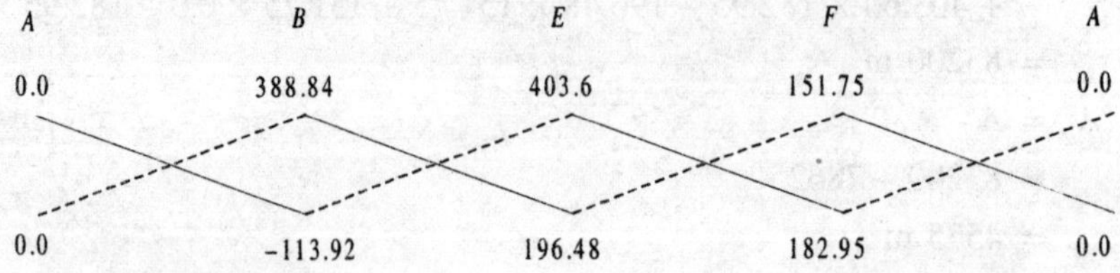

Check :

The area of $AGEF$ is

$$A_3 = \frac{1}{2} \times [0.0 \times (-105.40) - 0.0 \times 359.77 + 359.77 \times 196.48 - (-105.40)$$

$$\times 403.60 + 403.60 \times 182.95 - 196.48 \times 151.75 + 151.75 \times 0.0 - 182.95 \times 0.0]$$

$$= 78625 \text{ m}^2.$$

Thus

length of the cut off line EG = **305.05 m**

azimuth of the cut off line BG = **188°15′40″**.

Example 11.11

The area enclosed by a traverse shown in Fig. 11.30, is to be divided such that one-fourth of the enclosed area lies south of a line parallel to the x-axis. Compute the coordinates for the intersection of the dividing line with the traverse sides. The data for the traverse are given in Example 11.10.

Solution (Fig. 11.30):

Let the initial dividing line AG passes through A. Since AG is parallel to the x-axis, the y-coordinates of A and G will be same. Let the coordinates of A be (0, 150), then the coordinates of the other points are as under:

Point	X	Y
A	0.00	150.00
B	388.84	36.08
C	673.97	214.94
D	539.01	510.79
E	403.60	346.48
F	151.75	332.95
A	0.00	150.00

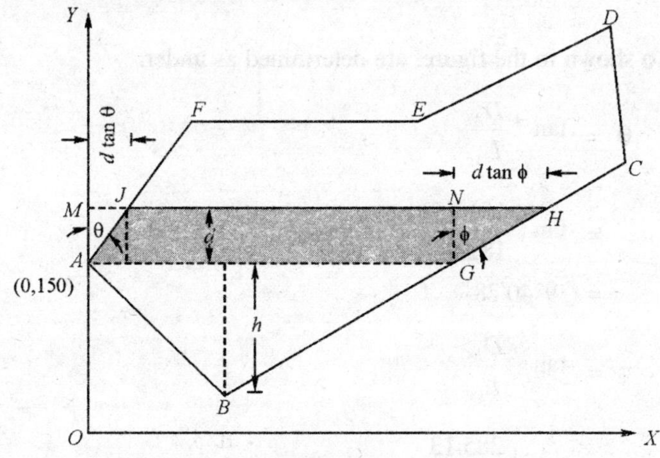

Fig. 11.30

We know that the coordinates of a point G (X_G, Y_G) lying on a line BC, can be determined from the following equation if the coordinates of B (X_B, Y_B) and C (X_C, Y_C) are known.

$$\frac{Y_G - Y_B}{Y_C - Y_B} = \frac{X_G - X_B}{X_C - X_B}$$

Since, $Y_G = Y_A = 150$

$$\frac{150 - 36.08}{214.94 - 36.08} = \frac{X_G - 388.84}{673.97 - 388.84}$$

or $X_G = 570.446$ m

Thus the coordinates of G are

$$X_G = 570.446 \text{ m}$$
$$Y_G = 150.000 \text{ m}$$

In triangle ABG

$$AG = X_G = 570.446 \text{ m}$$
$$h = (Y_G - Y_B) = 150.00 - 36.08 = 113.92 \text{ m.}$$

The area of the triangle ABG is

$$A_1 = \frac{1}{2} h\, AG$$
$$= \frac{1}{2} \times 113.92 \times 570.446$$
$$= 32493 \text{ m}^2.$$

The total area A of the traverse is 157250 m^2 and the required area A_2 is

$$A_2 = \frac{1}{4} A = \frac{1}{4} \times 157250 = 39313 \text{ m}^2$$

The area A_1 of the triangle ABG is too small by 39313 – 32493 = 6820 m^2 (= A_3). To increase the area of the triangle ABG, the dividing line is moved parallel to itself to position JH by a distance d from the original line.

The angles θ and ϕ shown in the figure, are determined as under:

$$\theta = \tan^{-1} \frac{D_{AF}}{L_{AF}}$$
$$= \tan^{-1} \frac{151.75}{182.95}$$
$$= 39°40'28''$$

$$\phi = \tan^{-1} \frac{D_{BC}}{L_{BC}}$$
$$= \tan^{-1} \frac{285.13}{178.86}$$
$$= 57°54'01''.$$

The area of the trapezoid *AJHG* is

$$A_3 = \text{Area } AMNG - \text{area } AMJ + \text{area } GNH$$

$$= dAG - \frac{1}{2} dd \tan\theta + \frac{1}{2} dd \tan\phi$$

$$2A_3 = 2dAG + d^2 (\tan\phi - \tan\theta)$$

or $(\tan\phi - \tan\theta)d^2 + 2dAG - 2A_3 = 0$

$$[\tan 57°54'01'' - \tan 39°40'28'']d^2 + 2 \times 570.446\, d - 2 \times 6820 = 0$$

$$0.7646909\, d^2 + 1140.892\, d - 13640 = 0$$

The solution of this quadratic equation is

$$d = \frac{-1140.892 \pm \sqrt{1140.892^2 + 4 \times 0.7646909 \times 13640}}{2 \times 0.7646909}$$

$$= 11.86 \text{ m.}$$

The departures and latitudes of line *JA* and *GH* are

$$D_{JA} = d \tan\theta = 11.86 \times \tan 39°40'28''$$

$$= 9.84 \text{ m}$$

$$L_{JA} = d = 11.86 \text{ m}$$

$$D_{GH} = d \tan\phi = 11.86 \times \tan 57°54'01''$$

$$= 18.91 \text{ m}$$

$$L_{GH} = d = 11.86 \text{ m}$$

The coordinates of the points *J* and *H* are

$$X_J = X_A + D_{JA} = 0.0 + 9.84 = \mathbf{9.84 \text{ m}}$$

$$Y_J = Y_A + L_{JA} = 150 + 11.86 = \mathbf{161.86 \text{ m}}$$

$$X_H = X_G + D_{GH} = 570.446 + 18.91 = \mathbf{589.36 \text{ m}}$$

$$Y_H = Y_G + L_{GH} = 150 + 11.86 = \mathbf{161.86 \text{ m.}}$$

The coordinates of the points *A*, *B*, *H*, *J*, and *A* in determinant form are

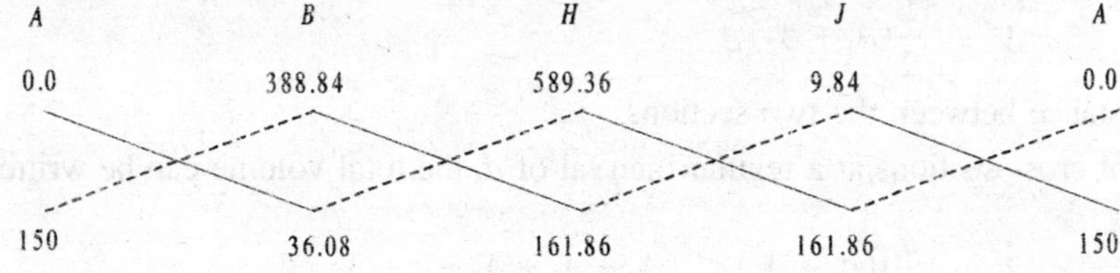

Check:

Area of *ABHJ* from Eq. (11.5), is

$$A_2 = \frac{1}{2} \times [0.0 \times 36.08 - 150 \times 388.84 + 388.84 \times 161.86 - 36.08 \times 589.36$$
$$+ 589.36 \times 161.86 - 161.86 \times 9.84 + 150 - 161.86 \times 0.0]$$

$$= 39313 \text{ m}^2.$$

11.9 VOLUMES

Earthwork operations involve the determination of the volumes of materials that must be excavated or embanked in an engineering project to bring the ground surface to a predetermined grade, and the setting of stakes to aid in carrying out the construction work according to the plans. The field work includes the measurements of the solids that make up the volumes, the setting of grade stakes, and keeping the field notes. The office work involves the computations of the measured volumes, and determination of the most economic manner of performing the work.

The units used for measurement in earthwork computations are metre (m), the square metre (m^2) and the cubic metre (m^3).

For the computation of volumes of some simple solids, formulae are given in Appendix-K.

Measurement of Volumes

Measurement of volumes may be made by one of the following methods:

1. From cross-sections
2. From spot levels
3. From contours.

The first two methods are generally employed in calculation of earthwork either in cutting or in embankment. Third method is used for the calculation of reservoir capacity.

Calculation of volumes from cross-sections

The volume of the earthwork between cross-sections taken along a route may be calculated by one of the following methods:

1. Average end-area (or trapezoidal) formula
2. Prismodial formula.

1. Volume by average end-area (or trapezoidal) formula

According to the end-area formula, the volume between two cross-sections having areas A_1 and A_2, is

$$V = \frac{1}{2}(A_1 + A_2)\, d \qquad \text{...(11.46)}$$

where d is the distance between the two sections.

For a series of cross-sections at a regular interval of d, the total volume can be written as

$$V = \frac{d}{2}[(A_1 + A_n) + 2(A_2 + A_3 + A_4 + \ldots + A_{n-1})]$$

$$= d\left[\frac{A_1 + A_n}{2} + A_2 + A_3 + \ldots + A_{n-1}\right] \qquad \text{...(11.47)}$$

where n is the number of segments in which the total length L between the end areas has been divided; *i.e.*, $L = nd$.

Although this relationship is not exact one when applied to many earthwork sections, it is the one most commonly used beause of the ease of its application, and because of the fact that the computed volumes are generally too great and thus the error is in favour of contractor.

2. Volume by prismoidal formula

When the more exact volume is required to be computed, the prismoidal formula given below, is used.

$$V = \frac{2d}{6}(A_1 + 4M + A_2) \qquad ...(11.48)$$

In Eq. (11.48), A_1 and A_2 are the two end cross-sections at a distance of $2d$, and M is the area of the middle section. In general, M will not be the mean of the two end areas. This formula is correct for determining the volumes of prisms, pyramids, wedges, and prismoids that have irregular end sections and sides that are warped surfaces. The prismoidal formula gives very nearly the correct volume of earthwork.

If the sections A_1, A_2, A_3, ... A_n are at a regular interval of d, the volume between the sections A_1 and A_3 will be

$$V_1 = \frac{2d}{6}(A_1 + 4A_2 + A_3)$$

$$= \frac{d}{3}[(A_1 + A_3) + 4A_2]$$

The volume between the section A_3 and A_5 will be

$$V_2 = \frac{d}{3}[(A_3 + A_5) + 4A_2]$$

Similarly, the volumes between other sections can be computed. The total volume will be sum of all the volumes. Thus,

$$V = V_1 + V_2 + V_3 + ... + V_n$$

$$= \frac{d}{3}[(A_1 + A_3) + 4A_2 + (A_3 + A_5) + 4A_4 + ... + (A_{n-2} + A_n) + 4A_{n-1}]$$

$$= \frac{d}{3}[(A_1 + A_n) + 4(A_2 + A_4 + ... + A_{n-1} + 2(A_3 + A_5 + ... + A_{n-2})] \qquad ...(11.49)$$

$$= \frac{d}{3} \text{ [Sum of the areas of end sections + 4 (sum of remaining even sections)}$$

$$\text{+ 2 (sum of remaining odd sections)}$$

Prismoidal correction

Since the average end-areas formula is not as accurate as the prismoidal formula for computations of volume, its accuracy can be increased by applying a correction called the *prismoidal correction.* It has been stated above that the volume calculated from the end-area formula is somewhat greater than that obtained by the prismoidal formula, therefore, this correction is always negative. Thus,

$$C_{pc} = \text{Volume by end-areas formula} - \text{volume by prismoidal formula}$$

$$= d(A_1 + A_2) - \frac{d}{3}(A_1 + 4M + A_2)$$

$$= \frac{2d}{3}(A_1 + A_2 - 2M) \qquad \text{... (11.50)}$$

where M is the area of the middle section.

For the different types of the sections discussed in Sec. 11.7, the height of fill or depth of cut, designated as h_M, at the midpoint of the formation for middle section, can be determined from the heights of the end sections. M can be computed from h_M.

For a level section from Eq. (11.34), the areas of the end sections are given by

$$A_1 = (b + sh_1)h_1 \text{ and } A_2 = (b + sh_2)h_2$$

Also $$h_M = \frac{h_1 + h_2}{2}$$

Therefore,

$$M = \left[b + s\left(\frac{h_1 + h_2}{2}\right)\right]\left(\frac{h_1 + h_2}{2}\right)$$

Thus, from Eq. (11.50), we have

$$C_{pc} = \frac{2d}{3}\left[(b + sh_1)h_1 + (b + sh_2)h_2 - 2\left\{b + s\left(\frac{h_1 + h_2}{2}\right)\right\}\left(\frac{h_1 + h_2}{2}\right)\right]$$

By rearranging and clearing the terms, we get

$$C_{pc} = \frac{d}{3}s(h_1 - h_2)^2 \qquad \text{...(11.51)}$$

In the similar manner, the formulae to compute the prismoidal correction can be obtained for other types of sections. The formulae for obtaining the prismoidal corrections for different sections are given below (*c.f.*; Sec. 11.7).

Level section

$$C_{pc} = \frac{2d}{6}s(h_1 - h_2)^2$$

Two-level section

$$C_{pc} = \frac{d}{6}s\left[\frac{n^2}{n^2 - s^2}\right](h_1 - h_2)^2 \qquad \text{...(11.52)}$$

Three-level section

$$C_{pc} = \frac{d}{6}s\left[\frac{n^2}{n^2 - s^2}\right](h_1 - h_2)^2 \qquad \text{...(11.53)}$$

Sidehill two-level section

$$C_{pc} = \frac{d}{12(n-s)} n^2 (h_1 - h_2)^2 \qquad ...(11.54)$$

Curvature correction

The average end-area method for calculating volumes is based on parallel end-areas, *i.e.*, the two cross-sections are normal to the centre-line of the route. When the centre-line is curved, the cross-sections are set out in the radial direction and, therefore, they are not parallel to one another. Hence volume computed on curves will have discrepancies, and need correction.

According to Pappus' theorem, a plane area revolving about an axis generates a volume equal to the product of the revolving area and the path generated by the centroid of the revolving area.

If an area A is revolved through a distance of L, the volume of the solid generated is

$$V = AL \qquad ...(11.55)$$

Fig. 11.31a shows two sections 1–1′ and 2–2′ in plan, having their centroids at a distance of e from the centre-line. The distance e is called eccentricity of the cross-sections. Fig. 11.31b is the side view of one of the sections.

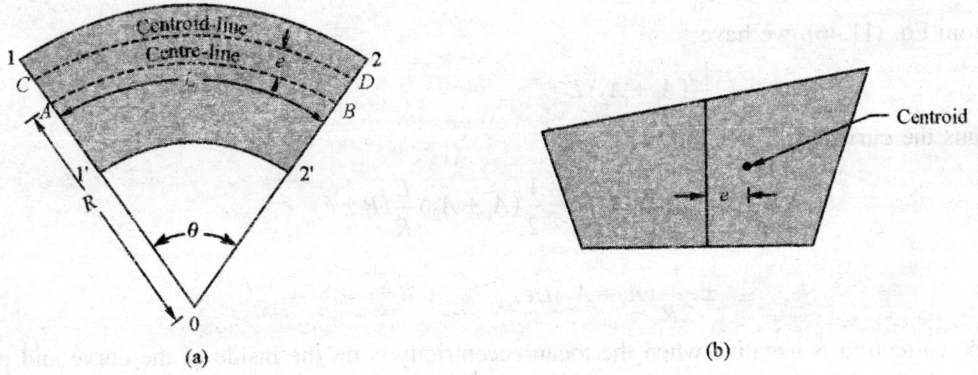

Fig. 11.31 Volume of the solid generated by revolving a section

If R is the radius of the curve with centre at O, the angle θ at the centre is given by

$$\theta = \frac{2\pi}{2\pi R} L = \frac{L}{R} \text{ radians} \qquad ...(11.56)$$

The length of the path CD traced by centroid is

$$L_c = \theta\,(R + e) \qquad ...(11.57)$$

From Eq. (11.56) and (11.57), we get

$$L_c = \frac{L}{R}(R+e)$$

As the centroid-line may lie on either side of the centre-line, in general

$$L_c = \frac{L}{R}(R \pm e) \qquad ...(11.58)$$

The eccentricity e is negative when it is inside the centre and centre-line, and positive when outside. The volume of the solid generated from Eq. (11.55), will be

$$V = A\,L_c$$

$$= \frac{AL}{R}(R \pm e) \qquad ...(11.59)$$

If the two cross-sections have different areas A_1 and A_2, and their eccentricities are e_1 and e_2 then the Eq. (11.59) is modified as

$$V = \left[\frac{A_1 + A_2}{2}\right]\frac{L}{R}(R \pm \bar{e}) \qquad ...(11.60)$$

where $\bar{e}$ = the means eccentricity $\left[\frac{e_1 + e_2}{2}\right]$

If the position of the centroid changes from one side of the centre-line to other side, the mean eccentricity $\bar{e}$ is obtained from the algebraic sum of e_1 and e_2.

If the volume by the average end-area formula for the two section A_1 and A_2, is V_0, and the curvature correction is C_e then

$$C_e = V_0 - V$$

From Eq. (11.46), we have

$$V_0 = \frac{1}{2}(A_1 + A_2)\,L$$

Thus the curvature correction is

$$C_e = \frac{1}{2}(A_1 + A_2)\,L - \frac{1}{2}(A_1 + A_2)\frac{L}{R}(R \pm \bar{e})$$

$$= \pm\frac{1}{2R}(A_1 + A_2)L\bar{e} \qquad ...(11.61)$$

The correction is negative when the mean eccentricity is on the inside of the curve and positive when on the outside.

The curvature correction can also be expressed as

$$C_e = \pm\frac{L}{2R}(A_1 e_1 + A_2 e_2) \qquad ...(11.62)$$

For the computation of curvature correction for different types of the sections, the formulae are given below (*c.f.*, sec. 11.6).

Level Section

No correction is needed, since the area is symmetrical about the centre-line, and, therefore,

$$C_e = 0 \qquad ...(11.63)$$

Two-level section

$$C_e = \frac{L}{6R}(w_1^2 - w_2^2)\left[h + \frac{b}{2s}\right] \qquad ...(11.64)$$

where R is the radius of the curve.

Sometimes a correction is applied to the area of the cross-section to get the equivalent areas and then use them in the prismoidal formula to get the corrected volume.

Three-level section

Correction to the area

$$C_{ae} = \frac{Ae}{R} \text{ per unit length} \quad ...(11.65)$$

where $$e = \pm\frac{w_1 w_2 (w_1 + w_2)}{3nA} \quad ...(11.66)$$

The size of the correction will depend on the sign of the eccentricity which is positive when outside the curve and negative when inside.

Sidehill two-level section

Correction to area

$$C_{ae} = \frac{Ae}{R} \text{ per unit length} \quad ...(11.67)$$

where $$e = \frac{1}{3}\left(w_1 + \frac{b}{2} - sh\right) \text{ for the larger area}$$

and $$e = \frac{1}{3}\left(w_1 + \frac{b}{2} + sh\right) \text{ for the smaller area}$$

ILLUSTRATIVE EXAMPLES

Example 11.12

A road embankment is 30 m wide at the top with side slopes of 2 to 1. The ground levels at 100 m intervals along a line AB are as under:

A 170.3, 169.1, 168.5, 168.1, 166.5 B

The formation level at A is 178.7 m with a uniform falling gradient of 1 in 50 from A to B. Determine the volume of earthwork by prismoidal formula. Assume the ground to be level in cross-section.

Solution:

The falling gradient from A to B is 1 in 50. Therefore, the fall at every 100 m will be

$$= \frac{1}{50} \times 100 = 2 \text{ m}$$

The formation level at A, 0 m = 178.7 m
The formation level at 100 m = 178.7 – 2.0 = 176.7 m
The formation level at 200 m = 176.7 – 2.0 = 174.7 m
The formation level at 300 m = 174.7 – 2.0 = 172.7 m

The formation level at B, 400 m = 172.7 – 2.0 = 170.7 m.

The height of the embankment at various section is given by

= Formation level – ground level

Thus,

The height at A, 0 m = 178.7 – 170.3 = 8.4 m

The height at 100 m = 176.7 – 169.1 = 7.6 m

The height at 200 m = 174.7 – 168.5 = 6.2 m

The height at 300 m = 172.7 – 168.1 = 4.6 m

The height at B, 400 m = 170.7 – 166.5 = 4.2 m.

From Eq. (11.34), the area of cross-section for a level section is given by

$$A = h\,(b + sh)$$

Area at A, 0 m = A_1 = $8.4 \times (30 + 2 \times 8.4) = 393.12$ m^2

Area at 100 m = A_2 = $7.6 \times (30 + 2 \times 7.6) = 343.52$ m^2

Area at 200 m = A_3 = $6.2 \times (30 + 2 \times 6.2) = 262.88$ m^2

Area at 300 m = A_4 = $4.6 \times (30 + 2 \times 4.6) = 180.32$ m^2

Area at B, 400 m = A_5 = $4.2 \times (30 + 2 \times 4.2) = 161.28$ m^2.

From Eq. (11.49), the volume

$$V = \frac{d}{3}[(A_1 + A_5) + 4(A_2 + A_4) + 2A_3]$$

$$= \frac{100}{3}\;[(393.12 + 161.28) + 4 \times (343.52 + 180.32) + 2 \times 262.88]$$

$$= \mathbf{105851\ m^2}.$$

Example 11.13

A road embankment 50 m wide at formation level with side slopes 1 to 1, and with an average height of 12 m, is constructed with an average gradient of 1 in 30 from contour 120 to 610 m. If the ground slope in the transverse direction is 10 to 1, calculate the volume of the earthwork.

Solution:

If the gradient of the road is 1 in m and the difference of levels between two points A and B, is Δh, the distance AB is given by

$$AB = m\,\Delta h$$

Therefore, the length of the road is

$$L = 30 \times (610 - 120) = 14700 \text{ m}.$$

Since the ground is sloping in the transverse direction, the cross-sections are two-level sections (*c.f.*, Fig. 11.21), their areas are given by Eq. (11.35).

Thus,

$$A = \frac{n^2 s}{n^2 - s^2}\left[h + \frac{b}{2s}\right]^2 - \frac{b^2}{4s}$$

It is given that

$$n = 10$$
$$s = 1$$
$$b = 50 \text{ m}$$
$$h = 12 \text{ m}$$

Thus,

$$A = \frac{10^2 \times 1}{10^2 - 1^2}\left[12 + \frac{50}{2 \times 1}\right]^2 - \frac{50^2}{4 \times 1}$$

$$= 757.83 \text{ m}^2.$$

The volume of the earthwork is

$$V = LA$$
$$= 14700 \times 757.83$$
$$= \mathbf{11140101\ m^3}.$$

Example 11.14

An embankment is to be constructed on a curve of radius 350 m. The specifications for the constructions are as below:

Formation width = 15 m

Side slopes = 2 to 1

Height of embankment at midpoint = 5 m

Ground downward slope towards the centre of the curve = 5 to 1

Calculate the curvature correction per 30 m length.

Solution:

The given data for a two-level section are

$$b = 15 \text{ m}$$
$$h = 5 \text{ m}$$
$$s = 2$$
$$n = 5$$
$$L = 30 \text{ m}$$
$$R = 350 \text{ m}$$

From Sec. 11.36, we have

$$w_1 = \frac{b}{2} + \frac{ns}{n-s}\left[h + \frac{b}{2n}\right]$$

$$w_2 = \frac{b}{2} + \frac{ns}{n+s}\left[h + \frac{b}{2n}\right]$$

Therefore,
$$w_1 = \frac{15}{2} + \frac{5\times 2}{5-2}\times\left[5 + \frac{15}{2\times 5}\right] = 29.17 \text{ m}$$

$$w_2 = \frac{15}{2} + \frac{5\times 2}{5+2}\times\left[5 - \frac{15}{2\times 5}\right] = 12.50 \text{ m}$$

From Eq. (11.64), the curvature correction for a two-level section is

$$C_e = \frac{L}{6R}\left(w_1^2 - w_2^2\right)\left[h + \frac{h}{2s}\right]$$

$$= \frac{30}{6\times 350}\times(29.17^2 - 12.50^2)\times\left[5 + \frac{15}{2\times 2}\right]$$

$$= \mathbf{86.83\ m^3}.$$

Example 11.15

Width of formation level of a certain cutting is 10 m and the side slopes are 1:1. The surface of the ground has a uniform transverse slope of 1 in 6. If the depth of cutting at the centre-lines of three sections 30 m apart, are 3 m, 4 m, and 5 m, determine the volume of earthwork involved in this length of cutting by (1) average end-area formula, and (2) prismoidal formula. Also calculate the prismoidal correction, and calculate the corrected volume obtained from average end-area formula.

Solution (Fig. 11.21):

The given data are

b = 10 m

h = 3 m, 4 m, 5 m

n = 6

s = 1

d = 30 m

From Eq. (11.35), the area of two-level section is

$$A = \frac{n^2 s}{n^2 - s^2}\left[h + \frac{b}{2s}\right]^2 - \frac{b^2}{4s}$$

$$A_1 = \frac{6^2\times 1}{6^2 - 1^2}\times\left[3 + \frac{10}{2\times 1}\right]^2 - \frac{10^2}{4\times 1}$$

$$= 40.828 \text{ m}^2.$$

$$A_2 = \frac{6^2\times 1}{6^2 - 1^2}\times\left[4 + \frac{10}{2\times 1}\right]^2 - \frac{10^2}{4\times 1}$$

$$= 58.314 \text{ m}^2.$$

$$A_3 = \frac{6^2 \times 1}{6^2 - 1^2} \times \left[5 + \frac{10}{2 \times 1}\right]^2 - \frac{10^2}{5 \times 1}$$

$$= 77.857 \text{ m}^2.$$

(1) By average end-area formula

From Eq. (11.47), we have

$$V_a = d\left[\frac{A_1 + A_3}{2} + A_2\right]$$

$$= 30 \times \left[\frac{40.828 + 77.857}{2} + 58.314\right]$$

$$= \mathbf{3529.70\ m^3}.$$

(2) By prismoidal formula

From Eq. (11.49), we have

$$V_P = \frac{d}{3}[(A_1 + A_3) + 4A_2]$$

$$= \frac{30}{3} \times [40.828 + 77.857 + 4 \times 58.314]$$

$$= \mathbf{3519.41\ m^3}.$$

From Eq. (11.52), the prismoidal correction for the two-level section is

$$C_{pc} = \frac{d}{6} s \left[\frac{n^2}{n^2 - s^2}\right](h_1 - h_2)^2$$

The correction between A_1 and A_2 is

$$C_{pc1} = \frac{d}{6} s \frac{n^2}{n^2 - s^2}(h_1 - h_2)^2$$

The correction between A_2 and A_3 is

$$C_{pc2} = \frac{d}{6} s \frac{n^2}{n^2 - s^2}(h_2 - h_3)^2$$

Total correction

$$C_{pc} = C_{pc1} + C_{pc2}$$

$$= \frac{d}{6} s \frac{n^2}{n^2 - s^2}[(h_1 - h_2)^2 + (h_2 - h_3)^2]$$

$$= \frac{30 \times 1}{6} \times \frac{6^2}{6^2 - 1^2}[(3-4)^2 + (4-5)^2]$$

$$= \mathbf{10.29\ m^3}.$$

The corrected volume obtained by the average end-area formula is

$$V = 3529.70 - 10.29$$
$$= \mathbf{3519.41\ m^3}.$$
$$= V_p$$

Example 11.16

The width at formation of a road is 12 m with side slopes of 1 in 1 in cutting and 1 in 2 in filling. The original ground has a cross-fall of 1 in 5. If the depth of excavation at the centre-lines of the two sections 50 m apart, are 0.4 m and 0.8 m, respectively, determine the volume of cutting and filling over this length.

Solution (Fig. 11.23):

For a sidehill two-level section from Eq. (11.38), area in cutting is

$$A_c = \frac{1}{2}\frac{\left[\frac{b}{2}+nh\right]^2}{n-s}$$

and from Eq. (11.39), area in embankment

$$A_e = \frac{1}{2}\frac{\left[\frac{b}{2}-nh\right]^2}{n-s}$$

It is given that

$$b = 12\text{ m}$$
$$h = 0.4\text{ m, } 0.8\text{ m}$$
$$n = 5$$
$$s_1 = 1\text{ in cutting}$$
$$s_2 = 2\text{ in embankment}$$

At the first section

$$A_{c1} = \frac{1}{2}\times\frac{\left[\frac{12}{2}+5\times 0.4\right]^2}{(5-1)} = 8.00\text{ m}^2$$

$$A_{e1} = \frac{1}{2}\times\frac{\left[\frac{12}{2}-5\times 0.4\right]^2}{5-2} = 2.67\text{ m}^2$$

At the second section

$$A_{c2} = \frac{1}{2}\times\frac{\left[\frac{12}{2}+5\times 0.8\right]^2}{5-1} = 12.50\text{ m}^2$$

$$A_{e2} = \frac{1}{2} \times \frac{\left[\frac{12}{2} - 5 \times 0.8\right]^2}{5-2} = 0.67 \text{ m}^2$$

The volume by average end-area formula

(*i*) For cutting

$$= \frac{8+12.5}{2} \times 50 = 512.50 \text{ m}^2$$

Prismoidal correction from Eq. (11.54), is

$$= \frac{d}{12(n-s)} n^2 (h_1 - h_2)^2$$

$$= \frac{50}{12 \times (5-1)} \times 5^2 \times (0.4 - 0.8)^2$$

$$= 4.17 \text{ m}^3$$

Corrected volume

$$V_c = 512.50 - 4.17$$

$$= \mathbf{508.33 \ m^3.}$$

(*ii*) For embankment

$$= \frac{2.67 + 0.67}{2} \times 50$$

$$= \mathbf{83.50 \ m^3.}$$

Prismoidal correction

$$= \frac{50}{12 \times (5-2)} \times 5^2 \times (0.4 - 0.8)^2$$

$$= 5.56 \text{ m}^2$$

Corrected volume

$$V_e = 83.50 - 5.56$$

$$= \mathbf{77.94 \ m^3.}$$

Calculation of volumes from spot levels

This method is suitable for large excavations. The volume of a barrow pit or of the excavation for the foundation of a building, is frequently found by dividing the surface area into triangles, squares or rectangles. The original ground surface elevations at the corners of these figures are usually determined by direct levelling. The final elevations are obtained either by repeating the levelling after excavation has been completed or, in the case of building foundations from the plans of the structure. The vertical depth of each corner is calculated by subtracting the final elevation from the original ground surface elevation.

The volume of any prism is taken as the horizontal area of the prism multiplied by the average corner depths.

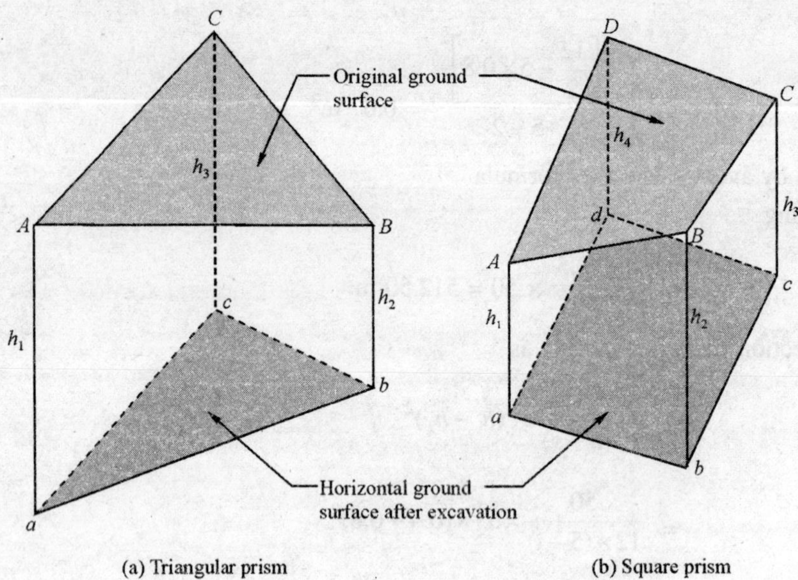

(a) Triangular prism

(b) Square prism

Fig. 11.32. Volume from the depth at the corners

If A is the area of the horizontal base of the prism and h_1, h_2, h_3, and h_4 represent the depths of the corners of the truncated prism, the volume of the truncated triangular prism (Fig. 11.32a) is

$$V = A\frac{(h_1 + h_2 + h_3)}{3} \qquad ...(11.68)$$

and the volume of the truncated square prism (Fig. 11.32b)

$$V = A\frac{(h_1 + h_2 + h_3 + h_4)}{4} \qquad ...(11.69)$$

The computations can be shortened by noting that some corner heights are common to more than one prism. The volume of the assembled truncated square or rectangular prism is

$$V = A\frac{(\Sigma h_1 + 2\Sigma h_2 + 3\Sigma h_3 + 4\Sigma h_4)}{4} \qquad ...(11.70)$$

where

Σh_1 = the sum of vertical depths common to one prism

Σh_2 = the sum of vertical depths common to two prisms

Σh_3 = the sum of vertical depths common to three prisms

Σh_4 = the sum of vertical depths common to four prisms.

ILLUSTRATIVE EXAMPLES

Example 11.17

The spot levels at the corners of the squares of size 25 m × 25 m, are shown in Fig. 11.33. If the area is to be brought to a finished grade elevation of 200.00 m, what would be the volume of the earthwork?

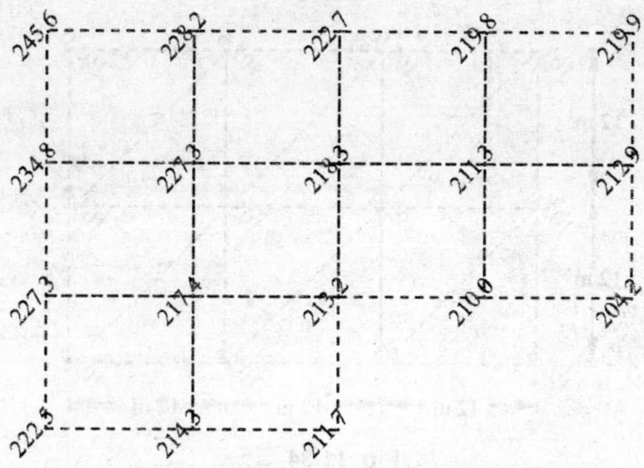

Fig. 11.33

The values 2456 is actually 245.6 and others are also like this but decimal is at the intersection of the lines, therefore not shown in the tigure.

Solution (Fig. 11.33):

The depth of the corners is equal to (h – 200.00), and their sums are as below:

$$\Sigma h_1 = 22.5 + 11.7 + 4.2 + 19.9 + 45.6$$
$$= 103.9 \text{ m}$$
$$\Sigma h_2 = 14.3 + 10.0 + 12.9 + 19.8 + 22.7 + 28.2 + 34.8 + 27.3$$
$$= 170.0 \text{ m}$$
$$\Sigma h_3 = 13.2 \text{ m}$$
$$\Sigma h_4 = 17.4 + 27.3 + 18.3 + 11.3$$
$$= 74.3 \text{ m.}$$

It is given that

$$A = 25 \times 25 = 625 \text{ m}^2.$$

Therefore, from Eq. (11.74), we have

$$V = A\frac{\Sigma h_1 + 2\Sigma h_2 + 3\Sigma h_3 + 4\Sigma h_4}{4}$$
$$= 625\times\frac{103.9+2\times170.0+3\times13.2+4\times74.3}{4}$$
$$= 121984 \text{ m}^3$$
$$\simeq \mathbf{122000\ m^3}.$$

Example 11.18

Determine the volume of the earthwork required for a tract of land shown in Fig. 11.34. The formation level is 101.00 m.

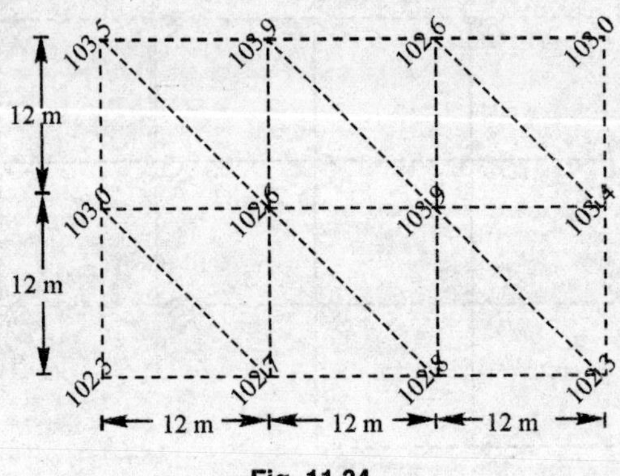

Fig. 11.34

The value 1035 is actually 103.5, and others are also like this but decimal is at the intersection of the lines, therefore not shown in the figure.

Solution (Fig. 11.34):

The height of each corner from the formation is obtained by subtracting the formation level from the spot levels and the same has been used to find Σh_1, Σh_2, Σh_3, etc., for the triangles.

$$\Sigma h_1 = 2.0 + 1.3 = 3.3 \text{ m}$$
$$\Sigma h_2 = 1.3 + 2.5 = 3.8 \text{ m}$$
$$\Sigma h_3 = 2.9 + 1.6 + 1.4 + 1.8 + 1.7 + 2.0 = 11.4$$
$$\Sigma h_4 = 0$$
$$\Sigma h_5 = 0$$
$$\Sigma h_6 = 1.6 + 2.9 = 4.5$$

and $$A = A = \frac{12 \times 12}{2} = 72 \text{ m}^2.$$

The volume of the earth work by triangular prisms is

$$= A\frac{(\Sigma h_1 + 2\Sigma h_2 + 3\Sigma h_3 + 4\Sigma h_4 + ...)}{3}$$

$$= 72 \times \frac{(3.3 + 2 \times 3.8 + 3 \times 11.4 + 6 \times 4.5)}{3}$$

$$= \mathbf{1730\ m^3}.$$

Calculation of volume from contours

Volume can also be determined using the contour lines drawn on a plan. This method gives approximate estimate of the volume since the contour interval is generally not sufficiently small to fully depict the irregularities of the ground. Also the ground slope between consecutive contours is not uniform. The general guideline for the contour interval is that it should not be more than 2 m on average ground, and 0.5 m on irregular ground. The method being approximate, it cannot compare with the determination of volumes using cross-sections, and therefore, is not much used except to determine the capacity of reservoirs, or to measure subaqeous excavation.

The contours are also used for the computation of earthwork on a specified gradient along a route.

Capacity of a reservoir

The plane containing any contour, represents a horizontal plane, and the area bounded by a contour is treated as the area of the cross-section. The vertical distance between any two adjacent cross-sections bounded by the contours, is equal to the contour interval. The area bounded by the contour is measured by a planimeter. Calculation of volume between any two contours can be done either by prismoidal formula or by end-area formula by adding the cubic contents between the successive contours (*c.f.*, Sec. 7.8).

In practice, the capacity of a reservoir is measured in terms of volume of water stored up to full reservoir level (F.R.L.) which is the level of water at its full capacity. In Fig. 11.35, the contour of 75 m has been marked as F.R.L. The contour interval being 5 m, the vertical distance h between the two adjacent contours, is 5 m. If the measured areas contained by the contours up to the face AB of the dam, be A_{75}, A_{70}, ... A_{45}, the reservoir capacity.

(*i*) by the average end-area formula is

$$V = h\left[\frac{A_{75} + A_{45}}{2} + A_{70} + A_{65} + A_{60} + A_{55} + A_{50}\right]$$

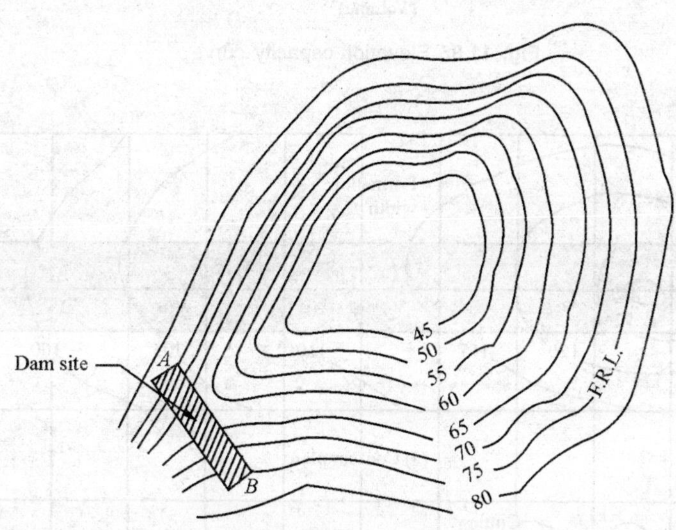

Fig. 11.35 Capacity of a reservoir

and (*ii*) by the prismoidal formula is

$$V = \frac{h}{3}[(A_{75} + A_{45}) + 4(A_{70} + A_{60} + A_{50}) + 2(A_{65} + A_{55})]$$

A curve, called *elevation-capacity curve* is generally drawn between the level of the water surface and the corresponding capacity of the reservoir to determine the capacity of the reservoir at a particular level of the water (Fig. 11.36).

Earthwork on a specified gradient

(*a*) L-section along a route AB can be plotted using a contour plan as shown in Fig. 11.37 (*c.f.*, Sec. 7.8). The line PQ at the required gradients having points at the predetermined elevations is drawn.

The depths of filling or cutting at various sections *a–a'*, *b–b'*, *c–c'*, etc., can be found from the L-section. The area of the cross-section is determined from the depth at the centre and side slopes. The volume of earthwork is then computed using average end-area formula or prismoidal formula.

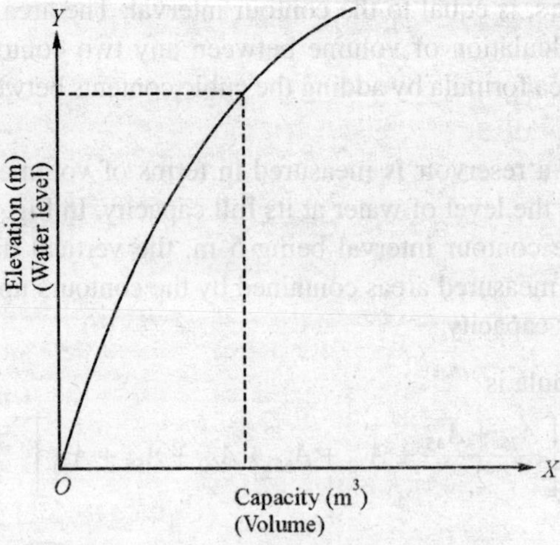

Fig. 11.36 Elevation-capacity curve

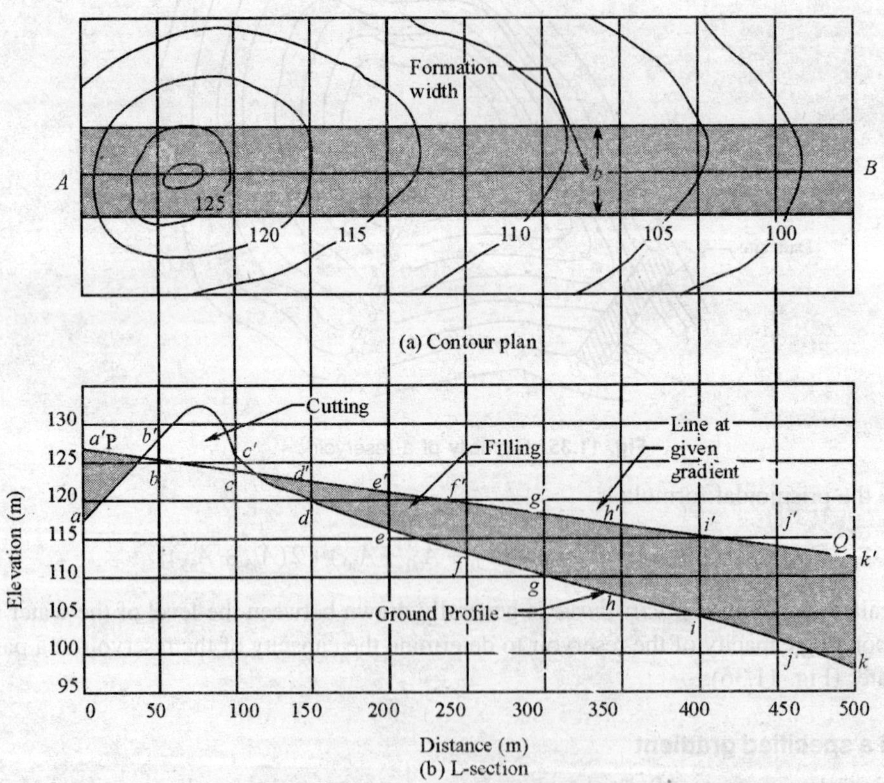

Fig. 11.37 Earthwork on a specified gradient along a route, formation width given

(*b*) If it is required to do earthwork excavation on a specified gradient and formation width is not given, then the earthwork computation are done as discussed below:

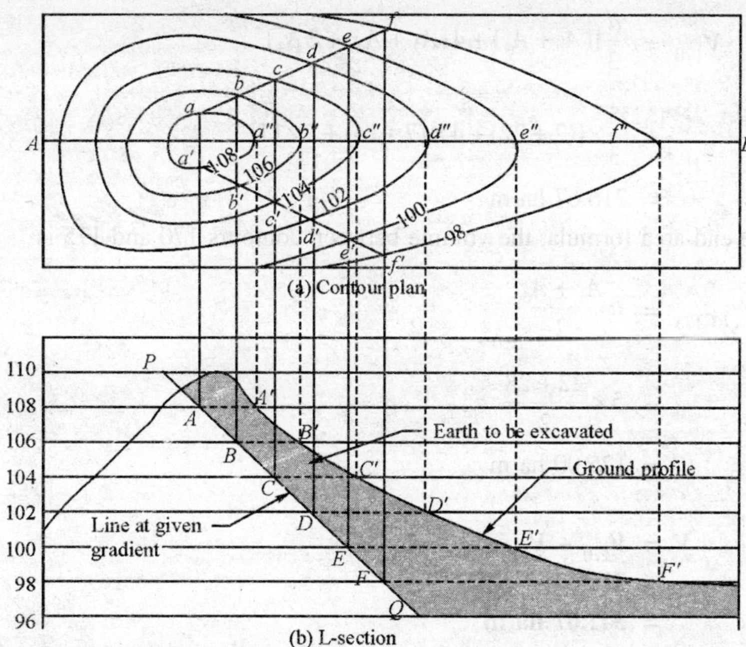

Fig. 11.38 Earthwork excavation on a specified gradient, formation width not given

In Fig. 11.38, the earth on the right side of the line *PQ* is to be excavated at the given gradient. Horizontal lines *AA*′, *BB*′, etc., are drawn through *A*, *B*, *C*, etc., to represent the horizontal planes through successive contours. Through the points *A*, *B*, *C*, etc., vertical lines are drawn to intersect the contours at *aa*′, *bb*′, *cc*′, etc. The areas are measured, and the volumes between two areas at a vertical distance of *d* which is contour interval, is computed using average end-area formula or prismoidal formula, and summed up together to get the total volume of the earthwork excavation. The ground surface shown as *abcdeff*′ *e*′*d*′*c*′*b*′*a*′ represent the face of the cutting in plan having finished gradient *ABCDEF*.

ILLUSTRATIVE EXAMPLES

Example 11.18

From a contour plan of a proposed reservoir area, the following data were found:

Contour (m)	150	155	160	165	170	175
Area* (ha)	2	7	11	14	22	28

*Enclosed by a contour

Determine (*i*) the capacity of the reservoir if the F.R.L. is 175.00 m, and (*ii*) the elevation of the water surface when the reservoir is at its half-capacity. The volume beow the contour of 150 may be ignored.

Solution:

(*i*) Using the prismoidal formula, the volume up to contour of R.L. 170 is

$$V_{170} = \frac{d}{3}[(A_1 + A_5) + 4(A_2 + A_4) + 2A_3]$$

$$= \frac{5}{3} \times [(2+22) + 4 \times (7+14) + 2 \times 11]$$

$$= 216.67 \text{ ha m}$$

and by average end-area formula, the volume between contours 170 and 175 is

$$V_{170\text{–}175} = h\frac{A_5 + A_6}{2}$$

$$= 5 \times \frac{22+28}{2}$$

$$= 125.00 \text{ ha m}$$

Total volume

$$V = V_{170} + V_{170\text{–}175}$$
$$= 216.67 + 125.0$$
$$= \mathbf{341.67 \text{ ha m}}$$

(*ii*) Half-capacity of the reservoir

$$= \frac{1}{2} \times 341.67$$

$$V' = \mathbf{170.84 \text{ ha m}}$$

As a first trial, let the half-capacity is between the R.L. of 165 and 170.

Capacity up to R.L. of 160

$$V_{160} = \frac{5}{3}[2 + 11 + 4 \times 7] = 68.33 \text{ ha m}$$

Capacity up to R.L. of 160 to 165

$$V_{160\text{–}165} = 5 \times \frac{(11+14)}{2} = 62.50 \text{ ha m}$$

Total capacity up to R.L. of 165

$$V_{165} = V_{160} + V_{160\text{–}165} = 68.33 + 62.50 = 130.83 \text{ ha m}$$

Capacity required above R.L. of 165

$$V'' = V' - V_{165} = 170.84 - 130.83 = 40.01 \text{ ha m}$$

Capacity up to R.L. of 170

$$V_{170} = 216.67 \text{ ha m}$$

Capacity between R.L. of 165 and 170

$$V_{165\text{–}170} = V_{170} - V_{165} = 216.67 - 130.83 = 85.84 \text{ ha m}$$

The elevation of the water surface when the reservoir is at its half-capacity

$$= 165 + 5 \times \frac{40.01}{85.84}$$

$$= \mathbf{167.33\ m.}$$

Example 11.19

The areas enclosed by contours of a hill and a lake situated side by side, are as under:

Hill	Contours (m)	100	110	120	130	140	150
	Area (m²)	5500	4000	2750	1500	500	0.0
Lake	Contours (m)	100	90	80	70	60	50
	Area (m²)	5000	3750	2500	1750	550	0.0

If the lake is to be filled upto 100 m level with the excavated earth from the hill, ascertain whether the excavated earth is sufficient or in excess. If in excess, upto what level the excavation is to done to just fill up the lake?

Solution:

The volume of the lake

$$V_{\text{Lake}} = \frac{10}{3}[5000 + 550 + 4 \times (3750 + 1750) + 2 \times 2500] + 10 \times \frac{(550 + 0.0)}{2}$$

$$= 111250 \text{ m}^3.$$

The volume of the earth from hill

$$V_{\text{Hill}} = \frac{10}{3}[5500 + 500 + 4 \times (4000 + 1500) + 2 \times 2750] + 10 \times \frac{(500 + 0.0)}{2}$$

$$= 114167 \text{ m}^3.$$

The volume of the earth required to fill up the lake is more by

$$= 114167 - 111250 = 2917 \text{ m}^3.$$

The volume of the earth between R.L. of 150 and 110 is

$$V_{150-110} = \frac{10}{3} \times [0.0 + 4000 + 4 \times (500 + 2750) + 2 \times 1500]$$

$$= 66667 \text{ m}^3.$$

The volume of the earth between R.L. of 110 and 100 is

$$V_{110-100} = 114167 - 66667$$

$$= 47500 \text{ m}^3.$$

The volume of the earth required to be excavated between R.L. 110 and 100 to make the total volume 111250 m³

$$= 111250 - 66667$$

$$= 44583 \text{ m}^3.$$

earth from R.L. of 110 is

$$0\times\frac{44583}{47500}$$

.3 m.

rface up to which excavation from the top is to be done to get the total

100 + (10 – 9.4)

100.6 m.

11.10 MASS DIAGRAM

A *mass diagram,* also called *mass-haul diagram,* is a curve between the cumulative volume of earthwork and the distance. It is a continuous curve whose ordinate represents the algebraic sum of the volumes of cutting and filling, and the abscissa represents the distance (Fig. 11.39b). The cumulative volume is the algebraic sum of the cutting taken as positive, and the filling taken as negative. If cuttings and fillings are on the same length of the longitudinal section, as in hillside roads, their difference only is used in the algebraic summation, and the sign of the greater volume is accepted in the computation.

It may also be noted that while computing volumes of the earthwork actually to be moved, due allowance is made for the swelling of the excavated material, and for the settlement and shrinkage (compaction) of the filled material. An ordinary soil may have an overall shrinkage (decrease) of about 10 to 20% when fully compacted. On the other hand, some rocks may have an overall bulking (increase) of 25 to 35%.

Basic Definitions

The following terms are associated with the excavation works in the engineering projects, and should be clearly understood.

Haul distance: It is the distance at any time between the working face of an excavation and the tip end of the embankment formed from the hauled material.

Average haul distance: It is the distance from the centre of gravity of a cutting to the filling.

Haul: It is equal to the total volume of the excavation multiplied by the average haul distance. It is also equal to the area between the mass curve and balancing line. The unit of haul is 1 station-metre where 1 station-metre = 1m^3 of material moved through one station (100 m).

Free-haul distance (F.H.D.): It is the distance up to which the hauling is done by the contractor free of charge.

Overhaul distance: If the excavated material from a cutting has to be moved a greater distance than the free-haul distance, the extra distance is known as overhaul distance.

Limit of economical haul (L.E.H.): It is the maximum limit of the haul distance beyond which it is not economical to use the material obtained from cuts. Beyond the limit of economical haul, it is more economical to waste the material or to take the material from the barrow pits than to haul it.

Balancing line: Any horizontal line drawn on the mass diagram is a balancing line because it balances the volume of cutting and filling. There is no difference in cumulative volume between two points where the balancing line cuts the mass diagram.

Barrow: It is the material needed for the embankment taken from barrow pits. [illegible] available from the excavation is not sufficient for the embankment, barrow pits are dug to tak[illegible] material.

Waste (spoil): It is the material excavated from cuts but not used for embankment.

Lead: It is the horizontal distance through which excavated material is moved from the cut to the required embankment. Generally, a lead of 30 m is included in the cost.

Lift: It is the vertical distance through which the excavated material from a cut is moved to the required embankment. Generally, a lift of 1.5 m is included in the cost.

Construction of Mass Diagram

The following steps are involved in the construction of a mass diagram:

1. Divide the length of route (road, railway) in separate sections of convenient distances.
2. Calculate the volume of earthwork of each section.
3. Plot the longitudinal section of each section of the route on a convenient scale (Fig. 11.39a).
4. Plot the volumes as ordinates and the distances as abscissa. The distances between the sections are kept the same as in the longitudinal section.
5. Plot the positive volumes above and negative volumes below, the base line.
6. Join the ends of the adjacent ordinates by a smooth curve to obtain the mass diagram (Fig. 11.39b).

The procedure of constructing a mass diagram will be more clear from the following illustrative example.

ILLUSTRATIVE EXAMPLE

Example 11.20

Draw a mass diagram for a road of a length 450 m. The details of the earthwork involved in cutting and in filling are tabulated below. The table also shows the cumulative volume of the earthwork.

Distance (m)	0		30		60		90		120		150		180		210
Cutting (+)		–		145		125		–		–		70		240	
Filling (–)		135		–		–		105		145		–		–	

Distance (m)	210		240		270		300		330		360		390		420		450
Cutting (+)		180		170		–		–		60		125		215		–	
Filling (–)		–		–		145		140		–		–		–		20	

Solution (Fig. 11.39):

Determine the cumulative volume of earthwork as given in the following table. Plot the cumulative volume as ordinates, and the corresponding distances as abscissa. Join ends of the adjacent ordinates by a smooth curve.

[illegible]	Volume (m^3)		Cumulative volume (m^3)
	Cutting (+)	Filling (–)	
[illegible]			0
		135	
[illegible]			– 135
	145		
[illegible]			+ 10
	125		
[illegible]			+ 135
		105	
120			+30
		145	
150			– 115
	70		
180			– 45
	240		
210			+ 195
	180		
240			+ 375
	170		
270			+545
		145	
300			+400
		140	
330			+ 260
	60		
360			+ 320
	125		
390			+ 445
	215		
420			+ 660
		20	
450			+640

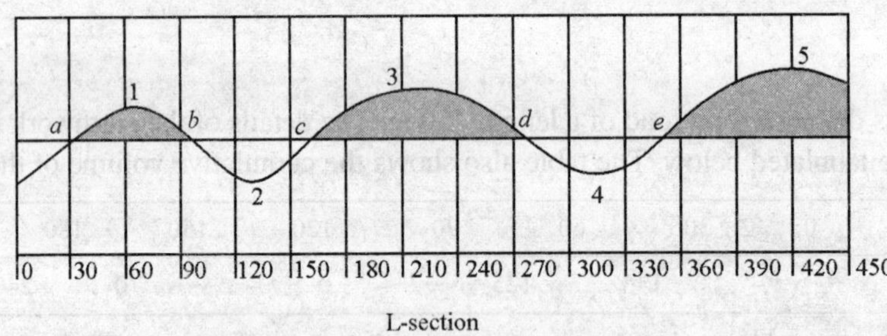

L-section
(a)

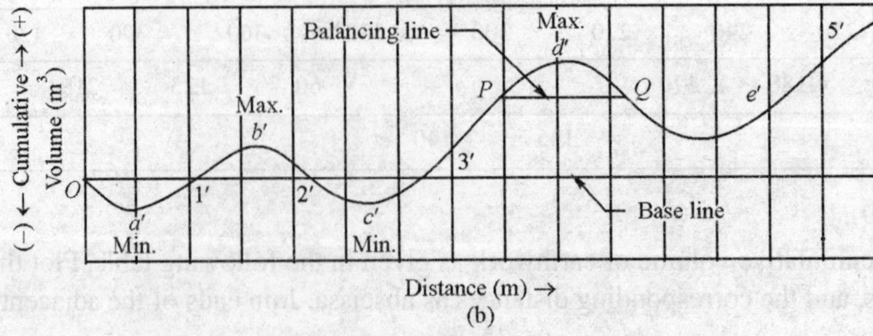

(b)

Fig. 11.39 Mass diagram

Characteristics of a Mass Diagram

A mass diagram has the following characteristics:

1. Upward slope of the curve in the direction of increasing abscissa indicates an excavated section and downward slope indicates an embankment.
2. The vertical distance between a maximum ordinate and the next forward minimum ordinate represents the whole volume of an embankment. The vertical distance between a minimum ordinate and the next forward maximum ordinate represents the whole volume of a cutting.
3. The vertical distance between two points on the curve which has neither a maximum nor a minimum points, represents the volume of earthwork between their abscissa, i.e., the chainage.
4. If the mass diagram curve cuts the base line at any two points in succession then the volume of cutting equals that of filling between these points, since the algebraic sum of the quantity between such points is zero.
5. Any horizontal line *PQ* (Fig. 11.39 b) drawn parallel to the base line and intersecting the curve at two points, indicates a length over which the volumes of cutting and filling will be equalized.
6. The area enclosed by a loop of curve and a balancing line, measures the haul in that direction.

Uses of Mass Diagram

A mass diagram may be used for the following purposes:

1. To find an economical scheme for distributing the excavated material by comparing a number of balancing lines.
2. To avoid the wastage of the material at one place, and borrowing at another place.
3. To overcome the difficulty of estimation of the proposed wastage, the designer may advise widening an embankment or a cutting where necessary.
4. To ascertain the cost of excavation and balancing one cubic metre as compared to balancing to waste one cubic metre plus that of excavating and hauling one cubic metre from the borrow pits.
5. To determine the most economical alternative of the utilization of the excavated material by comparing various alternatives.

QUESTIONS AND PROBLEMS

11.1 Write a short note on the use of areas and volumes. What are the factors which affect the accuracy of their determinations?

11.2 Discuss briefly the methods of determination of areas by field measurements.

11.3 Drive an expression to determine the area by coordinate method.

11.4 What do you mean by the following terms:

(*i*) Meridian distance (MD)

(*ii*) Double meridian distance (DMD)

(*iii*) Double parallel distance (DPD)

11.5 Derive the expressions to compute the area by

(*a*) Trapezoidal rule, (*b*) Simpson's rule.

11.6 What are the methods of determination of area from plan? Explain any one method with the help of a neat sketch.

11.7 What is a planimeter? Explain its working drawing a neat sketch of the instrument.

11.8 Describe the method of determining the two constants M and C of Amsler polar planimeter.

11.9 What is meant by "Area of zero circle" of a planimeter? How would you determine it?

11.10 What are the precautions to be taken while using a planimeter?

11.11 How the area of a plot is computed when the offsets are taken at equal intervals?

11.12 Differentiate between a two-level section and a three-level section drawing neat sketches.

11.13 Draw the sketch of a two-level section, and derive an expression for the area of cross-section.

11.14 Draw a sidehill two-level section and derive an expression for the area of cross-section when there is

(*i*) cutting at the centre-line,

(*ii*) filling at the centre-line.

11.15 Describe the method of determination of area of a multi-level section by the method of independent coordinates.

11.16 Taking a suitable example discuss the method of partitioning of land by a line running in a given direction.

11.17 Discuss the partitioning of a tract of land when the required area is to be cut off by a line through a given point.

11.18 Enumerate different methods of determination of volume of earthwork. Describe their merits and demerits.

11.19 Explain the methods of computation of volume by

(*i*) Average end-area formula.

(*ii*) Prismoidal formula.

11.20 What is prismoidal correction? Describe an expression for the prismoidal correction for a level section.

11.21 What is curvature correction? Derive an expression for curvature correction in terms of eccentricity of cross-section.

11.22 Discuss the methods of computation of volume of earthwork from spot levels when the area is divided into (*i*) triangle, (*ii*) squares.

11.23 Discuss various methods of computation of volume of earthwork from the contour plan.

11.24 Explain the method of computation of a capacity of a reservoir.

11.25 What is a mass diagram? How is it constructed, and what are its uses?

11.26 Define the following terms:

(*i*) Haul

(*ii*) Overhaul distance

(*iii*) Free-haul distance

(*iv*) Lead

(*v*) Lift.

11.27 Enumerate the characteristics of a mass diagram.

11.28 Calculate the side widths and area of the cross-section of an embankment with the following specifications:

Formation width = 20 m

Side slope = 2 to 1

Centre-height = 12 m

Transverse slope = 10 to 1

11.29 The following perpendicular offsets were taken at 10 m intervals from a survey line to an irregular boundary line:

2.95 m, 5.70 m, 4.00 m, 6.35 m, 8.25 m, 6.00 m, 3.30 m, 4.85 m, 5.70 m.

Calculate the area included between the survey line, the irregular boundary line, and the first and last offsets by (*a*) Average-ordinate rule, (*b*) Trapezoidal rule, and (*c*) Simpson's rule.

11.30 The following perpendicular offsets were taken from a survey line to an irregular boundary:

Chainage (m)	0	8	22	44	65	80
Offsets (m)	16.7	23.9	32.05	26.80	30.35	32.00

Calculate the area between the survey line, the boundary and the end offsets.

11.31 The following table gives the corrected latitudes and departures of the sides of a closed traverse *ABCD*:

Side	Latitude (m)		Departure (m)	
	N	S	E	W
AB	108	–	4	–
BC	15	–	249	–
CD	–	123	4	–
DA	0	–	–	257

Determine the area of the traverse by

(*a*) Coordinate method,

(*b*) Meridian distance (MD) method,

(*c*) Double meridian distance (DMD) method,

(*d*) Departure and total latitude method.

11.32 The adjusted coordinates of a closed traverse *ABCDE* are given below:

Line	*AB*	*BC*	*CD*	*DE*	*EA*
Latitude (m)	+ 155	+ 117	– 72	– 180	– 20
Departure (m)	– 33	+ 96	+ 162	– 31	– 194

Compute the area enclosed by the traverse by the departure and total latitude method, and check the result by any other method.

11.33 A planimeter was used to determine the area of a plan. When it traversed clockwise with the needle point inside the figure, the final and initial readings were 8.460 and 6.480, respectively. It was noted that the zero of the dial passed the fixed index twice in the counter clockwise direction. The multiplying and additive constants of the instrument are 100 and 20 cm^2, respectively. Compute the area of the plan.

11.34 Calculate the area of a figure from the following readings recorded by a planimeter with the needle point inside the figure:

Initial reading = 8.999

Final reading = 3.265

The instrument constants *M* and *C* are 100 and 25 cm^2, respectively. It was observed that the zero mark on the dial passed once the index mark in the counterclockwise direction.

11.35 A railway embankment is 8 m wide with side slopes of 15 to 1. The ground is level transversely. The centre-heights at 30 m interval are 0.76, 1.25, 1.40, 1.78, 1.73, 1.22, and 0.20 m. Compute the volume contained in this reach by the average end-area method and by the prismoidal formula.

11.36 For a railway in cutting, the width at the formation level is 10 m. The side slope in cutting is 1 to 1, and the original ground has a lateral slope of 11 to 1. Compute the volume of the cutting contained in a length of 260 m, the average depth at the centre-line being 2.5 m.

11.37 The width of a certain road at the formation level is 20 m, side slopes 1 in 1 for cutting and 1 in 2 for filling. The original ground transverse to the centre of the road, is 1 in 5. If the depth of excavation at the centre-line of three sections, 25 m apart, are 0.4, 0.8, and 1.2 m, respectively, compute the volume of the cutting and filling over the length of the road.

11.38 A rectangle *PQRS* forms the plan of a pit excavated for roadwork and *T* is the intersection of the diagonals *PR* and *QS*. The original and final levels of *P*, *Q*, *R*, *S* and *T* are as under:

Point	*P*	*Q*	*R*	*S*	*T*
Original level (m)	22.66	22.92	22.56	21.66	23.10
Final level (m)	18.07	17.97	18.33	18.33	18.15

If *PQ* and *QS* are 20 m and 31 m, respectively, determine the volume of the pit.

11.39 An excavation 30 m × 20 m at the bottom and 3 m deep is required to be made. The side slopes are 1:1. Assuming the surface to be level before excavation, calculate the volume of the cut.

11.40 An embankment 5 m at the formation level with side slopes of 2 to 1, has to be formed on a horizontal curve of radius 430 m. The transverse slope of the original ground is 5 to 1 downwards towards the concave side of the curve. Calculate the curvature correction for a length of 30 m if the centre-height is 2.5 m.

11.41 The areas within the contour lines at the side of a reservoir and the face of the proposed dam, are as follows:

Contour (m)	150.0	148.5	147.0	145.5	144.0	142.5	141.0	139.5	138.0
Area × 10^2 (m^2)	7065	6642	5509	4712	2886	1755	909	121	4

If the bottom level is 138.0 m and the F.R.L. is 150.0 m, determine the capacity of the reservoir.

12

HORIZONTAL AND VERTICAL CURVES

12.1 GENERAL

The horizontal alignment of a highway, railway, or canal consists of a series of straight lines and curves. The straight portions are called *tangents*. The curves are provided for smooth or gradual change in the direction due to the nature of the terrain, cultural features, or other unavoidable reasons. In highway practice, it is recommended to provide curves deliberately on straight routes to break the monotony in driving on long straight routes to avoid accidents.

The horizontal curve may be a simple circular curve or a compound curve. For a smooth transition between the tangents and the curves, a transition or easement curve is provided. The transition curves are spirals of third degree. The vertical curves are used to provide a smooth change in direction taking place in the vertical planes at the intersection of two grade lines. The curves joining the grade lines are generally parabolas of second degree.

12.2 HORIZONTAL CURVES

The horizontal curves can be circular or non-circular (transitional) curves. The horizontal circular curves are mainly of following three types:

1. Simple circular curve
2. Compound curve
3. Reverse curve.

The horizontal non-circular curves will be discussed separately.

Simple circular curve

A simple circular curve consists of a single arc of a circle. It is tangential to both the tangents or straight lines of the route (Fig. 12.1).

Compound curve

A compound curve consists of two or more circular arcs of different radii with their centers of curvature on the same side of the common tangent (Fig. 12.2). Compound curves are required when space restrictions preclude a signal circular curve, and when there are property boundaries.

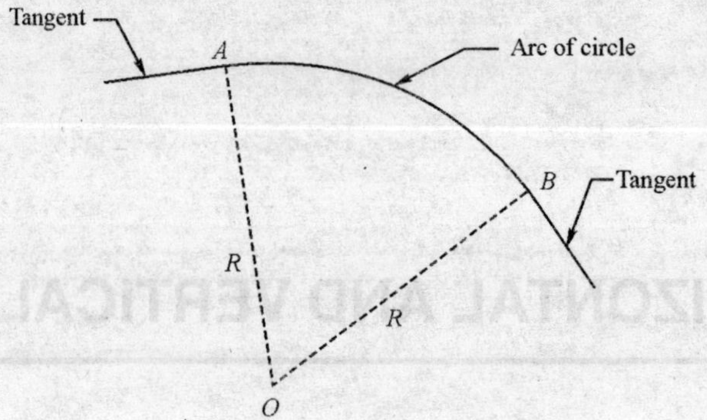

Fig. 12.1 Simple circular curve

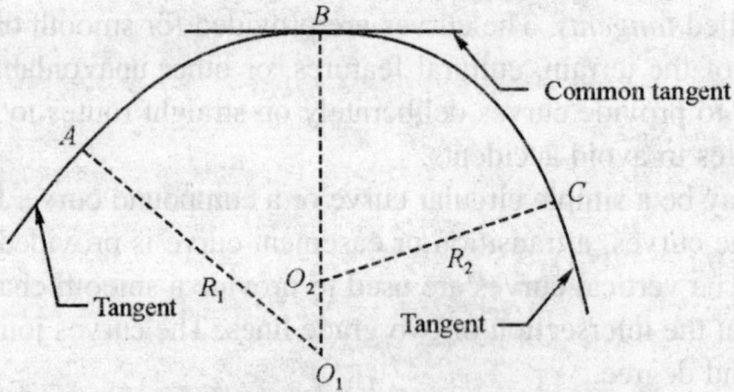

Fig. 12.2 Compound curve

Reverse curve

A reverse curve consists of two circular arcs of same or different radii, having their centers of curvature on the opposite sides of the common tangent (Fig. 12.3).

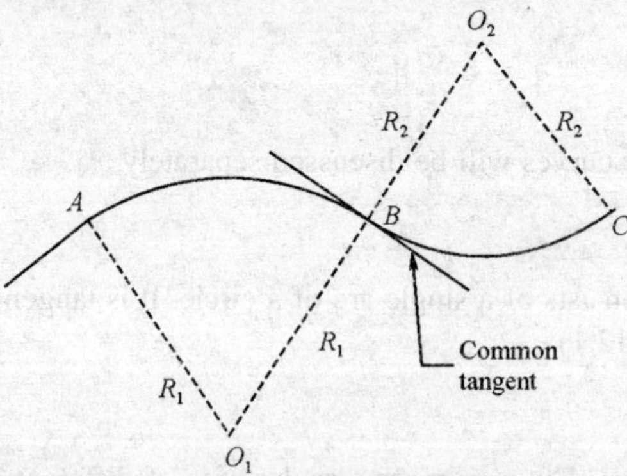

Fig. 12.3 Reverse curve

Other horizontal circular curves

The following horizontal curves are required under special field conditions.

Horse-shoe curve

It is a special case of a simple curve with a central angle exceeding 180° (Fig. 12.4).

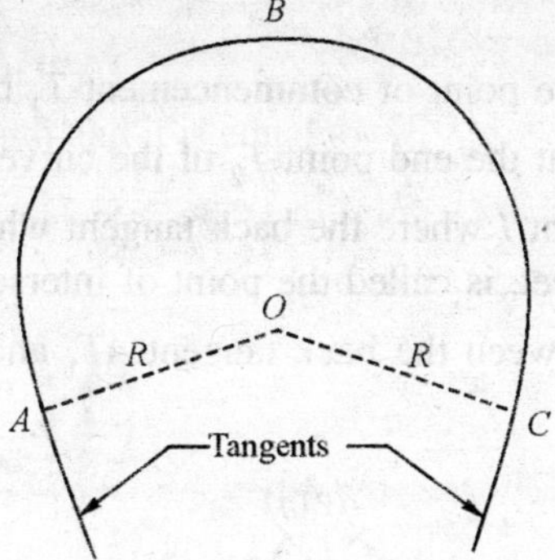

Fig. 12.4 Horse-shoe curve

Broken-back curve

A broken back curve has two circular arcs of the same or different radii connecting two straights, and separated by a small straight portion, tangential to both (Fig. 12.5).

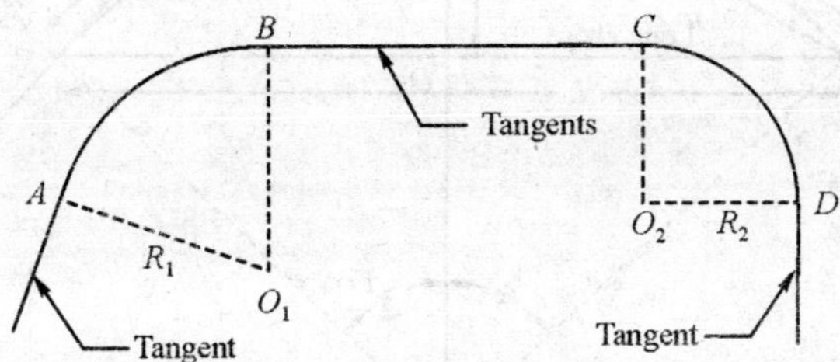

Fig. 12.5 Broken-back curve

Diversion or deviation curve

A diversion or deviation curve consists of two reverse curves, taking off from a straight and rejoining it at a certain distance (Fig. 12.6).

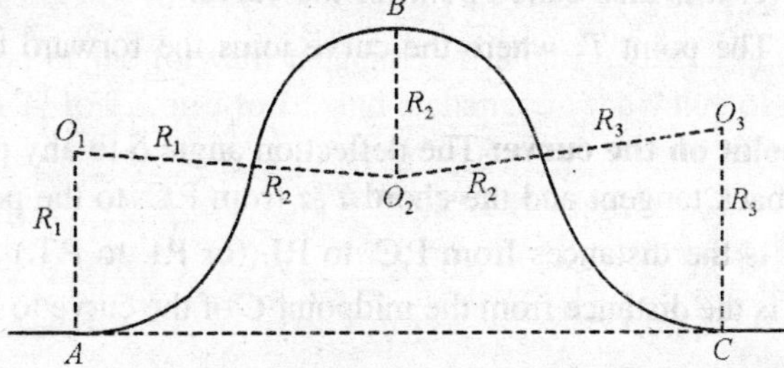

Fig. 12.6 Diversion curve

12.3 ELEMENTS OF A CIRCULAR CURVE

Fig. 12.7 shows a simple circular curve of radius R with its centre at O. A curve has the following element.

Back tangent: The tangent AT_1 at the point of commencement T_1 of the curve, is the back tangent.

Forward tangent: The tangent T_2B at the end point T_2 of the curve, is the forward tangent.

Point of intersection (P.I.): The point I where the back tangent when produced forward and forward tangent when produced backward meet, is called the point of intersection.

Intersection angle: The angle ϕ between the back tangent AT_1 and the forward tangent T_2B at I, is called the intersection angle.

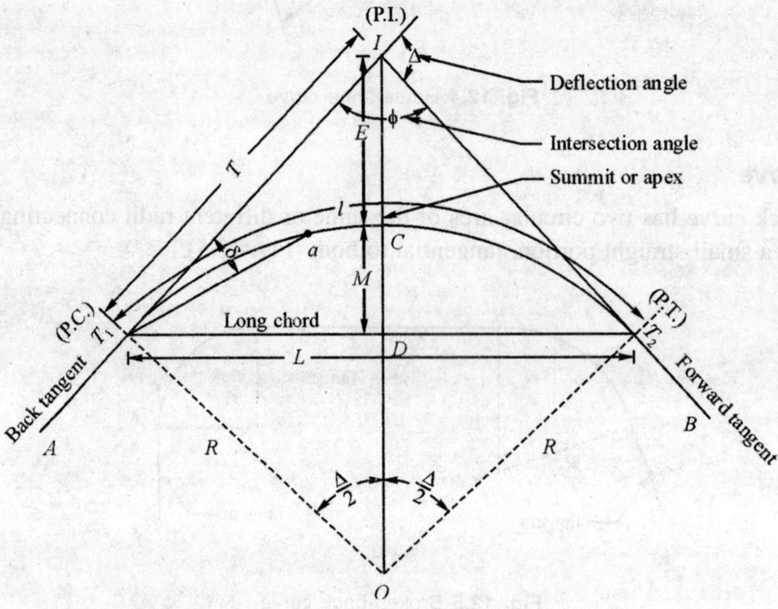

Fig. 12.7 Elements of a circular curve

Deflection angle of the curve: The angle Δ through which the forward tangent deflects, is called deflection angle of the curve. It may be either to the left or the right.

Point of commencement (P.C.): The point T_1 where the curve commences is called the point of commencement of the curve. It is also called point of the curve.

Point of tangency (P.T.): The point T_2 where the curve joins the forward tangent, is called point of tangency.

Deflection angle to any point on the curve: The deflection angle δ to any point a on the curve is the angle at P.C. between the back tangent and the chord T_1a from P.C. to the point.

Tangent distance (T): It is the distances from P.C. to P.I. (or P.I. to P.T.)

External distance (E): It is the distance from the midpoint C of the curve to P.I. It is also known as the apex distance.

Length of curve (l): It is the total length of the curve from P.C. to P.T.

Long chord (L): It is the chord joining P.C. and P.T.

Mid-ordinate (M): It is the ordinate from the midpoint of the long chord to the midpoint of the curve. It is also called the versine of the curve.

Normal chord (C): A chord between two successive regular pegs on the curve, is called a normal chord.

Sub-chord (c): When the chord is shorter than the normal chord, it is called a sub-chord. These generally occur at the beginning and end of the curve. These will be designated by c_f and c_l, respectively.

Right-hand curve: If the curve deflects to the right of the direction of the progress of survey it is called the right-hand curve.

Left-hand curve: If the curve deflects to the left of the direction of the progress of survey, it is called the left-hand curve.

12.4 GEOMETRICS OF A CIRCLE

Some of the important properties of a circle used in the computations for curve ranging, are given below (Fig. 12.8).

1. Length of tangents $T_1I = IT_2 = T = R\tan\frac{\Delta}{2}$
2. Long chord $T_1T_2 = 2R\sin\frac{\Delta}{2}$
3. The angle subtended by any chord at the centre is twice the angle between the chord and the tangent, i.e.,
$$\angle IT_1A = \frac{1}{2}\angle T_1OA$$
4. The angle subtended by a chord at any point on the circumference is equal to the angle between the chord and the tangent, i.e.
$$\angle AT_2T_1 = \angle IT_1A$$

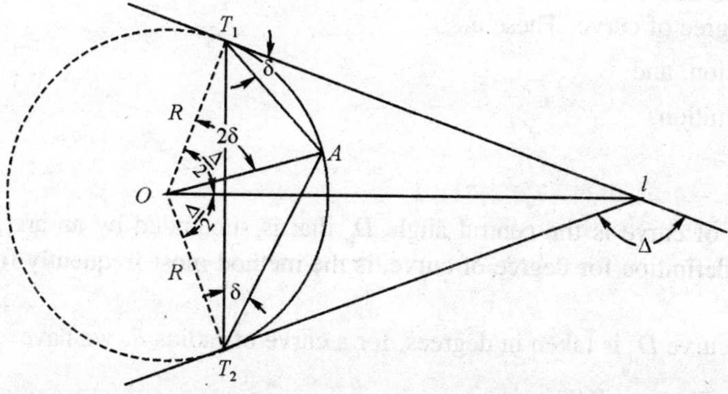

Fig. 12.8 Geometrics of a circle

12.5 DESIGNATION OF A CIRCULAR CURVE

The sharpness of curvature of a curve may be expressed in any of the following ways:

1. Radius of the curve
2. Degree of the curve.

Radius of curve

The curvature is defined by stating the length of radius. This method is often employed in subdivision surveys and sometimes in highway work.

In highways, the minimum radius of the curve is determined from the following formula:

$$R_{min} = \frac{V^2}{127(e+f)}$$

where

V = the speed of vehicles in km/h,

e = the maximum super elevation, and

f = the maximum friction (= 0.16).

In railways, R_{min} is determined using the following formula:

$$R_{min} = \frac{BV^2}{127e}$$

where

B = the gauge of the railway track (B = 1.676 m for broad gauge and 1.00 m for metre gauge), and

e = the maximum super elevation (e = 165 mm for broad gauge, and 90 mm for metre gauge).

Degree of curve

Here the curvature is expressed by stating the degree of curve D, which is traditionally defined as the angle subtended at the centre of the curve by an arc or a chord of specified length. Thus, there are two definitions of degree of curve. These are

(*i*) Arc definition, and

(*ii*) Chord definition.

Arc definition

Here the degree of curve is the central angle D_a that is subtended by an arc AB of 30 m length (Fig. 12.9). The arc definition for degree of curve, is the method most frequently followed in highway practice.

If the degree of curve D_a is taken in degrees, for a curve of radius R, we have

$$\frac{D_a}{30} = \frac{360°}{2\pi R}$$

or $$D_a = \frac{10800}{2\pi R} \text{ degrees}$$

$$= \frac{1718.9}{R} \text{ degrees } (\textit{approximate}) \qquad ...(12.1)$$

If the arc length is taken as 20 m then

$$D_a = \frac{1145.92}{R} \text{ degrees } (\textit{approximately})$$

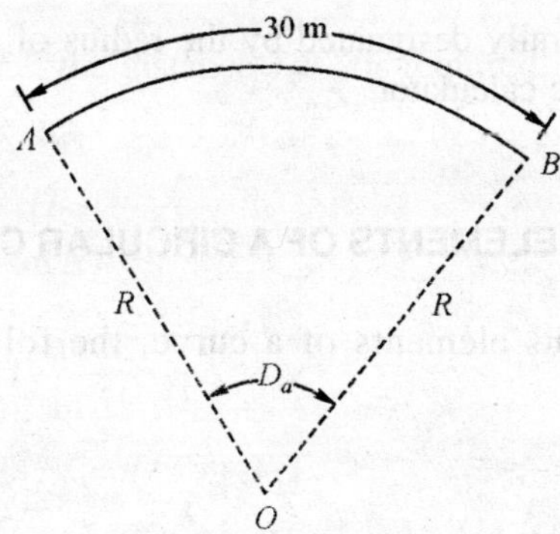

Fig. 12.9 Arc definition

Chord definition

The degree of curve may also be defined as the central angle of the curve that is subtended by a chord *AB* of 30 m length (Fig 12.10). This definition is followed almost invariably in railway practice.

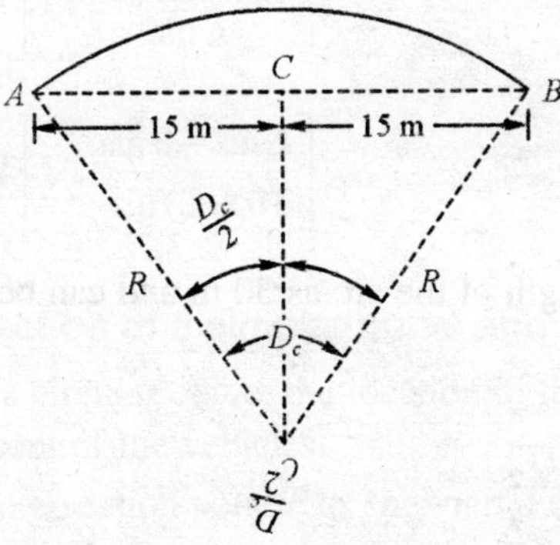

Fig. 12.10 Chord definition

From Fig. 12.10, we have

$$\sin \frac{D_c}{2} = \frac{AC}{AO}$$

$$= \frac{15}{R}$$

or $$R = \frac{15}{\sin \frac{D_c}{2}} \quad (exact) \qquad \text{...(12.2)}$$

Note that radius of curvature varies inversely as the degree of curve. A sharp curve has a large degree of curve whereas a flat curve has a small degree of curve.

To satisfy the requirements of safety at high speeds the curve should be as flat as economically feasible.

These days the curves are generally designated by the radius of curve as the calculations can be done conveniently with an electronic calculator.

12.6 FORMULAE FOR VARIOUS ELEMENTS OF A CIRCULAR CURVE

For the computation of the various elements of a curve, the following formulae may be used (Fig. 12.7).

Length of curve (l)

$$l = T_1CT_2$$

$$= \frac{2\pi R}{360}\Delta$$

$$= \frac{\pi R \Delta}{180} \qquad \text{...(12.3)}$$

Alternatively, from arc definition

$$\frac{D_a}{30} = \frac{\Delta}{l}$$

or $$l = \frac{30\Delta}{D_a} \qquad \text{...(12.4)}$$

Eq. (12.4) uses the specified length of the arc as 30 m and can be used if the curve is flat.

Tangent length (T)

$$T = T_1I = IT_2$$

$$= OT_1 \tan\frac{\Delta}{2}$$

$$= R\tan\frac{\Delta}{2} \qquad \text{...(12.5)}$$

Chainages of tangent points

The chainage of P.I. is generally known and thus,

$$\text{Chainage of } T_1 = \text{Chainage of } I - T$$

$$\text{Chainage of } T_2 = \text{Chainage of } T_1 + l \quad \text{...(12.6)}$$

Long chord (L)

$$L = T_1T_2$$

$$= 2OT_1 \sin\frac{\Delta}{2}$$

$$= 2R\sin\frac{\Delta}{2} \quad \text{...(12.7)}$$

External distance (E)

$$E = IC$$

$$= OI - OC$$

$$= R\sec\frac{\Delta}{2} - R$$

$$= R\left[\sec\frac{\Delta}{2} - 1\right] \quad \text{...(12.8)}$$

Mid-ordinate (M)

$$M = DC$$

$$= OC - OD$$

$$= R - R\cos\frac{\Delta}{2}$$

$$= R\left[1 - \cos\frac{\Delta}{2}\right] \quad \text{...(12.9)}$$

$$= R\,\text{versine}\frac{\Delta}{2}$$

The mid-ordinate of the curve is also known as the *versine* of the curve.

ILLUSTRATIVE EXAMPLE

Example 12.1

The chainage of the intersection of two straights having the deflection angle of 50° is 1680.50 m. If the radius of the curve is 450 m, calculate the following:

(*i*) tangent distance,

(*ii*) length of the curve,

(*iii*) chainages of P.C. and P.T.

(*iv*) length of the long chord

(*v*) degree of curve

(*vi*) apex distance, and

(*vii*) mid-ordinate.

Solution (Fig. 12.7):

(*i*) From Eq. (12.5)

$$T = R\tan\frac{\Delta}{2}$$

$$= 450\times\tan\frac{50°}{2}$$

$$= \mathbf{209.84\ m.}$$

(*ii*) From Eq. (12.3)

$$l = \frac{\pi R\Delta}{180}$$

$$= \frac{\pi\times 450\times 50}{180}$$

$$= \mathbf{392.70\ m.}$$

(*iii*) From Eq. (12.6)

Chainage of P.C. = Chainage of $I - T$

= 1680.5 – 209.84

= **1470.66 m.**

Chainage of P.T. = Chainage of P.C. + l

= 1470.66 + 392.70

= **1863.36 m.**

(*iv*) From Eq. (12.7)

$$L = 2R\sin\frac{\Delta}{2}$$

$$= 2\times 450\times\sin\frac{50°}{2}$$

$$= \mathbf{380.36\ m.}$$

(*v*) From Eq. (12.1)

$$D_a = \frac{1718.9}{R}$$

$$= \frac{1718.9}{450}$$

$$= \mathbf{3.82°.}$$

(*vi*) From Eq. (12.8)

$$E = R\left[\sec\frac{\Delta}{2} - 1\right]$$

$$= 450 \times \left[\sec\frac{50°}{2} - 1\right]$$

$$= \mathbf{46.52\ m.}$$

(*vii*) From Eq. (12.9)

$$M = R\left[1 - \cos\frac{\Delta}{2}\right]$$

$$= 450 \times \left[1 - \cos\frac{50°}{2}\right]$$

$$= \mathbf{42.16\ m.}$$

12.7 SETTING OUT A CIRCULAR CURVE

The methods of setting out a circular curve may be classified on the basis of the instruments employed, as below:

1. Tape method
2. Tape and theodolite method
3. Two theodolites method
4. Tacheometric method
5. Total station method.

Tape method

In this method no angular observations are taken and a curve is set out using a tape or a chain only. This method is generally employed for short length curves and where accuracy is not that important.

The curves can be set out using a tape or a chain by any one of the following four methods.

Offsets from the tangents

This method is used when the deflection angle and the radius of curvature both are comparatively small. In this method, the curve is set out by measuring offsets from the tangent. The offsets from the tangent can be either perpendicular to the tangent or they may be radial.

Perpendicular offsets method (Fig. 12.11)

Let the point 1 be on the curve and the perpendicular offset from the tangent T_1I to it at P be O_x. Let the distance of P from T_1 be x. Draw a line $Q1$ perpendicular to T_1O, intersecting OT_1 at Q.

From $\Delta Q1O$, we have

$$QO = \sqrt{(O1)^2 - (Q1)^2}$$

or $$R - O_x = \sqrt{R^2 - x^2}$$

or $$O_x = R - \sqrt{R^2 - x^2} \quad (exact) \qquad ...(12.10)$$

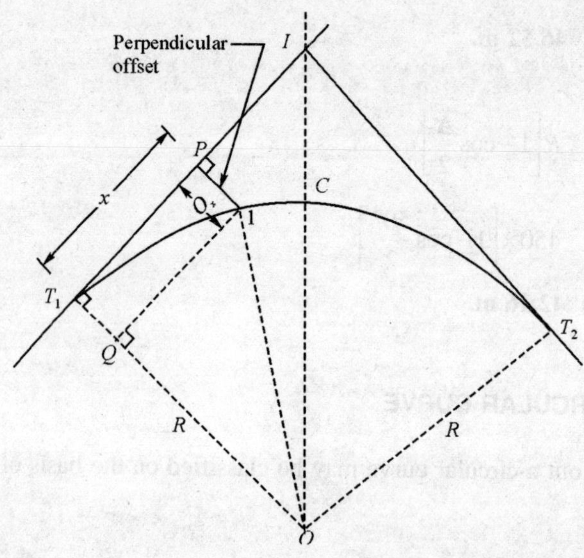

Fig. 12.11 Perpendicular offsets from tangent

From binomial theorem, we can write

$$O_x \simeq R - R\left(1 - \frac{x^2}{2R^2}\right)$$

$$\simeq \frac{x^2}{2R} \quad (approximate) \qquad ...(12.11)$$

Field operations

Before setting out a curve, a table of offsets for different values of x (e.g., 10 m, 20 m, 30 m, etc.) is made. Then from T_1 the distances x_1, x_2, x_3, etc., are measured along the tangent, and the corresponding offsets are measured on the perpendiculars to the tangent with the help of an optical square. Since the offsets of points equidistant from T_1 and T_2, are equal, the same table is used for offsets from both the tangents.

Radial offsets method (Fig. 12.12)

Let the radial offset to the point 1 on the curve, be O_x from the point P at a distance of x from T_1.

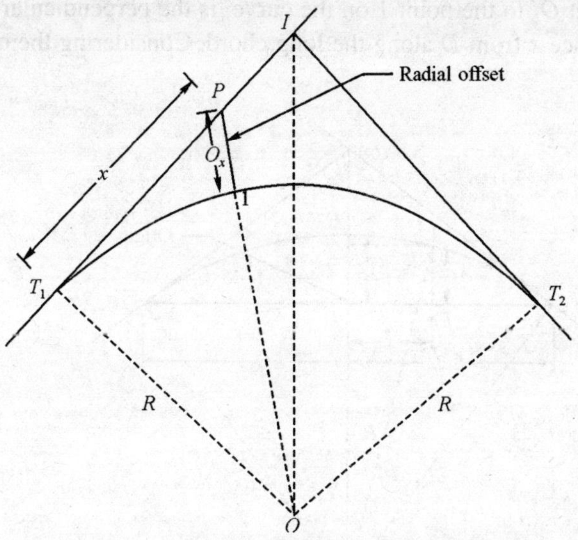

Fig. 12.12 Radial offsets

From ΔOPT_1, we get

$$OP = \sqrt{(OT_1)^2 + (T_1P)^2}$$

or
$$R + O_x = \sqrt{R^2 + x^2}$$

$$O_x = \sqrt{(R^2 + x^2)} - R \quad (exact)$$

$$= R\left(1 + \frac{x^2}{R^2}\right)^{1/2} - R$$

From binomial theorem, we can write

$$O_x \simeq R\left(1 + \frac{x^2}{2R^2}\right) - R$$

$$\simeq \frac{x^2}{2R} \quad (approximate) \qquad ...(12.12)$$

Field operations

The offsets for the different values of x are computed and tabulated. Then from T_1 the distances x_1, x_2, x_3, etc., are measured along the tangent, and the corresponding radial offsets are measured such that the points 1, 2, 3, etc., on the curve, lie on the lines joining the points and the centre of the curve.

Offsets from the long chord

The method is suitable for setting out circular curves of small radius, such as those at road intersections in a city, in kerb lines, or in boundary walls.

In Fig. 12.13, the offset O_x to the point 1 on the curve, is the perpendicular distance of 1 from the long chord T_1T_2, at a distance x from D along the long chord. Considering the origin at D, O_x is the y-coordinate of 1 at x.

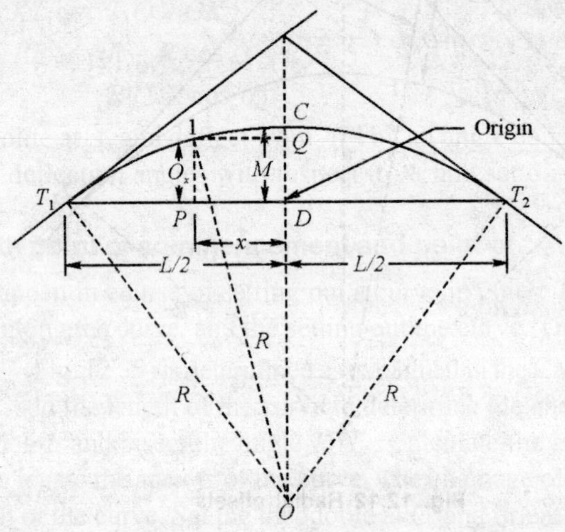

Fig. 12.13 Offsets from the long chord

$$O_x = QD$$
$$= QO - DO$$

From Δ $Q10$, we have

$$QO = \sqrt{O1^2 - Q1^2}$$

$$= \sqrt{R^2 - x^2} \qquad ...(12.15)$$

From Δ OT_1D, we have

$$DO = \sqrt{T_1O^2 - T_1D^2}$$

$$= \sqrt{R^2 - \left(\frac{L}{2}\right)^2} \qquad ...(12.16)$$

Thus

$$O_x = \sqrt{R^2 - x^2} - \sqrt{R^2 - \left(\frac{L}{2}\right)^2} \qquad ...(12.17)$$

Field operations

The long chord is divided into equal parts of suitable length. The offset corresponding to the distances from D along the long chord are measured perpendicular to the long chord with the help of an optical square. The points on the right side of CD are set out by symmetry.

Successive bisection of chords

The method being approximate, is suitable for small curves. It involves the location of points on the curve by bisecting the chords and erecting perpendiculars at the midpoint of the chords.

In Fig. 12.14, T_1T_2 is the long chord and D is its midpoint. C is the point of intersection of the line OD produced, with the curve, DC is the mid-ordinate, which from Eq. (12.9) is equal to

$$M = R\left[1-\cos\frac{\Delta}{2}\right]$$

At D, a perpendicular offset equal to M, is erected, and the position C is located. Now consider the chords T_1C and T_2C, locate their midpoints 1_0 and $1_0'$, respectively. Erect two perpendiculars at 1_0 and $1_0'$, and measure the offsets equal to 1_01 and $1_0'\,1'$, respectively.

The offsets 1_01 and $1_0'\,1'$ are computed from the following formula:

$$1_01 = 1_0'1'$$

$$= R\left[1-\cos\frac{\Delta}{4}\right]$$

In this manner, the points 1 and 1′ have been located on the curve.

By further successive bisections, the points 2, 3, 2′ and 3′ are located in a similar manner. The offsets 2_02, 3_03, $2_0'2'$, $3_0'3'$ are computed from the formula given below:

$$2_02 = 3_03 = 2_0'2' = 3_0'3'$$

$$= R\left[1-\cos\frac{\Delta}{8}\right]$$

Field operations

After locating T_1 and T_2, the midpoint D of T_1T_2 is obtained, by measuring T_1T_2. The perpendicular offset DC is set out at D with an optical square, and C is located. Measure T_1C, and T_2C, and locate their midpoints 1_0 and $1_0'$. The perpendicular offsets 1_01 and $1_0'1'$ are set out at 1_0 and $1_0'$, and the points 1 and 1′ are established on the curve. The process is continued till sufficient number of points on the curve are fixed.

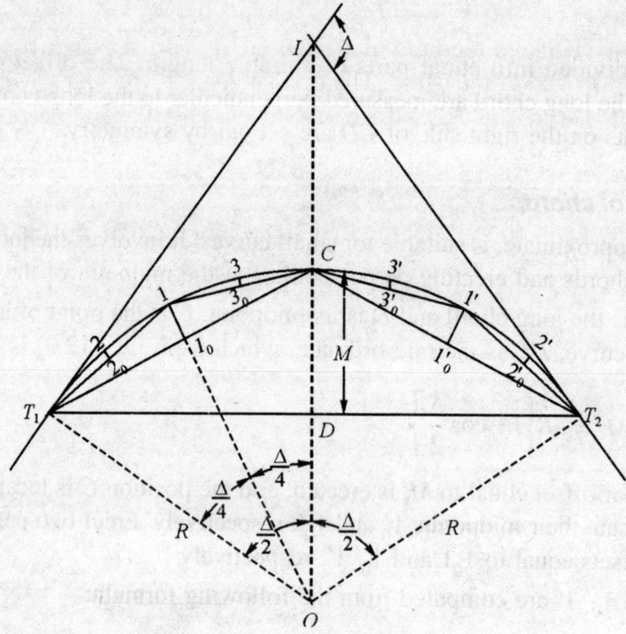

Fig. 12.14 Successive bisection of chords

Offsets from the chords produced

This method is commonly employed for highway curves when setting out is to be done by linear measurements only. The method is fairly accurate in plains when the linear measurements are possible. This method has advantage over the previously described methods that it can be used when the land between the tangent points T_1 and T_2 is inaccessible. On the other hand, the method has a drawback that the error in locating a point is carried forward to the other points.

The method is based on the assumption that for small chords, the chord length is equal to the arc length.

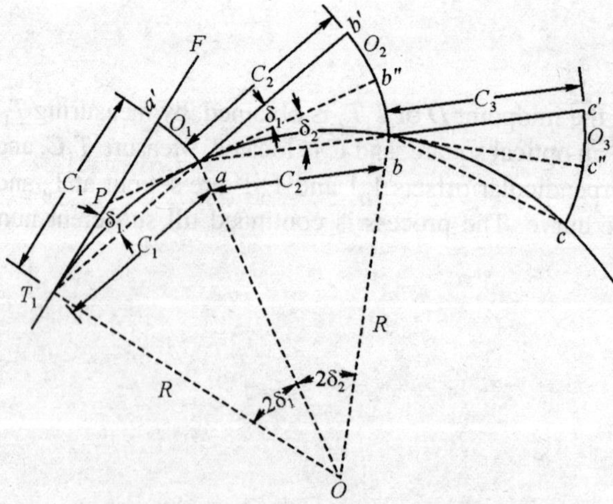

Fig. 12.15 Offsets from the chords produced

For setting out the curve (Fig. 12.15) it is divided into a number of chords normally 20 to 30 m in length. For the continuous chainage required along the curve, two sub-chords are taken, one at the beginning and the other at the end of the curve. The first sub-chord length is such that a full number of chainage is obtained on the curve near T_1, and the second sub-chord length near T_2 giving the desired chainage at T_2.

The offsets O_1, O_2, O_3, etc., are computed as under:

Let T_1F be the back tangent, and T_1a be the first sub-chord equal to c_f. Let the angle FT_1a be δ_1.

From $\Delta\ OT_1a$, we have

$$\angle OT_1a = 90° - \delta_1$$

$$\angle T_1Oa = 180° - 2\angle OT_1a$$

$$= 180° - 2\,(90° - \delta_1)$$

$$= 2\delta_1$$

Let
$$T_1a = C_1 = c_f = T_1O \cdot \angle T_1Oa$$

$$= R\ 2\delta_1$$

or
$$\delta_1 = \frac{c_f}{2R} \qquad \text{...(12.18)}$$

We have assumed that the arc aa' is equal to its chord length. Taking $T_1a' = T_1a = c_f$, and $\angle a'T_1a = \delta_1$, we have

$$aa' = c_f\,\delta_1$$

or
$$\delta_1 = \frac{aa'}{c_f} = \frac{O_1}{c_f}$$

From Eq. (12.18), we get

$$\frac{c_f}{2R} = \frac{O_1}{c_f}$$

or
$$O_1 = \frac{c_f^2}{2R} \qquad \text{...(12.19)}$$

where O_1 is the length of the first offset for the first sub-chord of length c_f.

To obtain the length of the second offset O_2, draw a tangent Pab'' at a cutting T_1F at P and bb', when produced, at b''. Since PT_1 and Pa are the two tangents on the curve between T_1 and a, the length PT_1 will be equal to Pa, and therefore,

$$\angle PT_1a = \angle PaT_1 = \angle b'ab'' = \delta_1$$

Since the Δ's $a'T_1a$ and $b'ab''$ are similar, being nearly isosceles triangles, we have

$$\frac{b'b''}{ab'} = \frac{a'a''}{a'T_1}$$

$$b'b'' = \frac{ab'\,a'a''}{a'T_1}$$

$$= \frac{C_2 O_1}{c_f}$$

Substituting the value of O_1

$$b'b'' = \frac{C_2}{c_f}\frac{c_f^2}{2R}$$

$$= \frac{C_2 c_f}{2R} \qquad ...(12.20)$$

From Eq. (12.19), we have

$$b'b'' = \frac{C_2^2}{2R} \qquad ...(12.21)$$

Since

$$O_2 = bb' = bb'' + b''b'$$

from Eqs. (12.20) and (12.21), we get

$$O_2 = \frac{C_2^2}{2R} + \frac{C_2 c_f}{2R}$$

$$= \frac{C_2}{2R}(C_2 + c_f) \qquad ...(12.22)$$

In a similar manner, we have

$$O_3 = \frac{C_3}{2R}(C_3 + C_2)$$

Since, normally all the chords excepting the two sub-chords, are the normal chords of equal lengths, *i.e.*, $C_2 = C_3 = C_4 ...= C_{n-1} = C$,

we have

$$O_{3 \text{ to } (n-1)} = \frac{C}{2R}(C + C)$$

$$= \frac{C^2}{R} \qquad ...(12.23)$$

where C is the length of a normal chord.

The offset for the second sub-chord is given by

$$O_n = \frac{c_l}{2R}(c_l + C_{n-1})$$

$$= \frac{c_l}{2R}(c_l + C) \qquad ...(12.24)$$

Field operations

Knowing the chainage of point of intersection, the deflection angle and the radius of the curve, the chainage of T_1 is computed, and T_1 is located on the back tangent. The lengths of the first and second sub-chords c_f and c_l arc also calculated from the chainages of T_1 and T_2. Calculate the length of the offsets O_1, O_2, O_3, ..., O_n.

Mark a' on T_1F at a distance of c_f. With the zero end of the tape or chain at T_1 and radius equal to c_f, draw an arc $a'a$, and cut off $a'a$ equal to O_1. Thus, the first point a on the curve is fixed. Now pull the tape forward in the direction of T_1a produced, and measure ab' equal to C_2 (*i.e.*, equal to C). Hold the zero of the tape at a, swing an arc of a radius equal to C, and cut off $b'b$ equal to O_2. Point b is thus fixed on the curve. Continue the process until T_2 is located by measuring c_l. The location of T_2 by taking the offset must agree with its already fixed position measuring IT_2 equal to the tangent length.

If it is found that the error in location of T_2 is more than 2 m, the whole work is repeated. If the error is less than 2 m, all the pegs are moved sideways by an amount proportional to the square of their distances from T_1 so that the error is distributed among all intermediate points of the curve.

ILLUSTRATIVE EXAMPLES

Example 12.2

The chainage of the intersection point of two straights is 1060 m, and the angle of intersection is 120°. If the radius of a circular curve is 570 m, and peg interval is 30 m, determine

(*i*) the tangent length,

(*ii*) the chainage at the beginning and end of the curve,

(*iii*) the length of the long chord,

(*iv*) the length of the sub-chords and chords, and

(*v*) the total number of normal chords.

Solution (Figs. 12.7 and 12.16):

The deflection angle Δ $= 180° - \phi$

$= 180° - 120°$

$= 60°$

(*i*) From Eqn. (12.5), the tangent length

$$T = R\tan\frac{\Delta}{2}$$

$$= 570 \times \tan\frac{60°}{2}$$

$$= \mathbf{329.09\ m.}$$

(*ii*) From Eq. (12.3), the length of the curve

$$l = \frac{\pi R \Delta}{180}$$

$$= \mathbf{596.90\ m.}$$

From Eqs. (12.6), we have

The chainage at the beginning T_1 of the curve

= Chainage of $I - T$

= 1060 – 329.09

= **730.91 m.**

and the chainage at the end T_2 of the curve

= Chainage of P.C. + l

= 730.90 + 596.90

= **1327.81 m.**

(*iii*) From Eq. (12.7), the length of the long chord

$$L = 2R \sin\frac{\Delta}{2}$$

$$= 2 \times 570 \times \sin\frac{60°}{2}$$

$$= \mathbf{570.00\ m.}$$

(*iv*) Since the peg interval is 30 m, the chainage of

$$T_1 = \frac{730.91}{30}$$

= 24 full chain length + 10.91 m

The length of the first sub-chord

c_f = (25 chain) × 30 – [(24 chain) × 30 + 10.91]

= **19.09 m.**

The chainage of T_2 = 1327.81

= 44 full chain lengths + 7.81 m

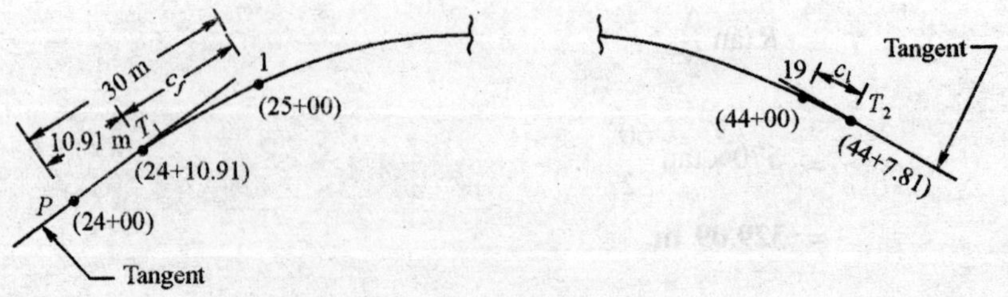

Fig. 12.16

The chainage of the last point on the curve having full chainage

$$= 44 \text{ chain} + 00 \text{ m}$$

Therefore, the length of second sub-chord

$$c_l = \mathbf{7.81\ m.}$$

(*v*) The number of normal chords

$$= \text{Chainage of the last peg} - \text{chainage of the first peg}$$

$$= 44 - 25$$

$$= \mathbf{19.}$$

Thus, the total number of chords

$$= 1 + 19 + 1$$

$$= \mathbf{21.}$$

Example 12.3

Two straight roads meet at an angle of 130°. Calculate the necessary data for setting out a circular curve of 15 chains radius between the roads by the following methods. The length of one chain is 20 m.

(*i*) Perpendicular offsets method

(*ii*) Radial offsets method.

Solution:

The radius of the curve

$$R = 15 \times 20 = 300 \text{ m}$$

The deflection angle

$$\Delta = 180° - \phi$$

$$= 180° - 130° = 50°$$

(*i*) Perpendicular offsets method (Fig. 12.17)

The distance x from T_1 along the tangent T_1I for fixing the apex C of the curve is determined from the $\Delta\ OQC$

$$x = QC = R\sin\frac{\Delta}{2}$$

$$= 300 \times \sin\frac{50°}{2}$$

$$= \mathbf{126.79\ m.}$$

The offset for C from Eq. (12.11) is

$$O_x = R - \sqrt{R^2 - x^2}$$

$$= 300 - \sqrt{300^2 - 126.79^2}$$

$$= \mathbf{28.11\ m.}$$

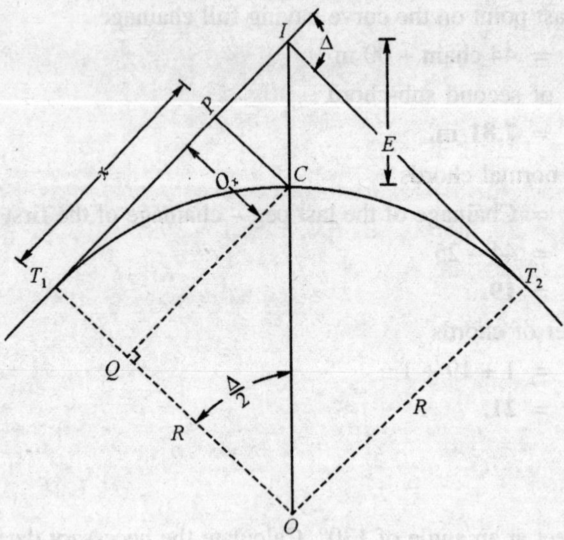

Fig. 12.17

Since the half of the curve is set out from T_1 and the other half from T_2, the values of x for which the offsets are to be calculated will be

$$x = 20, 40, 60, 80, 100, 120, \text{ and } 126.79 \text{ m.}$$

Therefore, the offsets are

$$O_{20} = 300-\sqrt{300^2-20^2} = \mathbf{0.67\ m}$$

$$O_{40} = 300-\sqrt{300^2-40^2} = \mathbf{2.68\ m}$$

$$O_{60} = 300-\sqrt{300^2-60^2} = \mathbf{6.06\ m}$$

$$O_{80} = 300-\sqrt{300^2-80^2} = \mathbf{10.86\ m}$$

$$O_{100} = 300-\sqrt{300^2-100^2} = \mathbf{17.16\ m}$$

$$O_{120} = 300-\sqrt{300^2-120^2} = \mathbf{25.05\ m}$$

$$O_{126.79} = \mathbf{28.11\ m} \quad \textit{(already computed)}$$

(*ii*) Radial, offsets method (Fig. 12.12)

In this case the distance x for the last point to locate the apex of the curve is equal to the tangent length. Thus for x equal to $x_c = T$, the offset O_{xc} will be equal to IC which is the external distance E.

From Eq. (12.5)

$$x = T = R\tan\frac{\Delta}{2}$$

$$= 300\times\tan\frac{50°}{2}$$

$$= 139.89 \text{ m.}$$

From Eq. (12.8)

$$O_x = E = R\left[\sec\frac{\Delta}{2} - 1\right] = 300\left[\sec\frac{50°}{2} - 1\right]$$

$$= 31.01 \text{ m.}$$

The values of x for which the offsets are to be calculated are

$$x = 20, 40, 60, 80, 100, 120, 139.89 \text{ m.}$$

From Eq. (12.13), the offsets are

$$O_x = \sqrt{(R^2 + x^2)} - R$$

$$O_{20} = \sqrt{300^2 + 20^2} - 300 = \mathbf{0.67\ m}$$

$$O_{40} = \sqrt{300^2 + 40^2} - 300 = \mathbf{2.65\ m}$$

$$O_{60} = \sqrt{300^2 + 60^2} - 300 = \mathbf{5.94\ m}$$

$$O_{80} = \sqrt{300^2 + 80^2} - 300 = \mathbf{10.48\ m}$$

$$O_{100} = \sqrt{300^2 + 100^2} - 300 = \mathbf{16.23\ m}$$

$$O_{120} = \sqrt{300^2 + 120^2} - 300 = \mathbf{23.11\ m}$$

$$O_{139.89} = \mathbf{31.01\ m} \quad \textit{(already computed).}$$

The other half of the curve is set out from T_2.

Example 12.4

Calculate the ordinates at 10 m intervals for setting out a circular curve of 200 m radius for a deflection angle of 60°. Use the method of offsets from the long chord.

Solution (Fig. 12.13):

From Eq. (12.7), the long chord T_1T_2 is equal to

$$L = 2R\sin\frac{\Delta}{2}$$

$$= 2 \times 200 \times \sin\frac{60°}{2}$$

$$= 200.00 \text{ m.}$$

From Eq. (12.9) the mid-ordinate is

$$O_0 = M = R\left[1 - \cos\frac{\Delta}{2}\right]$$

$$= 200\left[1 - \cos\frac{60°}{2}\right]$$

$$= 26.79 \text{ m.}$$

The value of x for half of the curve from D, are as

$$x = 10, 20, 30, 40, 50, 60, 70, 80, 90, 100 \text{ m.}$$

From Eq. (12.17), the offsets are

$$O_x = \sqrt{R^2 - x^2} - \sqrt{R^2 - \left(\frac{L}{2}\right)^2}$$

$$O_0 = \mathbf{26.79} \quad \textit{(already computed)}$$

$$O_{10} = \sqrt{200^2 - 10^2} - \sqrt{200^2 - 100^2} = \mathbf{26.54\ m}$$

$$O_{20} = \sqrt{200^2 - 20^2} - \sqrt{200^2 - 100^2} = \mathbf{25.79\ m}$$

$$O_{30} = \sqrt{200^2 - 30^2} - \sqrt{200^2 - 100^2} = \mathbf{24.53\ m}$$

$$O_{40} = \sqrt{200^2 - 40^2} - \sqrt{200^2 - 100^2} = \mathbf{22.75\ m}$$

$$O_{50} = \sqrt{200^2 - 50^2} - \sqrt{200^2 - 100^2} = \mathbf{20.44\ m}$$

$$O_{60} = \sqrt{200^2 - 60^2} - \sqrt{200^2 - 100^2} = \mathbf{17.58\ m}$$

$$O_{70} = \sqrt{200^2 - 70^2} - \sqrt{200^2 - 100^2} = \mathbf{14.14\ m}$$

$$O_{80} = \sqrt{200^2 - 80^2} - \sqrt{200^2 - 100^2} = \mathbf{10.10\ m}$$

$$O_{90} = \sqrt{200^2 - 90^2} - \sqrt{200^2 - 100^2} = \mathbf{5.40\ m}$$

$$O_{100} = \sqrt{200^2 - 100^2} - \sqrt{200^2 - 100^2} = \mathbf{0.00\ m.}$$

Example 12.5

Tabulate the values of ordinates for the points on a circular curve having a long chord of 120 m and a versine of 5 m. The ordinates are to be measured from the long chord at an interval of 10 m.

Solution (Fig. 12.13):

For $x = 0$, the ordinate is equal to the mid-ordinate M which is given as 5 m.

From Eq. (4.17), we get

$$O_x = \sqrt{R^2 - x^2} - \sqrt{R^2 - \left(\frac{L}{2}\right)^2} \quad ...(a)$$

or

$$O_0 = M = 5 = \sqrt{R^2 - 0^2} - \sqrt{R^2 - \left(\frac{120}{2}\right)^2}$$

or

$$5 = R - \sqrt{R^2 - \left(\frac{120}{2}\right)^2} \quad ...(b)$$

By rearranging the terms of (*b*), we get

$$R = \frac{3625}{10}$$

$$= 362.5 \text{ m.}$$

The ordinates for different values of x are computed from (*a*), by substituting values of x = 10, 20, 30, 40, 50 and 60 m, R = 362.5 m, and L = 120 m, and are given in Table 12.1.

Table 12.1

x (m)	0	10	20	30	40	50	60
O_x (m)	5.00	4.86	4.45	3.76	2.79	1.54	0.00

Example 12.6

The chainage of the intersection point of two straights is 110 + 50, and the deflection angle is 45°20′. A circular curve of 250 m radius is to be set out to connect the two straights. Calculate the necessary data for setting out the curve by the method of offsets from the chords produced. (Length of one chain = 20 m with 100 links, and peg interval = 20 m or 100 links).

Solution (Fig. 12.15):

Given data:

Chainage of I = 110 + 50 chains

Deflection angle Δ = 45°20′

Radius of curve R = 250 m

From Eq. (12.5), the tangent length

$$T = R\tan\frac{\Delta}{2}$$

$$= 250 \times \tan\frac{45°20'}{2}$$

$$= 104.41 \text{ m.}$$

From Eq. (12.3), the length of the

$$l = \frac{\pi R\Delta}{180}$$

$$= \frac{\pi \times 250 \times 45°20'}{180}$$

$$= 197.80 \text{ m.}$$

From Eq. (12.6)

$$\text{Chainage of } T_1 = \text{Chainage of } I - T$$

$$= 110 \times 20 + 50 \times 0.2 - 104.41$$

$$= 2105.59 \text{ m}$$

$$\text{Chainage of } T_2 = \text{Chainage of } T_1 + l$$
$$= 2105.59 + 197.80$$
$$= 2303.39 \text{ m.}$$

Since the chainage of T_1 is 2105.59 m, the chainage of the first full station is calculated as below:

$$\frac{2105.59}{20} = 105.2795 \text{ chains.}$$

Chainage of the next full chain station

$$= 106 \text{ chains}$$
$$= 106 \times 20$$
$$= 2120 \text{ m.}$$

Length of the first sub-chord

$$= 2120 - \text{chainage of } T_1$$

or $$c_f = 2120 - 2105.59$$
$$= 14.41 \text{ m.}$$

Since the chainage of T_2 is 2303.39 m, the chainage of the last full station is calculated as below:

$$\frac{2303.39}{20} = 115.1695 \text{ chains.}$$

The chainage of the last full chain station

$$= 115 \text{ chains}$$
$$= 115 \times 20$$
$$= 2300 \text{ m.}$$

Length of the second sub-chord

$$= \text{Chainage of } T_2 - 2300$$

or $$c_l = 2303.39 - 2300$$
$$= 3.39 \text{ m}$$

The number normal chords $$= \frac{(2300 - 2120)}{20}$$
$$= 115 - 106$$
$$= 9$$

Total number of chords $$= 1 + 9 + 1$$
$$= 11.$$

From Eq. (12.19)

$$O_1 = \frac{c_f^2}{2R}$$
$$= \frac{14.41^2}{2 \times 250}$$
$$= \mathbf{0.42 \text{ m.}}$$

From Eq. (12.22)

$$O_2 = \frac{20 \times (14.41 + 20)}{2 \times 250}$$

$$= \mathbf{1.38\ m.}$$

From Eq. (12.23)

$$O_{3\ \text{to}\ 10} = \frac{C^2}{R}$$

$$= \frac{20^2}{250}$$

$$= \mathbf{1.60\ m.}$$

From Eq. (12.24)

$$O_{11} = \frac{c_l(c_l + C)}{2R}$$

$$= \frac{3.39 \times (3.39 + 20)}{2 \times 250}$$

$$= \mathbf{0.16\ m.}$$

Tape and theodolite method

This method may be classified as:

(*a*) Setting out the curve from point of commencement (P.C.)

(*b*) Setting out the curve from point of intersection (P.I.).

Setting out the curve from point of commencement (P.C.)

The method popularly known as *Rankine's method* is also called the *tangential-angle method* or the *deflection-angle method.* The method is based on the principle that the deflection angle to any point on a circular curve is measured by the one-half the angle subtended by the arc from P.C. to the point. It is assumed that the length of the arc is approximately equal to its chord length.

The method is accurate, and is generally used for important highways and railways.

The curve is set out by driving pegs at a regular interval equal to the length of the normal chord except at the beginning, and the end of the curve where sub-chord lengths are used. The deflection angles are required to locate the position of the pegs on the curve. The formula for determining the deflection angles, is derived below.

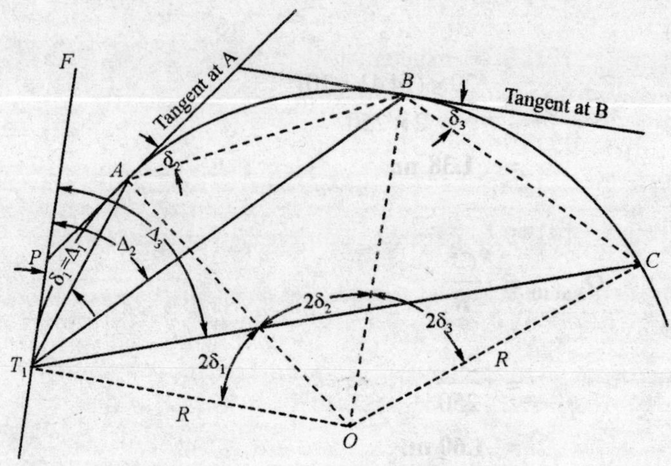

Fig. 12.18. Rankine's method of tangential or deflection angles

In Fig. 12.18, let the tangential angles for the points *A*, *B*, *C*, etc, be δ_1, δ_2, δ_3, etc., and Δ_1, Δ_2, Δ_3, etc, be the corresponding deflection angles of the points. T_1A, *AB*, *BC*, etc., are the first sub-chord c_f and the normal chords *C*, respectively.

From the property of a circle (c_f, Sec. 12.4),

$$\angle FT_1A = \frac{1}{2}\angle T_1OA$$

or

$$\delta_1 = \frac{1}{2}\angle T_1OA$$

or

$$\angle T_1OA = 2\delta_1$$

From $\Delta\, T_1OA$, we have

$$\frac{T_1A}{R} = \angle T_1OA$$

T_1A being the first sub-chord, we have

$$\frac{c_f}{R} = 2\delta_1$$

$$\delta_1 = \frac{c_f}{2R} \text{ radians}$$

$$= \frac{180^\circ c_f}{2\pi R} \text{ degrees}$$

$$= \frac{180\times 60 c_f}{2\pi R} \text{ minutes}$$

$$= 1718.9\frac{c_f}{R} \text{ minutes } (\textit{for the first sub-chord}) \quad ...(12.25)$$

$$\left.\begin{aligned}\delta_2 &= 1718.9\frac{C_2}{R}\text{ minutes}\\ \delta_3 &= 1718.9\frac{C_3}{R}\text{ minutes}\end{aligned}\right\}(\textit{for the normal chords})$$

$$\vdots$$

$$\delta_n = 1718.9\frac{c_l}{R}\text{ minutes}\quad(\textit{for the second sub-chord}) \qquad ...(12.26)$$

where c_f and c_l are the first and second sub-chords, and $C_2 = C_3 = C_{n\text{-}1} = C$, the normal chords. Thus

$$\delta_2 = \delta_3 = \delta_{n-1} = 1718.9\frac{C}{R}\text{ minutes}\,(\textit{for the normal chords}) \qquad ...(12.27)$$

Now, for the first chord T_1A, the deflection angle Δ_1 is equal to the tangential angle δ_1. Thus,

$$\Delta_1 = \delta_1 \qquad ...(12.28)$$

The deflection angle for B is Δ_2

or $$\Delta_2 = \angle FT_1B$$

From the property of a circle,

$$\angle FT_1B = \frac{1}{2}\angle T_1OB$$

or $$\Delta_2 = \frac{1}{2}(2\delta_1 + 2\delta_2)$$

$$= \delta_1 + \delta_2$$

From Eq. (12.28), we get

$$\Delta_2 = \Delta_1 + \delta_2$$

Similarly,

$$\Delta_3 = \delta_1 + \delta_2 + \delta_3$$

$$= \Delta_2 + \delta_3$$

and $$\Delta_n = \Delta_{n-1} + \delta_n \qquad ...(12.29)$$

Hence, the deflection angle for any chord is equal to the deflection angle for the previous chord plus the tangential angle for that chord.

Deflection angles in terms of the degree of curve

For the normal chord of 20 m and the degree of curve for a specified length of 30 m (Fig. 12.19)

The degree of curve D is defined for a chord length of 30°, therefore, if the chord length is 20 m, we have

$$\angle POQ = \frac{20}{30}D$$

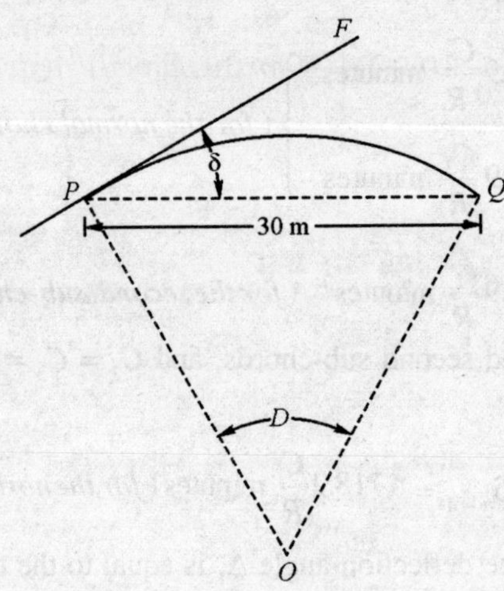

Fig. 12.19. Relationship between the degree of curve and the tangential angle

From the property of a circle, we have

$$\angle POQ = 2\delta = \frac{2}{3}D$$

or
$$\delta = \frac{D}{3}$$

Since, the normal chord is of 20 m length

$$\delta_2 = \delta_3 = \ldots = \delta_{n-1} = \delta = \frac{D}{3}$$

For the first and second sub-chords c_f and c_l, respectively, we have

$$\delta_1 = \frac{c_f}{20}\frac{D}{3} = \frac{c_f D}{60}$$

and
$$\delta_n = \frac{c_l}{20}\frac{D}{3} = \frac{c_l D}{60}$$

Therefore,

$$\Delta_1 = \delta_1 = \frac{c_f D}{60} \quad \textit{(for the first sub-chord)} \qquad \text{...(12.30)}$$

$$\Delta_2 = \Delta_1 + \delta_2 = \frac{c_f D}{60} + \frac{D}{3}$$

$$\Delta_3 = \Delta_2 + \delta_3 = \frac{c_f D}{60} + \frac{D}{3} + \frac{D}{3} = \frac{c_f D}{60} + \frac{2D}{3}$$

$$\Delta_{2 \text{ to } (n-1)} = \frac{c_f D}{60} + \frac{(n-1)D}{3}$$

or $$= \frac{D}{3}\left[\frac{c_f}{20} + (n-1)\right] \quad \textit{(for the normal chords)} \qquad ...(12.31)$$

and $$\Delta_n = \Delta_{n-1} + \delta_n$$

$$= \frac{D}{3}\left[\frac{c_f}{20} + (n-2)\right] + \frac{c_l D}{60}$$

$$= \frac{D}{3}\left[\frac{(c_f + c_l)}{20} + (n-2)\right] \quad \textit{(for the second sub-chord)} \qquad ...(12.32)$$

For the normal chord of 20 m and the degree of curve also for 20 m length (Fig. 12.19)

In this case $PQ = 20$ m, therefore,

$$\angle POQ = D$$

or $$\delta = \frac{D}{2}$$

$$\delta_1 = \frac{c_f}{20}\frac{D}{2} = \frac{c_f D}{40}$$

$$\delta_{2 \text{ to } (n-1)} = \frac{C}{20}\frac{D}{2} = \frac{D}{2}$$

Therefore,

$$\Delta_1 = \delta_1 = \frac{c_f D}{40} \quad \textit{(for the first sub-chord)} \qquad ...(12.33)$$

$$\Delta_2 = \Delta_1 + \delta_2 = \frac{c_f D}{40} + \frac{D}{2}$$

$$\Delta_3 = \Delta_2 + \delta_3 = \frac{c_f D}{40} + \frac{2D}{2}$$

$$\Delta_{2 \text{ to } (n-1)} = \frac{D}{2}\left[\frac{c_f}{20} + (n-1)\right] \quad \textit{(for the normal chords)} \qquad ...(12.34)$$

$$\Delta_n = \Delta_{n-1} + \delta_n$$

$$= \frac{D}{2}\left[\frac{c_f}{20} + (n-2)\right] + \frac{c_l D}{40}$$

$$= \frac{D}{2}\left[\frac{c_f + c_l}{20} + (n-2)\right] \quad \textit{(for the second sub-chord)} \qquad ...(12.35)$$

For the normal chord of 30 m and degree of curve also 30 m length

The formulae to calculate Δ_1, Δ_2, Δ_3 etc. for this case can be derived in a similar manner as above. Therefore,

$$\Delta_1 = \frac{c_f}{30}\frac{D}{2} \quad \text{...(12.36)}$$

$$\Delta_{2 \text{ to } (n-1)} = \frac{D}{2}\left[\frac{c_f}{30} + (n-1)\right] \quad \text{...(12.37)}$$

$$D_n = \frac{D}{2}\left[\frac{c_f + c_l}{30} + (n-2)\right] \quad \text{...(12.38)}$$

Field procedures

Rankine's method of tangential angles involves the use of a theodolite to lay off the deflection angles and a tape to measure the distances.

The point T_2 is located on the straight from its chainage, and a theodolite is set up at T_1 having the initial reading zero for the point *I*. Clamp the lower plate and unclamp the upper plate. Set the vernier to read the angle Δ_1. Measure the distance T_1A equal to the length of the first sub-chord c_f. Fix a peg at *A* when the peg is on the vertical hair of the cross hairs. This fixes the first point *A* on the curve.

To fix the second point *B*, set the vernier to read the deflection angle Δ_2, and measure the distance equal to the length of the normal chord *C*, keeping zero end of the tape at *A* so that *AB* is equal to *C*. The peg is fixed at *B* when it lies on the vertical hair of the cross hairs.

The above procedure is continued till the point of tangency T_2 is located. If there is no error in calculations, observations, and taping, the last point should finally coincide with the already fixed position of T_2.

It may be noted that in the case of a left-handed curve, each of the values Δ_1, Δ_2, Δ_3, etc., should be subtracted from 360° to obtain the required values to which the vernier is to be set to locate the points on the curve.

Setting out the curve from the point of intersection (P.I.)

This method also requires a theodolite to measure the angles and a tape to measure the distances. The method has advantage over the setting out from T_1, because once the instrument is set at *I* to determine the angle of intersection ϕ it can also be used at the same time for setting out the curve, and thus saving considerable time in setting up the instrument at T_1. However, the method has the disadvantage of pegs being not at full chain lengths.

In Fig. 12.20, to locate a point *A* on the curve, the angle α_A measured from the direction IT_1 at *I* and the distance from T_1 are required. Draw a perpendicular *AQ* to OT_1, intersecting OT_1 at *Q* and another *AP* to T_1I, intersecting T_1I at *P*.

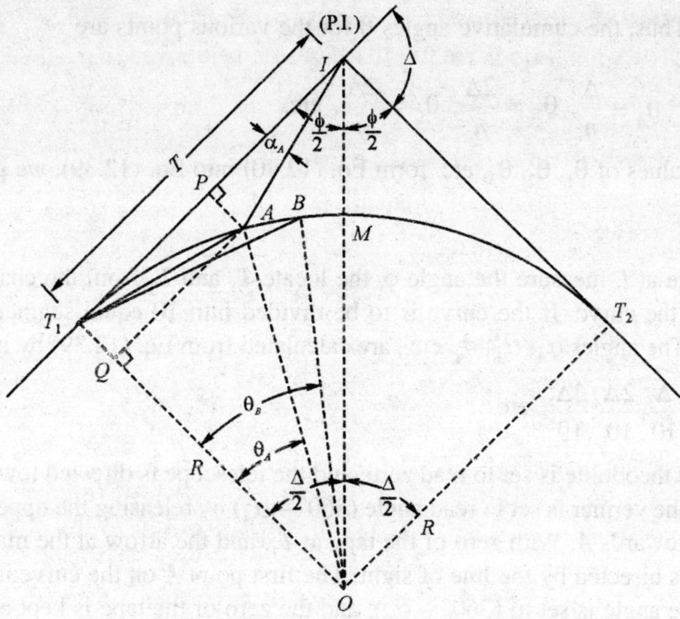

Fig. 12.20. Setting out the curve from P.I.

In Δ *PIA*, we have

$$\tan \alpha_A = \frac{PA}{PI}$$

$$= \frac{T_1Q}{T - T_1P}$$

$$= \frac{T_1O - QO}{T - AQ}$$

$$= \frac{R - R\cos\theta_A}{R\tan\frac{\Delta}{2} - R\sin\theta_A}$$

$$= \frac{1 - \cos\theta_A}{\tan\frac{\Delta}{2} - \sin\theta_A}$$

or in general, $$\alpha = \tan^{-1}\left[\frac{(1-\cos\theta)}{\tan\frac{\Delta}{2} - \sin\theta}\right] \qquad \text{...(12.39)}$$

To determine the value of θ, generally, the curve is divided in two n equal parts. If the length of the curve is l then the length of each segment will be $\frac{l}{n}$, and the angle subtended by each segment at the centre O will be $\frac{\Delta}{n}$. Thus, the cumulative angles θ for the various points are

$$\theta_A = \frac{\Delta}{n},\ \theta_B = \frac{2\Delta}{n},\ \theta_C = \frac{2\Delta}{n},\ \text{etc.} \qquad ...(12.40)$$

Substituting the values of θ_1, θ_2, θ_3, etc. form Eq. (12.40) into Eq. (12.39), we get α_A, α_B, α_C, etc.

Field Operations

Set up a theodolite at I, measure the angle ϕ, the locate T_1 and T_2 from the chainage of I, tangent length, and length of the curve. If the curve is to be divided into 10 equal segments, length of each segment will be $l/10$. The angles α_A, α_B, α_C etc., are calculated from Eq. (12.39) by inputting the values of θ_A, θ_B, θ_C, etc. as $\frac{\Delta}{10}, \frac{2\Delta}{10}, \frac{3\Delta}{10}$, etc.

The vernier of the theodolite is set to read zero, and the telescope is directed towards T_1. The lower plate is clamped, and the vernier is set to read angle $(360° - \alpha_A)$ by releasing the upper plate. The line of sight is now directed towards A. With zero of the tape at T_1, and the arrow at the mark $l/10$, the tape is swung till the aroow is bisected by the line of sight. The first point A on the curve is, thus located. For the second point B, the angle is set to $(360° - \alpha_B)$, and the zero of the tape is kept at A. The point B is located by following the above steps.

The above procedure is continued till the midpoint M of the curve is reached. The midpoint of the curve is located separately by calculating the mid-ordinate and α_M as $\left[90° - \frac{\Delta}{2}\right]$. The vernier reading to be set is $\left[360° - \left(90° - \frac{\Delta}{2}\right)\right] = \left[270° + \frac{\Delta}{2}\right]$. The other half of the curve is located by measuring angles α_A, α_B, α_C, etc. from the forward tangent IT_2.

Two-theodolites method

This method is employed for setting out a curve making angular measurements alone by two theodolites. The method is quite accurate. It is specially preferred when the ground is rough, and accurate chaining is not possible. Since, in this method each point is fixed independently, the error in setting out is not carried forward.

The method is based on the property of a circle described in Sec. 12.4, that the angle subtended by a chord at any point on the circumference of the circle is equal to the angle between the chord and the tangent. Thus, for the chord T_1A in Fig. 12.21.

$$\angle IT_1A = \angle T_1T_2A = \Delta_1$$

and for T_1B $\qquad \angle IT_1B = \angle T_1T_2B = \Delta_2$

The method requires setting up two theodolites, one at T_1 and the other at T_2. The computed deflection angles for the points A, B, C, etc., on the curve using the formulae given in Sec. 12.7 for Rankine's method of tangential angles, are directly used for setting out the curve by this method.

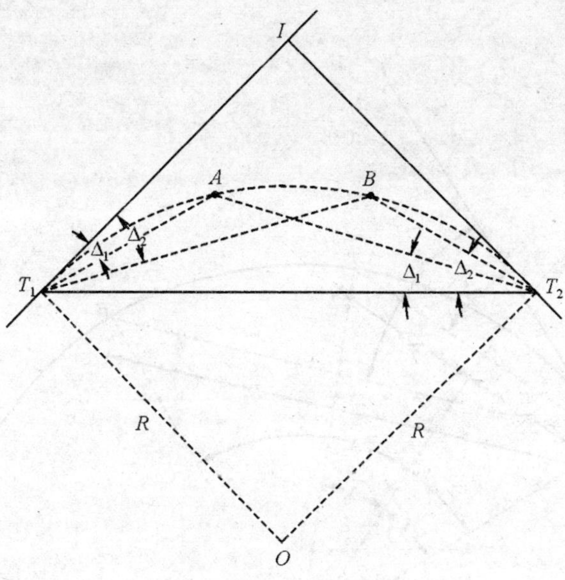

Fig. 12.21 Two-theodolites method

Field operation

Set up one theodolite at T_1 and the other at T_2. The theodolite at T_1 should read zero for the point I and the theodolite at T_2 should read zero for the point T_1. Set the first deflection angle Δ_1 on both theodolites. Thus their telescopes are in the direction T_1A and T_2A, respectively. Now the attendant is asked to move with a ranging rod in the line of the sight of one of the theodolites. The observer of the other theodolite finds the point where the ranging rod is intersected by the vertical hair of his theodolite. This point is the required location on the curve.

The second point is located by setting the second deflection angle Δ_2 on the two theodolites, and the location of the point on curve is determined by the procedure given above. The process is continued for locating the other points on the curve, till all the points are located on the ground.

Tacheometric method

In this method, the angular and linear measurements are made by using a tacheometer. The angular measurements are the deflection angles (*cf.*, Sec. 12.7), and the linear measurements are the distances of the points on the curve from the instrument station. The tacheometric method is less accurate than the Rankine's method because the linear measurements are not accurately measured with a tacheometer.

In Fig. 12.22, the points A, B, C, etc., are the points on the curve to be located. Let the deflection angles for these points be Δ_1, Δ_2, Δ_3, etc., and their distances from T_1 be L_1, L_2, L_3, etc. The angles subtended at O by the chords of lengths L_1, L_2, L_3, etc., will be $2\Delta_1$, $2\Delta_2$, $2\Delta_3$, etc. The point K is the midpoint of T_1A, therefore, $T_1K = KA = \dfrac{L_1}{2}$.

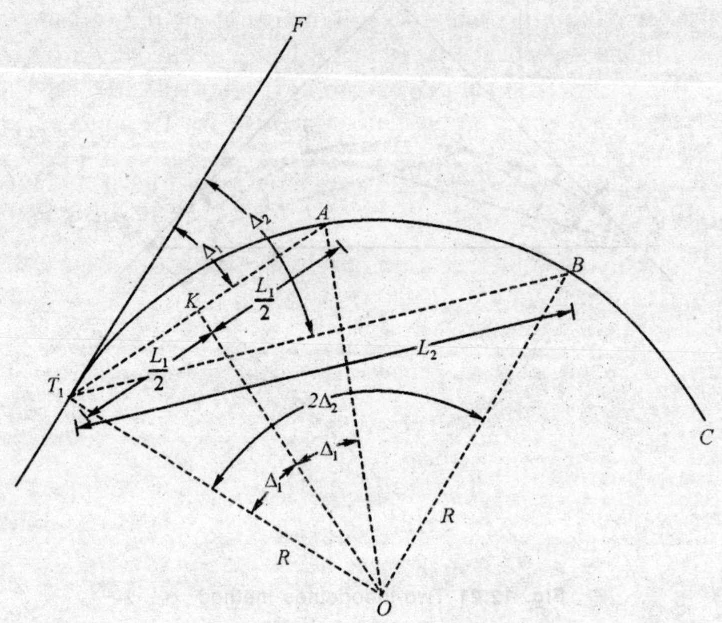

Fig. 12.22 Tacheometric method

From ΔT_1OK, we have

$$T_1K = R \sin \Delta_1$$

or

$$\frac{L_1}{2} = R \sin \Delta_1$$

$$L_1 = 2R \sin \Delta_1$$

Similarly,

$$L_2 = 2R \sin \Delta_2$$

In general,

$$L_n = 2R \sin \Delta_n \qquad ...(12.41)$$

In the case of horizontal line of sight, the horizontal distance L for the staff intercept s is computed from the following formula of tacheometry.

$$L = ks + C \qquad ...(12.42)$$

where

L = the horizontal distance,

k = the multiplying constant,

s = the staff intercept, and

C = the additive constant.

For the inclined sights with the inclination angle θ, Eq. (12.42) is modified as

$$L = ks \cos^2\theta + C \cos \theta \qquad ...(12.43)$$

Field operations

A tacheometer is set at T_1 with the line of sight towards I, and the vernier to read zero. The deflection angle Δ_1 is set for the first point A. The line of sight is directed towards A. The attendant is asked to keep the staff on the line T_1A, and move towards T_1 or away from T_1 till the required staff reading s_1 is obtained. The staff position is the position of the point A on the ground. The other points are located in the similar manner.

Total station method

A total station is an instrument which can make angular and linear measurements simultaneously. The values of the angles and distances are directly displayed on a display panel equipped with a keyboard for inputting the necessary data or for displaying the value of a required quantity.

The technique employed in this method is known as *radial-stake out technique.* The procedure is explained below.

The instrument is set up at any point P of known location (x_P, y_P) such that the points, A, B, C, etc., to be located on the curve, are visible (Fig. 12.23). Take a back sight to another point Q whose location (x_Q, y_Q) is also known. The azimuths of the line PQ will be

$$\theta = \tan^{-1}\left[\frac{x_Q - x_P}{y_Q - y_P}\right] \quad ...(12.44)$$

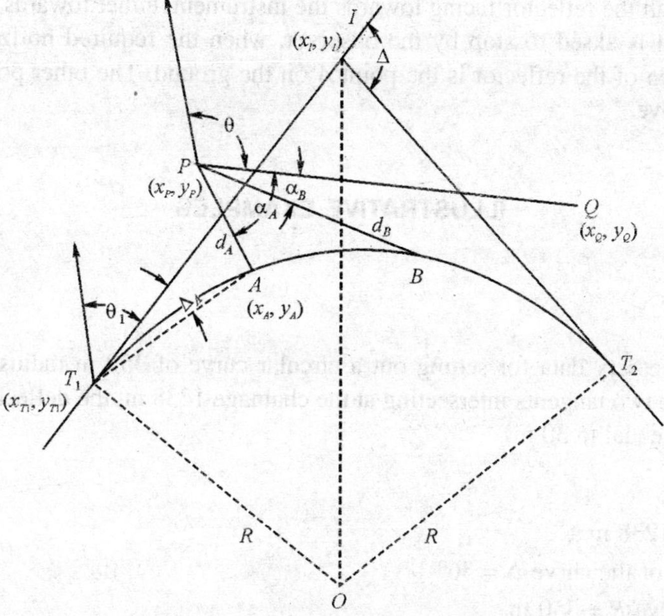

Fig. 12.23 Total station method

If the azimuth of the back tangent T_1I is θ_1, and the coordinates of I are (x_I, y_I), then the coordinates of T_1 are

$$x_{T1} = x_I - \left[R\tan\frac{\Delta}{2}\right]\sin\theta_1$$

$$y_{T1} = y_I - \left[R\tan\frac{\Delta}{2}\right]\cos\theta_1 \qquad \text{...(12.45)}$$

where Δ is the deflection angle of the curve.

The coordinates of the point A are

$$x_A = x_{T1} + (2R \sin \Delta_A) \sin (\theta_1 + \Delta_A)$$
$$y_A = y_{T1} + (2R \sin \Delta_A) \cos (\theta_1 + \Delta_A) \qquad \text{...(12.46)}$$

where Δ_A is the deflection angle for A.

To locate the point A from P, the distance PA and the angle QPA are required. These are computed as below:

$$d_A = \sqrt{[(x_A - x_P^2) + (y_A - y_P)^2]} \qquad \text{...(12.47)}$$

$$\alpha_A = \tan^{-1}\left[\frac{x_A - x_P}{y_A - y_P}\right] - \theta \qquad \text{...(12.48)}$$

Field operations

The instrument is set up at the point P with telescope directed towards the point Q, and the horizontal angle reading is set to zero. The telescope is rotated by an angle α_A and the attendant is asked to move on the line of sight with the reflector facing towards the instrument, either towards the point P or away from it. The attendant is aksed to stop by the observer, when the required horizontal distance d_A is displayed. The position of the reflector is the point A on the ground. The other points are fixed in the similar manner as above.

ILLUSTRATIVE EXAMPLES

Example 12.7

Calculate the necessary data for setting out a circular curve of 350 m radius by tangential-angle method to connect the two tangents intersecting at the chainage 1238 m, the deflection angle being 36°. Take the peg interval equal to 30 m.

Solution (Fig. 12.24):

Chainage of I = 1238 m

Deflection angle of the curve Δ = 36°

Radius of the curve R = 350 m

Length of the normal chord C = 30 m

The points to be located on the curve are 1, 2, 3, etc.

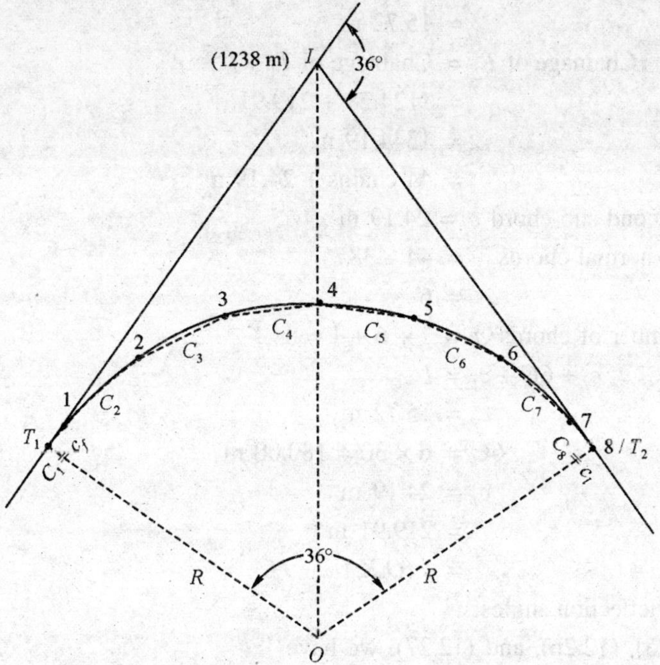

Fig. 12.24

From Eq. (12.5), we get

$$T = R\tan\frac{\Delta}{2}$$

$$= 350\tan\frac{36^\circ}{2}$$

$$= 113.72 \text{ m}$$

From Eq. (12.3), we get

$$l = \frac{\pi R\Delta}{180}$$

$$= \frac{\pi \times 350 \times 36}{180}$$

$$= 219.91 \text{ m}$$

From Eq. (12.6), we get

$$\text{Chainage of } T_1 = \text{Chainage of } I - T$$

$$= 1238 - 113.72$$

$$= 1124.28$$

$$= 37 \text{ chains} + 14.28 \text{ m}$$

$$\text{Chainage of the point 1} = 38 \text{ chains}$$

$$\text{Length of the first sub-chord} \quad c_f = 38 \text{ chains} - (37 \text{ chains} + 14.28 \text{ m})$$

$$= 1 \text{ chain} - 14.28 \text{ m}$$

$$= 30 - 14.28$$

$$= 15.72 \text{ m}$$

$$\text{Chainage of } T_2 = \text{Chainage of } T_1 + l$$
$$= 1124.28 + 219.91$$
$$= 1344.19 \text{ m}$$
$$= 44 \text{ chains} + 24.19 \text{ m}$$

Length of the second sub-chord c_l = 24.19 m

Total number of normal chords = 44 – 38 = 6

Check: Total number of chords $n = 1 + 6 + 1 = 8$

$$c_f + 6C + c_l = l$$
$$c_f = 15.72 \text{ m}$$
$$6C = 6 \times 30 = 180.00 \text{ m}$$
$$c_l = 24.19 \text{ m}$$

Total lengths = 219.91 m = l (*O.K.*)

Computation of deflection angles:

From Eqs. (12.25), (12.26), and (12.27), we have

$$\delta_1 = 1718.9 \frac{c_f}{R} = \frac{1718.9 \times 15.72}{350} = 77.20'$$
$$= 1°17'12''$$

$$\delta_{2 \text{ to } 7} = 1718.9 \frac{C}{R} = \frac{1718.9 \times 30}{350} = 147.33'$$
$$= 2°27'20''$$

$$\delta_8 = 1718.9 \frac{c_l}{R} = \frac{1718.9 \times 24.19}{350} = 118.80'$$
$$= 1°58'48''$$

From Eq. (12.29), we get

$$\Delta_n = \Delta_{n-1} + \delta_n$$
$$\Delta_1 = \Delta_0 + \delta_1 = 0 + 1°17'12'' = 1°17'12''$$
$$\Delta_2 = \Delta_1 + \delta_2 = 1°17'12'' + 2°27'20'' = 3°44'32''$$
$$\Delta_3 = \Delta_2 + \delta_3 = 3°44'32'' + 2°27'20'' = 6°11'52''$$
$$\Delta_4 = \Delta_3 + \delta_4 = 6°11'52'' + 2°27'20'' = 8°39'12''$$
$$\Delta_5 = \Delta_4 + \delta_5 = 8°39'12'' + 2°27'20'' = 11°06'32''$$
$$\Delta_6 = \Delta_5 + \delta_6 = 11°06'32'' + 2°27'20'' = 13°33'52''$$
$$\Delta_7 = \Delta_6 + \delta_7 = 13°33'52'' + 2°27'20'' = 16°01'12''$$
$$\Delta_8 = \Delta_7 + \delta_8 = 16°01'12'' + 1°58'48'' = \mathbf{18°00'00''}$$

Check:

$$\Delta_8 = \frac{1}{2} \times \text{deflection angle of the curve}$$

$$= \frac{1}{2} \times \angle T_1OT_2$$

$$= \frac{1}{2} \times 36°$$

$$= 18° \; (O.K.)$$

Example 12.8

Two tangents intersect at chainage 2380 m, the deflection angle being 50°30′. Compute the necessary data for setting out a 5.7° curve to connect the two tangents if it is intended to set out the curve by Rankine's method of tangential angles. Take the length of the normal chord as 30 m. Also tabulate the values of the deflection angles for setting out with theodolite having least count of 20″.

Solution:

Chainage of I = 2380 m

Deflection angle of the curve Δ = 50°30′

Degree of the curve D = 5.7°

Length of the normal chord C = 30 m

From Eq. (12.1)

$$D = \frac{1718.9}{R}$$

$$R = \frac{1718.9}{D}$$

$$= \frac{1718.9}{5.7}$$

$$= 301.56 \text{ m.}$$

From Eq. (12.5),

$$T = R \tan \frac{\Delta}{2}$$

$$= 301.56 \times \tan \frac{50°30'}{2}$$

$$= 142.22 \text{ m.}$$

From Eq. (12.3),

$$l = \frac{\pi R \Delta}{180}$$

$$= \frac{\pi \times 301.56 \times 50°30'}{180}$$

$$= 265.79 \text{ m}$$

Chainage of P.C. = Chainage of P.I. – T
= 2380 – 142.22
= 2237.78 m
= 74 chains + 17.78 m

Length of the first sub-chord c_f = 75 × 30 – (71 × 30 + 17.78 m)
= 12.22 m.

Chainage of P.T. = Chainage of P.C. + l
= 2237.78 + 265.79
= 2503.57 m
= 83 chains + 13.57 m

Length of the second sub-chord c_f = 13.57

Total number of normal chords
= 83 – 75
= 8

Total number of chords = 1 + 8 + 1
= 10

Check: $c_f + 8C + c_l = l$

$c_f = 12.22$

$8C = 8 \times 30 = 240.00$ m

$c_l = 13.57$ m

Total = 265.79 m (*O.K.*)

From Eqs. (12.36), (12.37), and (12.38), the deflection angles are

$$\Delta_1 = \frac{c_f}{30}\frac{D}{2}$$

$$\Delta_{2 \text{ to } 9} = \frac{D}{2}\left[\frac{c_f}{30} + (n-1)\right]$$

$$\Delta_{10} = \frac{D}{2}\left[\frac{c_f + c_l}{30} + (n-2)\right]$$

$$\Delta_1 = \frac{12.22}{30} \times \frac{5.7}{2} = 1°09'39''$$

$$\Delta_2 = \frac{5.7}{2} \times \left[\frac{12.22}{30} + (2-1)\right] = 4°00'39''$$

$$\Delta_3 = \frac{5.7}{2} \times \left[\frac{12.22}{30} + (3-1)\right] = 6°51'39''$$

$$\Delta_4 = \frac{5.7}{2} \times \left[\frac{12.22}{30} + (4-1)\right] = 9°42'39''$$

$$\Delta_5 = \frac{5.7}{2}\times\left[\frac{12.22}{30}+(5-1)\right]=12°33'39''$$

$$\Delta_6 = \frac{5.7}{2}\times\left[\frac{12.22}{30}+(6-1)\right]=15°24'39''$$

$$\Delta_7 = \frac{5.7}{2}\times\left[\frac{12.22}{30}+(7-1)\right]=18°15'39''$$

$$\Delta_8 = \frac{5.7}{2}\times\left[\frac{12.22}{30}+(8-1)\right]=21°06'39''$$

$$\Delta_9 = \frac{5.7}{2}\times\left[\frac{12.22}{30}+(9-1)\right]=23°57'39''$$

$$\Delta_{10} = \frac{5.7}{2}\times\left[\frac{12.22+13.57}{30}+(10-2)\right]=25°15'00''$$

$$\Delta_{10} = \frac{1}{2}\text{Deflection angle of the curve}$$

$$= \frac{1}{2}\times 50°30'$$

$$= 25°15'00''\ (O.K.)$$

The computed values are presented in Table 12.2 for a 20″ theodolite.

Table 12.2

Peg No.	Chainage (m)	Chord length (m)	Deflection angles	Deflection angles for theodolite setting
1	2250.00	12.22	1°09′39″	1°09′40″
2	2280.00	30	4°00′39″	4°00′40″
3	2310.00	30	6°51′39″	6°51′40″
4	2340.00	30	9°42′39″	9°42′40″
5	2370.00	30	12°33′39″	12°33′40″
6	2400.00	30	15°24′39″	15°24′40″
7	2430.00	30	18°15′39″	18°15′40″
8	2460.00	30	21°06′39″	21°06′40″
9	2490.00	30	23°57′39″	23°57′40″
10	2503.57	13.57	25°15′00″	25°15′00″

Example 12.9

Tabulate the data necessary for setting out a circular curve with the following specifications:

Angle of intersection = 144°

Chainage of the point of intersection = 1390 m

Radius of the curve = 300 m

The curve is to be set out from the point of intersection.

Solution (Fig. 12.20):

The deflection angle of the curve $\Delta = 180° - 144° = 36°$

From Eq. (12.3), the length of the curve

$$l = \frac{\pi R \Delta}{180}$$

$$= \frac{\pi \times 300 \times 36}{180}$$

$$= 188.50 \text{ m}$$

Let the curve be divided into ten equal segments. The length each segment will be $\frac{188.50}{10} = 18.85\text{ m}$.

The cumulative angles θ from Eq. (12.40) are

$$\theta_1 = \frac{36}{10} = 3.6°$$

$$\theta_2 = 2 \times \frac{36}{10} = 7.2°$$

$$\theta_3 = 3 \times \frac{36}{10} = 10.8°$$

$$\theta_4 = 4 \times \frac{36}{10} = 14.4°$$

$$\theta_5 = 5 \times \frac{36}{10} = 18.0°$$

Since half of the curve is to be set out in the similar manner as with respect to the forward tangent, only half of the data are required to be calculated.

The values of the angle α are given by Eq. (12.39)

$$\alpha = \tan^{-1}\left[\frac{1 - \cos\theta}{\tan\frac{\Delta}{2} - \sin\theta}\right]$$

Substituting the values of θ_1, θ_2, θ_3, etc., we get the values of α, and the same are tabulated in Table 12.3.

Table 12.3

Point No.	Chord lengths (m)	θ	α
1	18.85	3.6°	0°25′53″
2	18.85	7.2°	2°15′45″
3	18.85	10.5°	7°20′18″
4	18.85	14.4°	22°23′54″
5	18.85	18.0°	72°00′00″

12.8 FIELD PROBLEMS IN SETTING OUT THE CIRCULAR CURVES

The following are some of the field problems in setting out the circular curves. In urban areas more than one of these may occur simultaneously.

1. Passing the curve through a given point.
2. Curve tangential to three lines.
3. Shifting forward tangent parallel outward, radius unchanged.
4. Shifting forward tangent parallel outward, radius changed.
5. Changing the direction of forward tangent. P.T. unchanged.
6. Changing the direction of forward tangent, P.T. moved ahead.
7. Locating the intersection of a circular curve and a straight line.
8. Locating the intersection of two circular crves.
9. Curve not completely visible from the starting point.
10. An obstacle intervenes on the curve.
11. Point of intersection inaccessible.
12. Point of commencement inaccessible.
13. Point of tangency inaccessible.
14. Both point of commencement and point of intersection inaccessible.
15. Both point of commencement and point of tangency inaccessible.

Case-1: Passing the curve through a given point

Let the given point through which the curve has to pass is A as shown in Fig. 12.25. The curve has to be tangential to the two straights T_1I and IT_2. Therefore, the problem reduces to determining the degree or radius of that circular curve which satisfies these conditions. After determining the radius or degree of the curve, the curve may be set out by any one of the methods discussed in Sec. 12.7.

In $\Delta\ T_1OI$, we have

$$\angle T_1IO = 90° - \frac{\Delta}{2}$$

Therefore, $\angle AIO = \angle T_1IO - \angle PIA$

$$\text{or} \qquad \omega = 90° - \frac{\Delta}{2} - \alpha$$

where $\angle PIA = \alpha$

Also $\angle AOI = \angle T_1OI - \angle T_1OA$

$$\text{or} \qquad \lambda = \frac{\Delta}{2} - \theta$$

where $\theta = \angle T_1OA.$

From Δ *IAO*, we get

$$\angle IAO = 180° - (\lambda + \omega)$$

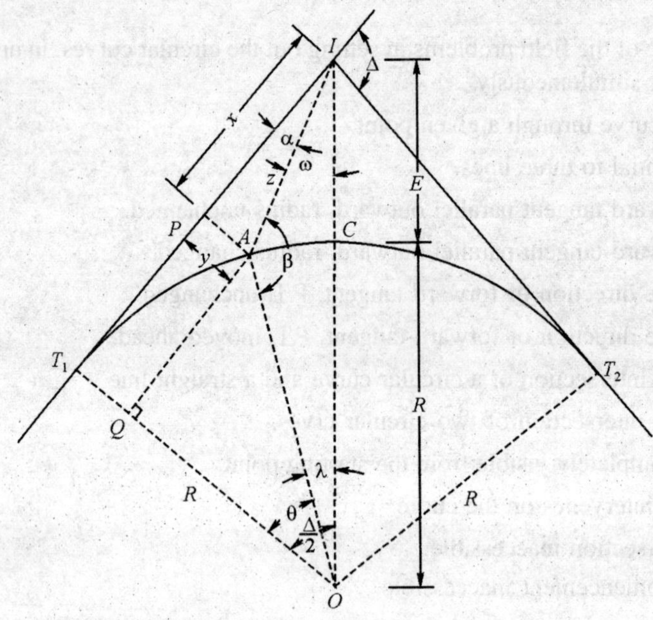

Fig. 12.25 Passing the curve through a given point

$$\text{or} \qquad \beta = 180° - \left[\frac{\Delta}{2} - \theta + 90° - \frac{\Delta}{2} - \alpha\right]$$

$$= 90° + (\theta + \alpha)$$

where $\angle AOC = \gamma.$

Solving Δ *IAO* by sine rule, we get

$$\frac{\sin\beta}{OI} = \frac{\sin\omega}{AO}$$

$$\text{or} \qquad \frac{\sin[90°+(\theta+\alpha)]}{(R+E)} = \frac{\sin\left[90° - \left(\frac{\Delta}{2} + \alpha\right)\right]}{R} \qquad ...(12.49)$$

From Eq. (12.8), we have

$$E = R\left[\sec\frac{\Delta}{2} - 1\right]$$

Therefore, $$R + E = R\sec\frac{\Delta}{2}$$

Now Eq. (12.49) becomes

$$\cos(\theta + \alpha) = \sec\frac{\Delta}{2}\cos\left[\frac{\Delta}{2} + \alpha\right]$$

$$= \frac{\cos\left(\frac{\Delta}{2} + \alpha\right)}{\cos\frac{\Delta}{2}}$$

or $$\theta = \cos^{-1}\left[\frac{\cos\left(\frac{\Delta}{2} + \alpha\right)}{\cos\frac{\Delta}{2}}\right] - \alpha \qquad \text{...(12.50)}$$

Let the distance of A from I along the tangent IT_1 and the perpendicular distance of A from IT_1 be x and y, respectively, then,

From Δ IPA, we get

$$\tan\alpha = \frac{y}{x}$$

or $$\alpha = \tan^{-1}\frac{y}{x} \qquad \text{...(12.51)}$$

By substituting the value of α from Eq. (12.51) into the Eq. (12.50), we get the value of θ.

Now, the radius of the curve is determined as under

$$T_1O = T_1Q + QO$$

$$R = y + R\cos\theta$$

$$= x\tan\alpha + R\cos\theta$$

$$R = \frac{x\tan\alpha}{1 - \cos\theta} \qquad \text{...(12.52)}$$

Case-2: Curve tangential to three lines

In Fig. 12.26, a circular is shown which is tangential to three lines T_1I, PQ and IT_2 at T_1, A, and T_2, respectively. The problem is to determine the radius of such a curve which is tangential to all the three lines.

Let the length of PQ be d, and the angles IPQ and IQP be α and β, respectively. The curve can be considered having two segments T_1A and T_2A. For the segment T_1A, the two tangents T_1P and PA meet at P, with deflection angle α, and for that of T_2A, the two tangents T_2Q and QA meet at Q, with deflection angle β.

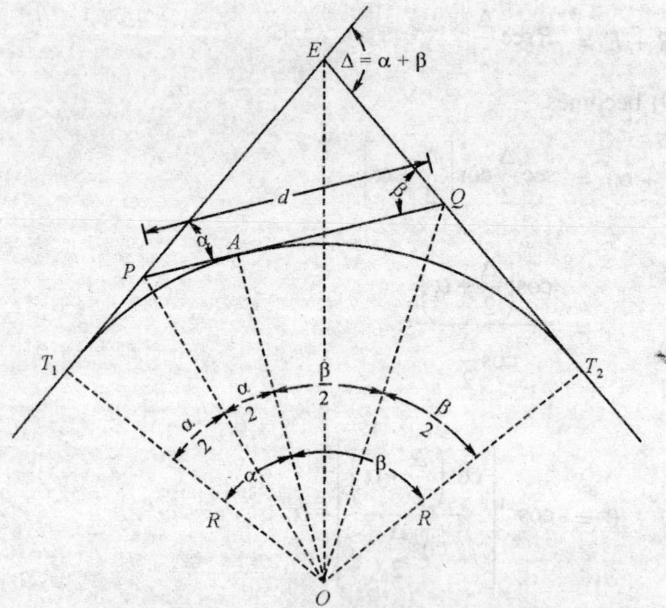

Fig. 12.26 Curve tangential to three lines

For the segment T_2A, the tangent length

$$T_1P = PA = R\tan\frac{\alpha}{2}$$

and for the segment T_2A, the tangent length

$$T_2Q = QA = R\tan\frac{\beta}{2}$$

We have

$$PQ = d = PA + QA$$

$$= R\left[\tan\frac{\alpha}{2} + \tan\frac{\beta}{2}\right]$$

Therefore,

$$R = \frac{d}{\tan\frac{\alpha}{2} + \tan\frac{\beta}{2}} \quad \text{...(12.53)}$$

Case-3: Shifting forward tangent parallel outward, radius unchanged

When a new straight is to replace the existing one by moving it parallel outward, without changing the radius of the curve, the existing curve is required to be relaid.

In Fig. 12.27, the firm line shows the elements of the original curve while the dashed lines and the letters with dash correspond to the condition when the forward tangent is shifted to new position $I'T'_2$ parallel to itself by a distance *d*.

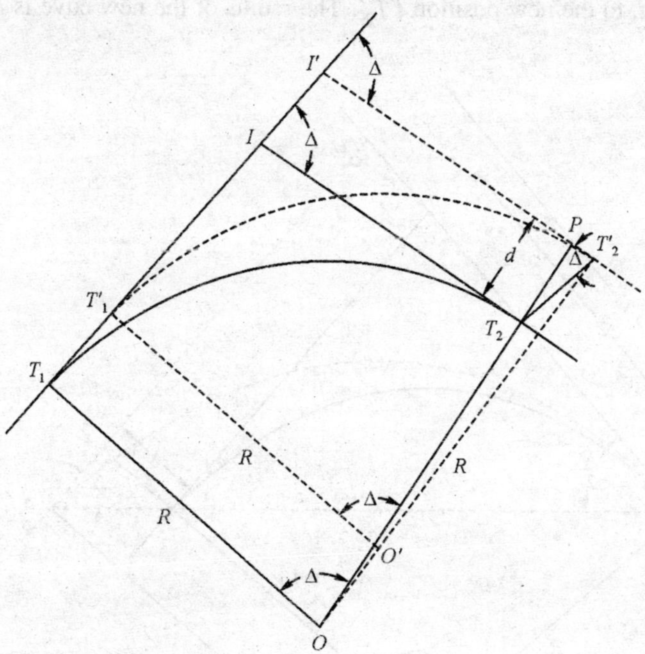

Fig. 12.27 Shifting forward tangent outward, radius unchanged

Thus, the perpendicular distance T_2P between the two positions of the tangents IT_2 and $I'T'_2$, is equal to *d*, and

$$T_1T_1' = OO' = T_2T_2' = II'$$

Since II' is parallel to T_2T_2',

$$\angle PT_2'T_2 = \Delta$$

From $\Delta\ PT_2'T_2$, we have

$$T_2T_2' = \frac{d}{\sin\Delta} \quad ...(12.54)$$

Thus,

$$\text{Chainage of the new P.I. I}' = \text{Chainage of the original P.I.} + \frac{d}{\sin\Delta} \quad ...(12.55)$$

$$\text{Chainage of the new P.C. } T_1' = \text{Chainage of the original P.C.} + \frac{d}{\sin\Delta} \quad ...(12.56)$$

If, however the forward tangent is shifted inward, Eq. (12.54) still holds good, but the chainage of the new P.C. will be obtained by subtracting $\dfrac{d}{\sin\Delta}$ from the chainage of the original P.C.

Case-4: Shifting forward tangent parallel outward, radius changed

Fig. 12.28 shows that the forward tangent IT_2 has been moved outward parallel to its original position by a distance d, to the new position $I'T_2'$. The radius of the new cuve is R'.

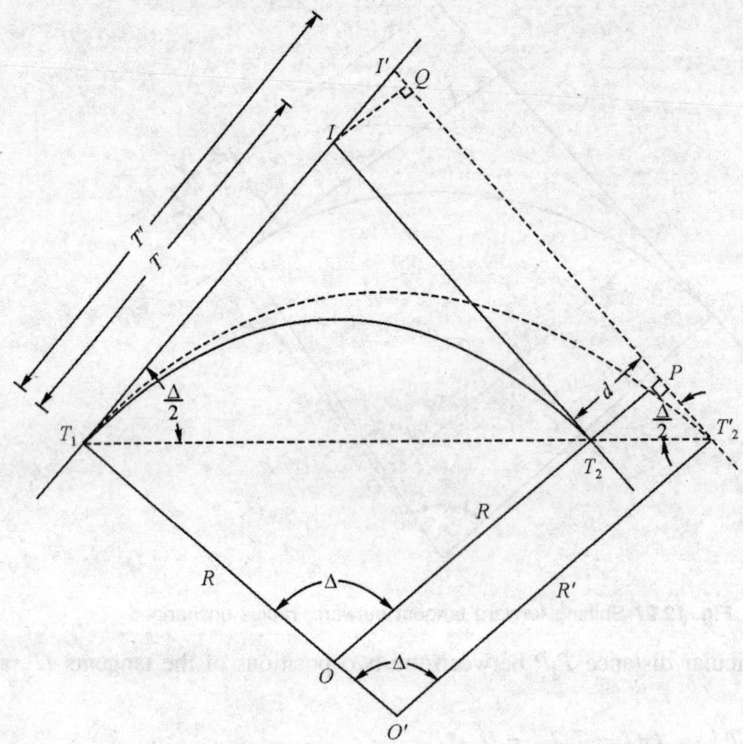

Fig. 12.28 Shifting forward tangent outward, radius changed

Since the angle $I'T_2'T_1$ is equal to $\dfrac{\Delta}{2}$, from $\Delta\ T_2PT_2'$, we have

$$T_2T_2' = \frac{d}{\sin\dfrac{\Delta}{2}} \qquad \text{...(12.57)}$$

From $\Delta\ II'Q$, we have

$$II' = \frac{d}{\sin(180°-\Delta)} = \frac{d}{\sin\Delta} \qquad \text{...(12.58)}$$

The new tangent length T_1I' is equal to

$$T' = T_1I + II'$$

$$= T + \frac{d}{\sin\Delta}$$

where T is the original tangent length and it is equal to

$$T = R\tan\frac{\Delta}{2}$$

Also, if the new radius is R', then

$$T' = R'\tan\frac{\Delta}{2}$$

Therefore

$$R'\tan\frac{\Delta}{2} = R\tan\frac{\Delta}{2} + \frac{d}{\sin\Delta}$$

or

$$R' = \frac{R\tan\frac{\Delta}{2} + \frac{d}{\sin\Delta}}{\tan\frac{\Delta}{2}}$$

$$= R + \frac{d}{\sin\Delta\tan\frac{\Delta}{2}}$$

Substituting $\frac{1-\cos\Delta}{\sin\Delta}$ for $\tan\frac{\Delta}{2}$, we get

$$R' = R + \frac{d}{1-\cos\Delta} \qquad ...(12.59)$$

In this case, the new position T_2' may be located by simply directing the theodolite set at T_1, towards T_2 and measuring the distance T_2T_2' along the line of sight.

Case-5: Changing the direction of forward tangent, P.T. unchanged

In Fig. 12.29, the direction of the forward tangent T_2A is changed to a new direction T_2A' by an angle θ. This causes a shift in T_1 to T_1', in I to I', and a change in the value of radius R to R'.

We have

$$\angle IT_2I' = \theta$$

$$\angle FI'T_2 = \angle I'IT_2 + I'T_2I$$

$$\Delta' = \Delta + \theta \qquad ...(12.60)$$

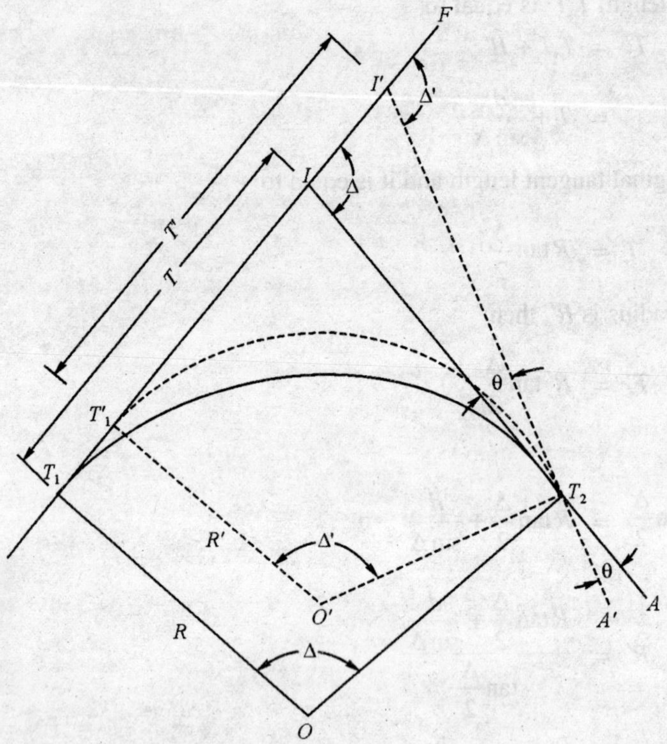

Fig. 12.29 Changing the direction of forward tangent, P.T. unchanged

Solving $\Delta I'IT_2$ by sine rule, we have

$$\frac{T_2I'}{\sin\Delta} = \frac{T_2I}{\sin(180°-\Delta')} = \frac{T_2I}{\sin\Delta'}$$

But $\quad T_2I = T_1I = T$

and $\quad T_2I' = T_1'I' = T'$

Therefore

$$\frac{T'}{\sin\Delta} = \frac{T}{\sin\Delta'}$$

or $$T' = T\frac{\sin\Delta}{\sin\Delta'} \qquad ...(12.61)$$

or $$R'\tan\frac{\Delta'}{2} = R\tan\frac{\Delta}{2}\,\frac{\sin\Delta}{\sin\Delta'}$$

or $$R' = \frac{R\tan\dfrac{\Delta}{2}}{\tan\dfrac{\Delta'}{2}}\,\frac{\sin\Delta}{\sin\Delta'} \qquad ...(12.62)$$

Substituting $\dfrac{1-\cos\Delta}{\sin\Delta}$ for $\tan\dfrac{\Delta}{2}$ and $\dfrac{1-\cos\Delta'}{\sin\Delta'}$ for $\tan\dfrac{\Delta'}{2}$, in Eq. (12.62),

we get
$$R' = R\frac{1-\cos\Delta}{\sin\Delta}\,\frac{\sin\Delta'}{1-\cos\Delta'}\,\frac{\sin\Delta}{\sin\Delta'}$$

$$= R\frac{1-\cos\Delta}{1-\cos\Delta'}$$

Substituting the value of Δ' from Eq. (12.60), we get

$$R' = R\frac{1-\cos\Delta}{1-\cos(\Delta+\theta)} \quad \text{...(12.63)}$$

By applying sine rule in $\Delta I'IT_2$, we get

$$\frac{II'}{\sin\theta} = \frac{IT_2}{\sin(180°-\Delta')} = \frac{IT_2}{\sin\Delta'}$$

or
$$I'I = IT_2\frac{\sin\theta}{\sin\Delta'}$$

$$= \frac{T\sin\theta}{\sin(\Delta+\theta)}$$

The amount by which T_1 is shifted to T_1' is determined as below:

$$T_1I' = T_1I + II'$$

$$= T + II'$$

and
$$T_1T_1' = T_1I' - T_1'I'$$

or
$$= T + II' - T'$$

$$= T + T\frac{\sin\theta}{\sin\Delta'} - \frac{T\sin\Delta}{\sin\Delta'}$$

$$= T\left[1+\frac{\sin\theta-\sin\Delta}{\sin\Delta'}\right]$$

$$= T\left[1+\frac{\sin\theta-\sin\Delta}{\sin(\Delta+\theta)}\right] \quad \text{...(12.64)}$$

Case-6: Changing the direction of forward tangent, P.T. moved ahead

Fig. 12.30 shows that the original forward tangent T_2A has been rotated by, an angle θ, causing shift in P.I. from I to I', and in P.T. from T_2 to T_2'. In this case the position of P.C. T_1 remains unchanged. Due to change in the direction of the forward tangent, the deflection angle has changed from Δ to Δ', and the radius of the curve from R to R'. The problem is to determine the location of T_2', and the value of the new radius R'.

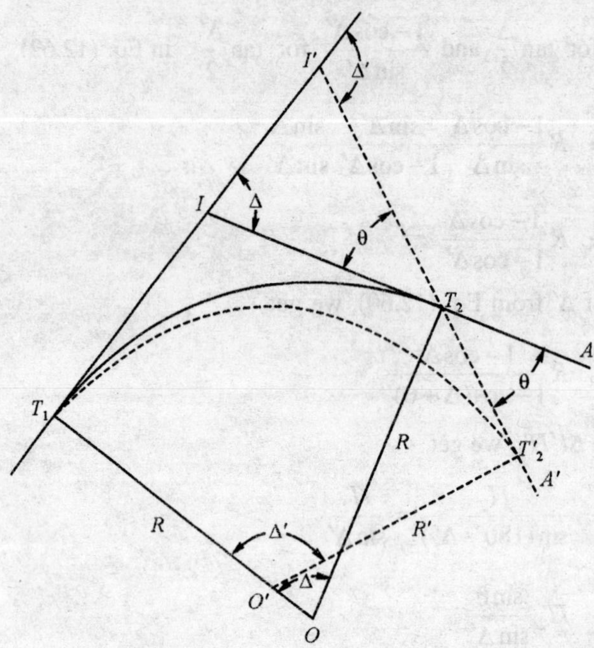

Fig. 12.30 Changing the direction of forward tangent, P.T. moved ahead

We have $\Delta' = \Delta + \theta$ ...(12.65)

$$\angle II'T_2 = 180° - \Delta'$$

By sine rule in $\Delta I'IT_2$, we get

$$\frac{II'}{\sin\theta} = \frac{IT_2}{\sin(180° - \Delta')} = \frac{IT_2}{\sin\Delta'}$$

$$II' = \frac{T\sin\theta}{\sin\Delta'} \quad ...(12.66)$$

We have $T_1I' = T_1I + II'$

$$= T + \frac{T\sin\theta}{\sin\Delta'}$$

or

$$T' = T\left[1 + \frac{\sin\theta}{\sin\Delta'}\right] \quad ...(12.67)$$

$$T = R\tan\frac{\Delta}{2}$$

$$T' = R'\tan\frac{\Delta'}{2}$$

Substituting the values of T and T' in Eq. (12.67), we get

$$R'\tan\frac{\Delta'}{2} = R\tan\frac{\Delta}{2}\left[1 + \frac{\sin\theta}{\sin\Delta'}\right]$$

$$R' = \frac{R\tan\frac{\Delta}{2}}{\tan\frac{\Delta'}{2}}\left[1+\frac{\sin\theta}{\sin\Delta'}\right]$$

From Eq. (12.65), we get

$$R' = \frac{R\tan\frac{\Delta}{2}}{\tan\frac{\Delta+\theta}{2}}\left[1+\frac{\sin\theta}{\sin(\Delta+\theta)}\right] \quad \text{...(12.68)}$$

To locate the position of T_2', the distance T_2T_2' is required.

By sine rule in $\Delta\, I'IT_2$, we get

$$\frac{I'T_2}{\sin\Delta} = \frac{IT_2}{\sin\Delta'}$$

or $$I'T_2 = T\frac{\sin\Delta}{\sin\Delta'}$$

Since, $$T' = I'T_2' = I'T_2 + T_2T_2'$$

$$T_2T_2' = T' - T\frac{\sin\Delta}{\sin\Delta'}$$

From Eq. (12.67), we have

$$T_2T_2' = T\left[1+\frac{\sin\theta}{\sin\Delta'}\right] - \frac{T\sin\Delta}{\sin\Delta'}$$

$$= T\left[1+\frac{\sin\theta-\sin\Delta}{\sin\Delta'}\right]$$

$$= T\left[1+\frac{\sin\theta-\sin\Delta}{\sin(\Delta+\theta)}\right] \quad \text{...(12.69)}$$

Case-7: Locating the intersection of a circular curve and a straight line

If a straight line intersects a circular curve, the location of the intersection is required to design the intersection for smooth movement of the vehicles.

Let the coordinates of the intersection point P as shown in Fig. 12.31, be (x_P, y_P). The coordinates of the two points A and B on the straight line, are given as (x_A, y_A) and (x_B, y_B), respectively.

If the coordinates of the centre O of the curve is (x_O, y_O), then the equation of a circle passing through P is

$$R^2 = (x_P - x_O)^2 + (y_P - y_O)^2 \quad \text{...(12.70)}$$

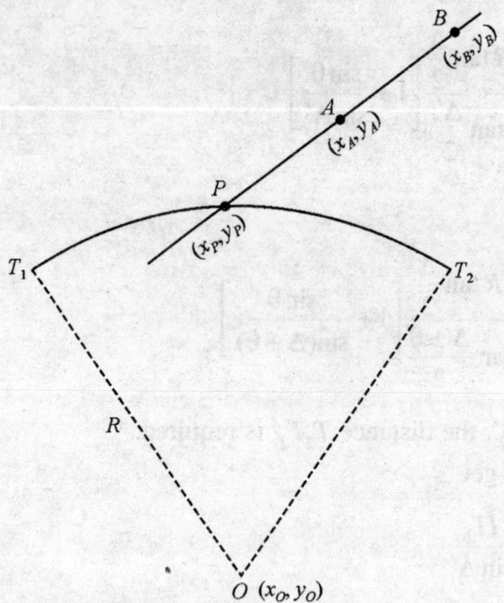

Fig. 12.31 Intersection of a circular curve and a straight line

where R is the radius of the curve.

The equation of the straight line passing through the two given points A and B is

$$y - y_A = \frac{y_B - y_A}{x_B - x_A}(x - x_A) \qquad \text{...(12.71)}$$

Solving the Eqs. (12.70) and (12.71), we get a quadratic equation for one of the unknowns as

$$a{y_P}^2 + by_P + c = 0 \qquad \text{...(12.72)}$$

whose solution is

$$y_P = \frac{-b \pm \sqrt{b^2 - 4ac}}{2a} \qquad \text{...(12.73)}$$

The value of x_P is obtained by substituting the value of y_P in Eqs. (12.70) or (12.71).

Case-8: Locating the intersection of two circular curves

In Fig. 12.32, the two circular arcs of radii R_1 and R_2 have their centres at O_1 and O_2, respectively. The coordinates of O_1 and O_2 are (x_{O1}, y_{O1}) and (x_{O2}, y_{O2}) respectively. The arcs intersect at P whose coordinates are (x_P, y_P).

The equations of the circles of radii R_1 and R_2, passing through P are

$$R_1^2 = (x_P - x_{O1})^2 + (y_P - y_{O1})^2 \qquad \text{...(12.74)}$$

and

$$R_2^2 = (x_P - x_{O2})^2 + (y_P - y_{O2})^2 \qquad \text{...(12.75)}$$

Solving Eqs. (12.74) and (12.75), we get the values of x_P and y_P.

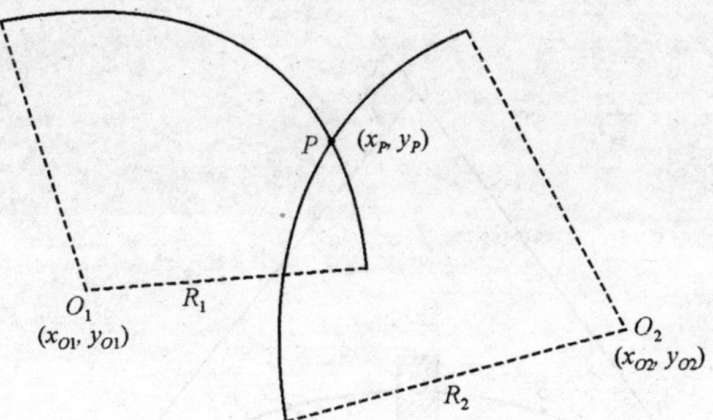

Fig. 12.32 Intersection of two circular arcs

Case-9: Curve not completely visible from the starting point

In Fig. 12.33, after fixing the points A, B, and C from T_1, it is not possible to fix the point D due to the obstruction at F, *i.e.*, after setting the angles Δ_1, Δ_2, and Δ_3, the angle Δ_4 could not be set for D. The following procedure may be used to fix D and further points on the curve.

Shift the instrument from T_1 to C, which is the last point set out from T_1. Set the vernier to read 0° and back sight on T_1 with the telescope inverted. Transit the telescope. The line of sight is now directed along T_1C produced. Unclamp the upper plate, and set the vernier to read the deflection angle Δ_4 for D, as if it were located from T_1, and locate the point D as usual.

The setting out of the curve is continued from C in the usual manner. Even if a further shift is required, precisely the same procedure is applicable provided an already set point is back sighted with the deflection angle corresponding to that point set on the horizontal circle.

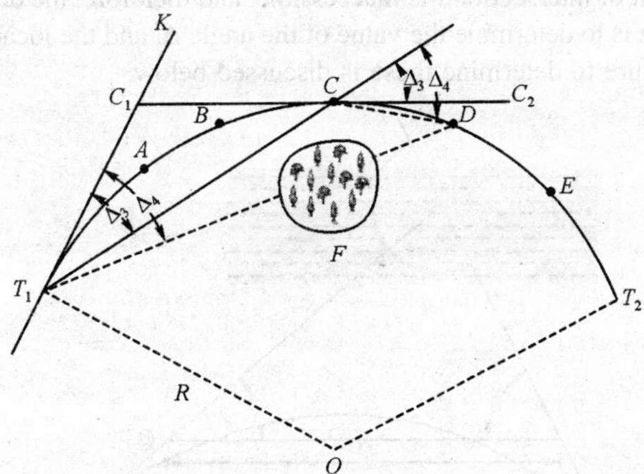

Fig. 12.33 Curve not completely visible from the starting point

Case-10: An obstacle intervenes on the curve

Let an obstacle, which cannot be chained across, intervenes on the curve as shown in Fig. 12.34. The location of the curve near the obstruction may have to be omitted until it is removed. However, further points can be fixed by the following procedure.

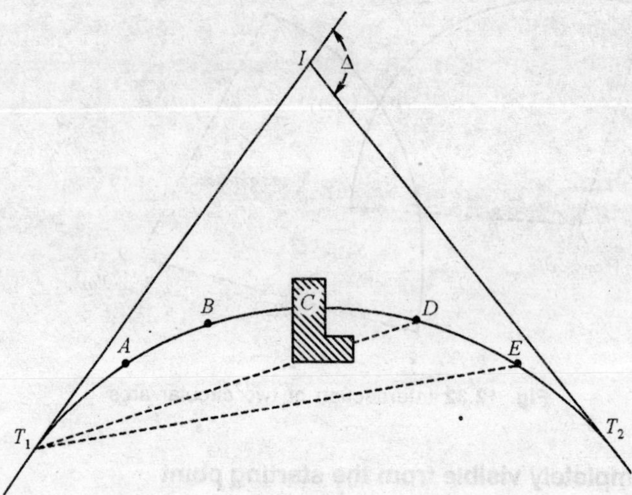

Fig. 12.34 An obstacle intervenes on the curve

After fixing the points A and B, it is found that the point C cannot be fixed due to the obstacle. Also, though the point D is clear of obstacle, it is not visible from T_1. Thus, the next point E, for which a clear line of sight from T_1 is obtained, is fixed by setting the corresponding deflection angle Δ_5, and measuring the distance T_1E which is equal to $2R \sin \Delta_5$.

The remaining points are fixed as usual from T_1. Alternatively, the points between T_2 and the obstacle, can be fixed from T_2.

Case-11: Point of intersection inaccessible

In Fig. 12.35, the point of intersection I is inaccessible, and therefore, the deflection angle Δ cannot be measured. The problem is to determine the value of the angle Δ, and the locations of T_1 and T_2 to set out the curve. The procedure to determine these is discussed below.

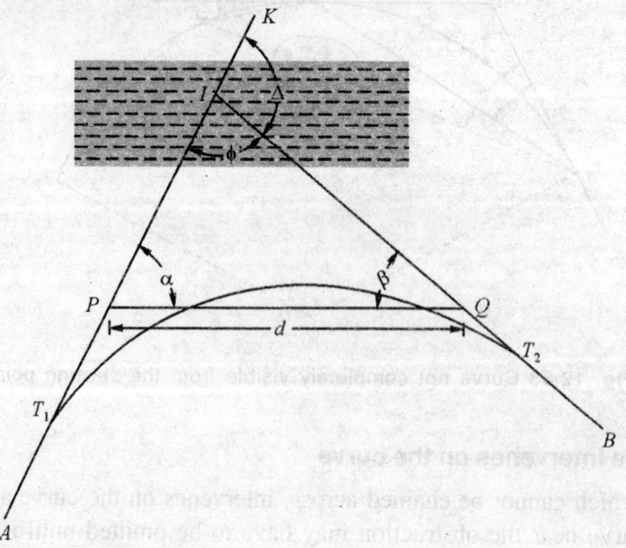

Fig. 12.35 Point of intersection in accessible

Two points P and Q are chosen at some convenient locations on the two tangents. The angles T_1PQ and PQT_2, and the distance PQ are measured. If there is no clear line such as PQ, a traverse has to be run around PQ, and the distance PQ, and the angles T_1PQ and PQT_2 are determined.

Let
$$PQ = d$$
$$\angle IPQ = 180° - \angle T_1PQ = \alpha$$
$$\angle IQP = 180° - \angle PQT_2 = \beta$$

From Δ PIQ, we get
$$\angle PIQ = \phi = 180° - (\alpha + \beta)$$
$$\angle KIQ = \Delta = 180° - [180° - (\alpha + \beta)]$$
$$= (\alpha + \beta) \qquad \text{...(12.76)}$$

Also by sine rule, we have
$$\frac{IP}{\sin\beta} = \frac{PQ}{\sin\phi} = \frac{IQ}{\sin\alpha}$$
$$IP = d\frac{\sin\beta}{\sin\phi}$$
$$= d\frac{\sin\beta}{\sin(\alpha+\beta)}$$
and
$$IQ = d\frac{\sin\alpha}{\sin(\alpha+\beta)}$$

The tangent length
$$T_1I = IT_2 = T = R\tan\frac{\Delta}{2}$$
$$= R\tan\frac{\alpha+\beta}{2}$$

Therefore, the distance
$$PT_1 = T - IP$$
$$= R\tan\frac{\alpha+\beta}{2} - d\frac{\sin\beta}{\sin(\alpha+\beta)} \qquad \text{...(12.77)}$$

and the distance
$$QT_2 = T - IQ$$
$$= R\tan\frac{\alpha+\beta}{2} - d\frac{\sin\alpha}{\sin(\alpha+\beta)} \qquad \text{...(12.78)}$$

Knowing the distances PT_1 and QT_2, the points T_1 and T_2 can be located.

Case-12: Point of commencement inaccessible

If the point of commencement T_1 is inaccessible as shown in Fig. 12.36, the procedure given below may be followed to determine its chainage. This is required to determine the length of the first sub-chord, and the position of the pegs on the curve.

Calculate the tangent length T, and measure it back along the tangent T_2I. Noting that P.C. falls in the obstacle, select a point P near the obstacle, and measure the distance PI.

Then

$$T_1P = T - PI$$

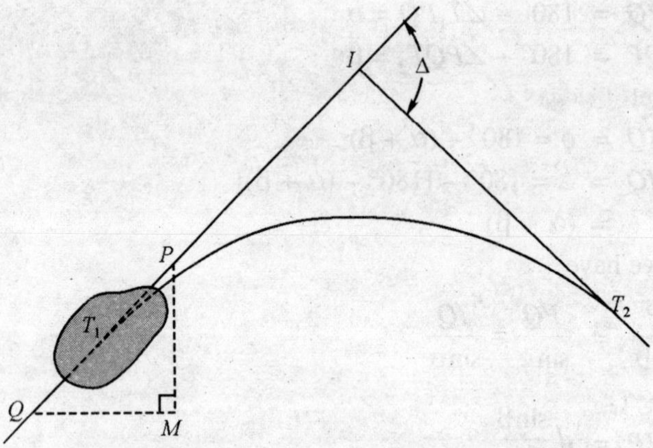

Fig. 12.36 Point of commencement inaccessible

Select another point Q on the tangent but on the other side of the obstacle, and determine its chainage. By any method of chaining past the obstacle (*e.g.*, the solution of the triangle PQM), compute the length PQ.

Now, the chainage of T_1 = Chainage of $Q + PQ - T_1P$

Thus, the chainage of P.C. is known.

The chainage of T_2 = Chainage of T_1 + length of the curve.

Case-13: Point of tangency inaccessible

In order to continue the work past the forward tangent when the point of tangency T_2 is inaccessible, it is necessary to know the chainage of a point Q past the obstacle as shown in Fig. 12.37. The chainage of Q may be determined as discussed below.

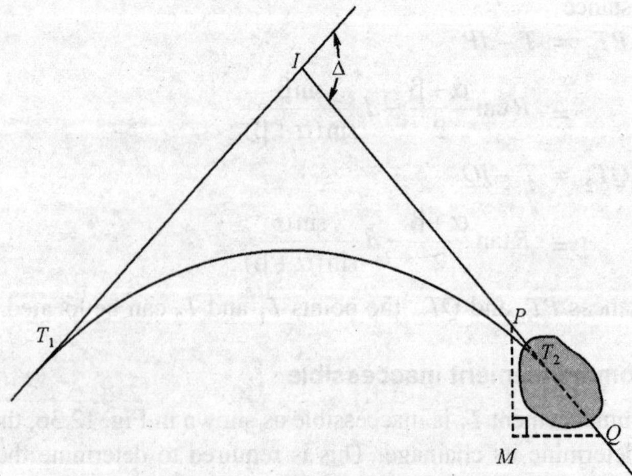

Fig. 12.37 Point of tangency inaccessible

Select a point P on the forward tangent close to the obstacle, and measure the distance IP. From the known chainage of I, we get

$$PT_2 = T - IP$$

Select another point Q on the forward tangent but to the other side of the obstacle, and compute the distance PQ by any method of chaining past the obstacle (*e.g.*, solution of triangle PQM). Since the chainage of T_2 is known,

The chainage of Q = chainage of $T_2 - PT_2 + PQ$

The first accessible full chainage peg on the forward tangent is located from Q.

Case-14: Both point of commencement and point of intersection inaccessible

When both point of commencement T_1 and point of intersection I are inaccessible as shown in Fig. 12.38, the setting out of the curve may be done as follows.

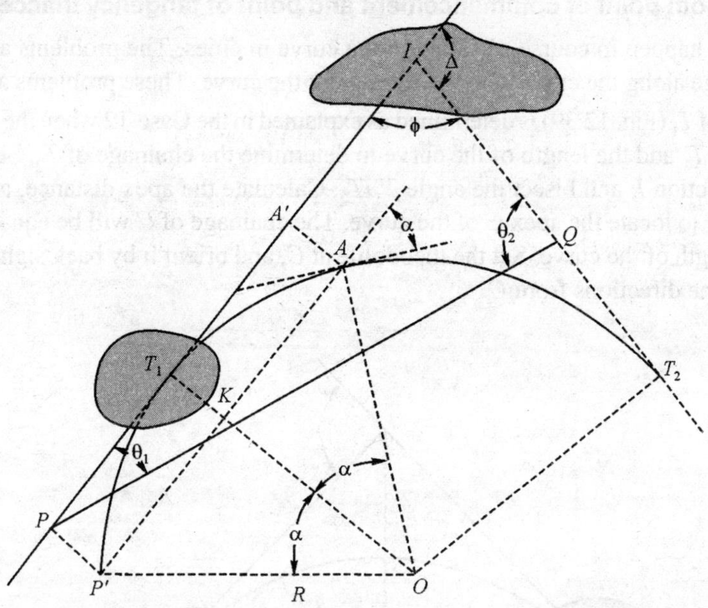

Fig. 12.38. Both point of commencement and point of intersection inaccessible

Select any point P on the back tangent. Take any convenient line PQ, and measure the angles IPQ and IQP, and its length.

Calculate the deflection angle Δ and the distance PT_1 as discussed in Case-11. Knowing the chainage of P and distance PT_1, the chainage of T_1 is determined. From the chainage of T_1 and the length of the curve, the chainage of T_2 is computed.

Let the curve be produced backward, and the perpendicular offset to it from P be PP'. Take a line $P'K$ parallel to the back tangent and equal to PT_1 in length, intersecting the curve at A when produced. We have

$$\sin P'OK = \frac{P'K}{P'O}$$

or $$\sin \alpha = \frac{PT_1}{R}$$

where $\alpha = \angle P'OK$

$$\alpha = \sin^{-1} \frac{PT_1}{R} \tag{12.79}$$

and $KT_1 = T_1O - OK$

or
$$PP' = R - R\cos\alpha$$
$$= R(1 - \cos\alpha) \tag{12.80}$$

Now, set a theodolite at A, and deflect from AP' by an angle equal to α for a tangent to the curve at A. Prepare a table of deflection angles with respect to A, and set out the whole curve from it.

Case-15: When both point of commencement and point of tangency inaccessible

This case may happen in course of setting out a curve in cities. The problems are to determine the continuous chainage along the curve, and the setting out the curve. These problems are solved as below.

The chainage of T_1 (Fig. 12.39) is determined as explained in the Case-12 when the P.C. is inaccessible. To the chainage of T_1 add the length of the curve to determine the chainage of T_2. Set up a theodolite at the point of intersection I, and bisect the angle T_1IT_2. Calculate the apex distance, and measure it from I along the bisector to locate the apex C of the curve. The chainage of C will be equal to the chainage of T_1 plus half the length of the curve. Set the theodolite at C, and orient it by back sighting to I and set out the curve in both the directions from C.

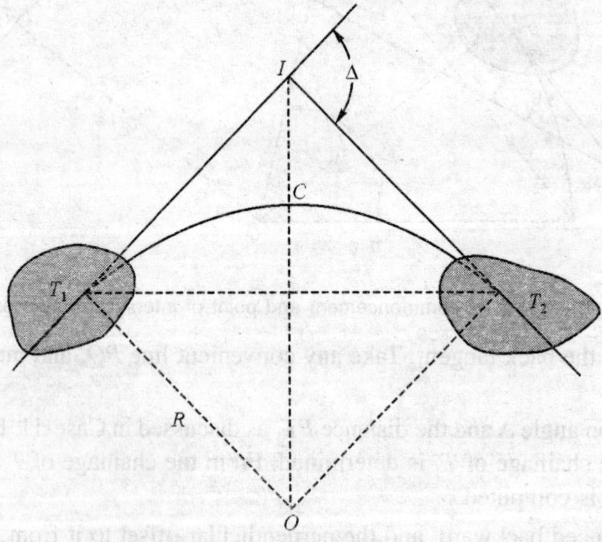

Fig. 12.39 Both point of commencement and point of tangency inaccessible

ILLUSTRATIVE EXAMPLES

Example 12.10

A simple circular curve is required to connect the two straights having an angle of intersection of 120°. The curve must pass through a point *A* which is located at a perpendicular distance of 8.08 m towards the curve from the back tangent, and at a distance of 150.96 m from the point of intersection along the back tangent. What would be the radius of such a curve?

Solution (Fig. 12.25):

It is given that

$$x = 150.96 \text{ m}$$
$$y = 8.08 \text{ m}$$
$$\text{D} = 180° - 120°$$
$$= 60°$$

From Eq. (12.51)

$$\alpha = \tan^{-1}\frac{y}{x}$$
$$= \tan^{-1}\frac{8.08}{150.96}$$
$$= 3°03'50''$$

From Eq. (12.50)

$$\theta = \cos^{-1}\left[\frac{\cos\left(\frac{\Delta}{2}+\alpha\right)}{\cos\frac{\Delta}{2}}\right] - \alpha = \cos^{-1}\left[\frac{\cos\,(30° + 3°03'50'')}{\cos 30°}\right] - 3°03'50''$$
$$= 11°32'08''$$

From Eq. (12.52)

$$r = \frac{x\tan\alpha}{1-\cos\theta} = \frac{150.96 \times \tan 3°03'30''}{1-\cos 11°32'08''}$$
$$= \mathbf{400.00\ m.}$$

Example 12.11

Two straights *AB* and *BC* intersect each other at *B*, the angle *ABC* being 120°. There are two points *P* and *Q* situated on *AB* and *BQ*, respectively, the distance *BP* being 142.26 m. A circular curve is required to be set out such that it is tangential to the two straights as well as to the line *PQ*. If the measured angles ∠*BPQ* and ∠*BQP* are 25° and 35°, respectively, what would be the radius of the curve?

Solution (Fig. 12.40):

Given that

$$BP = 142.26 \text{ m}$$
$$\angle BPQ = \alpha = 25°$$
$$\angle BQP = \beta = 35°$$
$$\angle PBQ = 120°$$

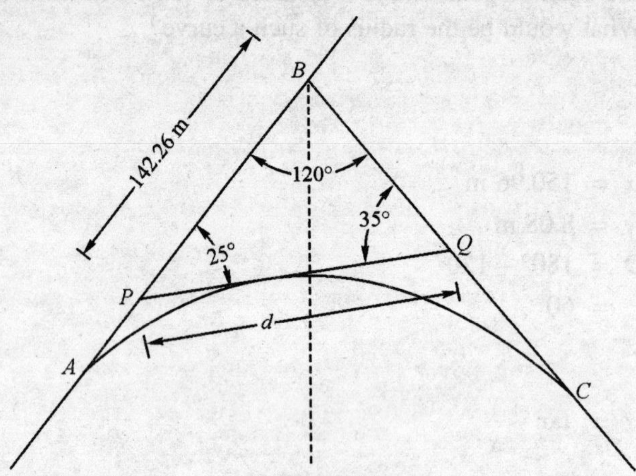

Fig. 12.40

From ΔBPQ, we have

$$\frac{PQ}{\sin PBQ} = \frac{PB}{\sin BQP}$$

or

$$PQ = d = \frac{PB \sin PBQ}{\sin BQP}$$
$$= \frac{142.26 \times \sin 120°}{\sin 35°}$$
$$= 214.79 \text{ m.}$$

From Eq. (12.53), we have

$$R = \frac{d}{\tan\frac{\alpha}{2} + \tan\frac{\beta}{2}}$$
$$= \frac{214.79}{\tan\frac{25°}{2} + \tan\frac{35°}{2}}$$
$$= \mathbf{400.00 \text{ m.}}$$

Example 12.12

Two straights AB and BC meet at an inaccessible point B. They are to be connected by a simple circular curve of 500 m radius. Two points P and Q are selected on AB and BC, respectively, and the following data are obtained:

$$\angle APQ = 157°22'; \angle CQP = 164°38'; PQ = 200 \text{ m}$$

Calculate the necessary data for setting out the curve by the method of deflection angles. The chain to be used is of 30 m in length, and the chainage of the point P is (57 + 17.30) chains.

Solution (Fig. 12.41):

(*i*) From the given data, we have

$$\text{Chainage of } P = 57 + 17.30 = 1727.30 \text{ m}$$

$$\alpha = 180° - 157°22' = 22°38'$$

$$\beta = 180° - 164°38' = 15°22'$$

$$\phi = 180° - (\alpha + \beta) = 142°00'$$

$$\Delta = \alpha + \beta = 38°00'$$

$$PQ = 200 \text{ m}$$

$$R = 500 \text{ m}$$

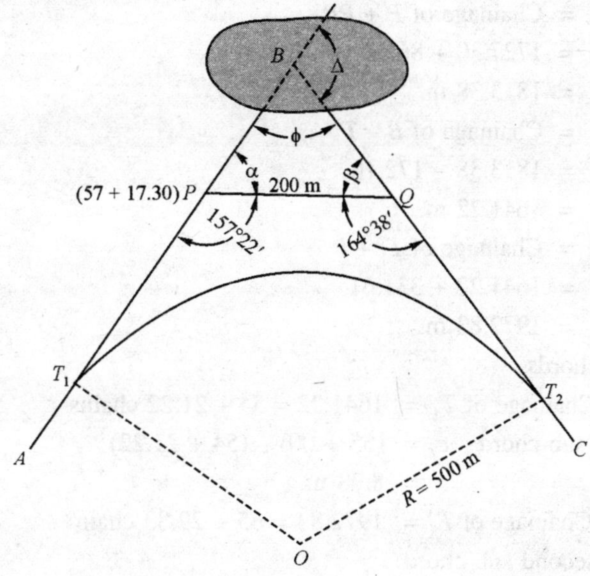

Fig. 12.41

Solving ΔBPQ by sine rule, we get

$$\frac{BP}{\sin\beta} = \frac{BQ}{\sin\alpha} = \frac{PQ}{\sin\phi}$$

$$BP = PQ\frac{\sin\beta}{\sin\phi} = \frac{200\times\sin 15°22'}{\sin 142°} = 86.08 \text{ m}$$

$$BQ = PQ\frac{\sin\alpha}{\sin\phi} = 200\times\frac{\sin 22°38'}{\sin 142°} = 125.01\,\text{m}.$$

(*ii*) From Eq. (12.5), the tangent length is.

$$T_1 = R\tan\frac{\Delta}{2}$$

$$= 500\times\tan\frac{38°}{2}$$

$$= 172.16\text{ m}.$$

(*iii*) From Eq. (12.3), the length of the curve is

$$l = \frac{\pi R\Delta}{180}$$

$$= \frac{\pi\times 500\times 38°}{180}$$

$$= 331.61\text{ m}.$$

(*iv*) Chainages

$$\begin{aligned}
\text{Chainage of } P &= 1727.30\text{ m}\\
\text{Chainage of } B &= \text{Chainage of } P + PB\\
&= 1727.30 + 86.08\\
&= 1813.38\text{ m}.\\
\text{Chainage of } T_1 &= \text{Chainage of } B - T\\
&= 1813.38 - 172.16\\
&= 1641.22\text{ m}.\\
\text{Chainage of } T_2 &= \text{Chainage of } T_1 + l\\
&= 1641.22 + 331.61\\
&= 1972.83\text{ m}.
\end{aligned}$$

(*v*) Length of sub chords

Chainage of T_1 = 1641.22 = 54 + 21.22 chains

Length of first sub-chord c_f = (55 + 00) – (54 + 21.22)

= 8.78 m.

Chainage of T_2 = 1972.83 = 65 + 22.83 chain

Length of the second sub-chord

c_l = (65 + 22.83) – (65 + 00)

= 22.83 m.

(*iv*) Number of normal chords of 30 m length

= 65 – 55 = 10

Total number of chords n = 1 + 10 + 1 = 12

Check: $c_f + 10\times C + c_l = l$

c_f = 8.78 m

$$10 \times C = 10 \times 30 = 300.00 \text{ m}$$
$$c_l = 22.83 \text{ m}$$
$$\text{Total length} = 331.61 \text{ m. } (O.K.)$$

(*vii*) From Eq. (12.1), the degree of curve is

$$D = \frac{1718.9}{R} = \frac{1718.9}{500} = 3°26'16.08''$$

(*viii*) From Eqs. (12.36), (12.37) and (12.38), we have

$$\Delta_1 = \frac{c_f}{60} D$$

$$\Delta_{2 \text{ to } (n-1)} = \frac{D}{2}\left[\frac{c_f}{30} + (n-1)\right]$$

and
$$\Delta_n = \frac{D}{2}\left[\frac{c_f + c_l}{30} + (n-2)\right]$$

Thus,

$$\Delta_1 = \frac{8.78}{60} \times 3°26'16.08'' = 0°30'11''$$

$$\Delta_2 = \frac{3°26'16.08''}{2} \times \left[\frac{8.78}{30} + 1\right] = 2°13'19''$$

$$\Delta_3 = \frac{3°26'16.08''}{2} \times \left[\frac{8.78}{30} + 2\right] = 3°56'27''$$

$$\Delta_4 = \frac{3°26'16.08''}{2} \times \left[\frac{8.78}{30} + 3\right] = 5°39'35''$$

$$\Delta_5 = \frac{3°26'16.08''}{2} \times \left[\frac{8.78}{30} + 4\right] = 7°22'43''$$

$$\Delta_6 = \frac{3°26'16.08''}{2} \times \left[\frac{8.78}{30} + 5\right] = 9°05'51''$$

$$\Delta_7 = \frac{3°26'16.08''}{2} \times \left[\frac{8.78}{30} + 6\right] = 10°48'59''$$

$$\Delta_8 = \frac{3°26'16.08''}{2} \times \left[\frac{8.78}{30} + 7\right] = 12°32'08''$$

$$\Delta_9 = \frac{3°26'16.08''}{2} \times \left[\frac{8.78}{30} + 8\right] = 14°15'16''$$

$$\Delta_{10} = \frac{3°26'16.08''}{2} \times \left[\frac{8.78}{30} + 9\right] = 15°58'24''$$

$$\Delta_{11} = \frac{3°26'16.08''}{2} \times \left[\frac{8.78}{30} + 10\right] = 17°41'32''$$

$$\Delta_{12} = \frac{3°26'16.08''}{2} \times \left[\frac{8.78 + 22.83}{30} + 10\right] = 19°00'00''$$

Check:

$$\Delta_{12} = \frac{1}{2}\Delta = \frac{38°}{2} = 19° (O.K.)$$

The results are presented in Table 12.4.

Table 12.4

Point on curve	Chainage chains	Length of chord (m)	Deflection angle	Theodolite reading	Remarks
T_1	54 + 21.22	—	—	—	The least count of the theodolite is 20″.
1	55 + 00	8.78	0° 30′ 11″	0° 30′ 20″	
2	56 + 00	30	2° 13′ 19″	2° 13′ 20″	
3	57 + 00	30	3° 56′ 27″	3° 56′ 20″	
4	58 + 00	30	5° 39′ 35″	5° 39′ 40″	
5	59 + 00	30	7° 22′ 43″	7° 22′ 40″	
6	60 + 00	30	9° 05′ 51″	9° 06′ 00″	
7	61 + 00	30	10° 48′ 59″	10° 49′ 00″	
8	62 + 00	30	12° 32′ 08″	12° 32′ 00″	
9	63 + 00	30	14° 15′ 16″	14° 15′ 20″	
10	64 + 00	30	15° 58′ 24″	15° 58′ 20″	
11	65 + 00	30	17° 41′ 32″	17° 41′ 40″	
T_2	65 + 22.83	22.83	19° 00′ 00″	19° 00′ 00″	

Example 12.13

A railway curve is to be tangential to each of the following lines:

Line	W.C.B.	Length (m)
AB	0°	–
BC	90°	220
CD	140°	–

Determine the following:

(*a*) Radius of the curve,

(*b*) Tangent lengths,

(*c*) Total length of the curve.

Solution (Fig. 12.42):

From the given bearings

$$\angle IBC = \alpha = 90°$$
$$\angle ICB = \beta = 50°$$
$$\angle BIC = \phi = 180° - (90° + 50°) = 180° - 140° = 40°$$
$$\angle KIC = \Delta = 180° - \phi = 180° - 40° = 140°$$

(*a*) From Eq. (12.53), the radius of the curve is

$$R = \frac{d}{\tan\frac{\alpha}{2} + \tan\frac{\beta}{2}}$$

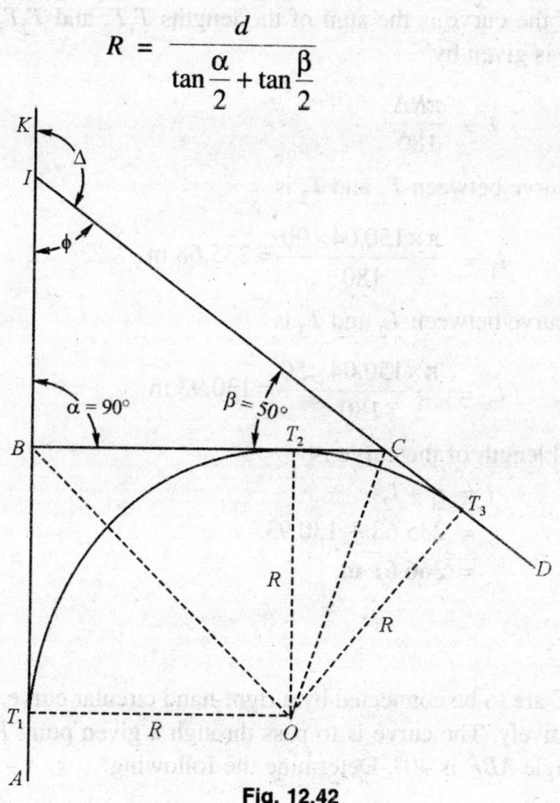

Fig. 12.42

It is given that

$$BC = d = 220 \text{ m}$$

$$R = \frac{220}{\tan\frac{90°}{2} + \tan\frac{50°}{2}}$$

$$= \mathbf{150.04 \text{ m.}}$$

(*b*) From Eq. (12.5), the tangent length is given by

$$T = R \tan\frac{\Delta}{2}$$

(*i*) For the curve between T_1 and T_2, the deflection angle is 90°, therefore

$$T_1B = BT_2 = 150.04 \times \tan\frac{90°}{2}$$

$$= \mathbf{150.04\ m.}$$

(*ii*) For the curve between T_2 and T_3 the deflection angle is 50°, therefore

$$T_2C = CT_3 = 150.04 \times \tan\frac{50°}{2}$$

$$= \mathbf{69.96\ m.}$$

(*c*) The total length of the curve is the sum of the lengths T_1T_2 and T_2T_3. From Eq. (12.3), the length of the curve is given by

$$l = \frac{\pi R \Delta}{180}$$

(*i*) The length of the curve between T_1 and T_2 is

$$l_1 = \frac{\pi \times 150.04 \times 90}{180} = 235.68 \text{ m}$$

(*ii*) The length of the curve between T_2 and T_3 is

$$l_2 = \frac{\pi \times 150.04 \times 50}{180} = 130.93 \text{ m}$$

Therefore, the total length of the curve is

$$l = l_1 + l_2$$

$$= 235.68 + 130.93$$

$$= \mathbf{366.61\ m.}$$

Example 12.14

Two straights *AB* and *BC* are to be connected by a right-hand circular curve. The bearing of *AB* and *BC* are 70° and 140°, respectively. The curve is to pass through a given point *P* which is at a distance of 120 m from *B*, and the angle *ABP* is 40°. Determine the following:

(*i*) Radius of the curve

(*ii*) Chainage of tangent points

(*iii*) Total deflection angles for the first two pegs.

The peg interval and the length of a normal chord are 30 m. The chainage of the point of intersection is 3000 m.

Solution (Fig. 12.43):

From the given data, we have

Bearing of $AB = 70°$

Bearing of $BC = 140°$

$BP = 120$ m

$$\angle ABP = \alpha = 40°$$

(*i*) The deflection angle is

$$\begin{aligned}\Delta &= \text{Bearing of } BC - \text{Bearing of } AB \\ &= 140° - 70° \\ &= 70°\end{aligned}$$

(*ii*) If $\angle POT_1$ is equal to θ, then

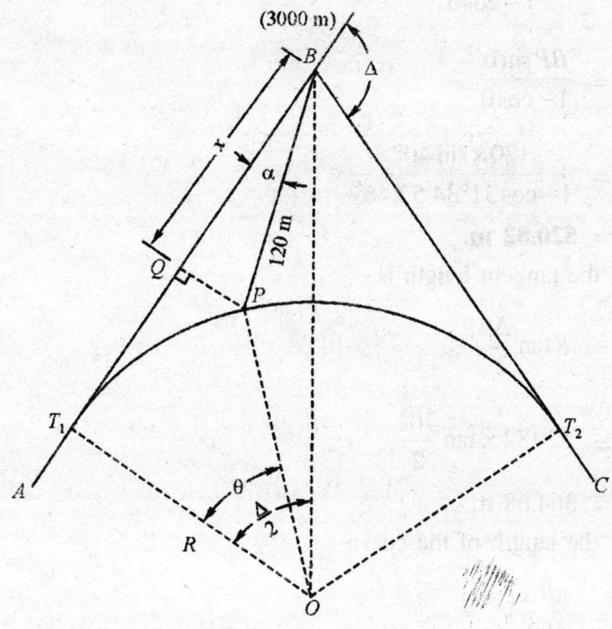

Fig. 12.43

From Eq. (12.50), we have

$$\theta = \cos^{-1}\left[\frac{\cos\left(\frac{\Delta}{2}+\alpha\right)}{\cos\frac{\Delta}{2}}\right] - \alpha$$

$$= \cos^{-1}\left[\frac{\cos\left(\frac{70°}{2}+40°\right)}{\cos\frac{70°}{2}}\right] - 40°$$

$$= 31°34'52.46''.$$

(*iii*) From Eq. (12.52), the radius of the curve is

$$R = \frac{x \tan\alpha}{1 - \cos\theta}$$

From Δ *PBQ*, we get

$$x = BP \cos\alpha$$

Therefore,
$$R = \frac{BP\cos\alpha \dfrac{\sin\alpha}{\cos\alpha}}{1 - \cos\theta}$$

$$= \frac{BP \sin\alpha}{1 - \cos\theta}$$

$$= \frac{120 \times \sin 40°}{1 - \cos 31°34'52.46''}$$

$$= \mathbf{520.82\ m.}$$

(*iv*) From Eq. (12.5), the tangent length is

$$T = R \tan\frac{\Delta}{2}$$

$$= 520.82 \times \tan\frac{70°}{2}$$

$$= 364.68 \text{ m}$$

(*v*) From Eq. (12.3), the length of the curve

$$l = \frac{\pi R \Delta}{180}$$

$$= \frac{\pi \times 520.82 \times 70}{180}$$

$$= 636.30 \text{ m}$$

(*vi*) Chainage of T_1 = Chainage of $B - T$
= 3000 – 364.68
= 2635.32
= (87 + 25.32) chains

Chainage of T_2 = Chainage of $T_1 + l$
= 2635.32 + 636.30
= 3271.62 m
= (109 + 1.62) chains.

(*vii*) Length of the sub-chord

First sub-chord c_f = (88 + 00) – (87 + 25.32)
= 4.68 m

(*viii*) Total deflection angles

From Eq. (12.26), $$\delta = \frac{1718.9\,C}{R}$$

For the first peg $$\delta_1 = \frac{1718.9 \times 4.68}{520.82} \text{ minutes}$$
$$= 0°15'27''.$$

For the second peg $$\delta_2 = \frac{1718.9 \times 30}{520.82}$$
$$= 1°39'01''.$$

Total deflection angles are

$$\Delta_1 = \delta_1 = \mathbf{0°15'27''}$$
$$\Delta_2 = \Delta_1 + \delta_2$$
$$= 0°15'27'' + 1°39'01''$$
$$= \mathbf{1°54'28''}$$

Example 12.15

On the basis of preliminary survey it was proposed to connect two straights having deflection angle of 114°, by a circular curve of 410 m radius. Later, however, it was decided to shift the forward tangent outward parallel to itself by a distance of 60 m. If the position of the original P.C. is not to be changed calculate (*i*) the new radius of the curve, and (*ii*) the chainages of the new P.I. The chainage of the P.C. is 6818.6 m.

Solution (Fig. 12.28):

The given data are

$$\Delta = 114°$$
$$R = 410 \text{ m}$$
$$d = 60 \text{ m}$$

Chainage of T_1 = 6818.6 m

(*i*) From Eq. (12.59), the new radius is given by

$$R' = R + \frac{d}{1 - \cos\Delta}$$
$$= 410 + \frac{60}{1 - \cos 114°}$$
$$= \mathbf{452.65 \text{ m.}}$$

(*ii*) Length of the new curve from Eq. (12.3) is

$$l' = \frac{\pi R' \Delta}{180}$$
$$= \frac{\pi \times 452.65 \times 114}{180}$$
$$= 900.63 \text{ m.}$$

(*iii*) From Eq. (12.5), the new tangent length is

$$T' = R' \tan\frac{\Delta}{2}$$

$$= 452.65 \times \tan\frac{114°}{2}$$

$$= 697.02 \text{ m.}$$

(*iv*) Chainage of the new P.I.

$$= \text{Chainage of } T_1 + T'$$

$$= 6818.6 + 697.02$$

$$= \mathbf{7517.62 \text{ m.}}$$

Chainage of the new P.T. $= \text{Chainage of } T_1 + l'$

$$= 6818.6 + 900.63$$

$$= \mathbf{7719.23 \text{ m.}}$$

Example 12.16

Two tangents connected by a circular curve of radius 400 m, have a deflection angle of 100°. It is proposed to change the position of the forward tangent by rotating it through an angle of 25°, thus changing the position of P.I. and P.T. only. Calculate the radius of the new curve.

Solution (Fig. 12.30):

It is given that

$$\Delta = 100°$$

$$R = 400 \text{ m}$$

$$\theta = 25°$$

From Eq. (12.68), the new radius is

$$R' = R\frac{\tan\frac{\Delta}{2}}{\tan\frac{\Delta+\theta}{2}}\left[1+\frac{\sin\theta}{\sin(\Delta+\theta)}\right]$$

$$= 400 \times \frac{\tan\frac{100°}{2}}{\tan\frac{100°+25°}{2}} \times \left[1+\frac{\sin 25°}{\sin(100°+25°)}\right]$$

$$= \mathbf{376.18 \text{ m.}}$$

Example 12.17

Taking the data from Example 12.16, calculate the new radius of the curve, if P.T. is unchanged and P.C. is changed. Also calculate the chainage of new P.I., P.C., and the original P.T. if the chainage of the original P.I. is 6818.8 m.

Solution (Fig. 12.29):

Given that

$$\Delta = 100°$$
$$R = 400 \text{ m}$$
$$\theta = 25°$$

From Eq. (12.63), the new radius is

$$R' = R\frac{1-\cos\Delta}{1-\cos(\Delta+\theta)}$$

$$= 400\times\frac{1-\cos 100°}{1-\cos(100°+25°)}$$

$$= \mathbf{298.34\ m.}$$

New deflection angle is

$$\Delta' = \Delta + \theta = 100° + 25° = 125°$$

The length of the new curve

$$l' = \frac{\pi R'\Delta'}{180°} = \frac{\pi\times 298.34\times 125}{180}$$

$$= 650.88 \text{ m.}$$

The tangent length of the original curve

$$T = R\tan\frac{\Delta}{2}$$

$$= 400\times\tan\frac{100°}{2}$$

$$= 476.70 \text{ m.}$$

The tangent length of the new curve

$$T' = R'\tan\frac{\Delta'}{2}$$

$$= 298.34\times\tan\frac{125°}{2}$$

$$= 573.11 \text{ m.}$$

From Eq. (12.64), we have

$$T_1T_1' = T\left[1+\frac{\sin\theta-\sin\Delta}{\sin(\Delta+\theta)}\right]$$

$$= 476.70\times\left[1+\frac{\sin 25°-\sin 100°}{\sin(100°+25°)}\right]$$

$= 149.54$ m.

Chainage of new P.C. (T_1') $=$ Chainage of $T_1 + T_1T_1'$

$= 6818.6 + 149.54$

$=$ **6968.14 m.**

Chainage of new P.I. (I') $=$ Chainage of $T_1' + T'$

$= 6968.14 + 573.11$

$=$ **7541.25 m.**

Chainage of the P.T. (T_2) $=$ Chainage of $T_1' + l'$

$= 6968.14 + 650.88$

$=$ **7619.02 m.**

Example 12.18

To connect two straights *AB* and *CB* by two right-handed circular curves separated by a straight *PQ*, 125 m long, the following measurements were made:

Bearing of *AB* = 35°

Bearing of *PQ* = 86°

Bearing of *BC* = 114°

Chainage of *B* = 1060.50 m

Total length of both the curves including the straight is 610 m. If the radius of the first curve is half that of the second, calculate the following:

(*a*) the radii of the curves

(*b*) the chainages of the point of tangencies.

Solution (Fig. 12.44):

(*i*) Deflection angle for the first curve

Δ_1 = Bearing of *PQ* – bearing of *AB*

$= 86° - 35°$

$= 51°$

Deflection angle for the second curve

Δ_2 = Bearing of *BC* – bearing of *PQ*

$= 114° - 86°$

$= 28°$

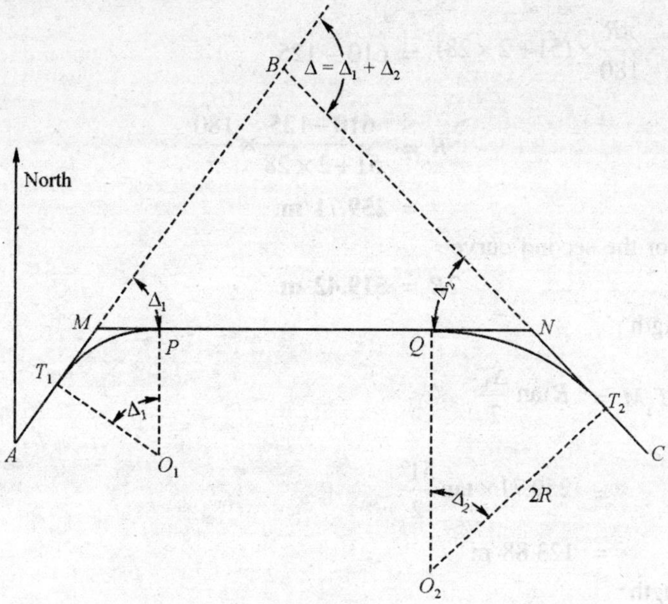

Fig. 12.44

Deflection angle for the straights *AB* and *BC*

$$\Delta = \Delta_1 + \Delta_2$$
$$= 51° + 28°$$
$$= 79°$$

(*ii*) Length of the first curve of radius *R*

$$l_1 = \frac{\pi R \Delta_1}{180}$$
$$= \frac{\pi R \times 51}{180}$$

Length of the second curve of radius 2*R*

$$l_2 = \frac{\pi(2R)\Delta_2}{180°}$$
$$= \frac{\pi(2R) \times 28}{180}$$

Total length of the curve

$$l = l_1 + l_2$$

But it is given that

$$l + PQ = 610 \text{ m}$$
$$l_1 + l_2 + PQ = 610 \text{ m}$$
$$\pi R \times \frac{51}{180} + \pi(2R) \times \frac{28}{180} + 125 = 610$$

$$\frac{\pi R}{180}\times(51+2\times28) = 610 - 125$$

$$R = \frac{610-125}{51+2\times28}\times\frac{180}{\pi}$$

$$= \mathbf{259.71\ m.}$$

and radius of the second curve

$$2R = \mathbf{519.42\ m.}$$

(*iii*) Tangent length

$$T_1M = R\tan\frac{\Delta_1}{2}$$

$$= 259.71\times\tan\frac{51°}{2}$$

$$= 123.88\ \text{m}$$

Tangent length

$$T_2N = 519.42\times\tan\frac{28°}{2}$$

$$= 129.51\ \text{m.}$$

We have

$$MN = MP + PQ + QN$$

$$= T_1M + PQ + T_2N$$

$$= 123.88 + 125.00 + 129.51$$

$$= 378.39\ \text{m.}$$

Solving Δ *BMN* by sine rule, we have

$$\frac{BM}{\sin\Delta_2} = \frac{MN}{\sin MBN} = \frac{MN}{\sin(180°-\Delta)}$$

$$BM = MN\frac{\sin\Delta_2}{\sin\Delta}$$

$$= 378.39\times\frac{\sin 28°}{\sin 79°}$$

$$= 180.97\ \text{m.}$$

$$BT_1 = BM + MT_1$$

$$= 180.97 + 123.88$$

$$= 304.85\ \text{m.}$$

(*iv*) Chainage of T_1 = Chainage of $B - BT_1$

$$= 1060.50 - 304.85$$

$$= \mathbf{755.65\ m.}$$

$$\text{Chainage of } P = \text{Chainage of } T + l_1$$

$$= 755.65 + \frac{\pi \times 259.71 \times 51}{180}$$

$$= 986.82 \text{ m.}$$

$$\text{Chainage of } Q = \text{Chainage of } P + PQ$$

$$= 986.82 + 125$$

$$= \mathbf{1111.82 \text{ m.}}$$

$$\text{Chainage of } T_2 = \text{Chainage of } Q + l_2$$

$$= 1111.82 + \frac{\pi \times (2 \times 259.71) \times 28}{180}$$

$$= \mathbf{1365.66 \text{ m.}}$$

Example 12.19

In order to layout a pond in a public park, two perpendiculars *PS* and *QR* of 50 m and 100 m length, respectively, were erected at either end of a line *PQ* of length 250 m. If the pond is to have straight sides *PQ* and *RS*, the ends being formed of circular arcs to which *PQ*, *RS*, and the end perpendiculars are tangential, determine:

(*a*) the radii of the sub-circular arcs, and

(*b*) the perimeter of the pond.

Solution (Fig. 12.45):

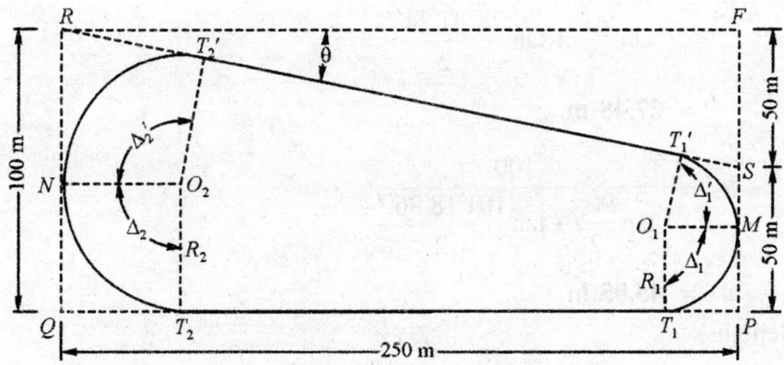

Fig. 12.45

(*i*) Dropping a perpendicular from *R* on the line *PS* produced, we get

$$PF = QR = 100 \text{ m}$$

$$SF = 50 \text{ m}$$

and $$RF = 250 \text{ m}$$

Let $\angle SRF$ be θ, then from Δ *SRF*, we have

$$\tan\theta = \frac{SF}{RF}$$

$$= \frac{50}{250}$$

$$\theta = 11°18'36''$$

(*ii*) Deflection angles

$$\Delta_1 = 90°$$

$$\Delta_1' = 90° - \theta$$

$$= 90° - 11°18'36''$$

$$= 78°41'24''.$$

$$\Delta_2 = 90°$$

$$\Delta_2' = 90° + \theta$$

$$= 90° + 11°18'36''$$

$$= 101°18'36''.$$

(*iii*) Radii of the curves

From Eq. (12.53), we have

$$R = \frac{d}{\tan\frac{\alpha}{2} + \tan\frac{\beta}{2}}$$

$$R_1 = \frac{50}{\tan\frac{90°}{2} + \tan\frac{78°41'24''}{2}}$$

$$= \mathbf{27.48\ m.}$$

$$R_2 = \frac{100}{\tan\frac{90°}{2} + \tan\frac{101°18'36''}{2}}$$

$$= \mathbf{45.05\ m.}$$

(*iv*) Tangent lengths

$$T_1P = PM = R_1 \tan\frac{\Delta_1}{2} = 27.48 \times \tan\frac{90°}{2} = 27.48 \text{ m}$$

$$MS = ST_1' = R_1 \tan\frac{\Delta_1'}{2} = 27.48 \times \tan\frac{78°41'24''}{2} = 22.53 \text{ m}$$

$$T_2Q = QN = R_2 \tan\frac{\Delta_2}{2} = 45.05 \times \tan\frac{90°}{2} = 45.05 \text{ m}$$

$$NR = RT_2' = R_2 \tan \frac{\Delta_2'}{2} = 45.05 \times \tan \frac{101°18'36''}{2} = 54.95 \text{ m}.$$

(*v*) Lengths of the curves

$$l_1 = T_1M = \frac{\pi R_1 \Delta_1}{180} + \frac{\pi \times 27.48 \times 90}{180} = 43.17 \text{ m}$$

$$l_2 = MT_1 = \frac{\pi R_1 \Delta_1'}{180} = \frac{\pi \times 27.48 \times 78°41'24''}{180} = 37.74 \text{ m}$$

$$l_3 = T_2N = \frac{\pi R_2 \Delta_2}{180} + \frac{\pi \times 45.05 \times 90}{180} = 70.76 \text{ m}$$

$$l_4 = NT_2' = \frac{\pi R_2 \Delta_2'}{180} = \frac{\pi \times 45.04 \times 101°18'36''}{180} = 79.66 \text{ m}$$

(*vi*) Perimeter of the pond

$$= T_1T_2 + \text{arc } T_2N + \text{arc } NT_2' + T_2'T_1' + \text{arc } T_1'M + \text{arc } MT_1$$

From Δ *FRS*, we get

$$\frac{RF}{SR} = \cos \theta$$

$$SR = \frac{RF}{\cos\theta} = \frac{250}{\cos(11°18'36'')} = 254.95 \text{ m}$$

$$\begin{aligned}
T_2'T_1' &= SR - (RT_2' + ST_1') \\
&= 254.95 - (54.95 + 22.53) \\
&= 177.47 \text{ m} \\
T_1T_2 &= PQ - (T_2Q + T_1P) \\
&= 250 - (45.05 + 27.48) \\
&= 177.47 \text{ m.} \\
\text{Perimeter} &= 177.47 + 70.76 + 79.66 + 177.47 + 37.74 + 43.17 \\
&= \mathbf{586.27 \text{ m.}}
\end{aligned}$$

Example 12.20

Two straights *AB* and *BC* having bearings of 40° and 100°, respectively, are to be connected by a 4° curve (for 20 m chord length). Due to inaccessible point of intersection, a traverse *APQR* is run, *R* being on the forward tangent. The lengths and bearings of the traverse lines are as follows:

Line	Length (m)	Bearings
AP	110	60°
PQ	90	130°
QR	180	30°

The chainage of *A* is 2118.2 m. What are the chainages of P.I., P.C., and P.T.?

Solution (Fig. 12.46):

In the closed traverse *APQR*, if the length and bearing of the line *AR* are known, the angles α and β can be determined, and then the length *AB* can be computed. From the known value of *AB*, chainages of P.I., P.C., and PT can be computed.

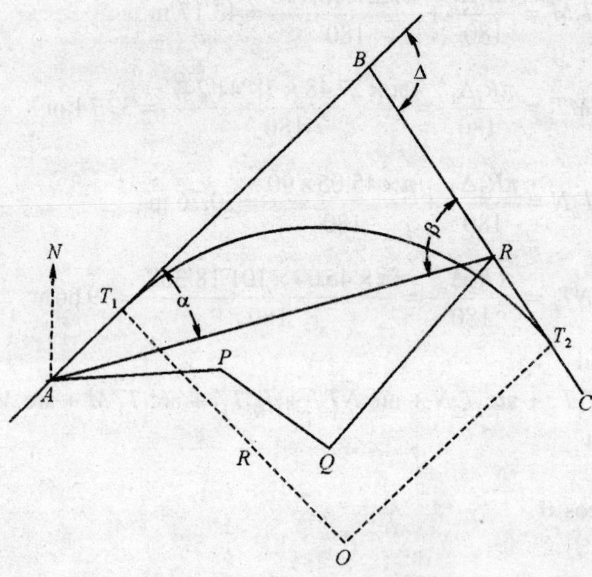

Fig. 12.46

(*i*) Latitude of *AP* $= L_{AP} = 110 \times \cos 60° = +55.00$ m

Latitude of *PQ* $= L_{PQ} = 90 \times \cos 130° = -57.85$ m

Latitude of *QR* $= L_{QR} = 180 \times \cos 30° = +155.88$ m

Latitude of *RA* $= L_{RA}$

Departure of *AP* $= D_{AP} = 110 \times \sin 60° = +95.26$ m

Departure of *PQ* $= D_{PQ} = 90 \times \sin 130° = +68.94$ m

Departure of *QR* $= D_{QR} = 180 \times \sin 30° = +90.00$ m

Departure of *RA* $= D_{RA}$

For the traverse *APQR*

$$\Sigma L = L_{AP} + L_{PQ} + L_{QR} + L_{RA} = 0$$

$$= 55.00 - 57.85 + 155.88 + L_{RA} = 0$$

$$L_{RA} = -153.03 \text{ m}$$

and

$$\Sigma D = D_{AP} + D_{PQ} + D_{QR} + D_{RA} = 0$$

$$= 95.26 + 68.94 + 90.00 + D_{RA} = 0$$

$$D_{RA} = -254.20 \text{ m.}$$

(*ii*) Bearing of *RA* $= \theta = \tan^{-1} \dfrac{254.20}{153.03}$

$= \text{S } 58°57'07''\text{W}$

Bearing of AR = N 58°57′07″E

(*iii*) Length of AR = $\sqrt{254.20^2 + 153.03^2}$

= 296.71 m.

(*iv*) $\angle BAR = \alpha$ = Bearing of AR – bearing of AB

$= 58°57'07'' - 40°$

$= 18°57'07''$.

$\angle BRA = \beta$ = Back bearing of BC – back bearing of AR

$= (180° + 100°) - (180° + 58°57'07'')$

$= 41°02'53''$.

We have,

$$\Delta = \alpha + \beta$$

$$= 18°57'07'' + 41°02'53''$$

$$= 60°$$

(*v*) From Δ *ABR*, we have

$$AB = AR\frac{\sin\beta}{\sin(180°-\Delta)}$$

$$= 296.71 \times \frac{\sin 41°02'53''}{\sin 120°}$$

$$= 224.99 \text{ m.}$$

(*vi*) Tangent length BT_1 is equal to

$$T = R\tan\frac{\Delta}{2}$$

But for 30 m chain $D = \dfrac{1718.9}{R}$

For a 20 m chain $D = \dfrac{1718.9}{R} \times \dfrac{20}{30}$

$$= \frac{1145.9}{R}$$

For a 4° curve the radius is

$$R = \frac{1145.9}{4}$$

$$= 286.48 \text{ m}$$

$$T = 286.48 \times \tan\frac{60°}{2}$$

$$= 165.40 \text{ m.}$$

and length of the curve

$$l = \frac{\pi R \Delta}{180}$$

$$= \frac{\pi \times 286.48 \times 60°}{180}$$

$$= 300.00 \text{ m.}$$

(*vii*) Chainage of P.I. = Chainage of $A + AB$
= 2118.2 + 224.99
= **2343.19 m.**

Chainage of P.C. = Chainage of P.I. – T
= 2343.19 – 165.40
= **2177.79 m.**

Chainage of P.T. = Chainage of P.C. + l
= 2177.79 + 300.00
= **2477.79 m.**

12.9 COMPOUND CIRCULAR CURVES

Compound circular curve has been defined in Sec. 12.2. Although compound curves can be manipulated to provide practically any vehicle path desired by the designer, they are not employed where simple curves or spiral curves can be utilized to achieve the same desired effect. Practically, compound curves are reserved for those applications where design constraints (topographic or cost of land) preclude the use of simple or spiral curves. They are usually found chiefly in the design of interchange loops and ramps. Smooth driving characteristics require that the larger radius be more than $1\frac{1}{3}$ times larger than the smaller radius.

Solutions to compound curve problems vary as several possibilities exist as to which of the data are known in any one given problem. All problems can be solved by use of sine law or cosine law or by the omitted measurement traverse techniques.

Elements of a Compound Curve

Figure 12.47 shows a two centred compound curve $T_1T_3T_2$ having two circular arcs T_1T_3 and T_3T_2 meeting at a common point T_3 known as the *point of compound curvature* (P.C.C). T_1 is the point of commencement (P.C.), and T_2 is the point of tangency (P.T.). The other elements such as tangent lengths, length of the curve, etc., for the smaller and larger curves, will be designated by the subscripts S and L, respectively, as below:

R_S, R_L = the radii of the curves

Δ_S, Δ_L = the deflection angles

Δ = the total deflection angles

l_S, l_L = the length of the curves

t_S, t_L = the tangent lengths

T_S, T_L = the tangent lengths on the sides of smaller and larger curves, respectively, for the compound curve.

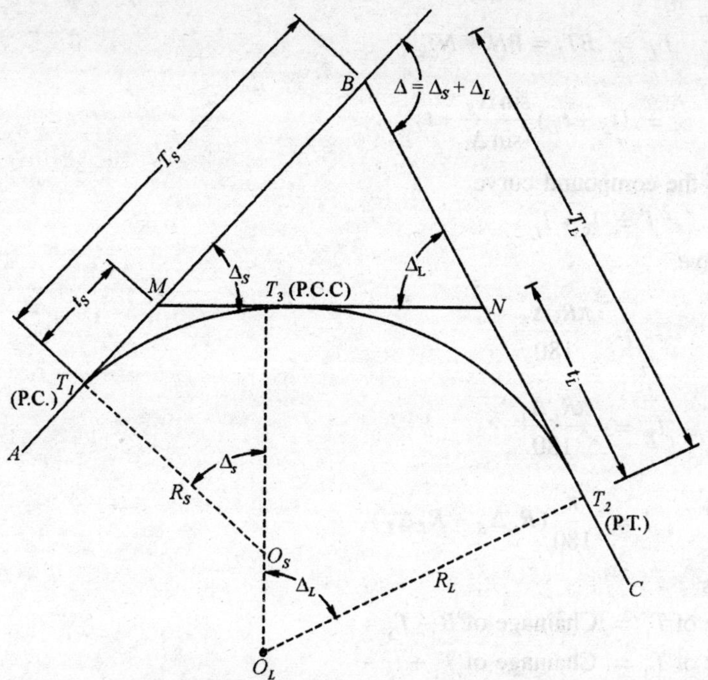

Fig. 12.47 Elements of a compound curve

(*i*) Tangent lengths for the circular curves

$$t_S = T_1M = MT_3 = R_S \tan\frac{\Delta_S}{2} \qquad (12.81)$$

$$t_L = T_3N = NT_2 = R_L \tan\frac{\Delta_L}{2} \qquad (12.82)$$

(*ii*) Total deflection angle

$$\Delta = \Delta_S + \Delta_L \qquad (12.83)$$

(*iii*) Tangent lengths for the compound curve

In Δ *MBN*, we have

$$MN = MT_3 + T_3N = t_S + t_L$$

$$BM = MN\frac{\sin\Delta_L}{\sin\Delta} = (t_S + t_L)\frac{\sin\Delta_L}{\sin\Delta}$$

$$BN = MN\frac{\sin\Delta_S}{\sin\Delta} = (t_S + t_L)\frac{\sin\Delta_S}{\sin\Delta}$$

Now,

$$T_S = BT_1 = BM + MT_1$$

$$= (t_S + t_L)\frac{\sin \Delta_L}{\sin \Delta} + t_S \quad (12.84)$$

$$T_L = BT_2 = BN + NT_2$$

$$= (t_S + t_L)\frac{\sin \Delta_S}{\sin \Delta} + t_L \quad (12.85)$$

(*iv*) Length of the compound curve

$$l = l_S + l_L$$

But we have,

$$l_S = \frac{\pi R_S \Delta_S}{180}$$

$$l_L = \frac{\pi R_L \Delta_L}{180}$$

or

$$l = \frac{\pi}{180}(R_S \Delta_S + R_L \Delta_L) \quad (12.86)$$

(*v*) Chainages

Chainage of T_1 = Chainage of $B - T_S$ (12.87)

Chainage of T_3 = Chainage of $T_1 + l_S$ (12.88)

Chainage of T_2 = Chainage of $T_3 + l_L$ (12.89)

or = Chainage of $T_1 + l_S + l_L$

Relationships Between Elements of a Compound Curve

The seven elements Δ, Δ_S, Δ_L, R_S, R_L, T_S, and T_L of a compound curve, are related to each other by mathematical relationships. When four of these including an angle are given the remaining three can be determined.

Usually, the two radii R_S and R_L are established from the lay out plan, and the angle Δ is measured in the field. The fourth quantity out of Δ_S, Δ_L, T_S and T_L, is determined from the plan according to the requirement. Calculation of the rest of the three is made as under.

In all, five cases may arise and the formulae for each case are detailed below.

Case-1: Given: Δ, R_S, R_L, and Δ_S (or Δ_L)

Required: Δ_L (or Δ_S), T_S and T_L

This is the most common case.

From Eq. (12.83), we have

$$\Delta_L = \Delta - \Delta_S \quad (12.90)$$

From Eqs. (12.84) and (12.85), we have

$$T_S = (t_S + t_L)\frac{\sin \Delta_L}{\sin \Delta} + t_S$$

$$T_L = (t_S + t_L)\frac{\sin \Delta_S}{\sin \Delta} + t_L$$

where t_S and t_L are given by Eqs. (12.81) and (12.82)

Case-2: Given: Δ, R_S, R_L and T_S

Required: Δ_S, Δ_L, and T_L

In Fig. 12.48, the shorter curve T_1T_3 is prolonged to a point E until the central angle at O_S is equal to Δ. The tangent to this curve at E is EB', and it will be parallel to the tangent BT_2. Drop a perpendicular $B'Q$ from B' on BT_2. Also prolong $B'E$ to meet O_LT_2 at P. Drop another perpendicular O_SK on O_LT_2 from O_S.

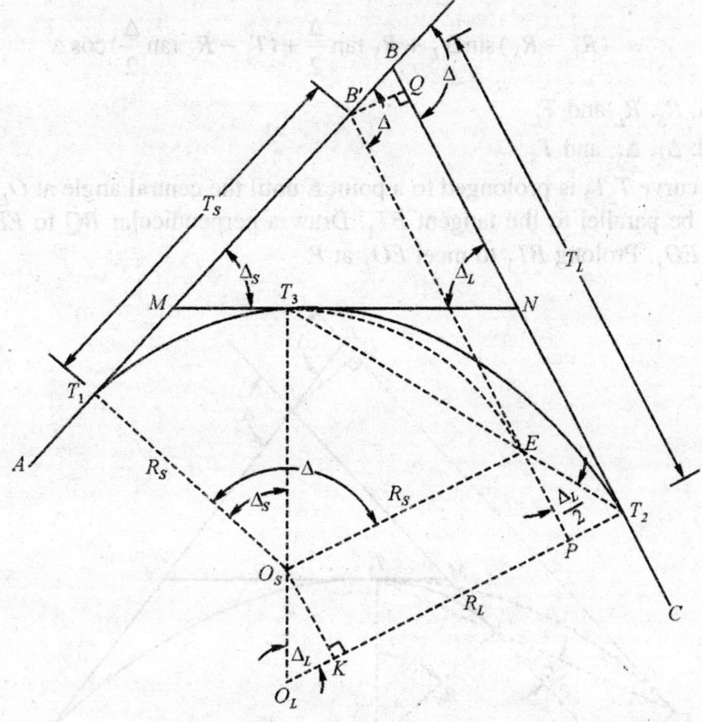

Fig. 12.48 Relationship between elemens of a compound curve

Now, $$T_1B' = B'E = R_S \tan\frac{\Delta}{2} \tag{12.91}$$

We have, $$\begin{aligned} T_2P &= B'Q = BB' \sin \Delta \\ &= (T_1B - T_1B') \sin \Delta \\ &= \left[T_S - R_S \tan\frac{\Delta}{2}\right]\sin \Delta \end{aligned} \tag{12.92}$$

Also, $$BQ = B'B\cos\Delta = \left[T_S - R_S \tan\frac{\Delta}{2}\right]\cos\Delta \tag{12.93}$$

Now, $O_LK = O_SO_L \cos \Delta_L = O_LT_2 - T_2P - PK$

or $(R_L - R_S) \cos \Delta_L = R_L - B'Q - R_S$

or $$\Delta_L = \cos^{-1}\left[1 - \frac{B'Q}{(R_L - R_S)}\right] \quad (12.94)$$

and $\Delta_S = \Delta - \Delta_L$

Also, $O_SK = EP = O_SO_L \sin \Delta_L = (R_L - R_S) \sin \Delta_L$ (12.96)

and $T_L = T_2B = T_2Q + BQ = PE + EB' + BQ$

$= O_SK + EB' + BQ$

$$= (R_L - R_S)\sin\Delta_L + R_S \tan\frac{\Delta}{2} + (T_S - R_S \tan\frac{\Delta}{2})\cos\Delta \quad (12.97)$$

Case-3: Given: Δ, R_S, R_L and T_L

Required: Δ_L, Δ_S, and T_S

In Fig. 12.49, the curve T_2T_3 is prolonged to a point E until the central angle at O_L becomes Δ. The tangent $B'E$ at E will be parallel to the tangent BT_1. Draw a perpendicular BQ to EB'. Draw another perpendicular O_SK to EO_L. Prolong BT_1 to meet EO_L at P.

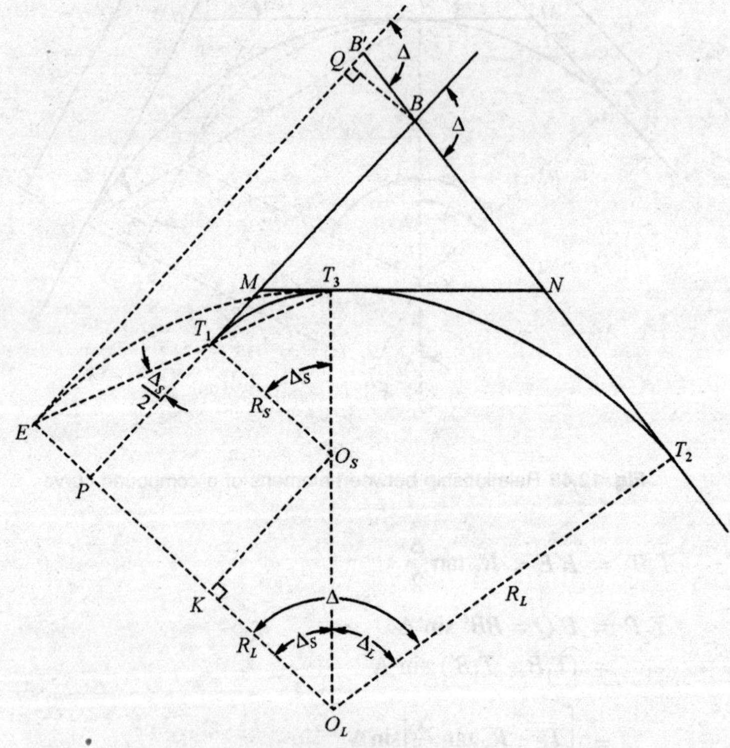

Fig. 12.49

Now, $EB' = B'T_2 = R_L \tan\frac{\Delta}{2}$ (12.98)

We have
$$PE = BQ = BB' \sin \Delta$$
$$= (T_2B' - T_2B) \sin \Delta$$
$$= \left(R_L \tan\frac{\Delta}{2} - T_L\right)\sin\Delta \quad (12.99)$$

Also,
$$B'Q = BB' \cos \Delta = \left(R_L \tan\frac{\Delta}{2} - T_L\right)\cos\Delta \quad (12.100)$$

Now,
$$O_LK = O_LE - EP - PK$$
$$= R_L - BQ - R_S$$
$$O_SO_L \cos \Delta_S = R_L - BQ - R_S$$
$$(R_L - R_S) \cos \Delta_S = (R_L - R_S) - BQ$$

or
$$\Delta_S = \cos^{-1}\left[1 - \frac{BQ}{R_L - R_S}\right] \quad (12.101)$$

and
$$\Delta_L = \Delta - \Delta_S \quad (12.102)$$

Now
$$O_SK = T_1P = O_SO_L \sin \Delta_S = (R_L - R_S) \sin \Delta_S \quad (12.103)$$

and
$$T_S = BT_1 = PB - PT_1$$
$$= EQ - O_SK$$
$$= EB' - B'Q - O_SK$$
$$= R_L \tan\frac{\Delta}{2} - \left(R_L \tan\frac{\Delta}{2} - T_L\right)\cos\Delta - (R_L - R_S)\sin\Delta_S \quad (12.104)$$

Case-4: Given: Δ, T_S, T_L, and R_S

Required: Δ_L, Δ_S, and R_L

Refer to Fig. 12.48.

Join T_3 and E, and prolong T_3E to pass through T_2. Evidently,

$$\angle T_2EP = \frac{\Delta_L}{2}$$

From Δ T_2EP, we get

$$\tan\frac{\Delta_L}{2} = \frac{T_2P}{EP}$$

From Eq. (12.92), we have

$$\Delta_L = 2\tan^{-1}\left[\frac{\left(T_S - R_S \tan\frac{\Delta}{2}\right)\sin\Delta}{O_SK}\right] \quad (12.105)$$

and
$$\Delta_S = \Delta - \Delta_L \quad (12.106)$$

From Eq. (12.96), we have

$$R_L - R_S = \frac{O_S K}{\sin \Delta_L} \tag{12.107}$$

We have

$$\begin{aligned} O_S K &= EP = PB' - B'E \\ &= T_2B - BQ - B'E \\ &= T_L - BQ - B'E \end{aligned} \tag{12.108}$$

From Eqs. (12.91) and (12.93), we get the values of $B'E$ and BQ and, therefore, O_SK is determined. Thus, from Eq. (12.105) Δ_L can be computed, and from Eq. (12.107), we get

$$R_L = R_S + \frac{O_S K}{\sin \Delta_L} \tag{12.109}$$

Case-5: Given: Δ, T_S, T_L and R_L

Required: Δ_S, Δ_L, and R_S

Refer to Fig. 12.49.

Join T_3 and T_1, and prolong T_3T_1 to intersect the prolonged curve T_2T_3 at E.

Evidently,

$$\angle ET_1P = \frac{\Delta_S}{2}$$

From $\Delta\, ET_1P$, we get

$$\tan\frac{\Delta_S}{2} = \frac{EP}{PT_1}$$

From Eq. (12.99), we have

$$\Delta_S = 2\tan^{-1}\left[\frac{\left(R_L \tan\frac{\Delta}{2} - T_L\right)\sin\Delta}{O_S K}\right] \tag{12.110}$$

and

$$\Delta_L = \Delta - \Delta_S \tag{12.111}$$

From Eq. (12.103), we get

$$R_L - R_S = \frac{O_S K}{\sin \Delta_S} \tag{12.112}$$

We have,

$$\begin{aligned} O_S K &= PT_1 = BP - BT_1 \\ &= QE - T_S \\ &= EB' - B'Q - T_S \end{aligned}$$

From Eqs. (12.98) and (12.100), we get the values of EB' and $B'Q$, and therefore, O_SK is determined. Thus, from Eq. (12.110) Δ_S is known, and from Eq. (12.112), we get

$$R_S = R_L - \frac{O_S K}{\sin \Delta_S} \tag{12.113}$$

Setting Out a Compound Curve

A compound curve being a combination of two (or more) simple circular curves, can be set out by any one method of setting out a simple circular curve discussed in Sec. 12.7. Generally, the Rankine's method of tangential angles in which a tape and a theodolite are used, is the most preferred method employed for setting out the compound curves.

The method discussed here is for a two-centred compound curve, and is also applicable when the number of circular curves are more than two. The first branch T_1T_3 is set out from T_1, and the second branch T_3T_2 from T_3 (Fig. 12.47). For setting out the curve, any four elements will be known, and the remaining three are determined by the formulae given in See. 12.9. Now the procedure for setting out is as follows.

Knowing T_S and T_L, the points T_1 and T_2 are located by linear measurements from P.I. Calculate l_S and l_L and then the chainages of T_1, T_3, and T_2. Calculate the deflection angles for the first curve using the Eq. (12.29). Set the theodolite at T_1, and set out the first branch of the curve.

Now shift the theodolite to T_3 (P.C.C.) and set it there. With vernier set to reading $\left(360°-\dfrac{\Delta_S}{2}\right)$, take a back sight on T_1, and plunge the telescope. The line of sight is thus oriented along line T_1T_3 produced, and if the theodolite is now swung through angle $\dfrac{\Delta_S}{2}$, the line of sight will be directed along the common tangent MN and thus, the theodolite is correctly oriented at T_3. Now set out the second branch of the curve using the computed deflection angles for this branch of the curve, till the point T_2 is reached.

Check the observations by measuring the $\angle T_1T_3T_2$ which should be

$$= \left[180°-\left(\frac{\Delta_S+\Delta_L}{2}\right)\right] \text{or} \left[180°-\frac{\Delta}{2}\right]$$

ILLUSTRATIVE EXAMPLES

Example 12.20

Two straights AB and BC are intersected by a line MN. The angles AMN and MNC are 145° and 140°, respectively. The radius of the first curve is 400 m, and that of the second curve is 600 m. Find the chainages of the tangent points, and the point of compound curvature, given that the chainage of the point of intersection is 5555 m.

Solution (Fig. 12.47):

Given that

$$\Delta_S = 180° - 145° = 35°$$
$$\Delta_L = 180° - 140° = 40°$$
$$\Delta = \Delta_S + \Delta_L = 75°$$

$$R_S = 400 \text{ m}$$
$$R_L = 600 \text{ m}$$
Chainage of B = 5555 m

(*i*) From Eqs. (12.81) and (12.82), we get

$$t_S = R_S \tan\frac{\Delta_S}{2} = 400 \times \tan\frac{35°}{2} = 126.12 \text{ m}$$

$$t_L = R_L \tan\frac{\Delta_L}{2} = 600 \times \tan\frac{40°}{2} = 218.38 \text{ m}$$

From Eq. (12.84), we have

$$T_S = BT_1 = (t_S + t_L)\frac{\sin\Delta_L}{\sin\Delta} + t_S$$

$$= (126.12 + 218.38) \times \frac{\sin 40°}{\sin 75°} + 126.12$$

$$= 355.37 \text{ m.}$$

(*ii*) Length of the curves

$$l_S = \frac{\pi R_S \Delta_S}{180} + \frac{\pi \times 400 \times 35}{180} = 244.35 \text{ m}$$

$$l_L = \frac{\pi R_L \Delta_L}{180} + \frac{\pi \times 600 \times 40}{180} = 418.88 \text{ m}$$

$$l = l_S + l_L = 244.35 + 418.88 = 663.23 \text{ m.}$$

(*iii*) Chainages

Chainage of T_1 = Chainage of $B - T_S$
= 5555 + 355.37
= **5199.63 m.**

Chainage of T_3 = Chainage of $T_1 + l_S$
= 5199.63 + 244.35
= **5443.98 m.**

Chainage of T_2 = Chainage of $T_3 + l_L$
= 5443.98 + 418.88
= **5862.86 m.**

Example 12.21

A compound curve is to connect two straights having a deflection angle of 90°. The lengths of the two tangents as determined from the plan are 340 m and 410 m.

Calculate the lengths of the arcs if the radius of the first curve is to be 300 m.

Solution (Fig. 12.48):

Given that

$$\Delta = 90°$$
$$T_S = 340 \text{ m}$$
$$T_L = 410 \text{ m}$$
$$R_S = 300 \text{ m}$$

The quantities to be determined are l_S and l_L. It is a Case-4 problem where Δ_S, Δ_L and R_L are required to be determined.

(*i*) From Eq. (12.108), we get

$$O_SK = T_L - BQ - B'E$$
$$= T_L - \left(T_S - R_S \tan\frac{\Delta}{2}\right)\cos\Delta - R_S \tan\frac{\Delta}{2}$$
$$= 410 - \left(340 - 300 \times \tan\frac{90°}{2}\right) \times \cos 90° - 300 \times \tan\frac{90°}{2}$$
$$= 110.00 \text{ m.}$$

From Eq. (12.105), we get

$$\Delta_L = 2\tan^{-1}\left[\frac{\left(T_S - R_S \tan\frac{\Delta}{2}\right)\sin\Delta}{O_S K}\right]$$
$$= 39°57'59''.$$

From Eq. (12.106), we have

$$\Delta_S = \Delta - \Delta_L = 90° - 39°57'59''$$
$$= 50°02'01''.$$

From Eq. (12.109), we have

$$R_L = R_S + \frac{O_S K}{\sin\Delta_L}$$
$$= 300 + \frac{110}{\sin(39°57'59'')}$$
$$= 471.25 \text{ m.}$$

(*ii*) Lengths of the arcs

$$l_S = \frac{\pi R_S \Delta_S}{180}$$
$$= \frac{\pi \times 300 \times 50°02'01''}{180}$$
$$= \mathbf{261.98 \text{ m.}}$$

$$l_L = \frac{\pi R_L \Delta_L}{180}$$

$$= \frac{\pi \times 471.25 \times 39°57'59''}{180}$$

$$= \mathbf{328.72\ m.}$$

Example 12.22

A 220 m length of straight connects two circular curves, both deflecting to the right. The radius of the first curve is 260 m, and that of the second curve is 195 m.The central angle for the second curve is 28°. If the two tangents are to be connected by a single circular curve between the P.C. and P.T. replacing the two curves and the straights, what would be the radius of the new curve? Assume that the two tangents of the earlier curves are equal in length. Also determine the following:

(*a*) Central angle of the new curve.

(*b*) Central angle of the first curve of radius 260 m.

Solution (Fig. 12.50):

Given that $AB = 220$ m

$R_1 = 260$ m

$R_2 = 195$ m

$\Delta_2 = 28°$

$T_1I = T_2I$

An essential condition to replace the two curves by a single curve without changing the direction of original tangents and also without shifting the original tangent points, is that the lengths of the two tangents T_1I and T_2I should be equal. Evidently, the central angle of the new curve will be equal to the deflection angle of the two tangents, *i.e.*, equal to Δ.

Since the new curve has to pass through T_1 and T_2, the point O which is the intersection of T_1O_1 and T_2O_2 produced, will be the centre of the new circular curve, say, having radius R.

Draw a perpendicular O_2C on AO_1, and join O_1 and O_2 by the line O_1O_2.

(*i*) From $\Delta\ CO_1O_2$, we get

$$O_1O_2 = \sqrt{O_1C^2 + O_2C^2}$$

$$= \sqrt{(O_1A - AC)^2 + AB^2}$$

$$= \sqrt{(O_1A - O_2B)^2 + AB^2}$$

$$= \sqrt{(260 - 195)^2 + 220^2}$$

$$= 229.40 \text{ m.}$$

$$\theta = \tan^{-1} \frac{O_1C}{O_2C}$$

$$= \tan^{-1} \frac{260 - 195}{220}$$

$$= 16°27'36''.$$

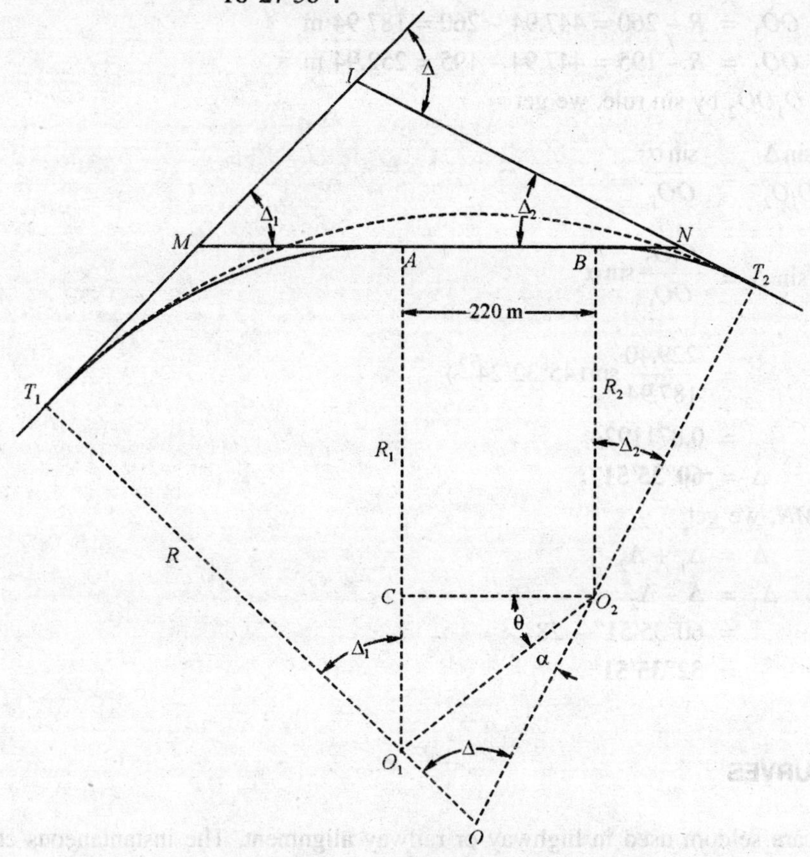

Fig. 12.50

(ii)

$$\angle O_1O_2T_2 = \theta + 90° + \Delta_2$$

$$= 16°27'36'' + 90° + 28°$$

$$= 134°27'36''.$$

$$\angle O_1O_2O = \alpha = 180° - \angle O_1O_2T_2$$

$$= 180° - 134°27'36''$$

$$= 45°32'24''$$

$$OO_1 = OT_1 - O_1T_1$$

$$= R - 260$$

$$OO_2 = OT_2 - O_2T_2$$

$$= R - 195$$

Applying cosine rule in Δ O_1OO_2, we get

$$OO_1^2 = O_1O_2^2 + OO_2^2 - 2O_1O_2\, OO_2 \cos\alpha$$

$$(R - 260)^2 = 229.40^2 + (R - 195)^2 - 2 \times 229.40 \times (R - 195) \times \cos(45°32'24'')$$

By rearranging and clearing the terms, we get

$$R = \mathbf{447.94\ m.}$$

(*iii*) $$OO_1 = R - 260 = 447.94 - 260 = 187.94 \text{ m}$$

$$OO_2 = R - 195 = 447.94 - 195 = 252.94 \text{ m}$$

Solving Δ O_1OO_2 by sin rule, we get

$$\frac{\sin\Delta}{O_1O_2} = \frac{\sin\alpha}{OO_1}$$

or $$\sin\Delta = \frac{O_1O_2}{OO_1}\sin\alpha$$

$$= \frac{229.40}{187.94}\sin(45°32'24'')$$

$$= 0.8711924$$

$$\Delta = \mathbf{60°35'51''.}$$

(*iv*) From Δ *IMN*, we get

$$\Delta = \Delta_1 + \Delta_2$$

or $$\Delta_1 = \Delta - \Delta_2$$

$$= 60°35'51'' - 28°$$

$$= \mathbf{32°35'51''.}$$

12.10 REVERSE CURVES

Reverse curves are seldom used in highway or railway alignment. The instantaneous change in direction occurring at the point of reverse curvature or point of reversed curve (P.R.C.) (Fig. 12.51) would cause discomfort and safety problems for all but the slowest speed. Additionally, since the change in curvature is instantaneous, there is no room to provide superelevation transition from cross-slope right to cross-slope left (*cf.*, Sec. 12.11). However, reverse curves can be used to advantage where the instantaneous change in direction poses no threat to safety or comfort.

Reverse curves are unavoidable in hilly roads where a loop of a curve in a valley is generally immediately followed by another loop round the shoulder of the ridge.

In cities where roads turn in different directions in succession or when roads approach a flyover, the reverse curves are frequently used.

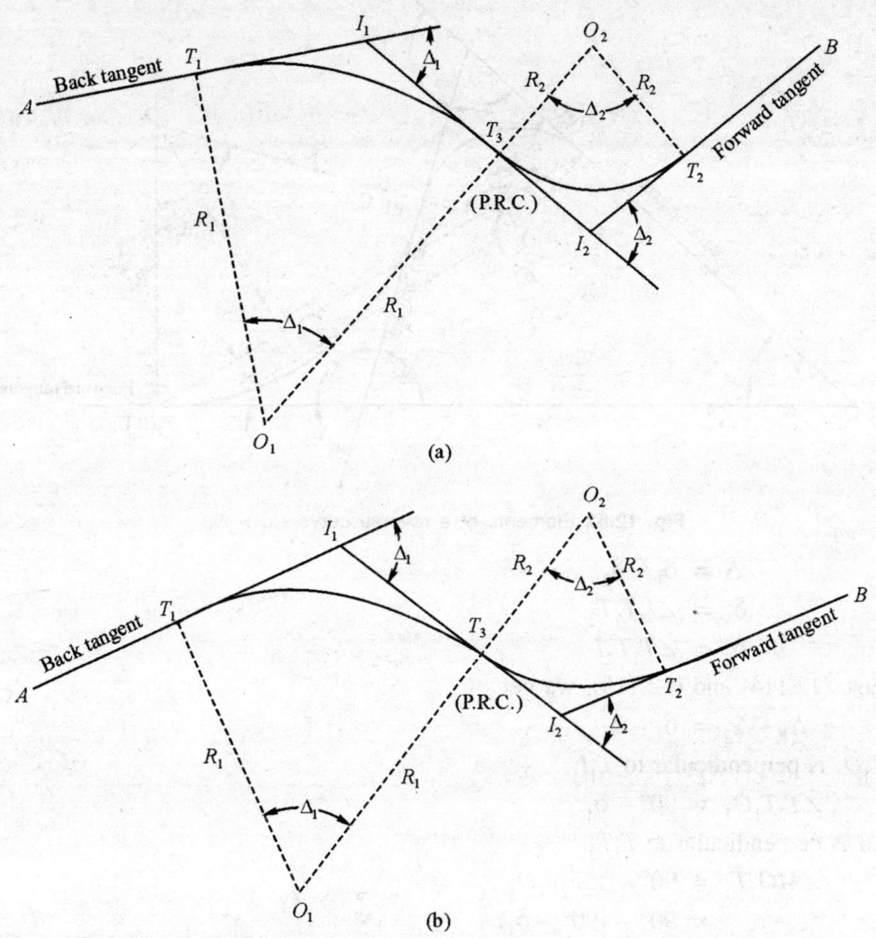

Fig. 12.51 Reverse curves (a) non parallel tangents; (b) parallel tangents

Elements of a Reverse Curve

As with compound curves, reverse curves also have six independent parameters (R_1, Δ_1, T_1, R_2, Δ_2, T_2); the solution technique depends on which parameters are unknown.

Fig. 12.52 shows a reverse curve between two straights AT_1 and T_2B having a total deviation of Δ at I. Let O_1 and O_2 be the centres of the two circular curves of radii R_1 and R_2, respectively, and Δ_1 and Δ_2 be their deflection angles or the central angles assuming Δ_1 greater than Δ_2.

Join the point T_1 and T_2, and draw perpendiculars O_1M and O_2N on T_1T_2 from O_1 and O_2, respectively. Draw a line O_1F parallel to T_1T_2 intersecting O_2N produced at F.

From $\Delta\ I_1II_2$, we have

$$\Delta_1 = \Delta + \Delta_2$$

or

$$\Delta = \Delta_1 - \Delta_2 \tag{12.114}$$

From $\Delta\ T_1IT_2$, we have

$$\delta_1 = \Delta + \delta_2$$

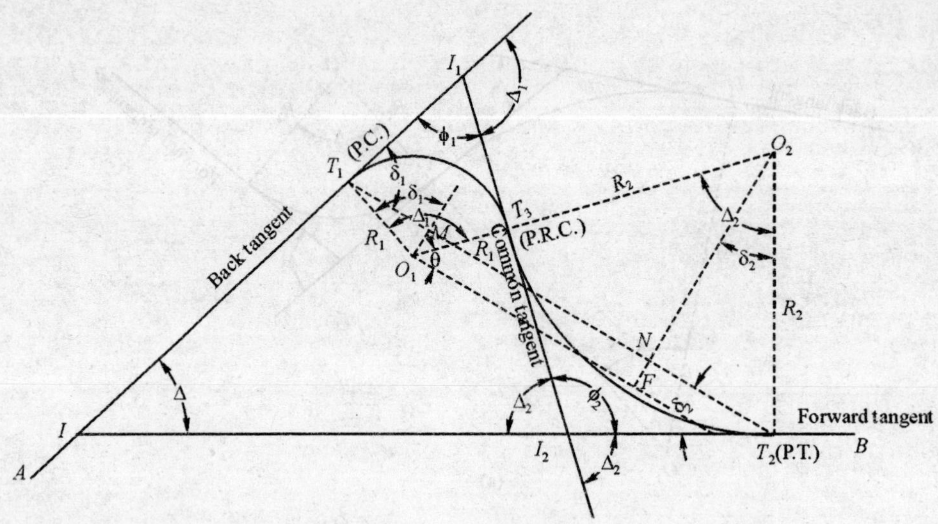

Fig. 12.52 Elements of a reverse curve ($\Delta_1 > \Delta_2$)

or $\quad \Delta = \delta_1 - \delta_2$ ...(12.115)

where $\quad \delta_1 = \angle I_1T_1T_2$

$\delta_2 = \angle T_1T_2I$

From Eqs. (12.114) and (12.115), we get

$$\Delta_1 - \Delta_2 = \delta_1 - \delta_2 \qquad ...(12.116)$$

Since T_1O_1 is perpendicular to T_1I_1,

$$\angle T_2T_1O_1 = 90° - \delta_1$$

and O_1M is perpendicular to T_1T_2,

$$\angle MO_1T_1 = 90° - \angle T_2T_1O_1$$
$$= 90° - (90° - \delta_1)$$
$$= \delta_1$$

Similarly, $\quad \angle NO_2T_2 = \delta_2$

Therefore, $\quad \angle NO_2T_3 = \angle T_2O_2T_3 - \angle NO_2T_2$

$$= \Delta_2 - \delta_2$$

and $\quad \angle MO_1T_3 = \angle T_1O_1T_3 - \angle MO_1T_1$

$$= \Delta_1 - \delta_1$$

Since, O_1M is parallel to O_2N,

$$\angle MO_1O_2 = \angle NO_2O_1$$

or $\quad \angle MO_1T_3 = \angle NO_2T_3$

$$\Delta_1 - \delta_1 = \Delta_2 - \delta_2 \qquad ...(12.117)$$

or $\quad \Delta_1 - \Delta_2 = \delta_1 - \delta_2$

which is same as Eq. (12.116)

Now from $\Delta\ T_1O_1M$, we have

$$T_1M = R_1 \sin \delta_1$$
$$O_1M = R_1 \cos \delta_1$$

and from $\Delta\ T_2O_2N$, we have

$$T_2N = R_2 \sin \delta_2$$
$$O_2N = R_2 \cos \delta_2$$

From $\Delta\ O_1O_2F$, we have

$$O_1F = O_1O_2 \sin (O_1O_2F)$$
$$= (R_1 + R_2) \sin (\Delta_2 - \delta_2)$$
$$O_2F = (R_1 + R_2) \cos (\Delta_2 - \delta_2) \quad ...(12.118)$$

Since, $MN = O_1F$

$$= (R_1 + R_2) \sin (\Delta_2 - \delta_2)$$

We have

$$T_1T_2 = T_1M + MN + NT_2$$
$$= R_1 \sin \delta_1 + (R_1 + R_2) \sin (\Delta_2 - \delta_2) + R_2 \sin \delta_2 \quad (12.119)$$

Since, $FN = O_1M$

$$= R_1 \cos \delta_1$$

we have $O_2F = FN + O_2N$

$$= R_1 \cos \delta_1 + R_2 \cos \delta_2$$

Equating the value of O_2F from Eq. (12.118), we get

$$(R_1 + R_2) \cos (\Delta_2 - \delta_2) = R_1 \cos \delta_1 + R_2 \cos \delta_2$$

or
$$\cos (\Delta_2 - \delta_2) = \frac{R_1 \cos\delta_1 + R_2 \cos\delta_2}{R_1 + R_2} \quad ...(12.120)$$

Since, from Eq. (12.117), we have

$$\Delta_1 - \delta_1 = \Delta_2 - \delta_2$$

$$\cos (\Delta_1 - \delta_1) = \frac{R_1 \cos\delta_1 + R_2 \cos\delta_2}{R_1 + R_2} \quad ...(12.121)$$

It has been assumed that Δ_1 is greater than Δ_2 so that $\Delta = \Delta_1 - \Delta_2$ is a positive quantity. In case Δ_2 is greater than Δ_1, we will have $\Delta = \Delta_2 - \Delta_1$ positive, and the point of intersection I will occur after the reverse curve as shown in Fig. 12.53.

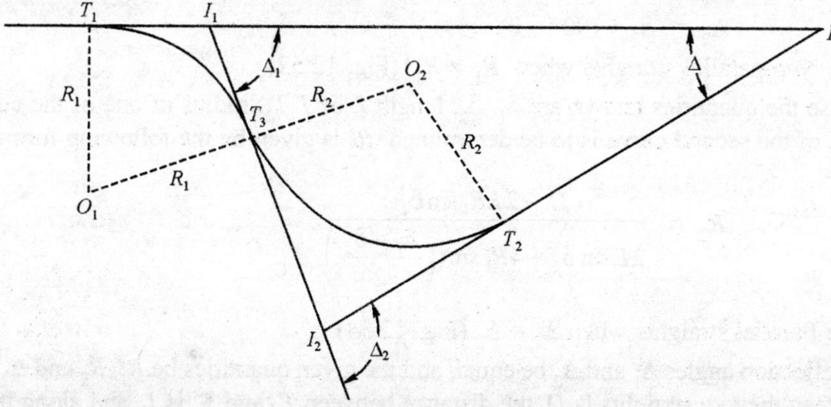

Fig. 12.53 Reverse curve between two non-parallel straights when $\Delta_2 > \Delta_1$ and $R_1 = R_2 = R$

Relationship Between Various Elements of a Reverse Curve

There are four cases depending on the quantities involved in the determination of unknowns. The first three cases are for non-parallel straights and the last fourth case is for parallel straights.

Case - 1: Non-parallel straights when $R_1 = R_2 = R$ (Fig. 12.53)

The quantities given are Δ_1, Δ_2 ($\Delta_2 > \Delta_1$), length d of the common tangent, and the chainage of the point of intersection I. The quantities to be determined are R, the chainages of T_1, T_2 and T_3. The formulae to determine these quantities are given below:

$$R = \frac{d}{\tan\frac{\Delta_1}{2} + \tan\frac{\Delta_2}{2}} \quad \text{...(12.122)}$$

$$\text{Chainage of } T_1 = \text{Chainage of } I - \left[R\tan\frac{\Delta_2}{2} + d\frac{\sin\Delta_2}{\sin\Delta}\right] \quad \text{...(12.123)}$$

where $\Delta = \Delta_2 - \Delta_1$

$$\text{Chainage of } T_3 = \text{Chainage of } T_1 + \frac{\pi R\Delta_1}{180} \quad \text{...(12.124)}$$

$$\text{Chainage of } T_2 = \text{Chainage of } T_3 + \frac{\pi R\Delta_2}{180} \quad \text{...(12.125)}$$

Case - 2: Non-parallel straights when $R_1 = R_2 = R$ (Fig. 12.52). The angles δ_1, δ_2, and the length L of T_1T_2 are known. It is required to determine the radius of the curves.

The radius of the curves in this case is given by

$$R = \frac{L}{\sin\delta_1 + 2\cos\theta + \sin\delta_2} \quad \text{...(12.126)}$$

where $\theta = \sin^{-1}\left(\frac{\cos\delta_1 + \cos\delta_2}{2}\right)$

$$\Delta_1 = \delta_1 + (90° - \theta) \quad \text{...(12.127)}$$

$$\Delta_2 = \delta_2 + (90° - \theta) \quad \text{...(12.128)}$$

Case - 3: Non-parallel straights when $R_1 \neq R_2$ (Fig. 12.52)

In this case the quantities known are δ_1, δ_2, length L of T_1T_2, radius of one of the curves, say R_1. The radius R_2 of the second curve is to be determined. R_2 is given by the following formula:

$$R_2 = \frac{L^2 - 2LR_1\sin\delta_1}{2L\sin\delta_2 + 4R_1\sin^2\left(\frac{\delta_1 - \delta_2}{2}\right)} \quad \text{...(12.129)}$$

Case - 4: Parallel straights when $\Delta_1 = \Delta_2$ (Fig. 12.54)

Let the deflection angles Δ_1 and Δ_2 be equal, and the given quantities be R_1, R_2 and Δ_1 ($= \Delta_2$). If the distance between the two straights is D, the distance between T_1 and T_2 is L, and along the straights it is H. For the length of T_1T_2 equal to L, D, H and L are given by

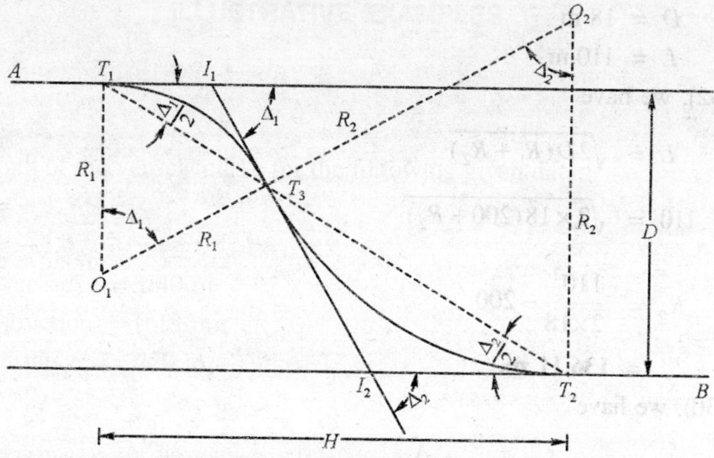

Fig. 12.54 Reverse curve between two parallel straights

$$D = 2(R_1 + R_2)\sin^2\frac{\Delta_1}{2} \qquad ...(12.130)$$

$$L = 2(R_1 + R_2)\sin\frac{\Delta_1}{2} \qquad ...(12.131)$$

or

$$= \sqrt{2D(R_1 + R_2)} \qquad ...(12.132)$$

$$H = (R_1 + R_2)\sin\Delta_1 \qquad ...(12.133)$$

Setting Out a Reverse Curve

A reverse curve is set out in the same way as a simple or compound curve. When the method of tangential angles is used, the values of the angles are calculated with respect to the first tangent for the first arc, and with respect to the common tangent for the second arc. Shifting of the instrument from the first tangent point to the junction, the back sighting and continuation are done in a manner similar to the method for simple curves. In the case of parallel straights, the setting out of reverse curve is even simpler whether it is set out by tangential angles or by offsets from long chords.

ILLUSTRATIVE EXAMPLES

Example 12.23

The first branch of a reverse curve has a radius of 200 m. Find the radius of the second branch so that the curve can connect parallel straights 18 m apart. The distance between tangent points is to be 110 m. Also calculate the lengths of the two branches of the curve.

Solution (Fig. 12.54):

Given that

$$R_1 = 200 \text{ m}$$

$$D = 18 \text{ m}$$
$$L = 110 \text{ m}$$

From Eq. (12.132), we have

$$L = \sqrt{2D(R_1 + R_2)}$$

$$110 = \sqrt{2 \times 18(200 + R_2)}$$

or
$$R_2 = \frac{110^2}{2 \times 18} - 200$$
$$= \textbf{136.11 m.}$$

From Eq. (12.130), we have

$$D = 2(R_1 + R_2)\sin^2 \frac{\Delta_1}{2}$$

$$\Delta_1 = 2\sin^{-1}\left[\sqrt{\frac{D}{2(R_1 + R_2)}}\right]$$

$$= 2\sin^{-1}\left[\sqrt{\frac{18}{2 \times (200 + 136.11)}}\right]$$

$$= 18°50'10''.$$

The length of the first branch of the curve

$$= \frac{\pi R_1 \Delta_1}{180}$$

$$= \frac{\pi \times 200 \times 18°50'10''}{180}$$

$$= \textbf{65.75 m.}$$

The length of the second branch of the curve

$$= \frac{\pi R_2 \Delta_2}{180}$$

$$= \frac{\pi \times 136.11 \times 18°50'10''}{180}$$

$$= \textbf{44.75 m.}$$

Example 12.24

A reverse curve is to be set out between two parallel straights 35 m apart. The line joining the two tangent points is 400 m.Calculate the necessary data for setting out the curve by offsets from a long chord at intervals of 20 m from the common tangent point. Take $R_1 = R_2$.

Solution (Fig. 12.55):

Given that $D = 35$ m

$T_1T_2 = 400$ m

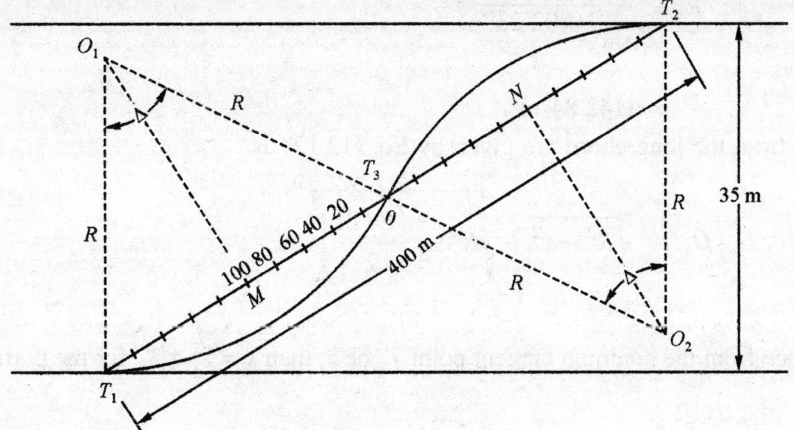

Fig. 12.55

Since $T_1T_2 = 400$ m, $T_1M = \frac{1}{4}T_1T_2 = \frac{1}{4} \times 400 = 100\,\text{m}$

From $\Delta\ O_1MT_1$, we get

$$T_1M = R\sin\frac{\Delta}{2} \qquad (a)$$

and from Eq. (12.130), we have

$$D = 2(R_1 + R_2)\sin^2\frac{\Delta_1}{2}$$

Since, $R_1 = R_2 = R$ and $\Delta_1 = \Delta_2 = \Delta$, we have

$$D = 4R\sin^2\frac{\Delta}{2} \qquad (b)$$

Dividing (*b*) by (*a*), we get

$$\frac{D}{T_1M} = 4\sin\frac{\Delta}{2}$$

or

$$\Delta = 2\sin^{-1}\frac{D}{4T_1M}$$

$$= 2\sin^{-1}\frac{35}{4 \times 100}$$

$$= 10°02'23''$$

$$100 = R \sin \frac{10°02'23''}{2}$$

or
$$R = \frac{100}{\sin \frac{10°02'23''}{2}}$$

$$= 1142.84 \text{ m.}$$

The offsets from the long chord are given by Eq. (12.17) as

$$O_x = \sqrt{R^2 - x^2} - \sqrt{R^2 - \left(\frac{(L/2)}{2}\right)^2}$$

If the distance from the common tangent point T_3 be x_t then $x = \frac{L}{4} - x_t$ for the portion between M and N.

Therefore,
$$O = \sqrt{R^2 - \left(\frac{L}{4} - x_t\right)^2} - \sqrt{R^2 - \left(\frac{L}{4}\right)^2}$$

$$= \sqrt{1142.84^2 - (100 - x_t)^2} - \sqrt{1142.84^2 - 100^2}$$

$$= \sqrt{1142.84^2 - (100 - x_t)^2} - 1138.46$$

Thus,

O_1 = 1.58 m for x_t = 20 m
O_2 = 2.80 m for x_t = 40 m
O_3 = 3.68 m for x_t = 60 m
O_4 = 4.20 m for x_t = 80 m
O_5 = 4.38 m for x_t = 100 m

The value of $x = x_t - 100$ for the portion between M to T_1 and N to t_2.

Therefore,
$$O = \sqrt{1142.84^2 - (x_t - 100)^2} - 1138.46$$

Thus,

O_6 = 4.20 m for x_t = 120 m
O_7 = 3.68 m for x_t = 140 m
O_8 = 2.80 m for x_t = 160 m
O_9 = 1.58 m for x_t = 180 m
O_{10} = 0.00 m for x_t = 200 m

The values of the offsets are tabulated in Table 12.5.

Table 12.5

T_1					←					T_3					→					T_2
200	180	160	140	120	100	80	60	40	20	0	20	40	60	80	100	120	140	160	180	200
0.001	1.58	2.80	3.68	4.20	4.38	4.20	3.68	2.80	1.58	0.0	1.58	2.80	3.68	4.20	4.38	4.20	3.68	2.80	1.58	0.00

Example 12.25

It is proposed to introduce a reverse curve between two straights *AB* and *CD* intersecting at *I* with $\angle CBI = 30°$ and $\angle BCI = 120°$. The reverse curve consists of two circular arcs *AX* and *XD*, *X* lying on the common tangent *BC*. If *BC* = 791.71 m, radius R_{AX} = 750 m, and chainage of *B* is 1250 m, calculate

(*i*) the radius R_{XD},

(*ii*) the length of arcs *AX* and *XD*, and

(*iii*) the chainage of *D*.

Solution (Fig. 12.56):

Given that

$$\Delta_1 = 30°$$

$$\Delta_2 = 180° - 120° = 60°$$

$$R_{AX} = 750 \text{ m}$$

$$BC = 791.71 \text{ m}$$

$$\text{Chainage of } B = 1250 \text{ m}$$

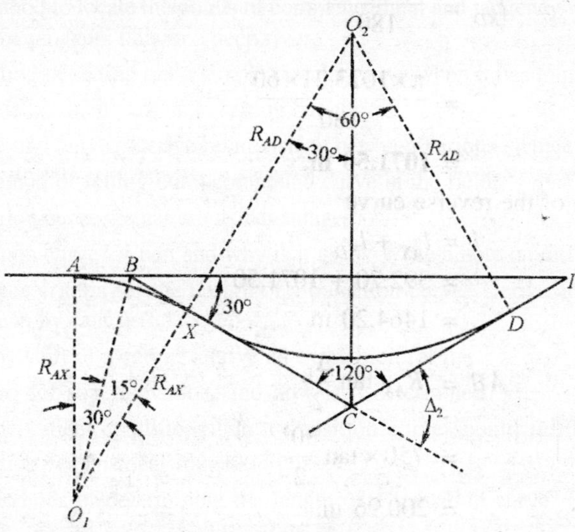

Fig.12.56

(*i*) From Eq. (12.5), the tangent lengths

$$BX = R_{AX} \tan\frac{\Delta_1}{2}$$

$$XC = R_{XD}\tan\frac{\Delta_2}{2}$$

But $$BC = BX + XC$$

or $$= R_{AX}\tan\frac{\Delta_1}{2} + R_{XD}\tan\frac{\Delta_2}{2}$$

or $$791.71 = 750\times\tan\frac{30^\circ}{2} + R_{XD}\tan\frac{60^\circ}{2}$$

or $$R_{XD} = \frac{791.71 - 750\times\tan 15^\circ}{\tan 30^\circ}$$

$$= \mathbf{1023.21\ m.}$$

(*ii*) From Eq. (12.3), length of the curve *AX*

$$l_{AX} = \frac{\pi R_{AX}\Delta_1}{180}$$

$$= \frac{\pi\times 750\times 30}{180}$$

$$= \mathbf{392.70\ m.}$$

(*iii*) and length of the curve *XD*

$$l_{XD} = \frac{\pi R_{XD}\Delta_2}{180}$$

$$= \frac{\pi\times 1023.21\times 60}{180}$$

$$= \mathbf{1071.50\ m.}$$

(*iv*) The total length of the reverse curve

$$l = l_{AX} + l_{XD}$$
$$= 392.70 + 1071.50$$
$$= 1464.20\text{ m}$$

$$AB = R_{AX}\tan\frac{\Delta_1}{2}$$

$$= 750\times\tan\frac{30^\circ}{2}$$

$$= 200.96\text{ m.}$$

Now chainage of *A* = Chainage of *B* – *AB*
= 1250.00 – 200.96
= **1049.04 m.**

Chainage of *D* = Chainage of *A* + length of the reverse curve
= 1049.04 +1464.20
= **2513.24 m.**

Example 12.26

Calculate the length of the reverse curve connecting two parallel straights 15 m apart, having the distance between the two tangent points 60 m along the straights, and (*i*) the radius R if $R_1 = R_2 = R$, and (*ii*) the radius R_2 if $R_1 = 55$ m.

Solution (Fig. 12.54):

$$\tan\frac{\Delta_1}{2} = \frac{D}{H} = \frac{15}{60} = 0.25$$

$$\Delta_1 = 2\tan^{-1} 0.25$$

$$= 28°04'21''$$

(*i*) For $R_1 = R_2 = R$, from Eq. (12.133), we have

$$H = 2R \sin \Delta_1$$

$$R = \frac{H}{2\sin\Delta_1}$$

$$= \frac{60}{2\times\sin 28°04'21''}$$

$$= \mathbf{63.75\ m.}$$

(*ii*) When $R_1 = 55$ m, from Eq. (12.133), we have

$$H = (R_1 + R_2)\sin\Delta_1$$

or

$$R_2 = \frac{H}{\sin\Delta_1} - R_1$$

$$= \frac{60}{\sin 28°04'21''} - 55$$

$$= \mathbf{72.50\ m.}$$

From Eq. (12.3), length of the curve is

$$l = \frac{\pi R\Delta}{180}$$

In the case of parallel tangents, $\Delta_1 = \Delta_2 = \Delta$, therefore when $R_1 = R_2 = R$, the total length of the curve will be $2l$, thus the total length of the curve

$$l = 2\frac{\pi R\Delta}{180}$$

$$= 2\times\frac{\pi\times 63.75\times 28°04'21''}{180}$$

$$= \mathbf{62.47\ m.}$$

Also, when R_1 = 55 m, R_2 = 72.50 m, the total length of the curve.

$$= (55+72.50)\times\frac{\pi\times 28°04'21''}{180}$$

$$= \mathbf{62.47\ m.}$$

Example 12.27

Two parallel railway lines are to be connected by a reverse curve, each section having the same radius. If the lines are 10 m apart, and the maximum distance between the tangent points measured parallel to the lines, is 50 m, what is the maximum allowable radius?

Solution (Fig. 12.54):

Given that D = 10 m

H = 50 m

$$\tan\frac{\Delta}{2} = \frac{D}{H} = \frac{10}{50} = 0.2$$

or $$\Delta = 2 \times \tan^{-1} 0.2$$

$$= 22°37'12''.$$

From Eq. (12.133), we have

$$H = 2\,R \sin \Delta$$

or $$R = \frac{H}{2\sin\Delta}$$

$$= \frac{50}{2\times\sin 22°37'12''}$$

$$= \mathbf{65.00\ m.}$$

12.11 TRANSITION CURVES

On a straight track its two edges are at the same level. But on a circular arc the outer edge is elevated depending on the radius of the curve and the speed of the vehicles expected, to avoid overturning of the vehicles due to centrifugal force acting on them while moving on circular path. Also there is an abrupt change in direction when the alignment changes from straight to circular curve, and *vice versa.*

The introduction of a transition curve or easement curve which is a non-circular curve between the straight and the circular arc as shown in Fig. 12.57, permits the gradual elevation of the outer edge or gradual introduction of *cant or superelevation* (raising the outer edge over the inner). At the same time it also permits gradual change of direction from straight to the circular curve, and *vice versa.*

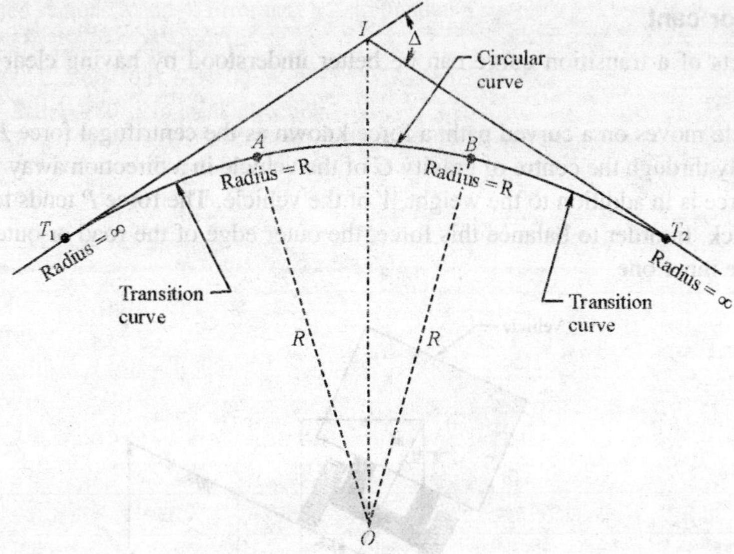

Fig. 12.57 Transition curves

Advantages of a transition curve

The introduction of a transition curve between a straight and a circular curve has the following advantages:

1. The chances of overturning of the vehicles and the derailment of trains are reduced considerably.
2. It provides comfort to the passengers while vehicles negotiating a curve.
3. The superelevation is introduced gradually in proportion to the rate of change of curvature.
4. It permits higher speeds at curves.
5. It reduces the wear on the running gears.

Requirements of a transition curve

A transition curve introduced between tangent and the circular curve should fulfil the following conditions:

1. It should be tangential to the straight.
2. It should meet the circular curve tangentially.
3. Its curvature should be zero ($R = \infty$) at the origin on tangent.
4. Its curvature should be equal to that of the circular curve at the junction with the circular curve.
5. The rate of change of curvature from zero to that of the circular curve should be the same as that of increase of cant or superelevation.
6. The length of the transition curve should be such that full cant or superelevation is attained at the junction with the circular curve.

Superelevation or cant

Various aspects of a transition curve can be better understood by having clear understanding of superelevation.

When a vehicle moves on a curved path, a force known as the centrifugal force P (Fig. 12.58) acts upon it horizontally through the centre of gravity G of the vehicle in a direction away from the centre of the curve. This force is in addition to the weight W of the vehicle. The force P tends to push the vehicle off the road or track. In order to balance this force, the outer edge of the road or outer rail on railways is raised above the inner one.

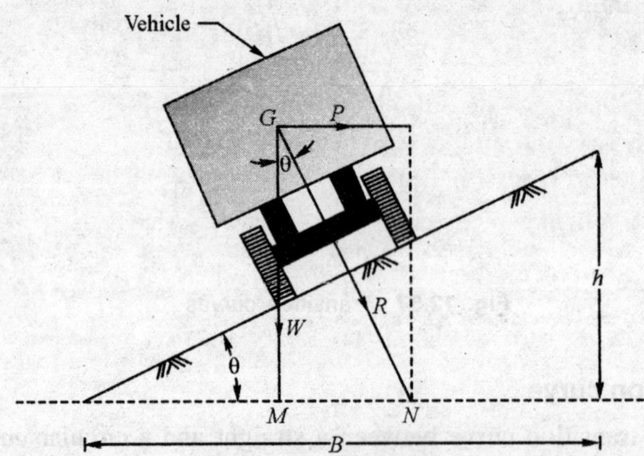

Fig. 12.58 Superelevation

The difference h in the top levels of outer and inner edges or rails, is called *superelevation* or *cant.* The amount of raising depends upon the radius of the curve, and the average speed of the vehicles.

From mechanics, centrifugal force P is given by

$$P = \frac{Wv^2}{gR} \qquad \text{...(12.134)}$$

where v = speed of the vehicle (m/s)

R = radius of the curve (m)

g = acceleration due to gravity (= 9.81 m/s^2)

From Eq. (12.134), we have

$$\frac{P}{W} = \frac{v^2}{gR} \qquad \text{...(12.135)}$$

Now, $$\tan\theta = \frac{h}{B}$$

or $$= \frac{MN}{MG}$$

or $$= \frac{P}{W}$$

$$\text{or} \qquad = \frac{v^2}{gR}$$

$$\text{or} \qquad \frac{h}{B} = \frac{v^2}{gR}$$

$$\text{or} \qquad h = \frac{Bv^2}{gR} \qquad \text{...(12.136)}$$

In Eq. (12.136), B is the horizontal distance between the two edges of a highway and the gauge of the railway track.

If the superelevation or cant provided in the case of railway tracks, is equal to that given by Eq. (12.136), it is called *equilibrium cant.* In that case, the load carried by both the wheels will be equal. In case the superelevation provided is less than the *equilibrium cant*, the track has a *cant deficiency*, and due to this deficiency, more weight will be carried by the outer wheel.

Maximum centrifugal ratio

The ratio $\frac{P}{W}$ in Eq. (12.135), is known as *centrifugal ratio*. It increases as R decreases. To avoid excessive inconvenience to slow-moving vehicles on curves, the maximum value of the centrifugal ratio is generally kept as 1/4 for highways, and as 1/8 for railways.

Thus, for roads

$$\frac{1}{4} = \frac{v^2}{gR}$$

$$\text{or} \qquad v = \sqrt{\frac{gR}{4}} \qquad \text{...(12.137)}$$

and for railways

$$\frac{1}{8} = \frac{v^2}{gR}$$

$$\text{or} \qquad v = \sqrt{\frac{gR}{8}} \qquad \text{...(12.138)}$$

Eqs. (12.137) and (12.138) give the maximum value of speed v for the vehicles to pass comfortably and safely over a curve of radius R.

The minimum value of radius R of the curve for the given speed v so that the vehicles can pass safely, is given by

$$\text{For highways } R = \frac{4v^2}{g} \qquad \text{...(12.139)}$$

$$\text{For railways } R = \frac{8v^2}{g} \qquad \text{...(12.140)}$$

Types of transition curves

There are mainly three types of transition curves:

1. Cubic spiral,
2. Cubic parabola, and
3. The lemniscate curve.

The cubic spiral and cubic parabola are best suited on railways, and the lemniscate curves on highways.

Equations of transition curves

1. Cubic spiral (Fig. 12.59)

The equation of a cubic spiral is

$$y = \frac{l^3}{6RL} \quad \text{...(12.141)}$$

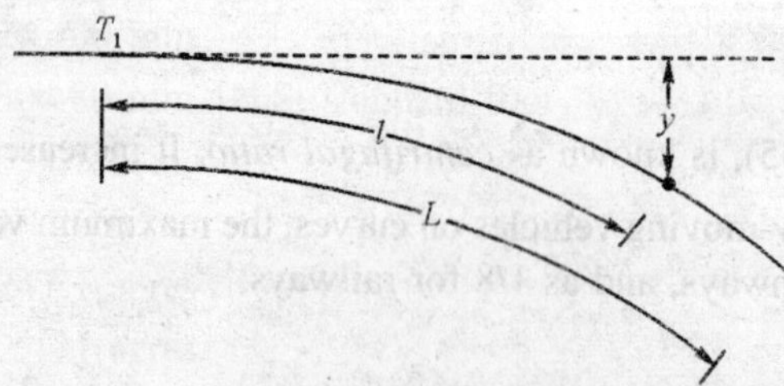

Fig. 12.59 Cubic spiral

where
y = perpendicular offset from the tangent
l = distance measured along the curve
R = radius of the circular curve
L = length of the transition curve.

2. Cubic parabola (Fig. 12.60)

The equation of a cubic parabola is

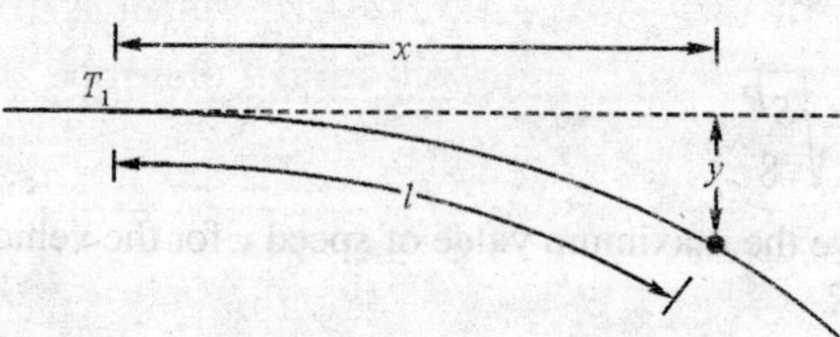

Fig. 12.60 Cubic parabola

$$y = \frac{x^3}{6RL} \quad \text{...(12.142)}$$

where
y = perpendicular offset from the tangent
x = distance measured along the tangent

R = radius of the circular curve

L = length of the transition curve.

3. The lemniscate curve (Fig. 12.61)

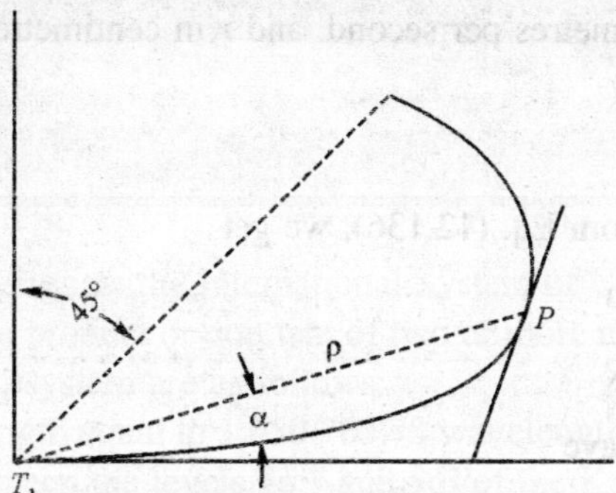

Fig. 12.61 Lemniscate curve

The equation of a Bernoulli's lemniscate curve is

$$\rho = k\sqrt{\sin(2\alpha)} \quad ...(12.143)$$

where

ρ = polar distance of any point

α = polar deflection angle for any point

k = constant.

Length of a transition curve

The length of a transition curve introduced between a straight and a circular curve, is calculated from one of the following considerations.

1. Arbitrary rate of superelevation

The length of a transition curve can be determined by providing superelevation at an arbitrary rate keeping in view the types of moving vehicles. The length L of the transition curve is given by

$$L = nh \quad ...(12.144)$$

The value of n may vary from 300 to 1200.

From Eq. (12.136), we get

$$L = \frac{nBv^2}{gR} \quad ...(12.145)$$

2. Time rate

By this criteria, the superelevation is applied at an arbitrary time rate of r units per second.

The time t taken by a vehicle to pass over the transition curve of length L with speed v is

$$t = \frac{L}{v} \text{ seconds}$$

The superelevation attained in this time is

$$h = tr = \frac{L}{v} r \text{ cm}$$

where L is in metres, v is in metres per second, and r in centimetres per second.

Therefore, $$L = \frac{vh}{r} \quad \text{...(12.146)}$$

Substituting the value of h from Eq. (12.136), we get

$$= \frac{Bv^3}{rgR} \quad \text{...(12.147)}$$

Taking v as V in km/hr, we have

$$L = \frac{BV^3}{46.66\, rgR} \quad \text{...(12.148)}$$

3. Rate of change of radial acceleration

In this method, the length of the transition curve is decided on the basis of the comfort of the passengers.

If α is the rate of change of radial acceleration, the radial acceleration a attained during the time vehicle passes over the transition curve, is given by

$$a = \alpha t = \alpha \frac{L}{v}$$

The radial acceleration is given by

$$a = \frac{v^2}{R}$$

Equating the two values of a, we get

$$\frac{\alpha L}{v} = \frac{v^2}{R}$$

or $$L = \frac{v^3}{\alpha R} \quad \text{...(12.149)}$$

where α is in m/sec^2/sec.

Taking v as V in km/hr, we have

$$L = \frac{V^3}{46.66\, \alpha R} \quad \text{...(12.150)}$$

The experience has shown that a rate of change of radial acceleration of 0.3 m/sec^2/sec passes unnoticed, and no discomfort is experienced by the passengers.

ILLUSTRATIVE EXAMPLES

Example 12.28

The maximum allowable speed on a curve is 60 km/hr, and the rate of change of radial acceleration is 0.3 m/sec²/sec. Calculate the length of the transition curve if the radius of the circular curve is 150 m.

Solution:

From Eq. (12.150), the length of the transition curve is given by

$$L = \frac{V^3}{46.66\alpha R}$$

$$= \frac{60^3}{46.66 \times 0.3 \times 150}$$

$$= \mathbf{102.87\ m.}$$

Example 12.29

A transition curve is required to be introduced between a straight and a circular curve of radius 320 m. Determine its length if

(*i*) the maximum superelevation is restricted to 0.1 m for a gauge of 1.0 m, and

(*ii*) the superelevation of 4 cm is provided on the distance covered by the vehicle in one second.

Solution:

From Eq. (12.136), we have

$$h = \frac{Bv^2}{gR}$$

Given that

$$h = 0.1 \text{ m}$$

$$B = 1.0 \text{ m}$$

$$R = 320 \text{ m}$$

Taking $g = 9.81 \text{ m/sec}^2$

$$0.1 = \frac{1.0 \times v^2}{9.81 \times 320}$$

or

$$v = \sqrt{\frac{1.0 \times 9.81 \times 320}{1.0}}$$

$$= 17.72 \text{ m/sec.}$$

From Eq. (12.146), we have

$$L = \frac{vh}{r}$$

The value of r given is 4 cm/sec or 0.04 m/sec. Therefore

$$L = \frac{17.72 \times 0.1}{0.04}$$

$$= \mathbf{44.30\ m.}$$

Example 12.30

What is the length of a transition curve if the maximum superelevation is restricted to 200 mm, and the superelevation is applied at the rate of 1 in 500?

Solution:

From Eq. (12.144), we have

$$L = nh$$

It is given that

$$n = 500$$

$$h = 0.2 \text{ m}$$

Therefore,

$$L = 500 \times 0.2$$

$$= \mathbf{100\ m.}$$

Ideal transition curve

When a vehicle moving on a straight takes a circular path, the superelevation is required to be introduced uniformly from zero to its maximum designed value so that the centrifugal force builds up gradually, and the lateral shock and discomfort are minimized. On the other hand, the speed of the vehicle is also kept constant. These requirements are fulfilled by

(*a*) increasing the centrifugal force at a constant rate, and

(*b*) varying the distance travelled along the transition curve, with time.

If a vehicle is moving with speed v on a transition curve, the distance l travelled in time t is given by

$$l = vt$$

or

$$t = \frac{l}{v} \qquad \text{...(12.151)}$$

If the centrifugal force P, given by Eq. (12.134), is to vary with time, then

$$P \propto t$$

From Eq. (12.151)

$$P \propto \frac{l}{v}$$

or $$\frac{Wv^2}{gr} \propto \frac{l}{v}$$

As W, g and v are constants,

$$\frac{1}{r} \propto l$$

At the end of the transition curve, we have $l = L$ and $r = R$, thus

$$rl = \text{a constant} = RL \qquad ...(12.152)$$

where L = length of the transition curve

R = radius of the circular curve.

Eq. (12.152) states the fundamental requirement of a transition curve that its radius of curvature (r) at any point, should be inversely proportional to its distance (l) from the beginning of the transition curve to that point. Curve fulfilling the above condition is an ideal transition curve. The curve represented by Eq. (12.152) is a *clothoid*, the *Glover spiral*, or the *Euler spiral.*

Intrinsic equation of an ideal transition curve

In Fig. 12.62, let

T = tangent point, the beginning of the transition curve

TA = initial tangent

B = any point on the transition curve

D = point of junction of the transition curve and circular curve

l = distance of B from T along the curve

L = distance of D from T along the curve

r = radius of the curve at B

α = angle which TB makes with the initial tangent

R = radius of the circular curve

ϕ = inclination of the tangent to the transition curve at B, to the initial tangent

Δ_S = spiral angle, the angle between the initial tangent and the tangent to the transition curve at D

x = x-coordinate of any point $B = TB_2$

X = x-coordinate of $D = TD_2$

y = y-coordinate of any point $B = B_2B$

Y = y-coordinate of $D = D_2D$

From Eq. (12.152), we have

$$rl = RL$$

or $$\frac{1}{r} = \text{curvature} = \frac{l}{RL}$$

But curvature $= \dfrac{d\phi}{dl} = \dfrac{1}{r}$

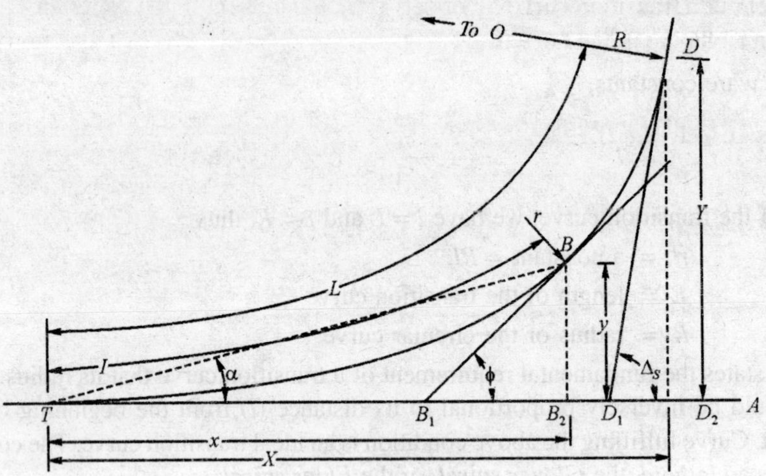

Fig. 12.62 Ideal transition curve

Therefore, $$\frac{d\phi}{dl} = \frac{l}{RL}$$

$$d\phi = \frac{l\,dl}{RL} \qquad \text{...(12.153)}$$

Integrating Eq. (12.153), we get

$$\phi = \frac{l^2}{2RL} + C$$

where C is the constant of integration.

When $l = 0$, $\phi = 0$, we have $C = 0$

thus $$\phi = \frac{l^2}{2RL} \qquad \text{...(12.154)}$$

Eq. (12.154) is the *intrinsic equation* of an ideal transition curve.

Expressing Eq. (12.154) as

$$l = \sqrt{2RL\phi}$$

$$= k\sqrt{\phi} \qquad \text{...(12.155)}$$

where $k = \sqrt{2RL}$

When $l = L$, $\phi = \Delta_S$, Eq. (12.154) becomes

$$\Delta_S = \frac{L}{2R} \qquad \text{...(12.156)}$$

Cartesian coordinates of the points on transition curve and polar deflection angles

In order to set out a transition curve by offsets from the tangent in the cartesian coordinate system, the x-axis is taken along the initial tangent TA (Fig. 12.62), and the y-axis in a direction perpendicular to TA, with origin at T.

Taking $k = \sqrt{2RL}$, the coordinates of any point B on the transition curve are given by

$$x = l\left[1 - \frac{l^4}{10k^4} + \frac{l^8}{216k^8} - \ldots\right] \quad \ldots(12.157)$$

$$y = \frac{l^3}{3k^2}\left[1 - \frac{l^4}{14k^4} + \frac{l^8}{440k^8} - \ldots\right] \quad \ldots(12.158)$$

The polar deflection angle α for any point B is given by

$$\alpha = \frac{l^2}{6RL} \text{ radians} \quad \ldots(12.159)$$

$$= \frac{1800}{\pi RL} l^2 \text{ minutes} \quad \ldots(12.160)$$

For small values of ϕ the following expression may also be used

$$\alpha = \frac{\phi}{3} \quad \ldots(12.161)$$

For $\phi = 15°$ the error in α is about 10″. For large values of ϕ, the following more exact equation is used.

$$\alpha = \frac{\phi}{3} - \delta \quad (\phi \text{ being in degree and } \delta \text{ in seconds}) \quad \ldots(12.162)$$

where $\delta = 3.095 \times 10^{-3}\,\phi^3 + 2.285 \times 10^{-8}\,\phi^5$.

Modification of the ideal transition curve

As the cartesian coordinates given by the Eqs. (12.157) and (12.158) are not simple, modifications are made to make them simpler for use.

Cubic spiral

Neglecting all the terms of Eq. (12.158), except the first one, we get

$$y = \frac{l^3}{3k^2}$$

Substituting the value of $k = \sqrt{2RL}$, we have

$$y = \frac{l^3}{6RL} \quad \ldots(12.163)$$

which is Eq. (12.141) of cubic spiral.

The cubic spiral is set out by chords and offsets from the initial tangent. If, however, the curve is set out by deflection angles, Eq. (12.160) is used.

Cubic parabola

Neglecting all the terms of Eq. (12.157), except the first one, we get

$$x = l$$

Substituting the value of l as x in Eq. (12.163), we get

$$y = \frac{x^3}{6RL}$$

which is Eq. (12.142) of cubic parabola.

The cubic parabola is the most widely used transition curve owing to the ease with which it may be set out by rectangular coordinates. It is almost identical with the clothoid and the lemniscate for deviation angle up to 12°. For small deviation angles, certain approximations made for calculations do not result in appreciable errors. However, for large deviation angles, it is necessary to express certain dimensions as infinite series, and hence, the great advantage of simplicity is then lost. In such cases clothoid or lemniscate should be used for better results.

Minimum radius of curvature of cubic parabola

The equation of the cubic parabola is

$$y = \frac{x^3}{6RL}$$

$$= Mx^3$$

where $$M = \frac{1}{6RL} \qquad \text{...(12.164)}$$

Differentiating Eq. (12.164), we get

$$\frac{dy}{dx} = 3Mx^2 = \tan\phi$$

or $$x = \sqrt{\frac{\tan\phi}{3M}}$$

$$\frac{d^2y}{dx^2} = 6Mx = 6M\sqrt{\frac{\tan\phi}{3M}}$$

$$= \sqrt{12M\tan\phi}$$

The radius of curvature is given by

$$r = \frac{\left[1+\left(\frac{dy}{dx}\right)^2\right]^{3/2}}{\frac{d^2y}{dx^2}}$$

$$= \frac{(1+\tan^2\phi)^{3/2}}{\sqrt{12M\tan\phi}}$$

$$= \frac{\sec^3\phi}{\sqrt{12M\tan\phi}}$$

$$= \frac{1}{\sqrt{12M\sin\phi\cos^5\phi}} \qquad \text{...(12.165)}$$

To make r a minimum, $\sqrt{12M\sin\phi\cos^5\phi}$ should be a maximum. Hence differentiating it, and equating to zero, we get

$$\cos^6\phi - 5\sin^2\phi\cos^4\phi = 0$$

or $$1 - 5\tan^2\phi = 0$$

or $$\tan\phi = \frac{1}{\sqrt{5}}$$

which gives $$\phi = 24°5'41''$$

Therefore, from eq. (12.161), we get

$$\alpha = \frac{\phi}{3} = 8°1'54''$$

Substituting the value of ϕ in Eq. (12.165), we have

$$r_{min} = \frac{1}{\sqrt{12M\sin 24°5'41''\cos^5 24°5'41''}} \qquad \text{...(12.166)}$$

$$= 1.39\sqrt{RL}$$

Hence the radius of curvature of the cubic parabola decreases from a value of infinity when $\phi = 0$ to a minimum value of $r = 1.39\sqrt{RL}$ when $\phi = 24°5'41''$.

Beyond this point the radius of curvature begins to increase again, and therefore, in no case, a cubic parabola should be used for the value of ϕ greater than $24°5'41''$ as it will not serve the required purpose of a gradual decrease in radius with an increase in length.

Characteristics of a transition curve

When a transition curve is introduced at the ends of a circular curve, the circular curve is required to be shifted from its original position in order to accommodate the transition. Alternatively, the circular curve can be located in the position without transitions if the two tangents are shifted outwards from the curve by an amount that would permit introduction of the transitions. Of these two approaches, the first, in which the circular curve is shifted is the common practice (Fig. 12.63).

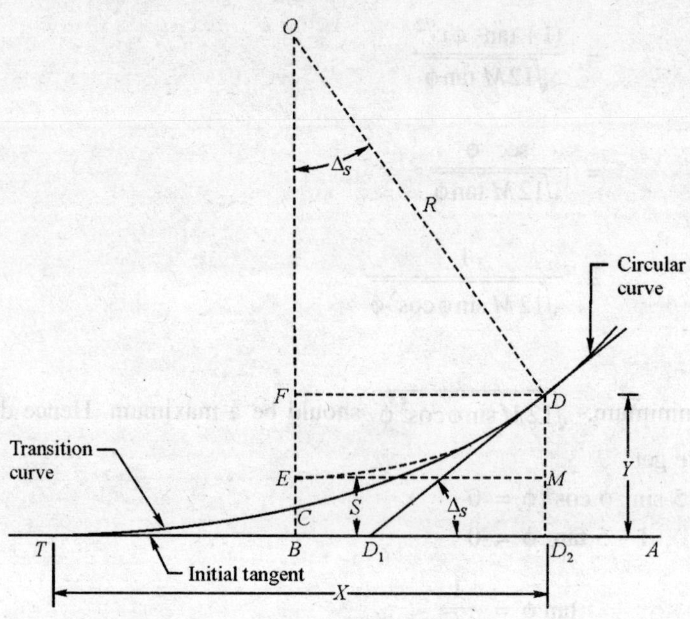

Fig. 12.63 Characteristics of a transition curve

Let

EM = the shift tangent to the circular curve at E, parallel to the initial tangent TA

S = BE = shift of the circular curve

L = TD = length of the transition curve

DD_1 = tangent common to the transition curve and the circular curve at D

DE = extended portion of the circular curve

TD_2 = X = x-coordinate of D

D_2D = Y = y-coordinate or offset of D

R = radius of the circular curve

O = centre of the circular curve

Δ_S = spiral angle

OE = perpendicular from O to the shift tangent

B = point of intersection of OE produced with TA

DF = line perpendicular to OB.

Since the tangent DD_1 makes angle Δ_S with the original tangent, $\angle BOD = \Delta_S$.

Now in Δ *EOD*, we have

arc $\quad ED = R\Delta_S$

From Eq. (12.156), we have

$$\Delta_S = \frac{L}{2R}$$

therefore,

$$ED = \frac{RL}{2R}$$

$$= \frac{L}{2}$$

When *CD* is very small, it may be taken equal to *ED*, thus

$$CD = \frac{L}{2} \qquad \text{...(12.167)}$$

Hence the shift BE bisects the transition curve at C.

Again

$$S = BE = FB - FE$$

$$= Y - R\,(1 - \cos \Delta_S)$$

$$= Y - 2R\sin^2 \frac{\Delta_S}{2}$$

When Δ_S is small, $\sin^2 \dfrac{\Delta_S}{2} = \dfrac{\Delta_S^2}{4} = \dfrac{L^2}{16R^2}$

and from Eq. (12.163), for

$$l = L$$

$$Y = \frac{L^2}{6R}$$

or

$$S = \frac{L^2}{6R} - \frac{L^2}{8R}$$

$$= \frac{L^2}{24R} \qquad \text{...(12.168)}$$

Also, BC = y-coordinate of C when $l = \dfrac{L}{2}$

$$= \frac{l^3}{6RL} = \frac{\left(\dfrac{L}{2}\right)^3}{6RL}$$

$$= \frac{1}{2}\frac{L^2}{24R}$$

From Eq. (12.168), we get

$$BC = \frac{1}{2}S \qquad \text{...(12.169)}$$

Hence the transition curve bisects the shift.

Formulae for various elements of transition curve (Figs. 12.63 and 12.64)

Total tangent length (*T*): The distance *TI* is known as the total tangent length, and it is given by

$$TI = BI + BT$$

From Δ *BOI*, we have

$$BI = (R + S)\tan\frac{\Delta}{2}$$

In Fig. 12.63, we have

$$\begin{aligned} BT &= TD_2 - BD_2 \\ &= X - FD \\ &= X - R\sin\Delta_S \end{aligned}$$

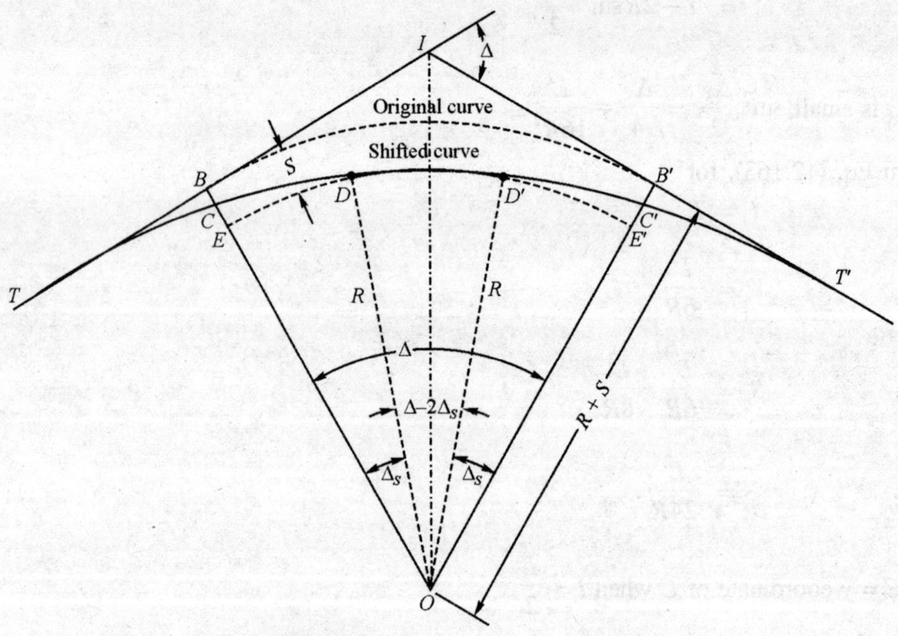

Fig. 12.64 A circular curve with end-transitions

Therefore, $TI = T_t = (R+S)\tan\frac{\Delta}{2} + (X - R\sin\Delta_S)$

Substituting $\sin\Delta s = \Delta_S \simeq \frac{L}{2R}$ and $X \simeq L$, and taking $\sin\Delta_S = \Delta_S$, we get

$$T = (R+S)\tan\frac{\Delta}{2} + \left[L - R\frac{L}{2R}\right]$$

$$= (R+S)\tan\frac{\Delta}{2} + \frac{L}{2} \quad ...(12.170)$$

Total length of the combined curve (l): The total length of the transition curve and the circular curve is given by

$$l = TD + DD' + D'T'$$

$$= L + \frac{\pi R(\Delta - 2\Delta_S)}{180} + L$$

$$= 2L + \frac{\pi R(\Delta - 2\Delta_S)}{180} \quad ...(12.171)$$

Alternatively, $l = TC + EE' + C'T'$

$$= \frac{L}{2} + \frac{\pi R\Delta}{180} + \frac{L}{2}$$

$$= L + \frac{\pi R\Delta}{180} \quad ...(12.172)$$

Length of long chord of the transition curve (L_t): The line joining the points T and D is the long chord of the transition curve. Its length is given by (Figs. 12.63 and 12.64)

$$L_t = \sqrt{TD_2^2 + D_2D^2}$$

$$= \sqrt{X^2 + Y^2}$$

Substituting $X \simeq L$ and $Y \simeq \frac{L^2}{6R}$ [from Eq. (12.163)], we get

$$L_t \simeq \sqrt{L^2 + \left(\frac{L^2}{6R}\right)^2} \quad ...(12.173)$$

$$\simeq \sqrt{L^2 + (4S)^2} \quad ...(12.174)$$

Chainages:

Chainage of T = Chainage of $I - T_t$

Chainage of D = Chainage of $T + L$

Chainage of D' = Chainage of D + length of the circular curve (l_c) ...(12.175)

Chainage of T' = Chainage of $D' + L$

Data required for setting out the combined curve

For setting out a combined transition curve and circular curve, the required data are obtained as explained below.

The data given are:

1. The deflection angle Δ between the tangents
2. The radius R of the circular curve
3. The length L of the transition curve
4. The chainage of the point of intersection I of the tangents.

The quantities required for setting out, are computed in the following steps:

1. Spiral angle [Eq. (12.156)]

$$\Delta_S = \frac{L}{2R}$$

2. Shift [Eq. (12.168)]

$$S = \frac{L^2}{24R}$$

3. Total tangent length [Eq. (12.170)]

$$T = (R+S)\tan\frac{\Delta}{2} + \frac{L}{2}$$

4. Length of the circular curve (Eq. 12.3)

$$l_c = \frac{\pi R(\Delta - 2\Delta_S)}{180}$$

5. Chainages of the salient points [Eqs. (12.175)]

   Chainage of T = Chainage of $I - T$

   Chainage of D = Chainage of $T + L$

   Chainage of D' = Chainage of $D + l_c$

   Chainage of T' = Chainage of $D' + L$

6. Length of the normal chords

   Generally, 10 m for the transition curve, and 20 m for the circular curve are used.

7. Lengths of the sub-chords

   It is calculated after knowing the chainages of salient points

8. Deflection angles

(*a*) For transition curve [Eq. (12.160)]

$$\alpha = \frac{1800 l^2}{\pi RL} \text{ minutes}$$

l is measured from the tangent point T. The deflection angle at the junction of the transition curve and the circular curve for $l = L$, is

$$\alpha_n = \frac{1800L}{\pi R}$$

As a check, α_n should be equal to $\dfrac{\Delta_S}{3}$.

(*b*) For circular curve [Eq. (12.25)]

$$\delta = \frac{1718.9\,c}{R} \text{ minutes}$$

where *c* is the length of the chord, and δ is the tangential angles from the tangent at *D*.

The total deflection angles are

$$\Delta_1 = \delta_1$$
$$\Delta_2 = \Delta_1 + \delta_2$$
$$\Delta_n = \Delta_{n-1} + \delta_n$$

As a check, Δ_n should be equal to $\dfrac{1}{2}(\Delta - 2\Delta_S)$.

Field operations for setting out a combined curve (Fig. 12.64)

By deflection angles

The first transition curve is set out from *T*, and the circular curve from the junction point *D* (Figs. 12.63 and 12.64). The second transition curve is then set out from *T'*, and the work is checked on the junction point *D'* which has been previously fixed from *D*.

The length of the transition curve is assumed or calculated as discussed in Sec. 12.11. The shift *S* is calculated from Eq. (12.168). The tangent point *T* is located by determining its chainage from Eq. (12.175). The other tangent point *T'* is located on the other tangent by measuring the total tangent length *T* from the intersection *I* of the two tangents. *T* is obtained from Eq. (12.170).

A theodolite is set up at *T*, the vernier *A* is set to zero, and *I* is bisected. The points on the transition curve are located from the computed deflection angles using Eq. (12.160) for the first sub-chord and normal chords. The last deflection angle for the transition curve should be equal to $\dfrac{\Delta_S}{3}$, and the perpendicular offset from the tangent *TI* should be equal to 4*S*. The distance to each of the successive points on the transition curve is measured from *T*.

Having laid the transition curve, the theodolite is shifted to *D*. After setting up and levelling, the vernier is set to read the angle $\left[360° - \dfrac{2}{3}\Delta_S\right]$ for a right-hand curve, and $\dfrac{2}{3}\Delta_S$ for a left-hand curve. Back sight is taken on *T*, and the telescope is rotated in azimuth by an angle $\dfrac{2}{3}\Delta_S$ till zero reading is obtained on the circle. In this position the telescope is directed along DD_1. On transiting the telescope now, the line of sight is directed along the tangent D_1D with reference to which the deflection angles of the circular curve have been calculated using Eq. (12.25). When the line of sight is thus correctly oriented, the reading on the circle will be zero. The vernier is set to the calculated deflection angles for the circular curve, and the points on it are located in usual way. For the last point D' of the circular curve, the last deflection angle should be equal to $\frac{1}{2}(\Delta - 2\Delta_S)$.

The other transition curve is set out from T' in the similar manner as the first is set out from T. The point D' set out from T' should be the same as already set out from D.

By tangential offsets

The length of the transition curve is assumed or calculated as discussed in Sec. 12.11, and the shift is calculated from Eq. (12.168). The tangent points T and T' are located as discussed in the method of setting out the curve by deflection angles above.

The offsets from tangent for the transition curve are calculated from Eq. (12.163), and for the circular curve from chords produced using Eqs. (12.19), (12.23) and (12.24). The points on the transition curve as well as on the circular curve are located by setting out the respective offsets.

If the distances are measured along tangent, the offsets in terms of shift can be calculated using the following formula.

$$y = \frac{4Sx^3}{L^3} \tag{12.176}$$

ILLUSTRATIVE EXAMPLES

Example 12.31

A railway curve of 1500 m radius is to be set out to connect two tangents. The design speed is 120 km/hr. Find a suitable length of transition curve, and the necessary shift of the circular curve.

Solution:

Given that

$$R = 1500 \text{ m}$$
$$V = 120 \text{ km/hr}$$

The length of a transition curve is given by Eq. (12.150) as

$$L = \frac{V^3}{46.66\alpha R}$$

Taking the rate of change of radial acceleration α equal to 0.3 m/sec²/sec, we get

$$L = \frac{120^3}{46.66 \times 0.3 \times 1500}$$
$$= 82.3 \text{ m}$$
$$\simeq \mathbf{83\ m.}$$

From Eq. (12.168), the shift of the circular curve is

$$S = \frac{L^2}{24R}$$

$$= \frac{83^2}{24 \times 1500}$$

$$= \mathbf{0.19\ m.}$$

Example 12.32

A transition curve of length 230 m joins a straight to a circular curve of radius 800 m. What is the angle turned by the transition curve, and what is the necessary shift? Also find the approximate offset to the transition at a distance of 150 m from the start along the tangent.

Solution:

Given that

$$L = 230 \text{ m}$$

$$R = 800 \text{ m}$$

The angle turned by the transition curve is the spiral angle Δ_S. From Eq. (12.156) it is given by

$$\Delta_S = \frac{L}{2R} \text{ radians}$$

$$= \frac{180L}{2\pi R} \text{ degrees}$$

$$= \frac{180 \times 230}{\pi \times 2 \times 800}$$

$$= \mathbf{8°14'11''.}$$

From Eq. (12.168), we have shift

$$S = \frac{L^2}{24R}$$

$$= \frac{230^2}{24 \times 800}$$

$$= \mathbf{2.76\ m.}$$

From Eq. (12.142), we have offset

$$y = \frac{x^3}{6RL}$$

$$= \frac{150^3}{6 \times 800 \times 230}$$

$$= \mathbf{3.06\ m.}$$

Example 12.33

A highway curve having a deflection angle of 78° is desired for a maximum speed of 120 km/hr, a maximum centrifugal ratio of 1/4, and a maximum rate of change of radial acceleration of 0.3m/sec^2/sec. The combined curve consists of two cubic spirals and a circular curve. Calculate

(*i*) the radius of the circular curve,

(*ii*) the length of the cubic spiral,

(*iii*) the total length of the combined curve, and

(*iv*) the chainages of all salient points if the chainage of the point of interesection is 3100 m.

Solution (Fig. 12.64):

It is given that

$$\Delta = 78°$$

$$V = 120 \text{ km/hr or } v = 33.33 \text{ m/sec}$$

$$\frac{v^2}{gR} = \frac{1}{4}$$

$$\alpha = 0.3 \text{ m/sec}^2\text{/sec}$$

Chainage of $I = 3100$ m

(*i*) The maximum centrifugal ratio is $\frac{1}{4}$, therefore,

$$\frac{v^2}{gR} = \frac{1}{4}$$

or

$$R = \frac{4v^2}{g}$$

$$= \frac{4 \times 33.33^2}{9.81}$$

$$= \mathbf{453 \ m.}$$

(*ii*) From Eq. (12.150), we have

$$L = \frac{V^3}{46.66 \alpha R}$$

$$= \frac{120^3}{46.66 \times 0.3 \times 453}$$

$$= 272.51 \text{ m}$$

$$\simeq \mathbf{273 \ m.}$$

(*iii*) From Eq. (12.156)

$$\Delta_S = \frac{L}{2R} \text{ radians}$$

$$= \frac{180L}{2\pi R} \text{ degrees}$$

$$= \frac{180 \times 273}{2 \times \pi \times 453}$$

$$= 17°15'53''.$$

The central angle of the circular curve is given by

$$= \Delta - 2\Delta_S$$

$$= 78° - 2 \times 17°15'53''$$

$$= 43°28'14''.$$

The length of the circular curve

$$l_c = \frac{\pi R(\Delta - 2\Delta_S)}{180}$$

$$= \frac{\pi \times 453 \times 17°15'53''}{180}$$

$$= \mathbf{136.5\ m.}$$

(*iv*) Total length of the combined curve

$$= 2L + l_c$$

$$= 2 \times 273 + 136.5$$

$$= \mathbf{682.5\ m.}$$

(*v*) From Eq. (12.168), we have shift

$$S = \frac{L^2}{24R}$$

$$= \frac{273^2}{24 \times 453}$$

$$= \mathbf{6.86\ m.}$$

From Eq. (12.170), we have

$$\text{Total tangent length} \quad T = (R + S)\tan\frac{\Delta}{2} + \frac{L}{2}$$

$$= (453 + 6.86)\tan\frac{78°}{2} + \frac{273}{2}$$

$$= 508.9 \text{ m.}$$

$$\text{Chainage of } T = \text{Chainage of } I - T$$
$$= 3100 - 508.9 = \mathbf{2591.1\ m.}$$
$$\text{Chainage of } D = \text{Chainage of } T + L$$
$$= 2591.1 + 273 = \mathbf{2864.1\ m.}$$
$$\text{Chainage of } D' = \text{Chainage of } D + l_c$$
$$= 2864.1 + 136.5 = \mathbf{3000.6\ m.}$$
$$\text{Chainage of } T' = \text{Chainage of } D' + L$$
$$= 3000.6 + 273 = \mathbf{3273.6\ m.}$$

Check:

$$\text{Chainage of } T' - \text{Chainage of } T$$
$$= 2L + l_c$$
$$3273.6 - 2591.1 = 2 \times 273 + 136.5$$
$$= 682.5 \text{ m} \quad (O.K)$$

Example 12.34

Two tangents *AB* and *BC* intersect at chainage (410 + 15), the deflection angle being 45°. It is proposed to insert a circular curve of 300 m radius with a transition curve of 90 m long at each end. Make all the calculations necessary for setting out the curve by the method of deflection angles using peg interval as 15 m on the transition curve, and 30 m on the circular curve.

Solution (Fig. 12.64):

It is given that the deflection angle $\Delta = 45°$, the radius of the circular curve $R = 300$ m, and the length of the transition curve $L = 90$ m = 3 chains.

(*i*) $$\text{Shifts} = \frac{L^2}{24R} = \frac{90^2}{24 \times 300} = 1.125 \text{ m}$$

(*ii*) $$\text{Total tangent length } T = (R + S)\tan\frac{\Delta}{2} + \frac{L}{2}$$
$$= (300 + 1.125)\tan\frac{45°}{2} + \frac{90}{2}$$
$$= 169.73 \text{ m}$$
$$= (5 + 19.73) \text{ chains.}$$

(*iii*) Spiral angle $$\Delta_S = \frac{L}{2R}$$
$$= \frac{180 \times 90}{\pi \times 2 \times 300}$$
$$= 8°35'40''.$$

(*iv*) Central angle for the circular curve
$$= \Delta - 2\Delta_S = 45° - 2 \times 8°35'40''$$
$$= 27°48'40''.$$

(*v*) Length of the circular curve

$$l_c = \frac{\pi R(\Delta - 2\Delta_S)}{180}$$

$$= \frac{\pi \times 300 \times 27°48'40''}{180}$$

$$= 145.62 \text{ m}$$

$$= (4 + 25.62) \text{ chains.}$$

(*vi*) Chainages

Chainage of T = Chainage of $I - T$
= (410 + 15) – (5 + 19.73)
= (404 + 25.27) chains.

Chainage of D = Chainage of $T + L$
= (404 + 25.27) + 3
= (407 + 25.27) chains.

Chainage of D' = Chainage of $D + l_c$
= (407 + 25.27) + (4 + 25.62)
= (412 + 20.89) chains.

Chainage of T' = Chainage of $D' + L$
= (412 + 20.89) + 3
= (415 + 20.89) chains.

Check:

Chainage of T' – Chainage of T = $l + 2L$

(415 + 20.89) – (404 + 25.27) = (4 + 25.62) + 2× 3

(10 + 25.62) = (10 + 25.62) (*O.K.*).

(*vii*) Deflection angles for the first transition curve:

Chainage of T = (404 + 25.27) chains

Chainage of the first peg on the transition curve = (405 + 00) chains

Length of the first sub-chord = (405 + 00) – (404 + 25.27)
= 4.73 m.

Length of the 15 normal chords is 15 m.

Length of the last sub-chord = 90 – (5 × 15 + 4.73)
= 10.27 m.

Length for the 1st point, l_1 = 4.73 m

Length for the 2nd point, l_2 = 15 + 4.73 = 19.73 m

Length for the 3rd point, l_3 = 15 + 19.73 = 34.73 m

Length for the 4th point, l_4 = 15 + 34.73 = 49.73 m

Length for the 5th point, l_5 = 15 + 49.73 = 64.73 m

Length for the 6th point, l_6 = 15 + 64.73 = 79.73 m

Length for the 7th point, l_7 = 10.27 + 79.73 = 90 m.

The deflection angle $\alpha = \dfrac{1800 l^2}{\pi RL}$ minutes

$$= \frac{1800 l^2}{\pi \times 300 \times 90} \text{ minutes}$$

$$= 0.021221\ l^2.$$

The total deflection angle

For 1st point, α_1 = 0.021221 × 4.73² = 0°0′29″

For 2nd point, α_2 = 0.021221 × 19.73² = 0°8′16″

For 3rd point, α_3 = 0.021221 × 34.73² = 0°25′36″

For 4th point, α_4 = 0.021221 × 49.73² = 0°52′29″

For 5th point, α_5 = 0.021221 × 64.73² = 1°28′55″

For 6th point, α_6 = 0.021221 × 79.73² = 2°14′54″

For 7th point, α_7 = 0.021221 × 90.00² = 2°51′54″

Check: $\alpha_7 = L$

$$= \frac{\Delta_S}{3} = \frac{8°35'40''}{3} = 2°51'54'' \ (O.K.).$$

(*viii*) Deflection angles for the circular curve

Chainage of D = (407 + 25.27) chains

Length of the first sub-chord

$$c_f = (408 + 00) - (407 + 25.27)$$
$$= 4.73 \text{ m}$$

Length of the normal chords

$$C = 30 \text{ m}$$

Chainage of D' = (412 + 20.89) chains

Length of the last sub-chord

$$c_l = (412 + 20.89) - (412 + 00)$$
$$= 20.89 \text{ m}$$

Number of the normal chords,

$$n = 412 - 408$$
$$= 4$$

Check:

$$c_f + nC + c_l = l$$
$$4.73 + 4 \times 30 + 20.89 = 145.62 \ (O.K.).$$

Deflection angles $\delta_n = \dfrac{1718.9\, c_n}{R}$ minutes

$$\delta_1 = \frac{1718.9 \times 4.73}{300} = 0°27'06''$$

$$\delta_2 = \delta_3 = \delta_4 = \delta_5 = \frac{1718.9 \times 30}{300} = 2°51'53.4''$$

$$\delta_6 = \frac{1718.9 \times 20.89}{300} = 1°59'41.6''.$$

Total deflection angles

$$\Delta_1 = \delta_1 = 0°27'06''$$
$$\Delta_2 = \Delta_1 + \delta_2 = 3°18'59.4''$$
$$\Delta_3 = \Delta_2 + \delta_3 = 6°10'52.8''$$
$$\Delta_4 = \Delta_3 + \delta_4 = 9°02'46.2''$$
$$\Delta_5 = \Delta_4 + \delta_5 = 11°54'39.6''$$
$$\Delta_6 = \Delta_5 + \delta_6 = 13°54'21.2''.$$

Check:

$$\Delta_6 = \frac{1}{2}(\Delta - 2\Delta_S)$$

$$= \frac{1}{2}(45° - 2 \times 8°35'40'')$$

$$= 13°54'20'' \text{ (O.K.)}.$$

(*ix*) Deflection angles for the second transition curve

Chainage of T' = (415 + 20.89) chains

Length for the 1st point, l_1 = 20.89 – 15 = 5.89 m

Length for the 2nd point, l_2 = 5.89 + 15 = 20.89 m

Length for the 3rd point, l_3 = 20.89 + 15 = 35.89 m

Length for the 4th point, l_4 = 35.89 + 15 = 50.89 m

Length for the 5th point, l_5 = 50.89 + 15 = 65.89 m

Length for the 6th point, l_6 = 65.89 + 15 = 80.89 m

Length for the 7th point D',

l_7 = 80.89 + 9.11 = 90 m.

The deflection angle $\alpha = \dfrac{1800 l^2}{\pi RL}$ minutes

Total deflection angles for the second transition curve to be set out from T'

For 1st point, α_1 = 0.021221 × 5.89² = 0°0'44"

For 2nd point, α_2 = 0.021221 × 20.89² = 0°09'16"

For 3rd point, α_3 = 0.021221 × 35.89² = 0°27'20"

For 4th point, α_4 = 0.021221 × 50.89² = 0°54'57"

For 5th point, $\alpha_5 = 0.021221 \times 65.89^2 = 1°32'08''$

For 6th point, $\alpha_6 = 0.021221 \times 80.89^2 = 2°18'51''$

For 7th point, $\alpha_7 = 0.021221 \times 90^2 = 2°51'54''$.

Check

$$\alpha_l = L = \frac{\Delta_S}{3} = \frac{8°35'40''}{3} = 2°51'54''\ (O.K.).$$

Example 12.35

Calculate the necessary data for setting out the combined curve in Example 12.34, by the method of tangential offsets.

Solution (Fig. 12.62 and 12.15):

The lengths l_1, l_2, ..., l_7 for the transition curves, and the length of the subchords for the circular curve have already been computed in Example 12.34.

(*i*) The offsets for setting out the transition curve from the tangent *TA* are given by

$$y = \frac{x^3}{6RL} = \frac{l^3}{6RL}$$

$$= \frac{l^3}{6 \times 300 \times 90}$$

$$= \frac{l^3}{162000}$$

Thus, $$y_1 = \frac{4.73^3}{162000} = 0.0007\,\text{m}$$

$$y_2 = \frac{19.73^3}{162000} = 0.05\,\text{m}$$

$$y_3 = \frac{34.73^3}{162000} = 0.26\,\text{m}$$

$$y_4 = \frac{49.73^3}{162000} = 0.76\,\text{m}$$

$$y_5 = \frac{64.73^3}{162000} = 1.67\,\text{m}$$

$$y_6 = \frac{79.73^3}{162000} = 3.13\,\text{m}$$

$$y_D = y_7 = \frac{90}{162000} = 4.50\,\text{m}$$

Check:

$$y_D = 4S = 4 \times 1.125 = 4.50 \text{ m. } (O.K.).$$

(*ii*) **Offsets from the chords for the circular curve**

$$O_n = \frac{C_n(C_{n-1}+C_n)}{2R} = \frac{C_n(C_{n-1}+C_n)}{600}$$

$$C_1 = c_f = 4.73 \text{ m}$$
$$C_2 = C_3 = C_4 = C_5 = 30 \text{ m}$$
$$C_6 = c_l = 20.89 \text{ m}$$

$$O_1 = \frac{c_f(0+c_f)}{600} = \frac{4.73^2}{600} = 0.04 \text{ m}$$

$$O_2 = \frac{C_2(c_f+C_2)}{600} = \frac{30\times(4.73+30)}{600} = 1.74 \text{ m}$$

$$O_3 = \frac{C_3(C_2+C_3)}{600} = \frac{30\times(30+30)}{600} = 3 \text{ m}$$

$$O_4 = \frac{C_4(C_3+C_4)}{600} = \frac{30\times(30+30)}{600} = 3 \text{ m}$$

$$O_5 = \frac{C_5(C_4+C_5)}{600} = \frac{30\times(30+30)}{600} = 3 \text{ m}$$

$$O_6 = \frac{C_6(C_5+C_l)}{600} = \frac{20.89\times(30+20.89)}{600} = 1.77 \text{ m}$$

(*iii*) **Offsets from the second tangent for setting out the second transition curve from** T'

$$y_1 = \frac{5.89^3}{162000} = 0.001 \text{ m}$$

$$y_2 = \frac{20.89^3}{162000} = 0.06 \text{ m}$$

$$y_3 = \frac{35.89^3}{162000} = 0.29 \text{ m}$$

$$y_4 = \frac{50.89^3}{162000} = 0.81 \text{ m}$$

$$y_5 = \frac{65.89^3}{162000} = 1.77 \text{ m}$$

$$y_6 = \frac{80.89^3}{169000} = 3.27 \text{ m}$$

$$y_{D'} = y_7 = \frac{90^3}{169000} = 4.5\,\text{m}$$

Check:

$$y_{D'} = 4S = 4 \times 1.125 = 4.5 \text{ m. } (O.K.).$$

Example 12.36

To connect a straight to a circular curve of radius 420 m, a transition curve is required, the gauge being 1.5 m between the rails, and the maximum superelevation restricted to 10 cm. The transition curve is to be desired for a velocity such that no lateral pressure is imposed on the rails when the rate of change of radial acceleration is 0.3 m/sec²/sec. Calculate the required length of the transition curve, and the design speed.

Solution:

Given that

$$R = 420 \text{ m}$$
$$B = 1.5 \text{ m}$$
$$h = 10 \text{ cm} = 0.1 \text{ m}$$
$$\alpha = 0.3 \text{ m/sec}^2\text{/sec}$$

From Eq. (12.136), the superelevation is given by

$$h = \frac{Bv^2}{gR}$$

Design speed

$$v = \sqrt{\frac{gRh}{B}}$$

$$= \sqrt{\frac{9.81 \times 420 \times 0.1}{1.5}}$$

$$= \mathbf{16.57 \text{ m/sec.}}$$

From Eq. (12.149), the length of the transition curve is

$$L = \frac{v^3}{\alpha R}$$

$$= \frac{16.57^3}{0.3 \times 420}$$

$$= \mathbf{36.11 \text{ m.}}$$

Spiralling compound curves

If the radii of the arcs of a compound curve in railways differ considerably, the superelevation at the junction point changes abruptly. To avoid this, transition curve is sometimes introduced between the arcs. Such spiralling is shown in Fig. 12.65. For the computations of various elements of the curve, the following procedure is adopted.

1. Calculate the superelevation h_1 and h_2 for the given design speed v corresponding to the two radii R_1 and R_2 of the circular curves from the expression

$$h = \frac{Bv^2}{gR}$$

2. Calculate the lengths L_1 and L_2 of the transition curves from the relation

$$L = nh$$

where n varies from 300 to 1200.

However, L_1 and L_2 can also be fixed by other criteria discussed in Sec. 12.11.

3. Calculate the shifts S_1 and S_2 for both the branches by relation

$$S = \frac{L^2}{24R}$$

The distance F_1F_3 between the tangents of the shifted curves is equal to $(S_1 - S_2)$. The transition curve at the common point of tangency is bisected at F_2, F_2 being equidistant from F_1 and F_3.

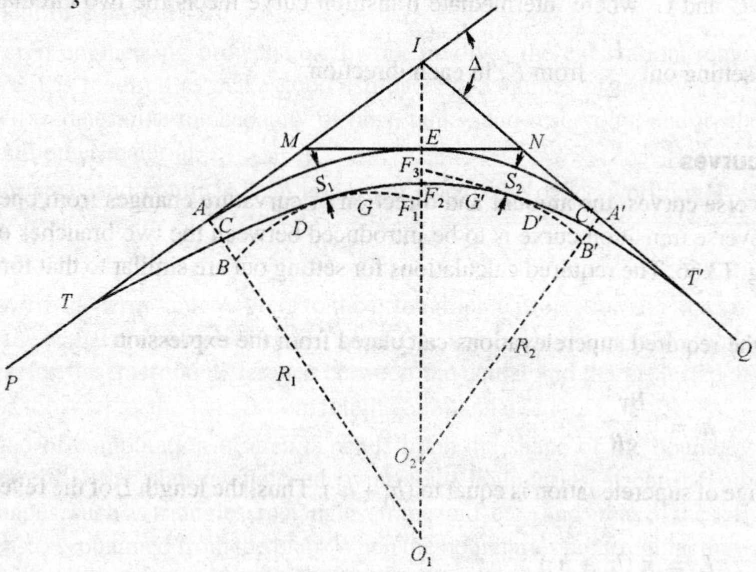

Fig. 12.65 Spiralling compound curves

4. The length L' of the transition curve required at the common point of tangency is given by the equation

$$L' = n(h_1 - h_2)$$

5. The chainage of T is computed in usual way from the known chainage of I and the tangent length TI. Then

$$\text{Chainage of } D = \text{Chainage of } T + L_1$$

$$\text{Chainage of } G = \text{Chainage of } D + \text{length of the first circular arc} - \frac{L'}{2}$$

$$\text{Chainage of } F_2 = \text{Chainage of } G + \frac{L'}{2}$$

$$\text{Chainage of } G' = \text{Chainage of } F_2 + \frac{L'}{2}$$

$$\text{Chainage of } D' = \text{Chainage of } G' + \text{length of the second circular arc} - \frac{L'}{2}$$

$$\text{Chainage of } T' = \text{Chainage of } D' + L_2$$

6. The first and last transition curves, and the two branches of the circular curves can be set out by the method discussed earlier.
7. The offsets for the common transition curve is approximately calculated from Eq. (12.176) in which S is replaced by $(S_1 - S_2)$ as below:

$$y = \frac{4(S_1 - S_2)}{L'^3}x^3$$

8. The points G and G' where intermediate transition curve meets the two circular curves, are located by setting out $\frac{L'}{2}$ from F_2 in each direction.

Spiralling reverse curves

In the case of reverse curves, the amount and direction of curvature changes from one value to the other, and hence, a reverse transition curve is to be introduced between the two branches of the reverse curve as shown in Fig. 12.66. The required calculations for setting out are similar to that for a compound curve.

If h_1 and h_2 are the required superelevations calculated from the expression

$$h = \frac{Bv^2}{gR}$$

then the greatest change of superelevation is equal to $(h_1 + h_2)$. Thus, the length L of the reverse transition curve is given by

$$L = n\,(h_1 + h_2)$$

where n = rate of superelevation.

Half of the length L is provided to each side of P.R.C.

The distance MN between the tangents of the two shifted arcs is $(S_1 + S_2)$.

The offset to the transition curve is calculated from the expression

$$y = \frac{4(S_1 + S_2)\,x^3}{L^3}$$

Setting out the end transitions, circular arcs, and junctions, is done using offsets or tangential angles. The usual procedures for the combined and compound curves are applicable here too.

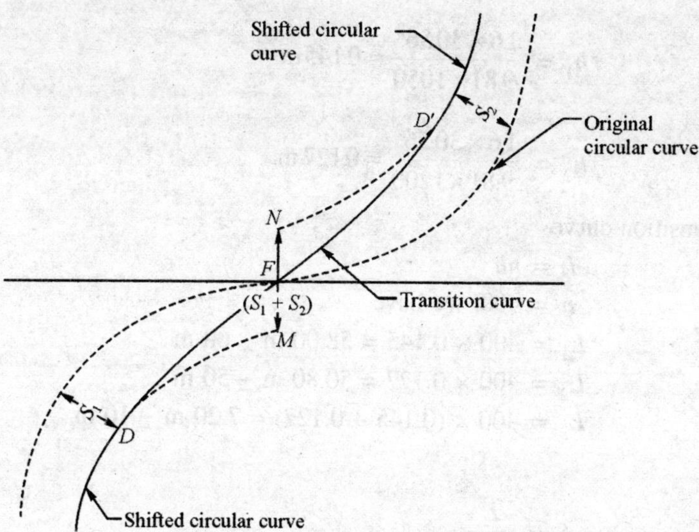

Fig. 12.66 Spiralling reverse curves

ILLUSTRATIVE EXAMPLE

Example 12.37

Two tangents *PI* and *QI* intersect at *I*. Two points *M* and *N* on tangents *PI* and *QI*, are selected so that angles *PMN* and *QNM* are 150° and 160°, respectively. It is proposed to introduce a compound curve tangential to *PI*, *MN* and *IQ*. The radii of the two branches of the curves are 1050 m and 1200 m, respectively. The maximum speed is 110 km/hr. Compute the necessary data for setting out the complete curve, if the transition curves are to be inserted between the two arcs, and at the junctions with the tangents *PI* and *QI*. The distance between the centres of rails is 1.6 m, and the chainage of *I* is 4550.00 m.

Solution (Fig. 12.65):

The data given are

$$\angle PMN = 150°$$
$$\angle QNM = 160°$$
$$R_1 = 1050 \text{ m}$$
$$R_2 = 1200 \text{ m}$$
$$V = 110 \text{ km/hr or } v = 30.56 \text{ m.sec}$$
$$B = 1.6 \text{ m}$$
$$\text{Chainage of } I = 4550 \text{ m}$$

(*i*) Superelevation $h = \dfrac{Bv^2}{gR}$

For 1st arc, $$h_1 = \frac{1.6 \times 30.56^2}{9.81 \times 1050} = 0.145\,\text{m}$$

For 2nd arc, $$h_2 = \frac{1.6 \times 30.56^2}{9.81 \times 1200} = 0.127\,\text{m}.$$

(*ii*) Length of transition curve

$$L = nh$$

Assuming $n = 400$, we have

$$L_1 = 400 \times 0.145 = 58.00\text{ m} \simeq 60\text{ m}$$
$$L_2 = 400 \times 0.127 = 50.80\text{ m} \simeq 50\text{ m}$$
$$L_3 = 400 \times (0.145 - 0.127) = 7.20\text{ m} \simeq 10\text{ m}.$$

(*iii*) Shift

$$S = \frac{L^2}{24R}$$

$$S_1 = \frac{60^2}{24 \times 1050} = 0.14\,\text{m}$$

$$S_2 = \frac{50^2}{24 \times 1200} = 0.09\,\text{m}.$$

(*iv*) Tangent lengths

$$\Delta_1 = 180° - 150° = 30°$$
$$\Delta_2 = 180° - 160° = 20°$$

$$ME = (R_1 + S_1)\tan\frac{\Delta_1}{2} = (1050 + 0.14)\tan 15° = 281.38\,\text{m}$$

$$EN = (R_2 + S_2)\tan\frac{\Delta_2}{2} = (1200 + 0.09)\tan 10° = 211.61\,\text{m}$$

$$MN = ME + EN = 281.38 + 211.61 = 492.99\text{ m}.$$

In $\Delta\, MIN$ by sine rule, we get

$$MI = \frac{492.99 \sin 20°}{\sin 130°} = 220.11\,\text{m}$$

$$NI = \frac{492.99 \sin 30°}{\sin 130°} = 321.78\,\text{m}$$

$$AI = AM + MI = ME + MI = 281.38 + 220.11 = 501.49\text{ m}$$
$$A'I = A'N + NI = EN + NI = 211.61 + 321.78 = 533.39\text{ m}$$

Chainage of A = Chainage of $I - AI$
$= 4550 - 501.49$
$= 4048.51$ m.

$$\text{Chainage of } T = \text{Chainage of } A - \frac{L_1}{2}$$

$$= 4048.51 - \frac{60}{2}$$

$$= 4018.51 \text{ m.}$$

$$\text{Chainage of } D = \text{Chainage of } T + L_1$$

$$= 4018.51 + 60$$

$$= 4078.51 \text{ m.}$$

$$\text{Spiral angle } \Delta_{S1} = \frac{L_1}{2R_1} = \frac{60}{2 \times 1050} \times \frac{180}{\pi} = 1°38'13''$$

Length of the first arc

$$l_1 = \frac{\pi R_1(\Delta_1 - \Delta_{S1})}{180} - \frac{L_3}{2}$$

$$= \frac{\pi \times 1050 \times (30° - 1°38'13'')}{180} - \frac{10}{2}$$

$$= 514.78 \text{ m.}$$

$$\text{Spiral angle } \quad \Delta_{S2} = \frac{L_2}{2R_2} = \frac{50}{2 \times 1200} \times \frac{180}{\pi} = 1°11'37''$$

Length of the second arc

$$l_2 = \frac{\pi R_2(\Delta_2 - \Delta_{S2})}{180} - \frac{L_3}{2}$$

$$= \frac{\pi \times 1200 \times (20° - 1°11'37'')}{180} - \frac{10}{2}$$

$$= 388.88 \text{ m.}$$

$$\text{Chainage of } G = \text{Chainage of } D + l_1$$

$$= 4078.51 + 514.78$$

$$= 4593.29 \text{ m.}$$

$$\text{Chainage of } F_2 = \text{Chainage of } G + \frac{L_3}{2}$$

$$= 4593.29 + \frac{10}{2}$$

$$= 4598.29 \text{ m.}$$

$$\text{Chainage of } G' = \text{Chainage of } F_2 + \frac{L_3}{2}$$

$$= 4598.29 + \frac{10}{2}$$

$$= 4603.29 \text{ m.}$$

$$\text{Chainage of } D' = \text{Chainage of } G' + l_2$$
$$= 4603.29 + 388.88$$
$$= 4992.17 \text{ m.}$$

$$\text{Chainage of } T' = \text{Chainage of } D' + L_2$$
$$= 4992.17 + 50$$
$$= 5042.17 \text{ m.}$$

Check:

$$\text{Chainage of } T' - \text{Chainage of } T = L_1 + l_1 + L_3 + l_2 + L_2$$
$$5042.17 - 4018.51 = 60 + 514.78 + 10 + 388.88 + 50$$
$$= 1023.66 \ (O.K.).$$

(*v*) Offsets

(*a*) For the first transition curve at 10 m interval using formula

$$y = \frac{4S_1x^3}{L_1^3} = \frac{4 \times 0.14}{(60)^3}x^3$$
$$= 2.5926 \times 10^{-6} \times x^3$$
$$= kx^3$$

where $k = 2.5926 \times 10^{-6}$

$$y_1 = k\,(10)^3 = 0.0026 \text{ m}$$
$$y_2 = k\,(20)^3 = 0.021 \text{ m}$$
$$y_3 = k\,(30)^3 = 0.07 \text{ m}$$
$$y_4 = k\,(40)^3 = 0.17 \text{ m}$$
$$y_5 = k\,(50)^3 = 0.32 \text{ m}$$
$$y_6 = k\,(60)^3 = 0.56 \text{ m.}$$

(*b*) Offsets for locating the other transition curves can be computed in a similar manner.

(*c*) The deflection angles or offsets can be computed for the circular curves by the method explained in Examples 12.34 and 12.35.

12.12 VERTICAL CURVES

When the grade line of a highway or railway changes grade such as while crossing low ridges or valleys, provision must be made for a vehicle to negotiate this transition smoothly, and to provide vision over the crest of a hill far enough ahead to give the driver of the vehicle ample time to react to a dangerous situation. A parabola is most commonly used as a vertical curve due to simplicity in calculations of offsets for setting the vertical curve. An important requirement of a vertical curve is that they should provide a constant rate of change of grade, and the parabola fulfils this requirement.

General equation of a parabola with its axis vertical, is

$$y = ax^2 + bx \quad ...(12.177)$$

Slope of the curve is given by

$$\frac{dy}{dx} = 2ax + b$$

and the rate of change of slope or grade is

$$\frac{d^2y}{dx^2} = 2a = \text{a constant} \quad ...(12.178)$$

Thus, the grade changes uniformly throughout the curve.

Types of vertical curves

The vertical curves may be classified as

1. Summit curves
2. Sag or valley curves.

Summit curves

If a vertical curve has its convexity upwards, it is called a summit curve. Depending upon the field conditions, a summit curve may be formed (*i*) be an upgrade followed by an equal or different down grade (Fig. 12.67a), (*ii*) by an upgrade followed by a flatter upgrade (Fig. 12.67b), or (*iii*) by a downgrade followed by a steeper down grade (Fig. 12.67c).

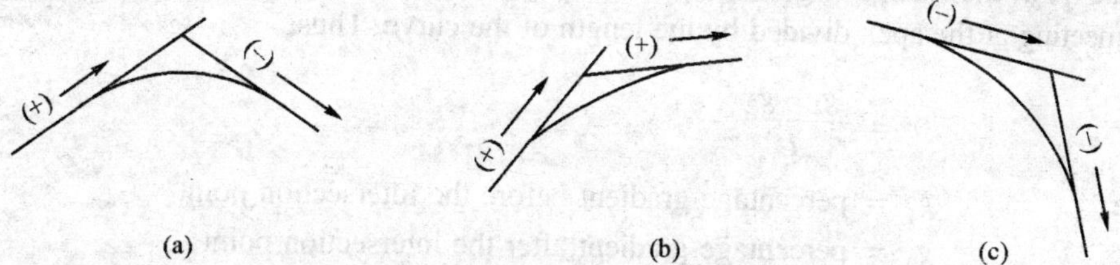

Fig. 12.67 Summit curves

Sag or valley curves

The vertical curve having its convexity downwards or when it is concave upwards it is called a sag or valley curve. A sag curve may be formed (*i*) by a down grade followed by an equal or different upgrade (Fig. 12.68a), (*ii*) by a downgrade followed by a flatter downgrade (Fig. 12.68b), or (*iii*) by an upgrade followed by a steeper upgrade (Fig. 12.68 c).

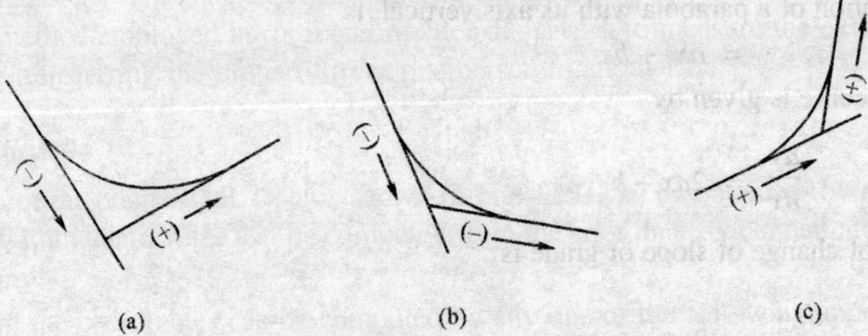

Fig. 12.68 Sag or valley curves

Gradient or the grade

The gradient may be defined as proportional rise or fall between two points along a straight line. it may be expressed in either of the following two ways:

1. Percentage (%)

   The gradient expressed as a percentage is the vertical rise or fall in a horizontal distance of 100 units. For example, a gradient of + 3% means that the slope rises by 3 m in every 100 m.

2. Ratio

The gradient expressed as a ratio is the ratio of the vertical rise or fall and the horizontal distances. For example, a gradient of 1 in 50 means that there is a rise of 1 m in 50 m.

Rate of change of gradient

The rate (r) of the change of gradient per chain length is equal to the algebraic difference of the two gradients meeting at the apex divided by the length of the curve. Thus,

$$r = \frac{g_1 - g_2}{L} \qquad ...(12.179)$$

where g_1 = percentage gradient before the intersection point

g_2 = percentage gradient after the intersection point

L = length of the vertical curve in chains.

Eq. (12.178) gives the rate of change of gradient, and it is constant for a parabolic vertical curve. The recommended values of the rates of change of gradient for railways are presented in Table 12.6.

Table 12.6 Rate of change of gradient

Type of railway	Curves at	
	Summit	Sag
(*a*) First class railways	0.3%	0.15%
(*b*) Second class railways or branch lines	0.6%	0.3%

ILLUSTRATIVE EXAMPLE

Example 12.38

A vertical curve has an upgrade of 2.5% followeed by a downgrade 0.5%. The recommended rate of change of grade is 0.15% per chain of 20 m. Calculate the length of the vertical curve.

Solution:

It is given that

$$g_1 = (+)\ 2.5\%$$
$$g_2 = (-)\ 0.5\%$$
$$r = 0.15\% \text{ per chain of 20 m (or 0.15\% per 20 m)}$$

From Eq. (12.179), we have

$$r = \frac{g_1 - g_2}{L}$$

$$L = \frac{g_1 - g_2}{r}$$

$$= \frac{2.5-(-0.5)}{0.15}$$

$$= 20 \text{ chains}$$
$$= 20 \times 20$$
$$= \mathbf{400\ m.}$$

Geometrics of a vertical curve

Generally, the vertical curves are flat, and therefore, instead of measuring the distances along the curve, they are measured horizontally, and the offsets are measured vertically from the tangent to the curve without introducing any appreciable error. Thus, the total length of a vertical curve is assumed to be its horizontal projection.

In Fig. (12.69), let O = beginning of the vertical curve and the origin of the cartesian coordinate system

OA = tangent having + g_1% slope

AB = tangent having – g_2% slope

P = any point on the curve having coordinates (x, y)

EP = h = vertical offset of P from the tangent.

Draw a line EF perpendicular to the x-axis, through P.

For a parabola, we have

$$\frac{dy}{dx} = 2ax + b$$

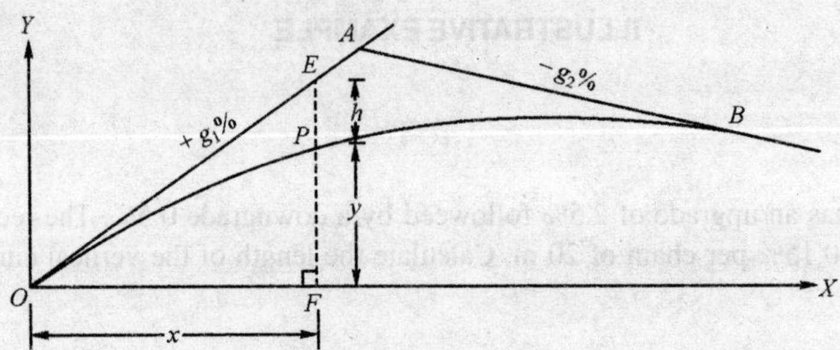

Fig. 12.69 Geometrics of a vertical curve

At $x = 0, \frac{dy}{dx} = +g_1$

Therefore, $g_1 = 2a\ (0) + b$

or $b = g_1$

Hence the equation of parabola becomes

$$y = ax^2 + g_1x \qquad \text{...(12.180)}$$

Now $EP = EF - PF$

$$h = g_1x - y$$

But from Eq. (4.180), we have

$$g_1x = y - ax^2$$

Hence, $h = y - ax^2 - y$

$$= -ax^2$$

or $= Cx^2$ ...(12.181)

or $= kN^2$ ...(12.182)

where $C = -a$

k = a constant.

N = the number of chords counted from O (total length $L = 2n$ chords, n being the number of chords on each side of the apex of the curve).

Eq. (12.182) shows that the difference in elevation between a point on a vertical curve and its corresponding point on the tangent, is proportional to the square of its distance from the point of tangency.

Determination of value of k

In Fig. 12.70, OC is the tangent OA produced, and the point C is vertically above B. The line AD is a horizontal line through A which is the point of intersection of the two tangents of OA and AB having grades of $+g_1$ and $-g_2$, respectively. The rise and fall corresponding to $+g_1$ and $-g_2$ per chord length of l, are $+e_1$ and $-e_2$, respectively. Let $2n$ be the total number of equal chords, each of length l, n on each side of apex.

Now, $OA = AC$

$$CD = ne_1$$

$$DB = -ne_2$$

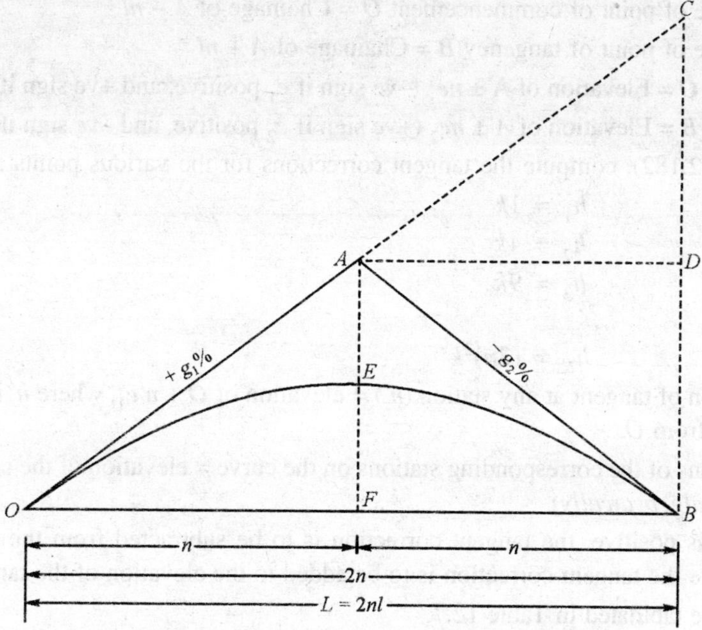

Fig. 12.70 Determination of constant k

But $\quad BC = CD + DB$

$$= ne_1 + n(-e_2)$$

$$= n(e_1 - e_2) \text{ (algebraically)}$$

From Eq. (12.182), we have

$$BC = kN^2 \text{ where } N = 2n$$

$$= k(2n)^2$$

$$4kn^2 = n(e_1 - e_2)$$

or

$$k = \frac{(e_1 - e_2)}{4n} \tag{12.183}$$

In the above equation, proper signs of e_1 and e_2 must be taken for obtaining the value of k.

Setting out a vertical curve

Points on vertical curves can be established by determining

(*i*) tangent corrections, or

(*ii*) chord gradients.

By tangent corrections

The tangent corrections h for various values of N are calculated from Eq. (12.182) knowing the value of k. The elevations of various points on the curve are computed as below (Fig. 12.70).

1. Let the elevation and chainage of the apex A be known, and the length of the curve on either side of the summit be n chords of equal length l. Then the length of the curve on either side of the summit = nl

2. The chainage of point of commencement O = Chainage of $A - nl$
   The chainage of point of tangency B = Chainage of $A + nl$
3. Elevation of O = Elevation of A $\pm ne_1$ (–ve sign if e_1 positive, and +ve sign if negative)
   Elevation of B = Elevation of $A \pm ne_2$ (+ve sign if e_2 positive, and –*ve* sign if negative)
4. From Eq. (12.182), compute the tangent corrections for the various points as

$$h_1 = 1k$$
$$h_2 = 4k$$
$$h_3 = 9k$$
$$\vdots \quad \vdots$$
$$h_N = (2n)^2 k$$

5. The elevation of tangent at any station (n') = elevation of $O + n'e_1$, where n' is the number of that station from O.
6. The elevations of the corresponding stations on the curve = elevation of the tangent + tangent correction (*algebraically*)

If the value of k is positive, the tangent correction is to be subtracted from the elevation of the tangent, and if negative the tangent correction is to be added to the elevation of the tangent.

The results may be tabulated in Table 12.7.

Table 12.7. Data for setting out the vertical curve

Station	Chainage	Tangent/grade elevation	Tangent correction	Elevation of the stations on the curve	Remarks

By chord gradients

The difference in elevation between the two ends of a chord is known as *chord gradient.* In this method, the elevation of a point on the curve is calculated by adding the chord gradient to the elevation of the preceding point.

In Fig. 12.71, M and N are two adjacent points on the curve. OA and AB are the two tangents of the curve at O and B, respectively, meeting at A. Through O, draw a horizontal line ON_2, and through M and N draw two vertical lines M_1M_2 and N_1N_2. Draw a horizontal line MN_3 through M, intersecting N_1N_2 at N_3.

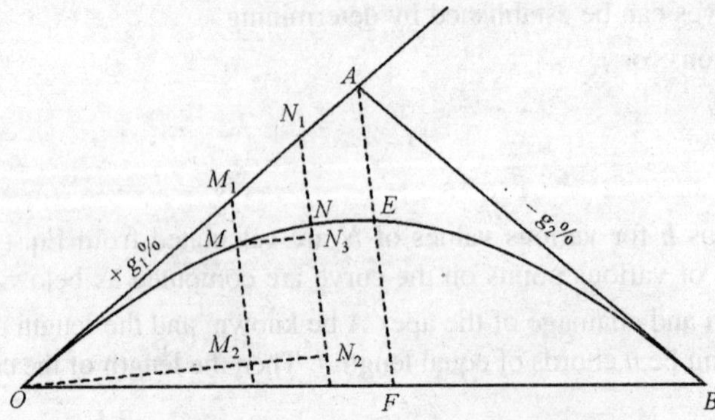

Fig. 12.71 Method of chord gradients

Let e_1 and e_2 be the rise and fall, respectively, of the tangents per chord length *l*. If *M* is the first station on the curve, then

$$M_1M_2 = e_1$$
$$M_1M = \text{tangent correction } h = kN^2$$
$$= k\,(1)^2 = k$$

First chord gradient = Difference in elevation between *M* and *O*

$$= MM_2$$
$$= M_1M_2 - M_1M$$
$$= e_1 - k$$

Similarly,

$$N_1N_2 = 2e_1$$
$$N_1N = \text{tangent correction}$$
$$= k2^2 = 4k$$
$$N_3N_2 = MM_2 = e_1 - k$$

Second chord gradient = Difference in elevation between *N* and *M*

$$= NN_3$$
$$= N_1N_2 - N_1N - N_3N_2$$
$$= 2e_1 - 4k - (e_1 - k)$$
$$= e_1 - 3k$$

Hence the *n*th chord gradient

$$= e_1 - (2n - 1)k \qquad \text{...(12.184)}$$

The elevation of different points on the curve, are calculated as below:

Elevation of 1st point = Elevation of tangent point *O* + 1st chord gradient

Elevation of 2nd point = Elevation 1st point + 2nd chord gradient

Elevation of *n*th point = Elevation of (*n* – 1)th point + *n*th chord gradient.

ILLUSTRATIVE EXAMPLES

Example 12.39

Calculate the value of the constant *k* for a vertical curve having upgrade 2.2% followed by a downgrade 1.8%, and the rate of change of grade is 0.04% per 20 m chain.

Solution:

Given that

$$g_1 = +2.2\%$$
$$g_2 = -1.8\%$$
$$r = 0.04\%$$

From Eq. (12.179), the length of the curve is

$$L = \frac{g_1 - g_2}{r}$$

$$= \frac{2.2-(-1.8)}{0.04}$$

$$= 100 \text{ chains}$$

We have

$$2n = L$$

$$n = \frac{L}{2} = \frac{100}{2} = 50 \text{ chains}$$

$$e_1 = \frac{g_1}{100} \times 20 = \frac{2.2}{100} \times 20 = 0.44$$

$$e_2 = \frac{g_2}{100} \times 20 = -\frac{1.8}{100} \times 20 = -0.36$$

From Eq. (12.183), we have

$$k = \frac{e_1 - e_2}{4n}$$

$$= \frac{0.44-(-0.36)}{4 \times 50}$$

$$= \frac{1}{250}.$$

Example 12.40

Two uniform grades 0.7% and – 0.8% are to be connected by a vertical curve having the chainage and elevation of the point of intersection of its two tangents as 3000 m and 330.00 m, respectively. Calculate the reduced levels of the various stations on the curve assuming the rate of change of grade to be 0.05% per 20 m chain.

Solution (Fig. 12.70):

It is given that

$$g_1 = 0.7\%$$

$$g_2 = -0.8\%$$

$$r = 0.05\% \text{ per 20 m chain}$$

R.L. of A = 330.00 m

Chainage of A = 3000 m

From Eq. (12.179), the total length of the curve is

$$L = \frac{g_1 - g_2}{r}$$

$$= \frac{0.7-(-0.8)}{0.05}$$

$$= 30 \text{ chains.}$$

Length on the either side of the summit is

$$= \frac{L}{2} = \frac{30}{2} = 15 \text{ chains}$$

$$= 15 \times 20 = 300 \text{ m}$$

Also $\qquad n = 15$

Chainage of O $\quad = \text{Chainage of } A - \frac{L}{2}$

$$= 3000 - 300$$

$$= \mathbf{2700 \text{ m.}}$$

Chainage of B $\quad = \text{Chainage of } A + \frac{L}{2}$

$$= 3000 + 300$$

$$= \mathbf{3300 \text{ m.}}$$

R.L. of the point of commencement O

$$= \text{R.L. of } A - \frac{g_1}{100} \times \frac{L}{2}$$

$$= 330.00 - \frac{0.7}{100} \times 300$$

$$= \mathbf{327.90 \text{ m.}}$$

R.L. of the point of tangency B

$$= \text{R.L. of } A + \frac{g_2}{100} \times \frac{L}{2}$$

$$= 330.00 + \frac{(-0.8)}{100} \times 300$$

$$= \mathbf{327.60 \text{ m.}}$$

R.L. of the point F

$$= \frac{1}{2}(\text{R.L. of } O + \text{R.L. of } B)$$

$$= \frac{1}{2} \times (327.90 + 327.60)$$

$$= 327.75 \text{ m.}$$

R.L. of the point E

$$= \frac{1}{2}(\text{R.L. of } A + \text{R.L. of } F)$$

$$= \frac{1}{2} \times (330.00 + 327.75)$$

$$= \mathbf{328.875 \text{ m.}}$$

Difference in R.L. between A and E

$$AE = 330.00 - 328.875$$
$$= 1.125 \text{ m}$$

Check:

$$e_1 = \frac{g_1}{100} \times 20 = \frac{0.7}{100} \times 20 = 0.14 \text{ m}$$

$$e_2 = \frac{g_2}{100} \times 20 = \frac{-0.8}{100} \times 20 = -0.16 \text{ m}$$

From Eq. (12.183), we have

$$k = \frac{e_1 - e_2}{4n}$$
$$= \frac{0.14 - (-0.16)}{4 \times 15}$$
$$= 0.005$$

From Eq. (12.182), we have

$$h = kN^2$$

Since for the full curve $N = 2n$, for half of the curve $N = n$, therefore

$$h_E = AE = kn^2$$
$$= 0.005 \times 15^2$$
$$= 1.125 \text{ m } (O.K).$$

The R.L. of the various points of the curve are computed as below:

(*a*) Tangential elevation for n'th station

$$H_{n'} = \text{R.L. of } O + n'e_1$$

(*b*) Tangential correction for n'th station

$$h_{n'} = k\,(n')^2$$

(*c*) R.L. of the n'th station

$$= H_{n'} - h_{n'}$$

R.L. of stations

$$\text{Station 1} = (327.9 + 1 \times 0.14) - 0.005 \times 1^2$$
$$= 328.04 - 0.005 = 328.035 \text{ m}$$
$$\text{Station 2} = (327.9 + 2 \times 0.14) - 0.005 \times 2^2$$
$$= 328.18 + 0.02 = 328.16 \text{ m}$$
$$\text{Station 3} = (327.9 + 3 \times 0.14) - 0.005 \times 3^2$$
$$= 328.32 - 0.045 = 328.275 \text{ m}$$

$$\vdots \qquad \vdots \qquad \vdots$$

$$\text{Station 15} = (327.9 + 15 \times 0.14) - 0.005 \times 15^2$$
$$= 330.00 - 1.125 = 328.875 \text{ m}$$

$$\vdots \qquad \vdots \qquad \vdots$$

$$\text{Station 30} = (327.9 + 30 \times 0.14) - 0.005 \times 30^2$$
$$= 332.10 - 4.5 = 327.60 \text{ m.}$$

The R.L.'s of the various points computed in a similar manner are presented in Table 12.7.

Table 12.7

Station No.	Chainage (m)	Tangent elevation (m)	Tangent correction (m)	R.L. of the station (m)	Remarks
0	2700	327.90	–0.0	327.900	Point *O* (*P.C*)
1	2720	328.04	–0.005	328.035	
2	2740	328.18	–0.020	328.160	
3	2760	328.32	–0.045	328.275	
4	2780	328.46	–0.080	328.380	
5	2800	328.60	–0.125	328.475	
6	2820	328.74	–0.180	328.560	
7	2840	328.88	–0.245	328.635	
8	2860	329.02	–0.320	328.700	
9	2880	329.16	–0.405	328.755	
10	2900	329.30	–0.500	328.800	
11	2920	329.44	–0.605	328.835	
12	2940	329.58	–0.720	328.860	
13	2960	329.72	–0.845	328.875	
14	2980	329.86	–0.980	328.880	
15	3000	330.00	–1.125	328.875	Point *E* (apex)
16	3020	330.14	–1.280	328.860	
17	3040	330.28	–1.445	328.835	
18	3060	330.42	–1.620	328.800	
19	3080	330.56	–1.805	328.755	
20	3100	330.70	–2.000	328.700	
21	3120	330.84	–2.205	328.635	
22	3140	330.98	–2.420	328.560	
23	3160	331.12	–2.645	328.475	
24	3180	331.26	–2.880	328.380	
25	3200	331.40	–3.125	328.275	
26	3220	331.54	–3.380	328.160	
27	3240	331.68	–3.645	328.035	
28	3260	331.82	–3.920	327.900	
29	3280	331.96	–4.205	327.755	
30	3300	332.10	–4.500	327.600	Point *B* (*P.T*)

Example 12.41

A –1.0% grade meets a +2% grade at station having elevation 320.050 m and chainage 460 m. A vertical curve of length 120 m is to be used to connect the two grades. If the peg interval is 10 m, calculate the R.L's of the points on the curve by (*a*) tangent corrections and by (*b*) chord gradients.

Also calculate staff readings for the pegs driven with their tops at the formation level of the curve if the height of instrument is 321.52 m.

Solution:

(*a*) By tangent corrections

The total number of stations at 10 m interval

$$= 2n = \frac{L}{10} = \frac{120}{10} = 12$$

or $n = 6$

$$e_1 = \frac{g_1}{100} \times 10 = \frac{-1.0}{100} \times 10 = -0.1 \text{ m}$$

$$e_2 = \frac{g_2}{100} \times 10 = \frac{2.0}{100} \times 10 = +0.2 \text{ m}$$

Elevation of the beginning of the curve

= Elevation of point of intersection – ne_1

= 320.050 – 6 × (– 0.1)

= 320.65 m

Elevation of the end of the curve

= Elevation of point of intersection

= 320.050 + 6 × (0.2)

= 321.250 m

Tangent correction with respect to the first tangent is given by

$$h = kN^2$$

where

$$k = \frac{e_1 - e_2}{4n}$$

$$= \frac{(-0.1) - (0.20)}{4 \times 6}$$

= – 0.0125

R.L's of the points on the curve

= Tangential elevation – tangent correction

= $H - h$

where H is the tangential elevation of a point.

R.L. of nth point on the cuve = R.L. of the beginning + $n'e_1 - k\,n'^2$

R.L. of 1st point = H for the 1st point – h for the 1st point

= 320.65 + 1 × (–0.1) – (–0.0125) × 1^2 = 320.563 m

R.L. of 2nd point = 320.65 + 2 × (–0.1) – (–0.0125) × 2^2 = 320.500 m

R.L. of 3rd point = 320.65 + 3 × (–0.1) – (–0.0125) × 3^2 = 320.463 m.

The values of R.L.'s for other points and the corresponding staff readings are tabulated in Table 12.8.

Table 12.8

Station No.	Chainage (m)	Tangential elevation (m)	Tangent correction (m)	R.L. of point on curve (m)	Ht. of instrument (m)	Staff reading	Remark
0	400	320.65	+0.0000	320.650	321.520	0.870	P.C.
1	410	320.55	+0.0125	320.563		0.958	
2	420	320.45	+0.0500	320.500		1.020	
3	430	320.35	+0.1125	320.463		1.058	
4	440	320.25	+0.2000	320.450		1.070	
5	450	320.15	+0.3125	320.463		1.058	
6	460	320.05	+0.4500	320.500		1.020	Apex
7	470	319.95	+0.6125	320.563		0.958	
8	480	319.85	+0.8000	320.650		0.870	
9	490	319.75	+1.0125	320.763		0.758	
10	500	319.65	+1.2500	320.900		0.620	
11	510	319.55	+1.5125	321.063		0.458	
12	520	319.45	+1.8000	321.250		0.270	P.T.

(*b*) By chord gradients

Elevation of the midpoint of the line joining the P.C. and P.T.

$$= \frac{1}{2} \times (320.65 + 321.25)$$

$$= 320.95 \text{ m}$$

Elevation of the apex of the curve

$$= \frac{1}{2} \times (320.05 + 320.95)$$

$$= 320.50 \text{ m}$$

From Eq. (12.184), the *n*th chord gradient is given by

$$= e_1 - (2n - 1)k$$

Chord gradients for

Point No. 1 $= -0.1 - (2 \times 1 - 1) \times (-0.0125) = -0.0875$

Point No. 2 $= -0.1 - (2 \times 2 - 1) \times (-0.0125) = -0.0625$

Point No. 3 $= -0.1 - (2 \times 3 - 1) \times (-0.0125) = -0.0375$

Point No. 4 $= -0.1 - (2 \times 4 - 1) \times (-0.0125) = -0.0125$

Point No. 5 $= -0.1 - (2 \times 5 - 1) \times (-0.0125) = -0.0125$

Point No. 6 $= -0.1 - (2 \times 6 - 1) \times (-0.0125) = -0.0375$

Point No. 7 $= -0.1 - (2 \times 7 - 1) \times (-0.0125) = -0.0625$

Point No. 8 = – 0.1 – (2 × 8 – 1) × (– 0.0125) = – 0.0875

Point No. 9 = – 0.1 – (2 × 9 – 1) × (– 0.0125) = – 0.1125

Point No. 10 = – 0.1 – (2 × 10 – 1) × (– 0.0125) = – 0.1375

Point No. 11 = – 0.1 – (2 × 11 – 1) × (– 0.0125) = – 0.1625

Point No. 12 = – 0.1 – (2 × 12 – 1) × (– 0.0125) = – 0.1875

R.L.'s of

Point 1 = 320.65 – 0.0875 = 320.563 m

Point 2 = 320.563 – 0.0625 = 320.500 m

Point 3 = 320.500 – 0.0735 = 320.463 m

Point 4 = 320.463 – 0.0125 = 320.450 m

Point 5 = 320.450 – 0.0125 = 320.463 m

Point 6 = 320.463 – 0.0375 = 320.500 m

Point 7 = 320.500 – 0.0625 = 320.563 m

Point 8 = 320.563 – 0.0875 = 320.650 m

Point 9 = 320.650 – 0.1125 = 320.763 m

Point 10 = 320.763 – 0.1375 = 320.900 m

Point 11 = 320.900 – 0.1625 = 321.063 m

Point 12 = 321.063 – 0.1875 = 321.250 m.

The R.L's of the points are same as given in Table 12.8 and, therefore, the staff readings for setting out the curve will be same as given in the table.

Example 12.42

A horizontal deck of a bridge meets a – 2.6% grade at chainage 2240 and elevation 226.715 m. A vertical curve of 18 metre length with 3 m peg intervals is to be introduced. Calculate the elevations of the points on the curve for setting out the curve.

Solution (Fig. 12.72):

Length of the station interval $l = 3$ m

$$\text{The number stations} = 2n = \frac{18}{3} = 6$$

$$n = \frac{6}{2} = 3$$

Chainage of O = Chainage of $A - nl$

= 2240 – 3 × 3 = 2231.00 m.

Chainage of B = Chainage of $A + nl$

= 2240 + 3 × 3 = 2249.00 m

R.L. of O is equal to the R.L. of A since OA is horizontal. Therefore,

R.L. of O = 226.715 m

$$\text{R.L. of } B = \text{R.L.of } A + \frac{g_2}{100} nl$$

$$= 226.715 + \frac{(-2.6)}{100} \times 3 \times 3$$

$$= 226.481 \text{ m.}$$

$$\text{R.L. of } F = \frac{1}{2}(\text{R.L.of } O + \text{R.L.of } B)$$

$$= \frac{1}{2} \times (226.715 + 226.481)$$

$$= 226.598 \text{ m.}$$

$$\text{R.L. of } E = \frac{1}{2}(\text{R.L.of } A + \text{R.L.of } F)$$

$$= \frac{1}{2} \times (226.715 + 226.598)$$

$$= 226.657 \text{ m.}$$

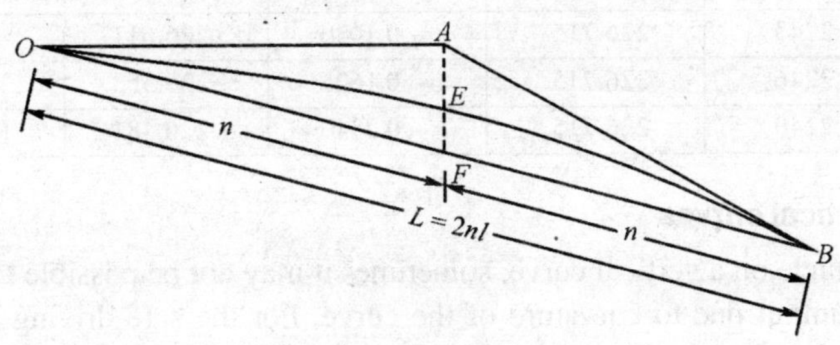

Fig. 12.72

Now,

$$e_1 = 0$$

$$e_2 = \frac{g_2}{100} \times l = \frac{-2.6}{100} \times 3 = -0.078 \text{ m}$$

$$k = \frac{e_1 - e_2}{4n}$$

$$= \frac{0 - (-0.078)}{4 \times 3}$$

$$= 0.0065 \text{ m.}$$

The tangent correction is given by

$$h = kN^2$$
$$= kn^2$$
$$h_1 = 0.0065 \times 1^2 = 0.0065$$
$$h_2 = 0.0065 \times 2^2 = 0.0260$$
$$h_3 = 0.0065 \times 3^2 = 0.0585$$
$$h_4 = 0.0065 \times 4^2 = 0.1040$$
$$h_5 = 0.0065 \times 5^2 = 0.1625$$
$$h_6 = 0.0065 \times 6^2 = 0.2340.$$

The tangential elevations of the first tangent for the various points will remain same as the tangent is horizontal. The calculated elevations of the various points are given in Table 12.9.

Table 12.9

Station No.	Chainage (m)	Tangential elevation (m)	Tangent correction (m)	R.L. of the curve point (n)	Remarks
0	2231	226.715	– 0.0000	226.715	Point *O*
1	2234	226.715	– 0.0065	226.709	
2	2237	226.715	– 0.0260	226.689	
3	2240	226.715	– 0.0585	226.657	Point *E*
4	2243	226.715	– 0.1040	226.611	
5	2246	226.715	– 0.1625	226.553	
6	2249	226.715	– 0.2340	226.481	Point *B*

Sight distance on vertical curves

While driving a vehicle on a vertical curve, sometimes it may not be possible to see the vehicles on the other side of the summit due to curvature of the curve. For the safe driving the curve should be designed such that a mnimum sight distance is available to the driver.

Sight distance is the length of the roadway ahead of the driver which is visible to the driver of the vehicle. It depends upon

(*a*) the stopping sight distance, and

(*b*) the overtaking sight distance

The length of the vertical curve should be sufficient to provide the minimum required sight distances.

Table 12.10 gives the minimum sight distances recommended by A.A.S.H.T.O (American Association of State Highway and Transport Officials) for different design speeds.

Table 12.10 Stopping sight distances

Design speed (km/hr)	48	64	80	96	112	128
Stopping sight distance (m)	61	84	107	145	183	229

Recommendations of the Indian Road Congress as per code IRC: 66–1976 are given in Table 12.11.

Table 12.11 Stopping sight distance on rural highways

Speed (km/hr)	20	30	40	50	60	80	100
Stopping sight distance (m)	20	30	45	60	80	120	180

To determine the minimum sight distance S, the following empirical formulae are sometimes used:

(*a*) For dual carriage ways

(*i*) $V < 60$ km/hr, $S = 2V - 30$ ...(12.185)

(*ii*) $V \geq 60$ km/hr, $S = 30 - V + 0.025V^2$ ...(12.186)

(*b*) For single carriageways

$S = 4.44\ V$ ...(12.187)

Sight distances at summit

There can be two cases: (*i*) the sight distance is less than the length of the curve ($S < L$), and (*ii*) the sight distance is greater than the length of the curve ($S > L$)

Case-1: $S < L$

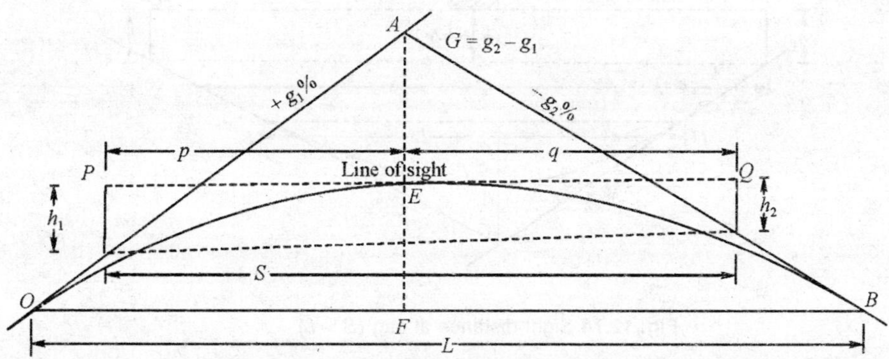

Fig. 12.73 Sight distance at summit ($S < L$)

In this case (Fig. 12.73), the length of the curve for a given sight distance, is determined from the following expression:

$$L = \frac{S^2(g_1 - g_2)}{200(\sqrt{h_1} + \sqrt{h_2})^2} \qquad \text{...(12.188)}$$

Case-2: $S > L$

In this case the length of the curve is given by

$$L = 2S - \frac{200(\sqrt{h_1} + \sqrt{h_2})^2}{(g_1 - g_2)} \qquad \text{...(12.189)}$$

In Eqs. (12.188) and (12.189), h_1 and h_2 are the heights of the driver's eye above the road level on the two sides of the apex of the curve. Taking $k = \dfrac{g_1 - g_2}{200L}$, h_1 and h_2 are given by

$$h_1 = kg_1^2$$

$$h_2 = kg_2^2$$

Sight distance at sag

In this case also there are two situations: (*i*) the sight distance is less than the length of the curve ($S < L$), and (*ii*) the sight distance is greater than the length of the curve ($S > L$).

In both the above cases, the minimum length of the curve is that length which will provide a specified sight distance underpass structures. It is assumed here that the point of intersection *A* of the curve is located vertically under the critical edge of the overhead structure restricting the view ahead (Fig. 12.74).

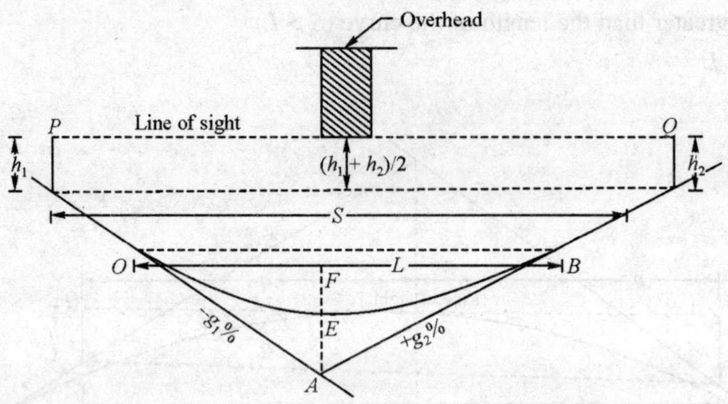

Fig. 12.74 Sight distance at sag ($S > L$)

Case-1: $S < L$

In this case the length of the curve for a minimum sight distance is given by

$$L = \frac{S^2(g_1 - g_2)}{(150 + 3.5S)} \qquad ...(12.190)$$

Case-2: $S > L$

In this case L is determined from the following expression

$$L = 2S - \frac{(150 + 3.5S)}{(g_1 - g_2)} \qquad ...(12.191)$$

ILLUSTRATIVE EXAMPLES

Example 12.43

Calculate the length of the vertical curve for the following given data:

Upgrade g_1 = + 1.5 %

Downgrade g_2 = – 1.0 %

Height of the driver's eye = 1.40 m

Height of the obstruction = 0.15 m

Minimum sight distance = 220 m

Solution:

From Eq. (12.188), the length of the curve is given by

$$L = \frac{S^2(g_1 - g_2)}{200(\sqrt{h_1} + \sqrt{h_2})^2}$$

$$= \frac{220^2 \times (1.5 + 1.0)}{200 \times (\sqrt{1.40} + \sqrt{0.15})^2}$$

$$= \textbf{245.3 m.}$$

Example 12.44

An upgrade of +2.0% meets a downgrade of –1.0%. If the height of the driver's eye is 1.45 m, the height of obstruction is 0.20 m, and the minimum speed of the vehicles is to be 110 km/hr, calculate the length of the curve.

Solution:

Assuming a dual carriageways from Eq. (12.186) for V = 110 km/hr, we have

$$\text{Sight distance } S = 30 - V + 0.025V^2$$

$$= 30 - 110 + 0.025 \times 110^2$$

$$= 225.5 \text{ m.}$$

From Eq. (12.188), the length of the curve is

$$L = \frac{S^2(g_1 - g_2)}{200(\sqrt{h_1} + \sqrt{h_2})^2}$$

$$= \frac{225.5^2 \times (2 + 1)}{200 \times (\sqrt{1.45} + \sqrt{0.20})^2}$$

$$= \textbf{279.7 m.}$$

Vertical curve passing through a given point

Let the point P be a given point as shown in Fig. 12.75, through which the vertical curve has to pass. Such points may be at a certain distance below an underpass structure or over the top of a culvert. Let the distance of P from the centre of the curve be x_0.

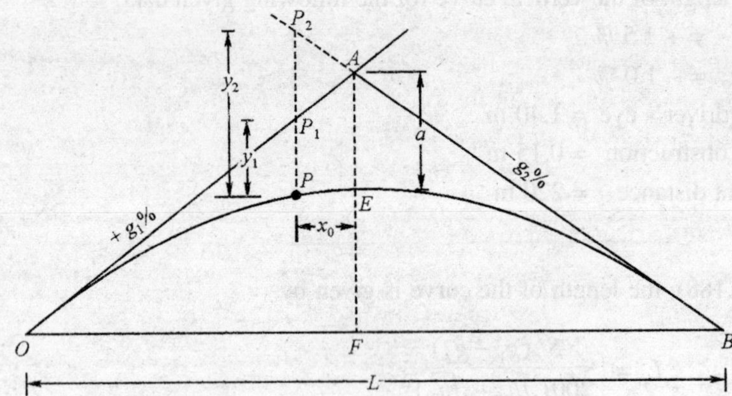

Fig. 12.75 Vertical curve passing through a given point

If y_1 and y_2 are the tangent offsets for both sides of the curve, and a is the distance of the apex E from the point of intersection A, then

$$y_1 = \frac{a}{\left(\frac{L}{2}\right)^2}\left[\frac{L}{2} - x_0\right]^2$$

and

$$y_2 = \frac{a}{\left(\frac{L}{2}\right)^2}\left[\frac{L}{2} + x_0\right]^2$$

Thus,

$$\frac{y_1}{y_2} = \frac{\left[\frac{L}{2} - x_0\right]^2}{\left[\frac{L}{2} + x_0\right]^2}$$

or

$$y_1\left[\frac{L}{2} + x_0\right]^2 = y_2\left[\frac{L}{2} - x_0\right]^2$$

or

$$L = \frac{2x_0(\sqrt{y_2} + \sqrt{y_1})}{(\sqrt{y_2} - \sqrt{y_1})} \qquad \text{...(12.192)}$$

Since the values of y_1, y_2 and x_0 are known, the length L of the curve can be determined.

ILLUSTRATIVE EXAMPLE

Example 12.44

A vertical curve is required to pass through a fixed point *P* of R.L. 190.00 m at 370.00 m chainage. The chainage of the point of intersection and its R.L. were measured as 335.00 m and 181.5 m, respectively. The gradients of the back tangent and the forward tangent, are –3.7% and +2.8%, respectively. Determine the length of the curve.

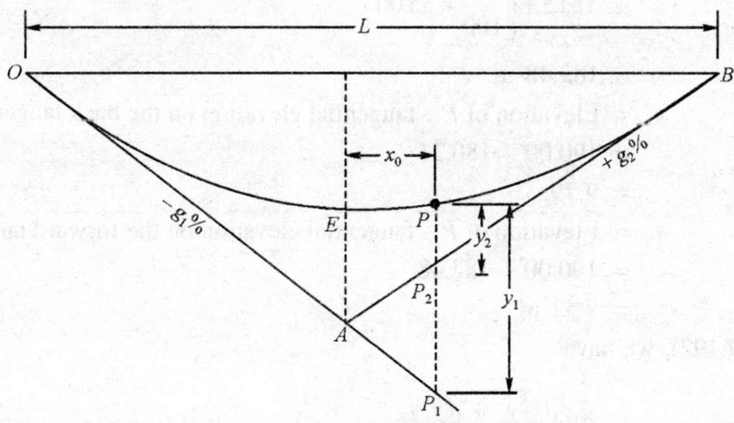

Fig. 12.76

Solution (Fig. 12.76):

Given that

$g_1 = -3.7\%$

$g_2 = +2.8\%$

R.L. of $A = 181.5$ m

Chainage of $A = 335.00$ m

R.L. of $P = 190.00$ m

Chainage of $P = 370.00$ m

Now,

$$x_0 = \text{Chainage of } A - \text{chainage of } P$$
$$= 335.00 - 370.00$$
$$= -35.00 \text{ m}$$

Tangential elevation at *P* on the back tangent

$$= \text{Elevation of } A + \left[\frac{g_1}{100} x_0\right]$$

$$= 181.5 + \left[\frac{-3.7}{100} \times 35.00\right]$$

$$= 180.21 \text{ m.}$$

Tangential elevation at P on the forward tangent

$$= \text{R.L. of } A + \left[\frac{g_2}{100} x_0\right]$$

$$= 181.5 + \left[\frac{2.8}{100} \times 35.00\right]$$

$$= 182.48 \text{ m.}$$

$$y_1 = \text{Elevation of } P - \text{tangential elevation on the back tangent}$$

$$= 190.00 - 180.21$$

$$= 9.79.$$

$$y_2 = \text{Elevation of } P - \text{tangential elevation on the forward tangent}$$

$$= 190.00 - 182.48$$

$$= 7.52 \text{ m.}$$

From Eq. (12.192), we have

$$L = \frac{2x_0(\sqrt{y_2} + \sqrt{y_1})}{(\sqrt{y_2} - \sqrt{y_1})}$$

$$= \frac{2 \times (-35) \times (\sqrt{7.52} + \sqrt{9.79})}{(\sqrt{7.52} - \sqrt{9.79})}$$

$$= \mathbf{1063.0 \text{ m.}}$$

QUESTIONS AND PROBLEMS

12.1 Write a short note on the use of curves in highways and railways.

12.2 What are different types of curves used in highways and railways? Describe each with neat sketches.

12.3 Explain the function of the following curves:

(*i*) Simple circular curve
(*ii*) Compound curve
(*iii*) Reverse curve
(*iv*) Transition curve
(*v*) Vertical curve
(*vi*) Broken-back curve

12.4 Draw a neat sketch of a circular curve, and show its various elements thereon.

12.5 Work out the relationships between the elements of a circular curve.

12.6 What is meant by degree of a curve? Derive its relationship with the radius of the curve.

12.7 What are the methods of designation of curve? Derive a relationship between the degree of a curve and its radius.

12.8 What do you understand by sub-chord and unit chord? How a suitable peg interval is selected in setting out the circular curves?

12.9 Describe the method of setting out a circular curve be perpendicular offsets from tangent.

12.10 Discuss various methods of setting out a horizontal circular curve with a tape.

12.11 Explain the procedure for setting out simple ciurcular curves with a tape and a theodolite.

12.12 Describe the method of setting out circular curves by offsets from chord produced.

12.13 Describe the method of setting out a simple circular curve by deflection angles using tape and theodolite.

12.14 Discuss the method of setting out a circular curve using two theodolites.

12.15 Derive the following relationship:

$$\delta = \frac{1718.9\,C}{R} \text{ minutes}$$

where δ = deflection angle of the chord
C = length of the chord
R = radius of the circular curve.

12.16 Discuss the method of setting out circular curves by the method of tacheometry. What are its advantages and disadvantages?

12.17 How would you set out a simple circular curve with a total station?

12.18 What are the methods of setting out simple curves? Explain Rankine's method of tangential angles for setting out curves.

12.19 Explain the method of setting out a simple circular curve from point of intersection.

12.20 Write a short note on the field problems in setting out curves.

12.21 Describe the method to locate the points of commencement and tangency when it is found that the point of intersection of the tangents falls in a deep river.

12.22 Discuss the method of setting out a simple circular curve when it has to pass through a given point.

12.23 Write a short note on the obstacles in setting out curves.

12.24 What is a compound curve? Derive relationships between various elements of a compound curve.

12.25 Describe the method of setting out a compound curve in the field.

12.26 What is a transition curve? What are its advantages?

12.27 What is a transition curve? When and why is it used? Write a note on different types of transition curve.

12.28 What are the basic criteria for the design of a transition curve? Derive an expression for superelevation. What do you mean by cant deficiency?

12.29 What is meant by shift of a curve? Derive an expression for it.

12.30 What is the need for superelevation, and how is it determined?

12.31 What are the theoretical conditions that a transition curve should fulfil?

12.32 Derive an equation for an ideal transition curve.

12.33 What are the methods of determining the length of a transition curve? Explain each in brief.

12.34 Derive an expression for the minimum radius of cubic parabola.

12.35 Explain the method of setting out a transition curve by

(*a*) tangent offsets

(*b*) deflection angles.

12.36 Prove that

(*a*) shift bisects the transition curve

(*b*) transition curve bisects the shift.

12.37 Derive expressions for the various elements of a transition curve.

12.38 Explain the spiralling of compound curves and reverse curves.

12.39 Explain the features of vertical curves.

12.40 When would you use a vertical curve?

12.41 What are different types of vertical curves? Discuss each with neat sketches.

12.42 Prove that a parabola provides a rate of change of grade at a uniform rate.

12.43 Discuss different methods of expressing gradient. Define the rate of change of gradient.

12.44 Prove that the difference in elevation between a point on a vertical curve and its corresponding point on the tangent, is proportional to the square of its distance from the point of tangency.

12.45 Explain the method of computing the length of a vertical curve.

12.46 Derive expressions for computing the tangent corrections and chord gradients in vertical curves.

12.47 Derive an expression of a vertical curve in terms of two gradients and length of the curve.

12.48 Explain the tangent correction and chord gradient methods of setting out vertical curves.

12.49 What is the sight distance? What is its importance in design of a vertical curve?

12.50 Discuss the method for the design of a vertical curve passing through a fixed point.

12.51 Given that the intersection angle of a two-degree curve is 120°, compute the various elements of a simple curve.

12.52 In setting out a circular curve it was found that it must pass through a point 16 m from the intersection point, and equidistant from the tangents. The deflection angle is 40°. The chainage of the point of intersection is 1000 m. Calculate

(*i*) the radius of the curve,

(*ii*) the degree of the curvature,

(*iii*) the chainage of the point of commencement, and

(*iv*) the chainage of the point of tangency.

12.53 Calculate the necessary data to set out a circular curve of 180 m radius between two roads having deflection angle of 44°40′.

12.54 Two straights having deflection angle of 48°30′ intersect at chainage of 111 + 40. Calculate the necessary data for setting out a curve of 250 m radius to connect the two straights. The chain used is 20 m in length, with 100 links. Take the peg interval as 20 m, and use the method of offsets from the chords produced.

12.55 Two tangents intersect at a chainage of 1190 m, the deflection angle being 36°. Compute the necessary data to set out a curve of radius 300 m by the method of deflection angles. Take peg interval as 30 m.

12.56 Two tangents having the angle of intersection of 139°30′, intersect at the chainage 1450 m. It is required to connect the two tangents by a circular curve of radius of 320 m. The curve is intended to be set out from the point of intersection. Calculate all the data necessary for setting out the curve.

12.57 Two straights *AB* and *BC* having bearings respectively of 100° and 160°12′, are to be connected by a right hand circular curve. The curve is to pass through a point *D* such that the *BD* is 47.66 m long and its bearing is 245°24′. Determine the radius of the curve.

If chainage of the point of intersection is 4447.50 m determine the tangential angles to be set out on a theodolite reading to 20″ for setting out the first two pegs on the curve at through chainage of 20 m.

12.58 The parallel sides of a trapezoidal plot of land are 600 m and 900 m, the other sides measure 1600 m each. Calculate the perimeter of the largest sized pond to be dug out, having its two ends circular.

12.59 The following data refer to a right-hand compound curve:

(*i*) Total deflection angle = 80°

(*ii*) Radius of the first arc = 200 m

(*iii*) Radius of the second arc = 250 m

(*iv*) Chainage of the point of intersection = 1504.80 m

(*v*) Deflection angle of the first arc = 50°

Determine the chainages of the point of curvature, the point of compound curve, and the point of tangency. Also find the remaining components of the curve. Compute the lengths of the sub-chords if the length of the normal chord is 20 m.

12.60 A compound curve consists of an arc of 33 chains radius followed by one of 42 chains radius and connects two straights with total deflection angle of 84°. The chainage of the point of intersection is 77.50 chains, and the starting point of the curve is chosen at 44.50 chains. Determine the chainages of the junction of the two arcs and also that of the end of the curve.

12.61 Two straights *AB* and *CD* both produced intersect at *V*. Angle *CBV* = 30°, and angle *BCV* = 120°. It is proposed to introduce a reverse curve consisting of two circular arcs *AT* and *TD*, *T* lying on *BC*. Length *BC* is 791.71 m, and radius of arc *AT* is 800 m, chainage of *B* is 1000 m. Calculate the radius of the arc *TD*, the length of the arc *AT*, the length of the arc *TD*, and the chainage of the point *D*.

12.62 Two straights AT_1 and CT_2 meet at *V*. It is proposed to introduce a reverse curve of common radius *R*, having T_1 and T_2 as tangent points. The angles AT_1T_2 and VT_2T_1 measured at T_1 and T_2 are 45°40′ and 25°20′, respectively. The distance T_1T_2 is equal to 700 m. Determine the common radius and the central angles for the two arcs.

12.63 A reverse curve *AB* is to be set out between two parallel railway lines, 30 m apart. If the two arcs of the curves are to have same radius, and the distance between the tangent points *A* and *B* is 180 m, calculate the radius. The curve is to be set out from *AB* at 10 m intervals along it. Compute the length of the offsets.

12.64 A transition curve is required for a circular curve of 250 m radius, the gauge being 1.55 m and maximum superelevation restricted to 15 cm. The transition is to be designed for a velocity such that no lateral pressure is imposed on the rails. The rate of gain of radial acceleration is 30 cm/sec^2/sec. Calculate the required length of the transition curve and the design speed.

12.65 A road bend which deflects 80° is to be designed for a maximum speed of 100 km/hr, a maximum centrifugal ratio of 1/4, and a maximum rate of the change of acceleration 0.3 m/sec^2/sec, the curve consisting of a circular arc combined with two cubic spirals. Calculate

(*i*) the radius of the circular arc,

(*ii*) the requisite length of transition,

(*iii*) the total length of the composite curve,

(*iv*) the chainage of the beginning of the transition curve,

(*v*) the chainage of the end of the transition curve, and

(*vi*) the chainage of the junctions of the transition curves with the circular arc.

Take chainage of the point of the intersection as 4000 m.

12.66 Calculate the length of the vertical curve for the following data:

(*i*) $g_1 = +1$ %, $g_2 = -1.5$ %, $h = 1.12$ m, and the sight distance is thrice the length of the vertical curve.

(*ii*) $g_1 = +1.5$ %, $g_2 = -2.5$ %, $h = 1.12$ m, and the sight distance is half the length of the vertical curve.

12.67 A parabolic vertical curve is to be set out to connect two uniform grades of + 0.8 % and – 1.2 %. If the rate of change of grade is – 0.25 % per 100 m, calculate the reduced levels of the first four pegs on the curve by the method of tangent correction if the R.L. of the point of intersection is 325.15 m, and its chainage is 1660.00 m. Take chain length as 20 m and peg interval as 40 m.

12.68 Design a vertical curve 260 m long connecting a rising gradient of 1 in 40 with a falling gradient of 1 in 80 which meet in a summit of R.L. of 120.50 m, and chainage of 3365.00 m. Take peg interval of 20 m. Calculate the elevations at full 20 m stations.

Answers to Numerical Problems

Chapter 1

1.7 125 m

Chapter 2

2.9 7.8635 m, $\pm 2.128 \times 10^{-4}$ m.

2.10 52.7″, ± 1.8562″, ± 0.1856 m, 16.17.

2.11 7701.3 cm^3, ± 405.7 cm^3.

2.12 ± 82 cm^3.

2.13 53322.41 m^2, ± 10.58 m^2.

2.14 28°49′30.70″, 12°00′19.54″, 139°10′09.76″, ± 2′34.97″, ± 1′58.70″, ± 3′27.97″.

2.15 8691.81 m^2, $\pm 3.859\ 10^{-6}$ m^2.

2.16 291236.62 m^2, ± 35.05 m^2.

Chapter 3

3.8 453.36 paces.

3.9 2014.98 m.

3.10 256.49 m.

3.11 49.59 m.

3.12 953.58 m.

3.13 0.19 m.

3.14 11.14″

3.15 128.34 m.

3.16 315.32 m × 750.75 m.

3.17 0.011 m.

3.18 0.0022 m.

3.19 29.999 m, 29.995 m.

3.20 3439.87 m.

Chapter 4

4.7 (*a*) 43°20′, 143°18′, 40°30′, 215°52′, 282°20′, 89°49′, 296°32′, 259°59′, 351°45′, 167°42′.
(*b*) 223°20′, 323°18′, 220°30′, 35°52′, 102°20′, 269°49′, 116°32′, 79°59′, 171°45′, 347°42′.

4.8 5°30′, 325°45′, 25°40′, 198°59′, 278°15′.

4.9 S 17°41′ E, *N* 80°27′ W, N 26°10′ W, *N* 5° 35′ *E*
117°14′ R, 54°17′ R, 31°45′ R.

4.26 112°23′12.5″.

4.27 48°42′02″, 34°14′25″.

Chapter 5

5.12 116.95 m.

5.13 835.53 m.

5.14 43.1 m.

5.15 46.34 m.

5.27 Affected stations R and S,
124°30′, 68°15′, 312°45′, 197°45′, 106°45′,
123°45′, 64°30′, 65°00′.

5.28 Affected stations 3 and 4, Error at 3 = – 15′, and at 4 = – 30′, 4°25′, 176°25′, 225°25′, 169°10′.

5.29 N 56°00′ E, *S* 66°30′E, *S* 24°00′ W, N 77°00′ W, N 62°30′ W.

5.30 F.B. – B.B. = 180°, No local attraction.

Chapter 6

6.27 (a) + 0.067 m, (b) + 0.026 m, (c) + 0.031 m.

6.28 1.054 m.

6.29 9.4 km.

6.30 27.2 km.

6.31 274.96 m.

6.32 *A* higher than *B* (Δh = 1.305).

6.33 605.059 m.

6.34 469.775 m.

6.35

Point	B.S.	I.S.	F.S.	Rise	Fall	R.L.	Remarks
1	1.195					92.545	A
2	0.445		2.375		1.180	91.365	
3	2.150		1.000		0.555	90.810	
4		0.720		1.430		92.240	B
5	1.465		0.260	0.460		92.700	
6	2.630		0.905	0.560		93.260	
7	2.140		0.975	1.655		94.915	
8			1.305	0.835		95.750	C
Σ	10.025	6.820	4.940	1.735			
Arith. check	10.025 – 6.820 = 4.940 – 1.735 = 95.750 – 92.545 = 3.205						

6.36

Point	B.S.	I.S.	F.S.	Rise	Fall	R.L.	Remarks
1	0.485					264.350	
2		1.020			0.535	263.815	
3		1.785			0.765	263.050	
4		3.395			1.610	261.440	
5	0.360		3.875		0.480	260.960	
6		1.305			0.945	260.015	
7		1.785			0.480	259.535	
8		2.675			0.890	258.645	
9		3.385			0.710	257.935	
10	1.835		3.885		0.500	257.435	
11		0.435		1.400		258.835	
12			1.705		1.270	257.565	
Σ	2.680		9.465	1.400	8.185		
Arith. check	2.680 – 9.465 = 1.400 – 8.185 = 257.565 – 264.350 = – 6.785						

6.37 B.S. 2.430, 2.800, 0.720,
F.S. 3.850, 1.340,
Rise 0.350, 0.790, 0.050
Fall 0.430, 0.550
R.L. 221.100, 220.400, 219.970, 220.320, 220.310, 221.410, 221.650, 221.700, 220.895
ΣF.S. = 12.260, ΣRise = 2.290, ΣFall = 2.490.

6.38 R.L. 160.32, 162.47, 163.22, 166.97, 166.46, 172.35
Embankment Point 1 (10.32 m), Point 2 (7.47 m), Point 3 (3.22 m), Point 4 (1.97 m), Cutting Point 5(3.54 m), Point 6 (2.65 m).

6.39 No.

6.40 Not acceptable.

6.41 (a) 27.50 m, (b) 16.50 m.

6.42 13.75″, 30 m.

6.43 0.029 m.

6.44 21.95 m, 18.79″.

6.45 (1) *B* lower than *A* by 1.241 m, (2) 198.759 m, (3) 8.5″.

6.46 2.745 m, – 0.005 m.

6.47 99.20 m, 7.31″.

6.48 Instrument needs adjustment, 1.800 m.

6.49 624.466 m.

6.50 240.65 m, 235.65 m.

6.51 348.905 m.

6.52 2164.98 m.

6.53 677.16 m.

Chapter 7

7.12 407275 m^3, 400117 m^3.

7.13 14031480 m^3.

7.14 (*i*) 195.35 m, (*ii*) 189.65 m.

Chapter 8

8.18 $k = 100$, $c = 0.3$ m.

8.19 $k = 100$, $c = 0.5$ m.

8.20 $k = 100$.

8.21 2.113 m.

8.22 170.6 m, 1496.655 m.

8.23 56.0 m, 1 in 95.

8.24 431.969 m, 159.721 m.

8.25 37.180 m, 331.355 m.

8.26 67.888 m, 49.358 m, 81.792 m.

8.27 202.120 m, 102.400 m.

8.28 521.528 m, 232.943 m, 251.736 m, 395.695 m.

8.29 1048.80 m

8.30 223.450 m, 0.001 m.

8.31 123.400 m, 138.988 m, 15.588 m, 530.264 m, 2°06′56″.

Chapter 9

9.14 712.714 m, 1045.708 m.

9.15 77.43 m, 180°

9.16 (*a*) *B* (E 741.88, N 1368.62), *C* (E 741.88, N 1718.62), *D* (E 937.95, N 2017.38), *E* (E 804.97, N 2300.00), *M* (E 902.49, N 1650.00),
(*b*) 174.65 m, 113°08′04″.

9.17 20594 m, 219°12′29.4″.

9.18 *B* (E 204.507, N 529.868), *C* (E 503.193, N 547.179), *D* (E 508.118, N 400.000).

9.19 (*a*) Lat. = 0.000 m, Dep. = – 139.000 m,
(*b*) 2.577 m, 302°38′30″.

9.20 Lengths *AB* = 60.00 m, *BC* = 64.35 m, *CD* = 49.84 m, *DA* = 81.58 m, Northings of *BC* = 45.50 m and *CD* = 36.15 m, Eastings of *AB* = 51.96 m and Westing of *CD* = 34.31 m.

Chapter 10

10.28 0.2 mm, Insignificant.

10.29 1 : 500.

10.30 0.09 mm.

10.31 (*a*) 140.641 m,
(*b*) 140.416 m.

Chapter 11

11.28 42.5 m, 28.33 m, 552.01 m^2.

11.29 418.7 m^2, 442.8 m^2, 447.8 m^2.

11.30 2269 m^2.

11.31 29221 m^2, 29221 m^2, 29221 m^2, 29221 m^2.

11.32 50820.5 m^2.

11.33 198 m^2.

11.34 926.6 cm^2.

11.35 2103 m^3.

11.36 8247.2 m^3.

11.37 1233.3 m^3, 311.7 m^3.

11.38 1974.2 m^3.

11.39 2304 m^3.

11.40 5.56 m^3 (negative since the ground slopes towards the concave side of the curve).

11.41 3614050 m^3.

Chapter 12

12.51 496.20 m, 859.45 m, 132,96 m, 115.14 m, 900.01 m.

12.52 249.31 m, 909.26 m, 1083.31 m.

12.53 73.95 m, 136.80 m, 14.60 m, 13.50 m, 140.32 m, 9.55°.

12.54 0.04 m, 0.98 m, 1.60 m, 0.38 m.

12.55 1°40′20″, 4°32′20″, 7°24′20″, 10°16′20″, 13°08′20″
16°00′20″, 18°00′40″.

12.56

Point no.	Chord length	θ	α
1	22.62	4°03′	0°28′47″
2	22.62	8°06′	2°30′19″
3	22.62	12°09′	8°02′48″
4	22.62	16°12′	23°49′23″
5	22.62	20°15′	69°45′00″

The above data is for half of the curve to be set out with respect to the back tangent. The same data are to be used for the remaining half of the curve for setting out with respect to the forward tangent.

12.57 271.53 m, 1°02′40″, 3°09′20″.

12.58 4037.03 m.

12.59 (T_1) 1330.18 m, (T_2) 1635.61 m, (T_3) 1504.71 m, (length of the larger tangent) 191.64 m, (First arc) 9.82 m, 4.71 m, (Second arc) 15.29 m, 15.61 m.

12.60 63.83 ch, 100.81 ch.

12.61 1000.00 m, 418.88 m, 1047.20 m, 2251.72 m.

12.62 299.20 m, 82°24′33″, 62°04′33″.

12.63 270 m, 0.0 m, 0.80 m, 2.10 m, 3.03 m, 3.59 m, 3.78 m, 3.59 m, 3.03 m, 2.10 m, 0.80 m, 0.00 m.

12.64 49 m.

12.65 (*i*) 315 m, (*ii*) 227 m, (*iii*) 666.8 m, (*iv*) 2061.4 m, (*v*) 2728.2 m, (*vi*) 2288.4 m, 2501.2 m.

12.66 (*i*) 72 m, (*ii*) 896 m.

12.67

Peg no	Chainage	R.L. (m)
0	1260	321.95
1	1300	322.27
2	1340	322.59
3	1380	322.91
4	1420	323.23

12.68

Peg no	Chainage	R.L. (m)
0	3225	122.5
1	3245	123.0
2	3265	123.5
3	3285	124.0

APPENDIX A

S.I. Units

"S.I." is the abbreviation used to designate the International System of Units (Systeme International d' Units) : it is a coherent system—the product or quotient of two or more units is the unit of the resultant quantity. The base units of the S.I. system are as follows:

Length: The *metre* is the unit of length equal to 1,650,763.73 wavelengths, in vacuum, of the radiation corresponding to the transition between the levels $2p^{10}$ and $5d^5$ of the Krypton-86 atom.

Mass: The *kilogram* is the unit of mass. It is equal to the mass of the international prototype of the kilogram.

Time: The *second* is the duration of 9,192,631,770 periods of the radiation corresponding to the transition between the two hyperfine levels of the ground state of the Caesium-133 atom.

Thermodynamic temperature: The *Kelvin* is the fraction 1/273.16 of the thermodynamic temperature of the triple point of water.

The base and other units of the S.I. System are tabulated as:

No.	Quantity	Unit	Symbol	Remarks
1.	Base units			
	Length	metre	m	
	Mass	kilogram	kg	1 kg = 1N/g
	Time	second	s	
	Electric current	ampere	A	
	Thermodynamic temperature	Kelvin	K	Celsius scale may be used for practical purposes
	Luminous intensity	candela	cd	
	Amount of substance	mole	mol	
2.	Supplementary units			
	Plane angle	radian	rad	
	Solid angle	steradian	sr	Solid angle subtended at the centre of a sphere by a surface area equal to the square of the radius.
3.	Derived Units			
	Force	newton	N	Force which produces an acceleration of 1 m/s^2 acting on a mass of 1 kg. Also, 1kgf = 1gN.
	Energy	joule	J	Work done by a force of 1N over a displacement of 1 m. 1J = 1Nm
	Power	Watt	W	Rate of work of 1 J/s
	Flux	Weber	Wb	
	Flux density	tesla	T	
	Frequency	hertz	Hz	1 Hz = 1 cycle/s
	Electric conductance	siemens	S	
	Pressure, Stress	Pascal	Pa	1 Pa = 1 N/m^2

General rules and conventions

Symbols

1. Full names of units, even when they are named after a person, are not written with a capital initial letter.
2. The symbol for a unit, named after a person, is written with an initial capital letter.
3. Symbols for other units are not written with an initial capital letter.
4. Symbols for units are always used in the singular.
5. No punctuation marks should be used within or at the ends of symbols for units.
6. A space is left between the numeral and the symbol.
7. A space is left between the symbols for compound units, *e.g.*, KW h; m N (m N would denote metre newton while mN would denote millinewton).
8. The denominators of compound units are expressed preferably in the base units, and not in their multiples or submultiples, e.g., MN/m^2 is preferred to N/mm^2.
9. The symbols of multiples and submultiples are to be used only conjointly with that of the unit and not with the full name of the unit, e.g., MW and not M Watt.

Prefixes

Multiples or submultiples involving the factor 1000 (or 10^{+3n}, n being an integer) are preferentially used for the purpose of international consistency. Common prefixes used are:

kilo (k) 10^3 milli (m) 10^{-3}
mega (M) 10^6 micro (μ) 10^{-6} (Normally, double prefixes are avoided.)
giga (G) 10^9 nano (n) 10^{-9}

S.I. units specifically used in surveying

(1) Unit Weight .... N/m^3 or kN/m^3
(2) Force .... N or kN
(3) Pressure, stress .... N/m^2 (Pa) or kN/m^2 (kPa)
(4) Velocity .... m/s
(5) Rate of flow .... m^3/s or 1/s
(6) Moment of force .... N m or kN m

Centesimal system of angle measurement

The graduations on the instrument range from zero to 400 gon, as against zero to 306° in sexagesesimal system. Subdivision in Centesimal system is carried out in steps of ten, and readings may be made to 0.0001 gon.

$$1 \text{ degree} = \frac{10}{9} \text{ gon} \qquad \left(1 \text{ degree} = \frac{400}{360} \text{ gon} = \frac{10}{9} \text{ gon}\right)$$

$$1 \text{ minute} = \frac{1}{54} \text{ gon} \qquad \left(1 \text{ minute} = \frac{400}{360 \times 60} = \frac{1}{54} \text{ gon}\right)$$

$$1 \text{ second} = \frac{1}{3240} \text{ gon} \qquad \left(1 \text{ second} = \frac{400}{360 \times 60 \times 60} = \frac{1}{3240} \text{ gon}\right)$$

Example: $53°07'10'' = 53 \times \frac{10}{9} + 7 \times \frac{1}{54} + 10 \times \frac{1}{3240}$

$= 58.8890 + 0.1296 + 0.0031 = 59.0217$ gon.

APPENDIX B

Greek Alphabets

Greek letter		Name	Equivalent	Sound when spoken
Α	α	Alpha	A	al-fah
Β	β	Beta	B	bay-tah
Γ	γ	Gamma	G	gam-ah
Δ	δ	Delta	D	del-tah
Ε	ε	Epsilon	E	ep-si-lon
Ζ	ζ	Zeta	Z	zay-tah
Η	η	Eta	E	ay-tay
Θ	θ	Theta	Th	thay-tah
Ι	ι	Iota	I	eye-o-tah
Κ	κ	Kappa	K	cap-ah
Λ	λ	Lambda	L	lamb-dah
Μ	μ	Mu	M	mew
Ν	ν	Nu	N	new
Ξ	ξ	Xi	X	zzEye
Ο	ο	Omicron	O	om-ah-cron
Π	π	Pi	P	pie
Ρ	ρ	Rho	R	row
Σ	σ	Sigma	S	sig-ma
Τ	τ	Tau	T	tawh
Υ	υ	Upsilon	U	oop-si-lon
Φ	φ	Phi	Ph	figh or fie
Χ	χ	Chi	Ch	kigh
Ψ	ψ	Psi	Ps	sigh
Ω	ω	Omega	O	o-may-gah

Metric Conversion

1 millimeter (mm)	=	1000 micrometers (mm) or microns (m).
1 centimeter (cm)	=	10 mm
1 meter (m)	=	100 cm
1 m	=	3.2808 ft = *39.37 in. (U.S. survey foot)
1 kilometer (km)	=	1000 m
1 km	=	0.62137 miles
*1 inch (in.)	=	25.400 mm
*1 foot (ft.)	=	304.80 mm }U.S. standard foot
1 sq. mm (mm^2)	=	0.00155 $in.^2$
1 m^2	=	10.76 ft^2
1 km^2	=	247.1 acres
1 hectare	=	2.471 acres
1 m^3	=	35.3 ft^3
1 litre	=	0.264 U.S. gal
1 gram (g)	=	0.035 oz
1 kilogram (kg)	=	2.20 lb
1 ton	=	907 kg = 2.00 kips
1 m/sec	=	3.28 ft/sec
1 km/hr	=	0.911 ft/sec = 0.621 mph
1 kg/m^3	=	0.0624 lb/ft^3
1 ton/m^3	=	0.0328 $lb/in.^3$

*Denotes exact value. All others correct to figures shown.

APPENDIX D

Some Important Numbers in Surveying

0.000 000 1 (or 2)	=	coefficient of expansion, Invar tape, per 1°F
0.000 004 848	=	sin 1″ = tan 1″
0.000 006 45	=	coefficient of expansion, steel tape, per 1°F
0.000 290 89	=	approx. sin 1′ = tan 1′ (0.000 29 or 0.000 3 convenient)
0.017 452 41 sin 0.017 455 06 tan	=	approx. sin 1″ = tan 1° = about 0.01¾ = radians in 1°
0.574	=	coefficient of combined curvature and refraction (ft/miles^2)
0.6745	=	coefficient for 50% standard deviation (i.e., probable error)
*1 in.	=	0.0254 m (U.S. standard foot, 1959)
*1 ft.	=	0.3048 m (U.S. standard foot, 1959)
1.15 miles	≃	1 minute (1′) of latitude ≃ 1 nautical mile
1.6449	=	coefficient for 90% standard deviation
3.141 592 654	=	π
*15° longitude	=	width of one time zone = 360°24 hr.
15°F	=	changes length of 100 ft steel tape by 0.01 ft.
20°C	=	standard temperature (Celsius) in taping = 68°F
*25.4 mm	=	1 in. (U.S. standard foot of 1959).
*50	=	Beaman arc reading for 0° vertical angle (30 in old arcs)
57°17′44.8′	=	1 radian (rad) = .57.295 779 51°
69.1 miles	≃	1° latitude
*400 gon	=	360°
490 lb/ft^3	=	density of steel for tape computations
*640 acres	=	one normal section of 1 mile^2
6076.10 ft.	=	1 nautical mile
*3600/3937	=	ratio U.S. yd/m for old legal (1866) and surveyor's foot

4,046.9 m^2	=	1 acre
10,000 km	=	distance from equator to pole (basis for length of metre)
*43,560 ft^2	=	1 acre
206,264.806 25 sec	=	1 radian = cot 1 sec = $180°/\pi$ in sec
299,792.5 km/sec	=	speed of light, and other electromagnetic waves, in vacuum
6,356,583.8 m	=	earth's polar semi-axis (Clarke ellipsoid 1866)
6,378,206.4 m	=	earth's equatorial semi-axis (Clarke ellipsoid 1866)
20,906,000 ft	=	mean radius of earth = 3960 miles
29,000,000 lb/in.^{2}	=	Young's modulus of elasticity for steel

* Denotes exact value. All others correct to figures shown.

APPENDIX E

Trigonometric Formulas for the Solution of Right Triangles

Let A = angle BAC = arc BF, and let radius $AF = AB = AH = 1$. Then,

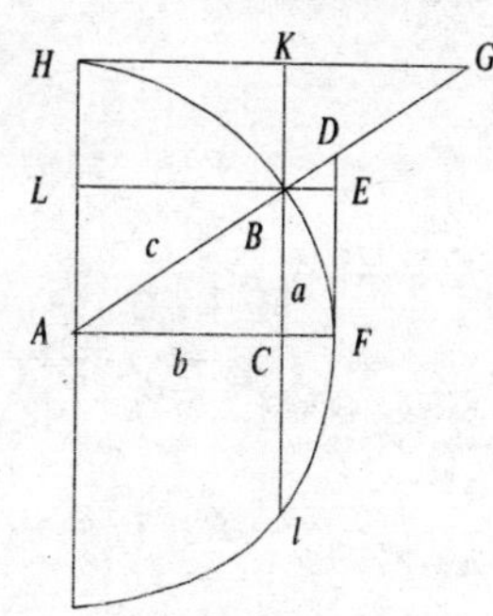

Fig. D-1

sin A	=	BC	csc A	=	AG
cos A	=	AC	sec A	=	AD
tan A	=	DF	cot A	=	HG
vers A	=	$CF = BE$	covers A	=	$BK = LH$
exsec A	=	BD	coexsec A	=	BG
chord A	=	BF	chord 2.A	=	$BI = 2\ BC$.

In the right-angled D ABC, let $AB = c$, $BC = a$, $CA = b$. Then,

1. $\sin A = \dfrac{a}{c}$
2. $\cos A = \dfrac{b}{c}$
3. $\tan A = \dfrac{a}{b}$
4. $\cot A = \dfrac{b}{a}$
5. $\sec A = \dfrac{c}{b}$
6. $\csc A = \dfrac{c}{a}$
7. $\text{vers } A = 1 - \cos A = \dfrac{c-b}{c} = \text{covers } B$
8. $\text{exsec } A = \sec A - 1 = \dfrac{c-b}{b} = \text{coexsec } B$
9. $\text{covers } A = \dfrac{c-a}{c} = \text{vers } B$
10. $\text{coexsec } A = \dfrac{c-a}{a} = \text{exsec } B$
11. $a = c \sin A = b \tan A$
12. $b = C \cos A = a \cot A$
13. $c = \dfrac{a}{\sin A} = \dfrac{b}{\cos A}$
14. $a = c \cos B = b \cot B$
15. $b = c \sin B = a \tan B$
16. $c = \dfrac{a}{\cos B} = \dfrac{b}{\sin B}$
17. $a = \sqrt{c^2 - b^2} = \sqrt{(c-b)(c+b)}$
18. $b = \sqrt{c^2 - a^2} = \sqrt{(c-a)(c+a)}$
19. $c = \sqrt{a^2 + b^2}$
20. $C = 90° = A + \mathrm{B}$
21. $\text{area} = \dfrac{1}{2}ab$

Trigonometric Formulas for the Solution of Oblique Triangles

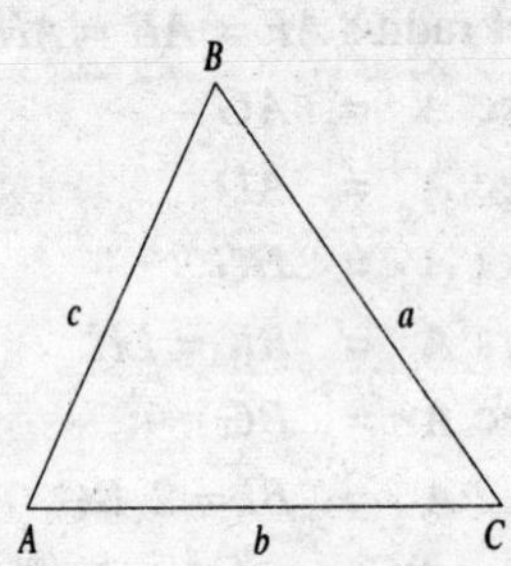

Given	Sought	Formula
A, B, a	C, b, c	$C = 180° - (A + B)$ $b = \dfrac{a}{\sin A} \times \sin B$ $c = \dfrac{a}{\sin A} \times \sin(A + B) = \dfrac{1}{\sin A} \times \sin C$
	Area	$\text{Area} = \dfrac{1}{2} ab \sin C = \dfrac{a^2 \sin B \sin C}{2 \sin A}$
A, a, b	B, C, c	$\sin B = \dfrac{\sin A}{a} \times b$ $C = 180° - (A + B)$ $c = \dfrac{a}{\sin A} \times \sin C$
	Area	$\text{Area} = \dfrac{1}{2} ab \sin C$

C, a, b	c	$c = \sqrt{a^2+b^2-2ab\cos C}$
	$\frac{1}{2}(A+B)$	$\frac{1}{2}(A+B) = 90° - \frac{1}{2}C$
	$\frac{1}{2}(A+B)$	$\tan\frac{1}{2}(A-B) = \frac{a-b}{a+b}\times\tan\frac{1}{2}(A+B)$
	A, B	$A = \frac{1}{2}(A+B)+\frac{1}{2}(A-B)$ $B = \frac{1}{2}(A+B)-\frac{1}{2}(A-B)$
	c	$c = (a+b)\times\frac{\cos\frac{1}{2}(A+B)}{\cos\frac{1}{2}(A-B)} = (a-b)\times\frac{\sin\frac{1}{2}(A+B)}{\sin\frac{1}{2}(A-B)}$
	Area	Area $= \frac{1}{2}ab\sin C$
a, b, c	A	Let $s = \frac{a+b+c}{2}$ $\sin\frac{1}{2}A = \sqrt{\frac{(s-b)(s-c)}{bc}}$ $\cos\frac{1}{2}A = \sqrt{\frac{s(s-a)}{bc}}$ $\tan\frac{1}{2}A = \sqrt{\frac{(s-b)(s-c)}{s(s-a)}}$ $\sin A = \frac{2\sqrt{s(s-a)(s-b)(s-c)}}{bc}$ $\cos A = \frac{b^2+c^2-a^2}{2bc}$
	Area	Area $= \sqrt{s(s-a)(s-b)(s-c)}$

APPENDIX G

Series

1. $(1+x)^n = 1 + nx + \frac{n(n-1)}{2!}x^2 + \frac{n(n-1)(n-2)}{3!}x^3 + \ldots$

   where 2! = factorial 2 = 2 = 2 × 1, etc.

2. $e^x = 1 + x + \frac{x^2}{2!} + \frac{x^3}{3!} + \ldots$

3. $e^{-x} = 1 - x + \frac{x^2}{2!} - \frac{x^3}{3!} + \ldots$

4. $\log_e (1+x) = x - \frac{x^2}{2} + \frac{x^3}{3} - \frac{x^4}{4} + \ldots$

5. $\log_e (1-x) = -x - \frac{x^2}{2} - \frac{x^3}{3} - \frac{x^4}{4} - \ldots$

6. $\sin x = \frac{x}{1!} - \frac{x^3}{3!} + \frac{x^5}{5!} - \frac{x^7}{7!} + \ldots$

7. $\cos x = 1 - \frac{x^2}{2!} + \frac{x^4}{4!} - \frac{x^6}{6!} + \ldots$

8. $\tan x = x + \frac{x^3}{3} + \frac{2}{15}x^5 + \frac{17}{315}x^7 + \ldots$

9. $\sinh x = \frac{e^x - e^{-x}}{2} = \frac{x}{1!} + \frac{x^3}{3!} + \frac{x^5}{5!} + \ldots$

10. $\cosh x = \frac{e^x + e^{-x}}{2} = 1 + \frac{x^2}{2!} + \frac{x^4}{4!} + \ldots$

APPENDIX H

Differential Calculus Formulae

1. $\dfrac{d}{dx}(x^n) = n\,x^{n-1}$

2. $\dfrac{d}{dx}(\sin x) = \cos x$

3. $\dfrac{d}{dx}(\cos x) = -\sin x$

4. $\dfrac{d}{dx}(\tan x) = \sec^2 x$

5. $\dfrac{d}{dx}(\cot x) = -\operatorname{cosec}^2 x$

6. $\dfrac{d}{dx}(\sec x) = \sec x \tan x$

7. $\dfrac{d}{dx}(\operatorname{cosec} x) = -\operatorname{cosec} x \cot x$

8. $\dfrac{d}{dx}(\text{arc} \sin x) = \dfrac{1}{\sqrt{1-x^2}}$

9. $\dfrac{d}{dx}(\text{arc} \cos x) = -\dfrac{1}{\sqrt{1-x^2}}$

10. $\dfrac{d}{dx}(\text{arc} \tan x) = \dfrac{1}{1+x^2}$

11. $\dfrac{d}{dx}(\text{arc} \cot x) = -\dfrac{1}{1+x^2}$

12. $\dfrac{d}{dx}(\text{arc} \sec x) = \dfrac{1}{x\sqrt{x^2-1}}$

13. $\dfrac{d}{dx}(\text{arc} \operatorname{cosec} x) = -\dfrac{1}{x\sqrt{x^2-1}}$

14. $\dfrac{d}{dx}(\log_e x) = \dfrac{1}{x}$

15. $\dfrac{d}{dx}(\log_a x) = \dfrac{1}{x}\log_a e$

16. $\dfrac{d}{dx}(e^x) = e^x$

17. $\dfrac{d}{dx}(a^x) = a^x \log_e a$

APPENDIX I

Integral Calculus Formulae

1. $\int x^n dx = \frac{x^{n+1}}{n+1} + c$

2. $\int \frac{dx}{x} = \log_e x + c$

3. $\int e^x \, dx = e^x + c$

4. $\int a^x \, dx = \frac{a^x}{\log_e a} + c$

5. $\int \sin x \, dx = -\cos x + c$

6. $\int \cos x \, dx = \sin x + c$

7. $\int \tan x \, dx = \log_e \sec x + c$

8. $\int \cot x \, dx = \log_e \sin x + c$

9. $\int \sec x \, dx = \log_e (\text{cosec } x - \cot x) + c$

10. $\int \text{cosec } x \, dx = \log_e (\sec x + \tan x) + c$

11. $\int \sec^2 x \, dx = \tan x + c$

12. $\int \text{cosec}^2 x \, dx = -\cot x + c$

13. $\int \frac{dx}{\sqrt{1-x^2}} = \text{arc } \sin x + c$

14. $\int \frac{dx}{\sqrt{a^2 - x^2}} = \text{arc } \sin (x/a) + c$

15. $\int \frac{dx}{\sqrt{1+x^2}} = \text{arc } \tan x + c$

16. $\int \frac{dx}{\sqrt{a^2 + x^2}} = \frac{1}{a} \text{arc } \tan (x/a) + c$

17. $\int \frac{dx}{\sqrt{x^2 \pm a^2}} = \log(x + \sqrt{x^2 \pm a^2}) + c$

APPENDIX J

Areas of Plane Figures

1. Square, $A = a^2 = d^2/2$
   where a is the side and d is the diagonal.
2. Rectangle, $A = a \times b$
3. Rhombus, $A = \dfrac{d_1 d_2}{2} = a^2 \sin \alpha$
   where a is the side, α is one of the angles, and d_1, d_2 are diagonals.
4. Parallelogram, $A = a \times h = ab \sin \alpha$
   where a and b are sides, α is one of the angles and h is the height.
5. Trapezoid, $A = \left(\dfrac{a+b}{2}\right) \times h$
6. Quadrilateral, $A = \dfrac{1}{2} d_1 d_2 \sin \alpha$
   where d_1 and d_2 are diagonals, and α is the angle between them.
7. Equilateral triangle, $A = \dfrac{1}{4} a^2 \sqrt{3}$
   where a is the side.
8. Any triangle, $A = \dfrac{1}{2} ab \sin C$, etc.
   Alternatively, $A = \sqrt{s(s-a)\,(s-b)(s-c)}$
9. Regular hexagon, $A = \dfrac{3\sqrt{3}}{2} a^2$
   where a is the side.

APPENDIX K

Surface Areas of Solids

1. Prism, $S = p \times h$
   where p is the perimeter and h is the height.
2. Right circular cylinder, $S = p \times h = 2\pi r \times h$
   where r is the radius.
3. Regular pyramid, $S = \frac{1}{2} p \times l$
   where l is the slant height.
4. Right circular cone, $S = \pi r \times l$
   where l = slant height
5. Sphere, $S = 4\pi r^2$
   where r is the radius.

APPENDIX L

Volume of Solids

1. Prism, $V = A \times h$

   where A is the area of the base.
2. Rectangular parallelepiped, $V = abc$
3. Circular cone, $V = \frac{1}{3}Ah = \frac{1}{3}\pi r^2 h$
4. Circular cylinder, $V = A \times h = \pi r^2 h$
5. Pyramid, $V = \frac{1}{3} A \times h$
6. Sphere, $V = \frac{4}{3}\pi r^3$
7. Truncated pyramid, $V = \frac{1}{3}(A_1 + \sqrt{A_1 A_2} + A_2) \times h$
8. Truncated circular cone, $V = \frac{1}{3}\pi h(r_1^2 + r_1 r_2 + r_2^2)$
9. Wedge, $V = \frac{1}{2} A \times h$
10. Spherical segment, $V = \pi h^2 \left(R - \frac{1}{3}h \right)$

    where R is the radius of sphere, and h is the height of segment.

APPENDIX M

Theorem of Circles

1. The angles *APB* and *AQB* on the same side of a chord *AB* are equal, and each is equal to one-half the angle *AOB* subtended at the centre. (Fig. L-la).

Thus, $\angle APB = \angle AQB = \dfrac{1}{2}\angle AOB = \theta$

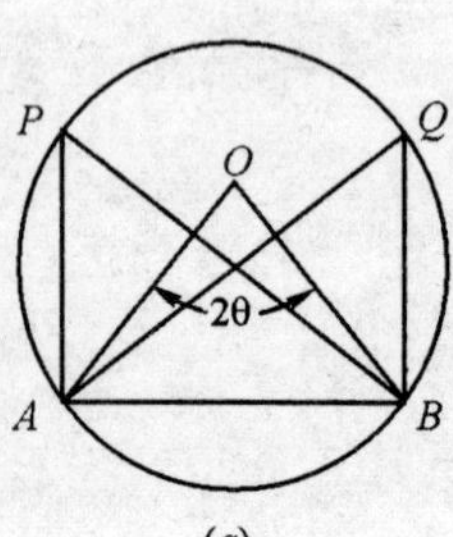

(*a*)

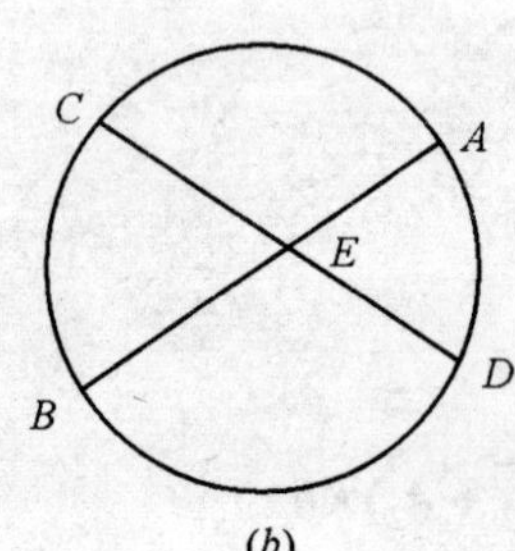

(*b*)

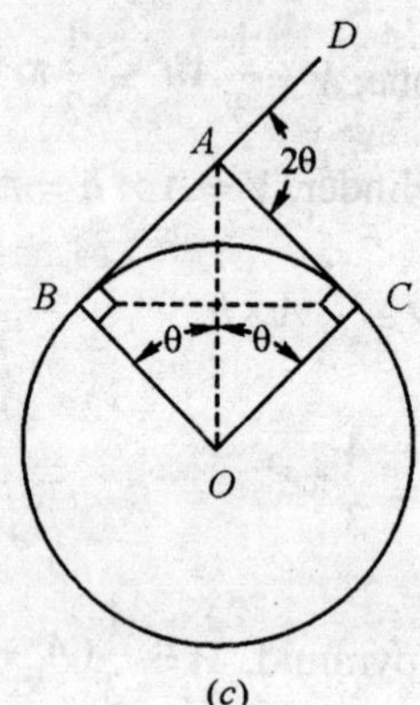

(*c*)

Fig. L-1

2. If *AB* and *CD* are two chords of a circle which intersect at *E* (Fig. L-1b),

$$AE \times EB = CE \times ED$$

3. If *AB* and *AC* are two tangents and *O* is the centre (Fig. L-1c).

$$AB = AC$$
$$\angle DAC = \angle BOC$$
$$\angle ABO = \angle ACO = 90°$$

4. If *AB* is a tangent and *BC* is a chord, (Fig. L-2a)

$$\angle ABC = \angle CDB = \theta$$

where *D* is any point on the circumference (Fig. L-2a)

5. If *AB* is a tangent and the line *ACD* is a secant (Fig. L-2b),

$$(AB)^2 = AC \times AD$$

6. If an arc AB subtends an angle θ degree at the centre O of a circle (Fig. L-2c).

$$\text{arc length } AB = \frac{\pi R\theta}{180°}$$

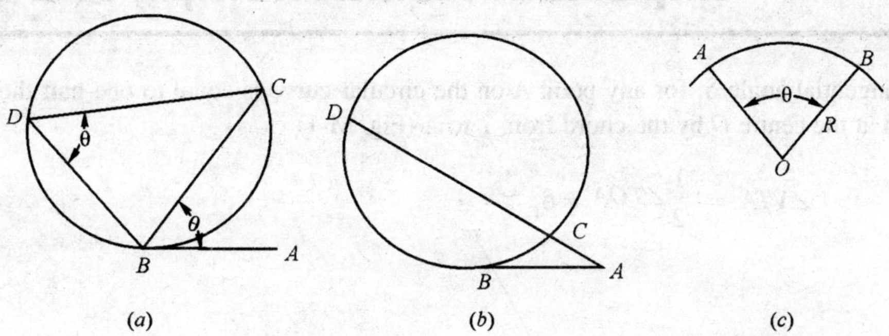

Fig. L-2

APPENDIX N

Important Relationships of a Circle

1. The tangential angle δ_1 for any point A on the circular curve is equal to one-half the angle subtended at the centre O by the chord from T to A (Fig. M-1)

$$\angle VTA = \frac{1}{2}\angle TOA = \delta_1$$

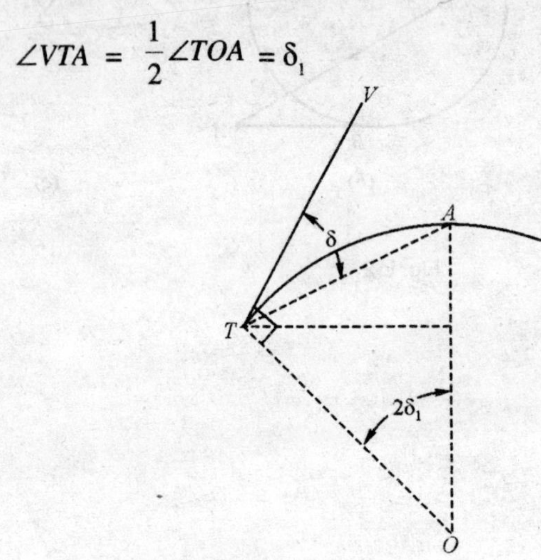

Fig. M-1

2. The deflection angle Δ to any point B on the circular curve is equal to the sum of the tangential angles from each chord upto that point (Fig. M-2)

$$\angle VTB = \frac{1}{2}\angle TOB$$

$$= \frac{1}{2}(\angle TOA + \angle AOB)$$

or
$$\Delta_2 = \frac{1}{2}(2\delta_1 + 2\delta_2)$$

$$= \delta_1 + \delta_2$$

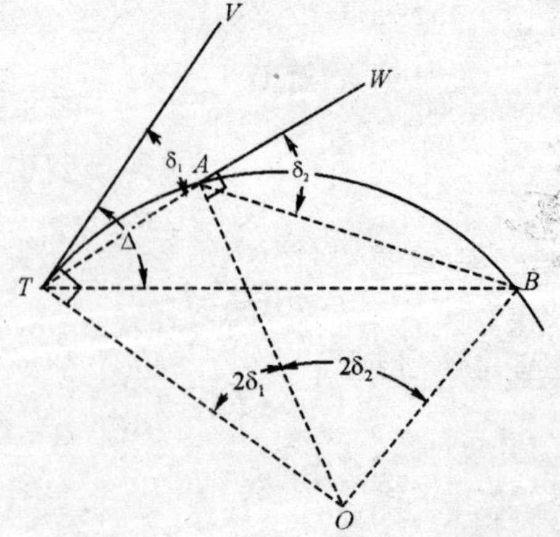

Fig. M-2

6. If an arc AB subtends an angle θ degree at the centre O of a circle (Fig. L-2c).

$$\text{arc length } AB = \frac{\pi R\theta}{180°}$$

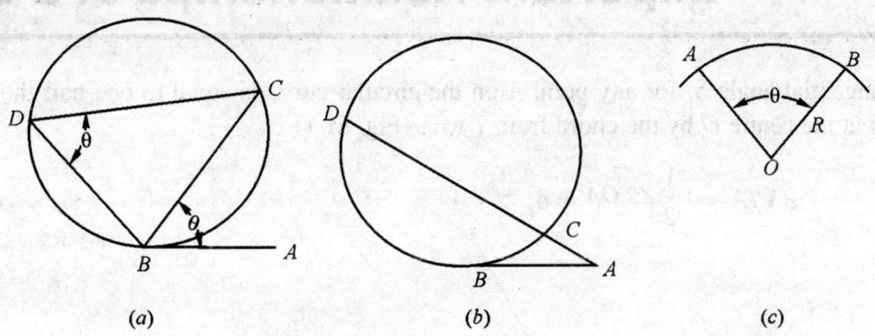

Fig. L-2

APPENDIX N

Important Relationships of a Circle

1. The tangential angle δ_1 for any point A on the circular curve is equal to one-half the angle subtended at the centre O by the chord from T to A (Fig. M-1)

$$\angle VTA = \frac{1}{2}\angle TOA = \delta_1$$

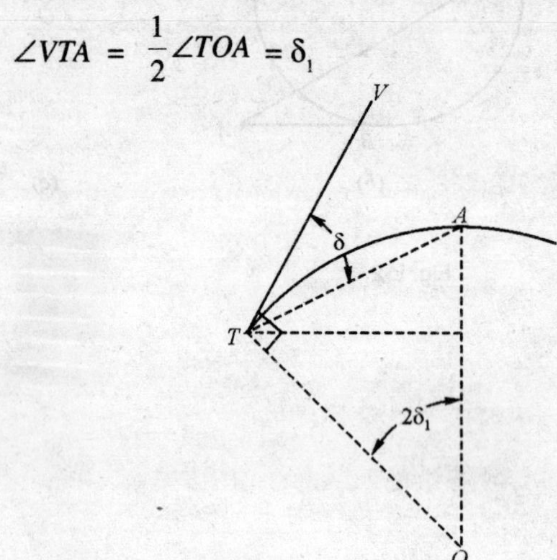

Fig. M-1

2. The deflection angle Δ to any point B on the circular curve is equal to the sum of the tangential angles from each chord upto that point (Fig. M-2)

$$\angle VTB = \frac{1}{2}\angle TOB$$

$$= \frac{1}{2}(\angle TOA + \angle AOB)$$

or $$\Delta_2 = \frac{1}{2}(2\delta_1 + 2\delta_2)$$

$$= \delta_1 + \delta_2$$

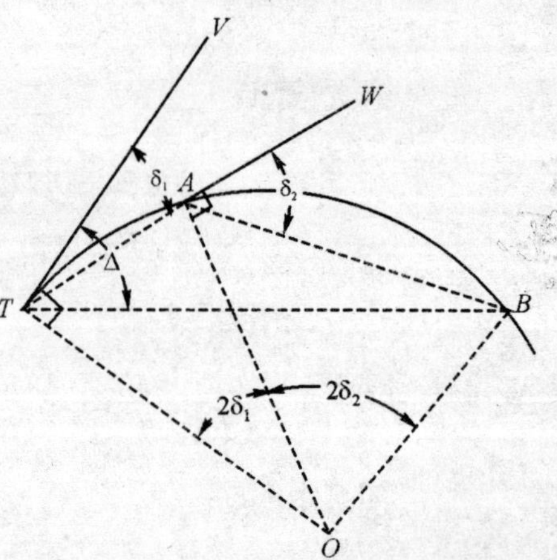

Fig. M-2

INDEX